The Cambridge Handbook of Sexual Development

The Cambridge Handbook of Sexual Development is a carefully curated conversation that brings together the top researchers in child and adolescent sexual development to redefine the issues, conflicts, and debates in the field. The handbook is organized around three foundational questions: first, what is sexual development? Second, how do we study sexual development? And third, what roles might adults – including the institutions of the media, family, and education – play in the sexual development of children and adolescents? As the first of its kind, this collection integrates work from sociology, psychology, anthropology, history, education, cultural studies, and allied fields. Writing from different disciplinary traditions and about a range of international contexts, the contributors explore the role of sexuality in children's and adolescents' everyday experiences of identity, family, school, neighborhood, religion, and popular media.

SHARON LAMB is Professor of Counseling Psychology in the Department of Counseling and School Psychology at the University of Massachusetts Boston, USA. Her current research focuses on sexual ethics as a basis for sex education and the moral reasoning of bystanders in "sketchy" sexual situations.

JEN GILBERT is Associate Professor of Education at York University, Canada. Her current research explores narratives of LGBTQ sexuality and gender in high schools and the problems and opportunities sexual health education poses for schooling.

The Cambridge Handbook of Sexual Development

Childhood and Adolescence

Edited by

Sharon Lamb
University of Massachusetts Boston

Jen Gilbert
York University, Toronto

CAMBRIDGE
UNIVERSITY PRESS

University Printing House, Cambridge CB2 8BS, United Kingdom

One Liberty Plaza, 20th Floor, New York, NY 10006, USA

477 Williamstown Road, Port Melbourne, VIC 3207, Australia

314–321, 3rd Floor, Plot 3, Splendor Forum, Jasola District Centre, New Delhi – 110025, India

79 Anson Road, #06–04/06, Singapore 079906

Cambridge University Press is part of the University of Cambridge.

It furthers the University's mission by disseminating knowledge in the pursuit of education, learning, and research at the highest international levels of excellence.

www.cambridge.org
Information on this title: www.cambridge.org/9781107190719
DOI: 10.1017/9781108116121

First published 2019

Printed in the United Kingdom by TJ International Ltd. Padstow Cornwall

A catalogue record for this publication is available from the British Library.

Library of Congress Cataloging-in-Publication Data
Names: Lamb, Sharon, editor. | Gilbert, Jen, 1971– editor.
Title: The Cambridge handbook of sexual development : childhood and adolescence / edited by Sharon Lamb, University of Massachusetts Boston, Jen Gilbert, York University, Toronto.
Description: Cambridge, United Kingdom ; New York, NY : Cambridge University Press, 2019. | Includes bibliographical references and index.
Identifiers: LCCN 2018025045 | ISBN 9781107190719 (hardback)
Subjects: LCSH: Children and sex. | Children – Sexual behavior. | Teenagers – Sexual behavior. | Sex. | Child development. | Adolescence.
Classification: LCC HQ784.S45 C36 2019 | DDC 613.9/51–dc23
LC record available at https://lccn.loc.gov/2018025045

ISBN 978-1-107-19071-9 Hardback
ISBN 978-1-316-64077-7 Paperback

Contents

Notes on Contributors

LOUISA ALLEN is a professor in the Faculty of Education and Social Work at the University of Auckland. She specializes in research in the areas of sexualities, young people and schooling, and innovative research methodologies that seek to engage hard-to-reach research populations. She has written six books in these areas, the latest of which is entitled *Schooling Sexual Cultures: Visual Research and Sexuality Education* (2017).

LAINA Y. BAY-CHENG is Associate Professor and PhD Program Director at the University at Buffalo School of Social Work. She concentrates her scholarship on exposing the normative, social, and material foundations of young women's sexual vulnerability and on advocating for conditions that enable young women's sexual agency.

JENNY BENGTSSON is a senior lecturer in childhood and youth studies in the Department of Education, Communication, and Learning at the University of Gothenburg, Sweden. Her research interests include issues of social justice in educational practices, childhood and sexuality, and sex education from preschool to upper secondary school.

DEEVIA BHANA is the DST/NRF South African Research Chair in Gender and Childhood Sexuality at the University of KwaZulu-Natal. She has published widely in the field of gender, childhood sexualities, and young masculinities. Her latest book is *Love, Sex and Teenage Sexual Cultures in South Africa: 16 Turning 17* (2018).

SANDRA BHATASARA is a senior lecturer and researcher in sociology at the University of Zimbabwe. She researches, writes, and publishes on the sociology of gender and sexuality, environment, and rural societies. She is also a women's rights activist, working with young women to promote feminist action research and transformative leadership on sexual and reproductive rights.

EVA BOLANDER is a senior lecturer in pedagogic practice in the Department of Social and Welfare Studies, Linköping University, Sweden. Her main fields of research and teaching include critical sexuality studies and intersectional perspectives on schooling and teaching materials. Bolander has extensive experience of researching sexuality education in Sweden using multiple methods.

Her work on the cultural intelligibility of condoms has been published in the journal *Sex Education: Sexuality, Society and Learning.*

ANNA BREDSTRÖM is a senior lecturer at the Institute for Research on Migration, Ethnicity and Society (REMESO) at Linköping University, Sweden. Her research is informed by feminist intersectionality theory, critical race theory, and science and technology studies. Her research focuses on bodies, health, and medicine, and she has vast experience of researching youth and sexuality. Her publications include work on HIV/AIDS policy, safer sex, and sex and alcohol, and she is particularly interested in developing methods for a critical multicultural sexuality education. Her work has been published in, among others, *Sexualities*, *European Journal of Women Studies*, *Nordic Journal of Migration Research*, and *Journal of Medical Humanities*.

ANA J. BRIDGES is Associate Professor of Clinical Psychology at the University of Arkansas. Her research focuses on mental health disparities and increasing access to treatment for vulnerable and underserved populations. She has authored numerous articles and book chapters investigating the role of pornography in sexual behavior and violence against women.

DEBORAH P. BRITZMAN is Distinguished Research Professor, Fellow of the Royal Society of Canada, and York Research Chair in Pedagogy and Psychosocial Transformations. Author of eight books and more than one hundred articles, Britzman's area of expertise is in psychoanalysis with education and the history of psychoanalysis. Her recent books are *Melanie Klein: Early Analysis, Play and the Question of Freedom* and A *Psychoanalysis in the Classroom: On the Human Condition in Education.*

ROSALIND S. CHOU is Associate Professor of Sociology at Georgia State University. She has authored three books: *The Myth of the Model Minority; Asian American Sexual Politics: The Construction of Race, Gender, and Sexuality*; and *Asian Americans on Campus.*

MANASE KUDZAI CHIWESHE is Senior Lecturer in the Institute of Lifelong Learning and Development Studies at Chinhoyi University of Technology in Zimbabwe and winner of the 2015 Gerti Hesseling Award for the best paper in African studies. His work revolves around the sociology of everyday life in African spaces, with special focus on promoting African ways of knowing, specifically in gender, sexuality, livelihoods, and leisure.

JENNIFER F. CHMIELEWSKI is a doctoral student in critical social/personality psychology at the Graduate Center, City University of New York. Her work explores the sexualized surveillance of women and girls and their lived experiences of embodiment, desire, and resistance at the intersection of gender, race, sexuality, and class.

MADDY COY is a lecturer in the Center for Gender, Sexualities, and Women's Studies Research at the University of Florida. Coy has worked in the field of violence against women as a practitioner, activist, researcher, and educator for 20 years. She has researched and published widely on violence against women, sexual exploitation, and sexualized sexism in popular culture.

CRISTYN DAVIES is a research associate in the Discipline of Child and Adolescent Health, Faculty of Medicine and Health, University of Sydney, and the Children's Hospital at Westmead. She has published widely, and across disciplines, in the areas of sexual and gendered citizenship, sexual health education for children and adolescents, HPV and the HPV vaccination, neoliberalism and governmentality, narrative and media studies, and innovative pedagogies and educational practice. Her co-authored book *Mediating Sexual Citizenship: Neoliberal Subjectivities in Television Culture* was released in 2018.

The late JOHN DELAMATER was Professor of Sociology at the University of Wisconsin–Madison. An expert in the sociology of human sexuality, he was co-author of the textbook *Social Psychology* and the textbook *Understanding Human Sexuality*.

LISA M. DIAMOND is Professor of Psychology and Gender Studies at the University of Utah. She studies the lifespan development of sexuality and sexual orientation, as exemplified in her award-winning 2008 book, *Sexual Fluidity*. Diamond is also co-editor of the *APA Handbook of Sexuality and Psychology* and has received awards for her work from the International Association for Relationship Research, the Society for the Scientific Study of Sexuality, and the Society for the Psychological Study of Social Issues.

JESSICA FIELDS is Professor of Sociology and Sexuality Studies at San Francisco State University and author of *Risky Lessons: Sex Education and Social Inequality*. With Laura Mamo, Nancy Lesko, and Jen Gilbert, she leads the Beyond Bullying Project, a community-based storytelling project that aims to understand and interrupt ordinary hostility in high schools to LGBTQ sexualities (funded by the Ford Foundation). Fields is currently writing her second book, *Problems We Pose: Feeling Differently about Qualitative Research*.

SARAH FLICKER is Associate Professor in the Faculty of Environmental Studies at York University, Toronto. Her research focuses on youth HIV prevention and support as well as environmental, sexual, and reproductive justice. More broadly, she is interested in community-based participatory methodologies and ethics. She is active on a variety of research teams that focus on adolescent sexual health with youth in Canada and South Africa. Her research has informed policy at the municipal, provincial, and federal levels. Flicker and her teams have won a number of prestigious awards for youth engagement in health research.

LORENA GARCIA is Associate Professor of Sociology and Latin American and Latino Studies at the University of Illinois at Chicago. She is author of *Respect*

Yourself, Protect Yourself: Latina Girls and Sexual Identity (2012). Her research interests are in the intersections of gender, sexuality, race/ethnicity, and class. Her work also focuses on US Latinxs and qualitative methods.

SARAH GARLAND-LEVETT is a master's graduate from the University of Auckland. Her research to date has focused on sexuality education policy in Aotearoa New Zealand. She has an interest in how critical, queer, feminist, and new materialist theories offer new possibilities for rethinking how sexuality education can be thought and taught in the interests of social justice.

JEN GILBERT is Associate Professor of Education at York University, Canada. Her current research explores narratives of LGBTQ sexuality and gender in high schools, and the problems and opportunities sexual health education poses for schooling.

PETAL GROWER is a PhD student in developmental psychology at the University of Michigan. Her work explores the complex links between media use, body image, and young women's sexual agency.

ALEXANDRA HAWKEY has an MPH and has recently submitted her PhD thesis. She is currently a research officer at the Translational Health Research Institute at Western Sydney University, Australia. She conducted her PhD research on the sexual and reproductive health of culturally and linguistically diverse women. Her areas of research interest are fertility, women's sexual health, contraception, menstruation, and menopause.

MIRANDA A. H. HORVATH is Associate Professor of Forensic Psychology and Deputy Director of Forensic Psychological Services at Middlesex University. She has extensive research experience, having conducted national and local multi-site/-team/-strand evaluation and research projects. Her research and publications focus on violence against women and children, sexualized media, and multiple-perpetrator rape. She is the co-editor of *Rape: Challenging Contemporary Thinking* (2009) and *Handbook on the Study of Multiple Perpetrator Rape: A Multidisciplinary Response to an International Problem* (2013).

LUCIE JARKOVSKÁ is Associate Professor at the Institute for Research in Inclusive Education at Masaryk University, Brno, Czech Republic. Her research interests include gender, education, sexuality, and anti-sex education movements. She works with nongovernmental organizations in Central Europe, promoting sex education and providing training for sex educators.

JENNIFER A. JOHNSON is Associate Professor and Chair of Sociology at Virginia Commonwealth University. She has published numerous articles and book chapters related to her research on the pornography industry, social network analysis, sexual and public health, and digital sociology. She is the lead editor of the journal *Sexualization, Media and Society*.

SHARON LAMB is Professor of Counseling Psychology in the Department of Counseling and School Psychology at the University of Massachusetts Boston, USA. Her current research focuses on sexual ethics as a basis for sex education and the moral reasoning of bystanders in "sketchy" sexual situations.

AUBREY LIMBURG is currently a PhD student in the Department of Sociology at the University of Colorado Boulder. Her research broadly focuses on gender and sexuality as related to health across the life course. Her current work examines the relationship between sexuality, health, and older adulthood.

KATIE MACENTEE is currently a Social Sciences and Humanities Research Council (SSHRC) postdoctoral fellow at York University, Toronto, in the Faculty of Environmental Studies. Her research interests include sexual health and HIV/AIDS education, transactional sex, girlhood, participatory visual methodologies, and cellphilms. She is co-editor of *What's a Cellphilm? Integrating Mobile Technology into Research and Activism* (2016).

SARA I. MCCLELLAND is Associate Professor at the University of Michigan in the Departments of Women's Studies and Psychology. Her research focuses on the expectations individuals develop for what they deserve to feel, experience, and avoid in their intimate lives. Recent work has addressed issues related to reproductive justice, sex education, and evidence of gender and sexual labor across the life span.

ALLISON MOORE is a senior lecturer in the Department of Social Sciences at Edge Hill University, Ormskirk, England. Her research interests lie in the sociology of sexuality and the regulation of sexuality, especially the regulation of youth sexuality. She is co-author of *Childhood and Sexuality: Contemporary Issues and Debates* (Moore & Reynolds, 2018) and has published a number of peer-reviewed journal articles. Her reading of childhood and sexuality is shaped by feminist analyses of gender and sexuality that explore the ways in which female behavior and sexual desire and expression is limited, contained, and regulated under heteropatriarchy.

JESSICA D. MOORMAN is a PhD candidate in the Department of Communication Studies at the University of Michigan and, in fall of 2018, will be joining the faculty of the University of Iowa as Assistant Professor in the School of Journalism and Mass Communication. Moorman's research explores how US Black adults make meaning of and are influenced by their representation in the media. Her current project explores how Black-oriented dating and relationship advice media contribute to single Black women's beliefs about gender and relationships, and their approaches to singlehood.

NELSON MUPARAMOTO is a PhD student at Rhodes University in the Department of Sociology. Muparamoto enjoys researching on sexualities both normative and non-normative. Currently he is focusing on the experiences of gays and lesbians in Zimbabwe, in which he explores what characterizes gay and lesbian identities in

Zimbabwe in an attempt to interrogate how they reinforce, modify, and challenge dominant social categories informed by the "global gay" culture.

MARIJKE NAEZER is a PhD student at Radboud University, the Netherlands, in the Department of Gender and Diversity Studies. She holds master's degrees in anthropology and gender studies, and has worked as a policy worker for the Dutch Women's Studies Association and the Dutch Association against Child Sexual Abuse. Moreover, she has worked as an independent researcher focusing on the theme of child sexual abuse. She recently submitted her PhD thesis "Sexy adventures: An ethnography of youth, sexuality and social media."

AOIFE NEARY is Lecturer in Sociology of Education in the School of Education, University of Limerick, Ireland. She held an Irish Research Council (IRC) Doctoral Scholar Award from 2011 until 2014 and has been an IRC New Foundations Awardee in 2013, 2014, 2015, and 2016. Drawing on feminist, queer, and affect theory, her work explores the politics of gender and sexuality as they are lived and configured in schools and society. She is author of *LGBT-Q Teachers, Civil Partnership and Same-sex Marriage: The Ambivalences of Legitimacy* (2017).

JANETTE PERZ is Director of the Translational Health Research Institute, Western Sydney University, Australia. She researches in the field of reproductive and sexual health with a particular focus on gendered experiences, subjectivity, and identity. She has undertaken a significant research program in sexual and reproductive health, including the experience of premenstrual syndrome (PMS) in heterosexual and lesbian relationships, the development of and evaluation of a couple-based psychological intervention for PMS, sexual well-being and reproductive needs in migrant and refugee women, and sexual and psychological well-being during menopause and midlife.

ALEKSANDRA PLOCHA is Assistant Professor in the Clinical Mental Health Counseling graduate program at Merrimack College in North Andover, Massachusetts. Her primary research area focuses on the intersection of three domains that are salient to college students: the developmental period of emerging adulthood, bereavement, and resilience. Her research examines how current operationalized definitions of resilience and available grief discourse impact the bereavement process, with the goal of better supporting students who have experienced the death of a loved one.

MARY LOU RASMUSSEN is located in the School of Sociology at the Australian National University. She is part of the Australian Research Council (ARC) Discovery Project, Queer Generations, investigating the experiences of two generations of LGBT young people in Australia. She leads an ARC Discovery investigating worldviews of Australian millennials. She is co-editor, with Louisa Allen, of *The Palgrave Handbook of Sexuality Education* (2017). Her monograph, *Progressive Sexuality Education: The Conceits of Secularism*, is now available in paperback.

JESSICA RINGROSE is Professor of Sociology of Gender and Education at the UCL Institute of Education, University College London. She is a co-chair of the International Gender and Education Association and co-coordinator of PhEmaterialism (Feminist Posthumanism and New Materialism Research Methodologies in Education) Network. Her research is about transforming sexualized media cultures, and activating gender and sexual equity in secondary schools. Her latest book, *Digital Feminist Activism: Girls and Women Fight Back against Rape Culture* (with Kaitlynn Mendes and Jessalynn Keller), is out in 2018.

CELIA ROBERTS is Professor of Gender and Science Studies in the Department of Sociology, Lancaster University, England. She also co-directs the Centre for Gender and Women's Studies. Roberts is the author of *Puberty in Crisis: The Sociology of Early Sexual Development* (2017) and *Messengers of Sex: Hormones, Biomedicine and Feminism* (2007), and is currently writing about fertility and stress biosensing.

KERRY H. ROBINSON is Professor of Sociology and the leader of Sexualities and Genders Research (SaGR) in the School of Social Sciences and Psychology at Western Sydney University, Australia. She has published widely in her field, with titles including: *Innocence, Knowledge and the Construction of Childhood: The Contradictory Relationship between Sexuality and Censorship in Children's Contemporary Lives* (2013) and co-authored *Diversity and Difference in Early Childhood Education: Issues for Theory and Practice* (Robinson & Jones Diaz, 2nd edn., 2016).

STEPHEN T. RUSSELL is Priscilla Pond Flawn Regents Professor of Child Development and Chair of the Department of Human Development and Family Sciences at the University of Texas at Austin. He is an expert in adolescent health, with a focus on sexual orientation and gender identity. He is a fellow of the National Council on Family Relations, an elected member of the International Academy of Sexuality Research, and was President of the Society for Research on Adolescence.

RITCH C. SAVIN-WILLIAMS, Professor Emeritus of Developmental Psychology at Cornell University, has written ten books on adolescent development, including *Mostly Straight: Sexual Fluidity among Men* (2017), *Becoming Who I Am: Young Men on Being Gay* (2016), and *The New Gay Teenager* (2005). Savin-Williams writes about the sexual and romantic development of youth, is a licensed clinical psychologist, and has consulted for media outlets such as MTV, 20/20, Oprah Winfrey, Today Show, National Geographic, and National Public Radio.

JULIA SINCLAIR-PALM is an instructor in Child Studies in the Institute of Interdisciplinary Studies at Carleton University, Ottawa, Canada. Drawing on feminist and queer theory, trans studies, and post-structuralism, her research examines how trans youth forge new identities, imagine futures, and navigate structural inequalities in the midst of these larger, and sometimes restrictive, narratives about trans lives. Her research interests include LGBT youth, educational policy, and theories of teaching and learning.

BRITTANY TAYLOR is currently a PhD student at Georgia State University in the Department of Sociology. She completed a master's degree in Women's and Gender Studies at the University of South Florida. Her research foci include health policy, substance use, HIV/AIDS, and intersectional applications with queer people of color (QPoC) health. Her current work involves tracing alcohol patterns among Black/African-American queer women in the South.

DEBORAH L. TOLMAN is Professor of Women and Gender Studies at Hunter College and Critical Social Psychology at the Graduate Center, City University of New York. Her research is on adolescent sexuality, specifically the "unmentionables" around pleasure as well as danger, agency, and prevention for girls. Tolman is the co-founder of SPARK – Sexualization Protest: Action, Resistance, Knowledge – and the author of *Dilemmas of Desire: Teenage Girls Talk about Sexuality*, which was awarded the 2003 Distinguished Book Award from the Association for Women in Psychology.

JANE USSHER is Professor of Women's Health Psychology in the Translational Health Research Institute, at Western Sydney University, Australia. She is editor of the *Routledge Women and Psychology* book series, and author of a number of books, including: *The Psychology of the Female Body, Women's Madness: Misogyny or Mental Illness?, Fantasies of Femininity: Reframing the Boundaries of Sex, Managing the Monstrous Feminine: Regulating the Reproductive Body, The Madness of Women: Myth and Experience*, and co-editor of the forthcoming *Routledge Handbook of Women's Sexual and Reproductive Health.*

L. MONIQUE WARD is Arthur F. Thurnau Professor of Psychology at the University of Michigan. Her research focuses on media contributions to sexual socialization, with particular attention to effects of sexual objectifying media. Her current research examines consequences of media sexualization, including consequences for women's sexual agency and for interpersonal violence. She has published more than 65 articles in peer-reviewed journals and served as a member of the American Psychological Association Task Force on the Sexualization of Girls.

LINDSEY WHITE is a doctoral student in counseling psychology at the University of Massachusetts Boston. She completed a master's degree in mental health counseling and a certificate in sexuality, women, and gender at Teachers College, Columbia University. Her current work focuses on sexual ethics and representations of gender diverse identities.

AMY C. WILKINS is Associate Professor of Sociology at the University of Colorado Boulder. Her current research focuses on identity transformations in the transition to college for first-generation, Black, and LGBQ young adults. Her research on gender, sexuality, and racial inequalities and identities has been published in journals such as *Sociology of Education, Gender & Society, Social Psychology Quarterly*, and *Signs*, and in a book, *Wannabes, Goths, and Christians: The Boundaries of Sex, Style, and Status* (2008).

Acknowledgments

Over the years that we have worked on sexual development, sex education, and sexuality, there have been many colleagues, professors, and students who provided us with insights and encouragement. Some of them have even contributed chapters to this volume. Some of them have not, but have inspired us nonetheless. Our deepest gratitude, however, goes to Jennifer Bethune, a PhD student, whose organizational skills, deep readings, and insightful questions certainly improved this volume and kept us on track to finish in a timely manner. Lee Iskander joined our editing team at a crucial moment and provided excellent support and smart readings. We are especially grateful to Janka Romero, our Cambridge University Press editor, who saw the need for this kind of handbook, one that looked at sexual development outside the typically pathologizing frameworks of juvenile justice or sexual victimization. We appreciate her vision, trust, and patience. We were lucky that our chapter authors were such good sports when we cajoled, challenged, and suggested new shapes for their chapters. We could not have done so if the raw material they provided wasn't supremely interesting, well written, and engaging.

Finally, Sharon thanks Jen Gilbert, delighting in this new friendship that came together through a suggestion from Jessica Fields, who perhaps knew how much she would love Jen's sense of humor, and knowing the fun we would eventually have when we met in person to share good food, wine, and stories. I (Sharon) appreciate Jen's continued focus on what is theoretically sound as well as meaningful, which helped me trust this volume would be special and useful. And Jen thanks Jessica Fields, whose love and companionship helped her stay grounded in the midst of the editing storm, and Sharon Lamb, whose work has long been important to her thinking. Thank you for the gift of collegiality and friendship – this volume reflects the boldness and bravery of your vision for sexuality research and education.

Introduction

Interdisciplinary Approaches to Sexual Development in Childhood and Adolescence

Jen Gilbert and Sharon Lamb

Young people come of age in an increasingly complex world. As they develop social and sexual identities, they navigate terrain familiar and new to them and to the adults in their lives: online bullying, easy access to pornography, proliferating sexual and gender categories, the risks of disease and pregnancy, and shifting religious and cultural norms about sexuality. These issues contribute to an anxious atmosphere around child and adolescent sexual development. The anxiety is not new – the relationship between sexuality and childhood has long been fraught (Angelides, 2004; Egan & Hawkes, 2008; Gittins, 1998; Kincaid, 1998). And, yet, the landscape for sexual development is changing – social media, new gender and sexual identities, and ongoing debates about sexuality, violence, and gender not only reshape the contexts in which children and youth experience and articulate their sexualities, these new "biopsychosocial" landscapes change sexual development itself (Roberts, Chapter 24). Young people enter puberty earlier and come out as gay, lesbian, bisexual, and trans before leaving school. They live in a hookup culture that detaches sex from long-term, monogamous relationships, even as they may enter college and university with less sexual experience than previous generations (Ethier et al., 2018). Young girls feel the weight of media sexualization, and then call out patriarchal cultures of harassment and violence they live in. The contributors to this volume chart this new landscape. In the face of enduring narratives that emphasize the risks and anxieties associated with sexuality for young people, they offer critiques, alternatives, and describe the political uses of those narratives.

As we write this introduction at the beginning of 2018, we are witnessing the landscape of sexual development shifting in new and important ways. We are living through a period of tremendous change: in the past year, the social media "#metoo" campaign invited women to share experiences of sexual violence, and a wave of accusations of sexual harassment against Hollywood celebrities, politicians, and athletes renewed conversations about feminism. So far, the repercussions of these accusations include new models of consent, and these have been taken up as powerful educational responses to entrenched gender norms. While this consequence is encouraging, questions remain. What will this social movement mean for children's understandings of intimacy and autonomy; teens' formation of and participation in alternative sexual cultures; adults' understanding and enactment of their role in the sexual development of young people? While social media campaigns interrogate the ambiguous and often-contested moral principles governing sexual behavior, creative production, collegiality, and intergenerational relationships, sexuality's entanglement with a host of ethical concerns in young people's development and well-being is clear. Perhaps the time for sex education as sexual ethics education has finally arrived.

A principled stance will be important as we face the new horizons heralded by these broad cultural shifts. The promise of the acceptance of sexual and gender diversity and the enthusiastic embrace of girls' sexual subjectivity in the West does not eradicate the risks of sexual development for children and adolescents around the world. Several of the contributors to this volume bring this international perspective to studies of sexual development that span nation and region while also reflecting local and regional contexts and concerns. Bhatasara, Chiweshe, and Muparamoto (Chapter 25) describe how the reality of child marriage eliminates girls' sexual choices; Bhana (Chapter 19) condemns the "corrective rapes" of lesbians in South Africa; MacEntee and Flicker (Chapter 18) discuss how girls' use of sex to obtain cell phones and other material goods can lead to violence, HIV infection, and stigma; and Sinclair-Palm (Chapter 13) reminds us of the bullying and harassment that continue to police trans youths' coming of age in North America.

The interdisciplinary approach of this collection complements its international perspective. We have gathered researchers from psychology, sociology, anthropology, gender and women's studies, education, and cultural studies. Each chapter draws on its authors' own research program to pose broad questions about children's and adolescents' sexual development in contemporary times. The questions are urgent and timely: How do new technologies inform young people's sexual identities, experiences, and expectations? How have shifts in everyday understandings of sexual and gender diversity transformed the meanings and experiences of children and youth – and what meanings and experiences remain entrenched? How do theories of sexuality from Freud, Foucault, and feminist and queer theory continue to influence empirical and theoretical studies of children and adolescents? How do nation, culture, and race shape young people's sexualities? How can formal and informal interventions – including, but not only, education – support the sexual development of children and adolescents?

These questions expand the scope of research on sexual development beyond concerns with normative trajectories. In envisioning and assembling this volume, we have been less concerned with outlining expected paths from sexual immaturity to maturity than with critiquing the possibility of a normative theory of sexual development. Even pleasure, an aspect of sexuality that feminists have often offered as an antidote to narratives of danger (Fine, 1988; Tolman, 2004) is suspect here; drawing on the work of others (Allen, 2014; Lamb, 2010; Quinlivan, 2014), several chapters interrogate pleasure's links to constraining developmental norms. For example, Garland-Levett and Allen (Chapter 26) provide an overview and an understanding of the way in which politics make the full embrace of a pleasure discourse complex and challenging. Some of the contributors to this volume, including Chou and Taylor (Chapter 12), and Bredström, Bolander, and Bengtsson (Chapter 27), contest norms of sexual development that too often center the experiences of White, heterosexual, middle-class, Western boys, while others continue to critique the hysteria and regulation surrounding girls' sexualities (Coy and Horvath (Chapter 23); Tolman and Chmielewski (Chapter 10)); they insistently expand understandings of sexual development to include the lives and experiences of young people who have been neglected – people of color, LGBTQ youth, and children and adolescents from non-Western countries.

Writing from different disciplinary traditions and about a range of international contexts, the volume's contributors have all dedicated their scholarly careers to understanding and advocating for children and adolescents' sexual health and well-being. They share a commitment to questioning developmental pathways and modifying theories of "sexual development," even as they also approach this task from a range of positions on the sexual development of children and adolescents. Readers will find – between chapters and within sections – significant debates about key questions in research on sexual development. For instance, while Naezer and Ringrose (Chapter 21) identify moments of resistance in young people's use of social media, Ward, Moorman, and Grower (Chapter 20) emphasize how media is dominated by gendered and heteronormative scripts. Conflicting perspectives between chapters are always generative, pointing not only to disagreement but also to those questions and issues that are most important to the field.

We have organized this volume around three questions that capture the stakes of these sites of conflict. First, what is sexual development? Second, how do we study sexual development? And, third, what roles might adults, including the institutions of the media, family, and education, play in the sexual development of children and adolescents? These questions point to broad differences between and within theoretical and disciplinary approaches to the study of sexual development; for example, the tension within psychology between biological understandings and a constructionist or narrative approach, the turn to the social construction of sexuality in sociology, and disagreements over the relative importance of including children's voices in research on their sexual development and differing opinions regarding how to interpret these voices. These questions also point to the continued growth of this field. We expect the study of youth and sexual development will return to these foundational questions again and again as scholars continue to map the continuities and discontinuities in children's and adolescents' lives.

What Is Sexual Development?

When we invited researchers to contribute to this handbook, we sent the title, "The Cambridge Handbook of Sexual Development: Childhood and Adolescence," and a brief description of what we hoped the collection might accomplish. Our hopes began with what we did not want to do – we did not want to attempt an authoritative volume that would falsely claim a sense of coherence to the field called "sexual development." Instead, as we described in that initial invitation, we wanted to "stage an interdisciplinary conversation amongst leading sexuality scholars," one that would "explore the role of sexuality in children's and adolescents' everyday experiences of identity, school, neighbourhood, religion, and popular media." We explained that the volume would, we hoped, open "sexual development" to the insights of scholars from the social sciences, humanities, and education.

What we did not do is tell contributors what we meant by "sexual development." And, in their responses to our invitation, contributors have not cleared this up. Across the chapters, authors use "sexual development" to describe a wide and contradictory range of behaviors, experiences, and feelings. Some locate the beginning of the study of sexual development with Freud and his observation – radical then and now – that sexuality begins at the birth. Psychoanalysis legitimized the study of sexuality in childhood by insisting that sexuality does not arrive with puberty but is a force – a drive – that is connected to life itself and that unfolds in a particular pattern across a lifetime. Tying instinct to physiological development and family dynamics, Freud laid out a theory of sexual development that offered the first norms of sexual development – norms that begged critique. Later theorists, including Foucault, asked how the sexual norms of a culture become embedded in the subject, shaping desires and identities.

The question of how cultural norms are entangled with sexual subjectivity lies at the heart of studies of sexual development, and that question necessarily spans this collection. Those contributors grounded in psychology and psychoanalytic theory tend to understand sexual development as a process in which internal drives or desires are expressed and modified by contact with the outside world, including family, school, culture, and religion. These scholars see sexuality as emerging from within the self (whether from physiology or intrapsychic dynamics), shaping how we encounter and connect with the world. The world may affect our desires, but there is something at the beginning – before the touch of the social.

Other contributors conceptualize sexuality as an effect of social processes, constructed so mightily that it is impossible to separate individuals from their social contexts and others within. These theorists, grounded in sociological traditions, claim that people's sexualities are formed in relation to the contexts in which they develop. The contexts include not only norms about gender, race, and sex but also varying versions of, and even the very possibility of, desiring. That is to say, desire is dependent on context as much as sexual identity and behavior, and it has the potential to be fluid, fixed, or anything in between. For these researchers, it does not make sense to speak of sexuality through some simple mechanism, such as socialization, or only in light of its coming into being in relation to others. They ask: Who are these others, and what comprises the social?

Many authors in this collection begin not by staking a claim in these disciplinary divides but instead in uncovering the possibilities that this conflict generates: while sexuality may be made at the intersection of biological, social, psychological, and discursive forces, it is impossible to distinguish between those effects. As Robinson and Davies argue, for example, our ideas about childhood and sexuality shape our relationships with actual children. Bay-Cheng's critique of neoliberal discourses of choice on young women's sexual agency asks readers to see sexual development as the internalization and refusal of gendered discourses (Chapter 9). Tolman and Chmielewski demonstrate how dominant norms about female sexuality, especially the stubbornly persistent sexual double standard, constrict young women's sense of sexual possibility. Those interested in new materialist theory – like Naezer and Ringrose, and Jarkovská and Lamb (Chapter 4) – use Deleuze and Guattari's concept of the assemblage to conceive of a sexuality without origin, maintained and changed through networks of discourses, bodies, and institutions in flux. Diamond (Chapter 5), Moore (Chapter 2), and DeLamater (Chapter 7) each argue in their chapters that investigating the interaction of these forces in children and adolescents' sexual lives requires new, dynamic theoretical models. As Diamond writes, those models must be "particularly suited to these phenomena because they focus explicitly on understanding how complex patterns of experience emerge, stabilize, change, and restabilize due to dynamic interactions between endogenous factors, such as genes, hormones, and brain organization, and exogenous factors, such as social environments and relationships." Even as the meanings of sexual development vary from chapter to chapter, the volume as a whole sees sexual development as dynamic – made at the intersection of social, psychological, and biological contexts.

The push to conceptualize new models of sexual development also emerges from researchers' discontent with normative psychological theories' failure to account for the experiences of sexual and gender minority children and adolescents and young people of color. Ritch Savin-Williams' work has been central to rewriting developmental pathways for young gay men. In his contribution to this volume (Chapter 8), Savin-Williams presents an overview of his research on the developmental milestones of young gay men, with a focus on how contemporary contexts, including expanding human and civil rights for LGBTQ communities in the United States, have affected identity work. Similarly, Julia Sinclair-Palm argues that the focus on gender in transgender youths' lives has led to a neglect of their sexualities. Trans youths' sexualities, she writes, are intersectional, shaped by gender but also race, class, age, ability, and citizenship. Other contributors also argue that axes of difference beyond gender and sexuality also matter for sexual development. As Ussher, Hawkey, and Perz explain (Chapter 6), histories of migration affect mothers' and daughters' interpretations and experiences of sexuality and sexual bodies; Wilkins and Limburg (Chapter 11) explore how White, working-class college students negotiate expectations about hooking up at university; and Chou and Taylor trace the effects of White supremacy on Asian-American adolescents' experience of masculinity and femininity. These researchers insist that theories of sexual difference are also theories of race, class, nation, and gender.

As particular theoretical orientations define their objects of study differently, they also reach different conclusions about the role of adults in supporting children and adolescents. Britzman (Chapter 16) cautions that sexuality resists symbolization and, thus, offers a way to read the wide variability in scholars' approaches to describing sexual development. The restless turn to various theoretical frameworks – sexual script theory, psychoanalysis, Foucault and discourse analysis, new materialist theory, dynamical systems theory, and figural and relational sociology – is evident in this volume. It is also, in part, a symptom of the difficulty of describing sexuality. As researchers of sexual development, a rigorous theoretical pluralism is necessary to understanding sexuality and development – experiences that are always on the move.

How Do We Study Sexuality?

Debates about the origins, meanings, and reach of sexuality raise a methodological question: How do we know what we know about sexual development? Historically, sexual development has been studied through psychological methods. As the history of psychology has shown, the framing of research – in other words, what is to be researched and what questions are to be answered – is an exercise in illuminating some areas and obscuring others, and, as a result, Jerome Kagan (2017) writes, the study of human development is still seriously constrained. McClelland echoes this cry in her chapter (Chapter 14), warning that power circumscribes the questions that can be asked and the discursive context that frames the objects of study and the production of knowledge. While recognizing the debt to psychological studies of human development, the chapters in this volume, taken together, make an argument for an interdisciplinary approach that draws on the theoretical strengths of the social sciences. Theories of sexual development are necessarily also theories of sociology, language, culture, and education. The chapters in this section of the volume show how the debates and methodological commitments of different disciplines contribute to an expansive and variegated understanding of sexual development.

Researching children and adolescents' sexual development is challenging for a number of reasons. Being curious about young people's sexualities carries risks for the researcher's reputation and professional standing (Fahs et al., 2017; Irvine, 2014). In her chapter, Bhana recounts the scrutiny and rejection her research encountered when she sought permission to study young people and LGBTQ sexuality in South Africa. Institutional review boards, especially, become professional gatekeepers that can be hostile to sexuality research (Allen, 2009). Russell's case study of advocacy for an LGBT-inclusive curriculum considers other roadblocks and the paths around them (Chapter 17). He shows the way building coalitions can bridge research and policy to promote proactive and positive practice. Fields and Garcia (Chapter 15) approach this issue from another angle. They argue that by recognizing love as a methodological stance and as the connection between adults and youth, sexuality research can move beyond an exclusive concern with risk and danger.

Even after receiving institutional permission to study the sexualities of young people, researchers may meet other obstacles. How will we invite children and youth to share their sexual thoughts, feelings, and experiences with us? The questions we ask, and the methods we choose, can shape what stories, feelings, and experiences we hear. The empirical studies represented in this volume wrestle with this question. As Lamb, White, and Plocha (Chapter 1) write in their survey of research on children's sexuality: "Sexual behavior tends to be carried out in private and thus is difficult to study. This is particularly true of childhood sexual behavior. Do we ask children? Do we ask their parents and teachers? Do we ask adults for their foggy or clear memories of childhood sexual practices?" The chapters that draw on interviews hold on to the promise that listening to individuals define, frame, and narrate their experiences will provide scholars with ample material to tease out the norms, discourses, and practices that structure ideas and experiences of sexuality. Lamb, White, and Plocha make clear the difficulty of asking children about their sexual play and games, while pointing to the limitations constraining what we learn about childhood sexuality by interviewing adults about their early experiences. Including young people's voices in qualitative research is a powerful approach, particularly in the realm of sex, sexuality, and sex education. And yet our contributors disagree with regard to what extent these voices are taken at face value. Even those youth who speak openly about their sexuality and sexual behavior are constrained by ideologies reproduced in their conversations. The young women in Bay-Cheng's research embrace a neoliberal discourse of choice when describing the constraining circumstances of their sexual lives, and the teen couple in Naezer and Ringrose's chapter reproduce a discourse of harm about online relationships, even when it was clear that their own online relationship contradicted this discourse.

Some contributors see method as crucial to what can and can't be said – that is, how we study sexual development will determine what we learn from children and adolescents about their sexualities. MacEntee and Flicker, for instance, wonder if participatory visual research methods will open up spaces for young people to reflect on their sexual identities in new ways. McClelland stretches the boundaries of research norms, asking investigators to use self-anchored ladders to study the marginalia of surveys to thicken survey design, and to bring back the classic Q method that asks participants to share and sort their feelings. These strategies uncover adaptations to injustice in the sexual lives of teens. Fields and Garcia's embrace of love in research provides a critique of "adultist" assumptions about young people's sexualities, as well as adultist assumptions about what they are willing to share. These researchers all see the relationship between researcher and participant as the context in which knowledge in sexuality research is both constrained and co-created.

Research about sexual development might always be constrained by a risk and danger perspective – the same perspective that constrains education. That is why, in Part III, we take care to balance chapters about how adults can address the risks awaiting young people with those that show how adults can play a part in welcoming a new discourse about sexuality.

What Roles Might Adults Play in the Sexual Development of Children and Adolescents?

From topics ranging from childhood innocence to heterosexual teen desire; from the sexualization of girls to the challenges of coming out as gay, sexual development often poses a problem for children and adolescents, and, by extension, for the adults in their lives. The chapters in this volume suggest adults have a strong role to play in children's and adolescents' development. However, we present this claim as a question – a question that comes up most concretely in debates about sexuality education but is implicit as well in research on institutions, including the families, media, and schools. What do children and adolescents need from adults as they grow up as sexual beings? And, just as crucially, what do adults need from children and adolescents in the name of "healthy" sexual development?

In many chapters, we meet the relational dependence that children and adolescents have on adults, including their parents. Gilbert (2014), playing with D. W. Winnicott's famous observation that "there is no such thing as a baby," argues, "there is no such thing as an adolescent. If you show me an adolescent, you certainly also show me parents, teachers, friends, peer groups, school, police, the fashion industry, the media, the mall, and so on" (p. 34). The sexual development of children and adolescents occurs in relation to adults, both because adults have themselves passed through childhood and adolescence, and because those same adults now bear responsibility for supporting young people who are in the midst of that transition.

This relational interdependence is reflected in chapters that place children's perspectives alongside their parents'. Ussher, Hawkey, and Perz find that menstrual stigma and the virginity imperative influence the way adolescent girls move in, feel, and live in their bodies, particularly when these constructions of sexuality are endorsed by their mothers. In Robinson and Davies' chapter (Chapter 3), parents' engagement with public discourses about children's sexuality affects their children's access to sexual knowledge and circumscribes the accounts of developing sexuality that children give. Some of the girls who experience early-onset puberty in Roberts' chapter (Chapter 24) appeared largely indifferent, as of yet, by their mothers' concerns, but will no doubt be affected over time by age- and biology-inspired norms that label some "on time" and others "off."

Questions of adult conceptualizations, involvement, trespass, and/or support come up explicitly across chapters that debunk myths about childhood innocence. These chapters unpack the idea that children have no sexuality of their own and that sexuality, when it arrives either through cultural representations, adult interference, or puberty, corrupts the purity of the child. Moore urges us to look at the lived sexualities of children at the micro level against the backdrop of policies and dominant constructions of their sexuality. Jarkovská and Lamb show how, in Slovakia, this myth has been put into the service of conservative movements to limit school-based sexuality education and oppose the civil and human rights of LGBTQ communities. Queer and trans sexualities are understood as especially corrosive to suggestable children and conservative backlash against LGBTQ rights is often done "in the name of the child" and in the name of one's country. If the child is innocent, then the adults' role is to protect that innocence against the premature emergence of a mature sexuality. However, these challenges to the discourse of childhood innocence have limits – Bhatasara, Chiweshe, and Muparamoto describe child "marriage" in Zimbabwe as an outcome of a rigidly patriarchal society that refuses to grant young girls a period of innocence, and, instead, perpetuates gender inequalities through practices like child unions.

However, as Jarkovská and Lamb argue in their chapter on childhood sexuality, when we critique the construction of childhood innocence, we are left with a problem – how can we describe our responsibility to protect children from harm without recourse to this conservative idea? They introduce the idea of vulnerability. If discourses of innocence demand that adults see children as empty, unsullied, or pure, the turn to vulnerability asks adults to consider how children, by virtue of their unequal position, their developing capacities, and their biological differences are vulnerable – both because they have less power than adults but also because they are developmentally different and some differences in some contexts make individuals vulnerable.

Turning our attention to adolescents, this idea of vulnerability is equally compelling. Young people are vulnerable because they navigate their sexual development through unequal relations of power with adults and through unequal gender relations. The developmental work of adolescence in numerous cultural contexts makes the transition from adolescence to adulthood risky. Some of the authors in this volume imagine a sexual adolescence that is free, empowering, and healthy, while at the same time describing the social and institutional challenges to making that emancipated sexuality a reality. For example, Bay-Cheng points out that the discourse of neoliberalism makes adolescents responsible for making "good choices," but argues that this way of conceptualizing autonomy releases adults and societies both from their responsibility for the supposedly "bad choices" and from setting up institutions and structures that support the so-called good choices. We hear in this discourse, as well, the "adultism" that Fields and Garcia speak of, a voice of control and judgment rather than affection and love. Wilkins and Limburg also look closely at the idea of "choice," which at first glance appears to support empowered, autonomous, sexual young people. The participants they study are heterosexual college students who make choices to opt in or out of hookup culture. Wilkins and Limburg claim that these choices aren't made in a vacuum, rather, they carry with them differential consequences dependent on gender and class. Tolman and Chmielewski mourn the concept of the empowered young women who accesses "the power of the erotic," a concept so powerfully and originally expressed by Audre Lorde. They show that today there is a renovated sexual double standard that renders teen women who have sex – the wrong kind of sex, too much sex, and too much of the wrong kind of sex – as "excessive" and, once again, "sluts."

The contributors who tackle the complexities of media in young people's lives conceptualize children and youth as both consumers and producers, navigating the real and virtual worlds of traditional media, pornography, and social media. These chapters focus on risk, but also on representation. Chou and Taylor, through their interview participants, draw attention to the exotification of Asian women and the castration of Asian men via media constructions of their sexuality. Coy and Horvath bring the questions of risk and representation to bear on their investigation of how young people are influenced by pornography, arguing that, while many young people turn to porn to satisfy their curiosity about sex, they are also affected by its rigidly heteronormative and sexist scripts. In their depiction of the porn industry's profit model, Johnson and Bridges (Chapter 22) remind the reader of the pecuniary connections between media and its consumers, and provide an unexpected example of how adults influence what kinds of access to knowledge teens do have. Exploring the complexities and contradictions that social media present for young people, Naezer and Ringrose rescue "media" from the risk and danger discourse to show the way a romance develops online, receptive and resistant to the available discourses of risk, intimacy, and sexuality.

Adults, of course, play a role in the sex education of children and adolescents, but together our chapters raise the question of whether sexuality can be educated? (Britzman, 1998) While most chapter authors would argue yes, the complications and roadblocks – and the difficulty in pinning a definition/meaning to sexuality – make this an impossible task, or at least one that can be undertaken only under the heavy burden of culture, country, policy, and politics. Sexuality education carries with it a sense of precarity – sexual development can easily go "wrong" depending on who is observing it, especially for young women, youth of color, and LGBTQ youth. This sense of precariousness, perhaps, is not something that is felt by individual children or adolescents but circulates around them, through social institutions, ideologies, and communities. What is the function of education then? Sex education has been criticized in the past for reproducing the *status quo* – a pitfall that contemporary research shows is difficult to escape. In Sweden, argue Bredström, Bolander, and Bengtsson, the sexually liberal norms endorsed by the country's progressive sexuality education curriculum create pressure to conform to a certain framework of sexuality. Rasmussen and Neary (Chapter 28) take up the idea that a teen pregnancy prevention program using robot babies could have unlikely and unbidden effects, increasing young peoples' respect for teen parents and normalizing a role they were warned against. This turn is one sex education theorists hope for, that the unpredictability of adolescents, and the emotional responses to sex education bring about a potential for sex education to be a space of transformation, resistance, and sexual agency.

The Context for Sexual Development

We began this introduction speaking about the internationality of this volume, but, in actuality, most of our chapters describe culture and context. Many chapter authors ask the reader to keep in mind the policies and politics that limit what can be known and what can be studied, to understand discourses of childhood innocence and adolescent excess in the context of nation and citizenship, laws that interfere with the rights of LGBT individuals, policies around marriage and sex education, gender inequality, and sexual violence. Within these national, social, and legal contexts, schools, especially, through programs, classes, and cultures of hookups or sexual harassment, provide their own context for learning. Media, too, is an ever-changing context that is both controlled and controlling when we consider the influences on developing sexuality and continues to cross borders, sharing solutions to restrictions around sexual development and new problems.

We offer these chapters not as a summary of canonical work in sexual development but as cross-conversations on questions that remain urgent. The brilliance of the chapters, in our opinion, lie in the way our authors take long standing questions and provide clever and creative approaches and ways of thinking about sexual development. We hope that educators will use these chapters to stimulate classroom conversations that go beyond the *status quo*, and to free new scholars to take up these questions in their own original ways that push the boundaries. From the ignoring of sex in childhood to the policing of sex in adolescence, from the sexual play and games in the early years to the hookups in college, from the campaigns for innocence to the campaigns to rule out inclusive sex education, there is much need for advocacy. But there is also a need for open, generous, and affectionate support to children and youth as we cast their experiences in research, scholarly writing, and volumes, like ours, that are yet to come.

References

Allen, L. (2009). "Caught in the Act": Ethics Committee Review and Researching the Sexual Culture of Schools. *Qualitative Research*, *9*(4), 395–410.

(2014). Pleasure's Perils? Critically Reflecting on Pleasure's Inclusion in Sexuality Education. In Allen, L., Rasmussen, M. L., & Quinlivan, K. (Eds.), *The Politics of Pleasure in Sexuality Education: Pleasure Bound*. London: Routledge.

Angelides, S. (2004). Feminism, Child Sexual Abuse, and the Erasure of Child Sexuality. *GLQ: A Journal of Lesbian and Gay Studies*, *10*(2), 141–177.

Britzman, D. P. (1998). *Lost Subjects, Contested Objects: Toward a Psychoanalytic Inquiry of Learning*. Albany: State University of New York Press.

Egan, D. & Hawkes, G. (2008). Imperiled and Perilous: Exploring the World of Childhood Sexuality. *Journal of Historical Sociology*, *21*(4), 355–367.

Ethier, K. A., Kann, L., & McManus, T. (2018). Sexual Intercourse among High School Students – 29 States and United States Overall, 2005–2015. *MMWR. Morbidity and Mortality Weekly Report*, *66*(5152), 1393.

Fahs, B., Plante, R. F., & McClelland, S. I. (2017). Working at the Crossroads of Pleasure and Danger: Feminist Perspectives on Doing Critical Sexuality Studies. *Sexualities*, *21*(4), 503–519.

Fine, M. (1988). Sexuality, Schooling, and Adolescent Females: The Missing Discourse of Desire. *Harvard Educational Review*, *58*(1), 29–53.

Gilbert, J. (2014). *Sexuality in School: The Limits of Education*. Minneapolis, MN: University of Minnesota Press.

Gittins, D. (1998). *The Child in Question*. New York: St. Martin's Press.

Irvine, J. M. (2014). Is Sexuality Research "Dirty Work"? Institutionalized Stigma in the Production of Sexual Knowledge. *Sexualities*, *17*(5–6), 632–656.

Kagan, J. (2017). *Five Constraints on Predicting Behavior*. Cambridge, MA: MIT Press.

Kincaid, J. R. (1998). *Erotic Innocence: The Culture of Child Molesting*. Durham, NC: Duke University Press.

Lamb, S. (2010). Feminist Ideals of Healthy Female Adolescent Sexuality: A Critique. *Sex Roles*, *62*, 294–306.

Quinlivan, K. (2014). "What's Wrong with Porn?" Engaging with Contemporary Painting to Explore the Commodification of Pleasure in Sexuality Education. In Allen, L., Rasmussen, M. L., & Quinlivan, K. (Eds.), *The Politics of Pleasure in Sexuality Education: Pleasure Bound* (78–94). London: Routledge.

Tolman, D. L. (2004). *Dilemmas of Desire: Teenage Girls Talk about Sexuality*. Cambridge, MA: Harvard University Press.

PART I

What Is Sexual Development?

Children

1 Are Children Sexual?

Who, What, Where, When, and How?

Sharon Lamb, Lindsey White, and Aleksandra Plocha

One of the most important criticisms of sex education initiatives, media reports about the sexualization of childhood, and government policies around childhood is that there is a presumption not only that children are inherently innocent, but also that they are not sexual (Egan & Hawkes, 2008; Hawkes & Egan, 2008; Robinson, 2013). That is, the presumption of childhood innocence is accompanied by, or supported by, a belief that sexual feelings, thoughts, activities, and preferences are exclusive to adulthood and are not common among, or appropriate for, children. Critics of an approach to childhood that conflates innocence with a lack of sexuality argue that children are indeed sexual, but rarely explain how, or they reduce the way they are sexual to examples of heteronormativity in children's talk of having "boyfriends and girlfriends" or making sexually harassing statements (Renold, 2007; Robinson, 2013; Robinson & Davies, 2015). Critics do this in order to make a point about heteronormativity of childhood discourse, and to show how the concept of innocence is used in an anti-LGBT conservative (Fischel, 2016; Robinson, 2013) or a racist agenda (Bernstein, 2010; Fields, 2012). But in so doing, they also reduce children's sexuality to something that seems to have very little to do with sex at all. Finally, those critics who aim to preserve sex and sexuality against protectionist claims almost always focus on adolescents or pre-adolescents (Renold et al., 2015) and thus unwittingly support the idea that children (individuals below the age of 11 or 12 years) are not sexual. They have simply moved the mark between innocence and knowingness down on a chronological developmental timeline, but kept the distinction.

But children are sexual, in almost every way that adults are sexual. One would never say that because children's cognitive capacities are different from adults, that they do not have them or that their cognitive capabilities are only developing. From the perspective of the child, they think, consider, question, and analyze, and the capacities of children at any particular age vary widely. Sexually, children have sexual feelings and desires. They have some sexual knowledge, depending on what they have seen of others, watched on screens, learned from other children, or participated in with others. The vast majority of children do not have sexual intercourse or bring other children to orgasm, thus drawing a distinct line between certain adult behaviors that represent being sexual, but some have found the pleasure of masturbation and some have had experiences in which they have touched other children and other children have touched them for sexual pleasure. We present this research later in this chapter.

When adults argue that children are innocent asexuals or that children have rights, they may at heart agree on one thing, that children are vulnerable, that children need protection. For the more conservative "childhood innocence" proponents, this is protection from corruption – the corrupting influence of sex. For those who would argue against their innocence, it is a need for protection from those who would deny children their rights to sex and sexuality. Both, are interested in protecting children from potentially exploitative adults, even if they see potential exploitation in different kinds of adults.

In this chapter, we review theories and research about childhood sexuality to affirm that children's sexuality not only exists but is an important organizing aspect of their emotional lives. We argue that children's sexualities may be different but as complex and complete as those of adults. Taking into account children's difference from adults, in terms of development and life experience, we attempt to disentangle innocence and (a)sexuality, and to argue for a resurrection of childhood innocence in the form of vulnerability. This perspective is in tension with an orientation toward childhood that conflates innocence with asexuality.

Surely protecting children from exploitation is a good thing. But Foucault (1978) warned of the growth of institutions to regulate and also of professionals who surveil childhood sexuality, adult experts who have expertise about behavioral norms and the circumstances around which knowledge about sex should be shared with children. As a result of this expert culture, any acknowledgment of children's sexual desires and behaviors is connected to an ideology around normativity and presented within a discourse of risk and prevention.

While advocates for a view of childhood that includes sexuality argue for children's and adolescents' right to a quality sex education and to pursue their preferences and interests, what is left undiscussed is what children do with their sexual feelings, thoughts, relationships, and behaviors. Is it unsavory or does it seem "perverted" to focus on the sexual lives of children except when such talk is medicalized or biologized? Perhaps. But in this chapter, we review some of the literature, from the biological to the sociological, that attempts to understand how and to what extent children are sexual beings, with an ear toward the kinds of discourses that make talking about children and sex permissible.

How do we capture the sexual diversity (diversity in thoughts, feelings, and behaviors) inherent to developing children's sexuality? From a postmodern perspective, which contextualizes norms within ideologies and histories of sexualities, how do we also keep the child central in our theorizing? While it is difficult to do research with children themselves on their sexual thoughts, feelings, fantasies, observations, and behaviors, we can look at studies of those who have observed and talked with children. And we can look at what has been deemed problematic in order to figure out the underlying "normal" it opposes.

Before looking at the actual research on childhood sexuality and childhood "abnormal" sexuality, we review theories of childhood sexuality. We then comment on the methods used to study childhood sexuality before presenting the empirical research. Following the empirical research we present narratives of childhood sexual experiences that speak to both the presence and complexity of childhood sexuality within childhood relationships. We finally look at influences on childhood sexuality, the world around children that shapes the form their sexuality takes. In the end, we hope to preserve the idea of childhood vulnerability but do away with the notion of innocence.

Theories of Childhood Sexuality

The biological perspective of childhood turns to hormones as the drivers of sexual development (Buchanan et al., 1992) and sexual identity (Bailey et al., 2000; Byne, 2007). The longstanding myth of the suddenly sexual adolescent relies on our understanding of the influx of hormones around age 11 or 12 years, which purportedly draws a line between childhood and adult sexuality. If hormones bestow an adult or adult-like sexuality to adolescents, within this theory any childhood sexuality will be seen as abnormal or "just play," "experimentation," and "practice" (Lamb, 2002; 2006).

Freud was interested in the biological aspects of sexuality but connected early sexuality to drives that made certain areas, according to development and an interaction with social and environmental demands, erogenous zones. Freud developed his Theory of Psychosexual Stages (Freud, 1976 [1905]) in which infants cathect various parts of the body connected to their relationships with their parents and others (the mouth when nursing; the anus during toilet training). Within his early Drive Theory, this concept of cathexis was a way to explain that energy from instinctual drives powered that investment in the particular body part for each phase of development. In early Freudian theory, early childhood was a particularly sexual period, as all human beings are born with sexual and aggressive drives to control. And during the development of the ego, the period Freud called "latency," there is a resting place, a time of relief from drives that prepares individuals for puberty and a return of the sexual drive in full force. There have been various critiques and reshapings of this theory, with particular attention to the idea that "latency" may be a way of explaining a period where sexual feelings are not permitted in families and in the culture (Friedrich et al., 1991; Lamb, 2002, 2006; Okami et al., 2002).

The ego psychologists who followed and built on Freudian theory, as well as the interpersonal group, and object relations theorists who also followed Freud all de-emphasized sexuality (Erikson, 1966; Flanagan, 2011). They emphasized the ways cultural context produces differences and relationships. Even more recent child analysts don't fully revive the idea of the sexual child. In their focus on children's development of a sense of self in relationship, any arousal or sexual experience is associated with whatever affect a caregiver bestows on such experiences. That is, sex and sexuality is defined in relationship with the mother. For example, Fonagy

(2008) and Fonagy and Target (2006) note in their observations that mothers ignore a baby's arousal, which may lead to a kind of sexual development in which a child will not understand this experience in relationship or fully integrate it into a self-state.

Another important theory of sexuality, Foucault's, found Freud to be treating sexuality as its own agent, with its own power, independent of whatever institutional power shapes and deploys it (Foucault, 1978). As Dorfman writes, for Foucault "power precedes sexuality" and sexuality is only one instance of power (2010, p. 158). Foucault also criticized psychoanalytic theory for not seeing its own discourse in the service of a regulating force, in its "dividing practice" of separating normal from pathological. Well-known analysts in the 1950s and 1960s saw homosexuality as pathological (Milchman & Rosenberg, 2018).

Foucauldian theory is used by many to understand power, normalization, and a hegemonic construction of childhood (Foucault, 1978). Looking at childhood sexuality in its historical context, Foucault showed how an analysis of discourse about sex, including the psychoanalytic discourse, can reveal ideology, ethics, and norms. Norms regulate what childhood sexuality is and isn't and are a part of a surveillance system that supports the status quo and "truth claims" about childhood sexuality. Discourse reveals ethics and ideology of the time (Foucault, 1978). Sexual pleasure "shorn of disguise" (1980, p. 191), according to Foucault, was one way in which individuals can escape the omnipresent press from institutions that regulate our being.

With regard to children in particular, he was concerned with three kinds of regulatory experiences: the institutions and concomitant discourses that imagine the child as an innocent in need of protection; the medical establishment that defined trauma and predicts harm; and whatever discourses encourage the self-surveillance around sexuality, pleasure, danger, and harm. His view is that childhood is managed – not only by parents but by society – and only pleasure can undo the ways in which sexuality is regulated (Foucault, 1978). In some ways, this conclusion echoes the complaint that ends Freud's *Civilization and Its Discontents* (1930), that society (through the superego), and self (through the ego), will never give permission for pleasure to reign.

Foucauldian discourse theory, which sees the regulation of sexuality implicit in ideologies, discourses, and institutions, doesn't exactly show the mechanism through which norms are internalized. Feminists Firth and Kitzinger (2007) took up Sexual Script Theory, which helps to explain the social construction of sex. It is a social learning theory developed by Gagnon and Simon (1973). Sexual Script Theory sees individuals as learning from observing and presents one view of how children learn what makes up sex, how one is sexual, and what one does when sexual. This kind of theory seems to apply to adolescents and young adults, given that there are no examples of sexual scripts for children in this literature. Guessing how script theory might be applied to childhood, it is possible to see children's play as repeating the adult sexual scripts they pick up through observation (Lamb & Coakley, 1993).

Pleasure and freedom are taken up by the field of anthropology, which has offered a view of childhood sexuality as culturally specific. Margaret Mead's (1961) study of a sexually free society, where the transition to adolescent sexuality is simple and not stormy, raised awareness in the 1960s that the way adolescent sexuality is conceptualized is dependent on culture, authority, power, and fear. Anthropologist Gilbert Herdt (2006) raised questions about gender identity and sexual abuse in his famous study of ritualized oral sex performed by young boys on older adolescents and men in a culture in New Guinea. He discovered that hetero-normative masculinity, for that culture, was supported through what they saw as the passing of seed from men to young boys through fellatio. Other anthropologists have discussed the cultural variability around the globe (Janssen, 2002; Martinson, 1994).

Developmental psychologists rely on theories that integrate nature and nurture arguments, but no one theory is used to understand sexual development. Developmentalists look for change over time and thus theoretically are likely to find that childhood sexuality is different from adolescent sexuality, and that these differences are supported culturally and biologically. Developmentalists also tend to look for stages and transitions, although this is a bias of developmental psychologists that Kagan (1984) has written a great deal about.

Methods of Studying Childhood Sexuality

Sexual behavior tends to be carried out in private and thus is difficult to study. This is particularly true of childhood sexual behavior. Do we ask children? Do we ask their parents and teachers? Do we ask adults for their foggy or clear memories of childhood sexual practices? Earlier work Lamb (first author) carried out involved asking adult college students if they recalled a childhood sexual experience with another child, and other scholars have done the same (Lamb & Coakley, 1993; Leitenberg et al., 1989; Okami et al., 1997). Some researchers have surveyed parents and adults who work with children (Fitzpatrick et al., 1995; Friedrich et al., 1998; Thigpen, 2009). Of course, the adults can only report on what they see and what they see misses the stories, feelings, and emotional life that are integral to the sexual experience of a child. These observations by adults are also subject to interpretation. Is what they saw considered sexual or a sexual game to the child participating (de Graaf & Rademakers, 2011)? Surveys often focus on sex acts rather than sexual feelings or experiences, adding up how many children were observed undressing together or showing each other their genitals (Haugaard, 1996; Haugaard & Tilly, 1988) which are arguably not sexual acts at all. Retrospective studies by adults are rare and contain biases. In reading narratives of childhood sexual play in games, it is possible to worry that some may have reinterpreted memories of play into memories of abuse and *vice versa* (Lamb, 2002).

Interview studies have explored the meaning of childhood sexual experiences (de Graaf & Rademakers, 2011; Tebele, Nel, & Michaelides, 2013). When Lamb interviewed adult women about their own childhood sexual experiences, she tried to ask questions in such a way as to gain a deeper understanding of what could have been sexual. The questions aimed at understanding how the thoughts, feelings, and bodily experiences remembered and experienced at the time helped a person to categorize some experiences as sexual.

Some research on early childhood relies on observations (de Graaf & Rademakers, 2011). It is harder for younger children to keep secrets and hide sexual behavior from those responsible for their well-being. But when surveys or observational studies find that sexual behavior declines after the age of 5 or 6 years, the findings are suspicious. There are few ways to find out whether the behavior declines, or if it is done more secretly or shared less with adults.

Are Children Sexual?

In this section we review the empirical studies that examine how children are sexual, beginning with children's sexual interest. Studying sexuality in childhood is difficult, in part, because we don't know what counts as sexuality and to what extent our ideas about sexual innocence inform what we study. Is the sexuality of children different than adults? (Many of these studies appear to be motivated by researchers' desires to understand adult sexuality in its nascent forms.) Do the sexual meanings we attach to certain behaviors have similar meanings for children? (Similar meaning is taken for granted in a number of these.) And what role does our attachment to childhood innocence, as an ideology, play in the development of our research methods and in the analysis of the data?

John Money (1986), using sexual scripts theory, described "love maps" as a way of understanding preferences in childhood. While he claimed that love maps could occur as early as 8 years old, once again, this research is limited by what younger and older children can and will share. Other research was aimed at discovering the roots of same sex or heterosexual attraction and perhaps at arguing for a biological basis, as in the work of Herdt and McClintock (2007). They propose that there are two kinds of puberty. One has to do with the adrenal glands, and occurs between the ages of 6 and 10 years. The second and more familiar puberty has to do with gonad development and changes. Adrenal puberty stabilizes attraction by the age of 10 years. And if one were to look at the sexual preferences, processes, and rites around the world, one would see that the age of 10 years is an important turning point. Other sexual interest researchers appear to point to the same age. For example, one study of 137 males found their first same-sex attraction was between the ages of 9.27 and 10.66 years (Remafedi, Farrow, & Deisher, 1993), while another found same-sex attraction beginning around the age of 8 years, although 30 percent recalled this feeling before elementary school (Savin-Williams, 1995).

As noted earlier, sexual behavior is harder to report on, particularly in cultures in which there is presumed childhood innocence, which has come to mean asexuality. Some reports focus on arousal and masturbation. An early report by Kinsey and associates reported orgasms in infants (1953), and this was substantiated by Rutter (1971) almost 20 years later. And the fact that male infants have erections and female infants have vaginal lubrication has been taken as evidence that they may have sexual responsivity (DeLamater & Friedrich, 2002; Martinson, 1976, 1994). But are these responses sexual? To consider these responses to be sexual, however, is quite telling; furthermore, the very limitation of what constitutes physiological sexual response to these two, potentially arbitrary, genital responses betrays a bias with regard to what is meant by "sex." Children masturbate in toddlerhood on through childhood; research supports this finding (Friedrich et al., 1991; Friedrich et al., 1998). Children also try to look at others undressing (Friedrich et al., 1998), although, once again, it seems unclear whether this should "count" as sexual behavior. And this study showed that mothers with more education were more likely to report sexual behaviors and see them as normal. Another study of 2–12-year-old African American children showed similar findings as Friedrich et al. (1998) regarding sexual behavior throughout this age period, but lower levels of masturbation (Thigpen, 2009). This author argued masturbation was also less pronounced in African-American adults. Unlike Friedrich's predominantly white sample, in his sample, the frequency of sexual behavior didn't decline or become more covert over the 10 years studied (Thigpen, 2009).

If a study of childhood sexuality stopped at masturbation, it would indicate a bias against children's capacities for play, pleasure, relationship, and fantasy. Why should those capacities be components of adult sexuality and not childhood sexuality? Few studies, however, look at childhood play and researchers sometimes reduce their definition of sexual play to touching or "I'll show you mine if you show me yours." One study of 233 parents in Ireland found that 36 percent of their sample engaged in sexual play (Fitzpatrick, Deehan, & Jennings, 1995). One study identified sexual experiences between peers in common childhood games played across South African cultures (Tebele, Nel, & Michaelides, 2013). Participants consisted of 16 Zulu individuals who reported sexual experiences situated within the games of *undize* (hide and seek), *icekwa* (touch and run), and *khetha* (choose the one you like). While most of the participants did not disclose how old they were when playing these games, a female participant reported masturbating and touching peers' genitals at the age of 9 years, and a male participant reported that he began touching and kissing girls at the age of 7 years.

Same-sex play and games have been considered by some researchers as signs of early non-heterosexual preferences (Rutter, 1971), while Kinsey et al. (1953) dismissed it as casual. Rutter (1971) also dismissed same-sex play occurs as a "transient phase" or an isolated event in 1 of 4 children.

Some researchers choose to talk to children rather than survey the adults around them. In her study of 377 urban children aged 6–12, Pluhar et al. (2005 as cited in Pluhar, 2007) found that 17 percent of the children surveyed had played games that involved boys and girls hugging or kissing each other. Of 11–12 year olds, she found that 10 percent had "made out," 6 percent had touched a boy's penis, and 5 percent had touched a girl's vagina.

Other researchers ask adults to look back and tell us about their childhood sexual experiences. Haugaard's (1996) sample of 600 undergraduates completed a survey showing that 59 percent of them had at least one sexual experience with another child during childhood. Of these, 38 percent of these were before age seven, 39 percent between the ages of seven and ten, and 35 percent during ages eleven and twelve.

Focus groups of children have proved to be a useful method of observing what children know about sex and how they formulate this sexual knowledge (Davies & Robinson, 2010; Robinson & Davies, 2015). Researchers have initiated discussions with children using media images from sources such as magazines and children's storybooks that depict cultural representations of gender, love, kissing, marriage, and family (Davies & Robinson, 2010; Robinson & Davies, 2014). Even in a group of children as young as 3–5 years old, children attempted to collaborate with peers to fill in knowledge gaps about sexuality and continued to independently assemble fragmented information into coherent narratives, with the resulting narratives often based in myth or partial truths (Davies & Robinson, 2010). The children's discussion also revealed that parents were often inaccurate in assessing their children's broad sexual understanding, sometimes by overestimating a child's ability to interpret relationships (e.g., misidentifying gay partners as friends), but more often by underestimating the amount of sexual knowledge that their child has gleaned from peers and media (Davies & Robinson, 2010).

This author, in Lamb and Coakley (1993) asked 128 undergraduate women specifically about different kinds of sexual play. In their study, 85 percent had played some sexual game in childhood and a quarter of these had shown their genitals to another child, 15 percent had touched another child's genitals while clothed, 17 percent while unclothed, 6 percent had used some object around the genitals in their play, and 4 percent had engaged in mouth-genital contact. The authors also asked about bullying (persuasion, manipulation, and coercion) and found that for these women, cross-gender play was more likely to involve persuasion, manipulation, and/or coercion.

As there is coercion and bullying in other kinds of children's play, one could expect there would also be some in sexual play. In one study of undergraduates' recollections, it was found that when there was coercion, predictably, the sexual play experience was less positive. But these findings also revealed that the kind of sex involved had little to do with how pleasurable or positive the experience was. If an experience involved genitals, it was neither more nor less positive, and thus the atmosphere of the play and, perhaps, the mutuality of it, was most related to how positive an experience it was (Haugaard & Tilly, 1988). And with regard to sexual play and games affecting long-term sexual adjustment, no correlation has been found (Leitenberg et al., 1989; Okami et al., 1997).

Research is thus particularly difficult with children, given we don't know what really counts as sexuality and use our adult perspectives and limited observations to make decisions about what to include and what not to include. We do not know if the sexual meanings we attach to certain behaviors have similar meanings for children nor what role our beliefs about childhood innocence, as an ideology, play in the development of our methods or in the analysis of data.

Sexual Stories from Childhood

Given the difficulties of empirically studying childhood sexuality, some researchers have collected narratives from adults about their childhood sexual experiences. More than a decade ago Lamb interviewed more than 100 women about their sexual experiences and sexual play and game experiences in childhood. These ranged from "chase and kiss," "I'll show you mine if you show me yours," and "playing doctor," games that individual women interviewed considered "normal," to games concerning Barbie dolls and games that mimicked adult experiences like playing "house," "school" with a sexual twist, going to a nightclub, or even pretending to be prostitutes. Individual women interviewed had a range of feelings about these games. Most of the stories of sexual play were with other girls, which troubled some adult heterosexual women; some recall couching same-sex play in heterosexual narratives, "You be the boy and I'll be the girl."

One of the important findings of this set of interviews was that the type of play seemed unrelated to the amount of guilt a woman held about that play at the time, when she was a girl, or later as an adult. That is, what many would consider an innocent story (e.g., of kissing) and what many would consider a more sexual story (e.g., involving genitals) seemed not to be related to how much guilt the woman expressed. The stories also revealed that children had sexual feelings of arousal – feelings that researchers had been wary to discuss or track earlier. For example, one woman described the "thrill" when she and a cousin slept together, pulled up their nightgowns, and touched bottom to bottom (butt to butt). Another woman recalled laying down on the floor, pretending to be a glamorous dead woman clad in a slip, an image she had seen appearing in her grandfather's detective magazines. When her cousins, playing at being detectives, entered a room to find her lying dead there, she reported being overcome with sexual feelings. In the interviews, participants conveyed sexual feelings through the following kinds of remarks: "We did wondrous things with her," "It was very thrilling," "It was titillating and fun … it was a feeling," and "It was very, you know, intoxicating … very arousing" (Lamb, 2004, p. 378). Some simply remarked, "I think I got sexually excited" (Lamb, 2004, p. 378).

Who could deny these feelings as sexual experiences of childhood even though what many adults call sex was clearly absent? The adult women also appeared confused about whether these experiences were sexual or "just play"; however, when any arousal was involved, they tended to worry that what they experienced was sex and that it was more adult-like with the presumption that children shouldn't feel those feelings.

I analyzed the feelings of guilt that many individuals spoke about in the interviews. Women seemed more likely to express guilt if there was arousal during the game, calling arousal "adult-like" or "more like a boy." Girls who experienced arousal saw themselves as quite different from other girls, stating the belief that girls were not supposed to be sexual or so actively sexual. They used words like "very bizarre" and made statements like, "I was a girl and I shouldn't want that." When a girl was more assertive in the play she would especially see herself as strange or male.

Outside of my research on the stories of childhood sexual play and games, very few researchers have looked at the nature of childhood sexual experiences with other children. One exception is Tebele et al. who also collected adults' recountings of childhood sexual games played with peers (Tebele et al., 2013) in the broader examination of early childhood sexual experiences. They found that adults reported experiences of kissing and touching as young as 7–9 years old. Of course, the age at which anything is remembered to have occurred is subject to distortions of memory and, in fact, difference in memory abilities at different ages.

There are few narratives of boys' sexual play and games. If boys are studied, it has been in the context of exploring histories of those who have gotten in trouble for sexual acting out (Flanagan, 2010) or are interested in hegemonic masculinity as it is expressed in boyhood (Cohan, 2009). Emma Renold examined how boys aged 10–11 years "performed" masculine sexuality at school and noted the way they publicize heterosexual relationships, harass girls, and talk publicly about sex (Renold, 2007). But these studies about boys appear to focus more on the way boys perform their gender roles rather than on their experience of sexuality as children.

Special Topics Relating to Childhood Sexual Development

Parental Influence on Development of Sexuality

While it is often assumed that peers have a great deal of influence on children's sexuality, it is important to explore parents and family members as well (Martin et al., 2007). Some scholars research parental communication (DiIorio et al., 2003; Grossman et al., 2016); however, few have explored sibling influence.

Studies indicate that many Americans believe parents ought to be the primary educators of children around sexuality (Pluhar et al., 2006), but parents do not tend to communicate with younger children, perhaps because they have been influenced by the notion of childhood innocence (DiIorio et al., 2003; Hutchinson & Cederbaum, 2011; Pluhar et al., 2008). When children reach middle-school ages, parents begin to communicate more (Byers et al., 2008). And those who have more liberal views toward sex education are likely to discuss topics in greater depth than those who do not (Byers et al., 2008). Those who became parents earlier in life are also more likely to communicate with their children about sex and to involve extended family in these discussions, perhaps in an attempt to diverge from their own experiences as adolescents who did not receive sufficient sex education in the home (Grossman et al., 2016). Mothers speak to daughters more than sons (Martin & Luke, 2010) about relationships, reproduction, and the morality of sexual behavior, but to both sons and daughters about abuse and pleasure. This mother–daughter communication has been considered to be a form of heterosexualization (Martin, 2009), including, not only information about sex, but primarily information about romance when speaking to their 3–6-year-old daughters. Fathers who discussed sex with their children generally discussed biology, delaying sex, and negative consequences (Wilson et al., 2010). Sons are more likely to be told to "have fun," whereas parental messages toward girls are more likely to promote abstinence, encourage being highly discriminatory in allocating sexual access, and to avoid and defend against sexual advances (Kuhle et al., 2014).

Few studies have explored the ways in which culture influences parental approaches to children's sexuality (Thigpen, 2012). Sociocultural factors should be considered given that most instances of child sexual behavior are observed and reported by caregivers. Thigpen (2012) suggested that African-American caregivers were less likely to report sexual behavior in their children due to awareness of historical patterns of perceptions of hypersexualization and pathologizing. Some research with Latino and Asian participants has indicated higher rates of implicit, indirect, or nonverbal parental messages, in contrast to Western pressures for open and direct communication (Raffaelli & Green, 2003; Wang, 2016). Wang (2016) argues that assessments of non-direct parent–child sexuality communication should focus on content rather than process in families in which direct parent-child communication is incongruent with cultural norms.

Sexual Abuse as an Influence on Childhood Sexuality

Too often those who study childhood and adolescent sexual development, exploring the potential for pleasure and agency, neglect to acknowledge the significant number of children who have experienced sexual harassment or abuse. This lack of interest among one set of researchers unwittingly supports another set seeking to discover the roots of problematic sexual behavior. "The vast majority of the extant research on sexuality and early childhood is tied to a social problem – childhood sexual abuse – while other aspects of sexuality in childhood are completely ignored" (Martin et al., 2007, p. 235). But there may not be such strong differences between sexually abused and non-sexually abused children and it is important to understand that the expectation of such may come from a belief that sexual abuse has damaged a child's innocence. Allen (2017) found that of those children with sexual behavior problems (SBPs), only 25 percent had been sexually abused. While children identified as having SBPs are more likely to have been sexually or physically abused as children (Letourneau et al., 2004), studies have repeatedly shown that many children with behavior problems have no known history of sexual abuse (Allen, 2017; Bonner et al., 1999; Friedrich et al., 2005; Hershkowitz, 2011;

Silvosky & Niec, 2002; Silvosky et al., 2007). Drach et al. (2001) found that of those children with SBPs, only 25 percent had been sexually abused.

There are also noted differences between the histories of children who sexually act out without involving other children and those whose actions are directed toward other children (i.e., interpersonal SBPs). A history of sexual abuse was found to be associated only with those children who sexually acted out without involving other children; experience of sexual abuse was not significantly associated with children who directed their SBPs toward others (Allen, 2017). Rather than sexual abuse, this latter group of children showed higher rates of physical abuse, posttraumatic stress, and externalizing behaviors (Allen, 2017). Thus, children who direct sexual behavior toward other children could be better understood as having a history of non-sexual trauma and general behavioral control problems.

Media Influences on Childhood Sexuality

Other chapters in this volume thoroughly describe media influences on children's sexuality; however, here it is important to point out that, while there is concern about the ways the media contributes to early sexualization, media also provides sex education. Children themselves interact with media, produce it, and have influence over it. Childhood sexuality *per se* is not depicted in media, but images and story lines that promote a way to be sexual when they are older lays the groundwork for heteronormativity and expectations of sexual harassment. Media also presents archetypes or stereotypes of sexual adults that children see, which inform them of ways to be sexual (Lamb & Brown, 2006). This is done through popular stars and musicians, lyrics, television, and movies.

Child SBPs

Children who haven't been sexually abused can show a wide range of what clinicians refer to as SBPs, ranging from compulsive masturbation to sexual coercion of other children (Chaffin et al., 2008). But children considered to have SBPs are a diverse group (St. Amand et al., 2008). They are not like adult sex offenders, nor are they likely to become them (Carpentier et al., 2006; St. Amand et al., 2008). They have experienced maltreatment or physical abuse, substandard parenting practices, exposure to sexually explicit media, and/or have lived in a highly sexualized environment (Friedrich et al., 2003; Hungerford et al., 2012; Lévesque et al., 2010; Waisbrod & Reicher, 2014). Showing a connection between trauma and SBPs, child behavior problems are positively associated with the severity and frequency of intimate partner violence events witnessed (Lieberman et al., 2005). Children who experience higher rates of traumatic events display higher levels of externalizing behavior problems (Grasso et al., 2013; Roberts et al., 2013), which can include interpersonal SBPs. Given the variety of sexual behaviors common to childhood, it might be better to see most children with SBPs as children with aggression or bullying problems who extend their behaviors to the sexual realm.

Conclusions

It is important to research children's sexuality for a number of reasons. The first pertains to documenting a sexual life of children so that the idea of childhood innocence can be supplanted with childhood vulnerability. We protect children because they have vulnerabilities, and not because they are sexual innocents damaged by exposure to adult sexual material. They are vulnerable in ways that are difficult to name without also evoking the Foucauldian notion of experts naming what is normal. And yet, children are not adults. They have, generally speaking, less cognitive abilities, less capacity to understand and manage their emotions, more fragile bodies, and different bodily abilities given their stage of development. The widespread idea that once a child has experienced sexual abuse, she or he is damaged for life, does considerable damage.

The second reason to document children's sexuality is to protect it. Children are entitled to play and explore in sexual ways if they do no harm to themselves and others. Research indicates that any harm that comes from sexual play and games has more to do with the child's perception that what they are doing is shameful or bad than from the play itself and from the way play reinforces gender stereotypes of passive females and boys always interested in sex.

There's plenty in adult sexuality that is problematic, but it is not the sex in and of itself. If children need protection from their own arousal or their exposure to adult sexuality, it is around that which is already a problem in the adult world: abuse, degrading porn, stereotypes, compulsive behaviors, lack of privacy, heteronormativity, disregard for bodies, objectification, and more. Studies of childhood sexuality from a protectionist perspective should focus on these kinds of harms rather than loss of innocence.

References

Allen, B. (2017). Children with Sexual Behavior Problems: Clinical Characteristics and Relationship to Child Maltreatment. *Journal of Child Psychiatry and Human Development*, *48*, 189–199. doi:10.1007/s10578-016–0633-8.

Bailey, J. M., Dunne, M. P., & Martin, N. G. (2000). Genetic and Environmental Influences on Sexual Orientation and Its Correlates in an Australian Twin Sample. *Journal of Personality and Social Psychology*, *78*, 3, 524–536.

Bernstein, R. (2010). *Racial Innocence: Performing American Childhood in Black and White*. New York: New York University Press.

Bonner, B. L., Walker, C. E., & Berliner, L. (1999). *Children with Sexual Behavior Problems: Assessment and Treatment. Final Report.* Washington DC: Administration of Children, Youth, and Families, DHHS.

Buchanan, C. M., Eccles, J. S., & Becker, J. (1992). Are Adolescents Victims of Raging Hormones? Evidence for Activational Effects of Hormones. *Psychological Bulletin, 111*, 62–107.

Byers, E. S., Sears, H., & Weaver, A. (2008). Parents' Reports of Sexual Communication with Children in Kindergarten to Grade 8. *Journal of Marriage and Family, 70*, 86–96.

Byne, W. (2007). Biology and Sexual Minority Status. In Meyer, I. H. & Northridge, M. E. (Eds.), *The Health of Sexual Minorities: Public Health Perspectives on Lesbian, Gay, Bisexual, and Transgender Populations* (65–90). New York: Springer.

Carpentier, M.Y., Silovsky, J. F., & Chaffin, M. (2006). Randomized Trial of Treatment for Children with Sexual Behavior Problems: Ten-Year Follow-Up. *Journal of Consulting and Clinical Psychology, 74*, 482–488.

Chaffin, M., Berliner, L., Block, R. et al. (2008). Report of the ATSA Task Force on Children with Sexual Behavior Problems. *Child Maltreatment, 13*(2), 199–218. doi:10.1177/1077559507306718.

Cohan, M. (2009). Adolescent Heterosexual Males Talk about the Role of Male Peer Groups in Their Sexual Decision-Making. *Sexuality & Culture, 13*, 152–177.

Davies, C. & Robinson, K. (2010). Hatching Babies and Stork Deliveries: Risk and Regulation in the Construction of Children's Sexual Knowledge. *Contemporary Issues in Early Childhood, 11*(3), 249–262.

de Graaf, H. & Rademakers, J. (2011). The Psychological Measurement of Childhood Sexual Development in Western Societies: Methodological Challenges. *Journal of Sex Research, 48*, 118–129.

DeLamater, J. & Friedrich, W. N. (2002). Human Sexual Development. *Journal of Sex Research, 39*(1), 10–14. doi:10.1080/00224490209552113.

DiIorio, C., Pluhar, E., & Belcher, L. (2003). Parent–Child Communication about Sexuality: A Review of the Literature from 1980–2002. *Journal of HIV/AIDS Prevention & Education for Adolescents & Children, 5*(3–4), 7–32. doi:10.1300/J129v05n03_02.

Dorfman, E. (2010). Foucault versus Freud: On Sexuality and the Unconscious. In Dorfman, E. & De Vlemnick, J. (Eds.), *Sexuality and Psychoanalysis: Philosophical Criticisms*, Leuven: Leuven University Press.

Drach, K. M., Wientzen, J., & Ricci, L. R. (2001). The Diagnostic of Sexual Behavior Problems in Diagnosing Sexual Abuse in a Forensic Child Abuse Evaluation Clinic. *Child Abuse & Neglect 25*, 489–503.

Egan, R. & Hawkes, G. (2008). Endangered Girls and Incendiary Objects: Unpacking the Discourse on Sexualization. *Sexuality & Culture, 12*(4): 291–311. doi:10.1007/s12119-008-9036-8.

Erikson, E. H. (1966). Eight Ages of Man. *International Journal of Psychiatry, 2*(3), 281–307.

Fields, J. (2012). Sexuality Education in the United States: Shared Cultural Ideas across a Political Divide. *Sociology Compass 6*(1), 1–14.

Firth, H. & Kitzinger, C. (2007). Reformulating Sexual Script Theory. *Theory and Psychology, 11*(2), 209–232.

Fischel, J. J. 2016. Pornographic Protections? Itineraries of Childhood Innocence. *Law, Culture and the Humanities 12* (2), 206–220. doi:10.1177/1743872113492396.

Fitzpatrick, C., Deehan, A., & Jennings, S. (1995). Children's Sexual Behaviour and Knowledge: A Community Study. *Irish Journal 0f Psychological Medicine*, *12*(3), 87–91.

Flanagan, L. M. (2011). Object Relations. In Berzoff, J., Flanagan, L. M., & Hertz, P. (Eds.), *Inside Out and Outside In: Psychodynamic Clinical Theory and Psychopathology in Contemporary Multicultural Contexts* (118–157). Lanham: Rowman & Littlefield.

Flanagan, P. (2010). Making Molehills into Mountains: Adult Responses to Child Sexuality and Behaviour. *Explorations: An E-Journal of Narrative Practice*, *1*, 57–69.

Fonagy, P. (2008). A Genuinely Developmental Theory of Sexual Enjoyment and Its Implications for the Psychoanalytic Technique. *Journal of the American Psychoanalytic Association*, *56*(1), 11–36. doi:10.1177/0003065107313025.

Fonagy, P. & Target, M. (2006). The Mentalization-Focused Approach to Self Pathology. *Journal of Personality Disorders*, *20*(6), 544–576.

Foucault, M. (1978). *The History of Sexuality.* New York: Pantheon Books.

(1980). *Power/Knowledge: Selected Interviews and Other Writings 1972–1977.* New York: Pantheon Books.

Freud, S. (1976 [1905]). *Three Essays on the Theory of Sexuality.* New York: Basic Books.

(1930). *Civilization and Its Discontents*. New York: W. W. Norton and Company, Inc.

Friedrich, W. N., Davies, W. H., Feher, E., & Wright, J. (2003). Sexual Behavior Problems in Preteen Children: Developmental, Ecological, and Behavioral Correlates. *Annals of the New York Academy of Sciences*, *989*, 95–104.

Friedrich, W., Fisher, J., Broughton, D., Houston, M., & Shafran, C. (1998). Mayo Clinic Study: Normative Sexual Behavior in Children: A Contemporary Sample. *Pediatrics*, *101*(4), e9.

Friedrich, W., Grambsch, P., Broughton D., Kuiper, J., & Beilke, R. (1991). Normative Sexual Behavior in Children. *Pediatrics*, *88*(3), 456–464.

Friedrich, W. N., Trane, S. T., & Gully, K. J. (2005). Letter to the Editor: Re: It Is a Mistake to Conclude that Sexual Abuse and Sexual Behavior Are Not Related. *Child Abuse and Neglect*, *29*, 97–302.

Gagnon, J. H. & Simon, W. (1973). *Sexual Conduct: The Social Sources of Human Sexuality.* Chicago: Aldine Pub. Co.

Grasso, D. J., Ford, J. D., & Briggs-Gowan, M. J. (2013). Early Life Trauma Exposure and Stress Sensitivity in Young Children. *Journal of Pediatric Psychology*, *38*, 94–103.

Grossman, J. M., Charmaraman, L., & Erkut, S. (2016). Do as I Say, Not as I Did: How Parents Talk with Early Adolescents about Sex. *Journal of Family Issues*, *37*(2), 177–197. doi:10.1177/0192513X13511955.

Hawkes, G. L. & Egan, R. D. (2008). Developing the Sexual Child. *Journal of Historical Sociology*, *21*, 443–465. doi:10.1111/j.1467-6443.2008.00345.x.

Haugaard, J. J. (1996). Sexual Behaviors between Children: Professionals' Opinions and Undergraduates' Recollections. *Families in Society*, *77*(2), 81–89.

Haugaard, J. & Tilly, C. (1988). Characteristics Predicting Children's Responses to Sexual Encounters with Other Children. *Child Abuse & Neglect*, *12*, 209–218.

Herdt, G. (2006). *The Sambia: Ritual, Sexuality, and Change in Papua New Guinea, 2nd edn.* Belmont, CA: Cengage Learning.

Herdt, G. & McClintock, M. (2007). The Magical Age of 10. In Tepper, M. S., Owens, A., Tepper, M. S., & Owens, A. (Eds.), *Sexual Health Vol. 1: Psychological Foundations* (183–203). Westport: Praeger Publishers/Greenwood Publishing Group.

Hershkowitz, I. (2011). The Effects of Abuse History on Sexually Intrusive Behavior by Children: An Analysis of Child Justice Records. *Child Abuse & Neglect*, *35*(1), 40–49.

Hungerford, A., Wait, S. K., Fritz, A. M., & Clements, C. M. (2012). Exposure to Intimate Partner Violence and Children's Psychological Adjustment, Cognitive Functioning, and Social Competence: A Review. *Aggression and Violent Behavior*, *1*, 373–382.

Hutchinson, M. & Cederbaum, J. A. (2011). Talking to Daddy's Little Girl about Sex: Daughters' Reports of Sexual Communication and Support from Fathers. *Journal of Family Issues*, *32*(4), 550–572. doi:10.1177/0192513X10384222.

Janssen, D. F. (2002). *Growing up Sexually: World Reference Atlas*. Retrieved from www2.hu-berlin.de/sexology/GESUND/ARCHIV/GUS/GUS_AFS.HTM.

Kagan, J. (1984). *The Nature of the Child*. New York: Basic Books.

Kinsey, A. C., Martin, C. E., Gebhard, P. H. et al. (1953). *Sexual Behavior in the Human Female*. Philadelphia: W.B. Saunders Co.

Kuhle, B. X., Melzer, D. K., Cooper, C. A. et al. (2014). The "Birds and the Bees" Differ for Boys and Girls: Sex Differences in the Nature of Sex Talks. *Evolutionary Behavioral Sciences*, *9*(2), 107–115. doi:10.1037/ebs0000012.

Lamb, S. (2002). *The Secret Lives of Girls: What Good Girls Really Do, Sex Play, Aggression, and Their Guilt*. New York: Free Press.

(2004). IV. Sexual Tensions in Girls' Friendships. *Feminism & Psychology*, *14*(3), 376-382.

(2006). *Sex, Therapy, and Kids: Addressing Their Concerns through Talk and Play.* New York: W. W. Norton & Co.

Lamb, S. & Brown, L. M. (2006). *Packaging Girlhood: Rescuing Our Daughters from Marketers' Schemes*. New York, NY: St. Martin's.

Lamb, S. & Coakley, M. (1993). Childhood Sexual Play and Games: Differentiating Play from Abuse. *Child Abuse and Neglect: the International Journal*, *17*(4), 515–26.

Leitenberg, H., Greenwald, E., & Tarran, M. J. (1989). The Relation between Sexual Activity among Children during Preadolescence and/or Early Adolescence and Sexual Behavior and Sexual Adjustment in Young Adulthood. *Archives of Sexual Behavior*, *18*(4), 299–313. doi:10.1007/BF01541950.

Letourneau, E. J., Schoenwald, S. K., & Sheidow, A. J. (2004). Children and Adolescents with Sexual Behavior Problems. *Child Maltreatment*, *9*(1), 49–61.

Lévesque, M., Bigras, M., & Pauzé, R. (2010). Externalizing Problems and Problematic Sexual Behaviors: Same Etiology? *Aggressive Behavior*, *36*, 358–370. doi:10.1002/ab.20362.

Lieberman, A. F., Van Horn, P., & Ozer, E. J. (2005). Preschooler Witnesses of Marital Violence: Predictors and Mediators of Child Behavior Problems. *Development and Psychopathology*, *17*, 385–396.

Martin, K. A. (2009). Normalizing Heterosexuality: Mothers' Assumptions, Talk, and Strategies with Young Children. *American Sociological Review, 74*(2), 190–207.

Martin, K. A. & Luke, K. (2010). Gender Differences in the ABC's of the Birds and the Bees: What Mothers Teach Young Children about Sexuality and Reproduction. *Sex Roles, 62*(3/4), 278–291.

Martin, K. A., Luke, K. P., & Verduzco-Baker, L. (2007). The Sexual Socialization of Young Children: Setting the Agenda for Research. In *Social Psychology of Gender* (231–259). Bingley: Emerald Group Publishing Limited.

Martinson, F. M. (1976). Eroticism in Infancy and Childhood. *Journal of Sex Research, 12*(4), 251–262. doi:10.1080/00224497609550945.

(1994). *The Sexual Life of Children*. Westport: Greenwood Publishing Group, Inc.

Mead, M. (1961). *Coming of Age in Samoa: A Psychological Study of Primitive Youth for Western Civilization*. New York: Morrow.

Milchman, M & Rosenberg, A. (2018) A Foucaultian analysis of psychoanalysis. *Accessed at* www.academyanalyticarts.org/milchman-foucauldian-analysis, Jan. 30, 2018.

Money, J. (1986). *Lovemaps: Clinical Concepts of Sexual/Erotic Health and Pathology, Paraphilia, and Gender Transposition in Childhood, Adolescence, and Maturity.* New York: Irvington.

Okami, P., Olmstead, R., & Abramson, P. R. (1997). Sexual Experiences in Early Childhood: 18-Year Longitudinal Data from the UCLA Family Lifestyles Project. *The Journal of Sex Research, 34*(4), 339–347.

Okami, P., Weisner, T., & Olmstead, R. (2002). Outcome Correlates of Parent–Child Bedsharing: An Eighteen-Year Longitudinal Study. *Journal of Developmental and Behavioral Pediatrics, 23*(4), 244–253.

Pluhar, E. (2007). Childhood Sexuality. In Tepper, M. & Owens, A. F. (Eds.), *Sexual Health Vol 1: Psychological Foundations* (155–181). Westport: Greenwood Publishing Group.

Pluhar, E., DiIorio, C., Jennings T., & Pines K. (2005). "Sexual possibility situations" and progressive heterosexual behaviors among children ages 6–12. Poster presented at the Annual Conference of the American Association of Sex Educators, Counselors and Therapists, May 10, 2005, Portland, OR.

Pluhar, E. I., DiIorio, C. K., & McCarty, F. F. (2008). Correlates of Sexuality Communication among Mothers and 6–12-Year-Old Children. *Child: Care, Health and Development, 34*(3), 283–290. doi:10.1111/j.1365-2214.2007.00807.

Pluhar, E., Jennings, T., & DiIorio, C. (2006). Getting an Early Start: Communication about Sexuality among Mothers and Children 6–10 Years Old. *Journal of HIV/AIDS Prevention in Children & Youth, 7*(1), 7–35. doi:10.1300/J499v07n01_02.

Raffaelli, M. & Green, S. (2003). Parent–Adolescent Communications about Sex: Retrospective Reports by Latino College Students. *Journal of Marriage and Family, 65*, 474–481.

Remafedi, G., Farrow, J. A., & Deisher, R. W. (1993). Risk Factors for Attempted Suicide in Gay and Bisexual Youth. In Garnets, L. D. & Kimmel, D. C. (Eds.), *Psychological Perspectives on Lesbian and Gay Male Experiences* (486–499). New York: Columbia University Press.

Renold, E. (2007). Primary School 'Studs': (De)constructing Young Boys' Heterosexual Masculinities. *Men and Masculinities, 9* (3), 275–297.

Renold, E., Danielle Egan, R., & Ringrose, J. 2015. Introduction. In Renold, E., Ringrose, J., & Danielle Egan, R. (Eds.), *Children, Sexuality and Sexualization* (1–21). Houndmills, Basingstoke: Palgrave Macmillan.

Roberts, Y. H., Ferguson, M., & Crusto, C. A. (2013). Exposure to Traumatic Events and Health Related Quality of Life in Preschool-Aged Children. *Quality of Life Research*, n22, 2159–2168.

Robinson, K. H. (2013). *Innocence, Knowledge and the Construction of Childhood: The Contradictory Nature of Sexuality and Censorship in Children's Contemporary Lives*. London: Routledge.

Robinson, K. H. & Davies, C. (2014). Doing Sexuality Research with Children: Ethics, Theory, Methods and Practice. *Global Studies of Childhood*, *4*(4), 250–263.

(2015). Children's Gendered and Sexual Cultures: Desiring and Regulating Recognition through Life Markers of Marriage, Love and Relationships. In Renold, E., Ringrose, J., & Egan, D. (Eds.), *Children, Sexuality and the 'Sexualisation of Culture* (174–190). London: Palgrave.

Rutter, M. (1971). Normal Psychosexual Development. *Journal of Child Psychology and Psychiatry*, *11*, 259–283.

Savin-Williams, R. C. (1995). An Exploratory Study of Pubertal Maturation Timing and Self-Esteem among Gay and Bisexual Male Youths. *Developmental Psychology*, *31*(1), 56–64. doi:10.1037/0012-1649.31.1.56.

Silovsky, J. F. & Niec, L. (2002). Characteristics of Young Children with Sexual Behavior Problems: A Pilot Study. *Child Maltreatment*, *7*, 187–197.

Silovsky, J. F., Niec, L., Bard, D., & Hecht D. B. (2007). Treatment for Preschool Children with Interpersonal Sexual Behavior Problems: A Pilot Study. *Journal of Clinical Child & Adolescent Psychology*, *36*(3), 378–391. doi:10.1080/15374410701444330.

St. Amand, A., Bard, D. E., & Silovsky, J. F. (2008). Meta-Analysis of Treatment For Child Sexual Behavior Problems: Practice Elements and Outcomes. *Child Maltreatment*, *13*(2), 145–166. doi:10.1177/1077559508315353.

Tebele, C., Nel, K. A, & Michaelides, M. J (2013). The Undize Phenomenon – South African Childhood Sex Games and Their Contributions to Early Sexual Experiences. *Journal of Psychology in Africa*, *23*(2), 323–326.

Thigpen, J. W. (2009). Early Sexual Behavior in a Sample of Low-Income, African American Children. *Journal of Sex Research*, *46*(1), 67–79. doi:10.1080/00224490802645286.

(2012). Childhood Sexuality: Exploring Culture as Context. In Carpenter, L. M. & DeLamater, J. (Eds.), *Sex for Life: From Virginity to Viagra, How Sexuality Changes throughout Our Lives* (43–106). New York: New York University Press.

Waisbrod, N. & Reicher, B. (2014). What Happened to Eric? The Derailment of Sexual Development. *Journal of Child Sexual Abuse*, *23*(1), 94–113. doi:10.1080/10538712.2014.864745.

Wang, N. (2016). Parent–Adolescent Communication about Sexuality in Chinese Families. *Journal of Family Communication*, *16*(3). doi:10.1080/15267431.2016.1170685.

Wilson, E., Dalberth, B., & Koo, H. (2010). "We're the Heroes!": Fathers' Perspectives on Their Role in Protecting Their Preteenage Children from Sexual Risk. *Perspectives on Sexual and Reproductive Health*, *42* (2), 117–124.

2 Toward a Central Theory of Childhood Sexuality

A Relational Approach[1]

Allison Moore

Introduction

In 1905, Sigmund Freud's *Three Essays on the Theory of Sexuality* was published. In it, he proposed a radical theory that fundamentally challenged prevailing norms and values with regard to gender and sexuality. He argued that the conventional view of sexuality that assumed the sexual instinct

> to be absent in childhood, to set at the time of puberty in connection with the process of coming to maturity and to be revealed in the manifestations of an irresistible attraction exercised by one sex upon the other; while its aim is presumed to be sexual union, or at all events actions leading in that direction [. . .] contain[s] a number of errors, inaccuracies and hasty conclusions. (Freud, [1905] 1977, p. 45)

For Freud, these errors, inaccuracies, and hasty conclusions are evident in three distinct manifestations of the sexual instinct: the widespread existence of homosexuality, which indicates that sexual drives are not limited to heterosexual genitality and reproduction; the expression of the sexual instinct through what Freud called 'perversions,' understood as sexual activities that extend "beyond the regions of the body that are designed for sexual union" (Freud, [1905] 1977, p. 623); and the presence of the sexual instinct in children, which can be seen in a wide range of autoerotic behaviors and led Freud to claim that children were polymorphously perverse. He rejected orthodoxy by positing that homosexuality was not a sign of degeneracy and that the perversions, deviations with respect to the sexual aim, can be understood as an extension rather than a rejection of 'normal' genitally focused sexual activities.

It is more than 100 years since the publication of this groundbreaking text and in, what Hawkes and Egan, (2008) term, the 'Anglophone West' many of the central tenets of Freud's psychosexual theory have been accepted, even if their psychoanalytical explanations have not. In many advanced liberal democracies in the Global North, homosexuality is seen as a legitimate lifestyle and same-sex relationships now enjoy state-sanctioned legitimation in many countries. There has been an

[1] The title of this chapter takes inspiration from Loyal & Quilley (2004).

increase in cultural representations of the sexual behaviors that Freud would have characterized as perversions, including BDSM (bondage, discipline, dominance, and submission) and fetishes. Of course, the extent to which this increased visibility represents little more than voyeurism and titillation rather than an acceptance of sexual diversity is debatable. While there are geographical variations with regard to the acceptance or even toleration of sexual diversity, it is hard not to agree with Jeffrey Weeks' claim that we are living in "the midst of a long, unfinished but profound, revolution that has transformed the possibilities of living sexual diversity and creating intimate lives . . . [which has been] overwhelmingly beneficial to the vast majority of people in the West" (Weeks, 2007, p. x).

However, there is one aspect of Freud's psychosexual theory that remains as controversial today as it was to his contemporaries in the early twentieth century – the idea of childhood sexuality. Indeed, there has been limited progress in theorizing childhood sexuality since Freud's assertion that "So far as I know, not a single author has clearly recognized the regular existence of a sexual instinct in childhood; and in writings that have become numerous on the development of children, the chapter on 'Sexual Development' is as a rule omitted" (Freud, [1905] 1977, p. 89). The notion of the sexual child is still considered oxymoronic. Sexuality continues to be assumed to be absent in childhood, to emerge at puberty, and gradually to evolve in a linear developmental path toward its normative culmination in heterosexual adulthood.

In the social sciences, social constructionism has been influential in challenging normative and naturalized assumptions of childhood and sexuality, illustrating that they are seen as antithetical as a result of the dominant constructions of childhood as a period of asexuality or presexuality and sexuality as the preserve of adults. While the significance of social constructionism for the study of childhood and sexuality should not be underestimated, it has had unplanned and unforeseen consequences. Social constructionist perspectives have underpinned much of the academic writing on sexuality since the 1970s and on childhood since the 1980s, but there is a real danger here that what is known and what is knowable about childhood and sexuality, particularly within the social sciences, must necessarily fall within a social constructionist framework. In the words of Burr (1995, p. 10), "We could say that 'social constructionism' itself has now achieved the status of an object . . . as an area of knowledge that has been 'discovered' rather than as an effect of social process." It might be argued, therefore, that "social construction has become a part of the very discourse that it presents itself as trying to undo" (Hacking, 1999, p. 36). However, while acknowledging the significant impact of social constructionism, this chapter will argue that there are other sociological tools available to social scientists to make sense of and understand the contemporary sexual world and children's relationship to it.

Drawing on the figurational sociology of Norbert Elias, this chapter will propose a "central theory" of childhood sexuality and argue that making sense of childhood sexuality in the twenty-first century in a way that empowers and enables as well as protects and safeguards children and young people requires a truly interdisciplinary approach. All too often, theories of both childhood and sexuality can be characterized by what Anne Fausto-Sterling (2000, p. 1) calls "duelling dualisms" of, for example, nature versus nurture, the individual versus society, and agency versus structure. The chapter will outline the defining features of Elias' figurational or relational sociology and consider its relevance to making sense of childhood sexuality. It will argue that as Elias' notion of figurations can be applied to the relationships and interdependencies of small groups of people as well as the interdependencies between the individual and the state (Quilley & Loyal, 2005), it can provide a framework for understanding the micro level of lived experiences of children and young people with regard to their sexual desires, expressions, and identities as well as the macro level of state legislation and policy, which are shaped by and, in turn, reinforce dominant constructions of childhood and sexuality.

Norbert Elias and Figurational Sociology: Toward a Central Theory

According to Dunning and Hughes (2013), Norbert Elias never published an explicit account of his central theory although the central tenets of it were evident through his teaching and conversations with colleagues over the years. That suggests that his central theory emphasizes the need "for theories based on meticulous, detailed and sensitive empirical observation couched at a level of synthesis sufficiently high to be applicable to a range of topics yet sufficiently down to earth to be clearly related to and relevant regarding the real-life experiences of humans" (ibid., p. 77).

In keeping with this, Elias rejected the grand theories of sociology that not only had a tendency to present social structures as objects external to the individual and, in so doing, "dehumanize" (Elias, 1978, p. 16) them and portray them as though they were separated by "some invisible barrier" (ibid., p. 15) but also tended to adopt "today-centred thinking" (Goudsblom, cited in Loyal & Quilley, 2004, p. 4), which failed to acknowledge the significance of long-term social transformations. For Elias, social change does not occur instantly or spontaneously but rather evolves gradually over generations. So, to make sense of contemporary attitudes toward sexuality, it is necessary to move beyond "today-centred thinking" (ibid.). What is required is a consideration of the continuities and discontinuities between contemporary attitudes and those of earlier epochs as well as a consideration of social, cultural, political, and economic developments that might have facilitated attitudinal change. With regard to sexuality, Elias (1994) traces the contemporary organization and regulation of sexuality back to the sixteenth century and the substantial changes that occurred in the way humans interacted with one another as a result of modernization. This was a period that saw a shift from independence to interdependence and the emergence of a highly differentiated division of labor. People lived in much closer proximity to one another and there was an increased awareness of our sense of selves in relation to others, which "arises from and feeds the sense of others' observation of us – one's visibility – the conscious awareness of which heightens the social and personal significance of our actions" (Hawkes, 1996, p. 20). In what Elias called 'civilizing processes,' behaviors that were considered inappropriate or uncivilized, including sexuality, came under greater surveillance and sex became relegated to the private sphere, "placed behind the walls in consciousness" (Elias, cited in Hawkes, 1996, p. 23).

At the same time, he was also critical of sociological approaches characterized by excessive individualism. For Elias, "[o]ne of the basic conditions of human existence is the simultaneous presence of a number of interrelated people" (Elias, 1991, p. 21). As a result, the individual cannot be understood outside of the material circumstances within which they live or the wider network of relationships within which they exist. The rejection of the reifying tendencies of macro sociology and the excessive individualism of some micro theories led to the development of Elias' figurational sociology, where the focus of analysis is not on structure/agency or individual/society but rather on "interdependent groups of individuals and the long-term transformations of the figurations they form with each other" (Loyal & Quilley, 2004, p. 5). Although not an uncritical advocate of Freud or psychoanalytic theory, Elias' figurational sociology owes much to Freud's work on the individual psyche (Lahire, 2013). Despite what he saw as the limitations of his theory, including its ahistoricity, the reification of the unconscious, and overemphasis on the sexual instinct, in his sociology Elias proposed "a processual reorientation of Freudian concepts,"[2] which connected the individual psyche with social processes in a dynamic and constantly evolving relationship.

Before considering the scope of Elias' figurational approach as a central theory of childhood sexuality, it is necessary to outline its defining characteristics. For Elias, all human relations are relations of interdependency or figurations. The individual cannot be understood in isolation from the interactions they have with others in their figurations, which, in turn, cannot be isolated from the wider social, cultural, and material conditions within which those figurations are formed. This relationality has a two-way dynamic. Social structures, themselves a product of social processes and human interdependency, may influence and shape an individual's life but they do not determine it. Similarly, individuals do exercise agency but are not the agents of their life as some contemporary, reflexive sociological theories would have us believe. From a figurational perspective, choice exercised by one person "becomes interwoven with those of others" (Elias, 1991, p. 49). Further, because our choices and subsequent actions are interwoven with choices and actions of others, Elias argued there was very little relationship between the intentions of our actions and the consequences of them. Planned action "unleashes further chains of actions, the direction and provisional outcome of which depend on the distribution of power and the structure of tensions within this whole mobile human network" (Elias, 1991, pp. 49–50). For Elias, this interdependency bridges the divisions between individual and society that had

[2] http://norberteliasfoundation.nl/blog/?p=345

beset sociological theory because it "connect[s] the psychological with the social, or habitus with social relations" (van Krieken, 1998, p. 49). Habitus or 'habit' has a long tradition in sociology and can be found in the work of the founding fathers, including Emile Durkheim and Max Weber (Camic, 1986). It was only during the mid-twentieth century that habitus was effectively "excised from the conceptual structure of the field [of sociology]" (Camic, 1986, p. 1039), primarily by the structural functionalist sociologists of this period. In contemporary sociology, it is Pierre Bourdieu's concept of habitus that is most widely used, but Elias also used a concept of habitus that had some overlaps with that of Bourdieu but also had clear differences. Habitus can be understood as unconscious, taken-for-granted, and routinized values, behaviors, and dispositions. For Elias, the unconsciousness of the habitus does not just refer to the fact that an individual does not consciously think about or is even aware of the motivations of their actions, but also refers to a much more explicitly Freudian sense of the unconscious of the psyche. He also suggested that habitus can be understood at both an individual and societal level. Where individual habitus refers to the personality of an individual formed through their specific life experiences and relations with others, social habitus refers to the values, behaviors, and dispositions of groups or figurations. As Elias adopted a relational view of social life, the individual and social habitus are inextricably linked. He argued that the individual habitus, no matter how much it is experienced subjectively, can only ever be understood as a variant of the social habitus, which he described as "the soil from which grow the personal characteristics through which an individual differs from other members of his society" (Elias, 1991, p. 182).

It is also important to highlight that Elias adopted not only a relational view of social life but also a processual view where figurations are dynamic. Therefore, habitus, individually experienced and collectively authored is always changing and evolving. However, while habitus is an ongoing process, shaped by our experiences and our relations with others, the significance of the habitus we acquire in our early life cannot be underestimated; "the web of social relations in which the individual lives during his more impressionable phases, during childhood and youth … imprints itself upon his unfolding personality" (Elias, cited in van Krieken, 1998, pp. 59–60).

Further, because social transformation usually occurs gradually and can take time to filter into our consciousness, figurations, and by extension the individual and social habitus, can tell us as much about the past as they do about the present; our "whole outlook on life continues to be psychologically tied to yesterday's social reality, although today's and tomorrow's reality already differs greatly from yesterday's" (Elias, cited in van Krieken, 1998, p. 61). Contemporary understandings of both childhood and sexuality and the concerns expressed over, for example, the sexualization of childhood and the impact of unfettered access to online pornography appear to be a product of the twenty-first century. However, they reflect much older constructions of childhood and sexuality, intersected with constructions of gender, race, and class (see Egan & Hawkes, 2009; Moore & Reynolds, 2017). The combination of relational and processual approaches allowed

Elias to theorize the relationship between psychogenesis (or the development of individual personality, socialization, and habitus) and sociogenesis (or changes in social relations at the level of the state or society at large).

Elias' relationality extends to his view of power, which avoids the characterization of power as a thing or entity owned by some and exercised over others. In this sense, he is not unlike Michel Foucault, who saw the exercise of power as a strategic game or power dynamic (Foucault, 1983), whereby "power is mobile; is exercised by degree rather than absolutely; and manifests in unexpected ways" (Kippax & Smith, 2001, p. 417). However, according to van Krieken (1998), where Elias, in particular, differs from Foucault's notion of power is in his conceptualization of resistance from below. For Elias (1978), power is a structural characteristic of all relationships, and he argued that in every interdependent relationship there exists what he called "power balances," whereby the extent to which individuals are able to exercise power over their individual decision making is always in proportion to functionality and dependence.

> In interdependent relationships, all individuals have a function but the importance attached to an individual's function and their level of dependence on others determines their ability to exercise power: In so far as we are more dependent on others than they are on us, more directed by others than they are by us, they have power over us, whether we have become dependent on them by their use of naked force or by our need to be loved, our need for money, healing, status, a career or simply for excitement (Elias, 1978, p. 93).

Further, while power, for Elias, can be exercised from below as well as from above, it "only applies to the *internal* dynamics of that relationship, but not to any capacity to transform it" (van Krieken, 1998, p. 64).

There is much in Elias' central theory that can be utilized in theorizing childhood sexuality. In particular, it is the requirement to examine the past in order to understand the present, the interdependency of social life, and the dissonance between the intentions of our actions and the unintended consequences that arise from them that provide new insights into making sense of the contested terrain of childhood sexuality in the twenty-first century.

Respice, Adspice, Prospice

The Latin maxim '*Respice, Adspice, Prospice*' means "examine your past, examine your present, examine your future" and this is where a central theory of childhood sexuality must begin because "present and future societies cannot be understood and explained without reference to past societies" (Elias et al., 1997, p. 366). Over recent years, a number of commentators have suggested that childhood is in crisis (see, for example, Postman's (1983) *The Disappearance of Childhood*, Furedi's (2001) *Paranoid Parenting*, Palmer's (2007) *Toxic Childhood*, Louv's (2008) *Last Child in the Woods*, and Leaton Gray & Phippen's (2017) *Invisibly Blighted*), under threat from the conditions of life in late modernity. It is perhaps in the area of sexuality that the fears over childhood are most acute (see, for example, Durham, 2008; Levin & Kilbourne, 2008; Olfman, 2008; Walter, 2011). Whether it is concerns over "precocious" sexual knowledge, sexual risk-taking behavior or the impact of digital technologies on children's gender and sexual identity, sexuality is portrayed as something dangerous to children and something that they must be protected from. Although the debates that arise from these concerns suggest that the organization of sexuality in the twenty-first century, and especially its representation in visual cultures, presents a new and pressing danger for children and young people, this is an example of what Elias called process-reduction or a "withdrawal to the present" (Elias, 1987, p. xv). For example, the heated discussions over the sexualization of childhood frequently cite developments in information and communication technologies, such as smart phones and greater accessibility to the Internet, as posing unprecedented dangers to children. However, while such developments may represent unique challenges to both children and adults, the cultural anxieties that underpin these concerns have a much longer lineage. Even the most cursory survey of the twentieth century highlights that the fears over the impact of the sexualization of culture on children should be "seen as a cyclical concern rather than a new phenomenon" (Kehily, 2010, p. 179). Each new development in technology, such as the emergence of home video players and computers, has resulted in concomitant moral panics over the effects of children's unfettered access to material deemed 'unsuitable' or 'age-inappropriate' by adults. Detaching oneself from the immediate context of the twenty-first century and adopting a long-term perspective illustrates that the present "forms but a moment within an ongoing process" (ibid., p. xvi). No matter how imminent the 'dangers' appear to be we must resist the "pressure toward a shortening of the time perspective" (ibid.). By looking to the past it is possible to identify connections between childhood, sexuality, and other social phenomena as well as continuities and discontinuities with the present day.

Although the twentieth century has been referred to as 'the century of the child' and in *The History of Sexuality – Volume 1: An Introduction* Foucault (1976) asserts that the production of sexuality as an object and body of knowledge can be traced back to the eighteenth century, it is possible to identify the roots of modern constructions of childhood and sexuality from the mid-sixteenth century. The French historian Philippe Ariès (1960) claimed that in the medieval era childhood did not exist and was not invented until the seventeenth century. Analyzing medieval writing about and portraits of children, as well as their clothing and pastimes, he suggested that prior to the seventeenth century children were portrayed as miniature adults who engaged in adult life as soon as they were considered physically mature enough, usually at around the age of seven. Notwithstanding the considerable criticism of his work for its focus on *representations* of childhood rather than the *reality* of children's lives, their place in the family, and the wider society in the medieval period (Pollack, 1983; Shahar, 1992), the seventeenth century was certainly a period in which broader social transformations impacted on the way that childhood was understood.

In *The Civilizing Process: History of Manners (Vol. 1)*, Norbert Elias (1994 [1939]) suggests that the increased proximity of people and the concomitant interdependency brought about by modernization during the mid-sixteenth century had a profound effect on behavior. The increased proximity of people led to an increased awareness of ourselves in relation to others which, in turn, placed greater significance on our actions and the consequences of them. In *The Civilizing Process* he examines how etiquette regarding behavior and deportment changed in a number of European societies during this period whereby "upper-class manners and affective sensibility . . . became generalized as a model for polite behaviour, gradually diffusing through wider strata of society" (Loyal & Quilley, 2004, pp. 9–10). Through his analysis of various treatises on manners it was evident that the behaviors that came under greatest scrutiny were those pertaining to bodily functions, like urination and defecation, and bodily impulses, including sexual impulses. 'Polite' and 'civilized' individuals were expected to show restraint in these areas and over time they were increasingly relegated to the private sphere and took place behind closed doors.

Prior to modernization, sex was not a private affair and certainly not something that was hidden from children. In part, this was due to the fact that domestic living arrangements were such that children would often hear conversations of a sexual nature, witness sex taking place, and be present during childbirth, but it was also because childhood had not yet been constructed as a period of asexuality. During modernity, sex, along with other activities of the body, became associated with shame and embarrassment evidenced in the "civilization of the sex drive" and the emergence of "a 'conspiracy of silence'" that surrounded sex whereby "[e]ven among adults it is referred to officially only with caution and circumlocution. And with children, particularly girls such things are, as far as possible, not referred to at all" for fear of "soiling of the childish mind" (Elias, 1994, p. 148). When adults did discuss sex with children it was as educators, guiding children in "the correct direction – or, more precisely, the direction desired by the educator" toward adult sexuality (ibid., p. 153).

The role of the adult as the conduit of sexual knowledge to the asexual child becomes formalized in the eighteenth and nineteenth century through what Foucault (1978) called the 'pedagogization of children's sex' a two-fold process of surveillance and regulation whereby Freud's polymorphously perverse child was acknowledged as 'normal' and yet, at the same time, children's expression of the sexual instinct was seen as contrary to nature, harmful, and, therefore, something that must be prohibited. The pedagogization of children's sex has to be seen in the context of the development in the modern era of "a completely new technology of sex" (Foucault, 1978, p. 116), which saw the appearance of a range of new authoritative voices in the area of sex and sexuality. The adult experts of children's sexuality came from the fields of medicine, sexology, psychiatry, education, and, of course, parents who were seen as the experts of their own children, although parents' expertise was and continues to be subordinate to the expertise of child 'professionals.' It was these adult experts who determined the parameters of children's sexuality, when it was acceptable for children and young people to become sexually active, what sexual knowledge they should be given and when, and what measures should be put in place to prevent the expression of children's sexuality until a 'developmentally appropriate' time.

What we see in the civilizing process that Elias identified in the sixteenth and seventeenth centuries are the roots of contemporary attitudes toward childhood and sexuality – that sexuality represents a pernicious danger to children and that girls are especially vulnerable. Further, the association of sex with shame and embarrassment has resulted in 'normal' sexual development being framed by shame; children learn that sex and sexuality should take place behind closed doors, masturbation is something that should be hidden and never discussed, and adults see any expression of sexual desire in children as something that is shameful and must be restrained or 'civilized.' The legacy of the pedagogization of children's sex is clearly evident in contemporary debates over childhood and sexuality. Those with the authority to 'know' children's sexuality continue to be adult experts and children's expertise remains marginalized. Responding appropriately to twenty-first-century concerns over childhood and sexuality necessitates a return to the past to ascertain what measures have been taken previously and whether those measures were beneficial for children or counterproductive.

Figurations of Social Life: Challenging the Adult–Child Dichotomy

Perhaps the overarching proposition of Elias' figurational sociology concerns the interdependency of social life. He argued that the concepts 'individual' and 'social' have come to be understood as representing "not merely differences but . . . an antithesis" (Elias, 1991, p. 155). However, detaching oneself from their contemporary usage and adopting a long-term perspective illustrates that there is nothing natural nor inevitable about this split and, indeed, the separation of the individual and the social is a relatively recent development in human history.

In order to explain the relationship between the individual and the social, Elias used the personal pronouns of 'I,' 'he,' 'she,' 'you,' 'we,' and 'they.' We use 'I' when referring to ourselves and 'we' when we are referring to those with whom we feel connected. 'He,' 'she,' and 'they' are applied to those individuals outside our group. He posited that in many so-called "developed societies . . . the differences between people, their I-identity, are valued more highly than what they have in common, their we-identity" (ibid., p. 156). It is possible to see the emphasis on the I-identity in contemporary sociological theories underpinned by notions of reflexivity whereby social structures such as class, gender, race, and ethnicity have lost their power to determine or even shape an individual's life. Freed from these shackles, it is claimed that individuals exercise choice, take calculated risks in an increasingly uncertain world, and engage in a 'reflexive project of the self' (Giddens, 1991) as the authors of their own life biography (see also Beck, 1992).

Elias referred to the privileging of the individual as an autonomous and isolated entity as *homo clausus* but suggested that a figurational model of social life based on interdependencies presents humans as *homines aperti*, open rather than closed, who "through their basic dispositions and inclinations, are directed toward and linked with each other in the most diverse ways" (Elias, 1978, pp. 14–15). As Roseneil and Ketokivi (2016) point out, there are clear similarities between Elias' figurational sociology and the relational psychoanalytical theory of the British object–relations tradition that characterized humans as fundamentally relationship seeking, which reflects his commitment to extending Freud's work.

Although interdependencies are the building blocks of social life, when it comes to children and their place in society, it is their *dependency on* rather than their *interdependency with* adults that is emphasized. Developmentalism, the process of observing and evaluating children through a developmental lens, continues to be the dominant paradigm through which childhood is understood. Within a developmental framework, the child is positioned as natural rather than social; an incomplete human being who progresses in a linear way through a set of incremental stages that correspond with increasing chronological age from a state of dependency toward adult independence and maturity. Of course, children *are* biologically immature and are dependent on adults for the satisfaction of their material needs for a relatively long period of their lives compared with other mammals. However, despite this dependence, it is more appropriate to think of an infant's relationship with the adults around her/him as relations of interdependency because they are biosocial in nature, based not only on meeting physiological needs but also social needs. "They [children] have to bond with others and others with them" (Dunning & Hughes, 2013, p. 51).

The consequence of a developmental framework that emphasizes children's dependence, their inabilities, and their differences to, rather than their similarities with, adults is that children and adults are seen as binary opposites; children are "a group apart . . . [they] are what adults are not" (James & James, 2004, p. 21). Within Elias' personal pronoun mode, children are positioned as the 'they' to the adult 'I'/'we.' His notion of established and outsider relations is also useful in making sense of how adults and children have been conceptualized as ontologically distinct categories and how that separation is perpetuated. In *The Established and the Outsiders* (1994), Elias and his collaborator John Scotson were interested in the power dynamics that defined community relations within a shared geographical location. Their research was concerned with how "members of groups which are, in terms of *power*, stronger than other interdependent groups, think of themselves in human terms as *better* than the others . . . [and] . . . What is more, in all these cases the 'superior' people may make the less powerful people themselves feel they lack virtue – that they are inferior in human terms" (Elias & Scotson, 1994, pp. xv–xvi, italics in original). The developmental paradigm is predicated on hierarchical power dynamics between adults and children whereby, because they are positioned as 'undeveloped' or 'developing' and adulthood is seen as the pinnacle of the developmental trajectory, children are characterized as not fully human, as human becomings rather than human beings.

The failure to see children and adults as having relations of interdependency (biosocial in nature and meeting physiological, psychological, and social needs of both adults and children) that sit within wider networks of figurations acts as a significant barrier to recognizing childhood sexuality. Representations of sex and the organization of sexuality have undergone profound transformations in the late twentieth and early twenty-first centuries, to the degree that some commentators would claim that we are living in a 'pornified' or hypersexual culture (see, for example, Attwood, 2009; McNair, 2002; Paassonen et al. 2007). Children continue to be positioned as though they are "untroubled and untouched by the cares of the (adult) sexual world to come" (Renold, 2005, p. 17), as though they live in an asexual bubble separated from the sexual world of adults by some invisible wall. But children do not live in an asexual world and here we are reminded of Elias' warning against reifying tendencies that present society and social structures as objects external to the individual. Although frequently characterized as "a special area of life" (Jackson, 1982, p. 2), sexuality is, in fact, anything but 'special'; it is ordinary, everyday, and mundane. Sex and sexuality are present in the fairy stories that children come into contact with, the films they watch, the games they play, the songs they listen to, and the performers who sing them. Sexuality is a social product and it extends far beyond sexual activities. It is experienced in multi-faceted ways and incorporates sexual and gender identities, as well as sexual desires and subjectivities.

Given how pervasive sexuality is in social life, the question that begs to be asked is how adults are able to maintain that children are untouched by the sexual world. This fallacy is perpetuated by two distinct but related aspects of the adult–child binary, which deny the similarities and, therefore, marginalize the interdependencies between them. First, as with all binary constructs, the continued existence of one of the pair relies on its opposite other; "the child . . . cannot be imagined except in relation to a conception of the adult but essentially it becomes impossible to generate a well-defined sense of the adult, and indeed adult society, without first positing the 'child'" (Jenks, 1996, p. 3). In order to maintain the adult–child dichotomy, the oppositional characteristics of the child in relation to the adult must be emphasized and any similarities are presented as anomalies. In relation to sexuality, it is possible to see how children's sexual identities, thoughts, and expressions become understood as anomalous to the status of childhood. A child with sexual knowledge beyond what is deemed 'appropriate' for their age might be determined to be precocious or as having developed 'abnormally.' At worst, the 'knowing' child (Robinson, 2012) risks losing the status of childhood and the protections it affords. This is problematized by Kitzinger (1997, p. 168), who suggests that "if the violation of innocence is the criterion against which the act of sexual abuse is judged then violating a 'knowing' child becomes a lesser offence than violating an 'innocent' child." We can find another example of the disruption of the adult–child binary in the teenage pregnant body because it is both/neither adult or child. To maintain the binary and the characteristics ascribed to adults and children, teenage pregnancy is typically portrayed as the product of ignorance or irresponsibility rather than a conscious and rational choice on the part of the young mother (Moore & Reynolds, 2017).

The second feature of the adult–child binary that perpetuates the notion of the asexual child is what Freud referred to as *infantile amnesia*; "the peculiar *amnesia* which, in the case of most people . . . hides the earliest beginnings of their childhood up to their sixth or eighth year" (1905, pp. 89–90). Freud claimed that our early years are never really forgotten but rather repressed from the unconscious mind to such an extent that our early sexual development is hidden from us as adults. Repressed memories do not disappear; they remain in our unconscious and their containment "requires a permanent expenditure of energy" (Freud, cited in Egan, 2013, p. 120). A recognition of the sexual child risks the resurfacing of adults' repressed memories of their sexual development and "collides with the revulsion that resides beneath a thin pellicle of repression and this creates more anxiety and another attempt at repression" (ibid.). Witnessing the polymorphously perverse child unencumbered by shame reminds adults of the polymorphous perversity of precivilized instincts, which, as a result of 'normal' sexual development, have now been restrained. In much the same way that object–relation theorists referred to 'splitting,' a process of "projective identification [which infants and adults engage in] to help defend against feelings of hatred, aggression and panic that they are unable to acknowledge as their own" (ibid., p. 121), so too can adults be seen to engage in a form of splitting to present children and adults as ontologically separate and distinct entities. In so doing, adults defend the repressed memories of their earlier sexual self, which, as civilized adults, they are unable to acknowledge.

Protecting Children from Sexuality: Planned Actions and Unintended Consequences

One of the key principles of Elias's sociology is that "although societies are composed of human beings who engage in intentional action, the outcome of the combination of human actions is most often *unplanned* and *unintended*" (van Krieken, 1998, p. 6). In other words, there is often little relationship between our planned and intentional actions and the consequences of them. However, this is not to suggest that social action is random, meaningless or completely uncontrollable. Elias uses a game model analogy, arguing that "As the moves of thousands of interdependent players intertwine, no single player nor group of players acting alone can determine the course of the game, no matter how powerful they may be" (Elias, 1978, p. 147). Elias' notion of unplanned order highlights the fluidity and indeterminacy of everyday practice and illustrates that while individuals are able to exercise agency they are, at the same time, constrained by their social position (Moore, 2010).

Understanding social life as the unplanned consequences of intentional action is a useful framework with which to make sense of childhood sexuality in the early twenty-first century. It warns us to exercise caution in uncritically accepting that the concerns raised over childhood sexuality and, in particular, premature sexualization, are purely contemporary responses to a contemporary 'problem.' Similarly, it encourages us to take a critical stance on proposals advanced to protect children from sexuality, especially in the form of greater surveillance and/or censorship, as they can have unplanned and unforeseen consequences for children. Frequently, measures to 'protect' children from sexuality involve varying degrees of censorship, including denying children access to sexual information and enforcing age related legislation with regard to sexual activity. Such measures are usually presented as necessary to protect children from exploitation and abuse but, an unintended consequence of them is that preventing children from learning about sexuality and becoming sexually literate can actually make them more vulnerable to abuse and exploitation. When combined with a processual approach that takes account of long-term social processes it allows us to see whether measures introduced in children's best interests throughout history have actually been beneficial for children.

Although the decisions and actions of *all* adults impact on the children with whom they have figurational relationships, it is perhaps in the areas of law and policy that the unintentional consequences of planned actions are most clearly evidenced. Where previously physical sexual immaturity and maturity served as the boundary between childhood and adulthood, in the twenty-first century that vague and variable demarcation has been replaced by "a plethora of rules and regulations that define sex as the exclusive realm of adults" (Gittins, 1998, p. 174). Such rules and regulations operate at an informal and formal level. At an informal level, the regulation of childhood sexuality takes place through custom and practice or, in Eliasian terms, the social habitus, which perpetuates and routinizes norms and values concerning what *is* and what *is not* acceptable for children and young people with regard to sexuality. The formal regulation of childhood sexuality utilizes the mechanisms of law and policy where the principle purpose of law can be seen as protecting the construction of childhood innocence by denying or limiting access to sexual knowledge (Lind, 1998) and social policy has a two-fold function; "to protect children *from* sexuality and pragmatically to acknowledge and deal *with* the consequences of the sexuality of young people" (Thompson, 2004, p. 88, emphasis in original).

Because of assumptions about the asexuality of children and their dependence on rather than interdependence with adults, the majority of law and policy is focused on protecting children from expressions of sex and sexuality and, primarily, from protecting them from abuse and exploitation. Of course, children *should* be afforded protection from those who would seek to exploit their vulnerabilities in the form of their comparative biological, psychological, and emotional immaturities in relation to most adults. However, the problem with a legislative framework couched almost exclusively in protectionism is that it becomes impossible to conceptualize a positive notion of childhood sexuality. By and large, the law positions sexuality in relation to children as 'freedom from' (freedom from harm, freedom from abuse) rather than 'freedom to' (freedom to sexual expression, freedom to sexual information). Even when law and policy appear to allow positive freedoms they are often underpinned by protectionism. For example, sex education, where is it provided for children and young people, is still dominated by a biomedical model of reproduction and information on how to protect oneself from unwanted pregnancy and sexually transmitted infections. A positive conception of sex education that prioritizes sexual consent and gender equality, and where sex and sexuality are equated with sensuousness and pleasure, is still, sadly, a long way off. Petchesky (2001, p. 125) suggests that "such negative constructions of sexual rights ... pervades human rights discourse in general." However, negative freedoms and positive freedoms are two sides of the same coin; "Sexual self-determination and sexual rights imply both the negative freedom against unwanted intrusions, violations and abuses, and also the positive capacity to seek and experience pleasures in a variety of ways and situations" (ibid., p. 131).

Denied tools, such as access to sex education that moves beyond prevention, to make sense of their sexuality in positive ways, children and young people grow up and internalize predominantly negative attitudes about sex; sex is something shameful that must be kept hidden behind closed doors and sex is something dangerous that we must protect ourselves and others from. If children are positioned outside of 'I'-'We' adult figurations and we deny the interdependencies between adults and children, this simply serves to reinforce the adult-child binary and perpetuates negative connotations of sex and sexuality which is ultimately counterintuitive. Law and policy underpinned by protectionism and negative freedoms from harm may be intended to protect children but can have unforeseen and unplanned consequences. If we accept Lind's argument that the law protects children as a group and childhood as a category by maintaining notions of innocence through denying or limiting access to sexual knowledge, then children can be left more vulnerable to abuse and exploitation. Without an understanding of their body and, especially, notions of bodily integrity, ownership and autonomy, they have limited knowledge to recognize abuse and an even more limited language to articulate what is happening to them. Further, sexual innocence is itself fetishized, sexualized, and exploited by abusers. As Kitzinger (1997, p. 164) claims, "A glance at pornography leaves little doubt that innocence is a sexual commodity ... If defiling the pure and deflowering the virgin is supposed to be erotic, then focusing on children's presumed innocence only reinforces their desirability as sexual objects" (See also, Dines, 2011). Finally, an unforeseen consequence of a protectionist approach can be to criminalize consensual sexual activity between young people who are under the statutory age of consent, which is put in place, ostensibly, to protect children from sexual exploitation by older adults. For example, in England and Wales the statutory provisions regarding the age of consent, along with the punishments meted out to those who violate the law, are enshrined in the Sexual Offences Act 2003 (SOA). The age of consent in the United Kingdom is sixteen and according to the SOA any sexual activity between individuals under the age of consent is a criminal offence and liable for prosecution. This applies regardless of whether all the parties involved have agreed to the activity willingly and consensually. Although actual prosecutions are relatively low (but not non-existent), there are 'knock-on' consequences of this measure of protection. If a 15-year-old boy and girl are in a sexual relationship but are aware that this is against the law, there is a disincentive with regard to accessing contraceptive and other sexual health services because it requires one or both of the parties to disclose that they have committed or intend to commit a criminal offence (Moore, 2010).

An awareness that planned actions can have unplanned consequences with respect to childhood sexuality is not, nor should it be seen as, a libertarian call for the retrenchment of children's rights to protection. However, it does require that their rights to protection are balanced with other rights so that their sexual subjectivities and identities are recognized. "In particular, it is necessary to recognise children's sexual identities from *their* perspectives rather than from the adult centred, protectionist perspective that currently frames dominant discourses of childhood and sexuality" (Moore, 2013, p. 170, italics added). Understanding children's sexual identities from their perspectives means avoiding the imposition of adult interpretations of their sexual behavior and asking children and young people themselves about their sexual subjectivities and identities.

Conclusion: Eliasian Sociology as a Central Theory of Childhood Sexuality?

According to Quilley and Loyal (2005), Elias' contribution to sociology falls into three related areas. First, his substantive body of historical studies which highlight the processual and figurational nature of social life and demonstrate the relationship between psychogenesis and sociogenesis. Second, his development of a "corpus of concepts providing the kernel of a unifying theoretical foundation for the discipline" (ibid., p. 825). Third, his contribution to a sociology of knowledge that locates sociology as "a linchpin in an encompassing human science" (ibid.) where knowledge is produced through the integration of a range of disciplines including, but not limited to, history, biology, and psychoanalytical theory. It is this legacy that makes Elias' work so appealing as a central theory of childhood sexuality.

The focus on interdependencies between adults and children reminds us that concerns expressed over childhood and sexuality in the twenty-first century "raise profound questions about the status of adult sexuality and its object" (Walkerdine, 2001, p. 16). Here, Walkerdine is referring to the sexualization of childhood innocence and "the eroticized child-woman of popular culture" (ibid., p. 23) but we might also consider the problematic status of adult sexuality in a sexualized culture in which sex has become commodified, fetishized, and objectified. Adults are right to express concerns over the impact that living in a hypersexualized society has on children but so too should they be concerned about how that impacts on adults; on the expression of sexual desires and on the relations, sexual or otherwise, between people. Elias also demonstrated how interdependencies or figurations were dynamic and changed over time. A processual approach encourages us to look to our past before we make decisions about how to respond to contemporary issues concerning childhood sexuality; "it is only a concern with the how and why of long-term processes which will provide us with the opportunity to acquire an orientation sufficiently broad and close to reality to enable us to decide whether short-term practical measures intended to remedy damage and disadvantage [in the present] do not in the longer term produce even greater damage and disadvantage" (Elias, et al., 1997, pp. 369–370).

Elias' call for a sociology of knowledge that is integrated also allows for a recognition of children as both sexual beings and sexual becomings. Gittins (1998, p. 176) suggests that "Freud 'gave back' to children their sexuality" but what adults frequently fail to recognize and which contributes to adults' anxieties, is that it is a '*childhood sexuality*' based on pleasures derived from and through the body. Laplanche and Pontalis (cited in Walkerdine, 2001) claim that languages of childhood sexuality and adult sexuality are different where the former is a language of tenderness and the latter is a language of passion. This leads Walkerdine (ibid., p. 28) to suggest that "there are two kinds of sexuality; an infant one about bodily pleasures and an adult one that imposes a series of other meanings on those pleasures." The imposition of adult sexuality combined with infantile amnesia which represses memories of childhood sexuality into the unconscious means that "adults either overestimate or underestimate children's sexual capacities" (Jackson, 1982, p. 78). Adults either deny the presence of sexuality in children or interpret anything remotely sexual "as if it were motivated by fully-formed sexual interests." One does have to subscribe to a developmentalist paradigm to acknowledge that there are differences between children and adults and that children, in general, are biologically, psychologically, and emotionally less mature than adults – although the closer to adulthood that children get the less certain these differences become. An integrated model of childhood sexuality, which Elias' theory lends itself to, which draws on notions of biological and psychosexual development facilitates an acceptance of the presence of childhood sexuality while simultaneously recognizing that it is different in form, expression and motivation to that of adults. Children, as with all human beings, are a process – "that is, we are born, mature and die" (Dunning & Hughes, 2013, p. 51). Using Elias' sociology to develop a central theory of childhood sexuality develops a deeper understanding of human sexuality in general which acknowledges that human sexuality is never static and changes over the life cycle and it is best to think of both children *and* adults as sexual beings as well as sexual becomings.

References

Ariès, P. (1960). *Centuries of Childhood.* Harmondsworth: Penguin Books.

Attwood, F. (ed.) (2009). *Mainstreaming Sex: The Sexualisation of Western Culture.* London: I. B. Taurus & Co.

Beck, U. (1992). *Risk Society.* London: Sage.

Burr, V. (1995). *An Introduction to Social Constructionism.* London: Routledge.

Camic, C. (1986). The Matter of Habit. *The American Journal of Sociology, 91*(5), 1039–1087.

Dines, G. (2011). *Pornland: How Porn Has Hijacked Our Sexuality.* Boston: Beacon Press.

Dunning, E. & Hughes, J. (2013). *Norbert Elias and Modern Sociology: Knowledge, Interdependence, Power, Process.* London: Bloomsbury.

Durham, M. G. (2008). *The Lolita Effect: The Media Sexualization of Young Girls and What We Can Do about It.* Woodstock: The Overlook Press.

Egan, D. (2013). *Becoming Sexual: A Critical Appraisal of the Sexualization of Girls.* Cambridge: Polity Press.

Egan, D. R. & Hawkes, G. (2009). The Problem with Protection: Or, Why We Need to Move towards Recognition and the Sexual Agency of Children. *Continuum: Journal of Media & Cultural Studies, 23*(3), 389–400.

Elias, N. (1978). *What Is Sociology?* New York: Columbia University Press.

(1987). *Involvement and Detachment.* Oxford: Basil Blackwell Ltd.

(1991). *The Society of Individuals.* New York: Continuum.

(1994). *The Civilizing Process.* Oxford: Blackwell Publishing.

Elias, N. & Scotson, J. L. (1994). *The Established and the Outsiders.* London: SAGE Publications.

Elias, N., van Krieken, R. & Dunning, E. (1997). Towards a Theory of Social Processes: A Translation. *The British Journal of Sociology, 48*(3), 355–383.

Fausto-Sterling, A. (2000). *Sexing the Body: Gender Politics and the Construction of Sexuality.* New York: Basic Books.

Foucault, M. (1978). *The History of Sexuality: Volume 1 an Introduction.* Harmondsworth: Penguin.

(1983). The Subject and Power. In Dreyfus, H. & Rabinow, P. (Eds.), *Michel Foucault: Beyond Structuralism and Hermeneutics.* Chicago: University of Chicago Press.

Freud, S. (1977). *Three Essays on the Theory of Sexuality.* London: Penguin Books Ltd, originally published in 1905.

Furedi, F. (2001). *Paranoid Parenting.* London: Allen Lane.

Giddens, A. (1991). *Modernity and Self-Identity: Self and Society in the Late Modern Age.* Cambridge: Polity.

Gittins, D. (1998). *The Child in Question.* Houndmills: Macmillan Press Ltd.

Hacking, I. (1999). *The Social Construction of What?* Cambridge, Massachusetts: Harvard University Press.

Hawkes, G. (1996). *A Sociology of Sex and Sexuality.* Buckingham: Open University Press.

Hawkes, G. & Egan, R. D. (2008). Landscapes of Erotophobia: The Sexual(ized) Child in the Postmodern Anglophone World. *Sexuality & Culture, 12*(4), 193–203.

Jackson, S. (1982). *Childhood and Sexuality.* Oxford: Blackwell.

James, A. & James, A. L. (2004). *Constructing Childhood: Theory, Policy and Social Practice.* Hampshire: Palgrave Macmillan.

Jenks, C. (1996). *Childhood*. London: Routledge.

Kehily, M. J. (2010). Childhood in Crisis? Tracing the Contours of 'Crisis' and Its Impact upon Contemporary Parenting Practices. *Media, Culture & Society, 32*(2), 171–185.

Kippax, S. & Smith, G. (2001). Anal Intercourse and Power in Sex between Men. *Sexualities*, *4*(4), 413–434.

Kitzinger, J. (1997). Who Are You Kidding? Children, Power, and the Struggle against Sexual Abuse. In James, A. & Prout, A. (Eds), *Constructing and Reconstructing Childhood* (165–189). London: Falmer Press.

Lahire, B. (2013). Elias, Freud and the Human Science In Dépelteau, F. & Landini, T. S. (Eds.), *Norbert Elias and Social Theory* (75–89). New York: Palgrave Macmillan.

Leaton Gray, S. & Phippen, A. (2017). *Invisibly Blighted: The Digital Erosion of Childhood.* London: UCL Institute of Education Press.

Levin, D. E. & Kilbourne, J. (2008). *So Sexy So Soon: The New Sexualized Childhood and What Parents Can Do to Protect Their Kids*. New York: Ballantine Books.

Lind, C. (1998). Law, Childhood Innocence and Sexuality. In Moran, L. et al. (Eds), *Legal Queeries: Lesbian, Gay and Transgender Legal Studies*. London: Cassell.

Louv, R. (2008). *Last Child in the Woods: Saving our Children from Nature-Deficit Disorder.* North Carolina: Algonquin Books of Chapel Hill.

Loyal, S. & Quilley, S. (2004). Towards a "Central Theory": The Scope and Relevance of the Sociology of Norbert Elias. In Loyal, S. & Quilley, S. (Eds), *The Sociology of Norbert Elias*. Cambridge: Cambridge University Press.

McNair, B. (2002). *Striptease Culture: Sex, Media and the Democratisation of Desire*. Abingdon: Routledge.

Mennell, S. (2011) 'Norbert Elias: Beyond Freud' http://norberteliasfoundation.nl/blog/?p=345.

Moore, A. (2010). 'I' and 'We' Identities – An Eliasian Perspective on Lesbian and Gay Identities. *Sociological Research Online*, *15* (4), www.socresonline.org.uk/15/4/10.html.

(2013) For Adults Only? Young People and (Non)participation in Sexual Decision Making. *Global Studies of Childhood 3*(2), 163–172.

Moore, A. & Reynolds, P. (2017), *Childhood and Sexuality: Contemporary Issues and Debates*. London: Palgrave Macmillan.

Olfman, S. (Ed.) (2008). *The Sexualization of Childhood.* Westport: Praeger Publishers.

Paassonen, S., Nikunen, K. & Saaenmaa, L. (2007). *Pornification: Sex and Sexuality in Media Culture*. Oxford: Berg.

Palmer, S. (2007). *Toxic Childhood: How the Modern World Is Damaging Our Children and What We Can Do about It.* London: Orion Books.

Petchesky, R. P. (2001). Sexual Rights Inventing a Concept Mapping an International Practice. In Blasius, M. (Ed.), *Sexual Identities Queer Politics* (118–139). Princeton: Princeton University Press.

Pollack, L. (1983). *Forgotten Children: Parent–Child Relations from 1500 to 1900.* Cambridge: Cambridge University Press.

Postman, N. (1983). *The Disappearance of Childhood*. London: W.H Allen.

Quilley, S. & Loyal, S. (2005). Eliasian Sociology as a 'Central Theory' for the Human Sciences. *Current Sociology*, *53*(5), 807–828.

Renold. E. (2005). *Girls, Boys and Junior Sexualities: Exploring Children's Gender and Sexual Relations in the Primary School*. London: Routledge Falmer.

Robinson, K. H. (2012). 'Difficult Citizenship': The Precarious Relationships between Childhood, Sexuality and Access to Knowledge. *Sexualities*, *15*(3/4), 257–276.

Roseneil, S. & Ketokivi, K. (2016). Relational Persons and Relational Processes: Developing the Notion of Relationality for the Sociology of Personal Life. *Sociology*, *50*(1), 143–159.

Shahar, S. (1992). *Childhood in the Middle Ages*. London: Routledge.

Thomson, R. (2004). Sexuality and Young People: Policies, Practices and Identities. In Jean Carabine, J. (Ed.), *Sexualities: Personal Lives and Social Policy* (85–122). Bristol: The Policy Press.

van Krieken, R. (1998). *Norbert Elias*. London: Routledge.

Walkerdine, V. (2001). Safety and Danger: Childhood, Sexuality and Space at the End of the Millennium. In Hultqvist, K. & Dahlberg, G. (Eds), *Governing the Child in the New Millennium*. Abingdon: Routledge.

Walter, N. (2011). *Living Dolls the Return of Sexism*. London: Virago.

Weeks, J. (2007). *The World We Have Won*. London: Routledge.

3 A Sociological Exploration of Childhood Sexuality

A Discursive Analysis of Parents' and Children's Perspectives

Kerry H. Robinson and Cristyn Davies

Introduction

The relationship between children and sexuality in many Western countries is precarious and controversial, impacting the kind of research that has been undertaken in the area of children's sexual subjectivities, especially in the social sciences. This research has been, and continues to be, highly regulated. Human sexuality has largely been constituted in universal biomedical and psychological discourses that view pubertal changes in adolescence as marking the beginning of sexual development. Children's physical maturity is considered to lead to a more heightened curiosity in sexuality as they reach puberty. Piagetian (Piaget, 1959, 1960) human development has been central to these scientific perspectives that reinforce an understanding of children as being too emotionally, cognitively, and physically immature to grasp concepts about sexuality, which have been widely viewed as 'adult knowledge.' As a consequence, the figure of the child has come to represent 'innocence,' especially sexual innocence, and is the focus of broad sociocultural, political, and legal regulatory practices in order to protect and prolong childhood innocence (Corteen & Scratton, 1997; Robinson, 2013). The discourse of childhood innocence has operated to reinforce the perspective in many Western countries that sexual development begins in puberty, impacting family and schooling practices about children's access to knowledge about sexuality throughout childhood and into adolescence.

There have been significant challenges to traditional biomedical discourses on children's sexual development starting in puberty. The most notable and controversial has been the works of Sigmund Freud in the early twentieth century (Freud, 1976 [1905]). Freud's theory asserts human sexuality starts at birth, that children have an active sexuality from this time, and that childhood experiences can influence adult sexuality. Although critiqued for his research methodologies, Freud provided an alternative to dominant thinking about human sexual development and children. Anthropological research on human sexuality, like the works of Margaret Mead in the 1930s (Mead, 1948 [1935]) and Clellan Ford and Frank Beach in the early 1950s (Ford & Beach, 1951), demonstrated the diversity of human sexual relationships and practices, highlighting the sociocultural foundations on which these were based.

Extending on these perspectives in more recent times, research has explored the social construction of human sexuality, arguing that sexual identity or sexual subjectivity is also shaped by sociocultural, political values and practices in which we live that change over time, rather than being universally determined in human biology (Butler, 1990, 1993; Foucault, 1984; Jagose, 1996; Weeks, 1985). Within this perspective, the social construction of sexuality is a life-long process that begins in the early years of life. Our discussion in this chapter is framed within a feminist poststructural and queer theoretical perspective that shifts beyond socialization theory to view children as powerful, agentic subjects, who are actively involved in the construction of their own gender and sexuality.

This chapter explores the discursive construction of children's sexual subjectivities within a sociocultural framework based on research conducted with Australian parents and children aged 3 to 11 years. A critical aspect of this research was to examine the sociocultural values and practices associated with children, the development of children's sexual subjectivities, and children's access to sexuality education in the home and in schools. First, we critically examine some of the key research on children's sexual development and the differing theoretical approaches that have contributed to understandings in this area. We address the tensions between biomedical and sociocultural discourses of sexuality and child development. Second, focusing on parents' narratives about children's access to sexuality education, we examine the differing and competing discourses that underpin their perspectives of children's sexual development. Third, we draw on children's narratives to explore the construction of children's sexual subjectivities in their everyday lives. Children's 'normal' healthy sexual development is generally constructed by adults as heterosexual. We consider the heterosexualization of children's sexual subjectivities through prevailing dominant discourses and everyday practices. Those children who step outside the boundaries of 'compulsory heterosexuality' generally find themselves the target of adult and peer regulatory practices.

Children's Sexual Development: An Overview of Major Research and Theoretical Frameworks

Across the disciplines, there are multiple ways of viewing sexuality. In traditional biomedical discourses, sexuality is perceived to emerge naturally around puberty alongside significant hormonal changes in children's bodies. Further, within these discourses there is an assumed, unquestioned link between the binary sexed body (male/female) and sexuality, with heterosexuality perceived as representative of 'normal' sexual development in young people. However, in more contemporary biomedical understandings of human sexuality, psychosocial discourses are central to constituting the sexual subject (Bennett & Robards, 2013;

Davies et al., 2018). That is, sexuality has a central role in young people's development and focuses on gender identity, gender roles, sexual attraction, function, and identity. The social context of sexual development includes desire for intimacy in relationships, curiosity, and perceived social status. Contemporary medical discourse understands that peers, family, social institutions, and culture impact young people's attitudes and beliefs with regard to sexuality (p. 194). Sociocultural, medical, and political discourses are historically located, changing across time and space.

Much of the knowledge that has prevailed about children's sexual development has come from research that was done with adults remembering their childhoods. Sigmund Freud's theory of infantile sexuality, developed in the late nineteenth and early twentieth centuries, is an example of this research approach (1976 [1905]). Freud's theory was highly controversial, not just in terms of the topic area, but also because it challenged biomedical theories that argued children's sexual development starts at puberty. His theories have been widely critiqued (e.g., ideas on female sexuality and homosexuality), especially in terms of the research methodologies that he used and his interpretations of the empirical evidence used to support his ideas (Freud, 1976 [1905]).

Danielle Egan points out, according to Freud, sexuality is "an evolving subjective experience that begins in earliest infancy and is formed at the intersection of the cultural, biological and biographical" (Egan, 2015, p. 108). Freudian discourse on children's sexuality argued that sexuality is not absent or dormant in childhood, rather children have an active sexuality that begins soon after birth, which needs to be expressed. Freud argued that children's first feelings connecting them to the world, especially to the mother, were sexual in nature. In the Freudian context, infantile sexuality is expanded to include any physical pleasurable sensation experienced by the child (e.g., stroking and cuddling), or conveyed in the processes of eating, drinking (e.g., breastfeeding), and toileting, and through emotions of tenderness and friendship (Goldman & Goldman, 1982). Freud viewed the sexual child as polymorphously perverse, autoerotic, bisexual, and primarily linked to pleasure (Egan, 2015). Before becoming aware of the social norms that persist around sexuality, children, according to Freud, have the ability to gain sexual gratification outside normative sexual behaviors. Children gained erotic pleasure and sexual gratification in parts of the body beyond their genitalia. Erotogenic zones of a child's body include not only the mouth, anus, and genitalia, but also the skin and mucous membrane associated with the ears, eyes, nose, and face.

Freud considered that there were three core stages in children's development that were central to children's experiences of pleasure: the oral stage, the anal stage, and phallic/genital awareness stage (Egan, 2015; Freud, 1976 [1905]; Goldman & Goldman, 1982). From birth, the oral stage is represented by the pleasure of feeding and the warmth and comfort of the parent's/carer's body. Weaning brings with it possible traumas or further pleasures. The anal stage is represented by expelling excrement and the shift to toilet training, both of which have associated social taboos that can impact parental attitudes and practices influencing experiences of pleasure or trauma. The phallic stage is represented by the child's awareness of the pleasure gained through stimulation of the genitals (e.g., bathing and cleaning activities). Masturbation among children is common, but is generally repressed due to enforcement of social mores stemming from cultural taboos. When children learn social norms, they generally suppress behaviors, which then become repressed (hidden, controlled). As a consequence, the latency period begins (around 5 years of age) and lasts to the start of prepubescence. During this period, Freud believed that sexual impulses are repressed and sexual energy is sublimated into other aspects of their lives, such as hobbies and sport. The last stage of Freud's theory of sexual development is puberty, at which point sexual intercourse (penis/vagina) becomes the focus. Freud believed that the suppression of sexuality in childhood was one of the causes of adult neurosis, including sexual deviancy. Unsuppressed psychosexual development in infancy, according to Freud, was the foundation of a healthy, mature heterosexual adult.

John H. Gagnon and William Simon (Gagnon, 1965, 1973; Gagnon & Simon, 1974; Simon & Gagnon, 1996) contested Freudian ideas of children's innate sexual desires and of repression, and also challenged the common-sense view of children as asexual, arguing sexuality was produced by the social rather than through inborn mechanisms in the child. Children's sexuality, according to Gagnon and Simon, is produced through social values and practices around sexuality and sexual knowledge. They argued that acts, feelings, and body parts only become sexualized through sociocultural scripts that instill them with sexual meaning. It is only when children have access to these social scripts that they start to constitute themselves as sexual beings. Gagnon and Simon identified three interacting scripts shaping everyday sexuality – cultural, interpersonal, and intrapsychic (Gagnon & Simon, 1974). Cultural narratives about what constitutes sexuality and what is appropriate sexual conduct are deployed and mediated through the interpersonal scripting of individuals through everyday interactions, sexual activities, and dialogues with others about sex. Intrapsychic scripting occurs at the level of individual desires and thoughts through an internal reflexive process of the self (Jackson & Scott, 2015). In their discussion of intrapsychic scripting, Stevi Jackson and Sue Scott (2015, p. 42) point out: "Unlike the psychoanalytic psyche, where desires originate largely in our unconscious, intrapsychic scripting is a process through which we reflexively interpret material from cultural scenarios and interpersonal experience through internal conversations with ourselves." Importantly, Gagnon and Simon argued that cultural scripts are interpreted and negotiated and may have different symbolic meanings for individuals. Within this perspective, individual sexual histories are open to interpretation and reinterpretation. Events in childhood, for example, are remembered through adult sexual understandings, taking on different meanings at that time. Adults' understanding of children's 'sexual' behavior is also viewed through the lens of adult sexual scripts and may not have the same meanings for children (Jackson & Scott, 2015).

In her pioneering book, *Childhood and Sexuality* (1982), Stevi Jackson applied Gannon and Simon's perspectives to children's and women's sexuality. In terms of childhood, Jackson argued that children only seem to be asexual because adults hinder their access to key aspects of cultural sexual scripts, making it difficult for them to acquire sexual knowledge and to fully understand their own sexual subjectivities. Jackson, as well as other contemporary researchers in this area (Davies & Robinson, 2010; Jackson & Vares, 2015; Kromidas, 2015), emphasize children are never totally excluded from cultural sexual scripts, but instead interpret, reinterpret, and negotiate those encountered in their everyday lives. Cultural sexual scripts (e.g., heterosexuality, marriage, romantic love, gender customs) are constituted within a variety of contexts like family, media, schooling, legal, and religious institutions (Blaise, 2005; Lamb, 2001; Renold, 2005). A perilous and volatile relationship developed around childhood and sexuality in which the discourse of 'childhood innocence' was central, not just to its constitution and maintenance, but also in relation to the regulation of broader societal practices around sexuality (Bhana, 2008, 2014; Davies & Robinson, 2013; Foucault, 1984; Robinson, 2013).

In the early 1980s, Ronald Goldman and Juliette Goldman (1982) conducted research on children's sexual thinking with children aged 5–15 years, across five countries, Australia, England, Canada, the United States, and Sweden. This research highlighted that children from very early ages are 'active sexual thinkers' (Goldman & Goldman, 1982, p. 5). The definition of 'sexual' used by Goldman and Goldman encompassed a broader understanding beyond biological discourses (e. g., sexual intercourse and other physical sexual acts), incorporating a range of sociocultural issues associated with sexuality, including gender identity and general differences and similarities between men/boys and women/girls; family and marriage; physical changes and differences in bodies; reproduction; social discourses about being childless and representations of gender; and sex education and sources of sexual knowledge. This broader perspective of sexuality is similar to what we have used in our research exploring children's sexual subjectivity. Goldman and Goldman (1982) argued that children's 'sexual socialization' is a process that starts from birth and is highly influenced by the cultures in which children live. In this process, Goldman and Goldman (1982) pointed out that children are actively seeking sexual knowledge, striving to understand it, and building their own knowledge (theories and hypotheses) based on their experiences and information received from various sources (e.g., family, media, friends, peers, school, religious teachings). Differences in children's sexual knowledge, thinking, and problem solving, according to Goldman and Goldman's research, were related to cultural and educational differences. Low-level thinking and problem solving was prevalent among the children, except among Swedish children. The differences across the children were perceived to be linked to adults' poor communication about sexuality with children. Children's low-level thinking and problem solving was considered to be primarily a result of adult inhibitions about using correct terminology and descriptions with children, resulting in children's use of sexual euphemisms and need to find explanations from limited, often false and mythical information with which they had been provided. Goldman and Goldman (1982) highlighted that false analogies often cause confusion in children.

The Swedish component of Goldman and Goldman's research also indicated that children were far more capable of understanding complex biological concepts much earlier than expected. For example, the Swedish children were able to display much earlier insights into the origins of babies and the role of males and females in the process, without intellectual confusion, than children from the English-speaking countries involved in the research. This was associated with an early sex education program and a less conservative cultural climate. The best strategies for enhancing children's sexual thinking, according to Goldman and Goldman (1982), is a sequential development of children's knowledge through specific programs involving home and school, parents and teachers, and appropriate research resources, including media. These programs and resources need to be based on up-to-date research about children's sexual thinking, not on perceptions of childhood that underestimate their abilities to comprehend sexuality issues.

Theoretical Framework

Feminist poststructuralist and queer theorists have critiqued fixed biological understandings of gender and sexuality, arguing that they are primarily fluid, dynamic, and socially constructed aspects of subjectivity (Butler, 1990; Foucault, 1984). Within these theoretical perspectives, we understand sexuality and gender as primarily constituted in sociocultural, historical discourses and subject to relations of power. This is also the case for the relationship between sexuality and childhood, which is a sociocultural, historical, and political construction, representing the values of the dominant cultures of the time (Jackson, 1982; Weeks, 1985). Within feminist poststructuralist and queer perspectives, the construction of gendered and sexual subjects, and the intersection of these with other aspects of subjectivity and identity (class, ethnicity, age, and so on), becomes central to relations of power (Butler, 2004; Foucault, 1984).

Pepper Schwartz and Dominic Cappello (2001) refer to sexuality as being the sum total of our sexual desire, behavior, and self-identity. Deborah Britzman (2000, p. 37) argued: sexuality is 'a human right of free association' and a *force* that is vital to human passion, interest, explorations, and disappointments. Children and young people in their own ways share in experiencing this *force* in their lives. We view sexuality as being experienced and expressed in multiple ways across the life span, which includes the lives of children. These theories challenge the binary construction of gender and its implications for normalizing and naturalizing certain performances of gender and sexuality identities, while rendering others unnatural and problematic (Butler, 2004). Heterosexuality and heteronormative performances of gender are constituted as the norm through which other performances of gender and sexuality are 'Othered.' Further, these theoretical perspectives are critical of discursive, taken-for-granted, normative assumptions about childhood, childhood innocence, and sexuality that perpetuate the belief that sexuality (and sexuality education) is irrelevant to children's lives. Children are active and agentic subjects in the construction of their subjectivities, including who they are as gendered and sexual beings.

Butler's notion of performativity and the heterosexual matrix are useful concepts in understanding the constitution of children's gender and sexual subjectivities. Butler (Butler et al., 1994, p. 33) argues performativity is the repetition of the performances of masculinity and femininity that constitutes and reconstitutes the masculine and feminine subject. That is, how and where masculinity and femininity are played out, culturally and historically, is the way in which masculinity and femininity are established, instituted, circulated, and confirmed. Performances of gender are relational – done for others around us so we are read as intelligible subjects (Butler, 1990; Davies, 2008).

The heterosexual matrix is defined by Butler as "a grid of cultural intelligibility through which bodies, genders, and desires are naturalised" (Butler, 1990, p. 151). It is a "hegemonic discursive/epistemic model of gender intelligibility that assumes that for bodies to cohere and make sense there must be a stable sex expressed through a stable gender (masculine expresses male, feminine expresses female) that is oppositionally and hierarchically defined through the compulsory practice of heterosexuality" (Butler, 1990, p. 151). Alsop, Fitzsimmons and Lennon (2002, p. 97) point out that "it is the 'epistemic regime of presumptive heterosexuality,' which drives our division into male and female, and which itself structures our understanding of biology." It is the presumption of heterosexuality as natural and normative that upholds the distinction of bodies into male and female.

Researching Children's Gender and Sexual Subjectivities: An Overview of Our Research

The two research projects on which this discussion is based examined the relationship between childhood and sexuality, with a focus on children's gendered and sexual cultures and their knowledge of sexuality, love, and relationships. The first research project was a pilot study (Davies & Robinson, 2010; Robinson, 2013; Robinson & Davies, 2008) undertaken in the state of New South Wales, and the second an Australian Research Council Discovery Grant (2011–2013) conducted in New South Wales and the state of Victoria (Robinson & Davies, 2015; Robinson, Smith, & Davies, 2017). Both projects investigated the sociocultural discourses operating around children's access to sexual knowledge; explored parents' approaches to speaking with their children about sexual knowledge; investigated children's understandings of intimate relationships (love, marriage, being in-love); and adults' and children's perspectives of sexuality and relationship education. Unlike the pilot study, which focused on children aged 3–5 years, the second, larger study targeted primary school-aged children aged 5–11 years and investigated children's understandings of respect, how parents approached educating children about respect, as well as educators' perspectives of sexuality and relationship education in primary schools. Separate surveys targeting parents and educators of primary school-aged children, which included short-answer questions on all the areas already identified, were also an addition in the larger project.

Across both projects, interviews were held with a total of 33 children and 31 individual interviews and 6 focus groups with parents. In addition, an online survey was completed by 342 parents. Children came from a diverse range of family structures (e.g., single-parent, same-sex, blended, and nuclear) and sociocultural and economic backgrounds, and were recruited from early childhood education settings, primary schools, parent/family organizations, social networking sites, snowballing, and through a recruitment organization. Parents consented to their children's participation and relevant educational and governing bodies granted ethics approval. In both projects, discussions with children and young people were initiated through the use of images from magazines, postcards, newspapers, and children's storybooks. The images were cultural representations of a range of areas including gender, marriage, love, kissing, family, and schooling. This methodology is useful to begin conversations with children and young people and to elicit their perspectives and ideas on their readings of the images and representations (Robinson & Davies, 2014). For younger children, it is a familiar approach, similar to storytelling activities that they encounter in their daily lives.

Initially a thematic analysis of the qualitative data from the surveys and interviews was undertaken. In addition, a secondary analysis was conducted using a Foucauldian discourse analytical approach. Discourse analysis provides a linguistic approach to an understanding of the relationship between language, knowledge, ideology, and power (Lupton, 1992). Through the discourses that emerge from parents' discussions of children's sexuality education, both in the home and in schools, we can identify the ideologies that are reproduced that reflect and privilege certain beliefs and values on childhood and sexuality. These discourses influence their practices with their children. Children's early learning about gender and sexuality through the cultural scripts, stemming from family, media, peers, and so on, are foundational to the development of children's sexual subjectivities. The following discussion examines competing discourses about childhood and sexuality and children's sexual development emerging from parents' perspectives of children's sexuality education.

Discourses of Childhood, Sexuality, Innocence, and Children's Sexual Development – Parents' Perspectives

Childhood Innocence and Child Development

Parent's perspectives of children's sexual development were generally constituted through a range of intersecting discourses about childhood, childhood innocence, child development, and sexuality. As expected, some parents' perspectives were framed in traditional biomedical understandings of childhood and sexuality, in which children were largely considered to be 'asexual' until they reached puberty. Within this context, children were articulated as being innocent, sexuality was understood to be an aspect of adult subjectivity, and consequently irrelevant and developmentally inappropriate for the child. Those that adhered to these discourses tended to consider that providing children with sexuality education would have adverse effects on children's emotional and cognitive development. The discourse of childhood innocence underpinned perceptions that children were 'too young' to engage with sexuality knowledge and, for some, it was important to prolong children's innocence for as long as possible (Corteen & Scraton, 1997; Robinson, 2013). Strictly regulating children's access to sexuality knowledge (e.g., at home, school, and in the media) was considered as being integral to this aim (Robinson et al., 2017). The following comments typified these perspectives:

> Kids need to remain kids as long as possible. Education makes them teenagers before they need to be. (46-year-old father, heterosexual, married, daughter aged 11 years)

> Too young at 6 years of age and I want my children to have a childhood before having this subject thrust upon them. (47-year-old father, heterosexual, married, daughter aged 6 years)

> My son is only 5 so I don't think it is relevant to him. (40-year-old mother, heterosexual, de facto relationship, son aged 5 years)

> I feel children are being exposed to information far too early and the innocence of childhood is being narrowed more and more. What is the hurry? (32-year-old mother, heterosexual, married, son aged 8 years)

The values and beliefs held by these parents, and the anxieties they experience, reflected in these comments, primarily emerge from the discourse of childhood innocence. Childhood innocence is generally considered to be naturally inherent, thus universal in the biological state of being a child. Indeed, a defining characteristic of childhood is the notion of being 'innocent' and 'vulnerable,' especially in terms of sexuality. However, the constitution of innocence in childhood is culturally determined; it varies across experiences of childhood, which are multiple (Robinson, 2013). Children's transgressions from 'childhood innocence' are largely constructed through adult perceptions of children having 'too much knowledge' of sexuality 'too early.' This also extends to children who engage in sexualized behaviors often considered inappropriate (e.g., touching genitals) being viewed as 'tainted' or 'sullied' – that is, no longer considered an appropriate child subject (Bond Stockton, 2009). The discourse of childhood innocence is framed in and reinforced through Piagetian theories of child development, which consider children as emotionally and cognitively immature (due to children's chronological age and stage of development) to comprehend complex and abstract concepts associated with adulthood and adult maturity.

The discourse of childhood innocence and children's perceived asexuality or latent sexuality have been central to the regulatory practices that have arisen around parents' approaches to children's sexuality education in the home. Some parents try to prolong an innocence in childhood by not using anatomical names of sexual body parts, but using euphemisms with children. This practice goes beyond sexual terms, but also includes knowledge of sexuality more generally. This practice can also be a result of fears around children using sexual terms publicly with other adults and other children – terms considered by some to be inappropriate for children.

Some parents fear being judged by other parents for being perceived to be transcending a culturally constructed boundary between what has been constituted as adults' knowledge and children's knowledge. In some instances, at the completion of focus groups, some parents privately shared that they talk to their young children about sexuality issues, but did not feel they could say this with other parents present, fearing that they would be considered 'bad' parents, in particular 'bad' mothers (Davies & Robinson, 2010). Mothers are traditionally the ones relegated as being responsible for caring for children, including talking to them about sexuality education. In the discourse of the bad mother, women are viewed to transgress from the social norms of good parenting, in this case, keeping children innocent. Some mothers in our research focus groups expressed the need to start conversations about sexuality much earlier in their children's lives than is generally accepted, especially if they had daughters, due to children's access to sexualized images in the media, advertising, and the Internet.

The discourse of the 'sexualization' of children, particularly girls, in the media, social media, and advertising, underpinned parental concerns about children's premature sexual activity. A parental key concern was that if children viewed sexually suggestive content in the media it would encourage sexual behaviors and practices. Parents felt that they could not totally control the messages that children received about gender and sexuality through these avenues, despite instigating strict regulations around children's access to these forms of communication. These concerns were echoed in the comments made by the following father of three girls:

> Due to technology (T.V, internet etc) kids are far more advanced in terms of their knowledge of sexuality. They are more inclined to experiment at a younger age than in the past and is important that they are also made aware of the consequences and meaning of such actions. (38-year-old father, heterosexual, living with partner, three daughters aged 11, 7, and 5 years)

What is often missing from the sexualization debates that prevail in Western cultures is a recognition of children's knowledge, sexual subjectivities, desire, and agency. Researchers have demonstrated that children are already actively building gendered and sexual cultures through their everyday interactions with peers in the early years of their lives (Davies, 1989; Jackson, 1982; Lamb, 2001; Thorne, 1993). Children are also far more capable of critical thinking than many adults give them credit for and often self-regulate their behaviors within the boundaries of what they view is possible as children. Children actively interpret, negotiate, and transform the discourses of gender, sexuality, and relationships they take up as their own (Renold 2005; Robinson & Davies, 2015).

Parents' Perspectives of Children's Sexual Development and Sexuality Education

For many parents sexuality was viewed to start at puberty, when a child's body shows signs of physical development and maturity. Sexuality was perceived to continue to develop from this point, paralleling the young person's physical and emotional development. Sexuality education was considered important at puberty, or just prior, in order for children to understand what was happening to their bodies or what biological changes were going to happen to them in the near future. These parents generally did not consider sexuality education relevant or appropriate for prepubescent children, viewing sexuality education primarily about sex, reproduction, and sexually transmitted infections. The sociocultural constitution of children's sexual subjectivities and building ethical and respectful relationships (e.g., developing understandings of consent) in the early years was generally not associated within sexuality education.

For many parents, children's sexual development was associated with the prevalent discourse of sex as dangerous. This perspective, coupled with the dominant discourse of teenagers being sexual risk takers, led to parental anxieties about future threats that their children might encounter, such as contracting a sexually transmitted infection and possible pregnancy. The following comments articulate these concerns:

> It's [sex education] part of growing up. There is a scientific aspect (ie: the human body is really amazing, this is how it works). There is a psychological aspect (your body will start changing, this is what is happening & why). There is a health aspect (there are some bad diseases, this is what they do, this is how you catch them), & reproductive aspect – this is how you make a child, & this is how you look after one during pregnancy and after birth. Year 5 & 6 [ages 9–12 years] kids should be aware of all of these. (44-year-old father, heterosexual, married, two boys aged 9 and 5 years)

> They need to know what they are going to go through as a teenager. How to protect themselves. And all the dangers – STDs, STIs. (Father, no age given, heterosexual, living with partner, three children: two daughters aged 6 and 10 years, and a son aged 6 years)

For many parents, their children's future teenage years were a source of anxiety and they articulated the importance of addressing the potential future dangers with their pubescent children. Despite considering such discussions to be important, many parents in our research found these talks too difficult to have with their children. Other parents only provided minimal sexuality education to their children (Robinson et al., 2017). The following comment by a mother highlights this point, when she spoke about her belief that girls in particular need to be educated about sexuality and their developing bodies, when they are nearing or reach puberty – represented by the onset of menstruation:

> I think that [sexuality education is important] after age 10 when the body starts developing, it needs to be explained. A great example to why is because a lot of parents do not bring it up with their children and are unaware of what happens to their bodies and have nobody to talk to. My daughter got her period in year 5 [9–10 years of age]. In the toilet one day her friend asked why she was taking so long and she said 'oh! I got my period' and her friend asked 'what's that?' My daughter was in absolute shock. (36-year-old mother, heterosexual, separated/divorced, two daughters aged 11 and 6 years, and a son aged 9 years)

This mother was concerned, as was her knowledgeable young daughter, that some girls are not educated about menstruation until they experience it, or informed incidentally by their peers. Parents' failure to address children's developing sexuality in the home early in children's lives is associated with a number of critical sociocultural and political issues: first, a denial of children's sexual subjectivity, based on the discourse of childhood innocence, incorporating notions of asexuality, and being 'too young'; second, parent's embarrassment with talking to their children about sexuality; and third, a reliance on schools to address sexuality education (Robinson et al. 2017).

Some parents expressed a counter discourse to that of sexuality education only being relevant at puberty, suggesting that age-appropriate sex education should start much earlier in children's lives. Children's sexual literacy was considered critical for building children's resiliencies, competencies, respectful relationships, understandings of consent, and awareness of self-protection. The following comments typify this perspective:

> It is never too early to learn age appropriate sexuality education both in terms of one's own sex and the opposite sex. Lack of appropriate knowledge in that area seems to lead to any or all of confusion, uncertainty, anxiety, misunderstanding, embarrassment and inappropriate behaviour toward others. (49-year-old father, heterosexual, single, a son aged 6 years)

> They should know how to protect themselves in order not to harm others. (36-year-old mother, heterosexual, married, two daughters aged 6 and 5 years)

Children's potential or actual inappropriate sexual behavior toward other children was a particular concern for these parents. There was a fear that children may not be able to control their sexual behaviors at the time of strong hormonal changes, peaking their curiosities. There was unease around children showing body parts and forcing other children to kiss them, as the following father comments:

> I feel that Year 5 [ages 9–10] or Year 6 [ages 11–12] in Primary is a good age to start . . . I was shocked to discover that an 8 year old asked my 8 year old daughter to try 'sex' . . . i.e. she started to kiss her on her lips and touch her body . . . I didn't realise until then how early it all starts for curious little minds. I feel that you need to discuss these issues early and prepare your child for distasteful scenarios . . .

> where they can confidently say 'no' to any unwanted advances. (45-year-old father, heterosexual, living with partner, two children: a son aged 9 years and a daughter aged 6 years)

Discourses of consent and protection were central to these parents' beliefs about children's development of sexual literacy. This scenario highlights parental concerns with children's use of gendered and sexual power over peers, and the importance of children developing skill sets and strategies to say no to unwanted attention. While the above scenario is focused on same sex power play between children, most parents expressed concern about boys' gendered and sexual power over girls. Parents stressed the importance of instilling in boys respect for girls and women early in their lives.

Parents raised the issue that children were reaching puberty earlier, resulting from children's early maturity both physically and socially; therefore, becoming more sexually aware and active sooner in their lives. Some made the point that it was a very different world today from the one they grew up in:

> I don't see the world as the same as when I was a little girl. Kids get mature & curious these days & sex education is very important for them to learn things & most importantly, protect themselves from the cruel world that we live in. (29-year-old mother, same-sex attracted, two children: a daughter aged 5 years and a son aged 3 years)

This parent mobilized the discourse of child protection that many parents associated with childhood and sexuality. Parents often expressed anxieties about children's vulnerability to sexual exploitation by peers or adults. Unlike parents who viewed sexuality education as inappropriate and compromising childhood innocence, some parents believed that sexuality education was critical in terms of building children's awareness and competencies in self-protection.

A less prevalent perspective voiced by parents was the view that prepubescent children were agentic sexual subjects (Robinson et al., 2017). Within this counter discourse to children as asexual and innocent, children's sexual development was considered to begin early in life. These parents' viewed children as having their own sense of sexuality, desire, and an active interest in bodies and behavior differences across the sexes. The following father of a 5-year-old daughter commented:

> I believe that children have their own experiences of desire/sexuality, and my child has an interest in body and behaviour differences. (44-year-old father, same-sex attracted, married, a daughter aged 5 years)

A mother of a 5-year-old son also remarked:

> Our child thinks his penis is something to urinate with and a play thing. I think little children should be able to enjoy their sexuality when they are that young, without being put upon thinking too much about it. (44-year-old mother, heterosexual, living with partner, son aged 5 years)

A mother of two daughters makes the following points:

> [Sexuality education is important] Because they are quite sexual little beings and have plenty of discussions/experiences surrounding their body parts. (36-year-old mother, heterosexual, married, two daughters aged 8 and 5 years)

These parents' mobilized the discourse of children as sexual subjects who are naturally aware and curious about their bodies at early ages. They highlighted that children embody desire and act on their feelings. In the broad sense of bodies, intimacies, relationships, desires, and emotions, sexuality is very much part of children's lives and the development of their identities (Bhana, 2014; Blaise, 2005; Renold, 2005; Robinson, 2013). Children take the cultural scripts (discourses) about gender and sexuality that they receive and make sense of these through the knowledge they have and their experiences in everyday life. The first mother's (with the 5-year-old son) comments also indicate that adults might make too much out of sexuality that is then imposed on children's experiences, with potential negative consequences. Adults can perceive and react to children's behaviors through adult eyes and experiences, which are often influenced by the social taboos that they have learnt about sexuality. As a consequence, sexual taboos can be reinforced in young children. In contrast, these parents create an environment in which children's sexual behaviors and curiosity are supported rather than stigmatized or denied. These discursive practices foster a positive relationship between parent and child regarding matters of sexuality. However, it can also lead to other parents judging their parenting practices, as pointed out previously.

Children's Sexual Knowledge and Parents' Discomfort

Children are given various levels of access to sexual knowledge, with most having minimal information, if any at all. Children are also given a great deal of misinformation or partial information around sexuality by parents, and peers, and often feel duped when they realize this is the case – the stork delivery story is still prevalent among some parents. In our research, most of the parents considered children's access to sexuality education to be important, with the best practice being a shared process between families and schools (Robinson et al., 2017). However, in most cases, parents and schools do not adequately provide children with comprehensive sexuality education, with both parties often relying on the other to provide this type of education. This has a great deal to do with the social taboos about sexuality, 'childhood innocence,' and the controversies often associated with children's sexuality education, particularly when it includes discussion of same-sex relationships, stemming from more conservative members in communities. Some parents position other people's children as a 'danger' to their own children. This is largely because they perceive these children to have 'too much' sexuality information. Within this discourse certain sexuality knowledge (e.g., intercourse, vaginal birth), considered adults' knowledge, instills fears in some parents that their children will be given this information by others, or through the media, thus compromising their children's innocence (Elliott, 2012; Robinson, 2013).

As we have argued elsewhere (Davies & Robinson, 2010), young children's sexual knowledge is most often pieced together from bits of information they are given by parents, siblings, peers, the media, and watching animals' behaviors. Children generally take this knowledge and build on it through their own world experiences and language in order to make sense of the information they are given. For example, children may be given some correct language and information, but parents or other adults often only provide partial information, stopping at a point that either becomes too embarrassing for the adult, or considered 'too much' information 'too early,' or 'too difficult' to explain for children to comprehend.

This process was demonstrated by 2-year-olds who explained the process of having babies. They were aware that the father has 'sperm' and the mother has the 'egg,' and continued to describe the process of the two combining to make a further egg, which 'hatches' and 'the baby comes out.' The children finished the incomplete story by building their understandings of the process of birth from what they already knew – their recognition of chicken eggs and the process of chickens hatching from the egg. Some parents acknowledged that explaining the birth process to children was one of the most difficult and embarrassing conversations, with some choosing not to discuss this process with children. In fact, one mother made it very clear that the best thing about her having a cesarian was that she would not have to explain a vaginal birth to her child and could say that the baby 'came out of her belly' (Davies & Robinson, 2010). This desexualized medical discourse of cesarian birth made it not only easier and less challenging for this mother to talk about birth with her child – shifting the discussion away from private sexual body parts and what happens during vaginal birth – but it also reinforced myths about babies coming out through a mother's belly button that some children believe is the case. Many of the myths that are associated with birth are more about parental discomfort and embarrassment about addressing sexuality and body issues with children.

The Sociocultural Discursive Construction of Children's Gender and Sexual Subjectivities in the Early Years

In recent years, researchers have demonstrated that the development of children's sexual subjectivities starts early in life, well before puberty (Egan & Hawkes, 2010; Epstein, 1995; Lamb, 2001). This body of work also points out that adults' perspectives of their child's understandings of sexuality can be very different from the reality in children's lives (Blaise, 2005, 2009; Robinson, 2013). Children interpret, negotiate, and reconceptualize sociocultural discourses about sexuality and gender they encounter in their everyday lives. The cultural scripts constituted in these discourses are enthusiastically played out in children's interactions with family members, peers, and other adults. Children are actively engaged in developing their sexual and gendered subjectivities (and influencing the development of other children's subjectivities) and in constructing their understandings of relationships, including those that are intimate and special.

Our research, as does other research in this area, highlights that children's perceptions of sexuality are primarily constituted through their understandings of gendered relationships and are largely heteronormative (Blaise, 2005; Renold, 2005; Robinson & Davies, 2015). Sharon Lamb's (2001) research points out that sexual games in childhood (e.g., 'I'll show you mine, if you show me yours' and 'Naked Barbies') were common secret stories relayed by women and girls. Lamb states, "Even at early ages, they [girls] incorporate into their sexual styles images of what they think adult female sexuality is about" (2001, p. 7). Cultural rituals, such as, mock weddings, marriage, mothers, fathers, and babies, doctors and nurses, and boyfriends and girlfriends are played out in children's everyday lives and are rehearsals of what children perceive to be central to their future roles as adults (Blaise, 2009; Lamb, 2001; Renold, 2006; Robinson & Davies, 2015). Children actively engage in having boyfriends and girlfriends from early ages and these relationships are central to children's everyday conversations with each other. In our opinion, these are more than 'pretend' but constitute 'special' relationships reflecting children's desires, feelings of love and being 'in-love' (Robinson, 2013).

Marriage, in particular, plays a significant role in children's sociocultural gender and sexual development, and is frequently viewed as a core part of children's right-of-passage into adulthood, the key mechanism to have babies, and the means through which intimacy (kissing, touching, expressions of love) is legitimized. The 'honeymoon' is a key part of the discourse of marriage as articulated by a 5-year-old girl in our research, responding to a photo of a boy and girl in a mock wedding scenario:

LI: They're gonna get married and go on a honeymoon.

RESEARCHER: What else happens when you get married? What happens when you get back [from the honeymoon]?

LI: A baby starts to grow.

As we have argued elsewhere (Davies & Robinson, 2010) children's learning often follows what is considered a rational linear formula – a procedure. In this case, 5-year-old Li demonstrates her learning of the heteronormative cultural script associated with traditional marriage – that is, one marries, goes on a honeymoon, returns home, falls pregnant, and a baby is born. Li highlights how for many children marriage and the honeymoon are linked to reproduction. The discourse of marriage is infused in children's lives through cultural narratives represented in family wedding photos, media, and children's literature. As one mother commented: "I look at it [the wedding photo] and I just see this replication of what is presented as the ideal relationship throughout the ages" (Robinson & Davies, 2015).

Children's play scenarios are framed within heteronormative gendered scripts and are legitimated by adults around them, as well as being central to early childhood education pedagogies in some places. Children play a central role in regulating the normative gendered behaviors of other children. For example, boys wanting to marry another boy was forbidden within children's mock wedding play scenarios among certain groups in our research. Such regulatory practices around the gender performances of their peers are frequently reinforced by teachers and families. While children's and young people's formal school curriculum is limited in terms of discussions of sexuality, schools are a central site in the everyday constitution of sexual and gender subjectivities (what is often considered the informal or hidden curriculum of schooling [Fields, 2008; Fields & Payne, 2016; Gilbert, 2014; Robinson, 2013]). Jen Gilbert (2014, p. xiv) argued: "Sexuality saturates educational spaces, objects and relations." Primary schools are no exception, with decades of research highlighting how curricula, teacher practices, and children's peer cultures constitute, reinforce, and perpetuate heteronormative discourses of gender and sexuality (Allen & Ingram, 2015; Renold, 2005; Robinson & Davies, 2008; Thorne, 1993). Maria Kromidas (2015, p. 161) in regard to her research with 10- and 11-year-olds in New York City pointed out:

> Within the school, sexuality was a thoroughly public text that was fully pedagogical. That is, it was subject to observation, analysis, scrutiny and debate. A large bulk of time and energy within the kids' informal interactional structures (in the playground, staircases, in 'free time' in the classroom) concerned sexuality.

Children are aware of the sociocultural taboos and regulations associated with sexuality and relationships (i.e., kissing, touching, being in-love) reinforced by family and school rules (e.g., 'No Kissing' rules at school, legitimized as a means of controlling germs). As a consequence, children often enact these relationships in secret. This is highlighted in the following comments by an 8-year-old girl, Meika:

RESEARCHER: What does it mean to have a special boyfriend or a girlfriend?

MEIKA: Like a special person in your life.

RESEARCHER: Do you know anyone . . . that has a girlfriend or a boyfriend?

MEIKA: No but – not that I know, but there's been this big, big, big, big rumour that this – I think they're both in Year six . . .
My friend told – well he's not actually my friend he's the boy that likes me in my class. He said he was spying on [girl's name] – that's the girl. He said that the boy kissed [girl's name].

RESEARCHER: At school?

MEIKA: Yeah. He said he witnessed it.

Meika highlights how these relationships can become a curiosity and fascination for other children, especially if children can be 'caught out' doing something considered not to be appropriate, like kissing, especially at school. Spying on children who were rumored to be having relationships was an exciting past time for some at school. This practice was also articulated by a 6-year-old boy, Ethan, from another school:

RESEARCHER: So, do you think that kids are allowed to kiss?

ETHAN: Well they are, but . . .

RESEARCHER You said that they shouldn't kiss in public?

ETHAN: Well it's just, they don't really like doing it in public at the school.They like going in secret places.

RESEARCHER: Do they?

ETHAN: People usually spy on them.

RESEARCHER: They just go off and hide in a cupboard or behind a tree or something?

ETHAN: Something bad, a guy named Greg blackmailed Patty. He saw them, he spied on them.

RESEARCHER: What do you mean blackmailed?

ETHAN: Where he was like, I won't tell if you give me something and that was something like an iPod touch thing.

RESEARCHER: What?

ETHAN: She gave it to him.

RESEARCHER: But why did she give it to him? What for? What was the reason?

ETHAN: So that he wouldn't tell anybody.

Within the context of childhood, discourses of secrecy and voyeurism associated with sexuality, become particularly powerful. Children are not just aware of the taboos associated with sexuality generally, but especially in relation to children's engagement with sexual behaviors. These discourses are reinforced in environments, such as schools, where rules strictly prohibit displays of intimacy or sexual behaviors (e.g., touching or kissing) between children or young people. These rules are regulated by teachers' surveillance (and children's surveillance) of children's and young people's behaviors. These discourses and discursive practices are in tension with school cultures that are infused with sexuality and are critical sites of children's and young people's sexual development, as discussed previously. As

Foucault (1984) has pointed out in *The History of Sexuality*, the enforced privacy, secrecy, and prohibitions associated with sexual behaviors (some more so than others) leads to a greater interest in the behaviors and an increased sense of titillation in observing or engaging in those behaviors. The discourse of secrecy and fears of being caught breaking the rules provides fertile ground for corruption and abuse.

Conclusion

Parents' perspectives of children's sexuality education can provide a glimpse of both sociocultural and traditional biomedical discourses that constitute understandings of children's sexual development. There are a range of competing discourses that underpin parents' perspectives, but the prevalence of the discourse of childhood innocence has significant influence, impacting values, beliefs, and practices in this area of children's lives. Of particular importance is the impact of the discourse of childhood innocence on the perception that children's sexual development starts at puberty, aligning with physical changes in children's bodies. However, we have argued in this chapter that children's sexual development is also constituted through sociocultural discourses – a process that starts well before puberty, early in children's lives. Exploring children's gendered and sexual cultures from the perspectives and everyday practices of children, demonstrates that they are actively involved in constituting their gender and sexual subjectivities early. From the sociocultural and heteronormative discourses that they take up and from interactions with peers, the media, families, and the broader society, children learn what it means to be a sexual being and the sociocultural expectations of what is viewed as the legitimate sexual subject. Much of children's education and knowledge building is done outside the gaze of adults, as children and young people learn the taboos and silences that exist around sexuality. The need to provide children with accurate and comprehensive sexuality and relationship education that begins early and built on by both families and schools is crucial to children's health and well-being and the development of their sexuality literacy and sexual citizenship.

References

Allen, L. & Ingram, T. (2015). "Bieber Fever": Girls, Desire and the Negotiation of Childhood Sexualities. In Renold, E., Ringrose, J., & Egan, D. R. (Eds.), *Children, Sexuality and Sexualisation* (141–158). London: Palgrave Macmillan.

Alsop, R., Fitzsimmons, A., & Lennon, K. (2002). *Theorizing Gender*. London: Polity.

Bennett, D. L. & Robards, F. (2013). What Is Adolescence and Who Are Adolescents? In Kang, M., Skinner, S. R., Sanci, L. A., Sawyer, S. M. (Eds.), *Youth Health and Adolescent Medicine* (pp. 3–19). Melbourne, Australia: I.P. Communications Pty. Ltd.

Bhana, D. (2008). Discourses of Childhood Innocence in Primary School: HIV AIDS Education in South Africa. *African Journal of AIDS Research*, *7*(1), 149–158.

(2014). *Under Pressure: The Regulation of Sexualities in South African Schools*. Braamfontein, South Africa: MaThoko's Books.

Blaise, M. (2005). *Playing It Straight!: Uncovering Gender Discourses in the Early Childhood Classroom*. New York: Routledge.

(2009). "What a Girl Wants, What a Girl Needs": Responding to Sex, Gender, and Sexuality in the Early Childhood Classroom. *Journal of Research in Childhood Education*, *23*(4), 450–460.

Bond Stockton, K. (2009) *The Queer Child, or Growing Sideways in the Twentieth Century*. Durham: Duke University Press.

Britzman, D. P. (2000). Precocious Education. In Talburt, S. & Steinberg, S. R. (Eds.), *Thinking Queer: Sexuality, Culture and Education*. New York: Peter Lang.

Butler, J. (1990). *Gender Trouble: Feminism and the Subversion of Identity*. New York: Routledge.

(1993). *Bodies That Matter: on the Discursive Limits of "Sex"*. New York: Routledge.

(2004). *Undoing Gender*. New York: Routledge.

Butler, J., Segal, L., & Osbo, P. (1994). Gender as Performance: An Interview with Judith Butler. *Radical Philosophy*, 67, 32–39.

Corteen, K. & Scraton, P. (1997). Prolonging "Childhood", Manufacturing "Innocence" and Regulating Sexuality. In Scraton, P. (Ed.), *Childhood in "Crisis"*. London: University College London Press.

Davies, B. (1989). *Frogs and Snails and Feminist Tails: Preschool Children and Gender*. Sydney: Allen and Unwin.

Davies, C. (2008). Becoming Sissy: A Response to David McInnes. In Davies, B. (Ed.), *Judith Butler in Conversation: Analysing the Texts and Talk of Everyday Life* (pp. 117–133). New York: Routledge.

Davies, C. & Robinson, K. H. (2010). Hatching Babies and Stork Deliveries: Risk and Regulation in the Construction of Children's Sexual Knowledge. *Contemporary Issues in Early Childhood*, *11*(3), 249–263.

(2013). Reconceptualising Family: Negotiating Sexuality in a Governmental Climate of Neoliberalism. *Contemporary Issues in Early Childhood*, *14*(1), 39–53.

Davies, C., Skinner, R. S., Odgers, H. L., Khut, G. P., & Morrow, A. (2018). The Use of Mobile and New Media Technologies in a Health Intervention about HPV and HPV Vaccination in Schools. In Grealy, L. D., Driscoll, C., & Hickey-Moody, A. (Eds.), *Youth, Technology, Governance, Experience: Adults Understanding Young Lives*. London and New York: Routledge.

Egan, R. D. (2015). Desexualizing the Freudian Child in a Culture of "Sexualization": Trends and Implications. In Renold, E., Ringrose, J., & Egan, R. D. (Eds.), *Children, Sexuality and Sexualization* (pp. 105–123). Basingstoke: Palgrave Macmillan.

Egan, D. R. & Hawkes, G. (2010) *Theorizing the Sexual Child in Modernity*. New York: Palgrave Macmillan.

Elliott, S. (2012). *Not My Kid: What Parents Believe about the Sex Lives of Their Teenagers*. New York: New York University Press.

Epstein, D. (1995). 'Girls Don't Do Bricks': Gender and Sexuality in the Primary Classroom. In Siraj-Blatchford, J. & Siraj-Blatchford, I. (Eds.), *Educating the*

Whole Child: Cross-Curricular Skills Themes and Dimensions. Buckingham: Open University Press.

Fields, J. (2008). *Risky Lessons: Sex Education and Social Inequality*. New Brunswick, NJ: Rutgers University Press, Series in Childhood Studies.

Fields, J. & Payne, E. (2016). Editorial Introduction: Gender and Sexuality Taking Up Space in Schooling. *Sex Education*, *16*(1), 1–7.

Ford, C. & Beach, F. (1951). *Patterns of Sexual Behavior*. New York: Harper and Brothers.

Foucault, M. (1984). *The History of Sexuality. Volume 1, An Introduction*. Hurley, R. (Trans.). Harmondsworth: Penguin.

Freud, S. (1976 [1905]). *Three Essays on the Theory of Sexuality*. Basic Books: New York.

Gagnon, J. (1965). Sexuality and Sexual Learning in the Child. *Psychiatry*, *28*, 212–228.

(1973). The Creation of the Sexual in Early Adolescence. In Groubard, S. (Ed.), *From Twelve to Sixteen*. New York: W.W. Norton.

Gagnon, J. & Simon, W. (1974). *Sexual Conduct*. London: Hutchinson.

Gilbert, J. (2014). *Sexuality in School: The Limits of Education*. Minneapolis: University of Minnesota Press.

Goldman, R. & Goldman, J. (1982). *Children's Sexual Thinking: A Comparative Study of Children Aged 5 to 15 Years in Australia, North America, Britain and Sweden*. London: Routledge and Kegan Paul.

Jackson, S. (1982). *Childhood and Sexuality*. Oxford: Basil Blackwell.

Jackson, S. & Scott, S. (2015). A Sociological History of Researching Childhood and Sexuality: Continuities and Discontinuities. In Renold, E., Ringrose, J., & Egan, D. R. (Eds.), *Children, Sexuality and Sexualisation*. London: Palgrave Macmillan.

Jackson, S. & Vares, T. (2015). New Visibilities? Using Video Diaries to Explore Girls' Experiences of Sexualized Culture. In Renold, E., Ringrose, J., & Egan, D. R. (Eds.), *Children, Sexuality and Sexualization*. London: Plagrave Macmillan.

Jagose, A. (1996). *Queer Theory: An Introduction*. New York: New York University Press.

Kromidas, M. (2015). "He's Cute, for Her": Kids' Entangled Pedagogies of Sexuality and Race in New York City. In Renold, E., Ringrose, J., & Egan, D. R. (Eds.), *Children, Sexuality and Sexualization* (pp. 159–173). London: Palgrave Macmillan.

Lamb, S. (2001). *The Secret Lives of Girls: What Good Girls Really Do – Sex Play, Aggression and Their Guilt*. New York: The Free Press.

Lupton, D. (1992). Discourse Analysis: A New Methodology for Understanding the Ideologies of Health and Illness. *Australian Journal of Public Health*, *16*(2), 145–150.

Mead, M. (1948 [1935]). *Sex and Temperament*. New York: Perennial/HarperCollins Publishers.

Piaget, J. (1959). *The Language and Thought of the Child* (3rd edn.). London: Routledge & Kegan Paul.

(1960). *The Child's Conception of the World*. London: Routledge & Kegan Paul.

Renold, E. (2005). *Girls, Boys, and Junior Sexualities: Exploring Children's Gender and Sexual Relations in the Primary School*. London: Routledge.

(2006). "They Won't Let Us Play . . . Unless You're Going Out with Them": Girls, Boys and Butler's "Heterosexual Matrix" in the Primary Years. *British Journal of Sociology of Education*, *27*(4), 489–509.

Robinson, K. H. (2013). *Innocence, Knowledge and the Construction of Childhood: The Contradictory Nature of Sexuality and Censorship in Children's Contemporary Lives*. London: Routledge.

Robinson, K. H. & Davies, C. (2008). Docile Bodies and Heteronormative Moral Subjects: Constructing the Child and Sexual Knowledge in Schooling. *Sexuality & Culture*, *12*(4), 221–239. doi:10.1007/s12119-008-9037-7

(2014). Doing Sexuality Research with Children: Ethics, Theory, Methods and Practice. *4*, *4*(4), 250–263.

(2015). Children's Gendered and Sexual Cultures: Desiring and Regulating Recognition through Life Markers of Marriage, Love and Relationships. In Renold, E., Ringrose, J., & Egan, D. (Eds.), *Children, Sexuality and 'Sexualization* (174–190). London: Palgrave.

Robinson, K. H., Smith, E., & Davies, C. (2017). Responsibilities, Tensions, and Ways Forward: Parents' Perspectives on Children's Sexuality Education. *Sex Education*, *17*(3), 333–347.

Schwartz, P. & Cappello, D. (2001). *Ten Talks Parents Must Have with Their Children about Sex and Character*. Rydalmere: Hodder Headline Australia.

Simon, W. & Gagnon, J. (1996). On Psychosexual Development. In Goslin, D. A. (Ed.), *Handbook of Socialization Theory and Research* (pp. 733–752). Chicago, IL: Rand McNally.

Thorne, B. (1993). *Gender Play: Boys and Girls in School*. New Brunswick: Rutgers University Press.

Weeks, J. (1985). *Sexuality and Its Discontents: Meanings, Myths, and Modern Sexualities*. London: Routledge.

4 Not Innocent, but Vulnerable

An Approach to Childhood Innocence

Lucie Jarkovská and Sharon Lamb

This chapter begins by examining the concept of childhood innocence, the critiques of the concept, and critiques about the political use of the concept. We go on to ask what about childhood innocence or similar concepts might be preserved in the area of sex education and childhood sexuality in general. We agree that using the concept of innocence to make claims on behalf of children has an insidious effect on discourse about children, not only because it positions children as helpless, incompetent, and entirely dependent on the will and decisions of adults but because it also supports political agendas harmful to children and other marginalized groups. The concept of innocence, as it is currently used across the globe with regard to sex and sexuality, also tends to be activated around certain (privileged) groups of children, while other kinds of children are neglected based on their race, class, ethnicity, or geopolitical location. We acknowledge, however, that the concept of innocence has historically also been closely connected with some policies and actions that were taken in order to make children's lives better. So, we argue that when critiquing the concept of childhood sexual innocence, scholars should be careful not to at the same time neglect the need for children´s protection. We suggest replacing the concept of innocence with the concept of vulnerability and use an example to describe how this might happen. In the end, searching for how to make an argument for actual vulnerabilities of children, we turn to what has been referred to as the "new materialism," which asks us to consider children in body and in consciousness, constructed by discourse but material circumstances as well, shaped by their interaction with other bodies, things, and people. This idea is often integrated with the Deleuze and Guattari´s concept of assemblages (Deleuze & Guattari, 2005; Renold & Ringrose, 2008), and the concept of assemblage protects but de-privileges human agency by seeing it as one of many parts of the assemblage where every component affects and is affected the others. We hope to show one need not romanticize children´s voices and children's agency as true or authentic in order to hold on to the idea that children are important, valuable, and can make worthwhile contributions to society.

This chapter has been written as part of the research project Diversifying Preschool Education in the Czech Republic: Inclusion, Exclusion and Social Inequalities, which has received funding from the Czech Science Foundation (registration no. GA16-18940S).

The Idea of Childhood Innocence

"What is it that is most appealing about children? Is it simply their physical beauty? Is it their openness to loving and being loved? Their playfulness, their innate humour? Beyond these things, in my view, children are beautiful because they possess something that we have all lost – the quality of innocence," writes journalist Tim Lott in *The Guardian* (2013). Not always was a child seen as a bearer of such qualities. Phillipe Ariès shows that the discourse of the innocent child emerged with Romanticism (Ariès, 1962), and while others have argued against the depiction of this era as the dawning of childhood itself (Kinney, 1995; Orme, 2001), the notion of innocence was important for that period. Before the Romantic era, the Christian child was said to be born into sin, gradually learning to become righteous (Najafi & Higonnet, 2003). The romantic child, on the other hand, was born innocent. Innocence was framed by purity, simplicity, sincerity, fragility, and lack of knowledge. As philosopher Joanne Faulkner puts it: "innocence is an empty trait, valued precisely as a deficit of experience, as if experience itself were corrosive of virtue" (2013). Those qualities make children lovable and in need of protection.

There are several explanations for this paradigmatic rupture that permitted these conceptualizations of innocence to flourish. The romantic period saw demographic changes and a decrease in infant mortality, secularization, and general changes in social organization of life with the rise of nuclear family and an emerging romantic worldview. Because romanticism admired the emotional, the mysterious, the unknown, the irrational, and the fantastic, and because it found nature and natural explanations superior to those associated with the grittiness of industry, the simplicity of an innocent child become a perfect counterpoise to complexities of turbulent industrial and social development of modern society. From the nineteenth century onward, the idea of children's innocence was not only related to nature but strongly related to children's sexuality. Their innocence became an argument for an absence of sexuality in children, and the lives of children, and the demand for such absence.

The idea of the innocent child who has to be shielded from the adult world encouraged a concern for their well-being and activism in favor of children´s rights. As Higgonet (1998) notes, sweetly sentimental pictures of girls and boys contrasted with darker images of real children's pain and suffering (1998) and sparked emotional responses that motivated adults to improve the children's living conditions. A variety of laws protecting the well-being of children at work, at school, or in the home were enforced in the United Kingdom (Health and Morals of Apprentices Act 1802, Acts addressing working conditions of children in cotton mills 1819, 1825, and 1829, Prevention of Cruelty to, and Protection of, Children Act 1889 and many others). In the United States and Britain, the social work movement used childhood innocence to argue for the foster care system.

Three Critiques of the Idea of Childhood Innocence

Over the past two decades scholars have taken a closer look at the idea of childhood innocence and how this idea has been used strategically to advance political agendas as well as how it has been used unknowingly in a way that works against its initial aim to protect children (Egan & Hawkes, 2010; James et al., 1998; Jenks, 1996; Jenkins, 1998; Kincaid, 1998). One criticism focuses on the way children are positioned as unknowing and unable to advocate for themselves. As such, they are denied agency, rights, and subjectivity, and adults speak *for* them and on behalf of them. This branch of criticism takes issue with the presumption that children – because of their innocence – would not and could not need to know more about sex.

A second criticism of the use of childhood innocence examines the way it can fuel moral panics. Institutions and public policy makers that construct children as innocent position them as in danger of corruption and thus in need of state protection. The image of an innocent child is useful to various political power players (Irvine, 2004; Robinson, 2008) and central to an argument that could lead to expansions of laws in a way that leads to collateral damage, for example, to LGBT rights (Fischel, 2016).[1]

A third criticism of the way the idea of childhood innocence has been used strategically is that it positions some children as innocent and others as invisible or always already corrupted. Critics have shown that this construction of innocence reproduces inequalities because the portrayal of innocence is racialized and classed (Bernstein, 2011; Fields, 2008), as it almost always features white middle-class children (Walkerdine, 1997, 2001). This was a criticism Fields (2008) leveled at parents she studied who were in conflict over sex education in North Carolina. Black girls and boys were understood to be more "knowing" and less innocent, and when pictured thus, the sex education to be offered appeared to condition or constrain this knowingness. In the same vein, boys are rarely positioned as innocent in the sex education wars in the United States over abstinence-only-until-marriage education (Lamb et al., 2013). They, like the girls of color in North Carolina, are assumed already knowing, sexual, and in danger of becoming pregnant or impregnating, and this knowingness is naturalized.

Historically, universal education and child labor laws, although motivated by factors other than childhood innocence, have also used childhood innocence to procure arguably tremendously positive privileges to developing children and sometimes the critique of the idea of childhood innocence can lose sight of the needs of actual children. As in the earlier examples, activists and policy makers may have used the romantic idea of childhood innocence, and may have believed in it, but it may also be true that they showed genuine concern for actual conditions of poor and working-class children facing severe consequences of industrialization

[1] For examples of how the childhood innocence is used in politics see below the section Slovakian referendum: conservative uses of "childhood innocence" APA Report: Progressive uses of "childhood innocence."

and fundamental societal change with rapid growth of cities, decline of community solidarity, decline of strong familial bonds, among others (Boone, 2005; Giroux, 1998). Later in this chapter we reconcile the critique of the childhood innocence concept with concerns about children that consider the pitfalls making the life of children difficult. Before we do so, we will examine the use of childhood innocence in conservative as well as progressive political projects.

Slovakian Referendum: Conservative Uses of "Childhood Innocence"

Once childhood became framed by the idea of innocence, children have been used strategically in political arguments. The use of children make these arguments more emotional and therefore persuasive. The potential of the trope of an innocent child to trigger emotions of sympathy or fear is used in both liberal as well as conservative struggles. Both sides may employ it with the honest belief they fight for children's well-being, or, more deceptively, to push through and legitimize other agendas.

Recently, images of endangered innocent children have been used by conservatives in movements that have been referred to in Europe as "anti-gender," as well as anti-LGBT movements on transnational levels across Europe (Maďarová, 2015; Schmincke, 2015). After decades of steady progress in terms of women's, transgender individuals,' and LGBT rights, several parts of Europe are facing new waves of backlash, manifested in resistance to a so-called gender ideology or gender theory, and deteriorations of support for gender equality agenda (Paternotte, 2015). In many countries (Slovakia, Hungary, Poland, Germany, and others) conservative campaigns against various issues as gay marriage, sex education, or equality policies are carried out. These conservative campaigns are examples of how the concern about children turns into moral panic, and the focus is shifted away from the child who needs protection to a chase for presumed perpetrator and a crusade against demonized social evil. Rather than careful analysis of actual harm, moral panics use the defamation of certain social groups for political mobilization. Childhood and innocence are typically utilized as a means through which the "good heteronormative adult citizenship subject is constituted and governed in conservative campaigns" (Robinson, 2012).

Sex panics revolving around the protection of childhood sexual innocence are deployed for political gain through fueling homophobia. In 2015, a referendum on banning same-sex marriage, adoptions by gay couples, and rejection of compulsory sex education was held in Slovakia. The plebiscite was initiated by a conservative organization, Alliance for Family (Aliancia za rodinu). The conservative group produced banners and posters featuring supposed children's voices – according to this campaign, children themselves are clear that they would vote against gay marriage, same-sex adoption, and compulsory sex education. A short video was produced by Alliance for Family and featured a gay couple who came to a family to pick up the child they wanted to adopt. In the video, the little boy looks at the couple – his potential fathers – and asks, confused: "And where is mommy?" In another video, underscored by moving music, suggesting sadness and trauma, the same boy poses a resentful question to another little boy (in the role of a viewer): "You would want to grow up in this [meaning a gay family]?" The gay couple is pictured as taking the child away from a family and family life. The way they are pictured looking at him and each other, it could be argued, signals that they might abuse him. The trope is used to trigger an emotional reaction of protection in order to gain political capital and unity around an idea that brings in various constituents across the conservative political spectrum.

Interestingly, these advertisements employ an idea of childhood agency, arguing that children's voices must be heard and if they are heard, they would fight for their right to remain innocent, that is, they would stay away from a world of sexual diversity and sexual rights. This agenda is symbolically linked to sex abuse and exploitation. This representation of an agentic child, although still innocent, is used to support a conservative agenda. As with the Romantic era, the child's voice is positioned as natural and unsullied, thus not partisan.

Emotional appeals regarding the innocent child have positioned women in particular as important protectors of children, which has had mixed outcomes. Used in this way, these appeals support conservative attempts to keep women out of the work force by enhancing the "job" of caregiving, which has been undervalued as it is typically not paid or well-paid work. The more children are at risk, the more valuable stay-at-home mothers' sacrifice is, in spite of the fact that stay at home mothers have less prestige, are poorer, and more at risk for future poverty because of divorce and lack of training to reenter the workforce. There exists a longstanding irony in the childhood innocence discourse that describes children as our most "precious asset," without ever acknowledging that caring for them is undervalued.

Conflating Innocence with Sexual Innocence

One of the reasons why the anti-LGBT propaganda can work when a moral panic is incited is because very real children are exploited, although less frequently by same-sex (LGBT) parents than mixed-sex (heterosexual) parents (Stevenson, 2000). Wouldn't all adults want to protect children from exploitation? This idea is currently used in some nations to argue against child marriage (see Chapter 25). There are laws and social-service systems and campaigns against abuse across the globe that are meant to teach adults that children are not permissible sexual partners. And, given the continuation of sexual exploitation and the spread of child pornography (Dines & Levy, 2013), giving up entirely on a campaign of protection may not be the best approach to combating this problem.

Innocence, in its depictions and uses, is often connected to perceptions of sexuality. Where sexuality is constructed for adults as something that is not only private but also somewhat "dirty," the immaculate innocence of childhood sexuality stands in opposition to it. This is not a modern construction. Childhood served as the projection of Judeo-Christian paradise. In the Biblical narration, Adam and Eve were innocent because they were unknowing. When they tasted the fruit of the Tree of Knowledge, they became conscious of their nudity and experienced shame – and lost paradise forever. In Christianity, sexuality is related to sin and possible defilement, and that is why it has no place in the paradise.

Sexuality in Western culture occupies a unique position within the list of potential risks and harms to children. The sexual abuse of children can be considered the worst form of exploitation and the sex offender one of the most hated individuals in society. The emotional appeal with regard to sexually abused children has been documented (Whittier, 2009), and, in spite of the public moral sentiment about sexual abuse, sexual abuse continues. Porn sites about underage girls and boys are some of the most popular sites around the world (Dines & Levy, 2013). Those outraged by cases of sexual child abuse may often ignore less "sexy" cases of child neglect, abandonment, inadequate nutrition, or poor education (Kincaid, 1998).

When childhood sexual innocence is considered today by those who would warn against sexualization by the media, it is almost always considered in relation to girlhood. Renold (2005) writes that boys are less easily situated in a state of "innocent minority," as masculinity is seen as already containing "the seeds" of sexual subjectivity. Duschinsky (2013a) writes that in some material written to address the problem of sexualization – for example, government reports – the warnings position boys and young men as harmed too but in a way that doesn't evoke a fall from innocence. Instead, sexualization appears to contribute to their becoming indiscriminately and even pathologically sexual. They are also portrayed as a potential sexual threat to girls through sexting, a modern cause of alarm. The whole discussion of girls becoming more and more sexualized, and boys being seen as agents enacting their sexuality in problematic but agentic ways, smacks of projection of a dichotomy that slices human experience in two. Girls in general are seen as exclusively vulnerable in depictions of sexuality in childhood and as objects in need of protection (while this rarely holds true for girls of color); boys hold that which is desired, freedom, and agency, and are also depicted as predators, which includes and is pronounced when boys of color are discussed (Brown et al., 2009; Lamb, 2010). As we write later, where there is the abject, or as Duschinsky writes, the injured, there needs to be the injurer – which is never us.

Are boys ever depicted as vulnerable? Priest scandals in various countries have brought to public attention that boys can be damaged by early sexual contact. But this narrative does not seem to be the same narrative of lost innocence. Present is a subtle and sometimes not so subtle homophobia (Russell & Kelly, 2003) where the pedophile is conflated with homosexuality in the media, and boys' sexual exploitation is seen as an initiation rather than abuse. As Cahill and Jones write (2002): when a man abuses a young girl, the problem is not heterosexuality. Few would characterize such abuse as a heterosexual act similar to consensual sex between an adult man and woman. Similarly, when a priest sexually abuses a boy, the problem is not homosexuality. The problem is child abuse.

The lack of interest in exploitation of boys is telling, and perhaps revealing, with regard to what raises concerns for girls. Girls have the triple risk of being sexualized, being seen as sexual when they are not, and being potential victims of sexual exploitation. These risks may be accurate but the way the facts of these risks are represented to the public presumes a figure of a girl imbued with qualities that are lost through sexual knowledge.

American Psychological Association Report: Progressive Uses of "Childhood Innocence"

Considerable writing and positioning of scholars occurred after the release of the 2007 American Psychological Association (APA) report on the sexualization of girls. The report introduced psychological and empirical research that together indicated that girls may be increasingly exposed to sexualized media and such exposure is harmful to their well-being. Although most of the research presented was on adolescent girls, anecdotal information was used to argue that when sexualized images and messages are omnipresent, younger girls get a message that they are valued primarily for their ability to become a good sexual object. Lamb and Brown (2006) began this argument in a book for parents that focuses on a qualitative thematic analysis of the objects, messaging, and marketing in girls' worlds. Their aim was to suggest that marketers and producers of media use standard stereotypes to influence girls to become consumers of girlhood, some of which are aimed at presenting girls as innocent, frail, and silly, and some of which presents girls' development as aiming toward a sexualized adolescence.

Critics responded to the APA report in full form, presenting criticism that it was not inclusive enough, and that the discourse in the report made sexualization appear to be just one more moral panic against sex. The latter critique was most likely connected to the overwhelming reliance on research on adolescent girls in the report, and the use of research literature that showed exposure to media was correlated with earlier and more frequent sexual activity, which, of course, begs the question, what is problematic about earlier sex?

One critique was that the girl to be saved from media in the report was pictured as White and middle class, although that argument was more of a hunch by critics regarding what images the report would elicit in its readers than supported by a close examination of the research, which did indeed include research on racialized and poor and working-class girls. While there were no pictures, except on the cover, and these were diverse images, the language used by researchers and the popular media that promoted the report, when subjected to a discourse analysis, betrayed for these critics class-based concerns connected to the idea of "respectability" (Egan & Hawkes, 2008; Renold & Ringrose, 2008; Skeggs, 2004). For example use of the word "prostitot" to describe what little girls looked like when dressed in sexualized clothing was said to evoke a class distinction to British critics, whereas, in the US context, it would be difficult to see that language as classed. Some of these arguments seemed more directly related to how the report, and any report, becomes popularized in the press, than the report itself.

A second argument is that media was taken in the report to be a monolithic big M force that only contributed problems to girls, ignoring the fact that girls make their own media and that there is much in the media that they use to resist overarching sexualized, heterosexist, and sexist messages (Gill, 2012; Hamilton, 2009). This argument goes on to say that looking at media as only a problem for girls rather than that which gives them power and a path toward participation denies them agency, subjectivity, and the capacity to think critically about what they are receiving (Gill, 2012).

A third criticism about the report found that it left little room to celebrate or even take notice of sexual development in childhood and adolescence. This criticism of the report and the public discourse around sexualization, in short, centered on how a concern for sexualization of girls appears to be combined with a concern for girls being sexual at all (Duschinsky, 2013a, 2013b). When this happens, the concerns for sexualization can sound like slut-shaming (Ringrose & Reynold, 2012) and that any form of childhood sexuality represented in girlhood is suspicious (Egan & Hawkes, 2010). This critique builds on the idea that what is really raising societal concerns is not that girls are being seen as sexual objects for grown men at too early an age, or that girls are being robbed of their opportunity to develop into whole human beings with many interests and attributes including their sexuality, but that there is something improper going on with the girls themselves. Sexualization discussions thus become discussions of girls and propriety, rather than girls and sexuality (Duschinsky, 2013a, 2013b). And the attention then is drawn to the girls themselves, for not acting respectably, or for being dupes of the media, rather than on media or marketers who spend billions of dollars promoting narrow views of girlhood that include sexualized views but other stereotypes as well that promote a neoliberal consumerism, for example, that of attractiveness. This again may have been an outcome of the report rather than a reflection of the report itself. As Duschinsky describes the process, it is both/and, the child is deployed as an unsavvy and vulnerable consumer and then redeployed by critics as a neoliberal subject:

> WHO but child is deployed as a consumer . . . a not yet savvy consumer . . . However, the child is re-deployed in "neo-liberal" discourses on sexualization in the subjectivation of responsible consumers and entrepreneurs, coding cultural and material inequalities as individual pathology and irresponsibility (2013a, p. 362).

Thus in Duschinsky's thinking, the Task Force report problematically pictured children as dupes, whereas the critics who mean to save childhood agency, set them up as neoliberal subjects, shoppers in the sexualized culture, making their own choices and, thus, in the end, responsible for them.

As noted earlier, critics of childhood innocence, while sometimes decrying the rise of sexist sexual messaging in societies, also recognize the slogan of "too sexy too soon" as imposing normative and regulatory messaging on girls regarding the timing of sexuality, the appropriateness of it, and the place for it, insinuating that there is a sexual purity, often written as sexual "health," that opposes a "dirty" sexuality, which must be preserved until an imaginary gate is opened. Boys are positioned as the salesmen of this "dirtier" sexuality, themselves no longer subjects but influenced and positioned by larger forces promoting patriarchy, pornography, and domination. The fallout from the kind of popularity this message received was that it was taken up within a larger discourse of middle-class parenting (where are the parents?) and "girls gone wild" (girls are different these days and doing most of the sexualizing to themselves). That is, the discussion was taken up into a neoliberal push toward individual choice and responsibility. The focus was no longer on institutions and ideologies but on individual families and girls, once again, as gatekeepers of innocence.

These various criticisms are important in that they show how quickly discourses can be taken up to be used against their ends, in this case feminist ends, how feminism can be co-opted, and how well-meaning scholars and researchers that focus on social-justice problems in relation to girls and boys can themselves fall into the trappings of using childhood innocence to their own ends. In this particular case, the report was undertaken from a feminist perspective to examine what could be considered an internalized sexism in which girls, who were developing sexually, were taken up and shaped by forces that would promote the patriarchal culture's status quo. The popular media turned the attention to shaping girls rather than reshaping the larger institutions of patriarchy and media control.

From Innocence to Vulnerability: Why Children Are Vulnerable

We thus agree that when the idea of "innocence" is brought into social or political discourse, we should be wary of two things: first, that the child may be co-opted to represent either damaged innocence or a conservative voice that cries out for its innocence; and, second, that positioned behind an innocent child is an adult corrupter who must be contained, whether LGBT or potential sex offender. But we propose that there is a third less nefarious risk when childhood innocence is introduced, and that is we can forget that children, in general, need protection.

Tropes of innocence work because of a shared understanding that children need protection. One can protect a child from numerous things, not only – or even most importantly – adult sexual exploitation. If innocence becomes the primary reason for protection and if sexual activity (even unwanted) becomes the primary way that innocence is corrupted, children who need the most may be ignored. As Robinson and Davies write (Chapter 3), real children are actively engaged in building knowledge around gender and sexuality and are more capable of critical thinking than adults believe. But the idea of childhood innocence will prevent adults from seeing children's agency, capacities, and understandings, and will lead to adults policing the boundaries around which children seek knowledge about sex and gender. Adult ideas of children's innocence set up taboos around which the children's curiosity and interests are silenced.

While Robinson and Davies introduce aspects of childhood that are ignored by those who would preserve an idealized notion of innocence, we should beware that discussion of such does not create a straw child, teeming with agency, choice, and adult cognitive and emotional capabilities. Such a version of the child would lead to a politics that supports doing away with the few resources that remain that help adults to care for children and protect their lives.

What is the harm from early sexuality? From too much knowing? And why should we be emotionally invested in protecting children from this? The harm clearly is not in losing their innocence as much as it is their vulnerability to exploitation from adults. And a second potential harm is that too much information can reproduce a kind of sexuality that overemphasizes performing sex for others' pleasure, or exploiting other people, and interfere with developing a healthy attitude toward sexuality and an ethical approach to other people.

We suggest that we need to maintain the concept of vulnerability that is tied to the idea of universal childhood development. Children have limited ways to exercise power or resist manipulation from adults who are stronger in their experience as well as physical power. Children have no other choice than to live in the world run by adults – they are subjected to laws, exposed to educational programs, and treated by a medical system all designed by adults. We need to recognize their minority position. However, this does not mean we deny children's voices. On the contrary, we support platforms that recognize children's voices and value their experience, while remaining wary of adult uses of these.

This call to remember the vulnerability of children could be compared with the calls for strategic essentialism for those who are considered the "other" in society, a call issued by Spivak in the 1980s (Spivak, 1990). Its use is justified when the aim is toward a "scrupulously visible political interest" (Fuss, 1995), in our case, the rights of children. It permits a group to be advocated for as one, based on some similarities that are historical, and in this case, developmental, while those who advocate need to take special care to not erase important differences based on class, culture, or race, nor reduce childhood to one overarching image (Grillo, 2013). In this way, what we are reminding the public of is NOT that children are not innocent, but that children are indeed in danger of many harms that come from policies that affect their lives as they live them in families, legal systems, amid global conflicts, and as they face various forms of prejudices that legitimate and rationalize a broad continuum of acts that are objectionable to children (Young-Bruehl, 2012).

And it is important to not erase children's own voices. When critics talk about children's voices, their agency, and the valuing of their experiences, what exactly is meant with regard to sex and sexuality? Do they cleverly conjure up 14- or 15-year-olds? Save for Robinson and colleagues' research in Australia, when do they use the example of a 6- or 7-year-old's experience and right to knowledge (Chapter 3)? It may be easier to do this when it comes to the area of LGBT rights and children's feelings and identification with gender and sexuality in a society that will make them feel "other" and question their thoughts and feelings. Some adults are beginning to offer protections to children with regard to these identities, whereas others continue to promote discrimination.

There is some romanticized projection that if we include children's voices, simply because they have been ignored in the past, we will discover what they need and what a healthy sexuality is. This viewpoint reproduces the same old belief in childhood innocence, purity, and authenticity. But, as Art Linkletter once said on a 1960s television hour, "Kids say the darndest things," and those voices, like adult voices, are tied to institutions and ideologies that may be harmful to their needs and existence. This is not to say that adults always know better and should ignore children's points of view, but adults have a special responsibility toward children's development, health, well-being, and fulfillment. And to the extent there are cultural and ethical guidelines for a "good" sexual life in adulthood, we have a responsibility to provide foundations for it through structures that we design for youth.

The other way children are "agents" isn't just as choosers but as responders to whatever adults put forth. This can be a problem in the sexualization literature – sometimes, in correlational or causal research, or in psychology research in general, individuals are positioned as "influenced" rather than mutually influencing. Hence Gill's (2012) important reminder that, while media is influencing adolescent girls, adolescent girls are influencing the media. Still, one must be wary of imposing the idea of the neoliberal chooser on these individual girls (Duschinsky, 2013a). To recognize children´s agency and to protect them does not need to be contradictory. Protecting children does not have to position them as passive recipients, nor weak, unknowing, or even innocent. They are vulnerable to certain harms that need to be addressed. Their harms may be particular to childhood and development as there are harms particular to various groups of people of different ages, abilities, backgrounds, and ethnicities.

Children's Vulnerability: An Example

Sam's Story

Sam was a third grader (around 9 years old). One day his mom found him in a strange mood. He did not want to talk to her, he seemed startled. His mom tried to talk to him, but he hid in his room. She did not know why, but he did not talk to her as much as before and seemed distant. She thought that maybe he was going through puberty. Later that month there was a parent's conference and Sam's class teacher told parents that, while working with tablets, some kids opened some porn websites. She was not sure if this happened accidently or because another child from the class searched for them on purpose. She apologized because there had obviously been a failure in the system that was supposed to block such websites on the school network. She asked parents to talk about this with their kids at home. Sam's mom opened the topic and Sam started to sob. He admitted he was looking at those pages. While he did not say that he felt guilty, it seemed clear that he did. He had looked at the pages with interest, was laughing at them with his schoolmates, and that what he felt the worst about was that he felt aroused and had an erection. When talking with his mom he broke into tears: "I was scared that I shouldn't hug you anymore." They then hugged each other and talked more.

It is easy to deconstruct simple stories like this one as a cautionary tale that positions children as vulnerable, parents as protectors, and pornography as bad. And one story can't encompass all the different stories that emerge as children have access to pornography. But without claiming this is a quintessential story, or even a typical one, an analysis of this simple story can help us have some sympathy for real families grappling with issues relating to pornography and vulnerability, and also to have an understanding of childhood sexuality through the lens of assemblages that we referred to in our introduction.

The concept of assemblages developed by Deleuze and Guattari (2005) emphasizes fluidity, exchangeability, connectivity, and multiple functionalities through entities, here the child. Assemblages can be imagined as relational networks, mixtures of the animate and inanimate that produce the world, and as discourse was argued to have constructed the child, assemblages that include discourse and ideologies as part of a relational network now do. This perspective de-privileges human agency, which does not mean that agency is not important. Instead, agency is seen as a part of the assemblage where every component affects and is affected by the others. Thus, agency is present but also affected by passivity, vulnerability, stasis, and constructed by ideology as well as material connections and the limits and affordances offered by the material world. We consider this approach as a way to protect against romanticizing children's voices and agency as true and authentic, acts we associate with the liberal response to conservative protectionism.

Childhood sexuality can be seen as an assemblage, an assemblage of discourses about childhood, technology that is part of their lives and extensions of their beings, schools that encase and transform children, parent–child (mother–son) relationships, ideas of sexuality and innocence, and bodies with their physical responsiveness. All of these parts of the assemblage are shaped by both culture and materiality. To apply this to our example, Sam has probably heard about where babies come from, he probably has heard about the fact that people make love for pleasure, but these pictures went beyond this. Sam was vulnerable to images that he saw on the Internet. And not just that, maybe if he hit those web pages in privacy he would quickly close them or he would take a look, but he would not face the pressure to engage actively and publically in an act of masculine performativity. By seeing the pictures that he was not looking for and especially by playing the tough-guy role among peers and experiencing the pleasure triggered by something that consciously he would not approve as good, he himself felt awkward. He was trapped in cultural dichotomy of pure and dirty and its relation to sexuality and physicality, and hugging his mom, the person he loved so much and who was so affectionate with him, suddenly felt just not right. A certain kind of representation of sexuality built a wall preventing Sam from being tender with his mother. His mother did not panic and was able to lead a meaningful talk with him about what happened, what it meant, and to reassure him that their relationship cannot be destroyed by such happenings. She was able to tell him that many people have the same excited feelings about those photos and they also feel a little or a lot guilty because they don't know the people in the photos and they don't know if there was some troubling experience connected to those photos for the people in them. She could emphasize her own values of privacy and sexuality, or talk about objectification, or share her feelings about intimacy, and at the same time say that looking at sex can be fun. She can also discuss how boys can bond together over looking at girls and women, or that there are different images that may be exciting to gay boys, opening up sexual identity as a topic of discussion.

This story is not suggesting that children should not watch pornography – although there are fine arguments that support this view. By retelling this story, we do not make a plea for an anti-porn campaign, which we fear will overextend in conservative ways that we have shown earlier. Instead, we try to understand the complexity of issues of childhood and sexuality in a contemporary world and show how children can be both confident subjects and vulnerable at the same time. Attempts to protect children are usually of a restrictive character – ban pornography, ban sex education, ban sexually explicit content in media and advertising, and ban the use of certain words. Adults are responsible for attending to children's vulnerabilities. Whatever the vulnerabilities, children need to know there are adults and sometimes other children who are older or more mature whom they can turn to for help, who will not judge them or condemn them for not being innocent or see them as ruined, in part, by their acts or viewings.

But how does a parent protect? If we take seriously that technology is a part of children's sexual "posthuman subjectivity," that the line where child ends and technology begins is blurred, both affecting the other in interaction, then the child's viewing of pornography, the images he remembers, and the potential to view pornography again become who he is, offering affordances, possibilities, and limitations. His relationship with his mother already exists but becomes newly a part of this assemblage of the technology/image-seen boy. Deleuze wrote about the ability to affect and be affected, to emerge in relation to various components of who one is and what one has experienced (1988). One might say that the assemblage of boy/technology/pornography has met the assemblage of boy/son-of-mother/part of family to be integrated in what Deleuze called a consistency. Two assemblages become a new assemblage, a unit. While Deleuze wrote about the wasp and the orchid becoming some symbiotic emergent unit, in this case, the mother reasserts the part she plays in the unit mother/son, which now is integrated into the assemblage of screen/boy.

It is important to remember that technologies are not only a part of children's sexual "posthuman subjectivities" (see Barad, 2003; Braidotti, 2013; Haraway, 1991) but a tool of global capital as well. For example, in marketing to children, the child consumer, an assemblage of imagined and actual capabilities of children, connected to technology and families, can mask the various vulnerabilities of children of particular ages, races, genders, and material conditions. Children are located in particular geopolitical spaces where some might personally have little power but the idea of who they are and their innocence becomes one component in an assemblage of conservative laws/bodies/policies in action. Politics, technology, media, and laws regarding privacy and criminalization, shape the emergent child cast as innocent or knowing depending on their nationality, skin color, and placement in the world.

That said, adults in most situations, cultures, and countries have more resources and ability to shape the institutions that frame their own and their children's lives. This brings with it the responsibility to guide and protect, to insert adult power into assemblages of emerging childhood. In Sam's case, we have shown an alternative to repression and panic around sex that has not proved as efficient in prevention. As assemblages look at individuals in relation to other individuals, institutions, structures, and objects, parents and responsible adults insert or reassert their position in children's lives. This is not an effort to protect against an essential vulnerability but to protect against potential vulnerabilities.

Conclusion

In the end, how do we protect the vulnerability of childhood without using the problematic trope of innocence and overemphasizing sexual knowledge as the example of loss of innocence? How do we take into consideration both that children are critical thinkers and making sense of the world as they grow, and that they are indeed also growing and developing and depend on adults in this work?

Children Develop

First we need to pay attention to needs at various developmental points. Adults would not conspire with first graders to not have any books in the classroom if that was their request, nor candy for lunch instead of something more healthy. And when providing sex education to tenth graders, while they may want to focus on the "how tos" of sex, it is responsible to include discussions of contraception and ethical training against coercion, because adults have some investment with regard to what will matter in their future, at this particular time in history and in this society. If the classroom decided, "We don't need to learn about coercion because we are all ethical beings," we would still want to teach about coercion.

Children Are Vulnerable

Second, we need to understand vulnerability intersectionally. Not all children are equally vulnerable. Different children have different vulnerability to being positioned as knowing and not knowing, and within certain geopolitical systems, some bodies are shaped and seen as in need of greater protection than others. In the United States, children of color are seen as less vulnerable. Globally, children in countries with fewer resources can surprisingly be seen as less in need of protection. This contextual and intersectional view needs to be a part of sex education and policy around sex education globally.

Children Can't Be Sexual Criminals

A recognition of childhood sexual rights would mean decriminalizing and depathologizing children who act out sexually. The notion of childhood innocence has a reverse side when children act out on other children in bullying ways. These acts need to be treated not as special sexual and corrupting acts, but within the realm of bullying.

Abandon the Trope of Innocence

Make it suspect to use photos of "innocent" children for causes such as trafficking and sexual abuse. Point out that innocence is used problematically and politically. Ferret out assumptions of "purity" and "respectability."

Understand Children's Capabilities for their Developmental Level (but do not glamorize or overrepresent agency)

We are not ready to give up the responsibility of adults toward children and are suspect of the glamorization of the agentic child – the neoliberal chooser who knows what is best for her or himself. The cry to listen to the voices of children/adolescents is a confirmation of a different kind of innocence, that they are all too knowing (the image of the wise child) and also that they know what is best so should be trusted. In this view, our adult protection can itself be corrupting. Liberals and scholars need to check ourselves with counter notions to childhood innocence, and reclaim an idea of development that focuses on vulnerability. The notion of vulnerability doesn't trade on sexual innocence and purity but leads us to fight for protections that children well deserve.

We hope this chapter has indicated that actual children may get lost in the process of progressives and conservatives use and critique of childhood innocence. Actual children aren't one age, they develop. And there's a materiality about development that is shaped by discourse but also stimulated and limited by what bodies and minds of developing children can do.

References

American Psychological Association (2007). *Report of the APA Task Force on the Sexualization of Girls.* Washington, DC: American Psychological Association.

Ariès, P. (1962). *Centuries of Childhood.* London: Jonathan Cape.

Bernstein, R. (2011). *Racial Innocence: Performing American Childhood from Slavery to Civil Rights.* New York and London: New York University Press.

Barad, K. (2003). Posthumanist Performativity: Toward an Understanding of How Matter Comes to Matter. *Signs*, *28*(3), 801–831.

Boone, T. (2005). *Youth of Darkest England: Working-Class Children at the Heart of Victorian Empire.* New York: Routledge.

Braidotti, R. (2013). *The Posthuman.* Cambridge: Polity.

Brown, L., Lamb, S., & Tappan, M. B. (2009). *Packaging Boyhood: Superheroes, Slackers, and Other Media Stereotypes*, New York: St. Martin's Press.

Cahill, S. & Jones, K. T. (2002). Child Sexual Abuse and Homosexuality: The Long History of the "Gays as Pedophiles" Fallacy. Retrieved October 3, 2002, from www.NGLTF.org.

Deleuze, G. (1988) *Spinoza: Practical Philosophy* (48–51). Translated by Robert Hurley. San Francisco: City Lights Books.

Deleuze, G. & Guattari, F. (2005). *A Thousand Plateaus.* Minneapolis: University of Minnesota Press.

Dines, G. & Levy, D. (2013, August 1). A rare defeat for corporate lobbyists. *Counterpunch.* www.counterpunch.org/2013/08/01/a-rare-defeat-for-corporate-lobbyists/.

Duschinsky, R. (2013a). Sexualization: A State of Injury. *Theory & Psychology*, *23*(3), 351–370. doi:10.1177/0959354312469732.

(2013b). The Emergence of Sexualization as a Social Problem: 1981–2010. *Social Politics: International Studies in Gender, State & Society*, *20* (1), 137–156. doi:10.1093/sp/jxs016.

Egan, R. & Hawkes, G. (2008). Endangered Girls and Incendiary Objects: Unpacking the Discourse on Sexualization, *Sexuality & Culture*, *12*(4), 291–311. doi:10.1007/s12119-008-9036-8.

(2010). *Theorizing the Sexual Child in Modernity.* Gordonsville: Palgrave MacMillan.

Faulkner, J. (2013). Vulnerability of "Virtual" Subjects: Childhood, Memory, and Crisis in the Cultural Value of Innocence. *Substance* *42*(3), 127–147. doi:10.1353/sub.2013.0029.

Fields, J. (2008). *Risky Lessons: Sex Education and Social Inequality.* New Brunswick and London: Rutgers University Press.

Fischel, J. J. (2016). Pornographic Protections? Itineraries of Childhood Innocence. *Law, Culture and the Humanities* *12*(2), 206–220. doi:10.1177/1743872113492396.

Fuss, D. (1995). *Identification Papers*, New York: Routledge.

Gill, R. (2012). Media, Empowerment and the "Sexualization of Culture" Debates. *Sex Roles* *66*(11–12), 736–745. doi:10.1007/s11199-011–0107-1.

Giroux, H. A. (1998). Nymphet Fantasies: Child Beauty Pageants and the Politics of Innocence. *Social Text*, no. 57, 31–53.

Grillo, T. (2013). Anti-essentialism and Intersectionality: Tools to Dismantle the Master's House. *Berkeley Journal of Gender, Law & Justice*, *10*(1), 16–30. doi:10.15779/Z38MC6W.

Hamilton, M. (2009). *What's Happening to Our Girls?* Melbourne: Penguin Group Australia.

Haraway, D. (1991). *Cyborgs, Simians and Women*. London: Free Association Books.

Higgonet, A. (1998). *Pictures of Innocence: The History and Crisis of Ideal Childhood*. London: Thames and Hudson.

Irvine, J. M. (2004). *Talk about Sex. The Battles over Sex Education in the United States*. Berkeley: University of California Press.

James, A., Jenks, C., & Prout, A. (1998). *Theorising Childhood*. Cambridge: Polity Press.

Jenks, C. (1996). *Childhood*. London: Sage.

Jenkins, H. (1998). Introduction: Childhood Innocence and Other Modern Myths. In Jenkins, H. (Ed.), *The Children's Culture Reader*. New York: New York University Press.

Kincaid, J. (1998). *Erotic Innocence: The Culture of Child Molesting*. Durham: Duke University Press.

Kinney, A. B. (1995). *Chinese Views of Childhood*. Honolulu, HI: University of Hawaii Press.

Kristeva, J. & Roudiez, L. S. (1982). *Powers of Horror: An Essay on Abjection*. New York: Columbia University Press.

Lamb, S. (2010). Feminist Ideals of Healthy Female Adolescent Sexuality: A Critique. *Sex Roles*, *62*(5/6), 294–306.

Lamb, S. & Brown, L. M. (2006). *Packaging Girlhood: Rescuing Our Daughters from Marketers' Schemes*. New York: St. Martin's Press.

Lamb, S., Graling, K., & Lustig, K. (2013). The Use and Misuse of Pleasure in Sex Education Curricula. *Sex Education: Sexuality, Society and Learning*, *13*(3), 305–318. doi:10.1080/14681811.2012.738604.

Lott, T. (2013, May 10). What exactly is the innocence of childhood. *The Guardian*.

Maďarová, Z. (2015). Love and Fear. Argumentative Strategies against Gender Equality in Slovakia In *Anti-gender Movements on the Rise?: Strategising for Gender Equality in Central and Eastern Europe* (33–42). Berlin: Heinrich Böll Stiftung.

Najafi, S. & Higonnet, A. (2003). Picturing innocence: An interview with Anne Higonnet. *Cabinet*, Issue 9. www.cabinetmagazine.org/issues/9/picturing_innocence.php.

Orme, N. (2001). *Medieval Children*. New Haven: Yale University Press.

Paternotte, D. (2015). Blessing the Crowds. Catholic Mobilisations against Gender in Europe. In Hark, S. & Villa, P.-I. (Eds.), *Anti-Genderismus. Sexualität und Geschlecht als Schauplätze aktueller politischer Auseinandersetzungen* (129–147). Bielefeld: Transcript Verlag.

Renold, E. (2005). *Girls, Boys and Junior Sexualities*. London: Routledge.

Renold, E. & Ringrose, J. (2008). Regulation and Rupture: Mapping Tween and Teenage Girls' "Resistance" to the Heterosexual Matrix. *Feminist Theory 9*(3), 335–360.

Ringrose, J. & Reynold, E. (2012). Slut-Shaming, Girl Power and "Sexualisation": Thinking through the Politics of the International SlutWalks with Teen Girls. *Gender and Education*, *24*(3), 333–343. doi:10.1080/09540253.2011.645023.

Robinson, K. H. (2008). In the Name of 'Childhood Innocence'; A Discursive Exploration of the Moral Panic Associated with Childhood and Sexuality. *Cultural Studies Review*, *14*(2), 113–129.

(2012). "Difficult Citizenship": The Precarious Relationships between Childhood, Sexuality and Access to Knowledge. *Sexualities 15*(3/4), 257–276. doi:10.1177/1363460712436469.

Russell, G. & Kelly, N. (2003). *Subtle Stereotyping: The Media, Homosexuality, and the Priest Sexual Abuse Scandal.* Amherst: The Institute for Gay and Lesbian Strategic Studies.

Schmincke, I. (2015). Das Kind als Chiffre politischer Auseinandersetzung am Beispiel neuer konservativer Protestbewegungen in Frankreich und Deutschland. In Hark, S. & Villa, P.-I. (Eds.), *Anti-Genderismus. Sexualität und Geschlecht als Schauplätze aktueller politischer Auseinandersetzungen* (93–107). Bielefeld: Transcript Verlag.

Skeggs, B. (2004). *Class, Self, Culture*. London: Routledge.

Spivak, G. C. (1990). *The Post-Colonial Critic: Interviews, Strategies, Dialogues.* New York: Routledge.

Stevenson, M. R. (2000). Public Policy, Homosexuality and the Sexual Coercion of Children. *Journal of Psychology & Human Sexuality, 12*(4), 8.

Walkerdine, V. (1997). *Daddy's Girl: Young Girls and Popular Culture.* London, Cambridge, MA: Harvard University Press.

(2001). Safety and Danger: Childhood, Sexuality, and Space at the End of the Millennium. In Hultqvist, K. & Dahlberg, G. (Eds.), *Governing the Child in the New Millennium*, (15–34). New York and London: Routledge Falmer.

Whittier, N. (2009). *The Politics of Child Sexual Abuse: Emotion, Social Movements, and the State*. Oxford: Oxford University Press.

Young-Bruehl, E. (2012). *Childism: Confronting Prejudice against Children.* New Haven: Yale University Press.

5 The Dynamic Expression of Sexual-Minority and Gender-Minority Experience during Childhood and Adolescence

Lisa M. Diamond

Considerable research has focused on the development of *sexual-minority* youths (those who express same-sex attractions) and *gender-minority* youths (those who deviate from conventional gender role expression and identity). How do these youth come to an awareness of their non-normative patterns of sexual attraction and gender expression? If one applies traditional, linear developmental models to these phenomena, one would expect that sexual- and gender-minority experiences and identities should unfold gradually during childhood and adolescence, beginning with a set of developmental precursors (such as early same-sex attractions or early gender nonconformity) that reliably predict the eventual expression of a gay, lesbian, bisexual, or transgender identity by the end of adolescence. Accordingly, considerable research has focused on identifying these developmental precursors and testing stage-based models of sexual- and gender-minority development (Bockting, 2014; Cass, 1979; Morgan & Stevens, 2008; Rosario et al., 2011; Troiden, 1989).

Yet these investigations have consistently found that sexual- and gender-minority experiences and identities do not unfold according to a uniform sequence of linear developmental stages. Rather, sexual- and gender-minority youths show diverse and variable developmental trajectories, sometimes involving abrupt onsets, offsets, reversals, and interruptions in sexual attractions and gender identification (Diamond, 2003; Diamond et al., 2011; Ekins & King, 1999; Ott et al., 2011; Savin-Williams, 1998; Steensma et al., 2013). I argue in this chapter for the use of *dynamical systems models* to understand sexual- and gender-minority experience and identity during childhood and adolescence. Dynamical systems approaches are particularly suited to these phenomena because they focus explicitly on understanding how complex patterns of experience emerge, stabilize, change, and restabilize due to dynamic interactions between endogenous factors, such as genes, hormones, and brain organization, and exogenous factors, such as social environments and relationships (Fogel & Thelen, 1987; Thelen et al., 1987;

Thelen & Smith, 1994). Dynamical systems models are not simply "improvements" upon conventional developmental approaches to sexual and gender variance but represent radical departures from traditional perspectives that put change – *in all of its forms* – at the center of our analytical frame. Traditional perspectives on sexual- and gender-minority youth have privileged one, and only one, type of developmental trajectory: one in which the child or adolescent gradually and progressively acknowledges and expresses same-sex desires or non-normative gender expression. Yet, as I review later, the reality is much more complex, including abrupt, non-linear, and sometimes recursive transformations and reorganizations at various points in development. If we fail to adequately model these experiences, we risk a fundamental misunderstanding of sexual and gender development, not only among sexual- and gender-minority youth but among *all* youth.

I begin with a brief review of research documenting the prevalence of complex change in sexual- and gender-minority experience during childhood and adolescence, noting the shortcomings of traditional deterministic models of development. I then introduce dynamical systems approaches and outline their usefulness for elucidating the factors underlying stability, change, and transformation in the expression of same-sex sexuality and gender variance during childhood and adolescence. I conclude by highlighting a number of potential directions for future research on the dynamic expression and experience of gender and sexuality in childhood and adolescence.

Diverse Developmental Expression of Same-Sex Sexuality

Developmental research on sexual orientation has been dominated by stage-based "coming out" models, which posit that sexual-minority youths represent a discrete and permanent class of individuals whose same-sex sexuality unfolds according to a series of ordered stages, beginning with early, vague interest in the same sex and progressing to clear-cut same-sex attractions, intensive questioning of one's sexual orientation, and eventual embrace of a lesbian/gay/bisexual identity label (reviewed in Cohen & Savin-Williams, 1996). Hence, these models reflect organismic assumptions about the basis of same-sex sexuality: the child's sexual orientation is viewed as fully formed at birth and simply waiting to emerge (Fausto-Sterling, 2012). Accordingly, developmental changes in the expression of same-sex sexuality are expected to follow one, and only one, pattern: progressive increases in expression and awareness.

Importantly, the development of *sexual orientation* (defined as an individual's underlying predisposition to experience sexual attractions for the same sex, the other sex, or both sexes) is not the same as the development of *sexual identity* (defined as an individual's conscious self-concept as lesbian, gay, bisexual, or heterosexual). This distinction dates back to Kinsey, who acknowledged in his groundbreaking studies of same-sex behavior that not all individuals engaging in such behavior viewed themselves as "homosexual," or viewed the behavior as important and self-relevant (Kinsey et al., 1948). For Kinsey, it was one's sexual response that was diagnostic of his/her sexual orientation, regardless of his/her self-concept. Yet many researchers studying sexual orientation in the 1970s and 1980s used sexual identity as a proxy for sexual orientation, by recruiting research participation on the *basis* of their sexual identity (i.e., advertising for "gay and lesbian participants" for research studies). The weaknesses of this approach were thrown into sharp relief during the AIDS crisis, when researchers and advocates realized that interventions targeted to "gay and bisexual men" would inevitably fail to capture the many individuals who engaged in same-sex behavior without identifying as gay or bisexual (it was for this reason that the terms "men-who-have-sex-with-men" and "women-who-have-sex-with-women" were coined). To this day, sexual identity and orientation continue to be viewed as distinct (albeit, obviously related) phenomena, with separate developmental trajectories.

Most research has focused on the development of *identity* rather than orientation. Extensive research in the late 1980s and early 1990s attempted to validate stage models of sexual identity development by asking openly identified gay, lesbian, and bisexual youths to recollect their earliest same-sex attractions and experiences, and to retrace the process by which they first began to question their sexual orientation (Cass, 1984; Coleman, 1981/1982; Troiden, 1989). Yet, over the years, these models have fallen out of favor because they fail to represent the diversity of sexual-minority youths' developmental trajectories (Diamond, 2008; Rosario et al., 2008; Savin-Williams, 2005). Some youths report becoming aware of their same-sex attractions as early as 9 or 10 years of age, whereas other youths do not report any awareness of same-sex attractions until late adolescence or even early adulthood, sometimes abruptly sparked by a single, transformative relationship (Golden, 1996; Savin-Williams, 1998, 2011). Some youths question their sexuality after pleasurably experimenting with same-sex sexual behavior, whereas others complete the entire process of sexual questioning and sexual-minority identification without ever having acted on their same-sex attractions (Dubé & Savin-Williams, 1999; Rosario et al., 2008).

Historically, long delays in awareness of same-sex attraction have been attributed to latency or "dormancy" (e.g., Saghir & Robins, 1973). From this perspective, an individual's same-sex attractions always existed but the social privileging of heterosexuality succeeded in blocking these feelings from awareness. Yet a number of in-depth interview studies have challenged the dormancy model. Although all of these studies have focused on adults, they have important implications for our understanding of children's and adolescents' experiences. For example, Loewenstein (1985) concluded from her research on more than 700 women that those reporting late-emerging same-sex attractions were undergoing genuine changes in their attractions, rather than a discovery of previously suppressed longing. Similarly, Kitzinger and Wilkinson (1995) interviewed women who underwent sudden and abrupt adult transitions to lesbianism, and many described these experiences in terms of sudden transformation, described in terms of "rebirth," a "quantum leap," a "conversion experience," or "emerging from a chrysalis" (Kitzinger, 1995, p. 100). To be sure, some individuals *do* describe "late-blooming" same-sex attractions in terms of previous repression and falsehood, as noted by Golden (1996) in her interview study of young women. Yet she cautioned against applying this interpretation to *all* individuals reporting the abrupt emergence of same-sex attractions. As one of her respondents straightforwardly stated, "Then I was heterosexual, and now I'm a lesbian" (p. 236).

Of course, an important problem with this body of research is its retrospective nature: adolescents and adults are asked to think back to early childhood experiences of sexual questioning and the accuracy of these recollections is impossible to discern. One notable study, however (Carver et al., 2004), directly asked children in grades 4 through 8 about their experiences of sexual questioning. Rather than asking respondents directly about same-sex desires or experiences, they asked children to report how confident they were that in the future, they would experience heterosexual attractions and participate in heterosexual relationships (such as falling in love with an other-sex partner). On this 4-point scale, boys' scores ranged from a mean of 3.3 (with an SD of 0.65) at grade 4 to a mean of 3.7 (with an SD of 0.48) in grade 8. Girls' scores did not appear to show the age-related increases observed in boys: Girls in grade 4 had a mean of 3.4 (with an SD of 0.58) and girls in grade 8 had a similar mean and standard deviation. These results (particularly the standard deviations) show that it is relatively common for children and young adolescents to question their heterosexuality. The authors attributed this to the increasing availability of media images and information regarding same-sex sexuality, which are likely to prompt children to reflect on their own heterosexuality and their own experiences with other girls and boys. As the authors note, some of these children may eventually adopt a sexual-minority identity, but most probably will not. Rather, they frame the process of sexual questioning not as "predictor" of future same-sex sexuality, but an important social-cognitive developmental experience in and of itself, which may bear its own unique and important relationship to the child's overall psychosocial developmental. Another strength of this study is that the authors assessed children's sexual questioning at two points in time: at the beginning and the end of the school year. The correlation between the fall and spring measures was significant ($r = 0.75$), but not perfect, suggesting that even over short spans of times, children's experiences and expectations regarding their heterosexuality show some malleability.

This, of course, runs counter to the traditional view that all individuals possess the same fundamental pattern of sexual attraction across their entire life span (colloquially summarized as "born that way"). Yet a growing number of longitudinal studies (reviewed in Diamond, 2016) show that the specific distribution of an individual's same- and other-sex attractions often shifts over time, especially among sexual minorities. Although it is rare for individuals to move all the way from exclusive same-sex sexuality to exclusive heterosexuality, "intermediate" transitions (from exclusive same-sex attractions to bisexual attractions, and *vice versa*) are extremely common.

Importantly, such emergent changes in patterns of sexual attraction should not be confused with *effortful* changes to extinguish same-sex attractions that some individuals seek through "reparative therapy," a form of therapy that is widely viewed to be both ineffective and psychologically damaging (APA Task Force on Appropriate Therapeutic Responses to Sexual Orientation, 2009). Rather, "naturally occurring" changes in sexual attraction appear to be attributable to a fundamental capacity for *fluidity* in human sexuality (Diamond, 2008). In addition, such changes do not appear to represent youthful confusion, or "coming out transitions," given they have been observed at all stages of life, and often occur many years after individuals' have already self-identified as lesbian, gay, or bisexual.

Organismic, stage-based models of sexual identity development have trouble explaining such findings regarding the developmental diversity of same-sex sexuality. What we need are developmental models capable of modeling the dynamic *interactions* between endogenous and exogenous factors that give rise to *nonlinear, discontinuous* changes in sexual expression, and which can trigger episodes of stabilization, destabilization, and restabilization at different points in time. As I discuss later, this is precisely the purview of dynamical systems theory. First, however, I review research on gender-minority development, which reveals similar problems with linear developmental models.

Diverse Developmental Expression of Gender Variance

Gender-minority youths (sometimes called *gender-variant, gender-nonconforming,* or *transgender* youths) are those whose psychological experience of gender or their outward gender presentation/behavior deviates from the sex to which they were assigned at birth. Gender variance can be mild (in the case of tomboys) or extreme (in the case of individuals who seek a complete gender transition). One of the most important developments over the past several decades of research on gender expression has been the increasing appreciation of the diversity of the gender-minority population (Devor, 2004; Ekins & King, 1999; Gagné et al., 1997; Halberstam, 2005; Roen, 2002). Whereas some gender-minority youths are distressed by, and seek to resolve and eliminate, discrepancies between their psychological experience of gender and the sex to which they were assigned at birth, others embrace nonbinary, fluid, or multiple gender identifications, and do not seek a clear cut identification as male or female (Diamond et al., 2011; Ekins & King, 1999; Gagné et al., 1997).

Furthermore, just as many sexual-minority youths undergo unexpected changes in their pattern of sexual attractions during childhood and adolescence, gender-minority youths often report changes in their gender identification and expression (Drummond et al., 2008; Steensma et al., 2011, 2013; Wallien & Cohen-Kettenis, 2008). Researchers thereby distinguish "persisters," who maintain their gender-nonconforming behavior and cross-gender identification over time, from "desisters," who eventually return to a pattern of gendered identification and behavior that conforms with the sex to which they were assigned at birth (Steensma et al., 2011, 2013). Yet even this basic categorization of persisters versus desisters oversimplifies the multiple developmental trajectories observed in gender-variant children. As argued by Steensma and Cohen-Kettenis (2015), there are additional potential pathways that emerge when one considers the timing and stability of a child's desistence and the potential role of sexual desire and relationships. Some children resolve their gender questioning in the course of adopting a gay, lesbian, or bisexual identity in adolescence or adulthood, whereas others resolve their gender questioning while maintaining a heterosexual identification. Some children desist from gender-variant behavior or identification only temporarily, eventually reengaging the questioning process in adulthood. Little is known about the factors driving these different pathways and whether they represent distinct and stable subtypes.

Transgender youths who openly embrace a fluid experience and expression of gender pose an inherent challenge to traditional assumptions that the normative and healthy endpoint of transgender identity development must involve the adoption of a stable, integrated, unambiguous identification as 100 percent male or 100 percent female (for reviews and critiques see Bornstein, 1994; Roen, 2002). After all, as early as 1987, the Diagnostic and Statistical Manual of Mental Disorders recognized a lack of coherent identity as a risk factor for poor mental health outcomes (American Psychiatric Association, 1987, as cited in Poston, 1990), and children who fail to develop a stable, psychological sense of gender (and who appear to be distressed as a result) may be formally diagnosed with gender dysphoria (American Psychiatric Association, 2000; Carroll et al., 2002; Levine et al., 1999). Yet there have been important conceptual and theoretical advances to gender and transgender identity development. For example, Denny's model (2004) de-emphasizes the rigid gender binary that characterizes conventional models of gender identity development, and instead presumes the existence of parallel gender continuums inclusive of male and female dimensions.

Despite these changes, psychologists tend to express ambivalence about whether it is healthy for youths to embrace a permanently liminal, flexible sense of gender, instead of moving progressively toward the goal of consistently identifying as male or female (reviewed in Mallon & DeCrescenzo, 2006). Yet there is no empirical data directly speaking to this question. In contrast to the extensive body of research on conventional gender identity development (Kohlberg et al., 1974; Martin & Ruble, 2004; Ruble et al., 2006, 2007), little research has focused on the basic developmental processes of transgender identity development in non-clinical populations (see Bockting, 2014, for a review), or has explored normative and resilient outcomes in this population.

In light of this developmental diversity and ambiguity, some researchers and clinicians have explicitly adopted a *gender affirmative model* of gender-minority experience and development, in which gender variance is viewed as a basic form of human diversity rather than a psychological disorder (Hidalgo et al., 2013). Gender affirmative approaches view gender variance as emanating from multiple interacting components, including biological factors, cultural factors, and cognitive-affective factors. Perhaps most important, gender affirmative approaches acknowledge the potential for fluidity in gender expression, meaning that gender identity and gender questioning may occur at multiple points across the life course, and may not necessarily resolve into a single and stable gender identification.

From a dynamical systems perspective, such diversity in sexual- and gender-minority trajectories is to be expected, and may be shaped by a wide range of interacting parameters, including the depth and duration of the youth's sexual and/or gender questioning, the cultural attitudes about gender and sexuality in the family, school, and community, the quality of the youth's relationships with other children and adults, access to information about sexual- and gender-minority experience, experiences of adversity or victimization, and experiences of support and nurturance. These influences are not additive factors to be entered into a regression equation neatly predicting the child's eventual sexual and gender identity, but dynamic, evolving, interacting forces that create changing constellation of motives, meanings, constraints, and opportunities. This is exactly what a dynamical systems approach can provide.

Introduction to Dynamical Systems Models

Dynamical systems models of social-behavioral phenomena belong to a larger class of theoretical approaches that seek to replace deterministic models of development with probabilistic, nonlinear, interactionist models that emphasize the interplay between biological and social factors over time (Fogel & Thelen, 1987; Granic & Patterson, 2006; Izard et al., 2000; Lewis, 2000; Thelen & Smith, 1994). Other examples of this approach include general systems theory, developmental systems theory, ecological perspectives, contextualism, transactionalism, and holistic-interactionism (reviewed in Granic, 2005). Dynamical systems models are particularly well-suited to explaining processes of nonlinear change, in which established patterns of thought, behavior, and experience undergo profound and abrupt disruption, recursion, and reorganization. Such nonlinear transformations are difficult – if not impossible – to explain with traditional linear models of development that set forth a uniform sequence of incremental, progressive stages leading inexorably to fixed endpoints. Such linear models do not capably represent the synergistic interactions among biological, interpersonal, and cultural factors across different developmental windows.

According to dynamical systems models, these interactions can create altogether novel psychological and behavioral phenomena – which may appear from the outside as sudden "jumps," "regressions," or "breaks" in development – via processes of systemic reorganization in underlying systems. These periods of reorganization are denoted "phase shifts" (Granic, 2005), and they are thought to occur when one or more of the parameters governing the system exceeds a critical threshold and provokes adjustment and realignment by the other parameters (Fogel & Thelen, 1987). During such phase shifts, existing patterns of thought and behavior dissolve and new forms of order and organization emerge to take their place.

Developmental psychologists were among the first to fully appreciate the potential usefulness of dynamical systems models for explaining both gradual and sudden changes in infants' and children's skills, abilities, traits, and experiences across a wide range of social, cognitive, emotional, and behavioral phenomena (Camras & Witherington, 2005; Fogel & Thelen, 1987; Granic, 2005; Lewis, 2000; Nowak et al., 2005; Smith & Thelen, 1993; Thelen et al., 1987; Thelen & Smith, 1994; Vallacher et al., 2005; van Geert & Steenbeek, 2005). Any human phenomena that involve complex, bidirectional interactions among endogenous factors (such as genes, hormones, maturational states, and traits) and exogenous factors (such as rearing conditions, socialization practices, interpersonal relationships, and cultural norms) are well-suited for a dynamical systems approach, and an emerging body of research on epigenetics and neural plasticity has begun to identify the critical mechanisms through which such bidirectional influences take shape. Thorough reviews of this literature are beyond the scope of this chapter (see Cicchetti & Curtis, 2006; Essex et al., 2013; Galván, 2010; Li, 2013; Meaney, 2010; Naumova et al., 2016; Rohlfs Domínguez, 2014; Roth & Sweatt, 2011), but, to briefly summarize, infants' and children's *direct engagement* with their social and sensory world (through touching and being touched, seeing, hearing, smelling, speaking, eating, learning, feeling, observing, etc.) *feeds back* through a variety of physiological channels to fundamentally organize and reorganize their developing brain and body, and to "turn on" and "turn off" a vast array of genes that direct subsequent development.

This body of research poses a fundamental challenge to the shopworn "nature/culture" dichotomy, given that it documents specific genetic and neurobiological processes through which our physical and psychological engagement with the "outside" environment is *directly incorporated* into our developing minds and bodies. In this view, culture does not simply "repress" or "encourage" inborn predispositions but gets "under the skin" to shape the fundamental transition from genotype to phenotype. As the child develops, and encounters a broader range of situational, social, cultural, and physical experiences, his/her phenomenology of gender and sexuality continues to shift and adapt, incorporating previous events and setting the stage for future experiences. As summarized by Fausto-Sterling (2012), there is no point in this trajectory at which we can say with certainty that the child or adolescent's sexual or gender expression has "finished" developing. Childhood and adolescence may be particularly ripe periods for organization and reorganization, but they are not the only ones, and the task for developmental psychologists is to identify the most important factors triggering stability and change during these periods.

Of course, cogent critiques of the nature/nurture dichotomy are nothing new to developmental psychologists (e.g., Ford & Lerner, 1992; Overton, 2013), so why is this dichotomy so difficult to dislodge when it comes to gender and sexuality? The social-political context of debates about the origin of sexual orientation may have played a key role. For more than 50 years, opponents of the rights of sexual and gender minorities have argued that such individuals are making deviant lifestyle choices that should be socially discouraged, and advocates for sexual and gender minorities have countered by arguing that sexual orientation (and, more recently, transgender experience) are fixed, biologically based traits that are fully formed and present at birth (reviewed in Diamond & Rosky, 2016). Following the logic of civil rights claims regarding race and ethnicity, it would be wrong to discriminate against sexual and gender minorities if they are "born that way." Hence, while the rest of developmental psychology moved on to nuanced, transactional models of the complex interbraiding between organisms and their environments over the life span, studies of sexual orientation have not generally followed suit. This is somewhat understandable, given that studies that *do* acknowledge a capacity for dynamic flexibility in same-sex sexuality over the life course are often cited by opponents of LGBT rights as reasons to *deny* civil rights protections to LGBT populations (e.g., McHugh, 2013), on the basis that LGBT status is not an immutable trait, like race or ethnicity. Yet researchers need not be cowed by the contentious political climate regarding LGBT rights: legal scholarship has demonstrated time and again that LGBT individuals need not be "born that way" in order to merit civil rights protections (Diamond & Rosky, 2016), and it is high time for scholars studying the development of gender and sexual minorities to adopt the more nuanced, dynamical approaches to development that these topics warrant.

Application to Gender and Sexuality

The past decade has seen an explosion of interest in neural plasticity and epigenetics, representing a growing appreciation in developmental psychology for probabilistic models of development that take more seriously the ongoing interplay between exogenous and endogenous influences. Yet, thus far, these dynamic, interactionist models of development have focused primarily on the dynamic biosocial shaping of infants' and children's emotions, cognitions, and stress regulation, and this approach has *not* been substantively applied to the topics of gender and sexuality (with some exceptions). This reflects the fact that within developmental psychology, gender and sexuality continue to be conceptualized as human "essences" that may be "pushed against," but not fundamentally changed by social/environmental factors. Dynamical systems models counter this view, arguing instead that gender and sexual identity are ongoing productions of dynamic and sometimes unpredictable person–environment interactions. As a result, there is no single point in time at which they are definitively "finished" and/or fixed, and no single precursor can uniformly predict future outcomes. Rather, both gender and sexual identity show equifinality and multifinality: equifinality denotes the fact that two individuals may arrive at similar gender or sexual identities through vastly different developmental trajectories, whereas multifinality denotes the fact that two individuals might follow similar developmental trajectories, but reach vastly different gender and sexual identity outcomes.

This perspective does not imply that gender and sexual identity are randomly variable. It simply suggests that when individuals (whether or not they are sexual- or gender-minorities) exhibit stable patterns of thought, behavior, and/or experience, these stable patterns cannot be interpreted as permanent and inevitable maturational achievements. Rather, all complex patterns remain subject to future change and realignment as a function of changing environments and situations (Fogel & Thelen, 1987). Some systems will prove relatively robust in the face of environmental perturbations, whereas others are more "softly assembled" (Thelen & Smith, 1998), meaning that they tend to be prone to reorganization due to changes in local parameters. Hence, whereas traditional deterministic models of gender and sexual identity have focused on disentangling the additive influences on each of these phenomena (i.e., genes, prenatal hormones, childhood experiences, and social and familial influences), dynamical systems approaches focus instead on understanding how these phenomena take a variety of different forms across different periods of development according to the complex, changing relationships among multiple interacting influences (Fogel, 1993).

Fausto-Sterling (2012) points out that most scientific and lay perspectives on same-sex sexuality and gender variance make a fundamental presumption that the primary driver of sexual and gender development is the child's internal, biologically based traits and systems (genes, hormones, and neurobiology). From this perspective, environmental factors may modify the *expression* of these traits but they are not expected to fundamentally change them. Yet dynamical systems theory, buttressed by the rapidly growing literature on neural plasticity and epigenetics, fundamentally challenges this view. Fausto-Sterling (2012) has outlined how processes of embodiment and neural plasticity may aid our understanding of children's developing sense and experience of gender: "Through its sensory and motor abilities the exterior layers of the body bring the world into the central nervous system. Neural plasticity lies at the heart of the matter. A toddler's mind emerges from experience in a particular body and particular world. The brain's very synapses form, take shape, die back, or reconnect in response to the world and body that envelops it" (p. 405). Applying this perspective to gender identity development, she notes that the children's ongoing physical interactions and psychological experiences with parents, peers, and culture fundamentally shape and reshape their experience of gender over time, as different brain/body systems couple and uncouple over time. In the end, gender is not a stable achievement but rather "a pattern in time" (p. 405) continually renegotiated on the basis of prior dynamics and current environmental affordances.

The phenomena of embodiment and plasticity are just as relevant for the development and expression of same-sex sexuality. Since the 1990s, a substantial body of work has demonstrated significant genetic influences on sexual orientation (reviewed in Bailey et al., 2016). Yet, these influences are probabilistic rather than deterministic (as evidenced by the fact that when one identical twin is gay, lesbian, or bisexual, the other twin is heterosexual about 70 percent of the time). Hence, although the phrase "born gay" has become common in colloquial discussions of sexual orientation, this phrase implies a level of fixity in the expression of same-sex sexuality that simply does not exist. One potential reason for such complexity may be the epigenetic regulation of sexual orientation (Ngun & Vilain, 2014; Rice et al., 2012). Epigenetics focuses on chemical mechanisms that alter the expression of genes at different points in the organism's life cycle in response to environmental influences. These environmentally released changes can have significant and lasting consequences for the phenotypic expression of genetically influenced traits, and can even be passed down to future generations, directly challenging traditional models of genetic inheritance. Recent studies using epigenetic models have proven more successful in explaining population variance in same-sex sexuality than studies using conventional genetic models (Ngun et al., 2015), and hence future research on the genetics of sexual orientation may increasingly focus on *environmentally released changes in gene expression*, and how these changes are passed down, rather than the simple presence or absence of certain genes at birth.

Hence, although individuals may be born with a predisposition for same-sex, other-sex, or bisexual attractions, environmental experiences play a fundamental role in shaping how these predispositions develop into phenomenology. At the current time, we know little about what sort of environmental influences may be relevant, but it is likely that a range of cognitive, emotional, and physical experiences play ongoing roles, including a child or adolescent's early experiences with sexuality and his/her process of making sense of these experiences (Hoffmann, 2012; Hoffmann et al., 2004). Along these lines, it is instructive to consider the progression of Vivienne Cass's thinking on sexual identity development over the years. She conducted some of the earliest and most influential work on sexual identity development (Cass, 1979, 1984), but by the 1990s she had come to reevaluate some of her initial theoretical assumptions about the independence between sexual identity and sexual orientation. In a startlingly forthright chapter reflecting on this issue (1990), Cass took herself to task for previously assuming that the process of developing a gay, lesbian, or bisexual identity was wholly separate from the initial emergence of a gay, lesbian, or bisexual orientation. Cass noted that over the years she had begun to doubt this primary assumption, and had arrived at a greater appreciation for the ways in which the process of cognitively questioning one's sexual identity – attaching different meanings to one's intimate experiences, experimenting with different types of same- and other-sex relationships, and reflecting on their rewards and implications – could reciprocally influence and shape one's fundamental experience of same-sex desire, therefore altering the development of sexual orientation itself. In her view, these processes of reciprocal influence occurred via straightforward learning and conditioning processes, "by narrowing opportunities for sexual/social/emotional expression, building attitudes that attach a fixed quality to identity and preference, reinforcing behaviors that are consistent with identity, and providing a system of rewards that encourages commitment to a particular mode of behavior" (p. 252). Just as individuals' subjective sexual experiences directly inform the identities they choose to adopt (i.e., I enjoy same- but not other-sex activity, therefore, I am gay), the adoption of a socially embedded identity can feed back to shape the quality of one's sexual experiences, providing a cognitive frame that may alter the very phenomenology of erotic pleasure – for example, either amplifying or dampening it – and also altering its representation in memory.

In essence, Cass is arguing that sexual desires, including the broader patterns of desire that we call "orientation," are not static properties but dynamic phenomena that take shape through ongoing interchanges between individuals' traits and propensities and their changing social, cognitive, and affective contexts. Hence, whereas Cass's original stage model of sexual identity development posited an inexorable, unidirectional progression from early same-sex attractions and sexual activity to eventual gay/lesbian/bisexual identity adoption, her newer formulation suggested a cascading, recursive process through which identity, context, desire, and behavior mutually shape one another over time, sometimes arriving at periods of stable erotic experience and identification but sometimes traversing through periods of re-questioning and destabilization. This is the precisely the sort of process that dynamical systems models seek to describe, reflecting a "cascade" approach to human development positing that early traits and experiences continuously feed forward to shape individuals' changing skills, capacities, and propensities over time. When applied to sexuality, this view suggests that sexuality represents both the "output" of prior development and the "input" for forthcoming experience. In essence, sexuality is a moving target, continuously reorganizing in response to an individual's cumulative succession of intimate feelings and experiences and the socially embedded meanings attached to these experiences. Some individuals' trajectories may gravitate toward increased stabilization, whereas other trajectories will repeatedly splinter, diversify, and reorganize.

Directions for Future Research

A chief goal for dynamical systems approaches to gender and sexual development is the identification of the key control parameters that inform children's and adolescents' expression of same-sex desire and gender variance, and to determine the conditions under which these parameters are pushed to the point of abrupt reorganization, denoted a "phase shift" (Granic, 2005). During phase shifts, previous patterns of thought, behavior, and experience (such as exclusive other-sex attractions or consistent gender role conformity) enter a period of flux and instability, and new patterns eventually take their place. The factors giving rise to these changes may be exogenous (such as the formation of specific relationships) or endogenous (such as adrenarche or gonadarche), and they may be large or small. Critically, reorganization of the system (perhaps manifested in the adoption of a gay/lesbian/bisexual/transgender identity) does not imply permanent stabilization. Rather, subsequent changes may introduce additional phase shifts and multiple episodes of reorganization. Hence, contrary to the longstanding view that gender and sexual identity reach maturity and permanence by adolescence, these phenomena instead exhibit "dynamic stability" (Fogel & Thelen, 1987), meaning that they may show relative stability over certain developmental epochs but remain subject to oscillation and readjustment depending on environmental influences. Charting the specific factors that give rise to both stability and change at different points in childhood and adolescence is a priority for future research.

Investigation of individual differences is another important topic for inquiry. Some children and adolescents recall highly stable patterns of same-sex attraction or cross-gender identification, beginning at an early age, whereas others show more variable patterns. In the language of dynamical systems, we would say that gender and sexuality are more "softly assembled" (Thelen & Smith, 1998) for some youth than others, meaning more prone to environmentally triggered reorganization. Currently, we do not know why there are such dramatic differences in the developmental trajectories of sexual- and gender-minorities. It is possible that this diversity reflects complex interchanges between genetic and environmental factors at different stages of development, and our growing understanding of epigenetics and neural plasticity may eventually help us to parse these influences. In order to make progress, we need to begin studying the development of gender and sexuality as early as possible in children's development, and to study the expression longitudinally. As argued by McClintock and Herdt (1996), sexual desire does not simply switch on at puberty but instead undergoes gradual development from childhood onward, reflecting a progressive interbraiding of biological, social, and psychological transitions. Yet, our base of knowledge on these experiences, their normative developmental time course, and their phenomenology (from the child's perspective) is woefully limited, given that cultural taboos have made it difficult for researchers to systematically study these experiences (Lamb, 2013). Yet, the research on childhood sexual questioning by Carver and colleagues (2004) shows that there are, in fact, sensitive and well-validated ways to assess children's phenomenology of sexuality and gender in a manner that could allow us, over time, to chart the factors that give rise to periods of flux and stability in children's and adolescents' experiences. Application of these techniques longitudinally is a priority for future research.

Finally, a crucial question for future research concerns whether dynamic variability in same-sex sexuality stems from – and is best represented by – fundamentally different theoretical and empirical models than dynamical variability in gender expression. Throughout this chapter, I have cited evidence for dynamical variability in both phenomena but this runs the risk of conflating these two distinct phenomena (a conflation that has a long history in research on these topics). The multiple interacting factors that give rise to non-normative sexual attractions do not neatly overlap with the multiple interacting factors that give rise to non-normative gender expression, and we must investigate each phenomenon independently in order to make sure that we do not inappropriately extrapolate findings from one domain to the other. The most important experience that is shared across sexual- and gender-minority individuals is their marginalization and ostracization from mainstream society, and because of this marginalization many sexual- and gender-minority individuals have formed powerful and life-sustaining community bonds. Yet, their core experiences are often quite different, and researchers applying dynamical systems perspectives to sexual- and gender-minority experience must remain mindful to these differences, and take care to develop and validate models that capably represent the unique time scales and control parameters for each phenomenon.

In the end, the most important "take-home message" of a dynamical systems approach concerns *equifinality and multifinality*: the notion that similar experiences (e.g., adolescent same-sex activity or adult gender variance) can branch onto notably different pathways and outcomes (heterosexuality, gay/lesbian/bisexual identification, mild or moderate gender nonconformity, or transgender identification), just as divergent experiences can eventually converge on the same pathway and outcome (i.e., some transgender adolescents report stable cross-gender identification from early childhood, whereas others report chronic oscillation between more masculine and feminine identities). From the standpoint of traditional approaches to sexual orientation and gender variance, both equifinality and multifinality are perplexing problems, since they suggest the impossibility of identifying reliable and valid predictors of a child's eventual sexual- or gender-minority status. Dynamical systems approaches prompt us to abandon our search for "predictors," and instead to attend to the interacting biosocial processes shaping both stability and change in the expression of gender and sexuality during childhood and adolescence. This is the only way to develop robust developmental models capable of representing the complexity of gender and sexual expression, capable of revealing their full range of developmental drivers, and capable of informing our understanding of the lived experiences of sexual and gender minorities at all stages of the life course.

References

American Psychiatric Association. (2000). *Diagnostic and Statistical Manual of Mental Disorders*, 4th edn. Washington DC: American Psychiatric Association.

APA Task Force on Appropriate Therapeutic Responses to Sexual Orientation. (2009). *Report of the Task Force on Appropriate Therapeutic Responses to Sexual Orientation*. Washington DC: American Psychological Association.

Bailey, J. M., Vasey, P. L., Diamond, L. M., Breedlove, S. M., Vilain, E., & Epprecht, M. (2016). Sexual Orientation, Controversy, and Science. *Psychological Science in the Public Interest*, *17*, 45–101.

Bockting, W. O. (2014). Transgender Identity Development. In Tolman, D. L. & Diamond, L. M. (Eds.), *APA Handbook of Sexuality and Psychology, Vol. 1: Person-based Approaches*. (739–758). Washington, DC: American Psychological Association.

Bornstein, K. (1994). *Gender Outlaw: Men, Women, and the Rest of Us*. New York: Routledge.

Camras, L. A. & Witherington, D. C. (2005). Dynamical Systems Approaches to Emotional Development. *Developmental Review*, *25*(3), 328–350.

Carroll, L., Gilroy, P. J., & Ryan, J. (2002). Counseling Trangendered, Transsexual, and Gender-Variant Clients. *Journal of Counseling & Development*, *80*(2), 131–138.

Carver, P. R., Egan, S. K., & Perry, D. G. (2004). Children Who Question Their Heterosexuality. *Developmental Psychology*, *40*(1), 43–53. doi:10.1037/0012-1649.40.1.43.

Cass, V. (1979). Homosexual Identity Formation: A Theoretical Model. *Journal of Homosexuality*, *4*, 219–235.

(1984). Homosexual Identity: A Concept in Need of a Definition. *Journal of Homosexuality*, *9*, 105–126.

(1990). The Implications of Homosexual Identity Formation for the Kinsey Model and Scale of Sexual Preference. In McWhirter, D. P., Sanders, S. A., & Reinisch, J. M. (Eds.), *Homosexuality/Heterosexuality: Concepts of Sexual Orientation* (239–266). New York: Oxford University Press.

Cicchetti, D. & Curtis, W. J. (2006). The Developing Brain and Neural Plasticity: Implications for Normality, Psychopathology, and Resilience. In D. Cicchetti, D. J. Cohen, D. Cicchetti, & D. J. Cohen (Eds.), *Developmental Psychopathology: Developmental Neuroscience*, Vol. 2, *2nd ed*. (pp. 1–64). Hoboken, NJ, US: John Wiley & Sons Inc.

Cohen, K. M. & Savin-Williams, R. C. (1996). Developmental Perspectives on Coming Out to Self and Others. In R. C. Savin-Williams & K. M. Cohen (Eds.), *The Lives of Lesbians, Gays, and Bisexuals: Children to Adults* (pp. 113–151). Fort Worth, TX: Harcourt Brace.

Coleman, E. (1981/1982). Developmental Stages of the Coming Out Process. *Journal of Homosexuality*, *7*, 31–43.

Denny, D. (2004). Changing Models of Transsexualism. In U. Leli & J. Drescher (Eds.), *Transgender Subjectivities: A Clinician's Guide*. (25–40). New York: Haworth Press.

Devor, A. H. (2004). Witnessing and Mirroring: A Fourteen Stage Model of Transsexual Identity Formation. *Journal of Gay & Lesbian Psychotherapy*, *8*(1), 41–67.

Diamond, L. M. (2003). Was It a Phase? Young Women's Relinquishment of Lesbian/Bisexual Identities over a 5-Year Period. *Journal of Personality and Social Psychology*, *84*, 352–364.

(2008). Female Bisexuality from Adolescence to Adulthood: Results from a 10 Year Longitudinal Study. *Developmental Psychology*, *44*, 5–14. doi:10.1037/0012-1649.44.1.5.

(2016). Sexual Fluidity in Males and Females. *Current Sexual Health Reports*. 8(4), 249–256. doi:10.1007/s11930-016-0092-z.

Diamond, L. M., Pardo, S. T., & Butterworth, M. R. (2011). Border Crossings: Transgender Experience and Identity. In Schwartz, S., Luyckx, K., & Vignoles, V. (Eds.), *Handbook of Identity Theory and Research* (629–648). New York: Springer.

Diamond, L. M. & Rosky, C. J. (2016). Scrutinizing Immutability: Research on Sexual Orientation and U.S. Legal Advocacy for Sexual Minorities. *Journal of Sex Research*, 53(4/5), 363–391. doi:10.1080/00224499.2016.1139665.

Drummond, K. D., Bradley, S. J., Peterson-Badali, M., & Zucker, K. J. (2008). A Follow-Up Study of Girls with Gender Identity Disorder. *Developmental Psychology*, *44*, 34–45. doi:10.1037/0012-1649.44.1.34.

Dubé, E. M. & Savin-Williams, R. C. (1999). Sexual Identity Development among Ethnic Sexual-Minority Male Youths. *Developmental Psychology*, *35*, 1389–1398. doi:10.1037/0012-1649.35.6.1389.

Ekins, R. & King, D. (1999). Towards a Sociology of Transgendered Bodies. *The Sociological Review*, *47*, 580–602. doi:10.1111/1467-954X.00185.

Essex, M. J., Boyce, W. T., Hertzman, C., et al. (2013). Epigenetic Vestiges of Early Developmental Adversity: Childhood Stress Exposure and DNA Methylation in Adolescence. *Child Development*, *84*(1), 58–75. doi:10.1111/j.1467-8624.2011.01641.x.

Fausto-Sterling, A. (2012). The Dynamic Development of Gender Variability. *Journal of Homosexuality*, *59*, 398–421. doi:10.1080/00918369.2012.653310.

Fogel, A. (1993). *Developing through Relationships*. Chicago: University of Chicago Press.

Fogel, A. & Thelen, E. (1987). Development of Early Expressive and Communicative Action: Reinterpreting the Evidence from a Dynamic Systems Perspective. *Developmental Psychology*, *23*(6), 747–761.

Ford, D. L. & Lerner, R. M. (1992). *Developmental Systems Theory: An Integrative Approach*. Newberry Park: Sage.

Gagné, P., Tewksbury, R., & McGaughey, D. (1997). Coming Out and Crossing Over: Identity Formation and Proclamation in a Transgender Community. *Gender & Society*, 11(4), 478–508.

Galván, A. (2010). Neural Plasticity of Development and Learning. *Human Brain Mapping*, *31*(6), 879–890. doi:10.1002/hbm.21029.

Golden, C. (1996). What's in a Name? Sexual Self-Identification among Women. In Savin-Williams, R. C. & Cohen, K. M. (Eds.), *The Lives of Lesbians, Gays, and Bisexuals: Children to Adults* (229–249). Fort Worth: Harcourt Brace.

Granic, I. (2005). Timing Is Everything: Developmental Psychopathology from a Dynamic Systems Perspective. *Developmental Review*, *25*(3), 386–407.

Granic, I. & Patterson, G. R. (2006). Toward a Comprehensive Model of Antisocial Development: A Dynamic Systems Approach. *Psychological Review*, *113*(1), 101–131.

Halberstam, J. (2005). *In a Queer Time and Place: Transgender Bodies, Subcultural Lives*. New York: NYU Press.

Hidalgo, M. A., Ehrensaft, D., Tishelman, A. C., et al. (2013). The Gender Affirmative Model: What We Know and What We Aim to Learn. *Human Development*, *56*(5), 285–290. doi:10.1159/000355235.

Hoffmann, H. (2012). Considering the Role of Conditioning in Sexual Orientation. *Archives of Sexual Behavior*, *41*(1), 63–71. doi:10.1007/s10508-012-9915-9.

Hoffmann, H., Janssen, E., & Turner, S. L. (2004). Classical Conditioning of Sexual Arousal in Women and Men: Effects of Varying Awareness and Biological Relevance of the Conditioned Stimulus. *Archives of Sexual Behavior*, *33*(1), 43–53.

Izard, C. E., Ackerman, B. P., Schoff, K. M., & Fine, S. E. (2000). Self-organization of Discrete Emotions, Emotion Patterns, and Emotion-Cognition Relations. In Lewis, M. D. & Granic, I. (Eds.), *Emotion, Development, and Self-organization: Dynamic Systems Approaches to Emotional Development.* (15–36). Cambridge: Cambridge University Press.

Kinsey, A. C., Pomeroy, W. B., & Martin, C. E. (1948). *Sexual Behavior in the Human Male*. Philadelphia: W. B. Saunders.

Kitzinger, C. (1995). Social Constructionism: Implications for Lesbian and Gay Psychology. In D'Augelli, A. R. & Patterson, C. (Eds.), *Lesbian, Gay, and Bisexual Identities over the Lifespan* (136–161). New York: Oxford University Press.

Kitzinger, C. & Wilkinson, S. (1995). Transitions from Heterosexuality to Lesbianism: The Discursive Production of Lesbian Identities. *Developmental Psychology*, 31, 95–104.

Kohlberg, L., Ullian, D. Z., Friedman, R. C., Richart, R. M., Vande Wiele, R. L., & Stern, L. O. (1974). *Stages in the Development of Psychosexual Concepts and Attitudes Sex Differences in Behavior.* Oxford: John Wiley & Sons.

Lamb, S. (2013). Childhood Sexuality. In Tolman, D. L. & Diamond, L. M. (Eds.), *APA Handbook on Psychology and Sexuality.* Washington, DC: APA Press.

Levine, S. B., Brown, G. R., Coleman, E., et al. (1999). The Standards of Care for Gender Identity Disorders. *Journal of Psychology & Human Sexuality*, *11*(2), 1–34.

Lewis, M. D. (2000). The Promise of Dynamic Systems Approaches for an Integrated Account of Human Development. *Child Development*, *71*(1), 36–43.

Li, S.-C. (2013). Neuromodulation and Developmental Contextual Influences on Neural and Cognitive Plasticity across the Lifespan. *Neuroscience and Biobehavioral Reviews*, 37(9, Part B), 2201–2208. doi:10.1016/j.neubiorev.2013.07.019.

Loewenstein, S. F. (1985). On the Diversity of Love Object Orientations among Women. *Journal of Social Work and Human Sexuality*, *3*(2/3), 7–24.

Mallon, G. P. & DeCrescenzo, T. (2006). Transgender Children and Youth: A Child Welfare Practice Perspective. *Child Welfare Journal*, *85*(2), 215–241.

Martin, C. L. & Ruble, D. (2004). Children's Search for Gender Cues: Cognitive Perspectives on Gender Development. *Current Directions in Psychological Science*, *13*(2), 67–70.

McClintock, M. K. & Herdt, G. (1996). Rethinking Puberty: The Development of Sexual Attraction. *Current Directions in Psychological Science*, *5*, 178–183. doi:10.1111/1467-8721.ep11512422.

McHugh, P. (2013). Brief of Amicus Curiae concerning the immutability of sexual orientations in support of affirmance on the merits, Windsor, 133 S. Ct. 2675 (Nos. 12–307).

Meaney, M. J. (2010). Epigenetics and the Biological Definition of Gene X Environment Interactions. *Child Development*, *81*(1), 41–79. doi:10.1111/j.1467-8624.2009.01381.x.

Morgan, S. W. & Stevens, P. E. (2008). Transgender Identity Development as Represented By a Group of Female-to-Male Transgendered Adults. *Issues in Mental Health Nursing*, *29*(6), 585–599.

Naumova, O. Y., Hein, S., Suderman, M., et al. (2016). Epigenetic Patterns Modulate the Connection between Developmental Dynamics of Parenting and Offspring Psychosocial Adjustment. *Child Development*, *87*(1), 98–110. doi:10.1111/cdev.12485.

Ngun, T. C., Guo, W., Ghahramani, N. M., et al. (2015). A Novel Predictive Model of Sexual Orientation Using Epigenetic Markers. Paper presented at the Annual Meeting of The American Society of Human Genetics, Baltimore.

Ngun, T. C. & Vilain, E. (2014). The Biological Basis of Human Sexual Orientation: Is There a Role for Epigenetics? *Advances in Genetics*, *86*, 167–184. doi:10.1016/B978-0-12-800222-3.00008-5.

Nowak, A., Vallacher, R. R., & Zochowski, M. (2005). The Emergence of Personality: Dynamic Foundations of Individual Variation. *Developmental Review*, *25*(3), 351–385.

Overton, W. F. (2013). A New Paradigm For Developmental Science: Relationism and Relational-Developmental Systems. *Applied Developmental Science*, *17*, 94–107.

Ott, M. Q., Corliss, H. L., Wypij, D., Rosario, M., & Austin, S. B. (2011). Stability and Change in Self-Reported Sexual Orientation Identity in Young People: Application of Mobility Metrics. *Archives of Sexual Behavior*, *40*(3), 519–532. doi:10.1007/s10508-010-9691-3

Poston, W. C. (1990). The Biracial Identity Development Model: A Needed Addition. *Journal of Counseling & Development*, *69*(2), 152–155. doi:10.1002/j.1556-6676.1990.tb01477.x.

Rice, W. R., Friberg, U., & Gavrilets, S. (2012). Homosexuality as a Consequence of Epigenetically Canalized Sexual Development. *The Quarterly Review Of Biology*, *87*(4), 343–368.

Roen, K. (2002). “Either/or” and “Both/Neither”: Discursive Tensions in Transgender Politics. *Signs*, *27*(2), 501–522. doi:10.1086/495695.

Rohlfs Domínguez, P. (2014). Promoting Our Understanding of Neural Plasticity by Exploring Developmental Plasticity in Early and Adult Life. *Brain Research Bulletin*, *107*, 31–36. doi:10.1016/j.brainresbull.2014.05.006.

Rosario, M., Schrimshaw, E. W., & Hunter, J. (2008). Predicting Different Patterns of Sexual Identity Development over Time among Lesbian, Gay, and Bisexual Youths: A Cluster Analytic Approach. *American Journal of Community Psychology*, *42*(3–4), 266–282. doi:10.1007/s10464-008-9207-7.

Rosario, M., Schrimshaw, E. W., & Hunter, J. (2011). Different Patterns of Sexual Identity Development over Time: Implications for the Psychological Adjustment of Lesbian, Gay, and Bisexual Youths. *Journal of Sex Research*, *48*(1), 3–15.

Roth, T. L. & Sweatt, J. D. (2011). Annual Research Review: Epigenetic Mechanisms and Environmental Shaping of the Brain during Sensitive Periods of Development. *Journal of Child Psychology and Psychiatry*, *52*(4), 398–408. doi:10.1111/j.1469-7610.2010.02282.x.

Ruble, D. N., Martin, C. L., & Berenbaum, S. A. (2006). Gender Development. In Eisenberg, N., Damon, W., & Lerner, R. M. (Eds.), *Handbook of Child*

Psychology, 6th ed.: Vol 3. Social, Emotional, and Personality Development. (858–932). Hoboken: John Wiley & Sons Inc.

Ruble, D. N., Taylor, L. J., Cyphers, L., Greulich, F. K., Lurye, L. E., & Shrout, P. E. (2007). The Role of Gender Constancy in Early Gender Development. *Child Development*, *78*(4), 1121–1136. doi:10.1111/j.1467-8624.2007.01056.x.

Saghir, M. T. & Robins, E. (1973). *Male and Female Homosexuality: A Comprehensive Investigation*. Baltimore: Williams & Wilkins.

Savin-Williams, R. C. (1998). *"... And Then I Became Gay": Young Men's Stories*. New York: Routledge.

(2005). *The New Gay Teenager*. Cambridge, MA: Harvard University Press.

(2011). Identity Development among Sexual-Minority Youth. In Schwartz, S., Luyckx, K., & Vignoles, V. (Eds.), *Handbook of Identity Theory and Research* (671–689). New York: Springer.

Smith, L. B. & Thelen, E. (1993). *A Dynamic Systems Approach to Development: Applications*. Cambridge, MA: The MIT Press.

Steensma, T. D., Biemond, R., de Boer, F., & Cohen-Kettenis, P. T. (2011). Desisting and Persisting Gender Dysphoria after Childhood: A Qualitative Follow-Up Study. *Clinical Child Psychology and Psychiatry*, *16*(4), 499–516. doi:10.1177/1359104510378303.

Steensma, T. D. & Cohen-Kettenis, P. T. (2015). More than Two Developmental Pathways in Children with Gender Dysphoria? *Journal of the American Academy of Child & Adolescent Psychiatry*, *54*(2), 147–148. doi:10.1016/j.jaac.2014.10.016.

Steensma, T. D., McGuire, J. K., Kreukels, B. P. C., Beekman, A. J., & Cohen-Kettenis, P. T. (2013). Factors Associated with Desistence and Persistence of Childhood Gender Dysphoria: A Quantitative Follow-Up Study. *Journal of the American Academy of Child & Adolescent Psychiatry*, *52*(6), 582–590. doi:10.1016/j.jaac.2013.03.016.

Thelen, E., Kelso, J. A. S., & Fogel, A. (1987). Self-Organizing Systems and Infant Motor Development. *Developmental Review*, *7*(1), 39–65.

Thelen, E. & Smith, L. B. (1994). *A Dynamic Systems Approach to the Development of Cognition and Action*. Cambridge, MA: MIT Press.

(1998). Dynamic Systems Theories. In Damon, W. & Lerner, R. M. (Eds.), *Handbook of Child Psychology: Volume 1: Theoretical Models of Human Development, 5th edn*. (563–634). Hoboken, NJ: John Wiley & Sons, Inc.

Troiden, R. R. (1989). The Formation of Homosexual Identities. *Journal of Homosexuality*, *17*, 43–73.

Vallacher, R. R., Nowak, A., & Zochowski, M. (2005). Dynamics of Social Coordination: The Synchronization of Internal States in Close Relationships. *Interaction Studies: Social Behaviour and Communication in Biological and Artificial Systems*, *6*(1), 35–52.

van Geert, P. & Steenbeek, H. (2005). Explaining after by before: Basic Aspects of a Dynamic Systems Approach to the Study of Development. *Developmental Review*, *25*(3), 408–442.

Wallien, M. S. C. & Cohen-Kettenis, P. T. (2008). Psychosexual Outcome of Gender-Dysphoric Children. *Journal Of The American Academy Of Child And Adolescent Psychiatry*, *47*(12), 1413–1423. doi:10.1097/CHI.0b013e31818956b9.

6 Sexual Embodiment in Girlhood and beyond

Young Migrant and Refugee Women's Discourse of Silence, Secrecy, and Shame

Jane Ussher, Alexandra Hawkey, and Janette Perz

Introduction

Historically, the sexual body has been conceptualized as a 'natural' object and the domain of biomedicine, leading to a focus on mapping normal adolescent development and functionality, as well as identifying disease and disorders (e.g., Omar, 2010). However, in recent decades, feminist scholars from the social sciences and humanities have turned their attention to sexual embodiment, the experience of living in, perceiving, and experiencing the world from the location of our sexual bodies and the ways in which our social environments "enter into and become entangled with our bodies" (Tolman et al., 2014, p. 761). Embodiment theories provide insight into how bodies are experienced and made sense of in relation to social structures and power. They also shed light on the ways in which cultural discourse and practice defines the boundaries of normality in relation to the sexual body (Foucault, 1978). Conceptualized as 'social inscription' (Grosz, 1994), the body is understood as a site within which social norms are enacted, and women's sexual subjectivity – their sense of a sexual self – is constructed and regulated (Bartky, 1999; Ussher, 1997). Women internalize social and cultural discourse associated with the body, and, through processes of self-policing, align themselves with cultural ideals of feminine embodiment, or risk being positioned as aberrant, deficient, or diseased (Bordo, 1993; Ussher, 2006). At the same time, discursive constructions of normative sexuality determine the sexual scripts that women are allowed to adopt, the ways in which sexual embodiment can be expressed, as well as the possibilities for resistance (Tiefer, 2004). This does not deny the material reality of the sexual body – but conceptualizes embodiment in a social context, reflexively constructed and reconstructed through sexual and social interactions (Jackson & Scott, 2002), with the processes of social inscription of the body having a psychical interior (Grosz, 1994). Within a material–discursive–intrapsychic theoretical framework (Ussher, 2000, 2011), this conceptualizes adolescent sexual embodiment as the interconnection between the corporeality of the leaking, bleeding, changing body; the construction of this same body within cultural discourse and practice; and women's intrapsychic negotiation of both corporeality and discourse.

Increasing evidence suggests that many young women have less than optimal experiences of sexual embodiment, leaving this population disempowered in the sexual domain (Tolman, 2009). Young women frequently report discomfort with their bodies, associated with difficulties in attaining positive sexual subjectivity, or sense of sexual self (Curtin et al., 2011). Within educational contexts, sex is generally framed within a discourse of abstinence or protection from male predators, producing a "missing discourse of desire," which denies young women's sexual subjectivity (Fine & McClelland, 2006). The reproductive body can be a source of shame, with the fecund woman positioned as the epitome of the 'monstrous feminine' (Ussher, 2006). This leads to menarche and menstruation being concealed to avoid stigma (Lee, 2009), and self-objectification, resulting from the positioning of the bleeding body as disgusting or dysfunctional (Roberts, 2004), and the critical scrutiny of the male gaze (Fredrickson & Roberts, 1997; Ussher, 1997).

Women's sexual embodiment is mediated by factors such as race, social class, sexual preference, and cultural background. Disempowerment and self-objectification may be exacerbated for young migrant and refugee women who originate from contexts that do not recognize or condone a woman's right over her sexual and reproductive health, and where women's sexuality is strictly regulated by religious or cultural discourse and practice. With the aim of improving sexual and reproductive health, the World Health Organization (WHO) encourages communities to "meet the special needs of vulnerable populations for reproductive health services, especially for adolescent . . . women" (World Health Organization, 2013). In order to implement effective policies that improve the sexual health of young women globally, research into the specific challenges facing young women migrating from different cultural and religious backgrounds has been recommended (Hankivsky & Cormier, 2009). This is the aim of this chapter: to explore the sexual embodiment of young migrant and refugee women living in Australia and Canada.

Examining sexual embodiment in young migrant and refugee women is important for a number of reasons. One of the outcomes of the adoption of a rights-based sexual health discourse in the West has been the widespread availability of sexual and reproductive health services for women, and sexuality education for young people, with positive implications for quality of life, mental health, and sexual well-being (Aggleton & Campbell, 2000; Chen et al., 2005; Stephenson et al., 2008). However, in Australia and Canada, the sexual health needs of young migrant and refugee women has been of increasing concern because they underutilize sexual health services (Botfield et al., 2016). This has a number of consequences. Cultural stigma surrounding the reproductive body can lead to lack of knowledge about menarche and menstruation, producing negative feelings associated with the unpredictability and shamefulness of sexual embodiment (Sommer et al., 2015; Teitelman, 2004). Young migrant and refugee women may be ill equipped to articulate their sexual rights (Martinez & Phillips, 2008), having little knowledge of, or access to, preventative sexual health measures (Salad et al., 2015), or contraception (Ngum Chi Watts et al., 2014).

This chapter will draw on the findings of a recent research study conducted in Australia and Canada to explore the material–discursive–intrapsychic context of young migrant and refugee women's sexual embodiment, and to examine the implications of our research, and those of others in this field, for sexual health practice and policy in relation to young women.

The Research Study

We conducted 84 individual interviews and 16 focus groups with 85 participants (total n=169), with the majority of participants (73%, n=124) interviewed in their first language by community interviewers. Participants were migrant and refugee women 18 years and over who had settled in Australia or Canada in the last 10 years, originating from various countries, including Afghanistan, Iraq, Somalia, and Sudan. Sri Lankan (Tamil), Indian (Punjab), and South Sudanese women were also included in the Australian sample and women from various South American (Latina) backgrounds in the Canadian sample to allow for analysis of sexual embodiment within and across cultural groups. Women practiced a range of religions, including Islam, Christianity, Sikhism, and Hinduism, and encompassed a range of social class backgrounds within their country of origin. All participants, except for one Latina woman, identified as being heterosexual and ranged from 18 to 70 years old, with a mean age of 35 years (for further details see Ussher et al., 2017). In this chapter, we draw on the accounts of younger women and on retrospective accounts of adolescent sexual embodiment given by adult women. We also consider how mothers shape their daughter's sexual embodiment and education.

In our analysis we adopted a material–discursive–intrapsychic theoretical approach (Gilbert et al., 2013; Ussher, 2000) in order to examine young women's experiences of sexual embodiment, the ways in which "our social and historical environments enter into and become entangled with our bodies" (Tolman et al., 2014, p. 761). Thematic decomposition was used to analyze the data (Stenner, 1993), a form of discourse analysis that attempts to separate a given text into coherent themes that reflect subject positions allocated to, or taken up by, a person (Davies & Harre, 1990). In this chapter, we will discuss three major discursive themes that were identified in our research, each associated with the regulation of women's sexual embodiment within cultural discourse and practice: "Embodying Stigma and Shame: Menstrual Silence and Secrecy," "Premarital Virginity Imperative: Regulating Sexual Knowledge and Practice," and "Resisting Shame and Secrecy: Menstrual Education and Rejection of the Chastity Imperative."

Embodying Stigma and Shame: Menstrual Silence and Secrecy

For many women, the regulation of sexual embodiment begins with menarche, a life transition that can be associated with stigma, silence, and secrecy (Lee, 2009; Martin, 1987). In addition to lack of preparation for menarche (Uskul, 2004), menstrual stigma and shame has been linked to increased sexual risk taking (Schooler et al., 2005) and embarrassment toward other reproductive functions, such as breastfeeding (Bramwell, 2001; Johnston-Robledo et al., 2007) and childbirth (Moloney, 2010), and is thus central to sexual embodiment. In our interviews, shame was associated with absence of menstrual education, shock at first blood, the positioning of postmenarcheal young women as sexual, and pubertal body changes.

The Unspeakable Body: Absence of Menstrual Knowledge and Education

Girls in the West seldom experience menarche with a complete absence of knowledge (Kissling, 1996), with mothers described as 'emotional anchors' during this time (Koff & Rierdan, 1995; Lee, 2008). In contrast, women interviewed in the present study across all cultural groups received little or no preparatory menstrual education, or support from their mothers. For while menstrual talk is typically avoided, even in a Western context (Kissling, 1996), menstruation was constructed as 'unspeakable' in the present study across all cultural groups. For example, "nobody tell me nothing . . . it's not only my mother . . . all mother[s], they didn't share"; "our mother's from the old generation so she didn't give me any information about it." In another example, when one woman questioned her mother about menstruation, her mother's response was, "don't worry about these stuff and never ask me questions like this again, it is not your business." Women were further denied information by being excluded from adult conversations that might have imparted menstrual knowledge, as one woman told us, "she [mother] said it is shame . . . when they speak about pregnancy or menstrual period, she said, go to other room." Such finding supports that of previous studies with migrant and refugee women (Al Omari et al., 2015; Costos et al., 2002), that across sociocultural settings menstruation continues to be discursively positioned as a shameful topic for mothers to discuss with their daughters, thus repeating intergenerational cycles of shame and secrecy (Bennett & Harden, 2014).

At the same time, many women described having felt discomfort in approaching their mothers with regard to information about menstruation, "I would be very embarrassed to talk with my mum"; "out of shame I couldn't, [I] didn't know how to approach her about it." Consequently, a number of women did not seek information about menstruation at all, "No, I did not ask anyone. I decided to deal with myself, I was shy to ask, I feel shame." This is because menstruation was positioned as "something dirty and something to feel bad about," or a sign of "dirt inside the body," a signifier of abject femininity (Kristeva, 1982) or the 'monstrous feminine' (Ussher, 2006). Similar to previous findings (Al Omari et al., 2015), women interviewed in our study were positioned as "naughty" or "disrespectful" if they spoke about menstruation in public: "if we share these things those girls are like naughty girls, so we never share anything." Consequently, this created a collective silence among young women to avoid being labeled as "bad" and resulted in women feeling ashamed to ask about their experience of menarche. Additionally, in some instances discussion of menstruation was considered too shameful to listen to, thus women engaged in self-policing (Foucault, 1979) to regulate their own reproductive health knowledge: "it was shameful for me to even listen to this kind of stuff." This confirms previous findings of self-policing reported by migrant women in relation to receiving sexual health education (Wray et al., 2014). Self-policing of essential health knowledge, such as menstrual education, might result in young women having limited understanding of their own sexual embodiment, leaving them unprepared for physical changes at menarche (Teitelman, 2004). This can place young women at risk of poor sexual and reproductive health, and have a negative influence on sexual subjectivity (Hawkey et al., 2017). It can also influence their relationships with other young women, as Chrisler argues, "stigma attached to women's bodies can divide women from each other and create conflict between 'good' and 'bad' women" (Chrisler, 2011, p. 8).

When information about menstruation was provided for women we interviewed, it predominantly occurred at the time of menarche, when such conversation was unavoidable. In parallel with previous research (Beausang & Razor, 2000; Uskul, 2004), the ways in which mothers reacted to girls at menarche was reported to have directly influenced a girl's experience of sexual embodiment. When mothers did educate their daughters about menstruation, discussions were commonly described as 'brief' or 'unemotional,' with a focus on menstrual rules, which can lead to girls feeling dissatisfied with their menarche experience and resentful toward their mothers (Costos et al., 2002; Uskul, 2004). For example, one woman told us, "my mother is an educated woman, she is a dentist, yet she summed the whole subject in five minutes and did not mention it again. She was shy to speak about such subject." Many women described topics covered by their mothers as being messages of warning, the need for concealment and practical management, with an absence of the physical and emotional care women needed. Such emphasis on menstrual rules and concealment may reflect the patriarchal influence over women and their menstruating bodies. A mother may feel responsible for conveying appropriate menstrual etiquette to their daughters, to ensure concealment and avoidance of public ridicule, particularly at the hands of men who 'must not know' about menstruation (Laws, 1990, p. 19). Participants told us: "I remember she didn't even give me a cuddle or comfort me. She just quietly put a very ugly and scary fabric inside my legs and told me to not tell anyone about it"; "she did not tell me anything about changing feelings, she told me very little and did not talk about it much." At the same time, some of the mothers interviewed disclosed being "shy" or "embarrassed" to talk with their daughters, or "unsure" when the right time was to address menstruation, for example: "until now I haven't said anything to her about it . . . I don't want her to experience the same as what I had . . . but I don't know when, and where and how." This demonstrates the influence of the discourse of the unspeakable body across generations. However not all experiences of menarche were negative. Women who were provided with adequate menstrual information prior to menarche described their first menstruation more positively: "I want to have it, it was okay because my mum used to explain for me. I used to see my aunties, yeah, it wasn't that bad"; "I knew about it before . . . I have a sister she is older than me and that's why, she told me, I didn't get surprised by that because I knew." These accounts reiterate how menarche experiences are shaped through the provision of menstrual education and familial support girls receive prior to and during menarche (Lee & Sasser-Coen, 1996). Girls who learn about the changes to expect in their pubertal bodies are more likely to develop positive feelings about sexual embodiment (Teitelman, 2004). While young migrant women of school age may learn about menstruation following migration, mothers still play an important part in supporting their daughters through menarche. For example, young women often prefer to learn about menstruation from their mothers (Sooki et al., 2016) and are more likely to have positive memories of their first period if they have emotionally engaged mothers (Lee, 2008). This emphasizes the need for support and education sessions for mothers to ensure they have a sound understanding of menarche as a reproductive and emotional transition, as well as providing an opportunity to counter negative discourses of menstruation through positive representations of menarche and menstruation. Education sessions could also promote the discussion of menarche and provide constructive methods to enable mothers to approach daughters about this sensitive topic (Hawkey et al., 2017).

The Abject Body: The Stigma of Menstrual Pollution

In the absence of any framework to make sense of menarche, young women associated their first menses with injury, guilt, and excrement, similar to reports from previous research conducted in a Western context (Cooper & Koch, 2007; Lee, 2009). Many participants reported having had no knowledge of menstrual bleeding or its function prior to menarche: "I didn't know what it was actually," "I thought I was the only girl who got it." When recounting their menarcheal experiences, some participants thought menstrual blood was feces or urine: "I had no knowledge about it. I thought I had diarrhoea with blood"; "I thought I peed myself." Others thought they had committed "a sin" or "done something wrong," or that they had injured themselves, as illustrated in the following accounts: "I was thinking that I might have torn my vaginal area," "I thought I must have ripped something in my belly." As a result, many of our participants reported distress when they first bled: "I was really scared, I will never forget my experience"; "I couldn't function like normally, I was very sad. I didn't ask questions and people didn't guide me." These constructions of menstrual blood as corporeal signification of the monstrous feminine (Ussher, 2006) can lead young women to feel humiliated and unclean, and might result in ongoing associations between menstruation and contamination (Lee, 2009).

Experiences of shame and feelings of 'dirtiness' toward menstrual blood are commonly reported by young women (Donmall, 2013; Lee & Sasser-Coen, 1996), and are thus not unique to participants in this study. Historically and cross-culturally menstrual blood has been discursively constructed as being poisonous, magical, and polluting (Fahs, 2016), and almost always positioned negatively (Bramwell, 2001). One explanation for this is because it exits the body from the vagina; a part of a women's body commonly represented as being unclean, shameful, and inherently sexual (Bramwell, 2001; Braun & Wilkinson, 2001). Menstrual stigma and shame could extend to influence how young women view and experience ongoing aspects of their sexual embodiment. For example, positioning menstruation as abject might mean women are reluctant to disclose menstrual cycle-related problems to their health care professionals, resulting in delayed diagnosis or treatment (Seear, 2009). It may also impact on a women's ability to discuss abnormal vaginal symptoms when seeking medical advice (Braun & Wilkinson, 2001). To provide culturally sensitive sexual health care for young women, it is essential that health care professionals are aware of cultural constructions of both the vagina and menstruation, particularly when considering the wider sexual embodiment of women (do Amaral et al., 2011).

Stigma and secrecy are also associated with reports of embarrassment at menarche; adolescent girls reported being "ashamed," as well as "shy" or "afraid" to disclose their first period, learning to conceal menstruation in isolation. Thus, young women said "I hide it [period], I was hiding one year and they didn't know it"; "I remember that for about a year, not even my mum knew that it was happening, because in Afghanistan, we have, you know, a sense of shame." Concealment of menstrual blood and self-surveillance was imperative: "I went to the toilet so many times ... checking everything is OK"; "I was worried people could see blood spots on my clothes." The imperative for concealment extended beyond menstrual blood to the menarcheal woman, with many participants describing practices of self-seclusion. This is illustrated in the following accounts: "I was so embarrassed I didn't want to show my face to anyone ... I locked myself in a room"; "No I didn't tell anyone I just put [on] pads and isolated myself. I can't look to my father and mother faces." These accounts confirm previous research findings that etiquettes of concealment act to prevent public knowledge of menstruation, and can result in young women experiencing shame associated with the fecund body (Beausang & Razor, 2000; Burrows & Johnson, 2005; Uskul, 2004). Such self-surveillance surrounding menstruation is likely to impact on a young woman's sexual embodiment and is energy consuming (Johnston-Robledo & Chrisler, 2011). Menstruation also complicates the social construction of a woman's body as being attractive and an object of desire (Ussher, 1997). Leaking bodies that 'smell' do not fit the ideal feminine standards of beauty, and thus the corporeality of the women's body must be repressed, contained, kept private, and outside the public gaze (Roberts & Waters, 2004; Ussher, 2006).

The Sexual Body: Nascent Fecundity and Sexuality

Menarche is a time of significant psychological and sociocultural adjustment, when young women transition from the identity of 'girl' to 'woman' within the patriarchal societies within which they live (Jackson & Falmagne, 2013). Menarche is discursively positioned as a marker of adulthood and reproductive maturity across many sociocultural contexts, signifying familial and public acknowledgment of a young woman's sexual embodiment (Lee, 1994; Ussher, 1989). In our research, a majority of women across all cultural groups described the sudden onset of bleeding as being a distinct point at which they transitioned into womanhood. For example, participants told us, "you start bleeding and you become a woman"; "the day when the period comes, like she becomes a woman." Although some women we interviewed positioned this transition positively, many reported that this new adult positioning was overwhelming or unwanted, as reported in previous research conducted with culturally diverse women (Orringer & Gahagan, 2010; Uskul, 2004). "I don't want to be . . . a big girl, I want[ed] to stay as a child . . . you need to change your manner, the way of sitting . . . you can't play outside with your friends . . . it's different" and "you can't play around like a child again ... I didn't like having to grow up." These accounts support the contention that the fecund body plays a key role in integrating young women into the social and sexual order, through ensuring that an 'appropriate' feminine subject position is adopted (Lee & Sasser-Coen, 1996; Ussher, 1989). For some young women, this resulted in a sense of lost childhood and negative attitudes toward menstruation, which can have implications for the way in which they experience sexual embodiment and sexual health (Teitelman, 2004).

Menarche is also a time in which young women's emerging sexuality is first discursively positioned as problematic (Lee, 1994; Teitelman, 2004). In this vein, 'becoming a woman' following menarche was aligned with women's nascent sexuality, and subsequent fear of pregnancy. Participants repeatedly disclosed being warned to "avoid boys," "be more careful," and "watch your steps" after menarche. Such cautionary advice was predominantly delivered by mothers and was frequently at the forefront of girls' menstrual education, as one woman said: "My mum always told me when you get the period, don't come closer to the men, don't sit with the men. If you sit with the men or talk closer to the men, you're going to fall pregnant . . . once I got it, I was scared of men because my mum always told me these stories." When one participant was asked what would happen if you "get closer" to men following menarche, her response was, "men can rape you and you can get pregnant and in my religion a woman is not supposed to get pregnant before she is married." However, warning messages received by young women were often difficult to understand, or they were given absent or incomplete information about the association between menstruation, sex, and pregnancy. As one participant commented, "they don't give any information . . . like any sexual relationship or anything . . . they won't tell." In addition to being told not to "go around with," "do a mistake," or "play with" boys, young women were given the erroneous impression that any contact with men can make you pregnant. As one young woman told us: "I didn't know that, because nobody tells us, nobody talk about it. We don't know how we get a baby." Some participants reported entering into engagement or marriage with inadequate information, as the following account typified, "I was 19 years when I got married. When I got engaged, I experienced a lot of tension how to find out if one is going to have a baby. Till 19 years I did not know anything." Others described learning the connection between menstruation, sexual intercourse, and pregnancy through sex education at school following migration: "I found out after a few years that my period and pregnancy were connected to each other when I came to Australia and I attended high school." This illustrates the potential influence of sexuality education for women's sexual knowledge, which may create greater space for young women's sexual agency and positive sexual embodiment.

A number of postmenarcheal girls did receive informal education about the association between menstruation and sexuality, primarily from sisters, aunts, and friends. However, some participants were given inaccurate information, as the following account illustrates, "I was told that now I have started bleeding, and if I sit on my brother's chair or maybe I wear his pants, I will become pregnant." Others were warned about contact with men, but didn't understand why "They say it's not good when the boy touches you . . . I didn't know the meaning of that." These beliefs served to regulate relationships between men and women, now that young women were capable of getting pregnant. In contrast, young women who had received sexuality education through schools, parents, or other family members, and knew about the association of menstruation with sexuality and fertility, positioned menarche as a welcome sign of normality: "I turned 16, exactly two days after, the period, it come to me, I was very happy, now was thinking I'm going to have kids because I have period." Such accounts were primarily from young women whose first menstrual period occurred after the majority of their peer group, suggesting that their education may have come from other young women.

Focusing on warning messages and the avoidance of men following menarche, with no concomitant explanation as to how menstruation is linked to pregnancy, has been found to be confusing for young woman (Costos et al., 2002) and might lead to fears that any expression of sexuality would lead to pregnancy and thus a loss of reputation (Ussher, 1989). This could have negative implications wherein young women associate their bodies and developing sexual embodiment with shame, danger, or victimization (Mason et al., 2013; Teitelman, 2004), with negative implications for constructions and experiences of the fecund body throughout adult life (Ussher, 2006).

Regulating the Pubertal Body: Regulating Young Women

Within androcentric societies, pubertal women learn quickly that their developing sexual bodies are objects of the male gaze and a signifier of sexuality (Lee & Sasser-Coen, 1996). As a consequence of such positioning, women from migrant communities commonly report being self-conscious of the sexualization of their bodies at menarche (Golchin Nayereh et al., 2012; Mason et al., 2013). Although women could attempt to conceal their menstruating bodies to avoid pubertal sexualization, breast development is an overtly visual signifier of adult sexual embodiment. In our interviews, the majority of women reported being self-conscious of their developing breasts and inherently positioned them as something that they must conceal from the public eye, as one woman told us, "I was mainly concerned about my breasts, I was very shy, and I was wearing loose clothes and was careful about that." In societies where women are encouraged to be sexually invisible to men other than their husband, the prospect of their breasts being an object of male desire can be experienced as shameful. This was reflected in accounts of women describing the pubertal growth of their breasts as anxiety provoking. For example, "I used sticky tape, scarves, and other things to tightly wrap my breasts close to my body in order to flatten them; I also used to hunch my back so they don't show"; "I was really embarrassed . . . when my breasts was coming, I was very shamed." Some Muslim women were expected to cover their bodies with long veils or headscarves: "once the girls are adults they cover themselves and you have to cover your whole body"; "I even started wearing a scarf at home so if a random person knocks at the door I was well dressed." The requirement for some young women to cover their bodies may reflect masculine constructions of sexuality in which men are positioned as lustful and unable to control their sexual desire, particularly if a women is unveiled (Sadr, 2012). Consequently, it is seen as a woman's responsibility to contain her sexual body, averting the male sexual gaze, and, thus, avoiding the discursive construction as 'woman' and 'sexual' within the public sphere. These young women are also engaging in self-objectification (Fredrickson & Roberts, 1997), wherein they have internalized social and cultural constructions of their bodies, judging themselves negatively as a result. These accounts of self-policing and self-judgment associated with pubertal development are contrary to those of young women in Western contexts. For example, the development of breasts is often seen as an 'asset' (Lee, 2009), and many young women are engaging in cosmetic surgery to enlarge their breasts (Sanchez Taylor, 2012), reflecting the increasing sexualization of adolescent girls and emphasis on breasts in the media (Evans et al., 2010). Our findings reinforce the viewpoint that we cannot generalize from the experience of White Western adolescents to all young women, and need to think about adolescent sexualization and sexual embodiment in relation to cultural difference, as well as sexuality, social class, and other axes of oppression (Gill, 2012).

The transition from 'girl' to 'woman' had material consequences, as menarche and pubertal changes signified marriageability for the majority of women in this study: "when the girls get their period they can be married to a man"; "In South Sudan, when the girl has the first period, that means you are considered as a woman . . . it's associated with marriage . . . you're going to get married and you are going to have babies." Marriage and pregnancy were immediate material outcomes of menarche for some women, particularly those who originated in Afghanistan. As one woman told us: "I remember my uncle's wife told my dad [that I had my first period] and that is how I got engaged and married by 14. Before knowing anything I was already a mother . . . I didn't get a chance to know when I was a girl, when I was a woman and when I was a mother." As is evident in this account, the majority of women did not position cultural norms of early marriage and childbirth positively. One woman reported that it caused her great anxiety, "I was scared because I knew that they are going to be forcing me to get married, and I wasn't prepared for it, I was scared to be a mum." Early marriage and childbearing also had consequences for the formation of a woman's sexual embodiment and the opportunities available to her. The above participant went on to say, "I had my first one [child] when I was 17 . . . you spend your time looking after the children, nothing else, [it's] not about you."

Marriage following menarche was to prevent women from engaging in unlawful practices, such as premarital sex or falling pregnant outside of wedlock (Raj et al., 2014; Schuler et al., 2006), and to protect young women from unwanted sexual advances of men. Many participants positioned the urgency of marriage following menarche as being a way to maintain family honor, "they are afraid for their honour on your own"; "after I got my period I have to get married because I might get pregnant." Without the protection of a husband to "take care of sexual things" women were deemed 'at risk' of being tempted into premarital sex and falling pregnant, a culturally intolerable act.

Premarital Virginity Imperative: Regulating Sexual Knowledge and Practice

Honor/Shame Discourse: Maintaining Sexual Innocence

Historically in the West, women's sexual embodiment has been framed within a Madonna–whore discourse (Ussher, 1997), which dictates that young, unmarried women who are 'good' engage in self-policing to contain and control their sexual desires (Fine & McClelland, 2006; Jackson & Lyons, 2013; Tolman, 2002). A sexual double standard allows men to be sexually active (Jackson & Cram, 2003), while women act as passive sexual gatekeepers within heterosexual relationships (Gagnon, 1990). Following a process of social change and feminist critique (Ussher, 1997; Vance, 1984), these patriarchal discourses have been challenged and resisted. The emergence of 'raunch culture' has led to the widespread cultural acceptance of a sexually liberated, savvy, and active young woman who is "up for it" in terms of sex outside of marriage (Evans et al., 2010, p. 115). However, young women who embrace 'raunch culture' and sexual agency may be vulnerable to social condemnation (Bishop, 2012), with agentic female sexuality positioned as sexual 'promiscuity' and the woman herself as a 'slut' or 'slag' (Bale, 2011; Jackson & Lyons, 2013). These labels, used by men to describe women, as well as between women, have historically worked to judge a women's worth in relation to their sexual relations with men (Attwood, 2007), they also objectify younger women, and act to control girls sexual behavior (Lees, 1993). Young Western women are made to negotiate these competing constructions of feminine sexuality in order to attain positive sexual subjectivity (Bishop, 2012; Gavey & McPhillips, 1999) and sexual embodiment (Bale, 2011; Stewart, 1999).

In our interviews with migrant and refugee women, there was little room for negotiation, with premarital sex positioned as being "unacceptable," "forbidden," or a "mistake" by nearly all participants interviewed, across cultural contexts, within an honor/shame discourse. Young women who are virginal function to maintain the honor of their families, while those who break this cultural code bring shame to their families. Participants told us; "nobody will respect her in society" and that, "if a woman had sex before marriage there is a very negative stigma that will follow her around . . . she is 'cheap', 'she is not worth it'." This stigmatization was said to result in a young woman becoming 'unmarriageable' or being 'sent back' to their family home if she transgresses the virginity imperative: "people start saying, she is a used woman, so I am not going to marry her into my family"; "we knew a few girls that didn't bleed [on their wedding night], and they were sent back"; "they kill them, families kill their daughters if they cause such a bad name to the family honour." These accounts suggest that the consequences of transgression of the virginity imperative, may act as a deterrent for young women's premarital sexual exploration, highlighting how cultural and religious discourse can regulate sexual embodiment.

No young or unmarried participants disclosed having had sex, suggesting the virginity imperative may continue to regulate young new migrant women's premarital sexual practice even following migration. The virginity imperative was a gendered practice (Hawkey et al., 2017b), with many women describing a sexual double standard in their communities – premarital sex was permitted for men but forbidden for women. For example women said: "my parents didn't mind them [brothers] to have relations, but for me I wasn't allowed"; "they have all these ridiculous sort of open-ended chances for men to redeem themselves . . . for a girl, they don't give you these concessions at all." Women's transgression of the virginity imperative put them at risk of severe material consequences, such as family exclusion, a loss of reputation, stigmatization, and violence. For example: "the reputation in the community would be like . . . this is a bad girl, they would brand people as bad and good girl." "[I]ts shame . . . men don't respect that girl, they call her names and they're not going to get married"; "people start saying, she is a used woman, so I am not going to marry her into my family." Other material dangers enmeshed with premarital sex included fear of infertility mentioned by Sudanese and South Sudanese women, as one woman told us; "if you have sex before marriage . . . you can't get kids . . . that's what they believe, and I believe it too." Pregnancy outside of wedlock was also constructed as being of significant concern discussed by women across cultural groups. One woman said, "any girl who falls pregnant before marriage . . . she will be isolated from the community . . . I witness that some girls fall pregnant, they didn't live [a] normal life after they had the baby." These accounts suggest that the consequences of transgression may act as a deterrent for women's premarital sexual exploration, highlighting how patriarchy and cultural or religious discourse can regulate unmarried women's sexual agency and sexual subjectivity (Hawkey et al., 2017b).

As a consequence of premarital sex being discursively constructed as culturally and religiously forbidden, within an honor/shame discourse, some young women described a process of self-regulation to maintain sexual innocence, such as refraining from thinking about sex: "oh my god it's bad [to think about sex] . . . we don't think like that"; "we never think sex before marriage, that's automatically with Muslim girls . . . it's not an important part of your life." This suggests that young or unmarried women may engage in self-policing of their sexual thoughts and desires in order to subscribe to the cultural ideals of an honorable woman, one who is chaste and naïve about sex (Tolman, 2009). Across cultural groups, the discussion of sex was also discursively positioned as "shameful" and "not allowed," particularly for young or unmarried women. This had material consequences in that women had limited opportunities to communicate about sex prior to marriage, as one participant said, "my mum was so embarrassed to tell me anything." Other women told us: "I can't ask my sister because I am a virgin"; "your mother would kill you if she heard that word [sex]." Such silencing may reflect wider cultural beliefs disclosed by migrant mothers, whereby it is thought that sexual knowledge may encourage sexual exploration (Ussher et al., 2012). Thus, within the patriarchal communities that they live, to protect their daughters from becoming 'unmarriable,' from social shame, and a loss of honor associated with premarital sex, mothers may avoid the sharing of sexual knowledge with their daughters.

These accounts are analogous to research with young Western women where dominant discourses of feminine sexuality have customarily been tied to a 'good girl' discourse, which idealizes the image of women who are passive, asexual, and not knowledgeable about sex (Harris et al., 2000; Jackson & Lyons, 2013; Tolman, 2002). However, this discourse has consequences for women's sexual knowledge, sexual agency, and sexual embodiment. Women who adopt gendered sexual scripts may have decreased sexual-risk knowledge, are less likely to advocate for themselves sexually, such as negotiate the use of contraception (Bennett, 2005; Curtin et al., 2011) and may have limited understanding of their own sexual desires and right to pleasure (Tolman, 2009). A lack of dialogue surrounding sex prior to marriage also results in women being vulnerable to negative embodied experiences of first sex (Ahmadi, 2003; Menger et al., 2015; Ussher et al., 2012). The discursive positioning of premarital sex as culturally and religiously forbidden may prohibit access to sexual health information and services for unmarried women, as being seen by other members of the community at sexual health clinics could result in public ridicule and family conflict (Beck et al., 2005; Rawson & Liamputtong, 2010; Rogers & Earnest, 2015).

Rejecting a Human Rights Sexual Health Discourse: Absence of Fertility Control and Sexual Health Knowledge

A human rights-based sexual health discourse has been embraced by international governing bodies (United Nations, 2014), legitimating women's sexual agency in the public sphere (Corrêa et al., 2008). This human rights discourse has also resulted in the widespread availability of sexual and reproductive health services and sex education for young women, with positive implications for quality of life, mental health, and sexual embodiment (Aggleton & Campbell, 2000; Chen et al., 2005; Stephenson et al., 2008). There was little evidence of adherence to this human rights discourse in our interviews, as knowledge or use of contraception was prohibited for young or unmarried women across cultural groups, because they were forbidden from being sexually active: "no, I don't know anything about it [contraception]"; "I have no idea about contraception"; "in biology they give us simple information about contraception," "[but] I'm not interested in this information." Lack of education was associated with misconceptions about contraception (Hawkey et al., 2017a). A number of women told us they believed that contraception would impact negatively on their reproductive function, causing "a blockage," making a woman "bleed to hell," or that "taking a pill every day will get to your blood." Others reported more generalized health consequences, saying it "affects your organs," "can give you some kind of sickness," or that "it creates a whole lot of other damages."

Absence of open discussion about sexual health also meant that some participants knew little about the existence or purpose of preventative sexual health measures, such as cervical screening. For example, one woman asked, "do we need to do it still? Is it important?" The participant went on to say: "Lack of knowledge is the main thing . . . we don't know what it is . . . how much is that important for us." Similarly, another woman stated about her lack of pap smear knowledge, "Yeah, I don't know anything about them, it's very shocking." Equally, few participants knew about the existence or function of the human papillomavirus vaccine, or held misconceptions about the vaccine: "I think maybe the injection itself is causing cancer." This lack of knowledge was positioned as a cultural norm, maintained by silence: "in my culture, we don't know anything about that . . . I've never come across [it], no."

Rejection of a human rights sexual health discourse serves to deny young women sexual agency, with implications for sexual embodiment during adolescence, which continues during adulthood. Inadequate contraception knowledge can lead to unwanted pregnancy (Rademakers et al., 2005), with negative psychosocial implications for women (Bunevicius et al., 2009; Tsui et al., 2010). Absence of education about sexually transmitted infections (STIs) and fertility control can lead to information being sought from unreliable sources, such as peer groups or the media (McMichael & Gifford, 2009; Rawson & Liamputtong, 2009), as well as engagement in risky behaviors (Rawson & Liamputtong, 2010). Delayed testing or screening may result in late diagnosis and treatment of cervical cancer (Manderson & Allotey, 2003; Mcmullin et al., 2005), HIV, or STIs (Fenton, 2001).

Resisting Shame and Secrecy: Menstrual Education and Rejection of the Virginity Imperative

Social constructionist and feminist theorists have argued that young women have the potential to resist traditional constructions of sexual embodiment (Jackson & Cram, 2003) through the mobilization of 'counter-stories' that position their sexuality and their bodies in more agentic ways (McKenzie-Mohr & Lafrance, 2014). As all of our participants were postpubertal women, accounts of shame, secrecy, and silence associated with menstruation were retrospective, illustrating the ways in which patriarchal family structures intersect with age and culture. However, very few women currently adhered to a discourse of menstrual shame, demonstrating the ways in which women can 'rewrite' or resist traditional or patriarchal constructions of sexual embodiment (Day et al., 2010; McKenzie-Mohr & Lafrance, 2014). The majority of participants described resistance to the cultural taboo surrounding discussion of menstrual blood in order to prepare their daughters for menarche, as evidenced in the following accounts: "It's very good to teach your daughters these things"; "I treat my daughters not like what my mother treated me ... I don't want them to be shocked like I was." This negotiation of menstrual shame and secrecy resistance was not without difficulty, however, as many women expressed concerns about the process of providing menstrual education. Some participants said they would rely on their daughter's school to start the conversation. Other women had discussed menstruation with their daughters, but avoided explanation of the association of menstruation and sexuality or fertility: "I told them it's normal to have that changing process in a woman's body. I bought them the things they need when they bleed . . . .But I do not talk to them about sex." This demonstrates the complexity of women's negotiation of cultural discourse associated with menstruation, with certain cultural taboos more difficult to resist (Hawkey et al., 2017).

Adherence to premarital sexual secrecy and silence was also not universal. A number of women gave accounts of resistance through seeking out sexual information before they were married, as one woman told us: "My mum and auntie, they don't allow us to read this book because it's about sex, it's about people asking the questions. In our age, they say it's not allowed, so when we buy it, we hide it. We read it and hide it, this book." Some women showed resistance to the silence around speaking about sex. For example; "I was close to being engaged with someone and I talked about it and how we were going to approach this, every detail I wanted to know ... I think I have knowledge, better than not knowing"; "sometimes I talk about it. I mean, my friends talk about it as well ... But it's a very intimate ... You don't talk about it to everyone." Many women positioned sex education as important: "I just think that sex education is very important for young girls as well as learning about periods." The acceptability of sex education in Australia and Canada contributed to this open communication, allowing women to let go of a sense of shame when talking to their daughters: "before I was thinking shame, I'm not feeling shame now. I answer them everything they are asking me . . . I feel more freedom. Before, there was something I'm hiding, I'm not hiding now." Several women were interested in finding out ways to approach talking about sex with their daughters as the following accounts highlight: "I would actually want to arm myself with all the right information so I could actually educate my daughter how she can go about those things"; "since I am a mother, I would like to have information about sexual education for kids and young people. I would like to have some advice or guidance on how to approach these kind of issues with my daughter."

A number of women resisted a discourse of sexual shame through challenging the virginity imperative (Hawkey et al., 2017b). Some participants said that sex before marriage could be acceptable if you were intending to marry the man, or that it should be a personal choice. For example, one woman said that "if it happens, it happens" when asked about her views on her daughter having premarital sex. The virginity imperative was also resisted through questioning of the sexual double standard wherein men could have sexual experience before marriage and women couldn't: "The Somali men, although they are not virgins, they like to have a virgin wife and that is not fair." Women's resistance to the chastity imperative was facilitated by secrecy and silence: "no-one knows, it's between you and your partner"; "that's up to you and god"; "I'm sure lots they have it [sex before marriage], but in a secret way"; "if it happens in our society, no-one will ever talk about it." This is evidence of silence and secrecy serving as a means of resistance, described in previous research as a "negotiated silence" (Kebede et al., 2014, p. 673).

These accounts of resistance demonstrate that women are not simply positioned within existing discourses, but can reposition themselves, variably adopting, resisting, negotiating, and tailoring discourses associated with sexuality to achieve a desired sexual embodiment (Day et al., 2010, p. 238). However, processes of patriarchal cultural, religious, and familial power serve to create limitations to ways in which young women can construct themselves and their options for resistance (Frosh et al., 2003).This means that *negotiation* of negative discourses associated with young women's sexual embodiment is often a more available strategy than resistance, but this can still be effective in achieving agency and empowerment (Day et al., 2010).

In accounts of negotiation women reproduced *and* resisted a discourse of sexual shame. As Catrina Brown has argued, the "both/and" position "honors women's agency and power while not minimizing the impact of oppressive social discourses and social relations" (Brown, 2007, p. 275). "Both/and" negotiation allows acknowledgment of the material consequences of transgression of a discourse of sexual shame *and* women's agency and power in negotiating a degree of sexual agency (Ussher et al., 2017). From this perspective, reproduction and resistance of discourse overlap rather than being discrete and separate processes (Day et al., 2010).

Conclusion: Implications for Conceptualizing Young Women's Sexual Embodiment

Negative discourses associated with young women's sexual embodiment are located in patriarchal cultural and religious ideologies, legitimating conjugal, familial, and institutional regulation of young women's sexual subjectivity and sexual lives. As a consequence of such patriarchal and religious ideologies, young women may internalize sexual shame, through a process of subjectification (Foucault, 1979), leading to self-surveillance and self-policing: not speaking or having knowledge about their developing sexual embodiment. This can have negative implications for young women's sexual rights, including their experience of agency in relation to their sexual and gendered subjectivity (Fahs, 2016), with consequences for their mental health (Fredrickson & Roberts, 1997; Ussher, 2011).

Our research demonstrates that it is important for researchers to consider the intersections of gender, culture, religion, and other categories of difference in shaping young women's sexual embodiment (Hankivsky & Cormier, 2009; Ussher et al., 2017), with a number of practical implications for sexual health service providers and educators. As a result of menstrual shame and stigma, many young women across cultural groups experienced menarche with a complete absence of knowledge about their bodies, and within patriarchal societies, particularly those who follow strict religious doctrine, women might be more likely to consider menstruation as shameful and polluting, resulting in negative attitudes toward the corporeality of their bodies (Hawkey et al., 2017). This research has demonstrated that some migrant and refugee women arrive in host countries with little or no knowledge of menarche and menstruation, highlighting the importance of appropriate menstrual education as a part of sexual and reproductive health education, for young girls and for mothers to transmit to daughters (Hawkey et al., 2017). This reinforces the importance of considering culturally specific experiences and constructions of menarche and menstruation given their possible implications on help seeking health behaviors and the wider sexual and reproductive health of migrant and refugee women.

Due to the virginity imperative, sexual and reproductive health services for young, unmarried migrant women need to be discrete and ensure confidentiality. Single women's prerogative to access sexual and reproductive health information and care, within a human rights perspective (World Health Organization, 2015), needs to be emphasized among migrant communities. Sexual health promotion and education for young migrant and refugee women needs to be culturally appropriate and spiritually significant, by acknowledging the complex realities associated with premarital sex within culturally diverse communities (Kebede et al., 2014; Mosavi et al., 2014). Specific religious principles could be drawn on to promote a sex-positive approach to sexual health education, strengthening women's sense of entitlement to sexual and reproductive health rights (Bennett, 2005). Health care professionals also need to be aware of the sociocultural constructions of virginity, in order to be responsive to young migrant and refugee women's questions and requests in relation to sexuality, preventative health measures, and contraception.

The establishment of migrant and refugee women's sexual and reproductive rights requires a combination of system improvements and services that benefit young women (Sen & Govender, 2015). This includes acknowledgment of the specific needs of young migrant and refugee women and the production of culturally safe health promotion strategies and sexual health resources (Botfield et al., 2016; Keygnaert et al., 2014). Sexual health promotion needs to be a key part of early resettlement for young migrant and refugee women (McMichael & Gifford, 2009). More specifically, there is a need for recognition of potential lack of knowledge in young women about the association between menstruation and fertility, a need for provision of information for community workers on menstruation to facilitate education of migrant and refugee women, and support for women in educating their daughters about menstruation (Hawkey et al., 2017). Misconceptions and absence of information about contraception need to be addressed, through the provision of resources and support in a range of modalities, in the language of different cultural groups, and young men involved in the discussion (Ngum Chi Watts et al., 2015). Difficulties experienced by unmarried women in obtaining information about contraception, and sex and sexual health need to be acknowledged (Salad et al., 2015).

Understanding the social and cultural sensitivities that many migrant and refugee women experience regarding discussion of sex or sexual concerns and the implications this has for sexual health and sexual rights will have benefits for provision of sexual health services and understanding of sexual embodiment. Resources on sexual rights and consent, STIs and screening, how to discuss sexual concerns with a health professional, as well as sexuality education for young people and their families, can address women's unmet needs in this sphere (Helmer et al., 2015). It has been suggested that sexuality education programs adapted to the specific cultural- and age-related contexts need to be introduced early within the resettlement process for both young people and their families (Dean et al., 2016). Overall, sensitivity to language and other barriers to sexual health service use need to be improved, with previous research suggesting a need for bilingual community-based interpreters or 'navigators' (Henderson & Kendall, 2011, p. 195).

In our research, resistance to patriarchal discourses that deny young women sexual agency and serve to reinforce sexual double standards was more evident in older women and those who had lived in Australia or Canada for a longer period, suggesting that acculturation, life experience, and confidence gained through adulthood may facilitate the 'rewriting' of traditional sexual scripts. However, as has been reported in previous research on young women's resistance of repressive sexual discourse, voices of resistance may be "muted and individual rather than collective" (Jackson & Cram, 2003, p.113), and thus every effort should be made by those working with young women to recognize and support attempts to disrupt repressive discourses associated with sexual embodiment and women's sexual rights.

In conclusion, this study demonstrated that young migrant and refugee women's sexual embodiment is experienced in the context of cultural discourses and practices, with implications for sexual knowledge, sexual behavior, and sexual health. In the context of migration, young women's sexual subjectivity is constructed and reconstructed through social interactions and negotiation of competing discourses associated with sexual embodiment. Researchers and health-service providers need to be aware of the cultural and religious constraints that may impede the development of migrant and refugee women's agentic sexual subjectivity, but also their capacity for resistance and negotiation.

Funding

The study described in this chapter was funded by Australian Research Council Linkage Grant LP130100087, in collaboration with Family Planning NSW, Community Migrant Resource Centre (CMRC), and Simon Fraser University.

References

Aggleton, P. & Campbell, C. (2000). Working with Young People – Towards an Agenda for Sexual Health. *Sexual and Relationship Therapy, 15*(3), 283–296. doi:10.1080/14681990050109863.

Ahmadi, N. (2003). Migration Challenges Views on Sexuality. *Ethnic and Racial Studies, 26* (4), 684–706. doi:10.1080/0141987032000087361.

Al Omari, O., Abdel Razeq, N. M., & Fooladi, M. M. (2015). Experience of Menarche among Jordanian Adolescent Girls: An Interpretive Phenomenological Analysis. *Journal of Pediatric and Adolescent Gynecology, 29*(3), 246–251. doi:10.1016/j.jpag.2015.09.005.

Attwood, F. (2007). Sluts and Riot Grrrls: Female Identity and Sexual Agency. *Journal of Gender Studies, 16*(3), 233–247. doi:10.1080/09589230701562921.

Bale, C. (2011). Raunch or Romance? Framing and Interpreting the Relationship between Sexualized Culture and Young People's Sexual Health. *Sex Education, 11*(3), 303–313. doi:10.1080/14681811.2011.590088.

Bartky, S., L. (1999). Skin Deep: Femininity as a Disciplinary Regime. In *Daring to Be Good: Essays in Feminist Ethics and Politics*. London: Routledge.

Beausang, C. C. & Razor, A. G. (2000). Young Western Women's Experiences of Menarche and Menstruation. *Health Care for Women International, 21*(6), 517–528. doi:10.1080/07399330050130304.

Beck, A., Majumdar, A., Estcourt, C., & Petrak, J. (2005). "We Don't Really Have Cause to Discuss These Things, They Don't Affect Us": A Collaborative Model for

Developing Culturally Appropriate Sexual Health Services with the Bangladeshi Community of Tower Hamlets. *Sexually Transmitted Infections*, *81*(2), 158–162. doi:10.1136/sti.2004.012195.

Bennett, C. & Harden, J. (2014). An Exploration of Mothers' Attitudes towards Their Daughters' Menarche. *Sex Education*, *14*(4), 457–470. doi:10.1080/14681811.2014.922862.

Bennett, L. R. (2005). *Women, Islam and Modernity: Single Women, Sexuality and Reproductive Health in Contemporary Indonesia*. New York: Routledge Curzon.

Bishop, E. C. (2012). Examining the Raunch Culture Thesis through Young Australian Women's Interpretations of Contradictory Discourses. *Journal of Youth Studies*, *15*(7), 821–840. doi:10.1080/13676261.2012.693597.

Bordo, S. (1993). *Unbearable Weight: Feminism, Culture and the Body*. Berkeley: University of California Press.

Botfield, J. R., Newman, C. E., & Zwi, A. B. (2016). Young People from Culturally Diverse Backgrounds and Their Use of Services for Sexual and Reproductive Health Needs: A Structured Scoping Review. *Sexual Health*, *13*(1), 1–9. doi:10.1071/SH15090.

Bramwell, R. (2001). Blood and Milk: Constructions of Female Bodily Fluids in Western Society. *Women & Health*, *34*(4), 85–96. doi:10.1300/J013v34n04_06.

Braun, V. & Wilkinson, S. (2001). Socio-cultural Representations of the Vagina. *Journal of Reproductive and Infant Psychology*, *19*(1), 17–32. doi:10.1080/02646830020032374.

Brown, C. (2007). Feminist Therapy, Violence, Problem Drinking and Re-Storying Women's Lives: Reconceptualizing Anti-Oppressive Feminist Therapy. In Baines, D. (Ed.), *Doing Anti-Oppressive Practice* (128–144). Halifax: Fernwood publishing.

Bunevicius, R., Kusminskas, L., Bunevicius, A., Nadisauskiene, R. J., Jureniene, K., & Pop, V. J. M. (2009). Psychosocial Risk Factors for Depression during Pregnancy. *Acta Obstetricia et Gynecologica Scandinavica*, *88*(5), 599–605. doi:10.1080/00016340902846049.

Burrows, A. & Johnson, S. (2005). Girls' Experiences of Menarche and Menstruation. *Journal of Reproductive and Infant Psychology*, *23*(3), 235–249. doi:10.1080/02646830500165846.

Chen, Y., Subramanian, S. V., Acevedo-Garcia, D., & Kawachi, I. (2005). Women's Status and Depressive Symptoms: A Mulitlevel Analysis. *Social Science and Medicine*, *60*, 49–60.

Chrisler, J. C. (2011). Leaks, Lumps, and Lines: Stigma and Women's Bodies. *Psychology of Women Quarterly*, *35*(2), 202–214. doi:10.1177/0361684310397698.

Cooper, S. C. & Koch, P. B. (2007). "Nobody Told Me Nothin": Communication about Menstruation among Low-Income African American Women. *Women & Health*, *46*(1), 57–78. doi:10.1300/J013v46n01_05.

Corrêa, S., Petchesky, R. P., & Parker, R. (2008). *Sexuality, Health and Human Rights*. New York: Routledge.

Costos, D., Ackerman, R., & Paradis, L. (2002). Recollections of Menarche: Communication between Mothers and Daughters Regarding Menstruation. *A Journal of Research*, *46*(1), 49–59. doi:10.1023/A:1016037618567.

Curtin, N., Ward, L. M., Merriwether, A., & Caruthers, A. (2011). Femininity Ideology and Sexual Health in Young Women: A focus on Sexual Knowledge, Embodiment, and Agency. *International Journal of Sexual Health*, *23*(1), 48–62. doi:10.1080/19317611.2010.524694.

Davies, B. & Harre, R. (1990). Positioning: The Discursive Production of Selves. *Journal of the Theory of Social Behaviour*, *20*, 43–65.

Day, K., Johnson, S., Milnes, K., & Rickett, B. (2010). Exploring Women's Agency and Resistance in Health-Related Contexts: Contributors' Introduction. *Feminism & Psychology*, *20*(2), 238–241. doi:10.1177/0959353509359761.

Dean, J., Mitchell, M., Stewart, D., & Debattista, J. (2016). Intergenerational Variation in Sexual Health Attitudes and Beliefs among Sudanese Refugee Communities in Australia. *Culture, Health and Sexuality*, 19(1), 17–31. doi:10.1080/13691058.2016.1184316.

do Amaral, M. C. E., Hardy, E., & Hebling, E. M. (2011). Menarche among Brazilian Women: Memories of Experiences. *Midwifery*, *27*(2), 203–208. doi:10.1016/j.midw.2009.05.008

Donmall, K. (2013). What It Means to Bleed: An Exploration of Young Women's Experiences of Menarche and Menstruation. *British Journal of Psychotherapy*, *29*(2), 202–216. doi:10.1111/bjp.12016.

Evans, A., Riley, S., & Shankar, A. (2010). Technologies of Sexiness: Theorizing Women's Engagement in the Sexualization of Culture. *Feminism & Psychology*, *20*(1), 114–131. doi:10.1177/0959353509351854.

Fahs, B. (2016). *Out for Blood: Essays on Menstruation and Resistance*. New York: Suny Press.

Fenton, K. A. (2001). Strategies for Improving Sexual Health in Ethnic Minorities. *Current Opinion in Infectious Diseases*, *14*(1), 63–69.

Fine, M. & McClelland, S. (2006). Sexuality Education and Desire: Still Missing After All These Years. *Harvard Educational Review*, *76*(3), 297–338.

Foucault, M. (1978). *The History of Sexuality: An Introduction*. London: Penguin.

(1979). *Discipline and Punish: The Birth of the Prison*. London: Penguin.

Fredrickson, B. L. & Roberts, T.-A. (1997). Objectification Theory: Toward Understanding Women's Lived Experiences and Mental Health Risks. *Psychology of Women Quarterly*, *21*(2), 173–206.

Frosh, S., Phoenix, A., & Pattman, R. (2003). Taking a Stand: Using Psychoanalysis to Explore the Positioning of Subjects in Discourse. *The British Journal of Social Psychology*, *42*, 39.

Gagnon, J. H. (1990). The Explicit and Implicit Use of the Scripting Perspective in Sex Research. *Annual Review of Sex Research*, *1*, 1–43.

Gavey, N. & McPhillips, K. (1999). Subject to Romance: Heterosexual Passivity as an Obstacle to Women Initiating Condom Use. *Psychology of Women Quarterly*, *23*, 349–367.

Gilbert, E., Ussher, J. M., Perz, J., Wong, W. K. T., Hobbs, K., & Mason, C. (2013). Men's Experiences of Sexuality after Cancer: A Material Discursive Intra-Psychic Approach. *Culture, Health & Sexuality*, *15*(8), 881–895. doi:10.1080/13691058.2013.789129.

Gill, R. (2012). Media, Empowerment and the "Sexualization of Culture" Debates. *Sex Roles*, *66*(11–12), 736–745. doi:10.1007/s11199-011-0107-1.

Golchin Nayereh, A., Hamzehgardeshi, Z., Fakhri, M., & Hamzehgardeshi, L. (2012). The Experience of Puberty in Iranian Adolescent Girls: A Qualitative Content Analysis. *BMC Public Health*, *12*(1), 698. doi:10.1186/1471-2458-12-698.

Grosz, E. (1994). *Volitile Bodies: Towards a Corporeal Feminism*. St Leonards: Allen and Unwin.

Hankivsky, O. & Cormier, R. (2009). *Intersectionality: Moving Women's Health Research and Policy Forward*. Vancouver: Women's Health Research Network.

Harris, A., Aapola, S., & Gonick, M. (2000). Doing It Differently: Young Women Managing Heterosexuality in Australia, Finland and Canada. *Journal of Youth Studies*, *3*(4), 373–388. doi:10.1080/713684386.

Hawkey, A., Ussher, J. M., & Perz, J. (2017a). "If You Don't Have a Baby, You Can't Be in Our Culture": Migrant and Refugee Women's Experiences and Constructions of Fertility and Fertility Control. *Women's Reproductive Health*, 5(2), 75–78. doi:10.1080/23293691.2018.1463728.

(2017b). Regulation and Resistance: Experiences and Constructions of Premarital Sexuality in the Context of Migrant and Refugee Women. *Journal of Sex Research*, doi:10.1080/00224499.2017.1336745.

Hawkey, A. J., Ussher, J. M., Perz, J., & Metusela, C. (2017). Experiences and Constructions of Menarche and Menstruation among Migrant and Refugee Women. *Qualitative Health Research*, *27*(10), 1473–1490. doi:10.1177/1049732316672639.

Helmer, J., Senior, K., Davison, B., & Vodic, A. (2015). Improving Sexual Health for Young People: Making Sexuality Education a Priority. *Sex Education*, *15*(2), 158–171. doi:10.1080/14681811.2014.989201.

Henderson, S. & Kendall, E. (2011). Culturally and Linguistically Diverse Peoples Knowledge of Accessibility and Utilisation of Health Services: Exploring the Need for Improvement in Health Service Delivery. *Australian Journal of Primary Health*, *17*(2), 195–201. doi:10.1071/PY10065.

Jackson, S. & Lyons, A. (2013). Girls' "New Femininity" Refusals and "Good Girl" Recuperations in Soap Talk. *Feminist Media Studies*, *13*(2), 228–244. doi:10.1080/14680777.2012.708511.

Jackson, S. & Scott, S. (2002). Embodying Orgasm: Gendered Power Relations and Sexual Pleasure. *Women & Therapy*, *24*(1–2), 99–110. doi:10.1300/J015v24n01_13.

Jackson, S. M. & Cram, F. (2003). Disrupting the Sexual Double Standard: Young Women's Talk about Heterosexuality. *British Journal of Social Psychology*, *42*(1), 113–127. doi:10.1348/014466603763276153.

Jackson, T. E. & Falmagne, R. J. (2013). Women Wearing White: Discourses of Menstruation and the Experience of Menarche. *Feminism & Psychology*, *23*(3), 379–398. doi:10.1177/0959353512473812.

Johnston-Robledo, I. & Chrisler, J. C. (2011). The Menstrual Mark: Menstruation as Social Stigma. *Sex Roles*, *68*(1), 9–18. doi:10.1007/s11199-011-0052-z.

Johnston-Robledo, I., Sheffield, K., Voigt, J., & Wilcox-Constantine, J. (2007). Reproductive Shame: Self-Objectification and Young Women's Attitudes toward Their Reproductive Functioning. *Women & Health*, *46*(1), 25–39. doi:10.1300/J013v46n01_03.

Kebede, M. T., Hilden, P. K., & Middelthon, A.-L. (2014). Negotiated Silence: The Management of the Self as a Moral Subject in Young Ethiopian Women's

Discourse about Sexuality. *Sex Education*, *14*(6), 666–678. doi:10.1080/14681811.2014.924918.

Keygnaert, I., Vettenburg, N., Roelens, K., & Temmerman, M. (2014). Sexual Health Is Dead in My Body: Participatory Assessment of Sexual Health Determinants by Refugees, Asylum Seekers and Undocumented Migrants in Belgium and the Netherlands. *BMC Public Health*, *14*(1), 1–13. doi:10.1186/1471-2458-14-416.

Kissling, E. A. (1996). Bleeding Out Loud: Communication about Menstruation. *Feminism & Psychology*, *6*(4), 481–504. doi:10.1177/0959353596064002.

Koff, E. & Rierdan, J. (1995). Early Adolescent Girls' Understanding of Menstruation. *Women & Health*, *22*(4), 1–19. doi:10.1300/J013v22n04_01.

Kristeva, J. (1982). *Powers of Horror: An Essay on Abjection*. New York: Columbia University Press.

Laws, S. (1990). *Issues of Blood: The Politics of Menstruation*. London: Macmillan Press.

Lee, J. (1994). Menarche and the (Hetero)sexualization of the Female Body. *Gender & Society*, *8*, 343–362.

(2008). "A Kotex and a Smile": Mothers and Daughters at Menarche. *Journal of Family Issues*, *29*(10), 1325–1347. doi:10.1177/0192513x08316117.

(2009). Bodies at Menarche: Stories of Shame, Concealment, and Sexual Maturation. *Sex Roles*, *60*(9–10), 615–627. doi:10.1007/s11199-008-9569-1.

Lee, J. & Sasser-Coen, J. (1996). *Blood Stories: Menarche and the Politics of the Female Body in Contemporary US Society*. London: Routledge.

Lees, S. (1993). *Sugar and Spice: Sexuality and Adolescent Girls*. London: Penguin

Manderson, L. & Allotey, P. (2003). Storytelling, Marginality, and Community in Australia: How Immigrants Position Their Difference in Health Care Settings. *Medical Anthropology: Cross-Cultural Studies in Health and Illness*, *22*(1), 1–21. doi:10.1080/01459740306767.

Martin, E. (1987). *The Woman in the Body*. Milton Keynes: Open University Press.

Martinez, A. & Phillips, K. P. (2008). Challenging Ethno-Cultural and Sexual Inequities: An Intersectional Feminist Analysis of Teachers, Health Partners and University Students' Views on Adolescent Sexual and Reproductive Health Rights. *The Canadian Journal of Human Sexuality*, *17*(3), 141–159.

Mason, L., Nyothach, E., Alexander, K., et al. (2013). "We Keep It Secret So No One Should Know" – A Qualitative Study to Explore Young Schoolgirls Attitudes and Experiences with Menstruation in Rural Western Kenya. *PLoS ONE*, *8*(11), e79132. doi:10.1371/journal.pone.0079132.

McKenzie-Mohr, S. & Lafrance, M. N. (Eds.). (2014). *Women Voicing Resistance: Discursive and Narrative Explorations*. London: Routledge.

McMichael, C. & Gifford, S. (2009). "It Is Good to Know Now . . . Before It's Too Late": Promoting Sexual Health Literacy amongst Resettled Young People with Refugee Backgrounds. *Sexuality & Culture*, *13*(4), 218–236. doi:10.1007/s12119-009-9055-0.

Mcmullin, J. M., De Alba, I., Chávez, L. R., & Hubbell, A. F. (2005). Influence of Beliefs about Cervical Cancer Etiology on Pap Smear Use among Latina Immigrants. *Ethnicity & Health*, *10*(1), 3–18. doi:10.1080/1355785052000323001.

Menger, L. M., Kaufman, M. R., Harman, J. J., Tsang, S. W., & Shrestha, D. K. (2015). Unveiling the Silence: Women's Sexual Health and Experiences in Nepal. *Culture, Health & Sexuality*, *17*(3), 359–373. doi:10.1080/13691058.2014.937462.

Moloney, S. (2010). How Menstrual Shame Affects Birth. *Women and Birth*, *23*(4), 153–159. doi:10.1016/j.wombi.2010.03.001.

Mosavi, S. A., Babazadeh, R., Najmabadi, K. M., & Shariati, M. (2014). Assessing Iranian Adolescent Girls' Needs for Sexual and Reproductive Health Information. *Journal of Adolescent Health*, *55*(1), 107–113. doi:10.1016/j.jadohealth.2013.11.029.

Ngum Chi Watts, M. C., Liamputtong, P., & Carolan, M. (2014). Contraception Knowledge and Attitudes: Truths and Myths among African Australian Teenage Mothers in Greater Melbourne, Australia. *Journal of Clinical Nursing*, *23*(15–16), 2131–2141. doi:10.1111/jocn.12335.

Ngum Chi Watts, M. C., McMichael, C., & Liamputtong, P. (2015). Factors Influencing Contraception Awareness and Use: The Experiences of Young African Australian Mothers. *Journal of Refugee Studies*, *28*(3), 368–387. doi:10.1093/jrs/feu040.

Omar, H. A. (2010). *Pediatric and Adolescent Sexuality and Gynecology: Principles for the Primary Care Clinician*. New York: Nova Science Publishers.

Orringer, K. & Gahagan, S. (2010). Adolescent Girls Define Menstruation: A Multiethnic Exploratory Study. *Health Care for Women International*, *31*(9), 831–847. doi:10.1080/07399331003653782.

Rademakers, J., Mouthaan, I., & de Neef, M. (2005). Diversity in Sexual Health: Problems and Dilemmas. *European Journal of Contraception & Reproductive Health Care*, *10*(4), 207–211. doi:10.1080/13625180500279847.

Raj, A., Gomez, C. S., & Silverman, J. G. (2014). Multisectorial Afghan Perspectives on Girl Child Marriage: Foundations for Change Do Exist in Afghanistan. *Violence against Women*, *20*(12), 1489–1505. doi:10.1177/1077801211403288.

Rawson, H. & Liamputtong, P. (2009). Influence of Traditional Vietnamese Culture on the Utilisation of Mainstream Health Services for Sexual Health Issues by Second-Generation Vietnamese Australian Young Women. *Sexual Health*, *6*(1), 75–81. doi:10.1071/SH08040.

(2010). Culture and Sex Education: The Acquisition of Sexual Knowledge for a Group of Vietnamese Australian Young Women. *Ethnicity & Health*, *15*(4), 343–364. doi:10.1080/13557851003728264.

Roberts, T. A. (2004). Female Trouble: The Menstrual Self-Evaluation Scale and Women's Self-Objectification. *Psychology of Women Quarterly*, *28*, 22–26.

Roberts, T. A. & Waters, P. L. (2004). Self-Objectification and that "Not So Fresh Feeling". *Women & Therapy*, *27*(3–4), 5–21. doi:10.1300/J015v27n03_02.

Rogers, C. & Earnest, J. (2015). Sexual and Reproductive Health Communication among Sudanese and Eritrean Women: An Exploratory Study from Brisbane, Australia. *Culture, Health & Sexuality*, *17*(2), 223–236. doi:10.1080/13691058.2014.967302.

Sadr, S. (2012). Veiled Transcripts: The Private Debate on Public Veiling in Iran. In Helie, A. & Hoodfar, H. (Eds.), *Sexuality in Muslim Contexts* (Vol. 182207). London: Zed Books.

Salad, J., Verdonk, P., de Boer, F., & Abma, T. A. (2015). "A Somali girl Is Muslim and Does Not Have Premarital Sex. Is Vaccination Really Necessary?" A Qualitative Study into the Perceptions of Somali Women in the Netherlands about the Prevention of Cervical Cancer. *International Journal for Equity in Health*, *14*(1), 1–13. doi:10.1186/s12939-015-0198-3.

Sanchez Taylor, J. (2012). Buying and Selling Breasts: Cosmetic Surgery, Beauty Treatments and Risk. *Sociological Review*, *60*(4), 635–653. doi:10.1111/j.1467-954X.2012.02127.x.

Schooler, D., Ward, L. M., Merriwether, A., & Caruthers, A. S. (2005). Cycles of Shame: Menstrual Shame, Body Shame, and Sexual Decision-Making. *The Journal of Sex Research*, *42*(4), 324–334. doi:10.1080/00224490509552288.

Schuler, S. R., Bates, L. M., Islam, F., & Islam, M. K. (2006). The Timing of Marriage and Childbearing among Rural Families in Bangladesh: Choosing between Competing Risks. *Social Science & Medicine*, *62*(11), 2826–2837. doi:10.1016/j.socscimed.2005.11.004.

Seear, K. (2009). The Etiquette of Endometriosis: Stigmatisation, Menstrual Concealment and the Diagnostic Delay. *Social Science & Medicine*, *69*(8), 1220–1277. doi:10.1016/j.socscimed.2009.07.023.

Sen, G. & Govender, V. (2015). Sexual and Reproductive Health and Rights in Changing Health Systems. *Global Public Health*, *10*(2), 228–242. doi:10.1080/17441692.2014.986161.

Sommer, M., Ackatia-Armah, N., Connolly, S., & Smiles, D. (2015). A Comparison of the Menstruation and Education Experiences of Girls in Tanzania, Ghana, Cambodia and Ethiopia. *Compare: A Journal of Comparative and International Education*, *45*(4), 589–609. doi:10.1080/03057925.2013.871399.

Sooki, Z., Shariati, M. Chaman, R. Khosravi, A. Effatpanah, M. & Keramat, A. (2016). The Role of Mother in Informing Girls about Puberty: A Meta-Analysis Study. *Nursing and Midwifery Studies*, *5*(1). doi:10.17795/nmsjournal30360.

Stenner, P. (1993). Discoursing Jealousy. In Burman, E. & Parker, I. (Eds.), *Discourse Analytic Research* (114–134). London: Routledge.

Stephenson, J., Strange, V., Allen, E., et al. (2008). The Long-Term Effects of a Peer-Led Sex Education Programme (RIPPLE): A Cluster Randomised Trial in Schools in England. *PLoS Medicine*, *5*(11), 1579–1590. doi:10.1371/journal.pmed.0050224.

Stewart, F. (1999). "Once You Get a Reputation, Your Life's Like ... 'Wrecked'": The Implications of Reputation for Young Women's Sexual Health and Well-Being. *Women's Studies International Forum*, *22*(3), 373–383. doi:10.1016/S0277-5395(99)00030-8.

Teitelman, A. M. (2004). Adolescent Girls' Perspectives of Family Interactions Related to Menarche and Sexual Health. *Qualitative Health Research*, *14*(9), 1292–1308. doi:10.1177/1049732304268794.

Tiefer, L. (2004). *Sex Is Not a Natural Act and Other Essays*. Cambridge, MA: Westview Press.

Tolman, D. (2002). *Dilemmas of Desire: Teenage Girls Talk About Sexuality*. Cambridge, MA: Harvard University Press.

(2009). *Dilemmas of Desire: Teenage Girls Talk about Sexuality*. Cambridge, MA: Harvard University Press.

Tolman, D., Bowman, C. P., & Fahs, B. (2014). Sexuality and Embodiment. In Tolman, D. L. & Diamond, L. M. (Eds.), *APA Handbook of Sexuality and Psychology: Vol. 1. Person-Based Approaches*, (759–804). Washington, DC: American Psychological Association.

Tsui, A. O., McDonald-Mosley, R., & Burke, A. E. (2010). Family Planning and the Burden of Unintended Pregnancies. *Epidemiologic Reviews*, *32*(1), 152–174. doi:10.1093/epirev/mxq012.

United Nations. (2014). *Sexual Health and Reproductive Rights: Articles 21,22 (1), 23 and 24 of the United Nationals Declaration on the Rights of Indigenous Peoples*.

Uskul, A. K. (2004). Women's Menarche Stories from a Multicultural Sample. *Social Science & Medicine*, *59*(4), 667–679. doi:10.1016/j.socscimed.2003.11.031.

Ussher, J. M. (1989). *The Psychology of the Female Body*. London: Routledge.

(1997). *Fantasies of Femininity: Reframing the Boundaries of Sex*. London/New York: Penguin/Rutgers.

(2000). Women's Madness: A Material-Discursive-Intra Psychic Approach. In Fee, D. (Ed.), *Psychology and the Postmodern: Mental Illness as Discourse and Experience* (207–230). London: Sage.

(2006). *Managing the Monstrous Feminine: Regulating the Reproductive Body*. London: Routledge.

(2011). *The Madness of Women: Myth and Experience*. London: Routledge.

Ussher, J. M., Perz, J., Metusela, C., et al. (2017). Negotiating Discourses of Shame, Secrecy, and Silence: Migrant and Refugee Women's Experiences of Sexual Embodiment. *Archives of Sexual Behavior*, *46*(7), 1901–1921. doi:10.1007/s10508-016-0898-9.

Ussher, J. M., Rhyder-Obid, M., Perz, J., Rae, M., Wong, T. W. K., & Newman, P. (2012). Purity, Privacy and Procreation: Constructions and Experiences of Sexual and Reproductive Health in Assyrian and Karen Women Living in Australia. *Sexuality & Culture*, *16*(4), 467–485. doi:10.1007/s12119-012-9133-6.

Vance, C. (1984). *Pleasure and Danger: Exploring Female Sexuality*. Boston: Routledge & K. Paul.

World Health Organization. (2013). Regional Framework for Reproductive Health in the Western Pacific. www.wpro.who.int/publications/docs/Regional_Framework_for_RH_14022013.pdf?ua=1.

(2015). Health and human rights. www.who.int/mediacentre/factsheets/fs323/en/.

Wray, A., Ussher, J. M., & Perz, J. (2014). Constructions and Experiences of Sexual Health among Young, Heterosexual, Unmarried Muslim Women Immigrants in Australia. *Culture, Health & Sexuality*, *16*(1), 76–89. doi:10.1080/13691058.2013.833651.

Adolescence

7 The Diversity of Adolescent Male Sexuality

John DeLamater

Introduction

This chapter attempts to capture the diversity of adolescent male sexuality. Let's begin by defining some key terms. First, *adolescence.* Although adolescence used to be equated with the teenage years, today adolescence researchers define it as extending from around age 10 years through the early 20s (Steinberg, 2008). This broader time span reflects both a trend over time toward pubertal changes occurring earlier and markers of adulthood, such as entering the workforce and marrying, occurring later. Adolescence involves numerous transitions and changes, including biological, psychological, and social transitions. Thus, we need a biopsychosocial perspective to incorporate the relevant influences on an adolescent's sexuality (DeLamater & Blumenstock, 2018).

Next, *sexuality.* Sexuality is complex; it includes sexual behaviors, sexual feelings, and sexual orientation (Fischer, 2016). Biology – genetics, hormones, physiology, the body – forms a substrate on which the complexity of sexuality is built (Hyde, 2005). Sexuality and sexual expression have a biological base. Beyond that, sexuality is influenced by psychological factors including attitudes, emotions, and the learned residues of past experience, and social factors including social norms and laws, and one's relationships, including (potential) partners and social networks.

Finally, *male*, which can be defined as a person with male sexual/reproductive structures, including penis, testes, seminal vesicles, and prostate. In the past decade, though, we have increasingly recognized the diversity of gender in contemporary society, as well as the fact that gender identity can differ from the biological sex of one's body. Although we continue to discuss gender as a binary of male or female, it would be a mistake to attribute essentiality to those categories (DeLamater & Hyde, 1998). At the same time, that binary is used in the reporting of all sorts of statistics and data relevant to this chapter, and so it will be used by default.

There are about 15.4 million males in the age range of 13 to 19 years in the United States (Howden & Meyer, 2011). Among children ages 0–17 years, in 2017, approximately 51 percent were White, 25 percent Hispanic, 14 percent Black, and 10 percent from other backgrounds (Childstats.gov, 2017).

The first research on adolescent sexuality to employ a biopsychosocial frame was conducted by Udry (1988). His goal was to integrate biological models of adolescent sexuality with sociological ones to predict the "transition to non-virginity," that is, first heterosexual intercourse. He identified four categories of predictor variables: age, hormones, pubertal development (consequences of hormones such as sexual development), and social controls including parental, peer, and religious influence. We will discuss his results later in the chapter. They provide evidence of the operation of both biological and social influences.

Sociosexual Development

Adolescence is a period of maturation both socially and sexually. I refer to the process involved as sociosexual development. Consistent with a biopsychosocial perspective, I will consider biological influences and then turn to psychological and social ones.

Biological Influences

Genetic factors; the original biological influences on the individual occur at conception. The specific combination of genes that are inherited influence many of the individual's characteristics. We know that the expression of many genes may be influenced by environmental pressures, but genes are involved in determining gender, race/ethnicity, and physical appearance, all of which affect one's sexuality.

Adrenarche, the maturation of the adrenal glands, occurs around 8–10 years of age, and leads to increased levels of androgens in both girls and boys (Del Giudice et al., 2009). The average age at which participants recalled first experiencing sexual attraction to another person was age 10 years, probably linked to the rise in androgens as a result of adrenarche (McClintock & Herdt, 1996).

Puberty refers to the process of physical changes by which the child's body becomes the body of an adult capable of reproduction. It is initiated by signals from the brain to the gonads (testes and ovaries), causing them to produce testosterone and estrogen, which in turn produce growth and maturation. (Note that boys and girls have testosterone and estrogen; the notion that testosterone is the "male" hormone and estrogen is the "female" hormone is no longer valid.) Puberty in boys typically begins about ages 11 or 12 years, and ends about ages 16 or 17 years. A surge in sexual interest occurs in many youth around puberty and continues throughout adolescence. This heightened sexuality may be caused by increases in the levels of sex hormones, the bodily/genital changes and awareness of them, or the US culture's emphasis on sexuality, for example, in the media (see later).

The changes that occur at puberty prepare the person for adult sexual expression (Fortenberry, 2013). Key elements of sexual anatomy and the hormonal basis of sexual functioning are developed at this time. There are four "hallmarks" of adult sexuality; puberty contributes to the development of each. Sexual desire generates increased attention to sexual stimuli; cognitive markers of desire, including sexual attraction and thoughts, emerge during adolescence. Sexual arousal, subjective and physiological, involves hormonal and neuropsychological attributes that develop during puberty. Sexual behavior becomes a focus of adolescent thought, including abstinence, masturbation, and partnered activities. Finally, sexual function, subjective aspects of sexual behavior, are important but their origins in adolescence have rarely been studied.

The *brain* plays a very important role in sexual functioning and behavior. Many changes in the brain occur during adolescence. Perhaps the most striking change is in maturation of the prefrontal cortex, a region that is crucial for psychological processes such as planning ahead, weighing risks, and controlling impulses (Steinberg, 2005, 2007, 2008). All of these processes are important for healthy sexuality. Yet, maturation of the prefrontal cortex is not complete until the mid-20s. Moreover, there is a shortage of research connecting brain maturation in adolescence directly to sexual outcomes. As one team of researchers noted, "Adolescence is a time of rapid change in neuroanatomy, yet it is not always clear how these changes translate into sexual response or behavior" (O'Sullivan & Thompson, 2014, p. 437).

As noted earlier, research by Udry (1988) exemplifies a biopsychosocial approach to adolescent sexuality. He studied 13–16 year olds, measuring hormone levels (testosterone, estrogen, and progesterone) and multiple psychological and sociological factors (e.g., their parents' educational level, whether they were in an intact family, the adolescent's responses on a self-report scale measuring sexually permissive attitudes, and the adolescent's attachment to conventional institutions such as involvement in school sports and church attendance). Overall, 35 percent of the boys in the sample had engaged in sexual intercourse. For boys, testosterone levels had a strong relationship to several measures of sexual activity (including intercourse, masturbation, and feeling "turned on"), but sexually permissive attitudes, a psychological variable, were also related to sexuality among boys, although they had a smaller effect than testosterone levels did. Overall, this study demonstrates the impact of biological factors (testosterone levels) as well as social psychological factors (attitudes). The study did not include measures of brain activity or brain maturation, so we cannot know what role these factors played.

Social Influences

Socialization is the process by which "individuals learn and re-create skills, knowledge, values, motives and roles appropriate to their positions in a group or society" (DeLamater et al., 2015, p. 66). Major socializing agents are parents, teachers, peers, and mass media.

One outcome that is especially consequential for sexuality is learning a *gender role*, the characteristics and behaviors expected of men and women. Traditionally in US society, men were expected to be competent – competitive, logical, able to make decisions easily, and ambitious. Gender role socialization begins early; parents treat the infant and socialize them as male or female based on the gender assigned at (or before) birth. Parents and other caregivers provide models for behavior, who children often imitate. When children enroll in pre/school, teachers take on the role of socializing agents. Teachers often organize work in classes by gender, use gendered language in interaction with students, and hold different expectations for boys and girls (Pascoe, 2007; Thorne, 1993). When school personnel have expectations similar to children's parents, this serves to reinforce parental socialization. When teachers hold different gender expectations, it can create conflicts for the child.

Other children – peers – are another influential socializing agent. Conformity to gendered expectations for dress, attitudes, and behavior is a major focus of peer interaction. Thorne (1993) documents various rituals and games that fourth graders used to teach and enforce gendered expectations. Both boys and girls take on the role of "gender police," making sure that other children behave appropriately. These practices continue into middle school (Eder, 1995), where boys and girls spend most of their time in homogeneous groups, enabling a high level of surveillance. It has also been observed in high school (Pascoe, 2007), although the tactics shift from direct confrontation and harassment to rumor and insults to reputation.

These pressures to conform can cause significant distress for those youth who do not identify with or accept the gender designation ascribed to them by others. These children may become a target for harassment and ostracism because of their gender nonconformity (Reisner et al., 2015).

A major developmental task of adolescence is learning how to manage physical and emotional intimacy in relationships with others (Hyde & DeLamater, 2017). Adolescents are curious about sex and seek out information about it. An important source are the mass media. In a survey of youth aged 14–16 years old, the most frequently named sources of information by males were friends (65 percent), mother (52 percent), media (50 percent), and teachers (48 percent) (Bleakley et al., 2009). On average, adolescents experience more than 11 hours of exposure to media per day (Rideout et al., 2010). The Internet contains plenty of sexual content. Sixty-six percent of boys aged 12–14 years old report viewing at least one form of sexually explicit media in the past year (Brown & L'Engle, 2009).

These portrayals represent *sexual socialization* by the media. The images, dialogue, plots, and characters provide insight and instruction into the initiation, management, and termination of intimate, sexual relationships (Ward et al., 2014). Youth learn scripts that may influence their sexual decision making and behavior. Researchers developed measures of a "heterosexual script" that included guidelines for male and female behaviors (Kim et al., 2007). In this script, masculinity is defined, in part, by sexual conquest and experience, by taking the initiative in relationships and aggressively seeking sexual intimacy, and by limiting emotional commitment. Femininity is defined as being chaste yet seductive, setting sexual limits, attaining status and power by objectifying oneself, and by seeking commitment. Researchers' analysis of prime-time network television programs indicated that there were 15.5 portrayals of elements of this script per hour. Many studies, both surveys and experiments, have documented relationships between the amount of sexual media consumed and adolescents' sexual attitudes and behaviors (Ward et al., 2014).

The gender role and sexual scripts learned by the child/adolescent become important *psychological influences* on the individual's sexuality, in the biopsychosocial perspective.

Ott (2010) conceptualized the development process as a transition to sex, "in which an individual is abstinent, goes through a period of becoming 'ready,' and transitions to a first sexual experience" (p. 56). She cited as evidence the fact that a multiethnic group of tenth graders chose "I was ready" as an important reason for engaging in intercourse. The process of determining whether one is ready involves social, emotional, and physical self-assessments, perhaps influenced by others' appraisals of the youth. Assessing oneself as ready may not lead immediately to behavior. Attitudes, learned scripts, and opportunities influence the actual transition as well.

Sexual Behavior

Masturbation

Masturbation does not require a partner, which is one reason it is the first sexual behavior that many persons engage in. Some gain experience with masturbation in childhood. Generally, boys start masturbating earlier than girls (Robbins et al., 2010). About 40 percent of boys (compared to 20 percent of girls) report orgasms from masturbation by age 12 years (Larsson & Svedin, 2002). Boys and girls tend to learn about masturbation in different ways. Typically, boys are told about it by their male peers, they see their peers doing it, or they read about. Self-discovery is easier for boys because the penis is an external organ and erections are visible and sensitive to stimulation. The experience of masturbation to orgasm is an important source of agency, or *sexual subjectivity*, the sense that one's sexuality is under one's control.

A survey of a nationally representative US sample in 2009 included 820 persons 14–17 years of age. By age fourteen, 63 percent of boys (and 43 percent of girls) had masturbated at least once. By age seventeen, the cumulative incidence was 80 (and 58) percent. Reported rates varied by ethnicity. Hispanic boys were most likely to report masturbation, Blacks were least likely to report the behavior (Rideout et al., 2010).

Not all youth masturbate. Some abstain by choice. In addition, some youth do not experience sexual desire and therefore may not be motivated to engage in any sexual behavior. These persons may not have the curiosity about sexual intimacy in adolescence that Ott (2010) argues is an important motive for making the transition to a sexually active person.

Same-Gender Sexual Activity

Same-gender sexual activity is a normal part of the sexual development of children. In childhood, children have a gender-segregated social organization, and children spend most of their time in close proximity to children of the same gender. Children work to actively create homogenous groups, as documented by Thorne (1993) and others. Thus, sexual exploration in this life stage is likely to be with partners of the same gender. These activities generally involve displaying the genitals, masturbation, and touching another's genitals. The script for these activities may be a medical one ("doctor" or "nurse").

A study of lesbian, gay, and bisexual youth found that participants reported their first experience of same-gender sexual attraction at age 10 or 11 years on average (Rosario, et al. 1996). Note that this age is comparable to that of the age of first heterosexual attraction discussed earlier.

The National Survey of Family Growth (NSFG) interviewed a national sample of 15–44-year-old persons in 2006–2008. Each was asked whether they had had any same-gender sexual contact. Among males, 1.7 percent of the 15–17 year olds, and 3.8 percent of the 18 and 19 year olds reported that they had. Among men 20 and older, 5.8 percent reported such contacts (Chandra et al., 2011). By race/ethnicity, among 15–19 year olds, 8.3 percent of Hispanics, 12.1 percent of Whites, and 10 percent of Black/African Americans reported any sexual contact with a same-gender partner. Note that these are "lifetime" experience measures, asking the person if they have ever experienced the behavior. Many of those reporting the contact may have only had it once in their lives.

Adolescence is the period during which one's identities become stabilized. The process of self-identification as a sexual minority person typically occurs between the ages of 14 and 21 (O'Sullivan & Thompson, 2014), and occurs at somewhat younger ages for boys. Many sexual-minority adolescents experience prejudice and rejection within their families or schools (Saewyc, 2011). Insults targeting minority adolescents and social ostracism are common forms of peer harassment in middle and high school. Nevertheless, many sexual-minority youth successfully navigate these difficulties and emerge at the end of adolescence with well-being comparable to their heterosexual peers (Saewyc, 2011).

The NSFG questioned respondents aged 18 years and older about their sexual identity. Among men aged 18 and 19 years, 1.8 percent of Whites, 1.2 percent of Black or African American, and 1.2 percent of Hispanics identified as homosexual or gay. There was no difference in the percentage identifying as bisexual by race, with 1.2 percent in each group.

Adolescence is also the period during which gender identity, one's sense of being male, female, or some other gender category, undergoes substantial development (Steensma et al., 2013). Many youth experience gender intensification, which is further development and elaboration of the assigned gender at birth. For a minority, it involves the development of a gender-variant identity. There are several events/experiences in late childhood and adolescence that may intensify concern about one's gender, including the maturation of the sexual parts of the body associated with puberty, intensified cultural and peer pressure to conform to gender-role norms, and increased time spent in gendered social contexts. These may encourage the adolescent to explore the possibility that he is *trans*.

Some children do experience *cross-gender sexual activity*. A study of Swedish high-school seniors asked them about consensual childhood sexual experiences (Larsson & Svedin, 2002). Eight percent of them recalled such an experience between the ages of 6 and 12 years; most occurred between the ages of 11 and 12 years, that is, probably after adrenarche. Nevertheless 17–44 percent (depending on the behavior) reported kissing and hugging, displaying their genitals, or another child touching their genitals between the ages of 6 and 10 years.

As boys and girls move into eighth and ninth grade, the gender segregation that is characteristic of childhood begins to break down. Youth begin to spend more time in mixed gender groups. The process of developing the skills and learning and practicing the scripts needed to sustain long-term relationships begins around ages 9–12 years, with a first boyfriend/girlfriend. Some of these early "relationships" are arranged by others and may involve little or no face-to-face interaction. Mixed gender social events and group "dates" provide an opportunity for communication and for peers to observe and instruct the person in sexual scripts. As the relationships evolve, youth begin to spend more time with their partner, including time away from others. These relationships provide the contexts in which the person develops the skills and learns and practices the scripts needed to sustain long-term intimate relationships.

A common view of romantic relationships in adolescence is that boys enter them with greater confidence, are less emotionally engaged, and exercise greater power over the relationship. Interviews with more than 1,300 adolescents, challenge that view (Giordano et al., 2006). Boys reported significantly lower levels of confidence in their ability to manage their romantic relationships. They also expressed levels of emotional engagement similar to girls and attributed greater power to the romantic partner.

Heterosexual Activity

Children learn very early that male–female pairings are the norm. That is, they learn *heteronormativity*, the belief that heterosexuality is the only pattern that is normal and natural. Intertwined with this view are beliefs that boys and girls are very different from each other, that boys should be attracted to girls and girls should be attracted to boys.

In adolescence, increasing numbers of boys and girls engage in heterosexual sexual activities. Generally, there is a progression beginning with kissing, then touching of breasts and genitals, perhaps to oral sex, and eventually to penile–

vaginal intercourse. This progression reflects the heterosexual script discussed earlier, often learned from the media and reinforced by the peer group. Variations in the sequence occur based on social class and race/ethnicity.

According to the NSFG data, among US boys aged 15–17 years, 23 percent report giving oral sex, 33 percent receiving oral sex, and 32 percent have participated in vaginal intercourse (Chandra et al., 2011). Among 18 and 19 year olds, the percentages are 55, 68, and 66, respectively. By age 24, 70 percent report giving oral sex, 78 percent have received oral sex, and 82 percent report intercourse. Among males aged 15–19 years, Hispanics are 7 percent less likely to report giving oral sex, and 6 percent more likely to report vaginal intercourse than Whites. Adolescents report a variety of reasons for engaging in intercourse, including relationship goals such as increased intimacy, sexual pleasure, and increased social status (Ott et al., 2006).

This sexual activity often occurs in the context of a romantic relationship (Collins et al., 2009). More than half of US teens say they have had a special romantic relationship within the past 18 months (Carver et al., 2003). Relationships with romantic partners provide opportunities to explore identity, develop future goals, learn communication and conflict resolution skills, and learn to enhance intimacy and sexuality. Partners may practice intimate self-disclosure, enhancing the depth of their relationship. On the negative side, they increase the likelihood of experiencing negative emotions – anxiety, jealousy, and depression. Power dynamics may be involved as well, as the partner becomes an important influence on attitudes and behavior.

First intercourse is a momentous experience for many people. In many cultures it is a symbol of having reached (reproductive) adulthood. In US culture it may also be a symbol of the young person's attractiveness and popularity. Few studies have assessed the influences on whether it is a positive or negative experience. Using data from 335 undergraduates, researchers found that an experience that was intentional (not spontaneous), involving people who were less committed to "traditional" gender roles and more satisfied with their bodies, produced more positive emotions (Smiler et al. 2005). Thus, carefully selecting the partner and setting for one's first experience may lead to more positive outcome. Compared with girls, boys are more likely to experience pleasure and anxiety, and less likely to experience guilt at the time of first intercourse (Sprecher, 2014).

Atypical Activity

Sometimes, sex occurs too early. In the United States, about 4 percent of adolescents have their first sexual intercourse before the age of 13 (Kann, et al. 2016). Among males. 5.6 percent report first coitus before the age of 13. By race, 3.5 percent of White, 12.1 percent of Black, and 6.8 percent of Hispanic boys report that experience. Experts agree that intercourse at the age of 15 or earlier is "early" sex, and that it carries a number of risks (Price & Hyde, 2009). Those who engage in intercourse early are more likely to not use a condom and to have sex with more than one partner. As a result, they are at increased risk of pregnancy and sexually transmitted diseases (STDs).

Survival sex is an atypical activity in the United States. "This term refers to transactional or commercial sex or exchange of sex for payment of some kind" (O'Sullivan & Thompson, 2014, p. 445). This has been studied primarily among homeless youth. Results from a survey of 1,625 homeless youth aged 10–25 years indicate that 9.4 percent had exchanged sex for money, food, drugs, clothing, or shelter (Walls & Bell, 2011). Survival sex was more likely to be reported by older, sexual-minority youth. There was no difference by gender.

Sometimes, sexual penetration is accomplished by force. Results from the 2015 Youth Risk Behavior Survey (Kann et al., 2016) indicate that 7 percent of the 15,713 ninth through twelfth graders reported being physically forced to have sexual intercourse when they did not want to. Three percent of males (and 10 percent of females) reported this experience. Among males, by race/ethnicity, 2 percent of Whites, 4 percent of Blacks, and 4 percent of Hispanics reported being forced. Another potential early experience is child sexual abuse. In the United States, 8 percent of men (and 25 percent of women) report some form of child abuse prior to the age 18. Among men, some perpetrators were adult men and others were adult women. Men reported that the most common types of perpetrators were a family friend (40 percent), and a relative (not father or mother). In the majority of cases, both for boys and girls, the activity involved only touching of the genitals. About 20 percent of cases involve forced sexual intercourse (Hébert et al., 2009).

Obviously, forced sexual activity can have life-long impacts on the person and his sexuality. These include avoidance of sexual relationships and activity, sexual dysfunctions, psychological distress such as depression, and posttraumatic stress disorder.

Asexuality

Some persons rarely or never engage in partnered sexual activity. According to the NSFG data, among males aged 15–17 years, 52.6 percent reported no sexual contact with another person. Of the 18 and 19 year olds, 22.9 reported no sexual contact in their lifetimes. Among males aged 20–24 years, the percentage was 13.0. By race/ethnicity, among 15–19 year olds, 42.8 percent of Whites, 28.1 percent of Blacks, and 36.7 percent of Latinos reported no sexual contact.

As noted in the discussion on masturbation, some of these persons are chaste by choice, choosing to remain abstinent. Others perhaps experience sexual desire and have attitudes and scripts that would facilitate sexual contact but have not met "M. Right," or are in circumstances that do not allow for sexually intimate relationships.

Some of these persons are *asexual*. Asexuality is defined as having no sexual attraction to another person. Researchers used data from the 2002 NSFG to estimate the prevalence of asexuality in the United States (Poston & Baumle, 2010). Interviews were conducted with persons aged 18–44 years. Responses to questions were used to construct three indices, assessing behavior, identity, and sexual attraction. Six percent of the males reported that they had never had sex in their lives. Almost 4 percent reported they were "something else" when asked their sexual orientation. Of all males, 0.9 percent gave the asexual response to all three. Asexual responses were associated with less education and less than full-time employment. Other research finds that some persons who identify as asexual are, or have been, in committed relationships, and may have engaged in various sexual activities.

The Adolescent Male Experience

The process of sociosexual development and the sexual experiences an adolescent boy may have in the contemporary United States are diverse. His sexual maturation is influenced by biological processes including the consequences of his unique genetic inheritance, adrenarche, and puberty, the effects of the hormones associated with these, and his developing brain. His development into a sexual person is influenced by the socialization he receives from parents or other adults, and possibly influenced by religious education. When he enters the education system, teachers become socializing agents and role models, from whom he may adopt attitudes, behaviors, styles of dress, and so on. Peers continue the gender role socialization process and also become "gender police," enforcing their expectations on the young person.

In the contemporary United States, the mass media are an especially impactful agent of socialization with regard to sexuality. They provide images of gendered adult behavior, adult relationships, and sexual activity that may have a powerful impact. Their power stems in part from the amount of exposure many adolescents experience, an average of 11 hours per day, and partly because they satisfy the youth's curiosity about sex and relationships. Research indicates that media portrayals perpetuate traditional gender role stereotypes, and portrayals of sexual behavior and relationships rarely have consequences such as pregnancy and STIs. Given the pervasiveness of these images, it is truly unfortunate that the images are unrealistic in ways that increase the risk of adverse outcomes for youth.

His sexual experiences will probably be numerous and diverse. There may be experiences of sex play in childhood, solitary or with others. Some of this activity may involve same-gender partners; other activities may involve partners with other characteristics. A minority of children will experience force or coercion as part of their early experiences, which will have lasting consequences, often negative. As they move into adolescence and gender and sexuality become increasingly salient, some males may question the gender ascribed to them by others. Other men may question the nature of their sexual attraction, moving toward attraction toward same gender partners or toward asexuality. For many men, their sexuality will develop along the traditional, typical path toward heterosexual expression, although it will do so with a pace and a pattern of contacts relatively unique to him. It will also vary according to his race/ethnicity. *Thus, there is amazing diversity of adolescent male sexuality in the contemporary United States!* The stereotype of the young male sexual predator is exactly that, a stereotype that is not borne out in the empirical data we have about real young men and their experiences.

Outcomes

Whatever the young man's sociodevelopmental trajectory, it lays the foundation for adult sexuality and relationships. He emerges from adolescence with at least a partly formed gender identity and sexual orientation. These will heavily influence choices about sexuality and relationships as he moves into adulthood. He will have learned sexual scripts and relationship skills that he may rely on for the rest of his life. The specifics of these will vary depending upon the mix of typical and atypical experiences he has had, his race/ethnicity, and his social class.

The data reviewed here support Fortenberry's (2013) view that adolescence is a period when the foundations of adult sexuality are laid down. The biological foundations of sexual desire have matured. Experiences with various kinds of persons and behaviors, and exposure to sexual scripts, will have channeled that desire toward specific kinds of persons, both physically and socially. Assuming typical biological maturation, the physiology of sexual arousal will function normally. Again, depending on socialization and experience, some stimuli will have acquired the ability to trigger that process. I have traced in some detail the kinds of experiences in childhood and adolescence that contribute to sexual behavior, and reviewed data on how preferences for behavior within intimate relationships may be influenced by typical and atypical experiences, as well as race/ethnicity. The combination of these will be the major influences on his sexual functioning.

I mentioned earlier the fact that media portrayals of sexual encounters rarely include negative outcomes. One of special concern is pregnancy. Available data focus on females. The teen pregnancy rate in the United States fell steadily from 1991 to 2013 (Guttmacher Institute, 2017). In 2013, it was 43 per 1,000 women aged 15–19 years old, representing 448,000 pregnancies. By race, the teen pregnancy rate in 2013 was 76 per 1,000 females aged 15–19 years among Blacks, 61 among Hispanics, and 30 among Whites. Most of those pregnancies are to women aged 18 and 19 years. It is likely that the fathers of most of these pregnancies were of similar race/ethnicity. Whether they were younger or older than 19 is unknown. A teenage male involved in a pregnancy faces a number of questions, some troubling, and undoubtedly experiences great stress. The experience may have life-long consequences, some of them unpredictable.

A second special concern is the risk of an STD. Young people aged 15–24 years acquire half of all new STDs annually (Centers for Disease Control and Prevention,

2017). In 2016, a total of 1,598,354 cases of *Chlamydia trachomatis* infection were reported to the Centers for Disease Control and Prevention (CDC). The rate of reported cases of chlamydia increased 4 percent among 15–19 years olds from 2015 to 2016. Among boys in this age range the number of reported cases increased 8.6 percent. In 2016, 468,514 new cases of gonorrhea were reported. The increase among boys in this age group, from 2015 to 2016, was 14.8 percent. In 2016, 27,814 new cases of syphilis were reported. Rates of primary and secondary syphilis increased 13 percent among persons 15–19 years of age. Among boys, the increase was 11.3 percent. While some of the increase reflects increased screening activity, especially among adolescents, some of it is due to increased incidence that is, an increase in unprotected penetrative sexual activity.

Statistics on rates by race are compromised by a sizeable number of reports to the CDC with missing information on race. The available data indicate that among 15–19-year-old boys, rates of all three are highest among Blacks, lowest among Whites, with Hispanic rates generally similar to White rates. Thus, the burden of these diseases is disproportionately borne by men in certain ethnic minority groups. The CDC points out that these differences in rates parallel differences in access to medical testing and care.

Conclusion

The outcomes of adolescent male sexuality are probably a combination of negative and positive for each individual man, depending on his experiences. Following from the biopsychosocial approach adopted in this chapter, sexual development for adolescent boys is influenced by biological factors such as hormones and brain maturation; by psychological factors such as identity development and attitudes; and by social factors such as peers.

The World Health Organization has defined sexual health as the goal. "Sexual health is a state of physical, mental and social well-being in relation to sexuality. It requires a positive and respectful approach to sexuality and sexual relationships, as well as the possibility of having pleasurable and safe sexual experiences, free of coercion, discrimination and violence" (World Health Organization, 2018) If we take this as the goal of the process of sexual maturation and development that occurs in adolescence, we have a way to go. Hopefully this review points to the directions in which we need to move.

References

Bleakley, A., Hennessy, M., Fishbein, M., & Jordan, A. (2009). How Sources of Information Relate to Adolescent's Beliefs about Sex. *American Journal of Health Behavior*, *33*, 37–48.

Brown, J. & L'Engle, K. (2009). X-Rated: Sexual Attitudes and Behaviors Associated with U.S. Early Adolescents' Exposure to Sexually Explicit Media. *Communication Research*, *36*, 129–151.

Carver, K., Joyner, K., & Udry, J.D. (2003). National Estimates of Adolescent Romantic Relationships. In Florsheim, P. (Ed.), *Adolescent Romantic Relationships and Sexual Behavior: Theory, Research, and Practical Implications* (291–329). New York: Cambridge University Press.

Centers for Disease Control and Prevention. (2017). *Sexually Transmitted Disease Surveillance 2016*. Atlanta: U.S. Department of Health and Human Services.

Chandra, A., Mosher, W. D., Copen, C., & Sionean, C. (2011). Sexual Behavior, Sexual Identity and Sexual Attraction in the United States: Data from the 2006–2008 National Survey of Family Growth. *National Health Statistics Reports*, 36, 1–36.

Childstats.gov. (2017). POP3: Race and Hispanic origin composition. www.childstats.gov/americaschildren/tables/pop3.asp.

Collins, W. A., Welsh, D. P., & Furman, W. (2009). Adolescent Romantic Relationships. *Annual Review of Psychology*, *60*: 631–652.

DeLamater, J. & Blumenstock, S. (2018). *Sexuality across the Life Course*. Oxford Bibliographies. Oxford: Oxford University Press. https://global.oup.com/academic/product/oxford-bibliographies-9780199799701?cc=us&lang=en&.

DeLamater. J. & Hyde, J.S. (1998). Essentialism vs. Social Constructionism in the Study of Human Sexuality. *The Journal of Sex Research*, *35*, 10–18. doi:10.1080/00224499809551913.

DeLamater, J., Myers D. J., & Collett J. L. (2015). *Social Psychology*. Boulder: Westview Press.

Del Giudice, M., Angeleri, R., & Manera, V. (2009). The Juvenile Transition: A Developmental Switch Point in Human Life History. *Developmental Review*, *29*, 1–31.

Eder, D. (With Evans, C.C. & Parker, S.) (1995). *School Talk: Gender and Adolescent Culture*. New Brunswick: Rutgers University Press.

Fischer, N. L. (2016). Sexualities. *Oxford Bibliographies*. Oxford: Oxford University Press.

Fortenberry, J. D. (2013). Puberty and Adolescent Sexuality. *Hormones and Behavior*, *64*, 280–287. doi:10.1016/j.yhbeh.2013.03.007.

Giordano, P.C., Longmore, M.A. & Manning, W.D. (2006). Gender and the Meaning of Adolescent Romantic Relationships: A Focus on Boys. *American Sociological Review*, 71, 260–287.

Guttmacher Institute. (2017). U.S. Rates of Pregnancy, Birth and Abortion among Adolescents and Young Adults Continue to Decline. www.guttmacher.org/news-release/2017/us-rates-pregnancy-birth-and-abortion-among-adolescents-and-young-adults-continue.

Hébert, M., Tourigny, M., Cyr, M., et al. (2009). Prevalence of Childhood Sexual Abuse and Timing of Disclosure in a Representative Sample of Adults from Quebec. *Canadian Journal of Psychiatry*, *54*, 631–636.

Howden, L. M. & Meyer, J. A. (2011). *Age and Sex Composition: 2010*. Washington, DC: U. S. Department of Commerce, U.S. Census Bureau.

Hyde, J. S. (Ed.) (2005). *Biological Substrates of Human Sexuality*. Washington, DC: American Psychological Association.

Hyde, J. S. & DeLamater, J. (2017). *Understanding Human Sexuality. 13e*. New York: McGraw-Hill Education.

Kann, L., McManus, T., Harris, W. A., et al. (2016), Youth Risk Behavior Surveillance – United States, 2015. *Morbidity and Mortality Weekly Report*, 65(6). U.S. Department of Health and Human Services: Centers for Disease Control and Prevention.

Kim, J. L., Sorsoli, C. L., Collins, K., Zylbergold, B. A., Schooler, D., & Tolman, D. L. (2007). From Sex to Sexuality: Exposing the Heterosexual Script on Prime-Time Television. *The Journal of Sex Research*, *44*, 145–157.

Larsson, I. B & Svedin, C-G. (2002). Sexual Experiences in Childhood: Young Adults' Recollections. *Archives of Sexual Behavior*, *31*, 263–274

McClintock, M. & Herdt, G. (1996). Rethinking Puberty: The Development of Sexual Attraction. *Current Directions in Psychological Science*, *5*, 178–183.

Ott, M. A. (2010). Examining the Development and Sexual Behavior of Adolescent Males. *Journal of Adolescent Health*, *46*, S3–S11.

Ott, M. A., Millstein, S., Ofner, S., & Halpern-Flesher, B. (2006). Greater Expectations: Adolescents Positive Motivations for Health. *Perspectives on Sexual and Reproductive Health*, 38, 84–89.

O'Sullivan, L. F. & Thompson, A. E. (2014) Sexuality in Adolescence. In Tolman, D. L. & Diamond, L. M. (Eds.), *APA Handbook of Sexuality and Psychology, Vol. 1: Person-Based Approaches* (433–486). Washington, DC: American Psychological Association, doi:10.1037/14193–015.

Pascoe, C. J. (2007). *Dude, You're a Fag: Masculinity and Sexuality in High School*. Berkeley: University of California Press.

Poston, D. L. Jr. & Baumle, A. K. (2010) Patterns of Asexuality in the United States. *Demographic Research*, *23*, 509–530.

Price, M. & Hyde, J. (2009). When Two Isn't Better Than One: Predictors of Early Sexual Activity in Adolescence Using a Cumulative Risk Model. *Journal of Youth and Adolescence*, *38*, 1059–1071.

Reisner, S. L., Greytak, E. A. Parsons, J. T., & Ybarra, M. L. (2015). Gender Minority Social Stress in Adolescence: Disparities in Adolescent Bullying and Substance Use By Gender Identity. *Journal of Sex Research*, *52*, 243–256.

Rideout, V. J., Foehr, U. G., & Roberts, D. F. (2010). *GenerationM^2: Media in the Lives of 8 to 18 Year Olds*. Menlo Park: Kaiser Family Foundation. www.kff.org.

Robbins, C., Fortenberry, J. D., Reece, M., Herbenick, D., Sanders, S., & Dodge, B. (2010). Masturbation Frequency and Patterns among U.S. Adolescents. *Journal of Adolescent Health*, *46*(Suppl 1), S36–S337.

Rosario, M., Meyer-Bahlburg, H. F. L., Hunter, J., Exner, T. M., Gwadz, M., & Keller, A. M. (1996). The Psychological Development of Lesbian, Gay, and Bisexual Youths. *The Journal of Sex Research*, *33*, 113–126.

Saewyc, E. (2011). Research on Adolescent Sexual Orientation: Development, Health Disparities, Stigma, and Resilience. *Journal of Research on Adolescence*, *21*, 256–272.

Smiler, A.P., Ward, L.M., Carruthers, A., & Merriweather, A. (2005). Pleasure, Empowerment, and Love: Factors Associated with a Positive First Coitus. *Sexuality Research and Social Policy*, *3*, 41–55.

Sprecher, S. (2014). Evidence of Change in Men's Versus Women's Emotional Reactions to First Sexual Intercourse: A 23-year Study in a Human Sexuality Course at a Midwestern University. *Journal of Sex Research*, *51*, 466–472.

Steensma, T. D., Kreukels, B. P.C., de Vries, A. L. C., & Cohen-Kettenis, P. T. (2013). Gender Identity Development in Adolescence. *Hormones and Behavior* 64, 288–297.

Steinberg, L. (2005). Cognitive and Affective Development in Adolescence. *Trends in Cognitive Sciences*, *9*, 69–74.

(2007). Risk-Taking in Adolescence: New Perspectives from Brain and Behavioral Science. *Current Directions in Psychological Science*, *16*, 55–59.

(2008). *Adolescence*, 8th edn. New York: McGraw-Hill.

Thorne, B. (1993). *Gender Play: Girls and Boys in School.* New Brunswick: Rutgers University Press.

Udry, J. R. (1988). Biological Predispositions and Social Control in Adolescent Sexual Behavior. *American Sociological Review*, *53*, 709–722.

Walls, N. E. & Bell, S. (2011). Correlates of Engaging in Survival Sex among Homeless Youth and Young Adults. *The Journal of Sex Research*, *48*, 423–436.

Ward, L.M., Reed, L., Trinh, S.L., & Foust, M. (2014). Sexuality and Entertainment Media. In Tolman, D. L. & Diamond, L. M. (Eds.), *APA Handbook of Sexuality and Psychology, Vol. 2: Contextual Approaches* (373–423). Washington, DC: American Psychological Association.

World Health Organization (2018). Sexual Health. www.who.int/topics/sexual_health/en/.

8 Developmental Trajectories and Milestones of Sexual-Minority Youth

Ritch C. Savin-Williams

Overview

It was not until the early 1970s that scientists – spearheaded by clinical and public health professionals – recognized and, in a sense created, a unique sexual population that was labeled *gay youth*. To find these youth, researchers recruited from locations and organizations that served the needs of compromised youth. Although the methodology was flawed, conclusions from these convenience samples were instrumental in founding a field of study. Not surprisingly, gay youth were perceived as having an exceptional developmental profile and consequently to be in dire need of immediate medical, psychiatric, and social interventions (Roesler & Deisher, 1972).

By contrast, over the past two decades an increasingly broad array of biological, social, and behavioral scientists has produced data on which to build a developmental perspective on sexual-minority youth.[1] This was possible primarily through social media recruitment and the inclusion of sexual status measures in large-scale surveys, giving researchers access to diverse and likely more representative populations of sexual-minority youth. A major consequence of the improved methodology was that many initial clinical findings were challenged, modulated, or, in some cases, repudiated (e.g., that one-third to half of sexual-minority youths attempt suicide, see Remafedi, 1987 vs. Savin-Williams, 2001a).

Although the early research has limited relevance for understanding contemporary sexual-minority youth, especially during their child and adolescent years, few social scientists produced data-based research that illuminated the developmental processes of same-sex sexual and romantic growth prior to adulthood. Presented in this chapter is this limited literature, which must, by its very nature, be suggestive rather than confirmatory regarding the qualities and experiences of millennial sexual-minority youths as they navigate from their first memories of same-sex sexuality to their self-acceptance, expression, and integration of that sexuality. It is

[1] Sexual-minority youth is used in this chapter to refer to all youths who have some degree of sexual and/or romantic attraction to the same sex – that is, are not exclusively heterosexual. They may not necessarily identify or behave as such, or even be aware that their sexual and romantic feelings, fantasies, crushes, and desires have meaning regarding who they are as an individual.

frequently a lengthy, nuanced process consisting of multiple developmental milestones that vary in order, intensity, timing, content, and significance across individuals. Relatively unknown are the critical casual agents that guide or determine the homoerotic life course and how that development varies across ethnicity, social class, region, and culture.

A differential developmental trajectories (DDTs) perspective is presented as a framework for understanding what is known regarding the timing and sequence of contemporary sexual-minority children and adolescents. This perspective does not assume that all sexual-minority youths follow a uniform developmental pathway as they progress from feeling different to self-acceptance and synthesis.

Differential Developmental Trajectories

Overview

A DDT framework remains faithful to the real-life experiences of sexual-minority children and adolescents, including their common and unique milestones, transitional incidents, fluidity, positive development, and pathways. More specifically, *differential* refers to the variability that is inherent within and across sexual-minority individuals in terms of their sexual and romantic orientations and identities. *Developmental* signifies sexual and romantic milestones and processes manifest during the life course. *Trajectories* indicate various sexual and romantic pathways occurring across time, both within and across individuals. Four critical assumptions are inherent in a DDT perspective.

First Tenet: Sexual-Minority Youths Are Foremost Youths

Sexual-minority youths share with other adolescents, regardless of their sexuality, basic developmental processes and outcomes. A central developmental principle seldom considered when the population includes sexual-minority youths is the degree to which such children and adolescents do *not* vary from heterosexual youths in their sexual and romantic development. They, too, live within similar historic and cultural contexts and within basic biological systems and constraints. During their childhood and adolescence, most experience and negotiate age-appropriate developmental transitions and milestones.

The anticipated conclusion of adolescence includes not only full physical and sexual maturity but also the cultivation of novel ways of thinking, the accumulation of knowledge, and the evolution of a system of ethical values and conduct. Educational and occupational futures are concerns they share with those who love and support them. More dynamically, youths of all sexualities must negotiate their interpersonal and social relationships, especially with family members and peers. And, although the gender of the fantasies and objects of desire differs, teens of all sexualities think about – perhaps obsess about – and explore arenas of sexual and emotional intimacy (asexuals may be the exception, to varying degrees). The desire to find friends, to locate dates, to engage with sex partners, and to meet others "just like me" or the "opposite of me" is not dependent on sexuality. Although these outcomes might well vary in form and substance depending on underlying sexual and romantic orientations, the basic goals and processes are similar.

Because most research paradigms assume a straight-versus-gay contrast, these fundamental developmental similarities are either ignored or minimized, and are thus unknown. To best understand how sexual and romantic orientations influence basic developmental milestones and trajectories, it is critical to understand the commonalities. The result is a greater appreciation for how sexual and romantic attractions matter in the lives of children and adolescents.

Second Tenet: Sexual-Minority Youths Are Unique

Sexual-minority youths are also unlike heterosexual youths in some aspects of their developmental trajectories. The presumed casual agents that separate sexualities could reside in the developing pre- and post-natal neuroendocrine systems and/or in the proximate and remote social and cultural environments that sexual minorities encounter during their childhood and adolescence. In particular, cultural heterocentrism (the assumption of heterosexuality) is manifested in the treatment of youths who display early signs of gayness. Thus, same-sex-attracted children and teens might well undergo psychological development in a manner at variance from other youths – both for biological and socialization reasons to varying degrees. The extent to which this is true and worthy of attention likely varies by race, class, ethnicity, geographical region, sex, and cohort – but at this point little is known about these intersections.

The magnitude of biological and socialization effects and whether they consist of creating one of a kind (separate sexual categories) or one of degree (a sexual/romantic continuum) is largely unknown because these issues are seldom systematically explored (Savin-Williams, 2016a). Related to this larger issue is whether the ways in which sexual and romantic development are similar or different vary among sexual-minority and straight youths.

Third Tenet: Sexual-Minority Youths Vary among Themselves

The presumptions of the first two tenets, of child/adolescent universals and sexual-minority variations, frequently conceal the degree to which individuals vary from others of their sexual/romantic status but are like others of a dissimilar sexual/romantic status. Here, the fundamental developmental issue is whether sexual-minority youths differ from each other in accordance with heterosexual teens – based on commonalities such as sex, gender, ethnicity, socioeconomic status, geography, and cohort – specific developmental milestones and processes that overwhelm potential orientation differences.

The result is distinctive trajectories that cut across sexual/romantic status. For example, growing up African American might align a sexual-minority youth more with African-American heterosexual youth in aspects of their developmental trajectories than with White, European sexual-minority youth. Thus, an African-American gay youth shares commonalities and differences with both White gay youth and Black straight youth and these, of course, interact with other confounds such as gender, social class, and immigration status. For example, young Mexican men who recently immigrated to the United States were more likely than those whose parents immigrated before they were born or as young children to have their first sexual contact with a same-sex cousin or friend rather than a member of the gay community (Carrillo & Fontdevila, 2011.

Most likely, the ways in which same-sex-oriented teens vary among themselves mirror to some degree divisions observed in the developmental histories of heterosexual teens. The range of shared subpopulation characteristics is boundless in scope and include factors that may be so pronounced as to trivialize differences across sexual and romantic orientations.

Fourth Tenet: Each Sexual-Minority Youth Is Exceptional

Because of orientation *and* background (both macro and micro, e.g., personality, temperament, family, community), every same-sex-attracted youth has distinctive developmental processes and milestones that are not shared by any other youth of any sexuality who has ever lived. This recognition implies that independent of scientific research each sexual-minority youth is an exception to preconceived categories and current data.

It is thus imprudent to characterize same-sex romantic and sexual desires as resulting in monolithic outcomes, for any orientation. It is the interaction between sexual and romantic orientations and personal and social variables that prevents easy characterizations. This level of analysis rarely exists but might well be the most promising approach to generate future hypotheses and research on sexual and romantic status. Relevant data are the life narratives and qualitative data provided by both scientific research and social media. Each sexual-minority youth is one of a kind.

Research Conundrums

Although youth usually experience their same-sex sexuality as newly energized with the onset of puberty, many have been aware of their same-sex attractions since their first memories (Savin-Williams, 2016b). This implies that the development of same-sex-attracted individuals is based on genetics and prenatal factors (LeVay, 2016). Yet, little research has been conducted on the postnatal, childhood *genesis* of same-sex sexual attractions, infatuations, erotic arousals, sexual behaviors, and crushes. This is not surprising, largely because it is consistent with the unstated perspective that sexuality during childhood is deemed "off-limits" to investigators, another consequence of the shroud of silence and denial regarding the sex lives of all children (Levine, 2002). It is considerably more acceptable to fathom a gay adolescent than a gay child. However, there is no sexual latency and no postnatal creation of a sexual-minority orientation. It is already present.

Thus, we know little about the first manifestations of homoeroticism except from the *recalled* memories of young adults who currently identify as a sexual minority and have disclosed this information to others. As such, our knowledge is subject to the problematic bias of retrospective recall. Although we have average ages of some milestones, the content, meaning, and significance of each remains mysterious. Even with the possibility of present-day research strategies, few scholars ask sexual minorities about their childhood sexuality. What is their earliest sexual memory? When did they first experience sexual desire? As a child, did they have sexual contact? In terms of early crushes, was it a boy, a girl, or both?

Of the many methodological shortcomings characteristic of nearly all research reported in this chapter, the most consequential is the recruitment of biased samples of sexual minorities – those sufficiently out to feel comfortable or motivated to volunteer for sex-oriented research. Whether these individuals represent the much larger number of non-volunteers is difficult to assess, but highly unlikely (Kuyper et al., 2016; Savin-Williams, 2001b). For example, they might well differ in their greater degree of atypical gender expression: it would have been more difficult for such youth to hide their sexuality and thus they were more likely to label themselves as "not straight" at an early age, making them eligible for sexual-minority research. Although, on average, sexual-minority individuals are more gender nonconforming, frequently neglected are the millions who are more-or-less gender typical.

Indeed, findings largely depend on where researchers recruit their population (e.g., gay community groups versus general population, see Kuyper et al., 2016); whether the sample is defined by sexual attraction or sexual identity (Bostwick et al., 2010; Savin-Williams, 2001b); and whether bisexuals and mostly straights are included as sexual minorities (Beaver et al., 2016; Doyle & Molix, 2016; Lea et al., 2014; Silva et al., 2016; Thomeer & Reczek, 2016; Wadsworth & Hayes-Skelton, 2015).

Feeling Different

Overview

Many, but not all, same-sex-attracted youth recall growing up feeling different from peers. This sense of divergence from other children can begin as early as first memories and usually intensifies with increased social contact. Children's first awareness of their same-sex sexuality is likely rooted in this differentness, linked to two aspects of their life that may or may not be distinctive: an awareness of being sexually/romantically attracted to same-sex others and having characteristics of the other sex (gender nonconformity).

Several early studies addressed this sense of differentness, the first conducted nearly four decades ago with San Francisco adults from diverse sexual backgrounds: "In grade school, to what extent did you think that you were different from others your age?" (Bell et al., 1981). About 20 percent of sexual-minority adults reported that they were "not at all" different from their peers. More telling, they were three times more likely than heterosexuals to feel "very much" different as children – and their gender-related reasons were considerably at odds from heterosexuals. For example, as girls, sexual-minority adults felt their interest in sports made them different from other girls; as boys, it was their *lack* of interest in sports. This sexual identity distinction was proportional rather than absolute as some heterosexual children also felt different because of their gender nonconformity. A second reason for feeling different, reported by 20 percent, was an awareness of having same-sex sexual interest but not opposite-sex sexual interest. Only 2 percent of heterosexuals reported this memory.

Similarly, Troiden (1979, 1989) noted that the initial stage of sensitization for pre-gay children was feeling marginalized, especially in gender terms – not acting or feeling like a typical girl or boy. At this age, they were only dimly aware that these feelings had relevance for their sexuality; as children, they usually became aware of how members of their sex were supposed to act earlier than they became aware about what it means to be sexually attracted to someone. Among men, Troiden found that the primary reasons for feeling different were gender inadequacies, effeminacy, lack of masculine interests, feeling alienated, and experiencing a warmth and excitement in the presence of other males. Feeling sexually attracted to the "wrong" sex was not initially felt as unnatural or bad, and was considerably less important than gender inappropriateness for feeling different. By adolescence, however, nearly all boys felt *sexually* different because of their prominent sexual interest in other boys, waning or non-existent sexual interest in girls, and sexual contact with boys.

Although other research conducted with those coming of age in the 1950s and 1960s reported similar results (Saghir & Robbins, 1973), investigators today seldom ask children and adolescents questions such as, "Did you feel different growing up?" and "How did you feel different?" Thus, whether these findings from a much older cohort characterize today's children and adolescents is unknown.

Same-Sex Sexual and Romantic Attractions

Perhaps the most reliable, yet underappreciated, early indicator of sexual-minority status is the emergence of distinctive same-sex sexual and romantic attractions. Developmentally, the ages during which youth first recall experiencing same-sex attractions are broad, extending from first memories in early childhood through adolescence. McClelland et al. (2016) discovered two age groups among girls for first awareness of same-sex attractions, before the age of 10 and between the ages of 16 and 22 years. If children experience same-sex attractions, it seldom disturbs them because the emotional component feels natural and exciting – that is until late childhood with the onset of adrenarche (McClintock & Herdt, 1996). This is when the adrenal glands increase their production of hormones, creating an upsurge in the intensity of sexual and romantic attractions. The resulting fascination with other girls or other boys is less a matter of the desire to emulate or act like them (gender nonconformity) but more the desire *to want* (or *to be wanted by*) same-sex others. How exactly this will happen usually waits for a later age.

After this enhancement of sexual and romantic eroticism during middle childhood, from a biological perspective, puberty and its dramatic escalation of hormones stamp passion onto these attractions (LeVay, 2016). With the infusion of pubertal hormones (gonadarche), denying the eroticism becomes more challenging. Previously defined friendships are converted into "something else" as the purity of infatuations is muddied with sexual desire. Crushes are energized and become more problematic as a youth inarticulately yearns for something more from others without knowing what that something is. "Puppy love" gives way to mini love affairs between two girls or two boys and curiosity intensifies about what another girl or boy "looks like naked."

Relative to boys, girls more frequently remembered their first same-sex attraction as an emotional attachment or crush, and boys, as a sexual thought, arousal, or behavior (Savin-Williams & Diamond, 2000). In part, this was confirmed and elaborated in a later qualitative study that reported three primary sources for first same-sex attraction among girls (McClelland et al., 2016, pp. 1384–1385):

1. Embodied self-experiences such as a fantasy, memory, or fleeting encounter or as visceral responses to other girls and women.
2. Relational memories emerging within a relationship with another girl that feels different from a friendship.
3. Social awareness of cultural meanings ascribed to how sexuality is supposed to be manifested through subtle cues delivered by social media, parents, and peers.

The degree to which these sex differences reflect biology or socialization is unknown. One usual explanation is based on the finding that women's sexuality is more dependent on environmental and situational factors, such as passionate interpersonal relationships with women and university courses with strong pro-feminist assignments (Diamond, 2008; Peplau, 2003). However, boys might be similarly disposed but they have been socialized to restrain expressing their romantic crushes, just as girls have been socialized to minimize their sexual desires.

It is also critical to recognize that recalling attractions to one's unpreferred sex is not solely the province of sexual-minority youth. At least 10 percent of straight-identified youth reports a small degree of same-sex sexuality and either maintains a self-label as straight or mostly straight (Savin-Williams, 2017; Savin-Williams & Vrangalova, 2013; Vrangalova & Savin-Williams, 2010). Among boys, Silva (2018) labeled some of these activities as "bud sex." Additionally, more than half of sexual-minority youth experience opposite-sex attraction and/or sex (Rosario et al., 1996). Developmentally, sexual attraction consistent with one's sexual orientation emerge earlier than attraction to the nonpreferred sex. Regardless, age of awareness of sexual and romantic attractions are inconsistently related to the timing of other developmental milestones, such as coming out to self and others. Acceptance of these attractions may be immediate or take years to enact (Savin-Williams, 2005).

Whereas several cross-sectional studies that relied on retrospective recounting of events that occurred a decade or more earlier indicated no secular trend in age of first same-sex attraction (Calzo et al., 2011; Floyd & Bakeman, 2006), other research reported that since the 1980s there has been a decline of about 4 years in the recalled age of first same-sex attraction. This observation is especially striking among girls, reflecting the growing recognition and acceptance of many aspects of their sexuality (Diamond & Savin-Williams, 2009; Maguen et al., 2002; Rosario et al., 1996).

The initial homoeroticism is seldom recognized as such, although, in retrospect, young adults realize it was a forbearer to their eventual romantic and sexual orientations. Same-sex crushes and arousals seldom dissipated but deepened over time and assumed new meanings. Thus, puberty does not create but merely strengthens preexisting sexual and romantic longings. Attempts to substitute heteroerotic desires through opposite-sex dating and genital contact fail to cancel the homoeroticism. What is irrefutable is that sexual and romantic desires and, sometimes, behavior exist long before parents and sex education classes are willing to talk about them (Josephs, 2015).

Gender Nonconformity

A second basis for feeling different involves gender expression – having characteristics and behaviors more typical of the other than your own sex. At the outset, it is important to note that many communal features and activities are gender neutral with cross-cultural confirmation, such as reading and bicycling, and, in these, children rarely differ based on their sexuality (Golombok et al., 2012; Grellert et al., 1982; Yu et al., 2010). However, gender-biased behavior emerges early, prior to preschool, and persists throughout the life course, strengthening during middle childhood and adolescence. Despite attempts to appear and act traditionally masculine or feminine, concealing atypical gender expressions is seldom subject to conscious control (Rule & Alaei, 2016).

Initially, being gender atypical is not likely to be particularly alarming to children because their fascination with acting like the opposite sex feels natural, a genuine aspect of themselves (Savin-Williams, 2005, 2016b). Eventually, however, consciousness of differentness evolves such that children perceive something is *not quite right*, and often undesirable. This message is delivered by the distress expressed by parents and peers who often interpret the gender nonconformity as the first sign of a budding homosexuality (Bos & Sandfort, 2015). Parents can be especially alarmed as they attempt to change their child's gender presentation to reduce peer harassment and, perhaps, with the hope that the child's sexuality will not solidify as gay (D'Augelli et al., 2008).

In attempting to recreate the childhood of same-sex-oriented individuals, a basic, cross-cultural research has longstanding support: "Homosexual individuals recall substantially more childhood cross-sex-typed behavior than do heterosexuals of the same sex" (Bailey & Zucker, 1995, p. 52). This covariation presumes that the same hormonal or genetic factors that alter the brain to create biologically atypical sexual attraction are also responsible for fashioning atypical feelings, perceptions, cognitions, temperaments, and play activities. Indeed, research has consistently found degrees of gender nonconformity in pre-gay children and gender conformity in pre-straight children to emerge relatively early (Rieger et al., 2008), likely in part because of early exposure to different levels of hormones that alter sexual differentiation of the brain (Cohen-Bendahan et al., 2005).

Across studies, relatively high levels of gender nonconformity during childhood predict high levels of gender nonconformity during adulthood and the link between homoeroticism and gender nonconformity has been documented not only for both sexes and at many ages but also in many cultures, including China, Brazil, India, Turkey, and Thailand (Stief, 2017), and among Asian and Hispanic Americans in the United States (Lippa & Tan, 2001). However, caution is necessary because what is considered gender atypical in the West does not always translate similarly across cultures. Gendered play activities and characteristics can be fluid, subject to change over time, such as girls playing rough-and-tumble team sports and boys engaging in artistic endeavors. Culturally, Stief (2017) noted in India, like the activo/pasivo distinction in Latin culture, panthi men are masculine in gender role and presentation but have same-sex sexual relations, as the insertive sex partner, with feminine-appearing hijra and kothi men, who are also sexually attracted to males.

These findings suggest that gender nonconformity is a stable trait, girls are predictably more gender atypical than boys, and the link between sexual orientation and gender nonconformity is more robust in men than women (Bailey & Zucker, 1995). Because Western society overvalues masculinity, girls are granted greater leeway in expressing masculinity and are thus less disparaged for engaging in sex or falling in love with other girls. This may be unfortunate for boys, with resulting detrimental consequences. Alanko and colleagues (2010, p. 89) noted "the gender atypical boys will to a greater extent stick out from other boys as peculiar and much more effort will be made to correct the behavior of gender atypical boys than girls."

Although the correlation between sexual and gender inversion is strong and significant, it is not perfect. Homoeroticism and gender expression differ by degree among sexual-minority youths, even to the point where many have heteroerotic desires and appear no different from heterosexual youths. For example, bisexuals and mostly straights are less likely than gays/lesbians to be gender atypical (Cohen, 2002; Savin-Williams & Vrangalova, 2013). In addition, not all sexual-minority children are more gender nonconforming than all heterosexual children; a wide range of gender expressions exists within all populations. Some lesbian girls are as feminine as straight girls and some gay boys are as masculine as straight boys (Rieger et al., 2008; Savin-Williams, 2016b). In addition, throughout their life course lesbians and gays show greater variability in gender nonconformity than heterosexuals (Rieger et al., 2008). Thus, there is considerable overlap in the distributions of gender behavior among heterosexual and sexual-minority children and adolescents.

Sexual Behavior

The average age of first post-childhood same-sex sexual activities is shortly after pubertal onset for boys and slightly later for girls (Savin-Williams, 2005). Usually ignored in the literature is specifying the types of sexual activities that transpire, the emotional reactions of the individuals to "having sex," the meanings of the sexual experiences for the individuals, and whether prepubertal "sex play" counts as first sex. Thus, little is known about the first sexual encounters other than the average age at which they occur.

Historically, the average age of first sex has not changed for sexual-minority boys but has decreased slightly for girls (Drasin et al., 2008; Maguen et al., 2002), and is nearly identical to that of heterosexual youths (Smiler, 2016). The onset of sexual activity precedes, co-occurs, or follows self-identification as a sexual minority and may be consistent with or contrary to that sexual identity. Regardless of sexuality, youth engage in early sex or delay sexual activity for various reasons, including not feeling ready, not liking the person, not emotionally attached to the person, and limited opportunities for sex (Heywood et al., 2016). Gay-identified virgins exist as do straight-identified youths, for similar reasons (Savin-Williams, 2016b).

First sex among contemporary sexual-minority youths typically occurs after, not before, the recognition that they are not totally straight. This might be due to an early awareness that same-sex attractions are paramount, independent of sexual encounters or crushes. In addition, cultural mores against adolescents of any sexuality having early sex (early dating is less stigmatized) and the shortage of readily available same-sex partners in middle and high school also influence the timing of sex. This developmental pattern has been characterized as identity-centric rather than sex-centric – embracing a same-sex awareness prior to experiencing same-sex behavior (Calzo et al., 2011; Drasin et al., 2008; Dubé, 2000; Floyd & Bakeman, 2006). Calzo et al. (2011) reported about one-quarter of gay youth had a same-sex experience prior to self-identification; typically, there was a 1-year gap between the two. Furthermore, across cohorts an identity-centric trajectory was more common among those who began their developmental milestones during adolescence rather than adulthood (Calzo et al., 2011; Floyd & Bakeman, 2006). Thus, early conceptual models of coming out (Troiden 1979) that viewed adolescent same-sex sexual experiences as serving to test or confirm a nonheterosexual identity, if true, then are apparently less accurate now. In this, contemporary sexual-minority youth are like heterosexual youth who seldom engage in sex as the basis for confirming their straight identity.

Most same-sex-oriented adolescents do not participate exclusively in same-sex behavior but have instances of sex with opposite-sex peers – usually prior to same-sex encounters. Reasons vary, including the desire to experiment or have fun, giving in to pressure while dating the nonpreferred sex, alcohol intoxication or substance use, and genuine heteroerotic desire (Diamond, 2008; Savin-Williams, 2005, 2016b). Although sexual fluidity among same-sex-oriented young women may explain their greater participation in heterosexual encounters, they are also frequently exposed to opposite-sex invitations. Nonetheless, most sexual-minority youth of both sexes engage in heterosexual sex, typically within a dating or friendship relationship (Diamond & Savin-Williams, 2009).

For youths who are exclusively same-sex oriented, the earlier they identify as lesbian or gay, the less likely they are to have heterosexual sex (Drasin et al., 2008). Although some straight-identified youth participate in same-sex encounters, those who are primarily homoerotic pursue such interactions with greater regularity and zeal and reportedly derive greater physical and emotional satisfaction from them (Vrangalova & Savin-Williams, 2010).

Reflecting heterosexual patterns of sexual behavior, same-sex-oriented young men are more likely than young women to report same-sex behavior, to have a greater number of sex partners, and to engage in such activities prior to heterosexual experiences. The first same-sex encounter among both sexes typically occurs with a friend or someone they are dating, although young men are more likely to have first sex within the context of a purely sexual encounter – this despite stated preferences, both before and after first sex, for relationship sex (Savin-Williams, 2016b; Smiler, 2016).

Self-Identification

Coming out to oneself – that is, recognizing one's same-sex attractions, crushes, fantasies, and sexual activities are meaningful statements about themselves – is a milestone most sexual-minority youths vividly recall. This is especially true for those who experience the realization as either terrifying or gratifying, and is less so for youths who have always known what their homoeroticism means for their sexuality and personal identity. The latter trajectory is becoming increasingly common as contemporary cohorts appreciate and name their sexuality, sometimes while still in middle school or, in some instances, in elementary school (Savin-Williams, 2016b).

Whereas boys may take years to process the meaning of their same-sex attraction and progress from comprehension to self-identification as a sexual minority, girls typically make the transition to self-recognition as a sexual minority far more quickly, although at a slightly older age (Maguen et al., 2002). It is not uncommon for girls to recognize, name, and disclose their homoeroticism within a few days or months, or even shortly after developing their first crush on another girl (Savin-Williams & Diamond, 2000).

One reason why gay boys take longer to identify as gay is that roughly half go through a "bisexual phase" (Savin-Williams, 2005, 2016b; Semon et al., 2017). A recent study indicated the reasons: it was "easier to think of themselves as bisexual than as completely homosexual," "They thought that others would accept them more readily as bisexual than as homosexual," and "They wanted a future with a wife and children" (Semon et al., 2017, p. 240). Both lesbian and gay young adults have genuine subjectively and objectively assessed sexual and romantic attractions and these individuals identify as "mostly gay/lesbian" (Savin-Williams et al., 2017; Semon et al., 2017). Young women differed from young men in two significant ways: far more identified as mostly lesbian or bisexual and far fewer assumed a bisexual identity as a passageway to a lesbian identity (Copen et al., 2016; Diamond, 2008).

Bisexual youths frequently take longer to reach developmental milestones. Perhaps because their sexual identity is more fluid over time and context or is dependent on person rather than sexual characteristics, naming their sexuality is less certain. They may question themselves more, have fewer sources of support from largely invisible sexual communities, and face greater disbelief from others who question the veracity of their neither straight nor gay claims (Rust, 2002). Calzo et al. (2011) found bisexuals were more likely than gays and lesbians to have a teenage- rather than a child-onset profile in their developmental trajectories. Self-identification averaged 1 year later than gays and lesbians (also see Maguen et al., 2002). Calzo and associates (2011, p. 1659) attributed the later bisexual developmental patterns "to the complexities of understanding and integrating attractions to both same- and other sex partners." They proposed the "recent increase in the visibility of bisexuality as a stable identity may mean that contemporary bisexual youth are more likely to self-identify as bisexual at younger ages, rather than adopt gay/lesbian or heterosexual identity labels first" (Calzo et al., 2011, p. 1669). Data supporting this hypothesis have not been reported.

Transcending conventional labels, sexual-minority individuals may redefine or create distinctive sexual identity categories or reject them altogether. Compared to baby boomers and Generation Xers, Vaccaro (2009, p. 131) found millennials "negotiate multiple identities instead of developing one singular identity." The cohort effect is clear: a growing constituency of youth is refusing categorical sex-based labels by embracing broadly defined notions of sexuality, gender, and romance (e.g., pansexual, gender fluid, bisexual homoromantic) and by describing their sexuality as an interaction between their erotic preferences and gender expression (Walton et al., 2016). Youths eschew traditional labels because they fear negative family or social repercussions, or they simply prefer to emphasize other aspects of their life that are more personally meaningful, such as their favorite video games. Still others dismiss traditional sexual classifications because they embody inaccurate or oppressive stereotypes (e.g., lesbians as butch; gay men as sissies; bisexuals as promiscuous) that they find abhorrent. Consequently, millennial youth might acknowledge their same-sex attraction and behavior but deny that they are gay, lesbian, or bisexual. Whether this is a passing historic phase or the beginning of a general trend of broadening recognized sexual identities is unknown, but likely the latter.

Another recent development is the visibility of youth who acknowledge, in addition to their predominant heterosexuality, a slight degree of same-sex sexuality. These individuals now have a heightened visibility and identity – *mostly straight* (Savin-Williams, 2017). Evidence for the validity of mostly straight as a sexual and romantic point along a spectrum is derived from five sources (Savin-Williams & Vrangalova, 2013). First, it has a unique sexual/romantic profile with youth reporting a small degree of same-sex sexuality. Second, mostly straights (males) have a distinctive physiological arousal pattern (a slight level of arousal to same-sex stimuli). Third, a significant number of individuals identify as mostly straight, especially women. The prevalence of mostly straights exceeds those who identify as gay, lesbian, or bisexual combined. Fourth, the identification is moderately stable over time. Fifth, a mostly straight identity has subjective relevance for young men and women.

A third recent trend is youth who consider their sexuality to be fluid, especially women and those who identify as bisexual or nonexclusive at some point in their lives (Dickson et al., 2013; Floyd & Bakeman, 2006; Savin-Williams et al., 2012). Diamond (2008) reported that most young women in her longitudinal study experienced several changes in their sexual identity, behavior, attraction, or relationships since childhood. Many felt sexual labels were limiting and individual characteristics trumped biological sex in determining romantic interest. Although some young women with same-sex interest or activity eventually embraced a straight label, they insisted their same-sex sexuality persisted. The same pattern is surfacing among young men who report fluidity in their sexual and romantic lives (Savin-Williams, 2017).

Finally, a growing number of nonheterosexual youth reject cultural mandates to label their sexuality. Because sexual identity labels do not correspond with or encompass the complexity and diversity of their sexual and romantic lives, they are "unlabeled." The mere construction of sexual identities reifies the labels across time and place and, most importantly, exaggerates artificial differences between them and their straight friends (Diamond, 2008; Muehlenhard, 2000; Savin-Williams, 2014). If mainstream straight youth are not required to assume a sexual identity, why should they be obligated to adopt one?

Disclosure

Coming out to others can be a protracted process with many disclosures to make, sometimes stretching throughout one's lifetime. During these times, youths face ongoing decisions regarding whether, when, and how to reveal their sexuality. Although a single-item question that assesses an overall degree of outness has been developed (Wilkerson et al., 2016), the potential audiences and the order in which friends, various family members, new acquaintances, and the "world" are told elicits varying degrees of considerations and techniques, with differential repercussions for the adolescent (Savin-Williams, 2005, 2016b). Should the individual be told face-to-face or by text? Will the person laugh, cry, celebrate, or abuse? Did the person already know or was it a shock?

For most sexual-minority youths, first disclosure occurs several years after coming out to self, although the two can be linked closely in time, even occurring simultaneously. The gap for girls is usually somewhat less than it is for boys. There is also a cohort effect: age of first disclosure – now averaging prior to high school graduation – is several years earlier than in previous generations (Calzo et al., 2011; Drasin et al., 2008; Floyd & Bakeman, 2006; Lucassen et al., 2014; Maguen et al., 2002). This earlier age is likely due to a more inviting, positive cultural context and supportive friendship networks for millennial youth not encountered by previous generations.

The advantages and disadvantages of being in or out of the closet can be profound and likely differ based on a host of factors, including personality characteristics, coping style, mental health, and the immediate environment. For example, Pachankis et al. (2015, p. 897) found that being open was associated with high levels of depression for men but not for women. Once men come out, they "experience discrimination that accompanies gender role violations," causing them increased anxiety and depression. Because women are given more leeway in their gender role expression, being out was not associated with depression. Rather, it was closeted women who were most anxious and depressed. Why? Perhaps because those not out were more likely to be in a heterosexual relationship, which was associated with negative mental health issues. Another explanation, not considered by the authors, is that boys acted out their depression by coming out about their sexuality, whereas depressed girls coped by internalizing their sexuality, keeping it to themselves.

The most common recipient of a first disclosure for both sexes was a best female friend. Next came another gay person, which is now more likely given the larger numbers who are out and hence available to receive a disclosure. A favorite sibling and a straight male best friend were also not uncommon. Parents, extended family members, school counselors, and religious leaders were rarely the first person told. When the object of first disclosure was carefully chosen, the reaction was nearly always positive, even celebratory. Again, there is a cohort effect: today's generation of Internet-consuming young adults routinely considers sexual diversity to be normative and thus typically nonplussed when friends come out to them (Savin-Williams 2005, 2016b). Friends frequently progress quickly from mild surprise or amused confirmation to support – perhaps with resolute determination to find a sexual or romantic partner for their friend.

Nonetheless, some youths resist disclosing because they fear being known as gay and the length and intensity of this struggle likely depends on their ethnicity, immigrant status, social class, and geographic region. Or, they are capable of concealing their sexuality because of their gender-conforming behavior or appearance; want to avoid hurting or disappointing friends, family, or former dating partners; or are unprepared to irrevocably box themselves in ("What if I later discover I'm not gay?"). The fear of losing friends is a critical argument for not disclosing. Although sexual-minority youths in Salt Lake City had smaller peer networks and some friendship loss, they were as connected with their remaining friends as their straight peers (Diamond & Lucas, 2004). Sexual-minority youths may expect, perhaps realistically or not, the detrimental effects of disclosure such as rejection, verbal harassment, and threats to physical safety (Huebner et al., 2004; Kosciw et al., 2010). This is less true today and indeed, among millennials, not being straight might draw friends, prestige, and hence "gay capital" (Morris, 2017).

Coming out to parents may be one of the last disclosures for sexual-minority youth, not because parents are deemed unimportant but precisely because of their importance. For example, parental disapproval of their son's self-expression, especially if he is insufficiently masculine during his early development, might negatively impact the boy's public self-consciousness. By highlighting their son's failure to act like other boys, parents create *greater* daily anxiety for him (Pachankis & Bernstein, 2012).

Youths who believe they must be certain about their sexuality before they initiate this highly significant disclosure delay coming out to parents. Others fear emotional rejection or financial withdrawal (e.g., no financial support for college). Surprisingly, even gay-affirming parents with gay friends and progressive politics might be among the last to learn about their child's sexuality. Their child might suspect that the parents believe that homosexuality is acceptable for others but not for their son or daughter.

Despite highly publicized instances of abuse, adolescents who disclosed to a parent (the mother was usually first) while living at home seldom faced an ongoing, severely negative response or expulsion – indeed, the clear majority received a neutral or positive response (Samarova et al., 2014; Savin-Williams, 2001c, 2016b). Parents were not always initially thrilled with having a gay child because they feared for the child's physical and medical safety, were concerned about what neighbors would think, or worried that their dreams of grandchildren were dashed. Parental reactions varied from celebration to rejection, but with time most eventually accepted what they had long suspected (Savin-Williams 2001c). Contemporary parents are likely becoming more accepting due to media portrayals of healthy sexual-minority youth, as well as the coming out of media figures, relatives, and friends.

Another method to come out publicly is to openly date someone of one's own sex – an occurrence that is dramatically increasing in today's cohort (Savin-Williams, 2005, 2016b). Sexual-minority youths recruited from gay-oriented organizations did not differ from heterosexual youths in the number of romantic relationships, especially those most out and thus most able to attract potential dating partners (Diamond & Lucas, 2004; also, see review by Connolly & McIsaac, 2009). Nonetheless, they were more likely to fear that they would not find the relationship they wanted, and young men faced obstacles in developing highly intimate same-sex relationships during their teen years, claiming (falsely) that most gay youth want sex rather than relationships (Savin-Williams, 2016b).

Unique challenges, however, confront bisexual youth who, as a group, are more likely than gay/lesbian youth to conceal rather than disclose their sexual status and thus to come out at a later age. If dating a member of the other sex, they might do so as a true expression of their sexuality or to hide their orientation (Schrimshaw et al., 2012). Young adult bisexual men were more likely to conceal their sexuality, not because they were uncertain about their identity or because they failed to accept their identity but because they wanted to avoid the stigmatizing reactions from others (Schrimshaw et al., 2018). Compared to lesbians, bisexual young women were also less apt to disclose their sexuality to others (Rosario et al., 2009). Perhaps because of their young age (14–21 years old) compared to lesbian girls, they had a later onset of first same-sex sexual attractions, arousals, and fantasies; were lower in their certainty, acceptance, and comfort of their sexual identity; possessed less positive attitudes toward homosexuality; were less involved in lesbian social activities; and were less comfortable with others knowing their sexuality.

Other sexual-minority youths, such as foreign nationals, members of conservative racial/ethnic or social class groups, and religious members of orthodox or evangelic religious communities also have unique concerns. For cultural reasons, they may be unable or unwilling to come out to family members; have covert sexual or romantic relationships with same-sex others; and have as their most urgent priority avoiding real or feared social admonishment. Although little is known about these mostly invisible youths, they face unique stressors in coming out to self and others as they reconcile their unacceptable sexuality through the lens of their primary family and social community (Barnes & Meyer, 2012; Dubé & Savin-Williams, 1999; Fisher et al., 2014). Beleaguered, they may be left alone to navigate their sexuality within the context of mostly White, gay subcultures in which the challenges of racism and classism are not acknowledged. For others, having supportive families and communities outweighs the disadvantages of coming out, at least during adolescence and young adulthood.

Despite limited empirical data, developmental psychologists generally believe that disclosing one's sexuality, when appropriately delivered, facilitates personal integrity, identity synthesis, and psychological health and reduces distress, anxiety, depression, and burn out, for both sexes (Juster et al., 2013). It is an act of self-empowerment and authenticity, and is a means for obtaining social support and interpersonal closeness (Legate et al., 2012). Through coming out, sexual-minority youth learn stigma management and develop strategies for coping with stressful encounters related to a marginalized identity. The age and conditions under which the benefits of disclosure outweigh the dangers are unknown. If the context is one in which a youth feels autonomous and supported, then the potential value of coming out is enhanced, "as individuals who disclosed more tended to experience greater wellness" (Legate et al., 2012, p. 150).

Self-Acceptance and Synthesis

Considered by many to be the final developmental milestones, few studies assess either sexual-identity acceptance or its synthesis with other aspects of personal identity among sexual-minority youth. Most likely, they can be achieved at any point in the life course – or never. Those who achieve synthesis recognize the importance of their sexuality but do not experience it as all-consuming or over-arching; it is simply one of many aspects of the self.

Considerable research supports the perspective that contemporary sexual-minority youth are as content with their lives as are heterosexual youth. For example, the clear majority of sexual-minority youths felt anywhere from indifferent to very good about their sexuality and less than 10 percent expressed a desire to be straight. If given the option, most would not take a magical pill to turn them straight. Despite public attitudes, sexual orientation is not strongly or directly related to quality of life or positive health indicators such as self-esteem or life satisfaction (Becker et al., 2014; Bostwick et al., 2010; Diamond & Lucas, 2004; Horowitz et al., 2001; Juster et al., 2013 Savin-Williams, 2005, 2016b). Most are content with their sexual and romantic orientations and do not define themselves solely in relationship to those orientations. Whether youth attach a sexual label to themselves is less important than acquiring the ability to accept and integrate their sexual and romantic selves with other essential elements of their life. Doing so enhances a sense of authenticity.

The Millennial Revolution

We have witnessed a proliferation of cultural recognition, positive social environments, and acceptance of sexual-minority youth (Dickson et al., 2013; Drasin et al., 2008; Savin-Williams, 2016b). One consequence has been an increase in the diversity and representative sampling of youth willing to participate in scientific research. This has allowed developmental scientists to investigate a plurality of young lives, a variety of developmental trajectories and outcomes, and nuanced snapshots of sexual-minority lives.

With these dramatic transformations, sexual-minority youth have been emancipated from their generational past (Cohler & Hammack, 2007). They have matured in a society that has become more accepting of sexual diversity and less tolerant of sexual prejudice (Pew Research Center, 2013; see Clements & Field, 2014, for UK data). For example, millennial youth frequently forego sexual confusion, know who they are prior to engaging in sex, and believe they are as "normal" as their straight friends (Savin-Williams, 2016b). Indeed, some have acquired "gay capital," which "inverts traditional understandings of gay youth as vulnerable and victimized due to their sexual minority status by showing that having a gay identity can act as a form of privilege in social fields where homophobia has diminished or disappeared" (Morris, 2017, p. 19 online). From this perspective, sexual-minority youth are not victims or survivors but victors. Indeed, some straight-identified youth now proclaim a "little bit of gayness" as a sign of identification with what they hold to be prestigious and advantageous (Savin-Williams, 2017).

Of course, not all sexual-minority youth have flourished as they continue to struggle with accepting their sexuality and its psychological and social burden well into adulthood. However, the proportion who experience a troubled life because of their same-sex sexuality is decreasing, almost certainly because their generation is far more comfortable with sexual and gender diversity (Savin-Williams, 2016b).

Conclusion

Although contemporary youth are at the vanguard in redefining themselves in capturing the essence of their sexual and romantic selves, academic research has not always kept pace. Researchers have been more conservative than sexual-minority youth in four critical ways.

1. Narrowly delineating sexual-minority youth by describing them solely based on their sexual attraction, sexual behavior, or sexual identity while ignoring other indicators such as sexual fantasy, nonintercourse sexual contact, infatuation, gender expressions, and romantic desires.
2. Defining sexual orientation categorically, labeling individuals as if there were only three types (straight, bisexual, gay/lesbian) rather than as points along a sexual/romantic spectrum. Sexual and romantic development is a continuously distributed individual characteristic.
3. Including research participants who are not representative or typical of sexual-minority youth and thus failing to recognize the inadequacy of prior research that characterized *gay* youth as a caricature progressing down a precarious and invariant developmental course (for critiques, see Savin-Williams, 2005 and Waidzunas, 2012). Whereas some youth navigate their lives with difficulty and, too often, tragically, others do so with remarkable "strength, courage, self-determination and the dignity with which they live their lives all-too-often in the setting of a disapproving culture or environment" (Garofalo, 2014, p. 200). That "disapproving culture" is shrinking rapidly.
4. Failing to collect data that highlights the normalization of sexual-minority youth, their positive attributes, and their diversity across populations and communities.

Developmental scientists are beginning to emphasize the *ordinariness* of sexual-minority youth as they discover that most are typical adolescents in their developmental trajectories, with positive as well as negative outcomes (Hammack, 2005; Harden, 2014; Morris, 2017; Morris et al., 2014; Savin-Williams, 2005, 2016b, 2017; Taulke-Johnson, 2008; Tolman & McClelland, 2011). Although sexual-minority children and adolescents undoubtedly face unique challenges and opportunities, similar to heterosexuals, the key elements for successfully traversing their lives include: "belonging to a community, creating families of choice, forging strong connections with others, serving as positive role models, developing empathy and compassion, living authentically and honestly, gaining personal insight and sense of self, involvement in social justice and activism, freedom from gender-specific roles, exploring sexuality and relationships, and enjoying egalitarian relationships" (Riggle et al., 2008, p. 210). That is, although sexual-minority youth have unique developmental trajectories, in large part because of their same-sex sexual and romantic selves, in most respects they are *typical youth* with similar developmental milestones and outcomes as straight youth.

References

Alanko, K., Santtila, P., Witting, K. et al. (2010). Common Genetic Effects on Childhood Gender Atypical Behavior and Adult Sexual Orientation. *Archives of Sexual Behavior*, *39*, 81–92.

Bailey, J. M. & Zucker, K. J. (1995). Childhood Sex-Typed Behavior and Sexual Orientation: A Conceptual Analysis and Quantitative Review. *Developmental Psychology*, *31*, 43–55.

Barnes, D. M. & Meyer, I. H. (2012). Religious Affiliation, Internalized Homophobia, and Mental Health in Lesbians, Gay Men, and Bisexuals. *American Journal of Orthopsychiatry*, *82*, 505–515.

Beaver, K. M., Connolly, E. J., Schwartz, J. A. Boutwell, B. B., Barnes, J. C., & Nedelec, J. L. (2016). Sexual Orientation and Involvement in Nonviolent and Violent Delinquent Behaviors: Findings from the National Longitudinal Study of Adolescent to Adult Health. *Archives of Sexual Behavior*, *45*, 1759–1769.

Becker, M., Cortina, K. S., Tsai, Y. M., & Eccles, J. S. (2014). Sexual Orientation, Psychological Well-Being, and Mental Health: A Longitudinal Analysis from Adolescence to Young Adulthood. *Psychology of Sexual Orientation and Gender Diversity*, *1*, 132–145.

Bell, A. P., Weinberg, M. S., & Hammersmith, S. K. (1981). *Sexual Preference: Its Development in Men and Women*. Bloomington: Indiana University Press.

Bos, H. & Sandfort, T. (2015). Gender Nonconformity, Sexual Orientation, and Dutch Adolescents' Relationship with Peers. *Archives of Sexual Behavior*, *44*, 1269–1279. doi:10.1007/s10508-014-0461-5.

Bostwick, W. B., Boyd, C. J., Hughes, T. L., & McCabe, S. E. (2010). Dimensions of Sexual Orientation and the Prevalence of Mood and Anxiety Disorders in the United States. *American Journal of Public Health*, *100*, 468–475.

Calzo, J. P., Antonucci, T. C., Mays, V. M., & Cochran, S. D. (2011). Retrospective Recall of Sexual Orientation Identity Development among Gay, Lesbian, and Bisexual Adults. *Developmental Psychology*, *47*, 1658–1673.

Carrillo, H. & Fontdevila, J. (2011). Rethinking Sexual Initiation: Pathways to Identity Formation among Gay and Bisexual Mexican Male Youth. *Archives of Sexual Behavior*, *40*, 1241–1254.

Clements, B. & Field, C. D. (2014). Public Opinion toward Homosexuality and Gay Rights in Great Britain. *Public Opinion Quarterly*, *78*, 523–547.

Cohen, K. M. (2002). Relationships among Childhood Sex-Atypical Behavior, Spatial Ability, Handedness, and Sexual Orientation in Men. *Archives of Sexual Behavior* 31, 129–143.

Cohen-Bendahan, C. C. C., van de Beek, C., & Berenbaum, S. A. (2005). Prenatal Sex Hormone Effects on Child and Adult Sex-Typed Behavior: Methods and Findings. *Neuroscience & Biobehavioral Reviews*, *29*, 353–384.

Cohler, B. J. & Hammack, P. L. (2007). The Psychological World of the Gay Teenager: Social Change, Narrative, and "Normality." *Journal of Youth and Adolescence*, *36*, 47–59.

Connolly, J. A. & McIsaac, C. (2009). Romantic Relationships in Adolescence. In Lerner, R. M. & Steinberg, L. (Eds.), *Handbook of Adolescent Psychology*, 3rd edn. (104–151). New York: Wiley.

Copen, C. E., Chandra, A., & Febo-Vazquez, I. (2016). Sexual Behavior, Sexual Attraction, and Sexual Orientation among Adults Aged 18–44 in the United States: Data from the 2011–2013 National Survey of Family Growth. *National Health Statistics Reports*, 88, 1–14.

D'Augelli, T. R., Grossman, A. H., & Starks, M. T. (2008). Gender Atypicality and Sexual Orientation Development among Lesbian, Gay, and Bisexual Youth: Prevalence, Sex Differences, and Parental Responses. *Journal of Gay & Lesbian Mental Health 12*, 121–143.

Diamond, L. M. (2008). *Sexual Fluidity: Understanding Women's Love and Desire*. Cambridge, MA: Harvard University Press.

Diamond, L. M. & Lucas, S. (2004). Sexual-Minority and Heterosexual Youths' Peer Relationships: Experiences, Expectations, and Implications for Well-Being. *Journal of Research on Adolescence 14*, 313–340.

Diamond, L. M. & Savin-Williams, R. C. (2009). Adolescent Sexuality. In Lerner, R. M. & Steinberg, L. (Eds.), *Handbook of Adolescent Psychology, 3rd edn* (479–523). New York: Wiley.

Dickson, N., van Roode, T., Cameron, C., & Paul, C. (2013). Stability and Change in Same-Sex Attraction, Experience, and Identity by Sex and Age in a New Zealand Birth Cohort. *Archives of Sexual Behavior*, *42*, 753–763.

Doyle, D. M. & Molix, L. (2016). Disparities in Social Health by Sexual Orientation and the Etiologic Role of Self-Reported Discrimination. *Archives of Sexual Behavior*, *45*, 1317–1327.

Drasin, H., Beals, K. P., Elliott, M. N., Lever, J., Klein, D. J., & Schuster, M. A. (2008). Age Cohort Differences in the Developmental Milestones of Gay Men. *Journal of Homosexuality*, *54*, 381–399.

Dubé, E. M. (2000). The Role of Sexual Behavior in the Identification Process of Gay And Bisexual Males. *Journal of Sex Research*, *37*, 123–132.

Dubé, E. M. & Savin-Williams, R. C. (1999). Sexual Identity Development among Ethnic Sexual-Minority Male Youths. *Developmental Psychology*, *35*, 1389–1399.

Fisher, C. M., Irwin, J. A., & Coleman, J. D. (2014). LGBT Health in the Midlands: A Rural/Urban Comparison of Basic Health Indicators. *Journal of Homosexuality*, *61*, 1062–1090.

Floyd, F. J. & Bakeman, R. (2006). Coming-Out across the Life Course: Implications of Age and Historical Context. *Archives of Sexual Behavior*, *35*, 287–296.

Garofalo, R. (2014). A Personal Reflection on the History of Population-Based Research with Sexual Minority Youths. *American Journal of Public Health*, *104*, 198–200.

Golombok, S., Rust, J., Zervoulis, K., Golding, J., & Hines, M. (2012). Continuity in Sex-Typed Behavior from Preschool to Adolescence: A Longitudinal Population Study of Boys and Girls Aged 3–13 Years. *Archives of Sexual Behavior*, *41*, 591–597.

Grellert, E. A., Newcomb, M. D., & Bentler, P. M. (1982). Childhood Play Activities of Male and Female Homosexuals and Heterosexuals. *Archives of Sexual Behavior*, *11*, 451–478.

Hammack, P. L. (2005). The Life Course Development of Human Sexual Orientation: An Integrative Paradigm. *Human Development*, *48*, 267–290.

Harden, K. P. (2014). A Sex-Positive Framework for Research on Adolescent Sexuality. *Perspectives on Psychological Science*, *9*, 455–469.

Heywood, W., Patrick, K., Pitts, M., & Mitchell, A. (2016) "Dude, I'm Seventeen . . . It's Okay Not to Have Sex by This Age": Feelings, Reasons, Pressures, and Intentions Reported by Adolescents Who Have Not Had Sexual Intercourse. *Journal of Sex Research*, *53*, 1207–1214.

Horowitz, S. M., Weis, D. L., & Laflin, M. T. (2001). Differences between Sexual Orientation Behavior Groups and Social Background, Quality Of Life, and Health Behaviors. *Journal of Sex Research*, *38*, 205–218.

Huebner, D. M., Rebchook, G. M., & Kegeles, S. M. (2004). Experiences of Harassment, Discrimination, and Physical Violence among Young Gay and Bisexual Men. *American Journal of Public Health*, *94*, 1200–1203.

Josephs, L. (2015). How Children Learn about Sex: A Cross-Species and Cross-Cultural Analysis. *Archives of Sexual Behavior*, *44*, 1059–1069.

Juster, R. P. Smith, N. G., Ouellet, E., Sindi, S., & Lupiendoi, S. J. (2013). Sexual Orientation and Disclosure in Relation to Psychiatric Symptoms, Diurnal Cortisol, and Allostatic Load. *Psychosomatic Medicine*, *75*, 103–116.

Kosciw, J. G., Greytak, E. A., Diaz, E. M., & Bartkiewicz, M. J. (2010). *The 2009 National School Climate Survey: The Experiences of Lesbian, Gay, Bisexual and Transgender Youth in Our Nation's Schools*. New York: Gay, Lesbian & Straight Education Network.

Kuyper, L., Fernee, H., & Keuzenkamp, S. (2016). A Comparative Analysis of a Community and General Sample of Lesbian, Gay, and Bisexual Individuals. *Archives of Sexual Behavior. 45*, 683–693.

Lea, T., de Wit, J., & Reynolds, R. (2014). Minority Stress in Lesbian, Gay, and Bisexual Young Adults in Australia: Associations with Psychological Distress, Suicidality, and Substance Use. *Archives of Sexual Behavior*, *43*, 1571–1578.

Legate, N., Ryan, R. M., & Weinstein, N. (2012). Is Coming Out Always a "Good Thing"? Exploring the Relations of Autonomy Support, Outness, and Wellness for Lesbian, Gay, and Bisexual Individuals. *Social Psychological and Personality Science*, *3*, 145–152.

LeVay, S. (2016). *Gay, Straight, and the Reason Why: The Science of Sexual Orientation, 2nd edn*. New York: Oxford University Press.

Levine, J. (2002). *Harmful to Minors: The Perils of Protecting Children from Sex*. Minneapolis: University of Minnesota Press.

Lippa, R. A., & Tan, F. D. (2001). Does Culture Moderate the Relationship between Sexual Orientation and Gender-Related Personality Traits? *Cross-Cultural Research*, *35*, 65–87.

Lucassen, M. F. G., Clark, T. C., Denny, S. J., et al. (2014). What Has Changed from 2001 to 2012 for Sexual Minority Youth in New Zealand? *Journal of Paediatrics and Child Health*, *51*, 410–418.

Maguen, S., Floyd, F. J., Bakeman, R., & Armistead, L. (2002). Developmental Milestones and Disclosure of Sexual Orientation among Gay, Lesbian, and Bisexual Youths. *Applied Developmental Psychology*, *23*, 219–233.

McClelland, S. I., Rubin, J. D., & Bauermeister, J. A. (2016). "I Liked Girls and I Thought They Were Pretty": Initial Memories of Same-Sex Attraction in Young Lesbian and Bisexual Women. *Archives of Sexual Behavior*, *45*, 1375–1389.

McClintock, M. K. & Herdt, G. (1996). Rethinking Puberty: The Development of Sexual Attraction. *Current Directions in Psychological Science*, *5*, 178–183.

Morris, M. (2017). 'Gay Capital' in Undergraduate Friendship Networks: An Intersectional Analysis of Class, Masculinity and Decreased Homophobia. *Journal of Social and Personal Relationships*. doi:10.1177/0265407517705737.

Morris, M., McCormack, M., & Anderson, E. (2014). The Changing Experiences of Bisexual Male Adolescents, *Gender and Education*, *26*, 397–413.

Muehlenhard, C. L. (2000). Categories and Sexuality. *Journal of Sex Research*, *37*, 101–107.

Pachankis, J. E. & Bernstein, L. B. (2012). An Etiological Model of Anxiety in Young Gay Men: From Early Stress to Public Self-Consciousness. *Psychology of Men and Masculinity*, *13*, 107–122.

Pachankis, J. E., Cochran, S. D., & Mays, V. M. (2015). The Mental Health of Sexual Minority Adults In and Out of the Closet: A Population-Based Study. *Journal of Consulting and Clinical Psychology*, *83*, 890–901.

Peplau, L. A. (2003). Human Sexuality: How Do Men and Women Differ? *Current Directions in Psychological Science* 12, 37–40.

Pew Research Center (2013). *A Survey of LGBT Americans: Attitudes, Experiences and Values in Changing Times*. Washington, DC: Pew Research Center.

Remafedi, G. (1987). Adolescent Homosexuality: Psychosocial and Medical Implications. *Pediatrics*, *79*, 331–337.

Rieger, G., Linsenmeier, J. A. W., Gygax, L., & Bailey, J. M. (2008). Sexual Orientation and Childhood Gender Nonconformity: Evidence from Home Videos. *Developmental Psychology*, *44*, 46–58.

Riggle, E. D. B., Whitman, J. S., Olson, A., Rostosky, S. S., & Strong, S. (2008). The Positive Aspects of Being a Lesbian or Gay Man. *Professional Psychology: Research and Practice*, *39*, 210–217.

Roesler, T. & Deisher, R. W. (1972). Youthful Male Homosexuality: Homosexual Experience and the Process of Developing Homosexual Identity in Males Aged 16 to 22 Years. *JAMA* 219, 1018–1023.

Rosario, M., Meyer-Bahlburg, H. F. L., Hunter, J., Exner, T. M., Gwadz, M., & Keller, A. M. (1996). The Psychosexual Development of Urban Lesbian, Gay, and Bisexual Youths. *Journal of Sex Research* 33, 113–126.

Rosario, M., Schrimshaw, E. W., Hunter, J., & Levy-Warren, A. (2009). The Coming-Out Process of Young Lesbian and Bisexual Women: Are There Butch/Femme

Differences in Sexual Identity Development? *Archives of Sexual Behavior*, *38*, 34–49.

Rule, N. O. & Alaei, R. (2016). Gaydar: The Perception of Sexual Orientation from Subtle Cues. *Current Directions in Psychological Science*, *25*, 444–448.

Rust, P. C. R. (2002). Bisexuality: The State of the Union. *Annual Review of Sex Research* 13, 180–240.

Saghir, M. T. & Robbins, E. (1973). *Male and Female Homosexuality*. Baltimore: Williams & Wilkins.

Samarova, V., Shilo, G., & Diamond, G. M. (2014). Changes in Youths' Perceived Parental Acceptance of Their Sexual Minority Status over Time. *Journal of Research on Adolescence*, *24*, 681–688.

Savin-Williams, R. C. (2001a). Suicide Attempts among Sexual-Minority Youth: Population and Measurement Issues. *Journal of Consulting and Clinical Psychology*, *69*, 983–991.

(2001b). A Critique of Research on Sexual-Minority Youths. *Journal of Adolescence*, *24*, 5–13.

(2001c). *"Mom, Dad. I'm Gay." How Families Negotiate Coming Out*. Washington, DC: American Psychological Association.

(2005). *The New Gay Teenager*. Cambridge, MA: Harvard University Press.

(2014). The New Sexual-Minority Teenager: Freedom from Traditional Notions of Sexual Identity. In Kaufman, J. S. & Powell, D. A. (Eds.), *The Meaning of Sexual Identity in the Twenty-first century* (5–20). Newcastle: Cambridge Scholars.

(2016a). Sexual Orientation: Categories or Continuum? Commentary on Bailey et al. (2016). *Psychological Science in the Public Interest*, *17*, 37–44.

(2016b). *Becoming Who I Am: Young Men on Being Gay*. Cambridge, MA: Harvard University Press.

(2017). *Mostly Straight: Sexuality Fluidity among Men*. Cambridge, MA: Harvard University Press.

Savin-Williams, R. C., Cash, B. M., McCormack, M., & Rieger, G. (2017). Gay, Mostly Gay, or Bisexual Leaning Gay? An Exploratory Study Distinguishing Gay Sexual Orientations among Young Men. *Archives of Sexual Behavior*, *46*, 265–272.

Savin-Williams, R. C. & Diamond, L. M. (2000). Sexual Identity Trajectories among Sexual-Minority Youths: Gender Comparisons. *Archives of Sexual Behavior* 29, 419–440.

Savin-Williams, R. C., Joyner, K., & Rieger, G. (2012). Prevalence and Stability of Self-Reported Sexual Orientation Identity during Young Adulthood. *Archives of Sexual Behavior*, *41*, 103–110.

Savin-Williams, R. C. & Vrangalova, Z. (2013). Mostly Heterosexual as a Distinct Sexual Orientation Group: A Systematic Review of the Empirical Evidence. *Developmental Review*, *33*, 58–88.

Schrimshaw, E. W., Downing, M. J., & Cohn, D. J. (2018). Reasons for Non-Disclosure of Sexual Orientation among Behaviorally Bisexual Men: Non-Disclosure as Stigma Management. *Archives of Sexual Behavior*, 47(1), 219–233.

Schrimshaw, E. W., Siegel, K., Downing, M. J., & Parsons, J. T. (2012). Disclosure and Concealment of Sexual Orientation and the Mental Health of Non-Gay-Identified,

Behaviorally Bisexual Men. *Journal of Consulting and Clinical Psychology, 81*, 141–153.

Semon, T. L., Hsu, K. J., Rosenthal, A. M., & Bailey, J. M. (2017). Bisexual Phenomena among Gay-Identified Men. *Archives of Sexual Behavior*, *46*, 237–245.

Silva, C., Chu, C., Monahan, K. R., & Joiner, T. E. (2016). Suicide Risk among Sexual Minority College Students: A Mediated Moderation Model of Sex and Perceived Burdensomeness. *Psychology of Sexual Orientation and Gender Diversity*, *2*, 22–33.

Silva, T. (2018). "Helpin' a Buddy Out:" Perceptions of Identity and Behaviour among Rural Straight Men That Have Sex with Each Other. *Sexualities*, *21*, 68–89. doi:10.1177/1363460716678564.

Smiler, A. P. (2016). *Dating and Sex: A Guide for the Twenty-First Century Teen Boy.* Washington, DC: American Psychological Association.

Stief, M. (2017). The Sexual Orientation and Gender Presentation of Hijra, Kothi, and Panthi in Mumbai, India. *Archives of Sexual Behavior*, *46*, 73–85.

Taulke-Johnson, R. (2008). Moving beyond Homophobia, Harassment and Intolerance: Gay Male University Students' Alternative Narratives. *Discourse: Studies in the Cultural Politics of Education*, *29*, 121–133.

Thomeer, M. B. & Reczek, C. (2016). Happiness and Sexual Minority Status. *Archives of Sexual Behavior*, *45*, 1745–1758.

Tolman, D. L. & McClelland, S. I. (2011). Normative Sexuality Development in Adolescence: A Decade in Review, 2000–2009. *Journal of Research on Adolescence*, *21*, 242–255.

Troiden, R. R. (1979). Becoming Homosexual: A Model of Gay Identity Acquisition. *Psychiatry* 42, 362–373.

(1989). The Formation of Homosexual Identities. *Journal of Homosexuality*, *17*, 43–73.

Vaccaro, A. (2009). Intergenerational Perceptions, Similarities and Differences: A Comparative Analysis of Lesbian, Gay, and Bisexual Millennial Youth with Generation X and Baby Boomers. *Journal of LGBT Youth*, *6*, 113–134.

Vrangalova, Z., & Savin-Williams, R. C (2010). Correlates of Same-Sex Sexuality in Heterosexually-Identified Young Adults. *Journal of Sex Research*, *47*, 92–102.

Wadsworth, L. P., & Hayes-Skelton, S. A. (2015). Differences among Lesbian, Gay, Bisexual, and Heterosexual Individuals and Those Who Reported an Other Identity on an Open-Ended Response on Levels of Social Anxiety. *Psychology of Sexual Orientation and Gender Diversity*, *2*, 181–187.

Waidzunas, T. (2012). Young, Gay, and Suicidal: Dynamic Nominalism and the Process of Defining a Social Problem with Statistics. *Science, Technology, & Human Values*, *37*, 199–225.

Walton, M. T., Lykins, A. D., & Bhullar, N. (2016). Beyond Heterosexual, Bisexual, and Homosexual: A Diversity in Sexual Identity Expression. *Archives of Sexual Behavior*, *45*, 1591–1597.

Wilkerson, J. M., Noor, S. W., Galos, D. L., & Rosser, B. R. S. (2016). Correlates of a Single-Item Indicator Versus a Multi-Item Scale of Outness about Same-Sex Attraction. *Archives of Sexual Behavior*, *45*, 1269–1277.

Yu, L., Winter, S., & Xie, D. (2010). The Child Play Behavior and Activity Questionnaire: A Parent-Report Measure of Childhood Gender-Related Behavior in China. *Archives of Sexual Behavior*, *39*, 807–815.

9 Bad Choices

How Neoliberal Ideology Disguises Social Injustice in the Sexual Lives of Youth

Laina Y. Bay-Cheng

Sexuality education in the United States is pursued on multiple fronts (e.g., in schools, online, through public service announcements) as a campaign on behalf of youth's current and future well-being, sexually and otherwise. It largely consists of urging, instructing, and warning them to make good choices and to avoid bad ones. However well-intentioned these efforts may be, they rest on the shaky foundation that individuals have the power to direct their life courses through choice alone. This faith is fueled in part by a neoliberal ideology that poses individuals as powerful agents who compete in a post-prejudice meritocracy and are held back only by their own deficits and mistakes. This narrative of unencumbered self-determination holds certain appeal, but it is a fiction for almost all youth; not because youth lack the agency or ability to make good choices but because they have such poor ones to pick from. In the current chapter, I argue that the rhetoric of good choices masks the reality of bad circumstances for many youth. This includes normative and material constraints that render many sexual choices illusory or impossible, thus little more than just "rights on paper" (Nussbaum, 2000, p. 54). I draw on Nussbaum's (see also Sen, 1999) *capabilities approach* to demonstrate the ways in which the neoliberal prescription of good sexual choices is fundamentally at odds with a social justice orientation to youth and youth sexuality.

Prescribing Choice: Neoliberal Ideology

Simple refrains premised on simplistic logic dominate our directives to youth about their current and future sexual well-being: make good choices and you'll be successful; make bad ones and you'll be sorry. There are a number of rhetorical substitutes and stand-ins for "good" choices. These might be morally, legally, or religiously right, responsible, healthy, safe, smart, informed, and so on. One widely used comprehensive sexuality education curriculum takes the injunction, "Making Proud Choices!" as its title. The parameters of what constitutes "good" vary according to the ideological bent of a program, but both comprehensive and abstinence-only programs offer such prescriptions. For the latter, this might entail abstinence from all partnered sexual activity or only from certain behaviors, whereas the former might sanction protected sexual activity as long as it occurs in a romantic, monogamous, long-term relationship. Variations in phrasing and boundaries aside, that there *are* good choices and that these are in an individual youth's control (and consequently are a matter of personal responsibility) is never in doubt. Also unquestioned is that the right choices will deliver desired outcomes: happiness, love, satisfaction, health, and success. Good sexual choices are good life choices. As averred on the abstinence-only website, www.mychoice2wait.org: "By choosing not to participate in at-risk behaviors, you are choosing FREEDOM"; and "It is ultimately your choice to protect your future" (for in-depth analyses of sexuality education discourses, see Fields, 2008; Jones, 2011; Kendall, 2012; Lesko, 2010).

Sexuality education's prescription of good sexual choices taps the cardinal principles of neoliberalism. In the United States, neoliberalism only recently surfaced in public discourse, though it now figures prominently in explanations of the dynamics and outcomes 2016's US presidential election and Brexit (e.g., Giroux, 2016; Klein, 2016; Norton, 2016). Neoliberalism refers to a body of policies aimed at the deregulation of all economic and social systems (e.g., trade and labor laws; social welfare programs). It is fueled by claims regarding the value – in both financial and philosophical terms – of free market competition. While the policy arm of neoliberalism is most commonly recognized, it also operates ideologically. Indeed, the dismantling of formal protections and safety nets was eased by an accompanying discourse championing self-interested liberty and ambition. Individual choice, as an expression of liberty, is at the core of neoliberal ideology, as is personal responsibility for any and all consequences of one's choices (Brown, 2003). Even beyond a means to specific ends, neoliberalism construes choice as a means to personhood. We are constituted and recognized as fully fledged agents and humans through the act of choosing and what we choose (Kelly, 2001). It is through our choice that we make our fortunes (or failures), our lives, and our selves. Individual choice thus functions almost as a superpower, creating self-determining agents who can be and have anything we desire given the requisite vision and fortitude.

Neoliberal ideology imbues choice with significant power, whether to confer rewards or to wreak havoc. It follows from this that the ability to distinguish good choices from bad ones and to follow through with the former are indispensable skills. Yet youth, depicted as lacking discipline, forethought, and caution (Lesko, 2001), are considered categorically inept in this regard. Consequently, the preponderance of youth sexuality interventions concentrate on instructing young people to become better choosers, both more discerning and more disciplined. Sexuality education campaigns train youth to become cost–benefit analysts and rational actors: by disseminating information about sexual functioning, risk-taking, and protective measures; by incorporating exercises to hone sexual planning, negotiation, and refusal skills; and by prompting youth to envision future lives of professional, material, and relational success to remind them of the need and reason to make the right sexual choices (e.g., Becker & Barth, 2000; Herrman & Waterhouse, 2012; see also, Elliott, 2014; Fields, 2008; Froyum, 2010; Kendall, 2012 Lesko, 2010).

Dominant constructions of youth also relegate them to a liminal status in which their worth is contingent, existing only in the form of future potential: who they might one day become or what they might one day have to offer (Ballet et al., 2011; Kelly, 2001; Lesko, 2001). Thus, policies and programs take as their goal the schooling of young people in disciplined and strategic decision making so that they do not squander their future potential on immediate gratification. In doing so, these approaches work to form youth not only into responsible sexual citizens but also into ideal neoliberal subjects who will strive, compete, and be duly rewarded.

This notion that youth can follow a sexual recipe for life success is reminiscent of the magical thinking underlying the "pan-optimism" (Lesko, 2010, p. 290) that sexual knowledge is an antidote for vulnerability or the prescription of a "prophylactic of talk" (Fields, 2008, p. 68) as a safeguard against sexual risk. Just as Lesko and Fields critique interventions aimed only at knowledge or communication skills, targeting decision making neglects the powerful interlocked forces that lie far beyond an individual's control. Interventions centered on altering youths' behavior, as though to protect them from themselves, pretend that an individual's impulsivity and shortsightedness are the primary threats to one's future success, not hostile, inequitable, and unreliable social and material conditions. This view, which focuses intently on developmental deficits, while ignoring contextual impediments, fuels the "responsibilization" of youth (Kelly, 2001; see also Elliott, 2014; Fields, 2008; Froyum, 2010; Goodkind, 2009). This echoes neoliberal ideology's denial of social injustice and its framing of inequalities as equitable (i.e., as a fair reflection of one's effort and talent, with a dose of arbitrary luck), with winners earning their rewards and losers deserving their struggles. According to this logic, the reasonable starting point for reducing or eliminating inequalities is to help individuals work harder, work better, and make the right choices.

Despite its appealing pretense of free, self-making agents, the rhetorical refrain of good choices rings immediately and unmistakably hollow in the context of youths' social, material, and legislative realities (Fine & McClelland, 2007; McClelland & Frost, 2014). Far from being able to choose their freedom, most young people have little more than "rights on paper," supposed choices that actually are imaginary, impossible, or imposed: (1) *Just World Choices* that make-believe a level playing field among equal competitors; (2) *Cinderella Choices* that are technically available but functionally impracticable; (3) the double bind of *Catch-22 Choices*; (4) normative and divisive *In-or-Out Choices*; and (5) *Forced Choices*, compelled by need and deprivation. This critical delineation of the options actually available to young people counters the neoliberal premise of so many sexuality education campaigns, that good choices will make you free (whether from danger or to succeed). Instead, they substantiate Brown's (2006) observation that "the choosing subject and the governed subject are far from opposites" (p. 705). Dissecting the variety and viability of options available to young people makes it possible to trace their sexual vulnerability back not to the bad choices they make but to the bad choices they are offered.

Just World Choices

Neoliberal ideology in general and its rhetoric surrounding choice in particular takes the existence of a just world for granted: that we live in post-prejudice meritocracy in which individuals are makers of their own fate and that, as Mychoice2wait.org stated, "It is ultimately your choice to protect your future." These convictions were explicit in the sexuality education delivered to young women in one US state's juvenile justice system. The program was an amalgam of the *Power of Choice* and *Big Decisions* curricula and included sessions entitled, "Creating the Future You Want" and "How to Make Your Choices Stick" (Herrman & Waterhouse, 2012). The pretense that one's future is a product of will and vision is repudiated by the unbridged gap between aspired ends and accessible means for marginalized youth, and by evidence of slowing social mobility and growing income inequality (Mitnik et al., 2016; Smeeding, 2016). College costs are rising; alternatives, such as for-profit vocational training programs have been exposed as costly and often fraudulent (Holland & DeLuca, 2016); fair wage and stable employment options are disappearing; and discriminatory and exclusionary practices in schools and workplaces continue unabated. Few youth are in the position to "create the futures they want," a proposal that is particularly absurd when addressed to those contending with compounded and complex disadvantages, as in the case mentioned earlier of girls involved in the juvenile justice or child welfare systems (e.g., Becker & Barth, 2000; Herrman & Waterhouse, 2012; for a critique of neoliberal self-improvement discourses in practice with young women, see Goodkind, 2009). To suggest that it is in one's power to "make choices stick" blatantly ignores other countervailing forces in youths' lives. As a focus group participant pointedly noted, when it comes to refusing unwanted sex and messages that girls just need to be more assertive and vocal: "[I]f that were the case, that a guy would believe 'no,' then there wouldn't be those rapes that you hear about. There wouldn't be all that stuff. Obviously 'no' doesn't mean 'no' to guys" (Bay-Cheng et al., 2011, p. 1183).

Nevertheless, sexuality educators repeatedly invoke scripted platitudes that, if you apply yourself to the right goals and resist the wrong temptations, you can be anything you want to be. The notion that the only thing youth have to fear is their own poor judgment reverberates throughout sexuality education campaigns' cautionary tales: people who drank too much (e.g., a public service announcement by the Pennsylvania Liquor Control Board was sharply criticized as attributing sexual assault to young women's drinking; Heldman, 2013); people who trusted too much or trusted the wrong person (e.g., a public service announcement by the Washington, DC Campaign to Prevent Teen Pregnancy showed a young African-American baby with the tagline, "He told his last baby mama he'd stay with her too."); people who got caught up in the moment and lost sight of their goals (e.g., a Candies Foundation public service announcement featuring Bristol Palin with the tagline, "I never thought I would be a statistic."). Victim-blaming discourses are typically and rightly critiqued, but just as important is how those who are victim-blamed and slut-shamed – often girls and women – are used as scapegoats and decoys for system injustice (Bay-Cheng, 2015). This supposes that lapses in judgment and discipline are the sources of their vulnerability (and targets for remediation), not institutionalized and interlocked forms of oppression. Yet, *Just World Choices* retain their allure for adult instructors and youth audiences alike, permitting us to maintain the psychological buffer of seeing ourselves as makers of our own destinies and our environment as the best and fairest of all possible worlds (Jost et al., 2004).

Cinderella Choices

A pillar of just world beliefs is the technical permissibility and theoretical availability of options: abortion is legal; minors in most states are entitled to sexual and reproductive health services; and condoms are sold in any number of stores or are provided for free at clinics. Just as Cinderella's stepmother does not absolutely forbid her from going to the ball, young people are not prohibited from sexual health care. Presumably, if they want something badly enough and are willing to take the necessary steps, it is theirs for the taking. And if they do not, then the responsibility is also theirs, and theirs alone (as in the cautionary tales discussed in the previous section). The illusion that a panoply of sexual choices are widely and freely available is propped up by popular media (e.g., Sisson and Kimport [2016] found that TV shows minimize barriers to abortion) and political rhetoric (e.g., Trump's simplistic statement in a television interview [Stahl, 2016] during the 2016 presidential campaign that women may just "have to go to another state" for abortion services). In fact, numerous and substantive obstacles make many forms of sexual health care unfeasible. Youths' access to sexual and reproductive health care may be prohibited or predicated on parental permission. Those living in under-resourced homes and communities may not have the money, time, or transportation to obtain them. Many may be functionally barred from services if they live with various disabilities and health conditions, with varying language and literacy abilities, and/or facing stigma and sanctions against their minority status(es) (e.g., sexual/gender identity expression; citizenship status; racial, ethnic, or religious identity; Fine & McClelland, 2007; for a useful analysis of how social policy frames sexual rights and well-being, see McClelland & Frost, 2014).

In the case of abortion, it may be federally permissible but made practically impossible for many women by financial cost, geographic distance, work schedules, caregiving responsibilities, stigmatizing or hostile environments, convoluted and opaque policies, and a slew of pending and enacted contingencies (e.g., required ultrasound viewings of a fetus, gestation period, burial/cremation requirements, waiting periods between seeking and receiving abortion services, hospital-admitting privileges for physicians; for up-to-date information about abortion access, see the Guttmacher Institute's website: www.guttmacher.org/state-policy

/laws-policies). Although some of these are only proposed and others have been overturned, this flurry of legislative attacks acts as a deterrent by amplifying the perception that abortion is a minority or fringe experience (it is not; Pew Research Center, 2016) and clouding the extent of women's sexual rights. All women are not equally impeded, of course: geographic, racial, and class disparities are substantial (Beckman, 2016; Dehlendorf et al., 2013; Ely et al., 2017) and likely to grow if threats to sexual and reproductive health care rights and providers are executed (Hasstedt, 2016). Nominal sexual rights that cannot be exercised are not simply worthless to individual women, they also cover up systemic bias and exclusion by propping up a façade of choice.

Catch-22 Choices

Also included in the battery of illusory choices are the products of the gendered double bind, damning both girls who do (have sex) and those who do not (Gavey, 2005; for an analysis of the classed intersections and implications of the double bind, see Hamilton & Armstrong, 2009). Femininity's imperatives to be other-focused and pleasing means that young women are socialized to oblige multiple, competing stakeholders: adult caregiving/instructional authorities; peers, ranging from close friends to the generalized other; and prospective sexual partners. Added to this in the supposed postfeminist era of girl power is the charge that young women also present as self-interested, self-promoting, and self-pleasing (Bay-Cheng, 2015; Gill, 2008; Gonick, 2006; Harris, 2004). While young women who convincingly play the part of neoliberal agents may skirt degradation as sluts, they are not necessarily warmly received (Bay-Cheng, 2015; Bay-Cheng, Bruns, & Maguin, 2018; Ringrose & Walkerdine, 2008).

Young women who experience coercion – to any degree and in any form – are also confined by another catch-22. If they explicitly claim their assault or exploitation, they risk being stigmatized for deflecting responsibility, making false accusations to cover their own regret, being attention whores, being weaklings, or for any simultaneous combination of these. There may be compelling psychological and moral grounds for women to assume some portion of responsibility for their experiences (Lamb, 2015). But it is important to recognize that these reasons may coincide with misplaced, outsized, and detrimental self-blame – for putting themselves in risky situations, for not "making choices stick," for going along with others and not being strong in themselves – in an attempt to salvage their credibility as neoliberal agents (Bay-Cheng & Eliseo-Arras, 2008; Stringer, 2014). No matter which route a young woman takes, she is likely to meet disbelief, ridicule, pity, and/or blame.

Many are well versed in the rhetoric of girls caught between competing norms and expectations, but it is equally important to attend boys'/men's entrapment by hegemonic masculinity. In fact, by neglecting to question and critique masculinity the way that we do femininity, we perpetuate both the relentless scrutiny of girls/women and the protective deflection of attention away from boys/men. Moreover, hegemonic masculinity comes at the cost not only to boys' and men's freedom of expression and relationships but of girls and women too, who bear so much of the brunt of men's socialization into dominance and aggression (Anderson & Umberson, 2001; Kimmel, 2002).

In-or-Out Choices

Gender remains a potent and defining social force, yet there are indications that the rules dictating sexuality are becoming more flexible. One commonly cited sign of progress on this front is the widening endorsement of sexual/gender diversity in public discourse, policies, and practices. This movement is long overdue and indisputably beneficial to many youth: popular and social media can offer positive role models and vital channels for identity exploration and community building (Craig et al., 2015; Fox & Ralston, 2016; Gomillion & Giuliano, 2011); marriage equality legislation has been found to attenuate suicidality among sexual-minority youth (Raifman et al., 2017); and school-based Gay–Straight Alliances can enhance students' well-being and safety (Ioverno et al., 2016; Marx & Kettrey, 2016; Poteat et al., 2013). Without discounting the significance of these progressive steps, the conditions of inclusion and acceptance of sexual/gender minorities warrant closer inspection. In fact, the embrace of sexual/gender diversity is often extended only to a specific subset of sexual/gender minorities and only on specific conditions, namely the homonormative expectation of assimilation into, or at least approximation of heteronormed relational scripts, roles, and institutions (Duggan, 2002).

These tandem heteronormative and homonormative forces find expression in research and advocacy, however well-intentioned, that stake claims of sexual/gender minorities' equal standing on their resemblance to their straight counterparts. For instance, van Eeden-Moorefield and colleagues (2011) point out that research attesting to how queer partners or parents are "just like" straight ones operate from the implicit premise that heterosexual/cisgendered relationships are a universal gold standard. This reifies heteronormativity and overlooks the distinct and successful alternative relational arrangements that sexual/gender minorities may create (Lamont, 2017; van Eeden-Moorefield et al., 2011). Attempts at "gaystreaming" (i.e., mainstreaming; Ng, 2013) queerness also circumvent homonormativity's interdependence with racism, classism, and transphobia (e.g., see Kennedy's [2014] critique of the film, "The Kids Are All Right"; Ng, 2013; Vitulli, 2010).

Universalizing discourses of sexual/gender minority experiences also mask the hostile conditions under which queer identities and relationships are forged, neglecting their distinct stressors and needs (van Eeden-Moorefield et al., 2011). For example, Mendelsohn's (2006) analysis of the mainstream reception of the acclaimed film, Brokeback Mountain, neutralized the film's depiction of queer oppression. The film, based on a short story, tracks the relationship – and its repercussions – between two closeted White men living in the rural US West during the mid-twentieth century. Marketers, reviewers, and audiences touted it as a same-sex Romeo and Juliet narrative. Yet, the film is not a love story and the protagonists are not star-crossed lovers doomed by a trivial (albeit tragic) familial grudge. To the contrary, the film is a study in how systemic oppression – founded on complex interrelations among time, place, sexuality, gender, and class – manifests, is internalized, and plagues individuals and those in their lives (Mendelsohn, 2006). Commentaries on the film as an illustration of the universality of love effectively drew attention away from its incisive social critique.

The apparent embrace of sexual/gender diversity feeds a congratulatory discourse of social progress, but critical analysis reveals its conditional and divisive undercurrents. Queer individuals, partners, families, and collectives face presenting themselves as "just like" their straight counterparts in order to be welcomed into – or just inside the periphery – the "charmed circle" (Rubin, 2011, p. 152) of sexual/gender normativity or else continue enduring stigmatization, violation, and deprivation (in social, emotional, and material terms). However, assimilation is not a viable option, even if it were a desirable one, for all queer people. Those relegated to the social margins, not only for their sexual and/or gender identity expression but also due to their race, ethnicity, class, ability, or other degraded statuses, remain outcast. The strings attached to sexual/gender minority inclusion demand that those who opt in leave behind those who do not or cannot (see Vitulli [2010] for an analysis of how homonormative compromises marginalize minorities within LGBTQ+ community). In-or-Out Choices come at the expense of those who cannot afford or abide the trappings of homonormativity. Thus, the inclusion of some exacerbates and masks the exclusion of others, fortifying an unjust *status quo* rather than challenging it.

Forced Choices

Finally, there are sexual choices that are foregone conclusions, compelled by factors that have little to do with sex and therefore are often excluded from discussions of youth sexuality. Mainstream discourse surrounding consent, for instance, centers on the choice between yes and no: Did she consent? Did she do so enthusiastically? This is an important and necessary conversation, but one that is relevant only if refusal is a viable option in the first place. It does not address the predicaments of young women who consent to protect themselves from greater violence (i.e., rape by acquiescence; Basile, 1999), to meet basic material needs (e.g., food or shelter), or to hold on to vital, yet scarce, emotional and relational lifelines (Watson, 2011). In an intersectional analysis of young women's experiences of unwanted sex, a collaborator and I detected meaningful differences between affluent and socioeconomically disadvantaged participants, with many of the latter linking their consent to prior trauma or hardship (e.g., poverty) and seeing it as a means to essential resources (Bay-Cheng & Bruns, 2016).

In an earlier study (Bay-Cheng & Fava, 2014), one participant's testimony exemplified how sexual consent may serve as a calculated life strategy. Stefanie was a 16 year old in group foster care with a boyfriend, Lawrence, whom she saw on weekends. Lawrence was a 20 year old with an apartment, a car, and a stable job. During the interview, she described consenting to fellatio with Lawrence even though she did not enjoy it (she called it "nasty"), and consenting to unwanted coitus even though she worried about pregnancy and sexually transmitted infections. But she also repeated two phrases: "I don't want to lose him" and, more plainly, "I can't afford to lose him." These were not romantic declarations but a stark report on her options. Given Stefanie's situation – aging out of foster care, no family or community ties to support her, and dim academic and employment prospects – Lawrence was her best bet for a chance at living independently and not in deep poverty. And since, as she put it, going down on him "wasn't the worst thing," this is what she did. Lawrence was pivotal to Stefanie's goals of upward mobility and self-advancement, the very ones that neoliberal ideology espouses. Without meaningful, viable access to education and employment, her assessment that she could not "afford" to lose him was correct. Young women such as Stefanie, or those who choose to have sex as a means to an essential end, are left out of most debates and discussions of consent. Their experiences do not register on surveys about rape or coercion. They say "yes" and choose sex but the conditions of their consent are nonetheless troubling and rife with injustice. But if, when diagnosing social problems, we look no further than whether something was chosen or not, these young women and the conditions that force their choices will go undetected and unabated.

Some of these so-called choices are compelled, whether by normative forces (In-or-Out Choices) or by impoverished circumstances (Forced Choices), while others are obstructed, again by normative forces (Catch-22 Choices) or impoverished – materially and politically speaking – circumstances (Cinderella Choices). In all cases, these are a far cry from the all-powerful, magical version of choice heralded by sexuality education campaigns. Instead, they are magical only in the sense that they are make-believe for many young people, especially those whose autonomy is already circumscribed by misogyny, racism, hetero- and cis-normativity, xenophobia, and economic injustice, among other vectors of oppression. The power to choose from a menu of prescribed options is hardly equivalent to having power over the choices available. Instead, an inflated discourse of choice acts as a screen that conceals powerlessness and onto which illusions of agency are projected. That "representations of choice can translate into a feeling of possibility," as Probyn (1993, p. 283) argued, is not a trivial or inconsequential matter. Indeed, tests of system justification theory demonstrate that believing ourselves to be self-determining subjects operating in a just world serves an important psychological purpose. It frees us from feeling culpable for others' lives and defends us from feeling impotent in our own (Jost et al., 2004). Our powerlessness is not just a matter of being susceptible to bad luck or natural forces; we do not simply lack control in an unpredictable world, we are deprived of it by more powerful others in an unjust system. Thus, to see system injustice is to see ourselves as victims who are not only powerless but also subordinate. Our psychological aversion to this low-status view of ourselves is exacerbated by prevailing neoliberal ideology and its categorical dehumanization of victims as pitied and/or despised (Bay-Cheng, 2015; Lamb, 1999; Stringer, 2014).

Neoliberalism is a fundamentally dehumanizing ideology because it is a capitalizing one, casting individuals as means to profitable ends and teaching individuals to see their own lives as a means to profitable ends. For youth, whose worth is contingent on future earning potential, this translates into pressure to make strategic choices in all life domains (including, but hardly limited to, sexuality) in order to maximize their future prospects. Neoliberal discourse is flooded by an enticing rhetoric of choice, effectively drowning out any debate over the viability of those choices in the first place.

Enabling Choice: Capabilities Approach

Nussbaum's *capabilities approach* (2000; see also Sen, 1999) is a sharp theoretical and political counterpoint to neoliberalism's decontextualized and misleadingly romanticized rhetoric of choice. The capabilities approach's central tenet is that all humans have equal dignity, irrespective of disparate "earning potential" or measurable successes. This diametrically opposes neoliberalism's view of individuals as means to profitable ends and its consequently prorated treatment of individuals in proportion to their predicted profitability (although the capabilities approach is not without its critics; e.g., Dean, 2009). The capabilities approach recognizes individuals as possessing varying aptitudes and abilities but nonetheless equally entitled to pursuing the same freedoms: life; bodily health; bodily integrity; senses, imagination, and thought; emotions; practical reason; affiliation; connections with other living beings; play; and control over one's environment. The role of social systems is to match all individuals' internal capabilities with the requisite means (i.e., what Nussbaum refers to as combined capabilities) needed to exercise their guaranteed freedoms:

> The various liberties of choice have material preconditions, in whose absence there is merely a simalucrum of choice. [. . .] In short, liberty is not just a matter of having rights on paper, it requires being in a material position to exercise those rights. And this requires resources. (p. 227)

This orientation toward social justice scrutinizes systems' obligations and provisions rather than individuals' behavior and responsibilities. It affirms the dignity of youth and their rights not just to prescribed, sanctioned (i.e., good) choices, but to a full range of volitional and actionable options.

The capabilities approach is explicitly and emphatically unconcerned with what individuals choose; its sole investment is in advocating for individuals' ability to do so. This is a crucial point since critiques of choice are often mistaken as criticisms of choosers or their choices (Evans & Riley, 2014; Probyn, 1993). Indeed, feminist inquiries into young women's sexualities are often stymied by reflexive, unfounded accusations that to question the reasons and ramifications of women's choices is to disrespect women's capacities for or rights to choice (Gill, 2008). As Nussbaum (2000) explains, to ask how preferences have been shaped by conditions (and by constraints and prescriptions) does not negate one's right to preferences in the first place. Rather than individuals' decisions or their decision-making abilities, the capabilities approach targets external impingements and inadequacies for remediation: "To secure a capability to a person, it is not sufficient to produce good internal states of readiness to act. It is also necessary to prepare the material and institutional environment so that people are actually able to function" (p. 235). This is a clear inversion of the neoliberal discourse of faux choices promulgated by sexuality education, in which we instruct youth in good sexual decision making absent any consideration of the social and material conditions of their lives.

The capabilities approach is also useful in revealing and rebutting the ways in which age and developmentalism are enlisted by neoliberal rhetoric. Its central premise that humans have dignity and worth as they are (i.e., this is not predicated on particular contributions or competencies) rejects the ageist notion that youths' value lies only in the potential of their future adult selves. It also contradicts conventional wisdom in the United States that youth should be prohibited from sexual information, care, services, discourse, and relationships because they are not emotionally or cognitively "ready" (for a comparative critique of US constructions of youth and youth sexuality, see Schalet, 2011). Instead of using individuals' limited internal capabilities (e.g., due to their stage of cognitive maturation) as grounds for restricting their choice, the capabilities approach uses these as grounds for increasing and enhancing external support to better enable their choice. Similarly, the capabilities approach sees the age-based structural disadvantages that diminish youths' control over their lives, make them subject to authorities and circumstances of others' making, and entail their dependence on adults for resources as even more reason to be vigilant in protecting youths' capabilities (Ballet et al., 2011; Nussbaum & Dixon, 2012).

The obstruction of youths' capabilities *vis-à-vis* sexuality – to varying extents depending on social identity and social location – should also be understood as a "corrosive disadvantage" (Wolff & De-Shalit, 2007, as cited by Nussbaum & Dixon, 2012) insofar as it can have cascading detrimental effects on future capabilities. A young woman denied access to sexuality information, services, support, and alternatives may be susceptible to a host of negative sexual experiences, the consequences of which may reverberate through the rest of her life. It is important to distinguish a capabilities-oriented understanding of negative sexual outcomes from the dominant discourse of sexual risk. According to the latter, risk originates in the developmental or personal shortcomings and the inherent danger of sex. The former, however, attributes some youths' disproportionate risk to negative sexual experiences to precursory deprivation and a systemic failure to ensure equally the capabilities of all youth.

The argument that young people are presented with false or fictitious choices does not negate that they may create alternatives for themselves or claim and wield significant power through their choices, nor does it presume youth to be unwitting dupes. Neoliberalism does not erase individuals' agency so much as misdirect and distort it into a solely self-serving, and therefore politically inert, force (Giroux, 2016). As I note in the final section, youth are essential to assembling critical collectives to resist neoliberalism's depoliticizing and divisive effects. My claim is that we cannot look to individual youth, either as problems or as solutions, while leaving their surrounding circumstances intact. I am concerned that the rhetoric of choice is a diversionary tactic, used to deflect attention away from social injustice, to lure individuals into taking responsibility for circumstances beyond their control, and then to scold them for bad, wrong, weak, or risky choices. I object to the pretense that all youth have all choices available to them, that their safety and futures can be secured through good, right, strong, and safe choices. Choice is a potent tool but it is not a magic wand that creates opportunities for fulfillment out of thin air and certainly not out of fundamentally unjust, impoverished circumstances. Choice is meaningful only when exercised in an unbounded, equally accessible field of options.

Postscript: Trumped Choice

Almost instantly upon the 2016 US presidential election, worry over virtually every marginalized and vulnerable group of Americans escalated. Since the inauguration, many of those worries have been realized with disorienting speed and in disoriented ways. Executive orders, legislative proposals, and pending judicial decisions have shifted the material and discursive ground underneath us such that rights to sexual and reproductive health care and protections against sexual assault are under explicit threat. This is no longer a matter of a rhetorical pretense of choice that is not matched by realistic viability; choices and rights of all sorts are simply being eliminated. The right-wing authoritarian nature of the Trump campaign and administration is alarming not only because it is so bald, but also because it is popular. Indeed, much of Trump's appeal is fueled by his unapologetic degradation of others.

Election postmortem analyses have also zeroed in on neoliberalism's explicit and immediate influence as well as its latent, decades-long influence in priming the United States for a president such as Trump (e.g., Bessner & Sparke, 2017; Giroux, 2017; Schram & Pavlovskaya, 2018). Beginning with the campaign, Trump was fashioned as an outspoken critic of neoliberal policies (e.g., North American Free Trade Agreement). He disputed the neoliberal claim of a post-prejudice United States but, importantly, he did so by inverting the usual argument against it (i.e., evidence of persistent biases against minoritized groups). He argued that we had not leveled the playing field but rather switched the advantage such that regular Americans (read: White, straight, Christian, cisgender, and male) were losing out domestically and globally. White-supremacist adherents articulated this fear at their August 2017 rally in Charlottesville in chants of "You will not replace us" (Spencer & Stolberg, 2017). However, critics point out the duplicity of Trump's rhetoric and his administration's actions: even as Trump criticizes neoliberalism, he is personally enriched by its policies and regularly deploys its ideology (Bessner & Sparke, 2017; Giroux, 2017; Klein, 2016; Schram & Pavlovskaya, 2018). He gives it voice with every repetition of his TV reality show tagline, "You're fired!" and reference to "winners" and "losers." Reflecting on neoliberal hegemony, Schram and Pavlovskaya describe Trump's embodiment of its trademark dehumanization and how he "fulsomely lived and breathed a cutthroat neoliberalism, perhaps even thoughtlessly, or even somatically, as if it were the only way to act in the world" (p. xviii).

The right-wing authoritarian momentum carrying the United States under the Trump administration is not a divergence from its neoliberal course. Neoliberal ideology and authoritarianism are bedfellows, with the former exalting competition, the latter ossifying the resulting hierarchy, and the former capitalizing the hierarchy, to the enrichment of those in power (Giroux, 2017). Neoliberal regimes carry out – and profit greatly from – punitive surveillance and suppression programs against minorities, all claims of unfettering liberty aside (Bessner & Sparke, 2017; Soss et al., 2011). Arguably, neoliberal impoverishment of our education, employment, and social welfare systems and concomitant erosion of collectivism paved the way for Trump's brand of authoritarianism (Giroux, 2017; Klein, 2016). Through the Trump administration and behind the diverting scenes it creates, economic and political power are being consolidated while individuals' and communities' capabilities are being collapsed. The neoliberal degradation of our material and relational conditions cuts our safety nets and pits us against each other, threatening to immobilize us as a citizenry.

Many speculate that Trump's presidency will be cut short by one means or another. But it is important to recognize that, just as Trump himself did not mastermind the conditions that precipitated his election, removing him from office will not eliminate the conditions that ushered him in. Countering the corrosive effects of neoliberal policies and ideology entails collective, critical action to ensure more than nominal "rights on paper" for all of us (Bessner & Sparke, 2017; Giroux, 2017; Schram & Pavlovskaya, 2018). Youth-driven initiatives, ranging from organized programs (e.g., the SPARK Movement) to impromptu actions (e.g., protests against sexist dress codes), demonstrate youths' vision and skill in resisting norms, policies, and practices that jeopardize their sexual rights and well-being. Sexuality education classrooms can also be springboards for critical, collective movement (Bay-Cheng, 2017). Progressive models of sexuality education reach beyond neoliberal rhetoric of self-interest and personal responsibility to explore the ethical and emotional complexities of sexuality and relationships (e.g., Lamb, 2010). They also reconfigure the curricular boundaries of sexuality education to engage youth in collaborative critical analyses of the social conditions that underlie sexual risk and obstruct sexual rights (Berglas et al., 2014;

Macleod & Vincent, 2014; Whitten & Sethna, 2014). If we are truly dedicated to ensuring youths' sexual development and well-being, and if we want them to make smart, healthy, responsible choices, then we need to stop offering them fake or forced ones. As vaunted as it is in American neoliberal ideology, real and meaningful choice is neither guaranteed nor magic. It is hard won and it must be well defended.

References

Anderson, K. L. & Umberson, D. (2001). Gendering Violence: Masculinity and Power in Men's Accounts of Domestic Violence. *Gender & Society*, *15*, 358–380. doi:10.1177/089124301015003003.

Ballet, J., Biggeri, M., & Comim, F. (2011). Children's Agency and the Capability Approach: A Conceptual Framework. In Biggeri, M., Ballet, J., & Comim, F. (Eds.), *Children and the Capability Approach* (22–45). London: Palgrave Macmillan.

Basile, K. C. (1999). Rape by Acquiescence: The Ways in which Women "Give In" to Unwanted Sex with Their Husbands. *Violence against Women*, *5*, 1036–1058. doi:10.1177/10778012990050090004.

Bay-Cheng, L. Y. (2015). The Agency Line: A Neoliberal Metric for Appraising Young Women's Sexuality. *Sex Roles*, *73*, 279–291. doi:10.1007/s11199-015-0452-6.

(2017). Critically Sex/Ed: Asking Critical Questions of Neoliberal Truths in Sex Education. In Allen, L. & Rasmussen, M. L. (Eds.), *Handbook of Sexuality Education* (343–376). London: Palgrave.

Bay-Cheng, L. Y. & Bruns, A. E. (2016). Yes, but: Young Women's Views of Unwanted Sex at the Intersection of Gender and Class. *Psychology of Women Quarterly*, *40*, 504–517.

Bay-Cheng, L. Y., Bruns, A. E., & Maguin, E. (2018). Agents, Virgins, Sluts, and Losers: The sexual typecasting of young heterosexual women. *Sex Roles*. Online first. doi: 10.1007/s11199-018-0907-7.

Bay-Cheng, L. Y. & Eliseo-Arras, R. K. (2008). The Making of Unwanted Sex: Gendered and Neoliberal Norms in College Women's Unwanted Sexual Experiences. *Journal of Sex Research*, *45*, 386–397. doi:10.1080/00224490802398381.

Bay-Cheng, L. Y. & Fava, N. M. (2014). What Puts "At-Risk Girls" at Risk? Sexual Vulnerability and Social Inequality in the Lives of Girls in the Child Welfare System. *Sexuality Research & Social Policy*, *11*, 116–125. doi:10.1007/s13178-013-0142-5.

Bay-Cheng, L. Y., Livingston, J. A., & Fava, N. M. (2011). Adolescent Girls' Assessment and Management of Sexual Risks: Insights from Focus Group Research. *Youth & Society*, *43*, 1167–1193. doi: 10.1177/0044118X10384475.

Becker, M. G. & Barth, R. P. (2000). Power through Choices: The Development of a Sexuality Education Curriculum for Youths in Out-of-Home Care. *Child Welfare*, *79*, 269–282.

Beckman, L. J. (2016). Abortion in the United States: The Continuing Controversy. *Feminism & Psychology*, *27*, 101–113. doi:10.1177/0959353516685345.

Berglas, N. F., Constantine, N. A., & Ozer, E. J. (2014). A Rights-Based Approach to Sexuality Education: Conceptualization, Clarification and Challenges. *Perspectives on Sexual and Reproductive Health*, *46*, 63–72.

Bessner, D. & Sparke, M. (2017). Nazism, Neoliberalism, and the Trumpist Challenge to Democracy. *Environment and Planning A*, *49*, 1214–1223.

Brown, W. (2003). Neo-liberalism and the End of Liberal Democracy. *Theory & Event*, 7. doi:10.1353/tae.2003.0020.

(2006). American Nightmare: Neoliberalism, Neoconservatism, and De-democratization. *Political Theory*, *34*, 690–714. doi:10.1177/0090591706293016.

Craig, S. L., McInroy, L., McCready, L. T., & Alaggia, R. (2015). Media: A Catalyst for Resilience in Lesbian, Gay, Bisexual, Transgender, and Queer Youth. *Journal of LGBT Youth*, *12*, 254–275. doi:10.1080/19361653.2015.1040193.

Dean, H. (2009). Critiquing Capabilities: The Distractions of a Beguiling Concept. *Critical Social Policy*, *29*, 261–273.

Dehlendorf, C., Harris, L. H., & Weitz, T. A. (2013). Disparities in Abortion Rates: A Public Health Approach. *American Journal of Public Health*, *103*, 1772–1779. doi:10.2105/AJPH.2013.301339.

Duggan, L. (2002). The New Homonormativity: The Sexual Politics of Neoliberalism. In Castronovo, R. & Nelson, D. D (Eds.), *Materializing Democracy: Toward a Revitalized Cultural Politics* (175–194). Durham, NC: Duke University Press.

Elliott, S. (2014). "Who's to Blame?" Constructing the Responsible Sexual Agent in Neoliberal Sex Education. *Sexuality Research and Social Policy*, 1–14. doi:10.1007/s13178-014-0158-5.

Ely, G. E., Hales, T., Jackson, D. L., Maguin, E., & Hamilton, G. (2017). The Undue Burden of Paying for Abortion: An Exploration of Abortion Fund Cases. *Social Work in Health Care*, *56*, 99–114. doi:10.1080/00981389.2016.1263270.

Evans, A. & Riley, S. (2014). *Technologies of Sexiness: Sex, Identity, and Consumer Culture*. New York: Oxford University Press.

Fields, J. (2008). *Risky Lessons: Sex Education and Social Inequality*. New Brunswick: Rutgers University Press.

Fine, M. & McClelland, S. I. (2007). The Politics of Teen Women's Sexuality: Public Policy and the Adolescent Female Body. *Emory Law Journal*, *56*, 993–1038.

Fox, J. & Ralston, R. (2016). Queer Identity Online: Informal Learning and Teaching Experiences of LGBTQ Individuals on Social Media. *Computers in Human Behavior*, *65*, 635–642. doi:10.1016/j.chb.2016.06.009.

Froyum, C. M. (2010). Making "Good Girls": Sexual Agency in the Sexuality Education of Low-Income Black Girls. *Culture, Health & Sexuality*, *12*, 59–72. doi:10.1080/13691050903272583.

Gavey, N. (2005). *Just Sex?: The Cultural Scaffolding of Rape*. New York: Routledge.

Gill, R. (2008). Culture and Subjectivity in Neoliberal and Postfeminist Times. *Subjectivity*, *25*, 432–445. doi:10.1057/sub.2008.28.

Giroux, H. (2016). Donald Trump and the Plague of Atomization in a Neoliberal Age [Blog post]. Retrieved from http://billmoyers.com/story/donald-trump-plague-atomization-neoliberal-age/.

Giroux, H. A. (2017). *America at War with Itself*. San Francisco: City Lights Books.

Gomillion, S. C. & Giuliano, T. A. (2011). The Influence of Media Role Models on Gay, Lesbian, and Bisexual Identity. *Journal of Homosexuality*, *58*, 330–354. doi:10.1080/00918369.2011.546729.

Gonick, M. (2006). Between "Girl Power" and "Reviving Ophelia": Constituting the Neoliberal Girl Subject. *NWSA Journal*, *18*, 1–23. doi:10.1353/nwsa.2006.0031.

Goodkind, S. (2009). "You Can Be Anything You Want, But You Have to Believe It": Commercialized Feminism in Gender-Specific Programs for Girls. *Signs*, *34*, 397–422. doi:10.1086/591086.

Hamilton, L. & Armstrong, E. A. (2009). Gendered Sexuality in Young Adulthood: Double Binds and Flawed Options. *Gender and Society*, *23*, 589–616. doi:10.1177/0891243209345829.

Harris, A. (2004). *Future Girl: Young Women in the Twenty-First Century*. New York: Routledge.

Hasstedt, K. (2016). Recent Funding Restriction on the U.S. Family Planning Safety Net May Foreshadow What Is to Come. *Guttmacher Policy Review*, *19*, 67–72.

Heldman, C. (2013). Pennsylvania Public Service Announcement Blames Rape Victims [Blog post]. Retrieved from https://thesocietypages.org/socimages/2013/03/21/pennsylvania-public-service-announcement-blames-rape-victims/.

Herrman, J. W. & Waterhouse, J. K. (2012). A Pilot Program to Address Healthy Sexual Behaviors among Girls in Juvenile Detention. *Journal of Child and Adolescent Psychiatric Nursing*, *25*, 224–231. doi:10.1111/jcap.12007.

Holland, M. M. & DeLuca, S. (2016). "Why Wait Years to Become Something?" Low-Income African American Youth and the Costly Career Search in For-Profit Trade Schools. *Sociology of Education*, *89*, 261–278. doi:10.1177/0038040716666607.

Ioverno, S., Belser, A. B., Baiocco, R., Grossman, A. H., & Russell, S. T. (2016). The Protective Role of Gay–Straight Alliances for Lesbian, Gay, Bisexual, and Questioning Students: A Prospective Analysis. *Psychology of Sexual Orientation and Gender Diversity*, *3*, 397–406. doi:10.1037/sgd0000193.

Jones, T. (2011). A Sexuality Education Discourses Framework: Conservative, Liberal, Critical, and Postmodern. *American Journal of Sexuality Education*, *6*, 133–175. doi:10.1080/15546128.2011.571935.

Jost, J. T., Banaji, M. R., & Nosek, B. A. (2004). A Decade of System Justification Theory: Accumulated Evidence of Conscious and Unconscious Bolstering of the Status Quo. *Political Psychology*, *25*, 881–919. doi:10.1111/j.1467-9221.2004.00402.x.

Kelly, P. (2001). Youth at Risk: Processes of Individualisation and Responsibilisation in the Risk Society. *Discourse*, *22*, 23–33. doi:10.1080/01596300120039731.

Kendall, N. (2012). *The Sex Education Debates*. Chicago: University of Chicago Press.

Kennedy, T. M. (2014). Sustaining White Homonormativity: The Kids Are All Right as Public Pedogogy. *Journal of Lesbian Studies*, *18*,118–132.

Kimmel, M. S. (2002). "Gender Symmetry" in Domestic Violence: A Substantive and Methodological Research Review. *Violence against Women*, 8, 1332–1363. doi:10.1177/107780102237407Lesko 2001.

Klein, N. (2016). It Was the Democrats' Embrace of neoliberalism that Won It for Trump [Blog post]. Retrieved from www.theguardian.com/commentisfree/2016/nov/09/rise-of-the-davos-class-sealed-americas-fate.

Lamb, S. (1999). *New Versions of Victims: Feminists Struggle with the Concept*. New York: NYU Press.

(2010). Towards a Sexual Ethics Curriculum: Bringing Philosophy and Society to Bear on Individual Development. *Harvard Educational Review, 80*, 81–105.

(2015). Revisiting Choice and Victimization: A Commentary on Bay-Cheng's Agency Matrix. *Sex Roles, 73*, 292–297.

Lamont, E. (2017). "We Can Write the Scripts Ourselves": Queer Challenges to Heteronormative Courtship Practices. *Gender & Society*, 31, 624–646.

Lesko, N. (2001). *Act Your Age!: A Cultural Construction of Adolescence*. New York: Routledge.

(2010) Feeling Abstinent? Feeling Comprehensive? Touching the Affects of Sexuality Curricula. *Sex Education, 10*, 281–297. doi:10.1080/14681811.2010.491633.

Macleod, C. & Vincent, L. (2014). Introducing a Critical Pedagogy of Sexual and Reproductive Citizenship: Extending the "Framework of Thick Desire". In Allen, L., Rasmussen, M. L., & Quinlivan, K. (Eds.), *The Politics of Pleasure in Sexuality Education* (115–135). New York: Routledge.

Marx, R. A. & Kettrey, H. H. (2016). Gay-Straight Alliances Are Associated with Lower Levels of School-Based Victimization of LGBTQ+ Youth: A Systematic Review and Meta-analysis. *Journal of Youth and Adolescence, 45*, 1269–1282. doi:10.1007/s10964-016-0501-7.

McClelland, S. I. & Frost, D. M. (2014). Sexuality and Social Policy. In Tolman, D. L. and Diamond, L. M. (Eds.), *APA Handbook of Sexuality and Psychology: Volume 2, Contextual Approaches* (311–337). Washington, DC: American Psychological Association.

Mendelsohn, D. (2006). An Affair to Remember. *New York Review of Books*. Retrieved from www.nybooks.com/articles/2006/02/23/an-affair-to-remember/?pagination=false.

Mitnik, P. A., Cumberworth, E., & Grusky, D. B. (2016). Social Mobility in a High-Inequality Regime. *ANNALS of the American Academy of Political and Social Science, 663*, 140–184.

Ng, E. (2013). A "Post-Gay" Era? Media Gaystreaming, Homonormativity, and the Politics of LGBT Integration. *Communication, Culture, & Critique, 6*. 258–283.

Norton, B. (2016). How Neoliberalism Fuels the Racist Xenophobia Behind Brexit and Donald Trump [Blog post]. Retrieved from www.salon.com/2016/07/01/how_neo liberalism_fuels_the_racist_xenophobia_behind_brexit_and_donald_trump/.

Nussbaum, M. C. (2000). *Women and Human Development: The Capabilities Approach*. Cambridge: Cambridge University Press.

Nussbaum, M. C. & Dixon, R. (2012). Children's Rights and a Capabilities Approach: The Question of Special Priority. *Cornell Law Review, 97*, 549–593.

Pew Research Center (2016). *As Election Nears, Voters Divided over Democracy and "Respect."* New York: Pew Research Center.

Poteat, V. P., Sinclair, K. O., DiGiovanni, C. D., Koenig, B. W., & Russell, S. T. (2013). Gay–Straight Alliances Are Associated with Student Health: A Multischool Comparison of LGBTQ and Heterosexual Youth. *Journal of Research on Adolescence, 23*, 319–330. doi:10.1111/j.1532-7795.2012.00832.x.

Probyn, E. (1993). Choosing Choice: Images of Sexuality And "Choiceoisie" in Popular Culture. In Fisher S. & Davis K. (Eds.), *Negotiating at the Margins: The Gendered Discourses of Power and Resistance* (278–294). New Brunswick, NJ: Rutgers University Press.

Raifman, J., Moscoe, E., Austin, B., & McConnell, M. (2017). Difference-in-Differences Analysis of the Association between State Same-Sex Marriage Policies and Adolescent Suicide Attempts. *JAMA Pediatrics*, *171*(4):350–356. doi:10.1001/jamapediatrics.2016.4529.

Ringrose, J. & Walkerdine, V. (2008). What Does It Mean to Be a Girl in the Twenty-First Century? Exploring Some Contemporary Dilemmas of Femininity and Girlhood in the West. In Mitchell, C. A. & Reid-Walsh, J. (Eds.), *Girl Culture: An Encyclopedia* (6–16). Westport: Greenwood Press.

Rubin, G. S. (2011). Thinking Sex: Notes for a Radical Theory of the Politics of Sexuality. In Rubin, G. S. (Ed.), *Deviations: A Gayle Rubin Reader* (137–181). Durham, NC: Duke University Press. (Original work published 1984).

Schalet, A. T. (2011). *Not Under My Roof: Parents, Teens, and the Culture of Sex*. Chicago: University of Chicago Press.

Schram, S. F. & Pavlovskaya, M. (2018). *Rethinking Neoliberalism: Resisting the Disciplinary Regime*. New York: Routledge.

Sen, A. (1999). *Development as Freedom*. New York: Oxford University Press.

Sisson, G. & Kimport, K. (2016). Depicting Abortion Access on American Television, 2005–2015. *Feminism & Psychology*, *27*, 56–71. doi:10.1177/0959353516681245.

Smeeding, T. M. (2016). Multiple Barriers to Economic Opportunity for the "Truly" Disadvantaged and Vulnerable. *Russell Sage Foundation Journal of the Social Sciences*, *2*, 98–122.

Soss, J., Fording, R. C., & Schram, S. F. (2011). *Disciplining the Poor: Neoliberal Paternalism and the Persistent Power of Race*. Chicago: University of Chicago Press.

Spencer, H. & Stolberg, S. G. (2017). White nationalists march on University of Washington. *New York Times*. Retrieved from www.nytimes.com.

Stahl, L. (Interviewer). (2016). The 45th president [Television broadcast]. In J. Fager (Executive Producer), *60 Minutes*. New York: CBS.

Stringer, R. (2014). *Knowing Victims: Feminism, Agency and Victim Politics in Neoliberal Times*. New York: Routledge.

van Eeden-Moorefield, B., Martell, C. R., Williams, M., & Preston, M. (2011). Same-Sex Relationships and Dissolution: The Connection between Heteronormativity and Homonormativity. *Family Relations*, *60*, 562–571.

Vitulli, E. (2010). A Defining Moment in Civil Rights History? The Employment Non-Discrimination Act, Trans-inclusion, and Homonormativity. *Sexuality Research & Social Policy*, *7*, 155–167.

Watson, J. (2011). Understanding Survival Sex: Young Women, Homelessness, and Intimate Relationships. *Journal of Youth Studies*, *14*, 639–655. doi:10.1080/13676261.2011.588945.

Whitten, A. & Sethna, C. (2014). What's Missing? Antiracist Sex Education! *Sex Education*, *14*, 414–429.

10 From Tightrope to Minefield

How the Sexual Double Standard "Lives" in Adolescent Girls' and Young Women's Lives

Deborah L. Tolman and Jennifer F. Chmielewski

SLUT: tramp; whore; floozy; harlot; hooker; hussy; prostitute; tart; vamp; broad; floozy; wench; trollop; minx; strumpet; nymphomaniac; broad; jezebel; skank; bimbo; chippie; doxy; hoochie; slag; cum dumpster; jizz can; nasty girl; slapper; blow job queen; slore; hoe; trash; cumbucket; walking blow job; hoebag; cumlover; fuck hole; cuntstinch; sperm burper; harlot; thot; jade; STD farm; slut bag; grisette . . .

(Payne, 2010; Urbandictionary.com, 2017)

Introduction

There is a viral meme, no-nonsense, stark, black lettering on a parchment background, that reads: "Slut [noun]: A woman with the morals of a man." Do a Google search of "slut" images and a plethora of memes playing with this idea cascade down the page: "I'm not saying she's a slut but . . . she gives away more pussy than an animal shelter; she's been banged more times than the first pipe on Flappy bird; if she walked in a sperm bank, her spit would be accepted; her favorite shade of lipstick is penis." "Slut" is an epithet and insult, suggesting a woman who has too much sex, with too many partners – who evidences the same bodily desires, needs, and/or interests in sex as a man – a girl or woman who has *wants* [or is imagined to want] in a visible, untethered, "unladylike" way.

"Slut" marks and mobilizes the sexual double standard (SDS) – the notion that men and boys are, and should be, [hetero]sexual fulcra of desires and that women and girls do not have strong sexual desires of their own; that passionless girls and women can restrain uncontrollable male sexual desire; that women and girls who embody this restrained or unimportant sexuality are good (selfless, pure or morally upstanding, appropriate, reliable gatekeepers), while those who suggest, demonstrate, or can be understood to have so-called morals of a man – un[fettered] sexual desire – are bad (selfish, immoral, not normal, unreliable gatekeepers). Infusing and leveraging the relations of power that drive and maintain persistent gender inequity (Butler, 1990; Foucault, 1978), the word "slut" is everywhere and nowhere. And yet there is in fact no such thing as a slut; slut is just a word in which meanings are invested. Slut is the discursive marker of the SDS; it does the work of producing, implementing, and maintaining it.

The SDS was, and remains, a powerful idea woven into female adolescent sexuality development. While a body of feminist theory and research has focused on the importance of pleasure, the possibilities of embodiment, and the portal of empowerment for three decades in adolescent female sexuality (i.e., Fine, 1988; Holland et al., 1994), a consistent drumbeat across race, ethnicity, geography and nation – even sexual orientation – is a persistently entrenched SDS. When girls learn about their sexuality from any and all sources, be it through relationships with parents and peers or the institutions of media and education, engagement with the SDS is not an option but a necessity. The ways in which that engagement happens vary, although, most frequently, girls develop the awareness, skills, and framework for experiencing and navigating their sexuality so as to sidestep, avoid, manipulate, or, in a small although growing number of cases, resist and refuse the SDS.

However, public discourse is flush with a postfeminist mantra that cisgender girls, especially those who are White and elite, and young women can – nay, must be – sexually empowered, in charge, knowledgeable, and "confident." Wouldn't this suggest that the SDS has been vanquished or rendered moot? Yet, at the same time, "slut-shaming" is an equally pervasive phenomenon. We suggest that the SDS remains in place but has changed, or, more accurately, shape shifted. Its fundamental purpose persists as an organizing force in stubbornly racist, classist, and sexist societies to keep girls and women from what Audre Lorde called "the power of the erotic," a force that enables and fuels unencumbered entitlement, passion, and the ability to live fully, to know, give, and bring one's entire self not only to sexuality but to the knowledge, hungers, and desires within which sexuality is interwoven (Lorde, 1984, p. 88). As we will elaborate later in this chapter, what was a tangible tightrope that girls could develop skills for traversing, off of which they were at risk of falling or being pushed, has now become for many an elusive minefield, a seemingly innocuous expanse that can erupt and injure without warning or respite. We begin this chapter by explaining the SDS and how it works; we will suggest and illuminate how the *traditional* SDS has undergone *renovation*; like a structure that is renovated, it is the surfaces that have changed, even if taken down to the studs. Its "bearing beams" are intact and continue to serve their purpose of scaffolding and holding up the original architecture, even as they seem to recede or disappear from view. In reviewing the research on the SDS for young women and girls, we will suggest that both versions of the SDS, traditional and renovated, are evident in the terrain that diverse adolescent girls traverse in their sexuality development. We will illuminate how this transition in the SDS is an *unacknowledged thread* through shifts in recent scholarship on the SDS, and how understanding the SDS as renovated enables us to make sense of fractured findings. We will then review how girls are pushing back, considering girls' resistance and thriving in the context of a renovated SDS.

The Modern History of the Traditional SDS

The *traditional* SDS depends upon two distinct and intersecting binaries. These binaries serve to control female sexuality through surveillance and a system of rewards and punishments. The first binary distinguishes "passive" female sexuality from "uncontrollable" male sexuality; the second binary, dependent on the first, separates girls and women into "good" and "bad" – those who comply and those who do not; those who are "respectable" and those who are "sluts." This system necessitates strict or, at the very least, discernable or intelligible binaries – the gender binary and the good/bad girl binary. These strict binaries are organized around beliefs and stereotypes about female and male sexuality and appropriate femininity and masculinity. Within this framing, women/girls are expected to contain and control their sexuality unless it is expressed within a "charmed circle" (Rubin, 1984) of monogamous and married heterosexuality. Traditionally, the charmed circle had been sexual expression focused solely on reproduction, virginity, and female passivity (assumed to be "normal") and male desire and pleasure through (vaginal) sexual intercourse within heterosexual marriage. Ultimately, the SDS works by meting out punishment and negative – sometimes devastating – consequences for girls and young women when they step outside of the charmed circle – being labeled a "bad" girl or woman – a slut (see earlier for the large lexicon) – who is in essence rendered undeserving of rights, respect, safety, or relationships. The SDS serves institutionalized heterosexuality (Rich, 1980) through a heterosexual matrix (Butler, 1990): demanding performance of particular forms of femininity (and masculinity); diminishing women's sexual freedom, curiosity, and power by demonizing it; and centering desirability in lieu of desire, thus enabling (heterosexual) men's sexual freedom and power in relationships and sexual encounters.

In order for the traditional SDS to function, male sexuality must be unequivocally understood as hard wired into a male body or biologically driven by hormones/testosterone. One could even argue that the "normal" developing boy's/man's sexuality is believed to be in some sense monstrous: he is overwhelmed by a desire that is heterosexual, uncontrollable, uncontainable, and must be satiated. His needs are physical; once incited, girls and women will be held responsible for managing them. Often taken as fact, these gendered concepts of sexuality are in fact *ideas* – social constructs – about boys and men that are imposed upon girls and women and boys and men themselves. In order for this system to work, girls cannot have desire or cannot/should not act on it except under "safe" conditions of a committed heterosexual relationship (Fine, 1988; Tolman, 2002).

From Traditional to Renovated: Emphasizing Excessive Female Sexual Desire

The SDS has always had the distinction of offering a noxious moral high ground for brutality, confusion, and suffering, and for conferring amnesty and perpetuating privilege for young men (Lamb et al., 2016). Previously, the traditional double standard and historical dichotomization of good girls who do not have or enact desire (virgins) and bad girls who do (sluts), meant that girls and women– at least those who were White, middle-class, and heterosexual – could, albeit with difficulty, strive to walk the tightrope of good girl status through abstinence or perceived abstinence until marriage or, more recently, a committed heterosexual relationship (Bay-Cheng, 2015). In this scenario, if a good girl falls off by failing to comply, she is transmogrified into a slut, joining those who never complied in the first place (Schippers, 2007). At the heart of this system is fear and thus restraint of excessive female sexuality.

Female sexuality that is not contained – and responsive and responsible to heterosexual male sexuality – is dangerous, out of control, morally reprehensible, or abnormal; it is deemed *excessive* (McClelland & Fine, 2008). Female sexual excess can be evidenced by having (oral, anal, or vaginal–penile) sex too young, too early, or at an "inappropriate" age, in unsanctioned relational or physical contexts of sexual encounters, having too many partners, or same-sex partners, or taking too much or demanding (any?) embodied pleasure. Excessive is the antithesis of respectable. The traditional SDS scaffolded a straightforward dynamic of excess, transgression, and consequences: too many partners, too much sexual behavior, too sexual outside of relationships, too much interest in sex brought on the expected moniker of "slut," social isolation, and even family shame. For Black and Latina girls, working-class and poor White girls, transgression played into stereotypes of hypersexuality and/or lack of or inability to have good judgment. What was judged excessive could be elusive – how many partners is too many? – yet, was relatively clear, even as no evidence was required for a girl to find herself labeled (Tanenbaum, 2000).

What has changed – what requires a renovation of the SDS – is the new demoralizing and confusing complexity layered on top of the traditional SDS – seeming to replace it but in actuality obfuscating its persistence. This new layer is a mandate to *seem but not be* appropriately excessive. The line of good and bad has been blurred by the fast pace of these *au courant* contradictions that require demonstrating or at least suggesting desire for (hetero)sex – but not *too much*. The notion that young women's, and especially girls,' sexual agency and desire simply "collect[s] danger" (McClelland & Fine, 2008, p. 92) now calls for renovation to account for these new wrinkles and expectations enforced by old punishments and consequences. What is missing from a renovated SDS – and thus retains the very notion of an SDS – is recognition that girls' and women's own pleasure and desire matters *for them*. Female desire and pleasure has itself been commodified to serve male pleasure, desire, and satisfaction; therefore, the appearance of desire and pleasure, rather than its importance for girls and women themselves, is the new mandate (Diamond, 2005; Tolman et al., 2015). Absent entitlement, a rallying cry of empowerment can ring hollow. Feminists have argued that excess is at the heart of female sexual pleasure and power, a critical dimension of sexual freedom; we suggest that *uplifting* containment of elusive (in)appropriate excess as definitional of a renovated SDS – an idea that is as contradictory as the practice itself – helps explain its ongoing power even as postfeminism has claimed victory. A renovated SDS maintains and integrates its intersectionality with race, ethnicity, class, ability, and sexual orientation; it too is applied unevenly and "unfairly" to women/girls who are "always already" lambasted as excessive, troubling but maintaining it (Chmielewski, 2017; Schippers, 2007). A renovated SDS leverages what remains intractable due to the intact bearing beams of its traditional forebear. A renovated SDS too has as its modus operandus the control, surveillance, assessment, punishment, and containment of female sexuality, in general, and desire, in particular, that is deemed excessive. It is the target of excessive female desire, which now takes new forms even as old norms and social practices shift, which we suggest is this bearing beam. The exact discourse that demands at least a performance of sexual agency and empowerment may in fact be a new regime of surveillance and control (Gill, 2008; McRobbie, 2009).

Recent moral panics about young women's sexuality show what a renovated SDS is by illuminating this reworking in action. A case in point is the "girls gone wild" phenomenon (Levy, 2006), in which college girls show (or fail to cover) their bodies and express their sexuality freely during spring break, only to be subjected to punishments and consequences for these actions after the fact, losing relationships, chastised by family, and suffering humiliation and shame. Another is an ongoing panic about the sexualization of girls and young women, with outsized anxiety about girls and young women dressing "scantily" and claiming sexual empowerment, performing desire in ways associated with male sexuality and bad girls/women (Chmielewski et al., 2017; Lamb et al., 2013). The implicit belief that when girls and women fail or refuse to change their behavior in the name of keeping male sexual desire under control – rape myth acceptance – remains a bedrock. This belief fuels anger and anxiety when female sexual desire and bodies erupt, which offers a partial explanation of how the SDS enables sexual harassment and assault (Hayes et al., 2016). But what caused this renovation?

The Normalization of Sexuality outside Marriage

As social norms and practices have changed, heterosexual marriage has become insufficient as systemic containment of female sexuality (England et al., 2008). Female sexuality is increasingly recognized as an aspect of normative psychosocial development, especially in adolescence (Horne & Zimmer-Gembeck, 2006; Tolman & McClelland, 2011); same-sex desire is increasingly recognized as part of the human condition rather than an aberration (Saewyc, 2011). While the standard of heterosexual marriage continues to apply in some places, cultures, and religious communities, research consistently shows that in the Anglophone West, premarital sex, especially (while) in a committed relationship can be acceptable for women (Crawford & Popp, 2003). This shift of cultural management and containment of sex makes sense: most sex in marriage is not associated with reproduction but is an expression of deep feelings of love and connection and now happens later in women's and men's development (Cohn et al., 2011); it assumes or even demands evidence of women's (hetero)sexual desire. Now that heterosexual marriage occurs later, "premarital sex" is almost anachronistic. In response, a renovated SDS is an updated system of control that continues to regulate girls' and young women's sexuality by labeling as "slut" any aspect of female sexuality that can be deemed (in)appropriately excessive. A renovated SDS is hidden in plain sight, written in invisible ink or lines of code that can materialize and metabolize unpredictably, yet its "stickiness" remains, a scarlet letter rendered branding tattoo – fueling its continued power (Ahmed, 2004; Tanenbaum, 2000, 2015; Tolman et al., 2015).

Neoliberal and Postfeminist Mandates for Sexual Empowerment

We now live in a postfeminist, neoliberal cultural climate that has introduced some complications and subsequent contradictions to the traditional good/bad girl binary. A renovated SDS is more complex and multifaceted. This shift was ushered in by the interloper into the good/bad girl binary – the *prude* – a young woman who does not comply with the feminine mandate of being – wanting to be desirable, interested in and focused on boys' and men's desire. The prude suggests a new form of poor or unpopular *choice* – not punished so much as disdained. The prude raises the profile of excess by being excessively devoid of interest in men's desire. But now young women's sexual engagements are *also* evaluated on the basis of a neoliberal conception of agency, what Laina Bay-Cheng (2015) calls "The Agency Line." This line assumes free will, entitlement to choice, and the prioritization of self-interest, and, is predicated on this ostensible freedom, and subsequent personal responsibility and accountability. Popular discourse now includes expectations for young women to be sexually agentic and desiring as well as desirable: "sexually empowered" young women, sexually savvy and agentic women who are "up for anything," and who are supposed to feel entitled to sexual freedom and pleasure within and outside committed relationships. This version of sexuality is individualized, depoliticized, and purportedly neutral across gender, sexuality, race, and class, obfuscating the continued structural barriers and challenges of sexism, heterosexism, and racism to girls' available sexual choices (Bay-Cheng, 2015). And so "bad" choices still await. They have simply shifted from having sex at all to making sexual choices that are, or appear to be, *excessive,* and girls are held responsible and accountable for making them under these confusing and often unfair and oppressive – and invisible – conditions. Girls and women are in a minefield of contradictory messages, mandates, and social repercussions for how they can and should look, act, feel, and make choices about their bodies and desires (Chmielewski et al., 2017). They must navigate the contradictory burden of "compulsory sexual agency" (Gill, 2008, p. 40), where they must *project* an empowered sexuality, and also *present* themselves as sexually desirable, *seem* appropriately excessive – but without *being* excessive and crossing over into "sluttiness."

The Persistence of the (Renovated) SDS

Combined with the shift in social practices related to sexuality – later marriage, same-sex marriage – and the intensification of sex as a commodity to consume and a sexualized self as a commodity to be/come – the SDS could have gone by the wayside or, as is the case, have been declared no longer in force or relevant. The neoliberal mandate for girls and young women to "achieve" the "right" amount, performance, and production of sexiness seems as if it is another death knell for the SDS – and it is often declared defunct. Yet the rampant moral panic about slut shaming, and the reality of its being part of young women's social worlds, lived experiences, and identity negotiation, underscores that declaration has not been realized. An (unacknowledged) renovated SDS remains at the heart of many moral panics about sexuality – especially the sexuality of adolescent girls – but is rarely itself the topic of discussion, questions, or critique. However, the question of how slut shaming is possible, even virulent, at a time when (some) girls and women are often positioned as being sexually empowered looms. Even as the SDS morphs, there is a persistent pattern of blaming the victim, denying and denigrating girls' and women's sexual agency, and assuming that men are either sexual predators or constantly trying to control their incessant sexual impulses. The hierarchical gender binary in which men's desire is privileged over women's remains steadfast; it was never unseated. Desire itself retains a residue of masculinity and abjection, cloaked in a flimsy claim of equal access.

Research on the SDS in Emerging Adulthood

We now report on research relating to the SDS, examining how it has been studied among young adults (mostly college students). While there is research documenting various dimensions of the SDS globally (i.e. Bordini & Sperb, 2013; de Meyer et al., 2017), we are reviewing studies from the Anglophone West. Most of this research considers and measures the traditional SDS, documenting how and where it exists within the current context of "hookup culture" where casual sex is normative, at least among adults and college students. In the questions asked and designs of studies, this research sits *within* the traditional SDS. The specter of a renovated SDS infiltrates, even motivates, much of this research but, as we will show, this scholarship falls short of a reconfiguration of the SDS itself, while illustrating the need for it.

Not surprisingly, research on the SDS among young adults has tended to ask whether or not it still exists, examines how (and by whom) it is perpetuated, and how it affects sexual well-being and relationships. These questions recognize that the traditional SDS is not operating in the same way as it once did yet at the same time seems not to have disappeared. Much of this research examines the phenomenon of casual sex and the emergence of "hookup culture" as a new arena in which casual sex is encouraged (purportedly for both men and women), which raises particular questions from the perspective of the traditional SDS. We might predict that as hookup culture is increasingly normative and expected, the SDS is fading. It is important to recognize that the *traditional* SDS infuses this scholarship as a conceptual underpinning: research attempts to document whether and how the traditional SDS exists in a postfeminist context.

From this vantage point, some researchers conclude that the traditional SDS continues, albeit in modified ways, increasingly focused on controlling other sexual behaviors (oral and anal sex), number of partners, and "correct" gendered sexual performance (e.g. sexual assertiveness and initiation; Bordini & Sperb, 2013; Jonason & Marks, 2009; Reid et al., 2011). In utilizing this perspective, it can seem as though the SDS is fading (Allison & Risman, 2013) – but findings about its persistence, especially among men, suggests something more is going on. Several quantitative studies find that the majority of college students do not personally endorse the traditional SDS, and some have actually suggested a reverse double standard may exist where female college students judge promiscuous male targets more harshly than they judge promiscuous female targets (Milhausen & Herold, 2002; Papp et al., 2015). However, the vast majority of studies indicates that casual sex is still less acceptable for women than men (Sprecher et al., 2013), and that men are more likely to endorse (Allison & Risman, 2013; Milhausen & Herold, 2002; Sprecher et al., 2013) and perpetuate the traditional SDS (Sanchez et al., 2012) than women. This research is ridden with contradictions and confusing findings.

We suggest that one explanation for this is that in these studies' investigations of the traditional SDS, findings do not account for contradictions embedded in a renovated SDS; findings reflect ongoing punishment in the face of observable changes in the SDS that a renovated SDS would predict. The consistent finding of men's greater endorsement of the SDS, and women believing that other women endorse the SDS even as they personally endorse gender equality in sexuality (Bordini & Sperb, 2013), offers a rupture for what the research is missing in its reliance on the traditional SDS.

Effects on Sexual Well-Being

The negative effects of the traditional SDS on women's sexual agency, pleasure, and well-being in their sexual experiences are well documented. The emerging research on these outcomes reflects resistance to the traditional SDS in repositioning it as harmful to women and a perspective that women are entitled to sexuality. Rudman and Fetterolf (2014) found that men who endorse the SDS report more hostile sexism and view sexuality as a female commodity for men, suggesting that men perpetuate it as a way to suppress female sexuality because they are resistant to gender equality. Other research has found traditional sexual scripts and gender roles (that are at the heart of the traditional SDS) are harmful for both men and women, but particularly women's ability to engage in sexual expression freely

(Sanchez et al., 2012). For instance, Woerner and Abbey (2017) found that traditional gender role beliefs are related to less sexual assertiveness and sexual pleasure, and less positive feelings about casual sex experiences for women. Women's endorsement of the traditional SDS is related to less sexual initiation, sexual assertiveness, sexual communication, and, thereby, less sexual satisfaction in their heterosexual dating relationships (Greene & Faulkner, 2005). Further, regardless of whether women personally endorse the traditional SDS for themselves, they tend to believe others endorse it, and, as a result, concern about men's judgments shapes their experiences, thoughts, and feelings about sex, both in and out of romantic relationships (Bordini & Sperb, 2013). This can leave them unable to directly communicate and engage (and acknowledge?) their desires (Jozkowski et al., 2017).

College women's choices of whether or not to engage in casual sex is impeded by the persistent and ever-looming "slut discourse" (Armstrong et al., 2014; Hamilton & Armstrong, 2009), and a fear of gaining a "reputation" keeps them from engaging in the sexual behavior they would like (Farvid et al., 2017). For instance, studies have shown that women refrain from engaging in casual sex with men (Conley et al., 2013) and initiating condom use in casual sex encounters to avoid stigma from male partners and being seen as too sexually assertive (Young et al., 2010). Some women discuss a need to refuse sex as a way to demonstrate their value to men in a context where men believe their role is to pursue women and try to coerce a yes from 'respectable women' (Jozkowski et al., 2017); if they say yes too easily, they may be excessive in their desire and slip (or be pushed) from respectable to slut. Other research examines how women continue to construct themselves and their sexuality in relation to the notion of the "slut." One study found that elite, White college young women construct themselves as "not sluts" by positioning others, who are of color and/or financially disadvantaged, as sexually excessive, making poor choices and living with the "self-imposed" consequences of a sexual reputation (Armstrong et al., 2014). Farvid and Braun (2017) found that college women's narratives about casual sex revealed that they saw sexual reputation as something other women have, retained a belief in the unacceptability of casual sex, and described how a slut is "made." We suggest that this research is motivated by resistance to the traditional SDS but also points to and sheds light on a renovated SDS in documenting ongoing complexities and tensions. We suggest that this renovated SDS accounts for these findings from research grounded in resistance to the traditional SDS by opening a window into the contradictions and difficulties experienced by college and adult women navigating the SDS in what is actually its renovated form.

Research on the SDS in Adolescence

Research with adolescents also primarily relies on the traditional conception of the SDS in its focus and measurement. The SDS in adolescence has similarities and resonances with its college-aged and emerging adult incarnations, but it is particularly virulently applied to teens. While emerging adulthood is a relatively short transition period (especially for college students), one of the key dimensions of adolescence is the development of adult sexuality. Research on teen sexuality is often about how it "works" in relation to other dimensions of adolescence. In adolescence, both the traditional and renovated SDS are salient and loom large. Children and adolescents are now developing in a culture where they are picking up on the way sexual women are talked about and which sexual interactions purportedly and sometimes do gain rewards or are condemned. The media, older siblings, parents, and even sex education are all highly influential in adolescents' sexual development (Collins et al., 2009), and often perpetuate the traditional SDS (Seabrook et al., 2017). Sexuality contents in popular media for teens (Aubrey, 2004), and news media for adults *about* teens, tend to emphasize negative consequences of sexuality for, and placing the responsibility for these consequences on, teenage girls (Chmielewski et al., 2017). Similarly, sex education from school and parents reinforces the notion that girls do not (or are not supposed to actually) desire and boys incessantly desire, which necessitates girls acting as gatekeepers (Bay-Cheng, 2003; Elliott, 2010).

With sexual feelings, emotions, interactions, explorations, and relationships intensifying in adolescence (Collins et al., 2009), the SDS is already embedded in the psychological and social (especially digitally mediated) lives of tweens (Jackson & Vares, 2011), and even girls (and boys) prior to puberty (Renold, 2005). Early developing girls are subjected to surveillance of and assumptions about their bodies and behavior; some suffer being labeled simply because their bodies have developed (White, 2002). A relational context that mimics marriage or could turn into it serves as a form of protection and/or as a screen from being visibly excessive (Tolman et al., 2015). However, when a relationship ends (and in adolescence, it almost always inevitably does), girls are vulnerable to the SDS; having been "sexually activated," and thus, by definition, available for sex or sexualized, they are always potentially excessive since they ventured out of the "safe space" of virginity (Tolman, 2002).

Effects on Sexual Well-Being

There is scholarship on adolescent girls that takes a resistant stance to the traditional SDS investigating its negative effects. Enactment of the SDS can already be discerned in adolescents' first sexual encounters (Sanchez et al., 2012). In middle school or early in high school, girls who have sex experience a decrease in their friendship networks, whereas boys experience pressure to become sexually active and gain an increase in peer acceptance if they have sex (Kreager et al., 2016). Endorsement and enactment of gendered expectations derived from the SDS are problematic because they are associated with a multitude of negative sexual and mental health effects (Sanchez et al., 2012). Some studies have found SDS endorsement to be associated with higher sexually transmitted infection/HIV infection risk (Bermúdez et al., 2010) and with early sexual initiation among both boys and girls (Goncalves et al., 2008). Other research asks how the traditional SDS is associated with women's sexual expression and satisfaction. For instance, endorsement of traditional gender roles leads to decreased sexual pleasure for both boys and girls (Sanchez et al., 2005). Specifically for girls, the sexual passivity associated with SDS endorsement is predictive of poor sexual functioning and lower sexual satisfaction (Kiefer & Sanchez, 2007), as well as more sexual problems (Sanchez & Kiefer, 2007). For boys, SDS endorsement has been related to rape myth acceptance (Truman et al., 1996). However, some research suggests that the traditional SDS is not monolithic but localized, possibly varying in intensity and practice, in line with shifts in the traditional SDS. In their study of racially diverse Ohio girls, Lyons et al. (2011) found that girls who have had more sexual partners but did not report a dip in popularity, desire for more friends, or lower self-esteem after a year, also identified accepting social networks and peer identity groups as key factors in buffering the effects of the SDS. What is missing from this body of work are the questions that emerge from a conceptual standpoint of a renovated SDS, such as how girls navigate conflicting demands to be and act sexy when girls' desire and actual sexual expression is always at risk of being labeled excessive. Below we discuss the small and burgeoning body of research that has opened the way toward understanding a renovated SDS.

Feminist Perspectives: Desire and Possibilities for Rupture

Feminist approaches to research have explored girls' sexuality and desire, and, by necessity, shed light on how and where the traditional SDS has been or is implicated in girls' and boys' experiences of desire and identity at the intersection of gender, race, class, and sexuality. This body of work constituted resistance to what was and continues to be an enormous literature on the risks predicting and associated with girls' sexual behavior (whether or not motivated by desire), including the risk of garnering a sexual reputation. As a whole, this research raised and answered questions about the SDS as problematic, and girls' sexuality and desire as normative. Over time, this research has incorporated a focus on the possibilities and pleasures of sexuality and girls' rights to their own embodied and unencumbered sexual desire. In 1988, Michelle Fine published the seminal paper, "*Sexuality Schooling, and Adolescent Females: The Missing Discourse of Desire*," an ethnography of an urban public high school, where she explored how discourses of disease, immorality, and danger perpetuated silence about "a missing discourse of girls' sexual desire" in schools. She observed that any sign or recognition of desire was suppressed – by girls themselves and by others (girls and boys) if it became evident – or simply absent (1988). Recognizing desire itself as the culprit, the animating force that brought controls into and onto girls' bodies and social lives, initiated a body of counter hegemonic research. This new research asked – and answered – very different questions about girls' experiences of their own sexual desire, their sexual subjectivity (sense of themselves as sexual people), their sexual agency (ability to know and act upon one's own desires or absence of desires), and new questions about positive dimensions of sexuality. In one of the earliest studies in this vein, Holland et al. (2004, originally published in 1998) found that (diverse) adolescent girls described unequal relationships and, in particular, that girls "collude[ed] with their male sexual partners in ... reproduce[ing] ... male power" (Holland et al., 2004, p.156). They dubbed this socialization process and effect "the male-in-the-head."

In other early research, Tolman (2002) identified that sexual desire posed dilemmas for girls; one pervasive reason was their negotiation of the SDS. Those fears manifested as worry about sexual reputation and being labeled a slut, being used by boys, being objectified, and not being recognized as subjects of their own sexual desire. This finding was consistent across urban and suburban, racially and sexually diverse participants. In particular, she found that some girls engaged in covert forms of resistance to ensure that evidence of their sexual desire – being witnessed as sexually assertive – was obscured or excused by the use of alcohol or curtailing sexual expression in a context where a boy or other girls might judge them as having crossed that ever-ambiguous line. This kind of dual agency – agency for pleasure and agency for protection – braided together to yield other costs, including, the effects of alcohol consumption, expending psychic energy, sexual frustration, or dissatisfaction, as well as benefits, including, acting on their desire, creating conditions for safety, exploring new experiences. Other girls were so concerned about the threat of a negative reputation that they described never feeling sexual desire – being disembodied – to eliminate any risk.

Quantitative measurements echo these findings and bridge scholarship anchored in the traditional SDS to a renovated form. Horne and Zimmer-Gembeck (2006) found that among adolescent girls and young adult women, sexual subjectivity, or the ability for girls and young women to experience (and feel entitled to experience) pleasure from and in their bodies, is connected to the resistance of patriarchal norms and the traditional double standard. Another study introduced a new measure for evaluating what we are calling a renovated SDS, the Scale for the Assessment of Sexual Standards among Youth (Emmerink et al., 2017). Among 465 diverse Dutch boys and girls (ages 16–20 years), higher gender investment was significantly associated with increased renovated SDS endorsement. For both boys and girls, increased feelings of entitlement to sexual pleasure through masturbation were significantly associated with less renovated SDS endorsement.

Qualitative research has suggested that embodiment may be an important tool for resisting both the traditional and renovated versions of the SDS (Tolman, 2002; Tolman et al., 2015). Piran (2017) traced how the SDS becomes a roadblock to the development of embodiment among girls. Maxwell and Aggleton (2012) found that adolescent girls connecting to their *feeling* bodies was central to sustaining sexual agency, enabling girls to determine what they like and want, as well as what they do not like or want, from their sexual experiences and relationships. And although girls' (and women's) masturbation is often still infused with shame, Bowman (2017) has found that some women who recall masturbating as children describe both embodied desires and pleasures and a continued sense of entitlement to them as adults.

Excess and the SDS for Girls of Color

Some research has investigated and documented how the SDS can operate in distinct ways for girls of color, poor girls, and queer girls. For instance, as Patricia Hill Collins (2004) has articulated, Black women (and girls) are "always already" assumed to be excessively sexual. As Fasula et al. (2014) have described, the SDS takes on a multidimensional form to regulate African-American girls based on this stereotype; thus, African-American girls are, like all other girls, navigating the SDS in relationship to the gender binary, but also in relation to Whiteness, and how their Blackness positions them as always at risk of being a slut predicated on White purity. For girls of color who are also queer, this evidence of desire is automatically excessive. Because it is directed at girls rather than boys, they face an added dimension when they combat a sexually predatory "slut" label from their straight peers who fear that they are always ready to prey on straight girls, regardless of their actual sexual behaviors (Chmielewski, 2017). Lamb and colleagues (2016) observed that African-American and Black girls, as well as Latina and Muslim girls, are learning to navigate their sexuality within discourses of respectability that has deep roots in these communities. This navigation is a form of resistance to "controlling images" of Black women's sexuality (Hill Collins, 2004); it is a refutation of the profound disrespect, assault, and objectification of African-American women under slavery. In Black communities, the articulation of respectability – perceived by others and enacted by the self – intersects with the SDS as a keen and particular vector of evaluation for Black adolescent girls situated in historical and cultural contexts. This discursive construction of African-American girls has been shown to be embedded in and to inform how mothers socialize their daughters in a more prohibitive way than their sons (i.e., Fasula et al., 2007).

The Complexities of Now: Managing a Renovated Sexual Double Standard

We live in a time when gender equity is now almost within reach in so many domains; once an anathema, "feminism" is *the* word of the year for 2017 (Merriam-Webster, 2017). As we write this chapter, we are seeing men every day being outed for sexual violence against women, and quickly ousted from their powerful positions (Almukhtar et al., 2017). The reality of sexual harassment and recognition and critique of White elite male privilege is now a widespread global dialogue. Women's sexuality and desire is increasingly considered normal and, in some circles, girls' developing sexuality, including desires, and curiosity about and enjoyment of pleasure, is recognized as a normative aspect of their psychosocial and physical development *to which they should be (although consistently do not feel) entitled.* Some girls use the word slut not only as an epithet but also as a term of endearment, a nickname, the residue of badness meant as a kind of rowdy backhanded compliment or redeployment of bad as good. Recent research is grounded in what we suggest is a renovated SDS (Chmielewski et al., 2017; Dobson, 2015). While feminists have debated how to understand what it means when girls describe themselves as sexually empowered (Bay-Cheng, 2012; Gavey, 2012; Gill, 2012; Lamb & Peterson, 2012; Tolman, 2012), we suggest that the widespread empowerment discourse is an effect of and contained by a renovated SDS. Rather than simply making a claim, not far from the surface is evidence that girls and women are navigating conflicting demands and punishments for excess in their various sexual experiences with boys/men (or anyone), constructing their identities in relation to other girls and the "slut discourse," and managing the (relatively) new terrain of social media and sexualized digital exchange.

How a Renovated SDS Complicates "Slut"

The 'slut' moniker persists, but its effects are complicated by this new context of a renovated SDS. Research illuminates how adolescent girls are actively constructing themselves in relation to other girls using the "slut discourse." Some research finds that girls are more willing to talk about their ongoing endorsement of other girls behaving as sluts in part by situating themselves as "not sluts" (Fjaer et al., 2015). These dynamics are not restricted to heterosexual girls: Payne (2010) has found similar processes among White lesbian adolescents in the US South. Yet the new context complicates the effect of the moniker "slut." Tanenbaum (2015) interviewed 55 adolescent girls and young women aged 14–22 years, diverse by race, ethnicity, and geography, to understand how the SDS operates. She reports how the moniker "slut" has both become complicated and at the same time still serves the purpose of surveilling teen girls' sexuality and compliance with norms of appropriate comportment and behavior. She identified two ways that they engaged with "slut" – the empowered "good slut" and the shameful "bad slut." Yet, as slut remains entangled with and serves a renovated SDS, utilizing the term yields negative consequences for girls who embraced it. With the proliferation of the moniker through media in general and social media in particular, she argues that every girl comes into contact with this term and its valences. While some young women identified as a sex-positive "good slut," all inevitably lost control of the word and experienced the punishment and control that the term exerts in upholding a renovated SDS. She found that girls felt that they "must be a little 'slutty' . . . but they can't be too much so" (p. 19). With the SDS still operating in renovated form, girls' and young women's efforts to navigate a neoliberal press to be "up for it," leaves them struggling with contradictions and limited options for navigating their sexuality development.

The SDS in the Digital Landscape

Finally, digital media platforms have also introduced new and more complex terrain where a renovated SDS circulates in girls' lives – in texts and images through technology and social media (Dobson, 2015; Ringrose et al., 2013). Ringrose et al. (2013) found that teen girls and boys performed current constructions that underpin a renovated SDS. Girls felt compelled to produce particular forms of "sexy" self-images at the same time that they say it is risky and can result in blame, shame, and a bad sexual reputation. They also found that some boys collected positive ratings from other boys when they were able to secure and share these images of girls, a new form of currency and value. A growing body of research documents how girls who sext (exchange of sexual images and/or text via technologies including smartphones and social media) are vulnerable to social exclusion, abuse, bullying, and psychological harm (Dobson, 2015; Walker et al., 2013). The constant engagement with digitally mediated, heterosexualized, classed, and raced norms normalizes a renovated SDS. Adult perceptions of girls' engagement in these sexualized norms in celebrity and digitally mediated cultures perpetuate the SDS, often ignoring girls' agency in the service of desire, at the same time as they emphasize girls' need to be agentic in the service of protection (Chmielewski et al., 2017; Lamb, et al., 2013).

Resistance and Thriving: Critical Consciousness, Activism and Rebuffing the SDS

Research shows that adolescents are questioning, and in many ways pushing back, against both traditional and renovated forms of the SDS, yet they often do so in individual ways, without social, educational, or community support (Ringrose et al., 2013). Even as adolescents want egalitarian relationships and express frustration about a persistent, confusing, and unfair SDS, their struggle is a missing critical consciousness that keeps in place these immense, although confusing, pressures ultimately to behave in accordance with gendered expectations (Tolman et al., 2016). Possibilities for resistance and thriving anchored in this missing link are articulated in feminist research and practice in sex education and activism with teens, especially girls. For instance, listening for what they call "*hidden* discourses of desire" (our italics, p. 82), McClelland and Fine (2008) found what they articulate as "release points" in focus groups with racially and ethnically diverse girls – moments when diverse girls' felt desire bumped up against those discourses and practices associated with a racialized understanding of the traditional SDS meant to rein them in – which McClelland and Fine suggest can be critical moments for collaborative disruption. These disruptions (vs. interventions) incorporate resistance and critical consciousness into traditional constructs of male and female sexuality, revealing individualistic solutions to be systemic racist, classed and homophobic gender inequality, the beating heart of the SDS.

Critically Conscious Sexual Education(s)

Feminist scholars and practitioners have argued that sex education must be sex positive *and* gender transformative, providing information not only about reproduction, disease, and risk reduction, but also possibilities of physical pleasure (i.e., the clitoris as part of anatomy and its functions (Fields, 2008), and about the vicissitudes of relationships and how to handle them realistically by addressing gender inequality and providing the tools to critique it and the SDS (Bay-Cheng, 2003; Fields, 2008). Sexuality education should be integrated throughout the school curriculum rather than segregated into a single class (Rogow & Haberland, 2005). We concur with McClelland and Fine's (2008) suggestion that "release points" can be identified, where desire and cultural containment can be critically assessed. Recognizing that the sexual double standard persists through renovation should guide the identification of such release points and, most importantly, the need for collaborative rather than individualistic recognition and rebuff of its presence and power. Adults (parents, teachers, and community leaders) can work to provide the tools for critical consciousness, to allow for the possibility that adolescent girls can be recognized as sexual people without being thought of as "sluts," along with the possibility that adolescent boys are driven by a desire for emotional intimacy rather than just sex (Way et al., 2018).

Activism: Levering Critical Consciousness

Activism, particularly by girls working collectively and also intergenerationally with women – where they can be encouraged, supported, and heard – has been effective in creating fissures for disruption and possibilities for mobilization (Brown, 2016). A teen girl for the feminist girls' activist initiative, SPARK, blogged about how girls' saying "Love Ya, Slut!" to each other is premature – without a critical analysis of its power, "slut" just becomes a more easily mobilized word (Ostrow, 2011). Activism and resistance in the form of art and performances can also be a visceral change agent (Edell, 2013). Katie Cappiello has found that girls performing *Slut: The Play* – written in consultation with girls – ignites awareness, sadness, outrage, and action to be more respectful of girls as sexual people in communities that perform it (personal communication, May 31, 2017). Her follow-up play, *Now That We're Men*, written in consultation with boys, examines how boys grapple with the SDS and expectations of masculinity. Another newer development is feminist clubs as a space where girls and women (and boys) can work together to challenge school policies and practices that may seem progressive by mandating a "slut-shaming free" climate but effectively suppress discussion or analysis of what slut shaming is, what is required to diminish it, and what girls and their allies can do to resist (Blackett, 2016; Brown, 2016).

The Slutwalks began in 2011 to draw attention to and protest (a still rampant) rape culture–blaming rape on the actions of girls and women (sexual behavior, dressing to show their bodies, embodying "sexiness," igniting men's uncontrollable sexual desire). They spread like a raging fire nationally and globally. This movement to "take back" the word "slut" – and to defy the SDS that it circulates – has been complicated and questioned. In the United States, African American women and other women of color have articulated how "taking back" a racialized word that in part depends on the abjection of Black women's bodies and sexuality is neither possible nor desirable and instead argue for more substantive action to reveal and refuse rape culture. A Slutwalk in postcolonial India garnered momentum that shocked the country; its meaning is localized, offering an accessible "feminism lite" to the general public by incorporating a pragmatic way for women to refuse to embody the "good" and "modest" (middle class) Indian woman whose task is not only to gatekeep and protect men but also the entire nation (Kapur, 2012).

The Women's March on January 21, 2017, the day after a "pussy grabbing" US president was inaugurated, may be ushering in push back against both the traditional and a renovated SDS. The effect of implicitly condoned sexual harassment in the workplace that the SDS enables is arguably undergoing a sea of change. #metoo, a hashtag denouncing sexual harassment and assault that surfaced in October 2017 and went viral in the wake of allegations against film producer Harvey Weinstein, had 12 million posts, comments, and reactions in the first 24 hours. All of these disruptions have provided a way or, at the very least, the outlines of a vision for creating resistant communities among women and girls and their allies, even as they have been rightly critiqued for their lack of focus on a missing discourse of the right to sexual expression and embodiment for girls and women – for their right to desire. The importance of engaging boys and men in these ways cannot be underestimated; gender inequity is the fuel and purpose of the SDS. Providing boys and men with the conditions and tools to recognize and resist stereotypes and harmful ideas about boys' and girls' sexuality is key; even more important is helping them understand and value what they are "trading" for toxic masculinity: knowledge and experience about their own emotions, even their own bodies, the pleasures of emotional connections, in essence, and their entitlement to their full humanity (Way et al., 2018).

Conclusion

McClelland and Fine (2008) observed that even as girls and women may struggle in various ways with their embodied sexuality, their "capacity to want" is discernable (p. 83). The potential for excess lives – and it is dangerous. While evidence of excess is being mobilized to keep girls' and young women's sexuality under control and under wraps, excess also has potent potential to fuel revelation and disruption of the structures and practices that serve to contain it, as we are now witnessing. In this chapter, we described how the traditional SDS was organized by two rigid intersecting binaries: normative male sexual desire is expected and monstrous and female desire is nonexistent or kept in check and girls/women who comply are "good" and those who do not are "bad." We articulated an emergent twist, a renovated SDS, that accounts for the newer realities that (heterosexual) marriage is no longer the boundary for teen girls' and young women's sexual desire and a postfeminist mandate for (some) girls and young women to be sexual in ways that are judged to be *(in) appropriately excessive*. We reviewed research on emerging adults and adolescents grounded in both of these versions of the SDS, illuminating how the SDS operates and also the ways in which the SDS is bad for girls and young women (and boys and young men). We traced the conceptual movement in this research from the traditional SDS, to questions about its existence, to resistance to it, and a shift to grounding inquiries in a renovated SDS. Finally, we reported on what is now a groundswell of activism and resistance to the SDS anchored in critical consciousness of its roots and offered some recommendations for how to proliferate these efforts. We began this chapter with a sampling of memes that reflect the persistence of the SDS. A less well circulated but still easily found meme underscores that resistance to the SDS is making headway in eroding it: What do you call a woman who has a lot of sex: her name. "Slut" is attacking women for their right to say yes; "friendzone" (a negatively valued term meaning turning down a sexual relationship with a male friend) for their right to say no. Girls' and young women's saying "no" will be, and is increasingly, believed when they can really say both yes and no.

References

Ahmed, S. (2004). Collective Feelings: Or, the Impressions Left by Others. *Theory, Culture & Society*, 21, 25–42.

Allison, R. & Risman, B. J. (2013). A Double Standard for "Hooking Up": How Far Have We Come toward Gender Equality? *Social Science Research*, *42*, 1191–1206.

Almukhtar, S., Gold, M., & Buchanan, L. (2017). After Weinstein: 47 men accused of sexual misconduct and their fall from power. *New York Times*. Retrieved from www.nytimes.com/interactive/2017/11/10/us/men-accused-sexual-misconduct-weinstein.html?_r=0.

Armstrong, E. A., Hamilton, L. T., Armstrong, E. M., & Seeley, J. L. (2014). "Good Girls": Gender, Social Class, and Slut Discourse on Campus. *Social Psychology Quarterly*, *77*, 100-122.

Aubrey, J. S. (2004). Sex and Punishment: An Examination of Sexual Consequences and the Sexual Double Standard in Teen Programming. *Sex Roles*, *50*, 505–514.

Bay-Cheng, L. Y. (2003). The Trouble of Teen Sex: The Construction of Adolescent Sexuality through School-Based Sexuality Education. *Sex Education: Sexuality, Society and Learning*, *3*, 61–74.

(2012). Recovering Empowerment: De-personalizing and Re-Politicizing Adolescent Female Sexuality. *Sex Roles*, *66*, 713–717.

(2015). The Agency Line: A Neoliberal Metric for Appraising Young Women's Sexuality. *Sex Roles*, *73*, 279–291.

Bermúdez, M., Castro, A., Gude, F., & Buela-Casal, G. (2010). Relationship Power in the Couple and Sexual Double Standard as Predictors of the Risk of Sexually Transmitted Infections and HIV: Multicultural and Gender Differences. *Current HIV Research*, *8*, 172–178.

Blackett, E. (2016). "I'm Allowed to Be Angry": Students Resist Postfeminist Education in Aotearoa/New Zealand. *Women's Studies Journal*, *30*, 38–52.

Bordini, G. S. & Sperb, T. M. (2013). Sexual Double Standard: A Review of the Literature between 2001 and 2010. *Sexuality & Culture*, *17*, 686–704.

Bowman, C. P. (2017). Persistent pleasures: Agency, social power, and embodiment in women's solitary masturbation experiences. Doctoral dissertation. City University of New York.

Brown, L. M. (2016). *Powered by Girl: A Field Guide for Working with Girl Activists*. Boston: Beacon Press.

Butler, J. (1990). *Gender Trouble: Feminism and the Subversion of Identity*. New York: Routledge.

Chmielewski, J. F. (2017). A Listening Guide Analysis of Lesbian and Bisexual Young Women of Color's Experiences of Sexual Objectification. *Sex Roles*, 77, 533–549.

Chmielewski, J. F., Tolman, D. L., & Kincaid, H. (2017). Constructing Risk and Responsibility: A Gender, Race, and Class Analysis of News Representations of Adolescent Sexuality. *Feminist Media Studies*, *17*, 412–425.

Cohn, D., Passel, J. S., Wang, W., & Livingston, G. (2011). Barely half of U.S. adults are married – A record low. Pew Research Center, Washington, DC. Retrieved from www.pewsocialtrends.org/2011/12/14/barely-half-of-u-s-adults-are-married-a-record-low/

Collins, W. A., Welsh, D. P., & Furman, W. (2009). Adolescent Romantic Relationships. *Annual Review of Psychology*, *60*, 631–652.

Conley, T. D., Ziegler, A., & Moors, A. C. (2013). Backlash from the Bedroom: Stigma Mediates Gender Differences in Acceptance of Casual Sex Offers. *Psychology of Women Quarterly*, *37*, 392–407.

Crawford, M. & Popp, D. (2003). Sexual Double Standards: A Review and Methodological Critique of Two Decades of Research. *Journal of Sex Research*, *40*, 13–26.

de Meyer, S., Kågesten, A., Mmari, K. et al. (2017). "Boys Should Have the Courage to Ask a Girl Out": Gender Norms in Early Adolescent Romantic Relationships. *Journal of Adolescent Health*, *61*, S42–S47.

Diamond, L. M. (2005). 'I'm Straight, but I Kissed a Girl': The Trouble with American Media Representations of Female–Female Sexuality. *Feminism & Psychology*, 15, 104–110.

Dobson, A. S. (2015). *Postfeminist Digital Cultures: Femininity, Social Media, and Self-representation*. New York: Palgrave MacMillan.

Edell, D. (2013). "Say It How It Is": Urban Teenage Girls Challenge and Perpetuate Stereotypes through Writing and Performing Theatre. *Youth Theatre Journal*, *27*, 51–62.

Elliott, S. (2010). Parents' Constructions of Teen Sexuality: Sex Panics, Contradictory Discourses, and Social Inequality. *Symbolic Interaction*, *33*, 191–212.

Emmerink, P. M., van den Eijnden, R. J., ter Bogt, T. F., & Vanwesenbeeck, I. (2017). A Scale for the Assessment of Sexual Standards among Youth: Psychometric properties. *Archives of Sexual Behavior*, *46*, 1699–1709.

England, P., Shafer, E. F., & Fogarty, A. C. (2008). Hooking Up and Forming Romantic Relationships on Today's College Campuses. *The Gendered Society Reader*, *3*, 531–593.

Farvid, P. & Braun, V. (2017). Unpacking the "Pleasures" and "Pains" of Heterosexual Casual Sex: Beyond Singular Understandings. *The Journal of Sex Research*, *54*, 73–90.

Farvid, P., Braun, V., & Rowney, C. (2017). "No Girl Wants to Be Called a Slut!": Women, Heterosexual Casual Sex and the Sexual Double Standard. *Journal of Gender Studies*, *26*, 544–560.

Fasula, A. M., Carry, M., & Miller, K. S. (2014). A Multidimensional Framework for the Meanings of the Sexual Double Standard and Its Application for the Sexual Health of Young Black Women in the US. *The Journal of Sex Research*, *51*, 170–183.

Fasula, A. M., Miller, K. S., & Wiener, J. (2007). The Sexual Double Standard in African American Adolescent Women's Sexual Risk Reduction Socialization. *Women & Health*, *46*, 3–21.

Fields, J. (2008). *Risky Lessons: Sex Education and Social Inequality*. New Brunswick, NJ: Rutgers University Press.

Fine, M. (1988). Sexuality, Schooling, and Adolescent Females: The Missing Discourse of Desire. *Harvard Educational Review*, *58*, 29–54.

Fjaer, E. G., Pedersen, W., & Sandberg, S. (2015). "I'm Not One of Those Girls": Boundary-Work and the Sexual Double Standard in a Liberal Hookup Context. *Gender & Society*, *29*, 960–981.

Foucault, M. (1978). *The History of Sexuality: Introduction* Vol 1. New York: Random House.

Gavey, N. (2012). Beyond "Empowerment"? Sexuality in a Sexist World. *Sex Roles*, *66*, 718–724.

Gill, R. (2008). Empowerment/Sexism: Figuring Female Sexual Agency in Contemporary Advertising. *Feminism & Psychology*, *18*, 35–60.

(2012). Media, Empowerment and the "Sexualization of Culture" Debates. *Sex Roles*, *66*, 736–745.

Goncalves, H., Behague, D. P., Gigante, D. P. et al. (2008). Determinants of Early Sexual Initiation in the Pelotas Birth Cohort from 1982 to 2004–5, Southern Brazil. *Revista de Saude Publica*, *42*, 34–41.

Greene, K. & Faulkner, S. L. (2005). Gender, Belief in the Sexual Double Standard, and Sexual Talk in Heterosexual Dating Relationships. *Sex Roles*, *53*, 239–251.

Hamilton, L. & Armstrong, E. A. (2009). Gendered Sexuality in Young Adulthood: Double Binds and Flawed Options. *Gender & Society*, *23*, 589–616.

Hayes, R. M., Abbott, R. L., & Cook, S. (2016). It's Her Fault: Student Acceptance of Rape Myths on Two College Campuses. *Violence against Women*, *22*, 1540–1555.

Hill Collins, P. (2004). *Black Sexual Politics: African Americans, Gender, and the New Racism*. New York: Routledge.

Holland, J., Ramazanoglu, C., Sharpe, S., & Thomson, R. (1994). Power and Desire: The Embodiment of Female Sexuality. *Feminist Review*, *46*, 21–38.

(2004). *The Male in the Head: Young People, Heterosexuality and Power*, 2nd edn. London: Tufnell Press (Original work published 1998).

Horne, S. & Zimmer-Gembeck, M. J. (2006). The Female Sexual Subjectivity Inventory: Development and Validation of a Multidimensional Inventory for Late Adolescents and Emerging Adults. *Psychology of Women Quarterly*, *30*, 125–138.

Jackson, S. & Vares, T. (2011). Media "Sluts": "Tween" Girls' Negotiations of Postfeminist Sexual Subjectivities in Popular Culture. In Gill, R. & Scharff, C. (Eds.), *New Femininities* (134–146). London: Palgrave Macmillan.

Jonason, P. K. & Marks, M. J. (2009). Common vs. Uncommon Sexual Acts: Evidence for the Sexual Double Standard. *Sex Roles*, *60*, 357–365.

Jozkowski, K. N., Marcantonio, T. L., & Hunt, M. E. (2017). College Students' Sexual Consent Communication and Perceptions of Sexual Double Standards: A Qualitative Investigation. *Perspectives On Sexual And Reproductive Health*, 44, 237–244.

Kapur, R. (2012). Pink Chaddis and SlutWalk Couture: The Postcolonial Politics of Feminism Lite. *Feminist Legal Studies*, *20*, 1–20.

Kiefer, A. K. & Sanchez, D. T. (2007). Scripting Sexual Passivity: A Gender Role Perspective. *Personal Relationships*, *14*, 269–290.

Kreager, D. A., Staff, J., Gauthier, R., Lefkowitz, E. S., & Feinberg, M. E. (2016). The Double Standard at Sexual Debut: Gender, Sexual Behavior and Adolescent Peer Acceptance. *Sex Roles*, *75*, 377–392.

Lamb, S., Graling, K., & Wheeler, E. E. (2013). 'Pole-arized' Discourse: An Analysis of Responses to Miley Cyrus's Teen Choice Awards Pole Dance. *Feminism & Psychology*, *23*, 163–183.

Lamb, S. & Peterson, Z. D. (2012). Adolescent Girls' Sexual Empowerment: Two Feminists Explore the Concept. *Sex Roles*, *66*, 703–712.

Lamb, S., Roberts, T., & Plocha, A. (2016). *Girls of Color, Sexuality, and Sex Education*. New York: Palgrave MacMillan.

Levy, A. (2006). *Female Chauvinist Pigs: Women and the Rise of Raunch Culture*. New York: Free Press.

Lorde, A. (1984). *Sister Outsider*. Freedom: The Crossing Press.

Lyons, H., Giordano, P. C., Manning, W. D., & Longmore, M. A. (2011). Identity, Peer Relationships, and Adolescent Girls' Sexual Behavior: An Exploration of the Contemporary Double Standard. *Journal of Sex Research*, *48*, 437–449.

Maxwell, C. & Aggleton, P. (2012). Bodies and Agentic Practice in Young Women's Sexual and Intimate Relationships. *Sociology*, *46*, 306–321.

McClelland, S. I. & Fine, M. (2008). Rescuing a Theory of Adolescent Sexual Excess: Young Women and Wanting. In Harris, A. (Ed.), *Next Wave Cultures: Feminism, Subcultures, Activism* (83–102). New York: Routledge.

McRobbie, A. (2009). *The Aftermath of Feminism: Gender, Culture and Social Change*. London: Sage.

Merriam-Webster (2017). Merriam-Webster's 2017 words of the year. Retrieved from www.merriam-webster.com/words-at-play/word-of-the-year-2017-feminism/feminism.

Milhausen, R. R. & Herold, E. S. (2002). Reconceptualizing the Sexual Double Standard. *Journal of Psychology & Human Sexuality*, *13*, 63–83.

Ostrow, C. (2011). Love ya, slut [Blog post]. Retrieved from www.sparkmovement.org /2011/04/07/love-ya-slut/.

Papp, L. J., Hagerman, C., Gnoleba, M. A. et al. (2015). Exploring Perceptions of Slut-Shaming on Facebook: Evidence for a Reverse Sexual Double Standard. *Gender Issues*, *32*, 57–76.

Payne, E. (2010). Sluts: Heteronormative Policing in the Stories of Lesbian Youth. *Educational Studies*, *46*, 317–336.

Piran, N. (2017). *Journeys of Embodiment at the Intersection of Body and Culture: The Developmental Theory of Embodiment*. Cambridge, MA: Academic Press.

Reid, J. A., Elliott, S., & Webber, G. R. (2011). Casual Hookups to Formal Dates: Refining the Boundaries of the Sexual Double Standard. *Gender & Society*, *25*, 545–568.

Renold, E. (2005). *Girls, Boys and Junior Sexualities*. London: Routledge Falmer.

Rich, A. (1980). Compulsory Heterosexuality and Lesbian Existence. *Signs*, *5*, 631–660.

Ringrose, J., Harvey, L., Gill, R., & Livingstone, S. (2013). Teen Girls, Sexual Double Standards and 'Sexting': Gendered Value in Digital Image Exchange. *Feminist Theory*, *14*, 305–323.

Rogow, D. & Haberland, N. (2005). Sexuality and Relationships Education: Toward a Social Studies Approach. *Sex Education*, *5*, 333–344.

Rubin, Gayle. (1984). Thinking Sex: Notes for a Radical Theory of the Politics of Sexuality. In Vance, C. S. (Ed.), *Pleasure and Danger: Exploring Female Sexuality* (267–319). London: Pandora.

Rudman, L. A. & Fetterolf, J. C. (2014). Gender and Sexual Economics: Do Women View Sex as a Female Commodity? *Psychological Science*, *25*, 1438–1447.

Saewyc, E. M. (2011). Research on Adolescent Sexual Orientation: Development, Health Disparities, Stigma, and Resilience. *Journal of Research on Adolescence*, *21*, 256–272.

Sanchez, D. T., Crocker, J., & Boike, K. R. (2005). Doing Gender in the Bedroom: Investing in Gender Norms and the Sexual Experience. *Personality and Social Psychology Bulletin*, *31*, 1445–1455.

Sanchez, D. T., Fetterolf, J. C., & Rudman, L. A. (2012). Eroticizing Inequality in the United States: The Consequences and Determinants of Traditional Gender Role Adherence in Intimate Relationships. *Journal of Sex Research*, *49*, 168–183.

Sanchez, D.T. & Kiefer, A.K. (2007). Body Concerns in and out of the Bedroom: Implications for Sexual Pleasure and Problems. *Archives of Sexual Behavior*, *36*, 808–820.

Schippers, M. (2007). Recovering the Feminine Other: Masculinity, Femininity, and Gender Hegemony. *Theory and Society*, *36*, 85–102.

Seabrook, R. C., Ward, L. M., Cortina, L. M., Giaccardi, S., & Lippman, J. R. (2017). Girl Power or Powerless Girl? Television, Sexual Scripts, and Sexual Agency in Sexually Active Young Women. *Psychology of Women Quarterly*, *41*, 240–253.

Sprecher, S., Treger, S., & Sakaluk, J. K. (2013). Premarital Sexual Standards and Sociosexuality: Gender, Ethnicity, and Cohort Differences. *Archives of Sexual Behavior*, *42*, 1395–1405.

Tanenbaum, L. (2000). *Slut!: Growing Up Female with a Bad Reputation*. New York: Harper Collins.

(2015). *I Am Not a Slut: Slut-Shaming in the Age of the Internet*. New York: Harper Perennial.

Tolman, D. L. (2002). *Dilemmas of Desire: Teenage Girls Talk about Sexuality.* Boston: Harvard University Press.

(2012). Female Adolescents, Sexual Empowerment and Desire: A Missing Discourse of Gender Inequity. *Sex Roles*, *66*, 746–757.

Tolman, D. L., Anderson, S. M., & Belmonte, K. (2015). Mobilizing Metaphor: Considering Complexities, Contradictions, and Contexts in Adolescent Girls' and Young Women's Sexual Agency. *Sex Roles*, *73*, 298–310.

Tolman, D. L., Davis, B. R., & Bowman, C. P. (2016). "That's Just How It Is": A Gendered Analysis of Masculinity and Femininity Ideologies in Adolescent Girls' and Boys' Heterosexual Relationships. *Journal of Adolescent Research*, *31*, 3–31.

Tolman, D. L. & McClelland, S. I. (2011). Normative Sexuality Development in Adolescence: A Decade in Review, 2000–2009. *Journal of Research on Adolescence*, *21*, 242–255.

Truman, D. M., Tokar, D. M., & Fischer, A. R. (1996). Dimensions of Masculinity: Relations to Date Rape Supportive Attitudes and Sexual Aggression in Dating Situations. *Journal of Counseling & Development*, *74*, 555–562.

Urbandictionary.com (2017). Slut. Retrieved December 20, 2017, from www.urbandictionary.com/define.php?term=slut.

Walker, S., Sanci, L., & Temple-Smith, M. (2013). Sexting: Young Women's and Men's Views on Its Nature and Origins. *Journal of Adolescent Health*, *52*, 697–701.

Way, N., Ali, A., Gilligan, C., & Noguera, P. (Eds.). (2018). *The Crisis of Connection: Roots, Consequences, and Solutions*. New York: New York University Press.

White, E. (2002). *Fast Girls: Teenage Tribes and the Myth of the Slut*. New York: Simon and Schuster.

Woerner, J. & Abbey, A. (2017). Positive Feelings After Casual Sex: The Role of Gender and Traditional Gender-Role Beliefs. *The Journal of Sex Research*, *54*, 717–727.

Young, M., Penhollow, T. M., & Bailey, W. C. (2010). Hooking-Up and Condom Provision: Is There a Double Standard? *American Journal of Health Studies*, *25*, 156–164.

11 Gender, Class, and Campus Sexual Cultures

White First-Generation College Students and the Transition to College

Amy C. Wilkins and Aubrey Limburg

In *American Hookup*, Lisa Wade (2017) describes "hookup culture" as pervasive in the lives of college students. Wade argues that what is new for contemporary college students is not casual sex but hookup *culture*: the idea that students *should* be having casual sex at the expense of other forms of relationships and of caring itself. The hookup – as a form of casual sexual behavior – is in fact much less common than the media hype has led us to believe (Weissbourd et al., 2017). Rather, it is the expectation that college students should hookup, should want to hookup, and should participate in the rituals that accompany hooking up, and the creation of an institutional space that enables casual sex and undermines other forms of relational intimacy, that Wade means when she talks about hookup *culture* (Wade, 2017). Thinking about hooking up as a culture alerts us to the ways its logic and imperatives pervade the lives of all college students, regardless of whether or not they want to participate. The logics of hookup culture favor White, privileged, heterosexual students. Other sorts of students have a much harder time making their way through hookup culture for a range of reasons: they do not have the material, cultural, or embodied resources to participate; or they are uninterested in or turned off by hookup culture. Whether one participates in hookup culture matters. Wade mentions but does not delve deeply into this point. Hookup culture is where students make friends and social connections. It's where they cultivate reputations as fun and easygoing. To not participate is to not only lose out on these key aspects of the college experience but to risk social isolation altogether. And social isolation is a prime factor in student attrition (Tinto, 1987).

In this chapter, we use interview data with White first-generation heterosexual-identified men and women attending Western University, a large residential public university in the US Mountain States, to examine the gendered implications of hookup culture and collegiate relationships for White first-generation students – students whose parents did not attend college. First-generation students are three times more likely to drop out of 4-year colleges in the first 3 years than students whose parents attended college (Dynarski, 2016). First-generation students experience the transition from adolescence to young adulthood differently from middle-class college students, and their experiences of collegiate sexual culture are important to helping us understand how and when sexuality may heighten these risks or operate as a protective factor.

Our approach to understanding sexual development is sociological, and thus emphasizes social contexts, identities, and interactions (Fields, 2008). Race, class, gender, and sexual identity all influence access to sexual experiences, sexual identities, and normative expectations (Fields, 2008; Garcia, 2012). Youth use sexuality to make identity claims – to construct and negotiate ideas about who they are and who they are not (Wilkins, 2008). In these ways, the development of one's sexual self is intimately connected with the development of other core identity features.

In the United States, young people leave high school as adolescents and enter residential college as young adults. Important development and cultural changes accompany these rapid role transitions, including the myth of new beginnings, the need to navigate new friendships and authority figures, increased but incomplete autonomy, and (often) movement out of the parental home. Both race and class mediate the ability to access the myths and resources associated with these transitions, such that White upper middle-class youth are best able to negotiate the delayed transition to adulthood currently idealized in US culture (Bettie, 2014; Settersten & Ray, 2010). Expectations about sexuality change rapidly with the transition to college. In high school, US parents more typically frown on the teen sleepover, and families and institutions alike treat adolescent sexuality as a social problem to be managed (Schalet, 2011). As late teenagers enter residential colleges such as the one in this chapter, they move rapidly into a new setting with new expectations of casual sexuality, limited adult surveillance, and changed forms of peer control (Wade, 2017).

The White first-generation men and women in our study opted out of hookup culture, but opting out caused women more problems than it caused men. When White first-generation women opted out, middle-class peers saw them as boring and they struggled to find other ways to make friends. Opting out seemed to undermine their likability as women. White first-generation men did not describe similar problems. Instead, opting out was compatible with their friendship-making strategies, and did not jeopardize their ability to construct successful masculine identities. In this chapter, we investigate how and why this happened.

What We Know about College Students and Hooking Up

Hookup culture has become the primary sexual script on college campuses (Bogle, 2008; Bradshaw et al., 2010; England et al., 2007; Glenn & Marquardt, 2001; Wade, 2017). The meaning of the hookup itself is (often deliberately) ambiguous (Currier, 2013), but it most broadly refers to casual sexual interaction (ranging from kissing to intercourse) where those involved do not expect continued emotional or intimate connection after a sexual encounter (England et al., 2007). Hookup culture is pervasive but hookup behavior is less so. College students *think* they should hookup a lot more than they actually do. In part, this is because they think that hooking up is part of what it means to be a college student, and, in part, this is because they overestimate how much their peers are hooking up (Wade, 2017; Weissbourd et al., 2017). Most college students of traditional age hookup at some point during college (Armstrong et al., 2012; England et al., 2007), but 40 percent report fewer than three hookup partners. Nonetheless, hookup culture matters because it creates expectations about normative sexual experiences and about how college students should think about sex and sexuality, and because it sets the standards for the more valued ways of being sexual in the context of college. It also matters because participation in hookup culture shape identities and social interactions in ways that transcend sexuality itself, influencing other aspects of the college experience.

Current literature has shown that women and men experience hookup culture in different ways, as the gendered double standard benefits men more than women, despite decreased stigma of more casual forms of sex (Allison & Risman, 2013; Armstrong et al., 2012; Armstrong et al., 2010; Bogle, 2008; England et al., 2007; Eshbaugh & Gute, 2008). Women continue to navigate competing expectations that they be relationally oriented, manage potential stigmatization as "sluts," and contend with expectations that they have more romantic feelings than men (Bogle, 2008; Hamilton & Armstrong, 2009; Wade, 2017). Nonetheless, because relationships also do not favor women, some feminists have been cautious about condemning hookups as more disadvantageous to women relative to relationships, or about suggesting that women always prefer relationships: the evidence indicates that women's desires and experiences are more complex (e.g., Hamilton & Armstrong, 2009; Wilkins & Dalessandro, 2013).

Research on men has found that the performance of heterosexual desire, conquest, and dominance is an important way of achieving a recognizable masculine identity (Connell & Messerschmidt, 2005; Kimmel, 2009; Pascoe, 2007; Smiler, 2008). In high school and college, men jockey for status through stories about heterosexual conquest (Pascoe, 2007), by "hunting" girls together (Grazian, 2007), or by demonstrating appropriate carelessness about the feelings of unattractive women (Sweeney, 2014; Wade, 2017). Masculinities scholar Michael Kimmel (2009) writes in *Guyland*: "If you're a guy, you have an 'endless loop' playing in your head: 'Gotta get laid, you're not a man, you're not a man unless you try for it, keep going, what's wrong with you?" Such an argument implies that collegiate men simply have no other options for the performance of a recognizable heterosexual identity. But, as we show in this chapter, they do.

Most research on hookup culture and hooking up has relied on the experiences of White, heterosexual, middle- to upper middle-class students at traditional residential universities (Heldman & Wade, 2010; Owen et al., 2010). While gender does not seem to affect participation rates in hookups (Owen et al., 2010; Paul et al. 2000), class and race do (Allison & Risman, 2014; Fielder et al., 2013; Kimmel, 2009; Owen et al., 2010). The scripts about hookup culture as a prominent and necessary component of the college experience seem only to be accessible to, and desirable for, some students.

First-generation college students have sometimes been included in research about hookup culture but their identities as first-generation college students have not been the central focus and is not often sufficiently considered to be an individual-level factor in determining participation in hookup culture. However, we know that first-generation college students differ from their peers in that they often face social and cultural challenges related to their transition from high school to college that result from experiences prior to entering college and differing experiences once in college (Terenzini et al., 1996). Moreover, students from working-class backgrounds are less likely to be oriented toward college as a time of sociability (Stuber, 2009), and to see college instead as a time to gain credits and credentials (Mullen, 2010). Thus, they do not tend to share middle-class students' normative orientation toward collegiate partying, a point we take up in this chapter.

These identities and experiences shape the ways first-generation students navigate higher education, and have implications for their experiences of collegiate sexuality. Moreover, collegiate hookup culture favors students with time, resources, and knowledge cultivated in upper middle-class and elite contexts. Thus, its logics and hierarchies necessarily disadvantage students from working-class backgrounds (Allison & Risman, 2014; Armstrong & Hamilton, 2013; Hamilton & Armstrong, 2009). As Allison and Risman (2014, p. 119) write, "[d] escriptions of hook-up 'culture' writ large reflect the sexual possibilities of privilege." Working-class students who live at home, for example, do not participate in the party culture in which hooking up is embedded. Although they may desire to act like "normal college students," living with their parents makes it hard for them to socialize in the ways other college students do, as they often have curfews, share family cars, and cannot bring peers home (Allison & Risman, 2014). But, beyond this, we know very little about how women and men from working-class backgrounds negotiate campus sexuality, or the implications of these negotiations for their experiences of college. Next, we will examine the experiences of White first-generation college men and women who attended a residential party school and lived on campus. White first-generation men and women both opted out of collegiate hookup culture, but we argue that gender mediates the outcome of these choices. For men, opting out was compatible with social integration, while, for women, it most often led to social isolation. In this chapter, we seek to explain why.

Methods

Data for this chapter come from a larger project investigating identities in the transition to college for three groups of college students: Black students, White first-generation college students, and LGBQ students. In conducting that research, Wilkins has interviewed more than 90 college students, conducted focus group interviews, focused surveys, and spent time talking with multiple campus actors.

This chapter focuses on the experiences of the eight White first-generation men and 11 White first-generation women in the study, but uses data from across the study to make sense of their experiences. Interviews with 11 first-generation students of color, some of whom were involved in other components of the study (e.g., some were Black; some identified as LGBQ), help shed light on the ways Whiteness shapes the particular experiences of the participants in this chapter.

White first-generation students were the most difficult participants to recruit for this study, in large part because they are invisible on the campus and they are neither networked with each other nor embedded in any "first-generation" campus organizations. Thus, participants did not recommend other participants for participation in the study. Instead, Wilkins recruited largely through word of mouth, classroom advertisements, and fliers in the Colleges of Engineering, Business, and Arts and Sciences. Participants were paid $30. Wilkins conducted the life course interviews lasting 60–90 minutes, and focused on the transition to college with an emphasis on peer relationships. Questions were broad and encouraged storytelling, and included, "Tell me about high school," "What was it like to come to college?" and "How did you make friends?" The interview protocol thus followed the direction of the stories participants told.

Analysis was inductive (Patton, 2005; Thomas, 2006), intersectional (Crenshaw, 1991; McCall, 2005), and comparative (Glaser & Strauss, 1967). By developing case studies of each participant, we focused on the ways they talked about party culture, sexuality, and relationships, but embedded those stories in their broader life story. We attended to contradictions and to silences to identify places where cultural expectations may not fit with their experiences or where participants may be experiencing discomfort. Such moments provide analytic insight into identities as they are lived and negotiated in everyday life (DeVault, 1990; Pugh, 2013). We used the case studies to develop analytic comparisons between White first-generation men and Black middle-class men (Wilkins, 2014), between White first-generation women and Black middle-class women, and between White first-generation women and men. These comparisons helped us understand the different ways race/class and gender mattered in women's experiences, facilitating the analysis. We then focused more systematically on class, developing a synthetic understanding of each group (see Wilkins, 2008).

Our study finds that White first-generation men are able to perform an alternative version of heterosexual masculinity, one that is assisted, in no small terms, by the simultaneous gendered performance of their (off-campus) girlfriends. The White first-generation women in our study (who are not, as you will see, the girlfriends of the White first-generation men), in contrast, enact more varied and more conflicted versions of heterosexual femininity. Men and women in both groups turn to long-term relationships in the face of a hookup culture that does not meet their needs. However, White first-generation women are more ambivalent about this strategy than are White first-generation men, who enter into heterosexual relationships later in their collegiate careers, and seem to experience more costs associated with them. Moreover, a number of first-generation White women avoid both relationships and hookup culture altogether, while almost all of the men in this study had long-term girlfriends. As is true more broadly, relationships serve women's needs less well than they do men's. In what follows, we first discuss the men's experiences before turning to the women's.

White First-Generation Men

In college, "partying" refers to a culture of heavy drinking, some drug use, and hooking up. Hookup culture is embedded in party culture (Armstrong & Hamilton, 2013; Grazian, 2007; Wade, 2017). Part of the ritual of collegiate drinking is seeking out partners for hookups. And part of the ritual of hooking up is drinking: drinking provides the lubrication and social cover needed to authorize hooking up (Wade, 2017). As first-generation students, both women and men entered college without a full understanding of the scope of collegiate partying. They had not been primed to party in the ways that many class-privileged students have been (Stuber, 2009). Moreover, partying can be troublesome for students without adequate resources, as it requires money to participate and time to recover, and because it almost inevitably impacts grades (Armstrong & Hamilton, 2013). It is thus a poor bet for first-generation students.

White first-generation men came to college clear that they didn't want to party. Like other White first-generation men, Sam did not want to party, in part, because he saw partying as antithetical to his collegiate goals. He says, "And the idea of like blurring that all out and doing something else just doesn't sound fun to me. And once you get started down that path, it's really easy to just kind of stick with it. And I figured I might as well, I'm here to learn and do my best, so." KJ worries that "when you drink you can become a different person." KJ tries to make light of it, but not being able to participate can be painful. He says, "I know if I were to try to go and get friends . . . And I know I would be judged for it, seeing as not having ten dollars every night to pitch [in] for a party. 'Cause I mean ten dollars is a lot." For KJ, avoiding partying is, in part, a way to avoid acknowledging that he does not have the requisite money to party and a way to sidestep possible judgment. Partying is not an option. Brendan describes the impact of not partying on his transition to college:

> I mean most of the schools that I went to, I fit in pretty well right away. And so it was weird for me to come here and not really fit in. Cause I don't, not to say that everybody here like smokes weed, and parties all the time or anything, but it's a big part of it. And I don't really do that.

As Brendan reveals, the decision not to party has consequences for White first-generation men's ability to create easy friendships with other students.

These consequences do not last long. The White first-generation men in our study found other ways to make friends, typically in the first semester, through common leisure activities such as hiking, pick-up basketball, and playing video games. Moreover, opting out of partying did not seem to tag them with socially debilitating labels. Although they often portrayed themselves as "boring," being boring was more socially acceptable for White first-generation men than for their female counterparts at Western.

Sam's story is illustrative. A senior now, Sam recalled his first year as disorienting. "Everybody knew everybody it seemed like. They had all been friends in high school." Sam didn't know anyone. He had gone to a small rural high school and did not have experience meeting new people. Still, he committed himself to the task. Speaking about the 120 people in his dorm, he said, "I just tried to meet all of them, and understand what they liked to do." He went room to room, and through this process he was asked to join an intramural basketball team. Eventually, he formed his own team. In this fashion, he created friendships. Basketball was good during the week, but it left his weekends empty. When I asked what he did on those, he said: "Not a whole lot, 'cause I still didn't party or anything. I would hang out in the dorm with people, and play videogames, and walk somewhere and get food. It wasn't real exciting but it was nice to relax after a hard week of class though." This strategy worked because Sam had asked to be in a substance-free dorm, but about halfway through the year, a lot of people in the dorm had changed their minds about remaining substance free, pulled by the lure of campus party and hookup culture. Sam did what almost every White first-generation man in this study did. He got a girlfriend.

Sam's girlfriend did not go to Western. She was still back home, and when she started college the next year she did not come to Western, but went to a lower-status regional. In this way, Sam's story was much like that of the other White first-generation men in this study. He was different, though, in that he began his relationship *after* he started college and not before. When the first White first-generation man Wilkins interviewed told her he was still dating his high school girlfriend, she was struck by the novelty of it. But interview after interview, she discovered that this is a common pattern among first-generation White men. The exception to this rule was Tim, who had dated an upper middle-class girl in high school. Like other class-privileged girls, she did not want a boyfriend when she started college (Armstrong & Hamilton, 2013). Most of the men's girlfriends attended lower-status regional schools, lived at home, and majored in fields like nursing that would allow geographic mobility after college. Many attended schools in their hometowns and lived back home, and thus they provided identity bridges, anchoring these men to their home communities while also supporting their goals of class mobility. By investing in feminized majors that would allow geographical mobility after college, women prioritized the men's career goals. Most of the men anticipated continuing their relationships post-college, and had no interest in "sowing their oats." This expectation did not appeal to them. Moreover, as we will discuss more later, the traditional, gendered assumptions built into these relationships supported White first-generation men's collegiate integration, buffered some of the class injuries of upward mobility, and protected them from potential hazards that could derail them. In this way, they were deeply stabilizing.

White first-generation men were not interested in dating other women. These were their first girlfriends, and, most hoped, their last. Sam explained, "Yeah, I mean there were several girls in my freshman year that I would hang out with a lot, and thought maybe I would want to date. And I probably could have, but I just realized that they weren't really what I was interested in. I don't know. I never dated as casually as people do I guess. Like I could tell before I went into that stage." I asked him why, and he said, "Just it meant more to me I guess, to be more serious." In this way, he portrayed himself as a different kind of guy relative to stereotypes of hookup culture. Sam likely did not have the skills to be successful in collegiate hookup culture, which privileges upper middle-class desires, tastes, and interactive proficiencies that he would not have acquired at home and did not have the money for. His girlfriend, from home, instead provided emotional stability, which he integrated into his heterosexual identity, using it to claim a more serious, committed heterosexual identity distinct from hookup masculinity.

As with other men, Sam's girlfriend solved problems for him. First, she filled his weekends. Because she attended college elsewhere, weekends were their time together. On weekends, he said, they went "on dates. Fun activities and we're going camping this weekend, and [we] do some homework." By spending time with his girlfriend on the weekend, Sam staved off any loneliness he might feel while other college men were participating in more expensive activities, or in the party culture in which he was disinterested.

Second, his relationship with his girlfriend provided him with intimacy that cushioned his class mismatch with the university. The men in this study downplayed their sense of class injuries, especially relative to the women (who also, for the most part, do not name their injuries as classed). Their greater ease was facilitated in part by other raced and gendered aspects of their experience (see Wilkins, 2014); there were simply more available options for White men to make friends and enact identities at the university than for other types of students. But girlfriends were also critical to alleviating their cross-class interactions in the university. Many of the men in this study drew on emotion work strategies that they had developed in high school to navigate potential class injuries that they faced at Western. For example, Danny described the way he drew on his high school experiences to cope with students' displays of wealth via cars: "And like it doesn't bother me at all, 'cause I used to see it all the time. Like all my really good friends, they have a lot of money and sometimes I even think I have money 'cause like that's where I've grown up." The men did not make direct links between their girlfriends and these experiences, but girlfriends likely supported these processes in three ways. They nourished the men's ability to do draining emotion work by providing them with restorative care; as class peers, they provide them with a respite from having to do cross-class interactive work; and they nourished their goals of class mobility. The following comments reveal these characteristics of their relationships. Sam explains that, to him, it was important "just to be with someone that cared about what you were doing and about the future, and wasn't just worried about what they were doing that weekend, and, I don't know, it's difficult to explain." Sam's comment, "it's difficult to explain" about something that seems in many ways straightforward reveals the ways in which he perceives his relationship to be out of step with expectations for collegiate relationships, a point we return to below. But it may also point to these unstated aspects of emotional sustenance. When I asked first-generation men what they liked about their girlfriends they said that they were "nice," "caring," and "listened to them." Enzo said, "I really like having a girlfriend. I like caring for someone. Someone caring for me." Patrick said that he and his girlfriend encouraged each other when college got difficult. "I guess we both were having a hard time with school. Both I guess supporting each other with how bad we were doing at one point." KJ described: "Yeah. So yeah, I mean I like it [being in a relationship]. It just keeps me out of trouble. We make each other happy." And "So she helps me remind me of who I am to become this person." In most of these comments, girlfriends provided particular kinds of care aimed at sustaining men's commitment to their university education. KJ's girlfriend, for example, kept him focused on his goals by "remind[ing] [him] who" he was "to become." Sam's girlfriend did homework with him and cared about his future. Patrick's girlfriend encouraged him to stay in school when he was struggling. In these ways, their girlfriends offer them not just intimacy but particular forms of support that kept them on their path to upward mobility.

Third, Sam's girlfriend provided him with a way to opt out of partying. Not only did she give him something to do when other college students were partying, she also provided him with an explanation for why he didn't party. Partying culture often entails hooking up, but Sam says, "I just . . . just don't . . . never wanted to do that." Indeed, he was surprised when I told him that I had done another study of college students in which a number of them reported moving between relationships and hooking up. He saw his relationship as a permanent solution to the "problem" of hooking up. He explained how his relationship with his girlfriend changed his social life, allowing him to confine his time spent socializing with men to weekdays, "and letting them [the men] do their own thing." People did sometimes try to get him to go out, he said, "and I'll go out, I'm just not. I don't want to get drunk or do something crazy." Having a girlfriend allowed him to manage these situations, avoiding them more often than not. Having a girlfriend meant he could confine most of his interactions with other men to weekday interactions, which is in fact what he did. Thus, Sam described a situation in which he was able to sustain friendships and a decent reputation while still opting out of the hookup scene.

Other men also revealed their experience in using their girlfriends to explain not partying. For example, when I asked Brendan about what he does with his friends, he said:

> I don't know. Just whatever. A lot of times we do study groups. Stuff like that. Just go over to people's houses, watch TV, hang out. Stuff like that. To be honest, I don't have a lot of time for it with the jobs and schools and stuff like that. I really don't, do that much. And then I usually see my girlfriend once or twice a week . . . I mean I don't go to parties to try to pick girls up or anything.

On the surface, Brendan's narrative seems like a simple description of the time constraints that limit his social participation, but it is more than that. It is also offers a well honed explanation for why he *can't* party. Without the final comment about his girlfriend, his explanation would probably suffice but it wouldn't work as well. The girlfriend provides an emotional and social explanation for his non-participation that made his explanation make more sense to the audience, and (imperfectly) propped up his masculinity. Patrick and Ben provided more succinct and more direct versions of these kind of explanations. Patrick said, "I've been dating the same girl so I'm not really interested in [hooking up]." And Ben explained that he had not hooked up with anyone because, "It sounds lame what I'm going to say . . . like I care about her a lot, you know." White first-generation men were adept at using this explanation to sidestep expectations that they participate in hookup culture and to do so with their heterosexuality intact. Girlfriends were better excuses for not partying than, say, studying, as they confirmed White first-generation men's heterosexuality in the absence of hooking up. This strategy, in turn, helped them view themselves, practice, and become particular sorts of heterosexual men: monogamous, steady, and committed. This form of heterosexuality made sense to them because it continued to be propped up by the forms of gendered support their girlfriends provided, and because they viewed other forms of masculine heterosexuality as costly.

Like Sam's earlier comment that his desire for feelings of care were "hard to explain," Ben's comment "it sounds lame" revealed his impression that his feelings of care were not normative for college men. The normative expectations of hookup culture – which idealizes sexual intimacy without emotional intimacy – limit the possibilities of caring relationships among undergraduate students (Wade, 2017). Because hookup culture is culturally predominant on college campuses, relationships are lower status, and perhaps especially so among men. Yet, as these men's stories also reveal, having a girlfriend signals heterosexuality and allows one to opt out of hookup culture, better than simply being unsuccessful in or uninterested in hookup culture. It allows them to be heterosexual *enough*. As Sam said, "Yeah, I mean everyone's happy for us, but I don't really know of anyone else who has [had a long-term girlfriend]." Yet, other men – Black men, gay men, first-generation men of color – Wilkins interviewed often wanted relationships but could not get them; thus, Sam and other White first-generation men's success at securing girlfriends may be unusual, but this feature could also bolster its utility in signaling the successful fulfillment of a particular kind of heterosexual self. The availability of stable heterosexual relationships helped White first-generation men see themselves as caring, committed, steady kinds of men, for whom a traditional kind of heterosexuality was a core and stable feature of their selves.

The men in this chapter cultivated images of themselves as unexciting (Wilkins, 2014), and their girlfriends helped with this. For example, Sam said, sounding like other White first-generation men, "I've just never really been that exciting." Being unexciting served Sam's purposes, helping him to opt out of party culture without seeming like he had been pushed out. As we have explained, Sam reported quickly getting into a relationship after entering college when he realized that the hookup scene wasn't his thing, and using his relationship to opt out of (most) expectations that he drink (which fall disproportionately on the weekend when he's with his girlfriend). It was at this point in the story that he hammered home that he wasn't exciting. Not being exciting meant not being interested in partying. He reiterated this point when he explained how he and his girlfriend spent their weekends together, saying "I mean it's exciting to me, but most people are like bummed if they don't party hard three times in one weekend." Sam's storytelling seemed defensive, but he was also proactive about claiming and using the identity. The next thing he said was, "I'm confident in what I do, and it's fun to me, and it doesn't really matter that much what other people think, I guess." Sam understood that high status men partied, but he did not want to do that. Being "unexciting" helped him to not party, and came with minimal social costs over which he seemed to feel some control. Having a girlfriend allowed him to claim – every weekend – that he was making an active choice to do something different and meaningful with his time.

White First-Generation Women

White first-generation women did not want to party either. Bailey explained that she did not "fall into like the social norms of like oh, let's go out and drink and stuff." And Ashley said, "I went out to the [party area] my first night here, and it just wasn't for me. I didn't like it there." These comments make it seem like it is simple for women to make different decisions about how to orient their social lives, but for most White first-generation women, opting out of the party scene came with social costs, as the following stories illustrate.

Like other first-generation students, Spring was unprepared for what college partying actually meant. "I mean, I guess that was one of the biggest shockers. I mean everyone was like yeah, [Western's]s a big party school. And I was like yeah, I get it, but I didn't drink in high school." Spring thought her high school's party scene and the collegiate party scene would be similar. In high school, she had not paid big social costs for not drinking. But she was wrong. Spring drew distinctions between herself and people who partied:

> Yeah, it's bizarre to me. I just think that college-age drinking – I'm pretty sure I mean it's literally about getting drunk and finding a mate at a completely primal level, you know. Because when you go to a party, that is the objective . . . like what guy are you going to hook up with? And that's not like at the top of my list. And that's not you know what I'm looking for.

Janae also crafted complex boundaries against women who partied. In her second year, she lived in what she described as a "party house" with eight women. Part of Janae's objection was that the partying interfered with her ability to focus on academics; she worried about its potential costs to her hard-won academic successes. Living in the house affected her grades and her focus. She recalled: "I was constantly nagging them about dishes, and cleaning up the keg from weeks ago, and stupid stuff like that. And they'd bring home sleazy guys. And I'd get mad at them. And it ... ended badly." Janae wrapped together concerns about sexuality, drinking, and cleanliness. Janae and other first-generation women called upon a gendered discourse that valued cleanliness and moral restraint in women. Men did not check other men in the same ways because these same things are generally not valued in men. Thus, it makes sense that White first-generation women believe they are calling on a legible cultural lexicon in launching these complaints. After all, a discourse valuing women's "purity" is pervasive (Valenti, 2010). But, in the context of collegiate hookup culture, using this discourse contributed to their marginalization. These women continued to use sexual restraint to evaluate their moral worth in college, rather than shifting to accommodate the new collegiate expectations.

How first-generation women used this discourse hurt them further. White first-generation women responded to other women's sexuality in ways that highlighted their disdain – they nagged, they yelled, they cried. These responses emphasized their own discomfort. They did this both because they often experienced other women's sexuality as personally disruptive and because they did not share the normative expectations of tolerance that their class-advantaged peers had brought with them to college. Instead, they had not learned the much more subtle collegiate rules for sanctioning women's sexuality which were nothing like those at play in many high schools. They also had less power to make their moral judgments stick. Armstrong et al. (2014) show that when working class women label class-privileged women "sluts," their judgments do not damage the reputations of the class-privileged women in the way that class-privileged women's judgments damage working-class women.

First-generation women's reactions also made them seem boring. Spring explained this process. Not wanting to party put her at a social disadvantage. "And then in the sense that I've never been a big partier or into the party culture, or drugs or drinking, or anything like that. I struggled a lot making friends, especially in the dorms because it's the norm that you go out every weekend and then some." Not only did it cut off a key route to meeting people, it also damaged her reputation. Her conflicts with her roommate made things worse because, as a partier, her roommate had made friends and Spring hadn't. Other women took her roommate's side, and saw Spring as a stick in the mud. She said, "As it became farther into the school year – people kind of started associating me with someone who really doesn't want to do anything, or like I'm boring or something like that. So I didn't meet as many people." As Spring explained it, being seen as boring further isolated her, as no one sought her out for non-party sorts of activities either. By the end of her freshman year, Spring was an outsider. Opting out of hookup culture was more consequential than it was for men. Unlike the men, these women did not view themselves as unexciting, but instead had that view imposed on them by other women, who judged their behavior as prudish and naïve, and who labeled them boring and marginalized them. For many women, these experiences sowed confusion because they did not understand how their heterosexual restraint had failed them. They resented having their sexual restraint labeled negatively, but their isolation and confusion meant that they often didn't have the same tools for transitioning into a positive alternative identity that the men had.

To solve their problems of isolation, about half of the White first-generation women began heterosexual relationships with class-matched men sometime after starting college (in contrast, all of the White first-generation men typically entered college in a relationship). The White first-generation women and men in this chapter did not date each other; the men were typically dating *their* high school sweethearts – women, as we described, who stayed behind and went to regional schools back home. In contrast, most of the women's relationships began later, usually a year or more after they had started college, and they dated men who also attended Western. First-generation women's relationships with their boyfriends provided them with important resources: because they understood what it was like to be first-generation, they offered some kinds of emotional support and companionship, and, many women experienced heterosexual norms as stabilizing at least in the short term. However, first-generation women experienced these relationships in diverse ways, with some viewing them as a constraint on their class mobility. For all of them, these relationships came with less of a payoff than men's relationships did.

Natalie had just broken up with her boyfriend of 3 years at the time of the interview. She explained that they had started dating after they struck up a conversation in front of the library. Unlike most other first-generation women, she had never lived with her boyfriend; instead, he lived in a neighboring city to save money and they saw each other a few times a week. Natalie was also different from most other first-generation women in that she had managed to sustain friendships with upper middle-class women throughout college, in large part because she was a triathlete, a sport that was not as cost prohibitive as many of the other club sports and through which she made friends early on. Nonetheless, Natalie described a continuous "gap in understanding" between herself and her friends around financial issues. Her boyfriend, also White first-generation, provided welcome relief from the interactive expectations required in her cross-class friendships with women. She said, "We had a lot of things in common that I don't have in common with my other friends. . . . I don't know we just "got" each other really well in those aspects." Yet, Natalie also described her relationship as difficult to balance with her other friendships, explaining, "It was also stressful, because there was this constant pull between my friends and him, 'cause we didn't share any mutual friends." Rather than try to integrate her boyfriend with her friendships, Natalie kept him separate. Natalie never explained why, but it is striking, given that she dated him for 3 years.

Amanda's story sheds light on the concerns Natalie might have faced. Like many Mexican students at Western, Amanda identified as White and positioned herself as more similar to the White students at Western than to the other Mexican students. She was thus particularly concerned with blending into the dominant White population at Western; to do so, she had to manage both her class background and her ethnicity. Her identity concerns were different in degree rather than kind from those of non-Hispanic White first-generation women, and, thus, they make more transparent the issues at stake more broadly for first-generation women.

Amanda and her boyfriend lived together, having moved in after her first year, when her grades had slipped. Like other first-generation women, she appreciated that he "kept me really grounded. . . . Like he knows the importance of finishing too, so he's just kind of been like another person to motivate me like my mom." He provided her with an explanation for not partying. They did "couple things" on weekends instead. However, she also felt tied down. "I guess I feel kind of domesticated in a sense. I'm not like you know I don't have the freedom to just have my own place really." She felt that early cohabitation marked her as different from other college students. "I definitely feel like what I'm doing is different. I don't really hear of other students my age or those other couples that we associate with living together." For example, other students called her "wifey," which she did not like. White first-generation men also remarked that others saw their early commitment as out of step with collegiate norms; co-residing exacerbated this effect in Amanda's case. Gender also did. Being "wifey" is not the same as being the man in a traditional relationship. Being the man accorded power, which is in keeping with men's status. Being "wifey" undermined and is at odds with more modern expectations that collegiate women be independent and focused on the self. Like the White first-generation men, both Natalie and Amanda felt that their collegiate relationships signaled a different kind of heterosexual self than other college students. The men embraced this difference as a sign of their maturity and commitment, but these women were ambivalent. They worried that it signaled the wrong kind of heterosexual self – one that was at odds with the class mobility they also hoped to achieve by being in college. These concerns become clearer next.

Amanda worried about her boyfriend's potential for blocking her upward mobility. She was frank about "his background." They were both first-generation Mexicans from the same town, but she viewed his family as less reputable than hers. She said, for example, "His background irritates me. [His] family [background], and I just try to picture my life like in 10 years, and you know do I want my children to have that type of grandfather and stuff like that. And I don't see it." Amanda peppered her lengthy confessions of her classed concerns with comments such as "I love him to death." Her boyfriend embarrassed her, and she felt bad about her embarrassment. She did not want him to threaten her long-term class project. Certainly, she worried about marrying him. One suspects that Natalie did not bring her boyfriend around her friends for similar reasons. He was the wrong kind of guy. First-generation men do not help first-generation women create heterosexual femininities that fit well in the university or that fit with their own visions of themselves as independent heterosexual women. Thus, for first-generation women, it is both the men themselves and the fact of the relationship that is out of step with their upper middle-class peers. These women were ambivalent about the development of too early heterosexual relationships; as they watched their class-privileged peers, they too embraced the importance of class-privileged patterns of heterosexuality that eschewed too early relational commitment and endorsed women's autonomy. Yet, the classed conditions of the university also made these relationships available as a critical resource in the absence of other kinds of educational resources.

Not all White first-generation women objected to early heterosexual commitment. Both Emily and Grace settled into cohabiting relationships with first-generation men that they seemed content with. Emily's boyfriend was from back home, atypical for the women in this chapter. After a bad experience with an affluent student she had met shortly after coming to campus, Emily used social media to regenerate her connections with people back home. Through Facebook chatting, she became involved with a somewhat older, class-matched friend from her home community in the rural Midwest. He decided to move out to be near her. To save money, they moved in together right away, and were still living together at the time of the interview. As her "best friend" – a role she stressed repeatedly – Robby provided her with the emotional support she needed to remain committed to her education at Western. After Robby moved in, Emily did not feel the need to develop other friendships, and she spent most of her time in school, working, or with him. Emily explained:

> It's gone fine. I've always been a really like patient and tolerant person. . . . Of course someone's not going to be perfect, and might leave the dishes, or might not do the dishes the way you like it. Or leave their dirty socks all over. Like oh well, it's so easy to deal with I think.

Emily's description of what made their relationship work is notable in contrast to those offered by the White first-generation men. Rather than highlight the ways they helped each other out, she noted the ways she had learned to put up with his irritating habits. Grace, who also lived with her older boyfriend, who had matriculated to Western after a stint in the military, and his friends, all men, sounded similar: "But it gets to the point where I can't stand it anymore and then I do everything. But no one's ever like oh, this is nice. I'll try and keep it clean longer." In return for their gendered labor, both women said, they appreciated that there was "no drama." They attribute not having drama to life with men, but it is likely an effect of not having to negotiate class differences in these relationships. The "drama" they were glad to leave behind had occurred in their attempts to interact with class-privileged women. Moreover, to assure that they do not have drama, these women describe learning to tolerate gendered inequities in their living situations. Thus, while the first-generation men described the benefits of the emotional and other support their girlfriends provided, the chief benefit these women described was "no drama." Moreover, these women describe providing other forms of gendered labor in addition to emotional support. The differences in these accounts reveal the ways these relationships, like most heterosexual arrangements, offer more to the men than to the women. The women who liked these arrangements best came to see themselves in quasi-married ways, imagining their heterosexual selves as different from, more mature and settled than, those of other campus women. These ways of thinking about themselves allowed them to revive their heterosexual differences from other campus women into a morally desirable identity.

White first-generation women who did not have boyfriends provide another point of comparison. Those women also sought to opt out of "drama." Describing herself as a "very drama-free person," Spring decided not to try to make friends on campus after her discouraging first year in which she had been marked as boring and a subsequent failed attempt at friendship building in year two. She said: "Like I know people in classes, but I don't really hang out with a lot of them outside of that. A lot of what I do – because I am busy – and I work a lot, and I go to school . . . a lot of what I do is like going to yoga classes with the people that I work with." Like other first-generation women, Spring described very thin on-campus social networks (the people she worked with were not college students), and these had consequences for her emotional, social, and academic trajectory. Spring continued to use sexual restraint as a moral yardstick to evaluate herself but she became more tolerant of others over time, saying things like "personal choice" and "not something we need to make a huge to do about." Opting out of drama can perhaps be seen as a preemptive way to claim being unexciting akin to the strategy adopted by the first-generation men, but it did not successfully position first-generation women in on-campus networks the way it did first-generation men. Thus, the women's stories revealed a series of imperfect solutions to the problem of being marked as boring.

Armstrong and Hamilton (2013) find that, while privileged women break off their high school relationships, working-class women often continue relationships with hometown boyfriends. In their study, women's boyfriends, who weren't in college themselves, were threatened by their girlfriends' success and often jeopardized women's educational goals. Contrastingly, for the women in this chapter, heterosexual relationships supported collegiate persistence by providing first-generation White women with an emotionally supportive partner who "got them" and cared about their collegiate success. In exchange for this class support, women traded deeper social networks and gender equality. Our findings are likely different, however, because the women in Armstrong and Hamilton's study would have already dropped out before making it into my study.

Women's relationships were an uneasy solution to the dilemmas they faced. For first-generation White men, girlfriends supported social integration, but, for women, boyfriends supported withdrawal from other campus social relationships. This seemed to be the case even in relationships that women experience as warm, supportive, and critical spaces of emotional support. Why were women's relationships, which they entered for similar reasons, so different? First-generation women could not use their boyfriends as a resource to remake their gendered identities in the same way that first-generation men could. Their boyfriends did not facilitate social relationships with class-advantaged women, while the men's relationships were compatible with their friendships with other men, providing men an explanation for why they didn't party while they nonetheless sustained their weeknight friendships. This difference occurred, in part, because men were less likely to cohabitate and, in part, because of gendered differences in the meaning of their committed roles. Women who sought an alternative to ongoing interactions with class-advantaged collegiate peers did not find this aspect of relationships stifling, but women who were more concerned about class mobility did.

Conclusion: Men, Women, Class, and Collegiate Sexuality

In many ways, the White first-generation women behaved in similar ways to the White first-generation men at Western: they chose not to party, and many had long-term relationships. Yet, their outcomes were starkly different. Rather than remaining integrated, they were isolated. Rather than being seen as regular, if unexciting, guys, with who other men might play a game of basketball or a video game, they were outcast as boring and prudish. Nina reports that she wasn't even invited to dorm events by her Resident Advisor, whose job it was to bring people in the dorm together! These different outcomes alert us to the important and complex ways gendered sexuality differently mediates men's and women's ability to navigate collegiate life beyond sexual relationships.

Why was not partying a bigger problem for women than men? Men's partying behavior, like women's, involves joint action (e.g., Grazian, 2007), but these women's stories indicate that their non-participation disrupted the joint production of collegiate fun in a more serious way. Two things, we think, contribute to these gendered differences. One is that, for women, the changes in expectations for gendered performances between high school and college are bigger for women than they are for men, and that first-generation women are much less likely than middle-class women to receive information via peer networks about those changes. In high school, expectations of feminine sexual restraint continue to predominate (Wilkins & Miller, 2017), but, in college, these expectations have changed, giving way to new, more complex expectations that (middle-class) women be more sexually experimental and oriented toward hooking up (Armstrong & Hamilton, 2013; Wade, 2017). Focus group data from this project reveals that women share this information with each other via social networks before coming to college but first-generation women do not share access to this information.

For men, however, regardless of actual behavior, expectations that men will *perform* a kind of sexually active (predatory) heterosexuality are relatively constant across educational contexts (Grazian, 2007; Pascoe, 2007; Sweeney, 2014). Thus, the first-generation men are not as surprised by the collegiate context and, furthermore, had already developed a set of skills for managing these expectations in high school by claiming identities as "normal" guys (see Wilkins, 2014 for further discussion). Among these skills is the preemptive claiming of an identity as "unexciting" as a means of opting out, rather than being pushed out. First-generation men did not have a subculture or separate group but instead used these "softer" collegiate masculinities to negotiate the campus culture more broadly. However, these relationships and flexibility were not available to all men. White heterosexuality enabled this strategy too. In Wilkins' broader data set, both Black men (heterosexual and gay) and gay men (White and of color), for different reasons, described few, if any, long-term relationships, although many desired them (see Wilkins, 2014). Moreover, the few first-generation men of color she interviewed also wanted girlfriends but were unsuccessful in finding them.

References

Allison, R. & Risman, B. J. (2013). A Double Standard for "Hooking Up": How Far Have We Come toward Gender Equality? *Social Science Research*, *42*(5), 1191–1206. doi:10.1016/j.ssresearch.2013.04.006.

(2014). "It Goes Hand in Hand with the Parties": Race, Class, and Residence in College Student Negotiations of Hooking Up. *Sociological Perspectives*, *57*(1), 102–123. doi:10.1177/0731121413516608.

Armstrong, E. A., England, P., & Fogarty, A. C. K. (2012). Accounting for Women's Orgasm and Sexual Enjoyment in College Hookups and Relationships. *American Sociological Review*, *77*(3), 435–462. doi:10.1177/0003122412445802.

Armstrong, E. A., Hamilton, L., & England, P. (2010). Is Hooking Up Bad for Young Women? *Contexts*, *9*(3), 22–27. doi:10.1525/ctx.2010.9.3.22.

Armstrong, E. A. & Hamilton, L. T. (2013). *Paying for the Party*. Cambridge, MA: Harvard University Press.

Armstrong, E. A., Hamilton, L. T., Armstrong, E. M., & Seeley, J. L. (2014). "Good Girls": Gender, Social Class, and Slut Discourse on Campus. *Social Psychology Quarterly*, *77*(2), 100–122. doi:10.1177/0190272514521220.

Bettie, J. (2014). *Women Without Class: Girls, Race, and Identity*. Berkeley: University of California Press.

Bogle, K. A. (2008). *Hooking Up: Sex, Dating, and Relationships on Campus*. New York: New York University Press.

Bradshaw, C., Kahn, A. S., & Saville, B. K. (2010). To Hook Up or Date: Which Gender Benefits? *Sex Roles*, *62*(9–10), 661–669. doi:10.1007/s11199-010–9765-7.

Connell, R. W. & Messerschmidt, J. W. (2005). Hegemonic Masculinity: Rethinking the Concept. *Gender & Society*, *19*(6), 829–859. doi:10.1177/0891243205278639.

Crenshaw, K. (1991). Mapping the Margins: Intersectionality, Identity Politics, and Violence against Women of Color. *Stanford Law Review*, *43*(6), 1241–1299.

Currier, D. M. (2013). Strategic Ambiguity: Protecting Emphasized Femininity and Hegemonic Masculinity in the Hookup Culture. *Gender & Society*, *27*(5), 704–727. doi:10.1177/0891243213493960.

DeVault, M. L. (1990). Talking and Listening from Women's Standpoint: Feminist Strategies for Interviewing and Analysis. *Social Problems*, *37*(1), 96–116.

Dynarski, S. (2016, February 19). How to help more college students graduate. *The New York Times*. Retrieved from www.nytimes.com/2016/02/21/upshot/how-to-help-more-college-students-graduate.html.

England, P., Shafer, E. F., & Fogarty, A. C. (2007). Hooking Up and Forming Romantic Relationships on Today's College Campuses. *The Gendered Society Reader*, *3*, 531–593.

Eshbaugh, E. M. & Gute, G. (2008). Hookups and Sexual Regret among College Women. *The Journal of Social Psychology, 148*(1), 77–90. doi:10.3200/SOCP.148.1.77-90.

Fielder, R. L., Carey, K. B., & Carey, M. P. (2013). Are Hookups Replacing Romantic Relationships? A Longitudinal Study of First-Year Female College Students. *The Journal of Adolescent Health : Official Publication of the Society for Adolescent Medicine, 52*(5), 657–659. doi:10.1016/j.jadohealth.2012.09.001.

Fields, J. (2008). *Risky Lessons: Sex Education and Social Inequality.* New Brunswick: Rutgers University Press.

Garcia, L. (2012). *Respect Yourself, Protect Yourself: Latina Girls and Sexual Identity.* New York: New York University Press.

Glaser, B. & Strauss, A. (1967). Grounded Theory: The Discovery of Grounded Theory. *Sociology the Journal of the British Sociological Association, 12*, 27–49.

Glenn, N. & Marquardt, E. (2001). *Hooking Up, Hanging Out, and Hoping for Mr. Right: College Women on Dating and Mating Today.* New York: Institute for American Values.

Grazian, D. (2007). The Girl Hunt: Urban Nightlife and the Performance of Masculinity as Collective Activity. *Symbolic Interaction, 30*(2), 221–243.

Hamilton, L. & Armstrong, E. A. (2009). Gendered Sexuality in Young Adulthood. *Gender & Society, 23*(5), 589–616. doi:10.1177/0891243209345829.

Heldman, C. & Wade, L. (2010). Hook-Up Culture: Setting a New Research Agenda. *Sexuality Research and Social Policy, 7*(4), 323–333. doi:10.1007/s13178-010-0024-z.

Kimmel, M. (2009). *Guyland: The Perilous World Where Boys Become Men* (1 Reprint edition). New York: Harper Perennial.

McCall, L. (2005). The Complexity of Intersectionality. *Signs: Journal of Women in Culture and Society, 30*(3), 1771–1800.

Mullen, A. L. (2010). *Degrees of Inequality: Culture, Class, and Gender in American Higher Education*. Baltimore: Johns Hopkins University Press.

Owen, J. J., Rhoades, G. K., Stanley, S. M., & Fincham, F. D. (2010). "Hooking Up" among College Students: Demographic and Psychosocial Correlates. *Archives of Sexual Behavior, 39*(3), 653–663.

Pascoe, C. J. (2007). *Dude, You're a Fag*. Berkeley: University of California Press.

Patton, M. Q. (2005). Qualitative Research. In *Encyclopedia of Statistics in Behavioral Science*. Hoboken, NJ: John Wiley & Sons, Ltd. doi:10.1002/0470013192.bsa514.

Paul, E. L., McManus, B., & Hayes, A. (2000). "Hookups": Characteristics and Correlates of College Students' Spontaneous and Anonymous Sexual Experiences. *The Journal of Sex Research, 37*(1), 76–88. doi:10.1080/00224490009552023.

Pugh, A. (2013). What Good Are Interviews for Thinking about Culture? Demystifying Interpretive Analysis. *American Journal of Cultural Sociology, 1*(1), 42–68.

Schalet, A. T. (2011). *Not Under My Roof.* Chicago: University of Chicago Press.

Settersten, R. & Ray, B. (2010). Not Quite Adults. *On the Frontier of Adulthood, 1*(1), 236.

Smiler, A. P. (2008). "I Wanted to Get to Know Her Better": Adolescent Boys' Dating Motives, Masculinity Ideology, and Sexual Behavior. *Journal of Adolescence, 31*(1), 17–32.

Stuber, J. M. (2009). Class, Culture, and Participation in the Collegiate Extra-Curriculum. *Sociological Forum, 24*, 877–900.

Sweeney, B. (2014). Party Animals or Responsible Men: Social Class, Race, and Masculinity on Campus. *International Journal of Qualitative Studies in Education*, *27*(6), 804–821. doi:10.1080/09518398.2014.901578.

Terenzini, P. T., Springer, L., Yaeger, P. M., Pascarella, E. T., & Nora, A. (1996). First-Generation College Students: Characteristics, Experiences, and Cognitive Development. *Research in Higher Education*, *37*(1), 1–22. doi:10.1007/BF01680039.

Thomas, D. R. (2006). A General Inductive Approach for Analyzing Qualitative Evaluation Data. *American Journal of Evaluation*, *27*(2), 237–246.

Tinto, V. (1987). *Leaving College: Rethinking the Causes and Cures of Student Attrition*. Chicago: University of Chicago Press.

Valenti, J. (2010). *The Purity Myth: How America's Obsession with Virginity is Hurting Young Women*. New York: Seal Press.

Wade, L. (2017). *American Hookup: The New Culture of Sex on Campus, 1st edn.* New York: W. W. Norton & Company.

Weissbourd, R., Ross Anderson, T., Cashin, A., & McIntyre, J. (2017). *The Talk: How Adults Can Promote Young People's Health Relationships and Prevent Misogyny and Sexual Harassment* (Making Caring Common Project). Cambridge, MA: Harvard Graduate School of Education.

Wilkins, A. C. (2008). *Wannabes, Goths, and Christians: The Boundaries of Sex, Style, and Status*. Chicago: University of Chicago Press.

(2014). Race, Age, and Identity Transformations in the Transition from High School to College for Black and First-Generation White Men. *Sociology of Education*, *87*(3), 171–187.

Wilkins, A. C. & Dalessandro, C. (2013). Monogamy Lite Cheating, College, and Women. *Gender & Society*, *27*(5), 728–751. doi:10.1177/0891243213483878.

Wilkins, A. C. & Miller, S. A. (2017). Secure Girls: Class, Sexuality, and Self-Esteem. *Sexualities*, *20*(7). doi:10.1177/1363460716658422.

12 Yellow Fever and Yellow Impotence

The Polarity of Asian-American Sexuality

Rosalind S. Chou and Brittany Taylor

Introduction

In a recent talk on a college campus about the book *Asian American Sexual Politics* (Chou, 2012), an Asian-American graduate student asked how Asian-American masculinity could be defined. The answer given was, quite simply, as marginalized people of color, Asian Americans do not get to define themselves. Meanings are externally imposed for Asian Americans in the position where race, gender, sexuality, and class intersect, are positioned relative to others, always under the lens of White supremacy. These meanings have particular implications for Asian-American adolescents and how they define their viewpoints on sexuality. Actions, movements, and bodies are compared relative to all other bodies, and what is unspoken is how normal and central Whiteness is to both masculinity and femininity. There has been a long tradition whereby bodies and sexual behaviors of people of color define what is abnormal, exotic, oversexualized, or dysfunctional. White sexuality, beginning with White boyhood, is the unspoken "normal" or standard sexuality.

The children's story of Goldilocks and the Three Bears is a metaphor for how sexuality is raced for developing Asian-American children and adolescents. Goldilocks is in search of various items (bed, chair, and food) that are "just right." When she is seeking out porridge to eat, one bowl is "too hot," another "too cold," and she wants one that is "just right." This is similar to the ways in which male sexuality is constructed on a racial hierarchy in the United States; however, it is the construct of Whiteness that is "just right."

The normalization of White sexuality has grave implications for individuals who have multiple intersecting marginalized positions (e.g., race, gender, and sexual orientation) and are not guided or protected by Whiteness. How sexuality is to be performed and how its performance has been dictated has numerous effects for Asian-American adolescents. In order to appropriately address the sexual development of Asian American adolescents, it is necessary to first unpack the oppressive structures that are in place concerning their race and gender.

Literature Review

Gender, race, and sexuality can be conceptualized as social constructions. A social construction is a concept that indicates how ideas, groups of people, and other social occurrences or phenomena are crafted by society itself. Gender, for example, is not real but becomes real when deployed in social settings. The idea of "doing gender" (West & Zimmerman, 1987) refers to a performance inherent to various social settings, and has been applied to the well-known gender binary of masculinity and femininity. The ways in which gender is performed begins at a very early age. Prior to birth, the expectation of gender is performed through the use of specific colors to indicate the sex of a baby. These expectations are reinforced in other social areas to indicate accepted norms of masculinity and femininity. Straying from these accepted norms could result in the individual being ostracized or perceived as deviant.

Race is also conceptualized as a social construction. It is shown that there is no biological basis for racial identity as we depict it today other than the social norms created as demarcation lines (Omi & Winant, 2015). These socially constructed racial hierarchies have implications for how bodies are perceived and treated in our society. Asian Americans occupy a racial identity that is not situated within the duality of Black and White relations; that is, Asian Americans are not Black but they still do not receive White privilege and are marginalized (Ancheta, 2010). The cultural identity connected to Asian-American sexuality today follows from the sociohistorical conception of Asia as the colonized "Oriental," where Asia as a whole is conceptualized as a monolithic, homogenous culture instead of multiple countries with unique cultures (Said, 1978). The reinforcement of Asian culture as "Oriental" by Western colonizers has arguably informed assumptions about race, sexuality, and gender roles for Asian Americans (Said, 1978).

Asian-American adolescents' identity is also deeply embedded within the concept of the "model minority status" (Kiang et al., 2016; Yoon et al., 2017). The model minority status perceives Asian Americans as docile beings, overly prioritizing educational achievement, and submissive to the demands of Whiteness (Wu, 2002). Asian Americans are considered the exemplary minority group in which other racial groups are to be compared. Within the White racial frame, the concept of a model minority is perceived as a positive anecdote to the Asian-American experience due to its proximity to Whiteness. Rather, as Chou and Feagin (2015) argue, the model minority myth serves to support an assumption that Asian Americans fare much better due to the pressures of assimilation. It is often used politically to deny support and to contribute to pro-assimilation arguments. The lived reality of a model minority status does not provide resiliency, nor does it protect Asian Americans from racism (Chou & Feagin, 2015; Ong et al., 2013). The perpetuation of the model minority stereotype also correlates to an increase in negative psychological effects for Asian-American adults (Gupta et al., 2011).

While race, gender, and sexuality are all separate social constructions, considerable overlap exists. Taking the intersections of race, gender, and sexuality into consideration, Asian-American adolescent sexuality becomes much more complicated. Patricia Hill Collins (2005) suggests that as a result of these intersecting identities, African-American women and men are engaged in unique "Black sexual politics." These politics are defined

> . . . as a set of ideas and social practices shaped by gender, race, and sexuality that frame all men and women's treatment of one another, as well as how individual men and women are perceived and treated by others. Because African Americans have been so profoundly affected by racism, grappling with racism occupies a prominent place within Black sexual politics (p. 7).

Similarly, Asian Americans have been affected by racism. The effects of this racism remain relatively invisible in the dominant racial discourse, even among academics (Chou & Feagin, 2015). Hill Collins (2005) contends that "such politics lie at the heart of beliefs about Black masculinity and Black femininity, of gender-specific experiences of African Americans, and of forms that the new racism takes in the post-civil rights era" (Hill Collins, 2005, p. 7). As demonstrated by the respondents, racialized gender-specific experiences are a reality for Asian Americans.

Asian Americans face a reality of imposed stereotyping regardless of nation of ancestry, class, sexuality, or gender. In the media Asian-American adolescents are exposed to, "Asian males yield to the sexual superiority of the white males who are permitted filmically to maintain their sexual dominance over both white women and women of color" (Espiritu, 2008, p. 104). This is eerily parallel to the social reality of Asian-American men. Among all other races and genders, Asian-American women have the highest outmarriage rates. The majority of Asian-American women who outmarry have White male partners (Nemoto, 2006). For heterosexual interracial couples of Asian-American women and White men, the relationship is significantly impacted by colonialism and racialized gender power differentials (Nemoto, 2006). There is a strained relationship between Asian-American women and men as the media construct and portray the men as the most undesirable and incapable sexual partners. As Espiritu (2008) notes,

> Both Western film and literature promote dichotomous stereotypes of the Asian woman: either she is the cunning Dragon Lady of the servile Lotus Blossom Baby (Tong, 1994, p. 197). Though connoting two extremes, these stereotypes are interrelated: both eroticize Asian women as exotic "others" – sensuous, promiscuous, but untrustworthy. Whereas American popular culture denies "manhood" to Asian men, it endows Asian women with an excess of "womanhood," sexualized them but also impugning their sexuality (p. 105).

These omnipresent controlling images in the media exacerbate the "oriental fetishism" Asian and Asian-American women face (Prasso, 2005). Controlling images affecting both Asian-American men and women exist "to define the white man's virility and the white man's superiority" (Kim, 1990, p. 70). At the core of this imaging is hegemonic Whiteness and masculinity. The necessity to define White male virility and superiority through demeaning images of Asian Americans is essential in retaining White supremacy. These images are not contemporary inventions of Hollywood.

The construction of Black and Latino men as sexual predators is prevalent in the media (Vargas, 2010). They are represented as hypersexual with insatiable appetites. The representations show Black teenage boys and men having an uncontrollable urge for White women, in particular, and this is implied for Latinos who are characterized having an abundance of offspring. On the other end of the spectrum, Asian-American men (especially of East Asian descent) are constructed as hyposexual, meaning they are lacking in sexuality. Instead of sexuality existing within a dichotomy, Asian-American masculinity is assumed as an effeminate, unipolar lack of sexual expression. The cultural notion of Asian-American men as desexualized is yet another mechanism of White supremacy to ensure Asian masculinity is not a perceivable threat to Whiteness. Asian-American men are situated within the structure of Whiteness under the assumption that they are not attractive since they are not White, in contrast to Black and African-American men who are fetishized due to assumptions related to their physical attributes (Hill Collins, 2005). Asian-American men are not considered White since they lack the appropriate signifiers of hegemonic masculinity (Connell & Messerschmidt, 2005), while still remaining oppressed due to the racialization of their sexuality (i.e., perceived, at times, as hypersexualized). This figurative "castration" (Eng, 2001) of Asian-American men has detrimental effects on their overall well-being and position in society. The forced removal of one's presumed masculinity and associated manhood ultimately situates Asian men in a space of disempowerment. While the stereotypes have changed over time, the attempted regulation of East Asian male bodies through the belittlement of their penises has *everything* to do with race, specifically maintaining White supremacy. While "white fear of black sexuality is a basic ingredient of white racism" (West, 2001, as cited in Hill Collins, 2005, p. 87), Whites' ridicule of the sexuality of Asian men is another ingredient.

Yellow Fever: Asian-American Femininity

Asian-American adolescent girls are exoticized under the belief that their race automatically forces them into sexualized territory via the White male gaze. This gaze seeks to demonstrate that Asian-American adolescents, women, and femininity in general are only validated through a racialized lens. Asian-American women are therefore at a double disadvantage as their bodies are constantly surveilled within the White racial frame while simultaneously embodying the "model minority status" (Chou & Feagin, 2015). Due to this double bind, Asian-American women are often erased from popular media representation. When cultural references or representations are made, Asian-American women are generally symbolized in a racist dichotomy of negative sexual imagery. These images depict either hyperarousal through the stereotype as a 'dragon lady,' or as submissive and docile

(Espiritu, 2001; Prasso, 2005), as witnessed in the film, *Memoirs of a Geisha*. Some television shows, such as *Gilmore Girls*, highlight the experiences of Asian-American adolescent girls who are forced into assimilationist roles as a way to satisfy the "model minority" myth while also being restricted from engaging with their sexuality. In *Gilmore Girls*, Japanese-American actress Keiko Agena plays Lane Kim, a South Korean teenager living in a predominately White, small-town neighborhood. Most notably, Lane's mother is depicted as an overly strict, Christian Korean mother who forces Lane to remain studious over interacting with typical heterosexual teenage events, such as dating or sexual practices. Lane's character is ultimately a symbolic definition of how the media frames Asian-American adolescent girls and women with the model minority. The White racial framing of Asian-American women goes beyond embodiment and has direct consequences on how Asian-American women's bodies are portrayed and thus assimilated into Western culture.

Furthermore, Asian women often feel compelled to identify with the White beauty standard as a way of passing or reconstructing their identities. The Western beauty standard is a cultural reinforcement of the racist underbelly within a capitalist system. Asian-American women often feel obligated to reconstruct their bodies and physical characteristics to match the White Western beauty standard (Javier & Belgrave, 2015). Many Asian-American women report seeking eyelid reconstruction surgery, known as blepharoplasty, to minimize the appearance of hooded eyelids as a way to appear whiter (Chou & Feagin, 2015; Kaw, 1993). This discrepancy in body image is experienced globally, with Chinese women reporting cosmetic surgeries and enhancements due to internalizing White standards (Lindridge & Wang, 2008; Luo, 2013; Zhang, 2012). By producing and selling specific makeup products that are not marketed for Asian women, the beauty standard reinforces a specific White image.

Research has attempted to highlight a current wave of sexual resistance among Filipino-American women by reconstructing the colonized narrative of the hypersexualization of Asian-American women (Espiritu, 2001). Instead of internalizing or embracing the supposed provocativeness of White women, Filipina women are reinforcing more conservative sexual viewpoints, such as the heavy emphasis to retain one's virginity (itself a social construction) until marriage (Espiritu, 2001). Filipina-American adolescents therefore embrace sexual maturity from within a narrative of resisting Whiteness, yet must still grapple with restrictive sexual norms.

The media continues to incur detrimental effects for Asian-American adolescents, primarily due to the lack of positive representation. This arguably impacts how Asian-American adolescent girls develop and negotiate their sexuality. In a survey of Asian, Black, and White female college students in Michigan, Asian respondents (n=54) were reported as having disparities concerning their bodies, as well as identifying with dominant social trends, that is, Whiteness (Evans & McConnell, 2003). The current Western beauty standard idealizes, not just Whiteness, but a specific kind of white female body. The reinforcement of acculturation therefore implies a racialized sexualization of Asian-American adolescent girls, which can lead to an increase in sexual partners during adolescence (Hahm et al., 2006; Tong, 2013). The combination of societal demands surrounding sexual stereotypes of Asian women, inhabiting a model minority status, and the reinforcement of a White, idolized beauty standard inevitably places a detriment on the sexual development of Asian-American adolescent girls. While there are some positive representations of Asian-American women resisting stereotypes of Asian women, Asian-American adolescent girls and women are still hypersexualized and also represented as passive and submissive. Comedians such as Mindy Kaling have recently integrated discussions of body image and sexuality on their show, *The Mindy Project* (Lamb et al., 2016). Due to the continued implied passivity and lack of positive representation, a deeper emphasis must be placed on disrupting this narrative.

Yellow Impotence: Asian-American Masculinity

Similar to the impact of the Western beauty standard for Asian-American women, Asian-American men are also inundated with negative media representation. Examples of these negative images are found with William Hung's viral performance on American Idol (Gangnam style with Psy), and racist caricatures of Asian men on *Breakfast with Tiffany's*. They are laughable buffoons who do not stand a chance with a woman. The high school character of Long Duk Dong in the popular 1980s film, *Sixteen Candles*, illustrates how Asian-American male adolescents are shown for comedic relief instead of perceived as attractive. This juxtaposition masks the middle position of White men's sexuality, sitting quietly in between the prefixes of hyper (over, excess) and hypo (under) as the norm. These images further depict their sexual expression as a comedic act that derives perverse pleasure from mocking displays of masculinity. Even though Asian-American boys and adolescents are inundated with negative imagery within the media, new characterizations are becoming more mainstream. Indian-American actor Aziz Ansari's recent roles in *Parks and Recreation*, as well as his romantic comedy, *Master of None*, depict male Indian-Americans in less asexual, more positive roles – albeit not without the focus on comedic relief. In a study of 30 popular magazines in the United States, researchers found that Asian men are vastly underrepresented in both "men's" magazines, such as Maxim, as well as "women's" magazines, such as Vogue and Cosmopolitan (Schug et al., 2017). The results from this study are consistent with the overall lack of positive representation of Asian-American men in the media and reinstates Asian male sexuality as unattractive or completely devoid of sexual desire.

Due to the consistent framing and emphasis of Asian male sexuality as impotent, Asian-American adolescent boys inevitably internalize these images. Asian-American adolescent boys are presented with a duality concerning their identities. They may feel compelled to try and embrace hegemonic masculinity for visibility purposes and subsequently benefit from a patriarchal system (Chan, 2001).

The influence of hegemonic masculinity is present when discussing sexual messages (and subsequent sexual behaviors) among Asian-American adolescent boys, especially compared to Asian-American adolescent girls. In a study of cross-sectional studies on Asian-American college students (n=312), researchers found that Asian-American boys were given messages that were generally accepting of casual sex (Trinh et al., 2014). In the same study, Asian-American adolescent girls were found to receive opposite messages, and instead were given messages on abstaining from sexual encounters (Trinh et al., 2014). Even though Asian-American males are perceived as hyposexual via negative media images, their sexuality is not nearly as threatened as it is for Asian-American adolescent girls. It is within this duality that many Asian-American adolescent males are given mixed social messages regarding their sexuality.

Asian-American Queerness

An additional key component to the sociological study of sexuality is the damaging impetus of heteronormativity. Heteronormativity is a social structure that claims (and thereby reproduces) heterosexuality as the ideal or hegemonic sexual framework. This oppressive structure reinforces heterosexuality as the only acceptable sexuality by actively working to situate itself in legal structures, such as the institution of marriage; as well as health care, where physicians must take cultural competency courses that highlight queer sexual behaviors. Sexual identity and behaviors that exist outside the design of heteronormativity are perceived as abnormal.

Asian-American men as a whole are perceived as being void of sexuality or sexual desire; this is further mirrored in queer spaces that center Whiteness and masculinity. Queerness intensifies the already negative racial stereotyping of gay men. If Asian-American men are constructed as hypomasculine, Asian-American gay men are often marginalized, subordinated, hypomasculinized man.

Gay, male Asian-American adolescents learn at a young age that not only are they rendered sexless due to misconceptions about their race but also face racialized perceptions about their sexuality. Gay Asian-American male adolescents are often found to actively participate in the model minority concept in order to avoid being bullied over their complex identity of being Asian American and gay (Ocampo & Soodjinda, 2016). As they age, Asian-American gay males encounter dating apps that are replete with racist comments that intentionally alienate Asian-American men (Riggs, 2013). Gay Asian-American men also encounter a unique form of racialized objectification within the queer community by those referred to as "rice queens" (Han et al., 2014; Kumashiro, 1999). "Rice queens" are White gay men from the United States whose fetishization of Asian men is deeply rooted in colonialism (Kumashiro, 1999).

Research has also indicated that many gay Asian Americans inevitably internalize the racist sexual scripts and stereotypes they are forced to endure (Chou, 2012; Wilson & Yoshikawa, 2004), especially as a way to pass in certain settings

(Choi et al., 2011). As many adolescents look to media or pornographic material to understand sexual scripts, gay men of color are no exception. David Eng asserts that it is imperative to take Asian-American men's racial formation into account in order to understand how their sexuality has been constructed (Eng, 2001). There is a racial castration process that takes place where Asian-American men are stripped of all sexual elements. Gay Asian men are almost always perceived as "bottoms" in gay male pornography, meaning they are the receptive partner in same-sex sexual scenarios (Fung, 2005; Nguyen, 2014). Even in the porn industry, they are searching for their penises (Fung, 2005). The East Asian-American representation is far from complimentary, however, even more alarming is the almost complete lack of representation of Southeast, South Asian, and Pacific Islander Americans in the media. These sexual scripts are indicative of the aforementioned castration of Asian-American masculinity, and the sexualized racism experienced by gay Asian-American men is systemic with clear intentions to maintain White masculinity as the gay *status quo*.

With regard to queer Asian-American girls and adolescents, there is a dearth of research that accurately captures queer Asian-American women's sexuality. Some second-generation "out" South Asian-American lesbians report experiences of marginalization within their families and surrounding communities due to heteronormative cultural expectations for immigrants (Bacchus, 2017). In a study of 50 Asian-American queer women, 32 percent of respondents indicated feelings of invisibility that are often reflective of media representation (Sung et al., 2014). As we have outlined, there is a clear discrepancy surrounding the sexual development of Asian-American adolescents that encompasses both heterosexual and queer identities.

Themes in Asian-American Sexuality

In this chapter, we use data from 74 interview participants and 47 survey respondents in order to discuss what models of sexuality are available for Asian and Asian-American children and adolescents. Our participants self-identify as 66 women and 54 men; one self-identifies as "female-bodied gender queer." The 111 respondents self-identify ethnically as: Taiwanese, Chinese, Indian, Filipino, Korean, Malaysian, Vietnamese, Hmong, Pakistani, Bangladeshi, Japanese, Thai, and multiracial Americans, ranging in age from 18 to 71 years. These data were collected from 2006 to 2013 and the survey was distributed electronically in a social research laboratory on a college campus.

From this sample a number of themes arose and we focus on three for this chapter: (1) racialized, gendered, and sexualized stereotypes; (2) the performance of "body work" to meet the White standard of beauty; and (3) the effects of stereotypes and body work on the sexual development and sexual politics for Asian-American adolescents.

Controlling Images and Externally Imposed Stereotypes

As noted already, there are limited representations of Asian-American women in the media. The images that do exist are rigid and subordinate to the constructions of a hegemonic femininity associated with White womanhood. This othering can cause internalized conflict and affect self-image. Furthermore, the normalization of negative body imagery can inevitably impact one's sexual development or sexual practices through girls' relationships to their body. Fareena struggled with self-esteem when she went to an all-White school:

> I remember I hated myself in the sixth grade. Hated myself. And that was the time I went to all white, all very rich white. I remember that the type of girls that all the boys started liking didn't look like me, you know, being a brown woman. Issues of body hair came in to play. I have body hair that other girls don't have. I have to pluck my eyebrows and other girls don't have to. It looks dirty on me. And there is this concept of dirt. I had real issues of just wanting to purge, physically purge things out of me. You know, my elbows are darker, my knees are darker, when I scar I leave a brown mark instead of a pink mark that fades. And all that is looked at as dirty or ugly or scarred and not simply like a part of life. So, I felt very dirty. And I was also curvier than the other girls at the time. I started puberty in the fourth grade. By sixth grade, I didn't look a lot different from this. And I felt fat. All the other girls were skinny. I felt I didn't have muscles the way the other girls did. I was really into sports at the time. And I felt puny and couldn't athletically compete like them. And there is an attraction with athletic girls. You know, the girl's basketball team or track team. There'd be this camaraderie with the boys' basketball team because we had to travel together and do things like that. There are a lot of hookups. No one wanted to hookup with the lone brown girl.

Fareena's use of words such as "hated," "dirty," and "ugly" highlight the internalization of racist constructions of beauty. In contrast to the Whites, Fareena, as the brown girl, occupies the inferior half of the White/non-White binary. But African Americans have greater access to magazines, books, television channels, and movies that convey the message that "Black is beautiful." Certainly, there are still hierarchical problems with some of these media depictions involving body size, skin color, and objectification of female bodies, but they do offer alternative ideologies for young African-American women. Asian-American women do not have easy access, and, in the options that they do have, largely light-skinned women of East Asian descent are displayed. South Asian Americans have fewer resources. Even with some of the anti-hegemonic resistance movements in Black-owned media, White standards of beauty pervade.

For South Asian-American women, there are also numerous assumptions and controlling images regarding their sexuality, as Indira explains.

> We don't get to be who we are. We're perceived, our identities are perceived and then placed on us. So when East Asian women experience being overly exotified, it becomes this like there's the overtone of a cunning woman who is going to manipulate you with her exotic ways. And I think South Asian women experience that as well, but it will come out in way that is intertwined with our culture identity.

> So, for example, I'll get the or I used to in college, "Hey do you know about the *Kama Sutra*? I can *Kama Sutra* you." What does that mean? I think that there's these notions of spirituality and sexuality get intertwined in an erotic way that kind of leads to a hypersexualization of South Asian women.

The imagined or longed-for hypersexuality of South Asian women by White men greatly contrasts the sentiment within the South Asian community that constructs sex, as Fareena put it, as a "punishment" for women. Fareena understood that in her community sex is not something that is supposed to be enjoyed. It is simultaneously sacred and joyless (Bacchus, 2017). This contrasts with the interest in the *Kama Sutra* taken from exotic stereotypes of Indian women. The *Kama Sutra*, since the colonization of India, has been the "white man's sex manual with 'exotic' women." In the mid-1800s, it was common for English men to have Indian mistresses and "in the British imagination and in their daily lives Indian women were sexualized in ways scholars recognize as the typical colonial gaze: Indian women were defined as seductive, sensual, and exotic" (Nagel, 2003, p. 151). This remark about the *Karma Sutra* exoticizes and dehumanizes Indria, and imagines her sexuality to be very different from what she understands as part of her culture.

Stereotypes of White-constructed manhood also may affect Asian-American adolescents. In the film *Tough Guise*, Jackson Katz asserts, "There are millions of male trauma survivors walking around today, men who were bullied in adolescence" (Katz, 1999). There is a great societal cost to the normalization of male violence. The effect of violence on Asian-American men has not been thoroughly researched. As one respondent, Indira, poignantly states, "American history has isolated the Asian man in that way to not be able to speak. And I think an accumulation of that can only result in deep harm."

Irwin Tang (2005), a Chinese-American writer, has a great deal of experience with racialized violence at school. Irwin speaks from his own personal experiences, since he was bullied for a number of years in middle and high school. While Irwin experienced physical threats and harm, he notes that the unspoken acts of racism he endured daily from his White classmates as an "other" or "outsider" was extremely powerful. Irwin describes being able to be both negatively and positively influenced by representations of Asian Americans, and the contrasting aspects of Asian and White masculinity. These racialized constructions of Asian-American men have affected how Irwin has constructed his own identity:

> I started having this sort of my own very twisted understanding of Asian masculinity, Asian men, and hatred [of] Asian men as people who I wish I didn't have to be associated with. I followed the Hitler complex. And it was very, very weird. It was rolled into all sorts of just extreme feelings about everything. Obsessive thoughts about my girlfriend, about my self, about news, I guess these feelings got projected onto construed people that I thought were inferior, Asian men. I wish that they would all die. Disappear or something like that and it was very, very strange. It took me a long time to get over . . . You know, psychological issues, I was prescribed Lithium for a while and I didn't like it. It's a combination of all those

> things. Certainly it was worsened by the insecurities and such that are complicated by being an Asian American male born in America and having grown up here.

Emasculating racist imagery and interactions accumulate up over time and can have detrimental effects, as in Irwin's case. Hegemonic ideologies continue to thrive because "contemporary forms of oppression do not routinely force people to submit. Instead, they manufacture consent for domination so that we lose our ability to question and thus collude in our own subordination" (Hill Collins, 2005, p. 50). Collusion with one's oppression exacerbates fighting and eliminating it. If Asian Americans adopt hegemonic ideologies as truth, the racial *status quo* remains unchallenged. Irwin had a very difficult time conceiving of himself as a masculine being, and internalized hegemonic ideology about his body:

> That was freshman year of high school. Um, I mean I think I had a very un-masculine body. I was real thin and stuff I think I was almost like transgendered in some sense because my sense of myself was certainly not that I was macho or very masculine at all and it didn't help that when I was very young in elementary school and middle school and stuff like that something people would think that I was a girl because I had kind of poofy hair. I think even I had a hard time conceiving of Asian men – maybe myself – as being a man. Like using that word "man." Like I think I still have a hard time calling myself "man." (Chou, 2012)

Even when a participant in our study seemed to appreciate Asian women's beauty, one could detect a norm of internalized Whiteness. Jeremy, a Bangladeshi American in his 30s, repeated a few times that he "truly believed" the statements he was making about attractiveness, that Asian-American women, whether South, East, or Southeast Asian in origin, were just "naturally" more attractive. Additionally, he used the term that women outside of his race were "out of his league." Here he is placing clear boundaries, or conjuring images of a hierarchy of women to which he has access to some, but not others. Jeremy has internalized the constructions of exotic Asian female beauty and the lack of attractiveness of Asian men; "attractive" women of other races are unapproachable. Jeremy states:

> Indian [South Asian] men are so physically ugly for the most part. No. No. We really are. It's just if you look at our women and you look at our men, our woman are clearly more attractive. Even the ones that are with Indian men are on the grand scale a lot more attractive than we are ... I think Indian men don't outmarry because I don't think Indian men have the confidence to approach people of another race. We feel like it's out of our league for the most part. I'm talking about the race in America as a whole, whereas women they [Asian American women] get approached all the time. More often than not, Indian men will date Indian women. But if they date outside the race, outside the Indian box, they [the non-Indian women] are not very good-looking, nine times out of ten ... I mean I have two uncles who married white women and they're pretty gross. I have one uncle that married three times and this computer is more attractive than my uncle's wives. That's just the truth. When we pick white, they're not white, they look busted.

In essence, Jeremy is stating that beauty is Whiteness. He considers the women his uncles have chosen as partners unattractive and thus "they're not white, they look busted." While his statement is sexist and problematic, he again highlights the racial boundaries when it comes to dating and partnerships. Jeremy has internalized these White supremacist concepts where he makes sweeping statements about "all Indian men." The adoption of the White racial frame further complicates Asian-American sexual politics. The stereotypes of Asian-American men as sexualized bodies leaves for politically charged conceptions of self and others.

Body Work

The most frequent Asian and Asian-American plastic surgeries are procedures to Anglicize their facial and other body features. Reports show a sharp increase in cosmetic surgery for Asian Americans, the most common procedures for women are eyelid surgery and nose reshaping. The nose surgery involves a nose bridge operation that changes a flatter-looking Asian nose into a protruding more European-type nose. Thus, much cosmetic surgery is directed to make Asian women look more like a common White view of ideal female beauty. Charlotte, a Chinese American in her 40s recalls wanting to be different physically in high school:

> I remember in high school, meeting one girl who was also Chinese. Assimilation was the name of the game. I remember she and I talked, and all she wanted to have was blonde hair and blue eyes and to be named Chris, and all I wanted to have was regular brown hair and regular brown eyes and be named Janet. We would just talk about how all we wanted to do was be like everybody else.

Charlotte was one of many respondents who expressed a desire to have different features that met the White standard of beauty. The desire to perform body work to fit an ideal standard of beauty was not reserved for Asian-American women. Glenn describes an Asian-American friend who he believes is a model of Asian-American masculinity.

> I have a former student slash friend now, born in Singapore and raised in the U.S., who is a personal trainer. He exhibits what I call the ideal Asian American type. He's very masculine. He's very built. He acts in a very American way. If you paint him white, he is completely American. Not saying that Asian Americans are not Americans. I think there is a misunderstanding that Asian Americans are not Americans because they're not *American*. Americans are supposed to be white. At the same time, I think black is also understood to be a part of the American model. Now Latino men are moving into the mainstream. But Asian men are lagging behind. They are not there yet. So it's the assumption that they're not quite American, yet. I think that he represents what I would say a lot of heterosexual Asian American men would like to become . . . He's the kind of Asian American I would like to become. I don't think I have the physical characteristics that he has. He's big, huge. He's slightly taller than me. He really trains himself to develop the physique that is competitive with other "Americans" – white, Latino, black . . . Bruce Lee had a great body, but he's lean, very lean. He's not really muscular. He's lean and tall. I would say the body types are a little different. Asian men are lean and toned, not muscular. Lean and toned aren't what is most desirable.

Glenn's friend is a representation of an Asian-American male conforming to Whiteness. What Glenn describes is a person working hard to shape and form a body associated with non-Asian men. Glenn is arguing that to become truly American, Asian Americans must not act Asian, something he does not clearly describe. Glenn puts a great deal of emphasis on constructions of Whiteness and Asianness. Glenn's friend attempts to access Whiteness by doing "body work," but, instead of plastic surgery, he uses the gym to shape his body in what is perceived as White and male. While both Charlotte and Glenn are adults, their experiences with racialized perceptions of their bodies highlights the myriad struggles Asian-American children and adolescents experience due to internalizing negative ideas.

Sexual Politics

Partnerships are political. The way we choose partners or even have the ability to "choose" is based on a number of sociopolitical factors tied to our identities. Although media portrayals sell us ideas about romantic love that knows no bounds, we are, in fact, bound by conscious and unconscious meanings and definitions that affect our decisions for partnership. Reality television shows to find "love" like *The Bachelor* are crude, yet sociologically significant, examples of how the search for love is based on class, age, race, constructions of beauty, and weight. Individuals who have an element of "freedom" to choose a partner must contend with these dimensions of attraction that are not necessarily based on animal urges, but economic and sociopolitical hierarchies.

Asian-American adolescents are met with an imposed gender ideology where power relations of race, class, gender, and sexuality permeate individual consciousness. The White racial frame can place psychological boundaries on what partners Asian-American adolescents think that they can access. This ideology tells them how they should think about their own bodies, relationships, and sexuality. This racial hierarchy is also articulated indirectly through racial preferences of the Asian-American female respondents. Alex, a Chinese-American third-year student at an elite university, describes her attraction to "Caucasian guys" over "Asian boys":

> . . . I think I'm just more attracted to Caucasian guys just in general I don't know Asian boys I find very attractive but Asian men tend to be very androgynous in their features and I can't date a guy that's prettier than me and Asian boys tend to be prettier than me. I don't know but for some reason they're not like I don't see them as handsome I see them as pretty and when a boy is prettier than me it's kind of like a blow to your ego. So I find them attractive but I don't think I'd ever want to date any of them.

Alex phrases her preference for White males over Asian males in terms of masculinity. She refers to Asian males as "prettier" than her and "androgynous" in their features and not handsome. She is able to compliment males as "pretty" and simultaneously deny them masculinity. That is, her adjectives negate the masculinity of Asian males and clearly paint them in feminine terms. Alex reinforces White hegemonic masculinity, not only by relegating Asian and Asian-American males to a subordinate position of femininity but also by preferring White males to Asian and Asian-American males.

The Asian-American respondents who were currently enrolled in college at the time of the interviews said they were interested in finding romantic partners but also seemed to recognize certain racial limitations and boundaries in their love lives. The Asian-American female respondents' racial preferences insinuate the influence of racial hierarchy in romance. Like Alex, Diana, a Chinese-American female senior, explains her preference for White men:

> I look for predominantly white males as partners, specifically those who are over 5'10" in height, with similar education level, and are career ambitious. I prefer white men because they are more independent and don't have a tendency to be as needy as Asian men in relationships ... in general, I prefer white men because they're more aggressive in all aspects of life, more independent, and are more readily seen as successful. I also feel more attractive when I'm dating someone white though it's hard to explain why. I guess in a way, I'm more proud to show off my white boyfriend than my Asian boyfriend. I just feel slightly more judged when I'm dating someone Asian, and feel more prized when I'm dating someone white.

Diana preference stems from hegemonic masculinity. White men are "more aggressive" and "more independent" – essentially more masculine – whereas Asian men are "needy" and subordinated. Diana admits she "feels more attractive dating someone white." Although she says, "it's hard to explain why," she goes on to say she "feels more prized when I'm dating someone white." In essence, she benefits from White privilege and power in having a White partner.

This dynamic can create tension with Asian-American heterosexual adolescent boys who are seeking out partnership across the life course. Respondents look to the media to help explain and make sense of their world. What they often find is that faces like theirs are lacking. We see how these images play out in the lives of the respondents as they try to define themselves and have relationships with others, where Diana and Alex choose not to date Asian-American men. Our Asian-American male respondents notice the imbalance in how sexually attractive they appear in the media. Brent observes:

> Women fit some image of Asian in white Western society ... Sure some exotic hottie. That sort of thing doesn't exist for Asian men in the western world. For the most part, from what I've seen, there are no sort of Asian men sex symbols. There might be, but I don't think there are. Asians in the media, they don't occupy that sort of role. Where as of course Lucy Liu does, you know, or any very attractive Asian female. So you might as well not even have a dick as a man here sometimes.

These constructions play out in the LGBTQ community as well. Glenn, a Malaysian American who identifies as gay, he finds that Asian-American heterosexual men are not the only ones burdened with weak media constructions. He also sees similar obstacles for Asian-American gay men:

> I think Asian gay men are screwed in some way, too. Even though there is a small community of "rice queens." Non-Asian gay men who like Asian men. They are gay. So they are called "queens" and they like "rice." So they are called Rice Queens. There is a small community of gay men who seek out Asian men. But there are stereotypes about them, too. Some stereotypes, from when I was in California, they are usually losers. They can't find partners of their own race. Or non-Asian gay men. That's why they are like, 'I'll just be with Asians because they are easier.' Another stereotype is that all gay Asian men are bottoms, so the assumption is that they are easy targets because they are the leftover. So if you can't find your own type or a more-macho gay man, go to the Asian gay men. Because they are all bottoms. So if you're a top or if you want a fuck, then just talk to the gay Asian men. They are easier. They're submissive. Easy targets. I think these two assumptions draw gay men to Asian men, which I totally reject. That has been my experience about what has been portrayed in both the traditional mainstream media as well as in gay media – that Asian men are portrayed as feminine, weak, passive bottoms. And in a way, asexual.

Glenn has a gay friend of many years, whom he mentored as a resident assistant in his college dorm. Glenn served as a support while the friend was coming out. Even though his resident knew that he was gay, Glenn was never seen as a sexual being:

> Basically, he very honestly told me, 'I've always seen you as asexual. I don't see you as anything else in the gay world. I would just walk right past you. When I go to the gay club, looking for targets, looking for a one night stand, a date, a boyfriend, whatever, I would probably just walk right by you and I wouldn't register anything because Asian men are asexual to me.' He's a white American, born and raised in Nebraska.

This racist stereotyping has had an impact on Glenn's self-esteem and his choice of partners. He colluded with the system and internalized that he was not capable of getting partners besides "rice queens." Glenn explains:

> You usually get a lot of attention from Rice Queens. It's not really what I want, because I want to fit in. I'm still hoping for that ideal situation where my race and my color don't factor in. Or the assumption of my penis size doesn't get into the equation where they calculate, 'What's my chance of getting this person?' I think things have become better. When I was younger, I was acting in a way that was still operating in that assumption. Feeding into the machine. I was consciously contributing to that cycle, to those assumptions. The cycle that the only types of people that you can date or sleep with are Rice Queens, who are losers. So, if you can't get laid elsewhere, they come to you. I think that was the assumption. I think now I am consciously breaking out of that and having other types of successes.

While Glenn is finding other successes, he still has to contend with an LGBTQ community that may or may not see him as equal man and an equal potential partner.

> I do recognize that people see me as an Asian, so there's obviously racism intersected in the gay culture. I feel like I do get turned away sometimes because I'm Asian. Personally, I don't care. Well, I do care, but I get over it real quick. I think being gay plus being Asian, having those two together, actually reinforces another stereotype. It gets deeper and more complex.

Our partnership choices may become limited with how we view ourselves as individuals. If we believe that members of an entire race are "out of our league" then we limit our own possibilities. It is a self-fulfilling prophecy. White racist ideologies create those boundaries. In the not-so-distant past, there were legal boundaries and deadly consequences to crossing the color lines romantically; the message is still conveyed through media and the "castrating" of Asian-American men. As long as William Hung gets airtime, the longer we delay racial progress. All men and women are not created equal. White racist imagery shapes individuals, families, communities, and nations. The White racial frame, whether consciously or unconsciously, affects White racist imagery. These controlling images, whether used consciously or unconsciously, affects Asian-American sexual politics. It influences who we deem attractive, who we approach, and with whom we choose to partner.

Conclusion

Race, class, gender, nationhood, and sexuality are tangled interlocking systems of power, domination, and oppression. Racial and gender inequality is maintained by everyday practices. For individuals, racialization and gendering begins before birth, extends and is most overt during childhood. Asian-American bodies are bombarded with ethnosexualized messages and images from both their most intimate familial relations and their surrounding environment. Cultural values are built into the gendering. Asian Americans learn very quickly that, because of their race, they are inferior to Whites, and assumptions are made about them not only based on race but also gender and sexuality. These hegemonic lessons can be unlearned and in our study of Asian-American college students, some resisted these racialized stereotypes. Beth, a Chinese-American sophomore, says:

> Don't give a shit about what white people think you are supposed to do. Asians are not "supposed" to do anything. We operate with all the same rights, freedoms, desires, fears, sexual urges, despair, [and] anger as white people – and, yes, even in dating and hooking up. You can have as much sex or as little sex or no sex with whomever you want. Asian women are just as beautiful as white women. Asian men are just as sexy as white men. Believe it, live it.

Beth recognizes and rejects Asian-American racial boundaries that White ideology has created and attempts to remove expectations on sexualized racism and beauty. Her counter-narrative attempts to free Asian Americans from subordination to Whites by recognizing that Asian-Americans' rights, emotions, and desires have value.

We contend that Asian-American sexuality is formed in ways that perpetuate White privilege, particularly for White men. This formation begins in adolescence with lasting effects across the life course for Asian Americans. Controlling images of both Asian-American men and women exist "to define the white man's virility and the white man's superiority" (Kim, 1990). Again, at the core of these Asian portrayals is the strength of White hegemonic masculinity. Defining White male virility and superiority through demeaning representations of Asian Americans is essential in retaining the existing racial structure. It is apparent that the maintenance of White supremacy through controlling images and stereotypes of Asian Americans as gendered and sexualized bodies is a sobering reality for our respondents. While all people go through a gendered and sexualized process in society, the intersecting racial identity for people of color introduces racial domination into the mix.

The additional struggle with defining one's own racial identity is difficult enough for any individual, regardless of gender identity or sexuality. There are societal forces consistently imposing identity on us all based on gender, sexuality, class, race, ability, and many others. However, consideration of *power* and *domination* must constantly be centralized in this analysis to get a clear picture of how oppression is operating. Asian Americans, while perhaps seen as "nearly white," are not free from gendered, racialized treatment. This racialized and gendered process is not static and has direct implications on the sexual development of Asian-American adolescents. The sexual stereotyping of people of Asian descent has mutated throughout American history, changing based on the needs and interests of Whites (Chou, 2012).

We encourage further critical research that puts issues in historical context and further examines constructions of race, ethnicity, gender, and sexuality, especially for Asian-American adolescents. By further unpacking these intersecting identities and their relationship to power and domination, we can dismantle controlling images and resist externally imposed meanings and definitions that are harmful to the sexual development of Asian-American adolescents.

References

Ancheta, A. (2010). Neither Black nor White. In Wu, J. Y. S. and Chen, T. (Eds.), *Asian American Studies Now: A Critical Reader*. (21–34). New Brunswick: Rutgers University Press.

Bacchus, N. (2017). Shifting Sexual Boundaries: Ethnicity and Pre-marital Sex in the Lives of South Asian American Women. *Sexuality & Culture*, *21*, 776–794. doi:10.1007/s12119-017-9421-2.

Chan, J. (2001). *Chinese American Masculinities: From Fu Manchu to Bruce Lee*. New York: Routledge.

Choi, K., Han, C., Paul, J., & Ayala, G. (2011). Strategies for Managing Racism and Homophobia among U.S. Ethnic and Racial Minority Men Who Have Sex with Other Men. *AIDS Education and Prevention*, *23*(2), 145–158.

Chou, R. & Feagin, J. (2015). *The Myth of the Model Minority: Asian Americans Facing Racism*, *2nd edn*. Boulder: Paradigm Publishers.

Chou, R. (2012). *Asian American Sexual Politics*. Plymouth: Rowman & Litlefield Publishers, Inc.

Connell, R. W. & Messerschmidt, J. W. (2005). Hegemonic Masculinity: Rethinking the Concept. *Gender & Society*, *19*(6), 829–859. doi: 10.1177/0891243205278639.

Eng, D. (2001). *Racial Castration: Managing Masculinity in Asian America*. Durham, NC: Duke University Press.

Espiritu, Y. L. (2001). 'We Don't Sleep around Like White Girls Do': Family, Culture, and Gender in Filipina American Lives. *Signs: Journal of Women in Culture & Society* *26*(2), 415–40.

(2008). *Asian American Women and Men: Labor, Laws, and Love, 2nd edn*. Lanham: Rowman & Littlefield Publishers, Inc.

Evans, P. C. & McConnell, A. (2003). Do Racial Minorities Respond in the Same Way to Mainstream Beauty Standards? Social Comparison Processes in Asian, Black, and White Women. *Self and Identity*, *2*, 153–167. doi:10.1080/15298860390129908.

Fung, R. (2005). Looking for My Penis: The Eroticized Asian in Gay Video Porn. In Ono, K. A. (Ed.), *A Companion to Asian American Studies* (235–253). Malde: Blackwell Publishers.

Gupta, A., Szymanski, D. M., & Leong, F. T. L. (2011). The "Model Minority Myth": Internalized Racialism of Positive Stereotypes as Correlates of Psychological Distress, and Attitudes toward Help-Seeking. *Asian American Journal of Psychology*, *2*(2), 101–114.

Hahm, H. C., Lahiff, R., & Barreto, R. (2006). Asian American Adolescents' First Sexual Intercourse: Gender and Acculturation Differences. *Perspectives on Sexual & Reproductive Health*, *38*(1), 28–36.

Han, C., Proctor, K., & Choi, K. (2014). I Know a Lot of Gay Asian Men Who Are Actually Tops: Managing and Negotiating Gay Racial Stigma. *Sexuality & Culture*, *18*, 219–234.

Hill Collins, P. (2005). *Black Sexual Politics*. New York: Taylor & Francis Group.

Javier, S. & Belgrave, F. (2015). An Examination of Influences on Body Dissatisfaction among Asian American College Females: Do Family, Media, or Peers Play a Role? *Journal of American College Health*, *63*(8), 579–583.

Katz, J. (1999). *Tough Guise: Violence, Media and the Crisis in Masculinity*. Northampton, MA: Media Education Foundation.

Kaw, E. (1993). Medicalization of Racial Features: Asian American Women and Cosmetic Surgery. *Medical Anthropology Quarterly*, *7*(1), 74–89.

Kiang, L., Witkow, M., & Thompson, T. (2016). Model Minority Stereotyping, Perceived Discrimination and Adjustment among Adolescents from Asian American Backgrounds. *Journal of Youth & Adolescence*, *45*, 1366–1379. doi:10.1007/s10964-015-0336-7.

Kim, E. H. (1990). "Such Opposite Creatures": Men and Women in Asian American Literature. *Michigan Quarterly Review*, *29*(1), 68–93.

Kumashiro, K. (1999). Supplementing Normalcy and Otherness: Queer Asian American Men Reflect on Stereotypes, Identity, and Oppression. *International Journal of Qualitative Studies in Education*, *12*(5), 491–508.

Lamb, S., Roberts, T., & Plocha, A. (2016). *Girls of Color, Sexuality, and Sex Education*. New York: Springer.

Lindridge, A. & Wang, C. (2008). Saving 'Face' in China: Modernization, Parental Pressure, and Plastic Surgery. *Journal of Consumer Behavior*, *7*, 496–508. doi:10.1002/cb.267.

Luo, W. (2013). Aching for the Altered Body: Beauty Economy and Chinese Women's Consumption of Cosmetic Surgery. *Women's Studies International Forum*, *38*, 1–10.

Nagel, J. (2003). *Race, Ethnicity, and Sexuality*. New York: Oxford University Press.

Nemoto, K. (2006). Intimacy, Desire, and the Construction of Self in Relationships between Asian American Women and White American Men. *Journal of Asian American Studies*, *9*(1), 27–54.

Nguyen, T. H. (2014). *A View from the Bottom: Asian American Masculinity and Sexual Representation*. Durham, NC: Duke University Press.

Ong, A., Burrow, A., Fuller-Rowell, T., Ja, N., & Sue, D. (2013). Racial Microaggressions and Daily Well-Being among Asian Americans. *Journal of Counseling Psychology*, *60*(2), 188–199. doi:10.1037/a0031736.

Ocampo, A. & Soodjinda, D. (2016). Invisible Asian Americans: The Intersections of Sexuality, Race, and Education among Gay Asian Americans. *Race, Ethnicity, and Education*, *19*(3), 480–499.

Omi, M. & Winant, H. (2015). *Racial Formation in the United States*. New York: Routledge.

Prasso, S. (2005). *The Asian Mystique: Dragon Ladies, Geisha Girls, and Our Fantasies Of the Exotic Orient*. New York: Public Affairs.

Riggs, D. (2013). Anti-Asian Sentiment amongst a Sample of White Australian Men on Gaydar. *Sex Roles*, *68*, 768–778.

Said, E. (1978). *Orientalism*. New York: Random House.

Schug, J., Alt. N., & Lu, P. (2017). Gendered Race in Mass Media: Invisibility of Asian Men and Black Women in Popular Magazines. *Psychology of Popular Media Culture* *6*(3), 222–236.

Sung, M. R., Szymanski, D., & Henrichs-Beck, C. (2014). Challenges, Coping, and Benefits of Being an Asian American Lesbian or Bisexual Woman. *Psychology of Sexual Orientation and Gender Diversity*, *2*(1), 52–64.

Tang, I. (2005). *How I Became a Black Man and Other Metamorphoses*. Austin, TX: IT Works.

Tong, B. (1994). *Unsubmissive Women: Chinese Prostitutes in Nineteenth-Century San Francisco*. Norman, OK: University of Oklahoma Press.

Tong, Y. (2013). Acculturation, Gender Disparity, and the Sexual Behavior of Asian American Youth. *Journal of Sex Research*, *50*(6), 560–573.

Trinh, S., Ward, M., Day, K., Thomas, K., & Levin, D. (2014). Emergent Peer and Parent Sexual Messages to Asian American College Students' Sexual Behaviors. *Journal of Sex Research*, *51*(2), 208–220. doi: 10.1080/00224499.2012.721099.

Vargas, D. (2010). Representations of Latina/o Sexuality in Popular Culture. In Asencio, M. (Ed.), *Latina/o Sexualities: Probing Powers, Passions, Practices, and Policies*. (117–136). New Brunswick: Rutgers University Press.

West, C. & Zimmerman, D. H. (1987). Doing Gender. *Gender and Society*, *1*(2), 125–151.

Wilson, P. & Yoshikawa, H. (2004). Experiences of and Responses to Social Discrimination among Asian and Pacific Islander Gay Men: Their Relationship to HIV Risk. *AIDS Education and Prevention*, *16*(1), 68–83.

Wu, F. (2002). *Yellow: Race in America beyond Black and White*. New York: Basic Books.

Yoon, E., Adams, K., Claswson, A., Chang, H., Surya, S., & Jérémie-Brink, G. (2017). East Asian Adolescents' Ethnic Identity Development and Cultural Integration: A Qualitative Investigation. *Journal of Counseling Psychology*, *64*(1), 65–79. doi:10.1037/cou0000181.

Zhang, M. (2012). A Chinese Beauty Story: How College Women in China Negotiate Beauty, Body Image, and Mass Media. *Chinese Journal of Communication*, *5*(4), 437–454. doi:10.1080/17544750.2012.723387.

13 Conceptualizing Sexuality in Research about Trans Youth

Julia Sinclair-Palm

Introduction

Young people often first learn about their gender and sexuality from their parents. These lessons are typically framed within a cisgender and heteronormative lens, with the assumption that gender development is teleological and that young people are not sexual beings until they reach puberty. Trans and gender-nonconforming youth do not identify with the gender they were assigned at birth and often find it tricky to navigate and understand the relationship between their gender and sexuality. Trans youths' experiences are absent from much of the research about sexuality (Bauer et al., 2009; Bettcher, 2013; Galupo, Davis, et al., 2014), and when they are studied, researchers focus on gender to the exclusion of sexuality or they are lumped in with LGB youth and their experiences are assumed to be similar.

Historically, sexuality has been conceptualized through labels and measurements, and research participants are tasked with reporting their desires for particular sex and gender designations (Dozier, 2005; Lev, 2004; van Anders, 2015). Traditional conceptualizations and theories of sexual identity development argue that sexual orientation is stable after adolescence (Bell et al., 1988; Money, 1988), although recent research proposes that sexuality is fluid (Diamond, 2008; Katz-Wise, 2015; Kinnish et al., 2005; Ott et al., 2011). Much of the research on sexuality has focused on the experiences of cisgender (non-transgender) individuals and fails to consider the complexity of trans people's sexuality and range of sexual identities (Katz-Wise et al., 2016). However, in the past 30 years, researchers have begun to explore how trans adults understand their sexual desires and sexual identity (Bockting et al., 2009; Bockting & Coleman, 1991; Dargie et al., 2014; Devor, 1993; Diamond et al., 2011; Hines, 2007), in addition to the ways their sexuality might change over time and is influenced by their gender identity (Galupo, Mitchell et al., 2014; Kuper et al., 2012; Meier et al., 2013; Rowniak & Chesla, 2013). For example, it is often assumed that trans men transition to become heterosexual men, however, studies have found that at least 25 percent describe themselves as gay, bisexual, or queer (Clements-Nolle et al., 2001; Grant et al., 2011). The limitations of language to capture the sexual experiences and identities of trans people, often leads them to endorse nonbinary and/or multiple sexual identities such as bisexual, pansexual, and queer (Dargie et al., 2014; Galupo, Bauerband et al., 2014; Galupo, Henise et al., 2016; Kuper et al., 2012).

Drawing on trans studies and queer theory, I conceptualize sexuality as more than a combination of our gender, sexual identity, and sexual desires. Rather, sexuality is shaped by the stories others tell about us and we tell about ourselves, by the social contexts we are immersed in, and the ways we navigate and relate to our body. In this chapter, I explore how sexuality is conceptualized in research about trans youth. I use the term "trans" throughout this chapter as a way to acknowledge, describe, and "encompass all manifestations of transness" (Cromwell, 2001, p. 263; Noble, 2006), including, but not limited to: transgender, transsexual, gender queer, and "diverse gender variant practices" (Aizura, 2006, p. 291). I use the term youth to describe people between the ages of 15 and 25 years old. I find that literature about young trans people's sexuality can be organized into three themes: a medicalized discourse about trans youth, the construction of their trans identity development and the social contexts influencing how trans youth navigate and negotiate their sexuality. I conclude with suggestions for future research and argue that research about the sexual development of trans youth must include an analysis of gender. I begin with a discussion of how our understanding of trans youth has been influenced by a history of research about sexuality and how trans youths' lives and sexuality are conceptualized in recent studies.

Framing Research about Trans Youth

Research about trans people began in the 1800s, when early psychiatrists and sexologists, including Karl Ulrichs (1994), Richard von Krafft-Ebing (2006), Magnus Hirschfeld (1991), Sigmund Freud (1962), David Cauldwell (2006), and Harry Benjamin (1954), developed the initial theories defining and describing the bodies, experiences, and identities of gender-variant people. These theories invented the transsexual, constructing a language to describe the transsexual, a framework for diagnosing the transsexual, and subsequently creating a cure to rid them of their sexual perversion. Furthermore, this early research influenced the questions future researchers asked about trans people and the ways researchers encounter, recognize, and explore sexuality in the lives of trans people. For example, Ulrichs' description of himself as having a "female soul in a male body," characterizes the misalignment metaphor that many trans people use today to describe the relationship between their body and gender (1994, p. 363). Being "born in the wrong body" is a phrase that continues to shape how current researchers and medical providers understand the embodied experiences of trans people. Trans youth use this narration of their gender to advocate for the use of puberty blockers (Pyne, 2017) and this rationale for their transition is supported by government bodies, medical institutions, and schools (American Psychological

Association, 2013; National Association of School Psychologists, 2014; Ontario Human Rights Commission, 2014).

Early research by sexologists has also influenced medical and psychological discourses about trans people that concentrate on theorizing the origins of transsexualism (Cohen-Kettenis & Pfäfflin, 2003; Zucker et al., 1997), developing techniques and treatments for "fading" trans people of their gender-variant behavior (Meyer-Bahlburg, 2002; Zucker, 2004), and exploring the relationship between sexual orientation to various gende-related characteristics (Bailey & Zucker, 1995; Doorn et al., 1994; Tsoi, 1990). In this research, there is a lack of an analysis of the ways sexuality plays a role in the lives of trans people and any reference to their pleasures and desires are pathologized. In response to unethical techniques like aversion therapy, there have been studies offering therapies that are characterized as more affirming and adaptive for families with transgender children, designed to prevent gender variant youth from developing a damaged self-esteem and building a positive identity no matter what gender and sexual identity they are (Menvielle & Tuerck, 2002; Pleak, 1999).

Over the past decade, there has been an increasing number of studies about LGBT youth, and yet these studies rarely report on the experiences of those who are gender non-conforming or do not include a representative sample size of transgender youth (D'Augelli & Patterson, 2001; Mallon, 1998; Savin-Williams & Cohen, 1996). When trans youth are lumped into research about young lesbian, gay, and bisexual people, their status as a gender minority becomes conflated with their sexuality and their sexual desires are denied or misunderstood. Dean Spade (2004) critiques the consolidation of identities in the term LGBT, calling it instead "LGB-fake-T" (p. 53) to draw attention to the absence of trans issues and trans people in the use of the category LGBT. Susan Stryker (2008) draws attention to the ways that by listing "T" with "LGB" transgender becomes an orientation and that the inclusion of trans in LGBT privileges the expression of sexual identity over gender identity (p. 148). Although trans youth are often linked to the lesbian, gay, and bisexual community, many identify as heterosexual and the ways trans youth understand and navigate their heterosexuality is absent from much of the research about LGBT youth.

Some researchers and youth-led community projects use the term queer to describe the diverse sexual and gender identities and experiences of the populations they are working with. Queer comes to stand in for those who identify as LGB and the sexual and gender diversity of those who do not identify as LGB. In some cases, trans youth are included in the umbrella term queer. For example, in an edited collection about queer youth cultures, Susan Driver (2008) uses the term "queer youth" to "signify young people who identify in ways that exceed the boundaries of straight gender and/or sexual categories" (p. 2). In *Imagining Transgender*, David Valentine (2007) discusses how the term queer is often used in place of the category LGBT in order to "stress the commonalities of experience across particular identity formations" (note 17). However, as Valentine notes, some trans people argue that the term queer does not describe their heterosexual identity and that the use of the term queer to describe some LGBT people "undermines the notion of fixed subjectivities and identity which are so central to many transgender (as well as lesbian and gay) identities" (note 17). Although LGB, queer, and trans youth bodies of literature overlap and explore similar issues, the experiences of LGB, queer, and trans youth can differ quite drastically and yet young people often have multiple gender and sexuality identities. Trans youth are increasingly using multiple terms and identities to describe their sexuality and gender, and future research needs to respond to the new language trans youth are using. The development of new words tells us something about the limitations of language and how trans youth are navigating their sexuality in the face of intelligibility and misrecognition

In addition to these tensions in language, research about trans people is often limited in a number of ways. First, the majority of representations and research about trans people are from transsexuals who have sought counseling or services from gender-identity clinics (Lewins, 1995). Second, most medical literature about trans people is about Anglo, White, and European-American transsexuals who were born male-bodied (see Bailey & Zucker, 1995; Tsoi, 1990; Winter, 2002). These demographics influence how sexuality is conceptualized in narratives about trans youth. These narratives rest on a linear story of identity development, in which the youth describes having always been gender non-conforming and always knowing they were trans. Lastly, the majority of research about trans people has been conducted by non-trans people in the social sciences (Green, 1999; Prieur, 1998), where, historically, trans people have been oppressed and pathologized. These limitations shape the research that has been conducted on trans youths' sexuality and also offers a place from which to imagine new directions in the field of trans youth studies.

While there have been significant problems with the way researchers have explored trans youth, there have also been a few important findings. Current research about trans youth describes them as having higher rates of discrimination, violence, substance abuse, homelessness, and suicide ideation than their gender-conforming peers (Kosciw & Cullen, 2001; O'Shaughnessy et al., 2004; Sember et al., 2000). There have also been some recent studies on the sexual and romantic experiences of trans youth and on how their gender-affirming treatment affects their sexual health (Bungener et al., 2017; Veale et al., 2015). In a recent Canadian study, Veale and colleagues (2015) report that of the 923 young trans people they surveyed, 69 percent of those aged between 14 and 18 had been in a romantic relationship. Based on a large quantitative survey completed by 137 Dutch trans young people aged between 10 and 17 years, Bungener and colleagues (2017) explored topics ranging from sexual experiences, romantic experiences, sexual orientation, and sexual satisfaction. The results of the study were compared with a group of similar-aged young Dutch people, in addition to the sexual experiences reported by trans girls and trans boys who participated. The majority of trans youth reported that they had been in love; however, only half had been in a romantic relationship and only a few (5 percent) had engaged in sexual activity. Overall, the findings were that young trans people are sexually and romantically less experienced than the general population; however, there are a number of ways to understand this information. Many trans people, including young trans people, feel uncomfortable in their body (Prosser, 1998; Pyne, 2017), and this can affect their negotiation of sexual experiences. Trans youth are also often unable or not ready to engage in gender-affirming interventions, and this may limit their desire and comfort in sexual relationships. This finding might also point to the heteronormative and cisgender assumptions inherent in frameworks for thinking about sexual development.

Other exceptions to the lack of research and information about trans youths' sexuality can be found in the few books targeted toward trans and gender-diverse young people that address issues such as relationships, intimacy, and sex (Kuklin, 2014; Rainess, 2015; Testa et al., 2015). For example, in *Beyond Magenta* (Kuklin, 2014), a book documenting the lives of six transgender teenagers, a teen named Christina discusses her sexual relationships, how taking estrogen impacted her sex drive, and her feelings about her body. In this next section, I explore some of the medical discourses shaping how researchers conceptualize trans youths' sexuality.

Medical Discourses about Trans Youths' Sexuality

There has been a recent growth in the number of people who identify as trans, inciting more researchers to explore the formation of the trans subject and the existence of trans people. Some researchers attribute the increase in the number of people who identify as trans to the feminist and lesbian/gay liberation movements (Coogan, 2006; Heyes, 2000). There has also been research about the diversity among trans identities (Ekins & King, 1999, 2006; Valentine, 2007) and the historical presence and representation of gender variance throughout different cultures (Bullough & Bullough, 1993; Feinberg, 1996; Herdt & Boxer, 1993). Recent work in the field of trans studies also explores the increasing accessibility of medical transitioning for trans people and the greater number of options gender-variant people have in figuring out their gender, opening up different ways for trans people to transition and consider the complexity of their gender (Castañeda, 2014). Medical discourses about trans youth offer debates about the ways young trans people are diagnosed and treated by the medical system.

Despite the ways medical discourses have pathologized and oppressed trans people, paradoxically they have also lent legitimacy to the experiences of trans people and are always in the process of rewriting how the medical community describes and labels trans people. The *Diagnostic and Statistical Manual of Mental Disorders* (DSM) is the most common classification system of mental disorders used by mental health professionals in the United States. In the most recent version of the DSM, the DSM-5, the diagnostic name "gender identity disorder" is replaced with the term "gender dysphoria" (American Psychiatric Association, 2013).

The DSM-5 was met with backlash in both the United States and internationally because of the way some common behaviors and emotions are categorized as mental health disorders (Pearson, 2013). The World Professional Association for Transgender Health (WPATH) prefers the term gender dysphoria "to reflect that a diagnosis is only needed for those transgender individuals who at some point in their lives experience clinically significant distress associated with their gender variance" (WPATH, 2011, p. 6). This change in terminology reflects a shift in conceptualizing gender as "disordered" to understanding gender as both biologically based and socially constructed, and places the focus on the distress with one's body rather than conformity with societal gender norms (Lev, 2013). This new terminology also reframes the diagnosis so that it is no longer necessarily a lifetime diagnosis. Although this diagnosis allows some trans people to access greater health care and resources, it also contributes to an unequal relationship between the mental health field and trans people because it maintains the gatekeeper status of the medical institution.[1] For trans people to access hormones or other forms of medical services they need approval and permission from a therapist.

Recently, there has been a push for children who are diagnosed with gender dysphoria, are questioning their gender, or do not identify with the gender they were assigned at birth to be receive hormone-suppression therapy and cross-sex hormones therapy (Spack et al., 2012). Debates about the use of puberty blockers offer a compelling look into how the medical community, parents, and media conceptualize the sexual subjectivity of trans youth. Puberty blockers are seen as a way to delay development or buy young trans people time to decide what they want their body to look like and how they want to express their gender identity. Castañeda (2014) describes how within medical discourse, "hormone suppression therapy puts the pubertal process 'on hold' while cross-sex hormones begin a partial process of transition that can be halted up to a point without permanent cross-sex effects" (p. 60). Within discussions about puberty, blockers seems to be both a wish to give young gender-variant people more agency and simultaneously a question about when a young person understands their gender and can make a decision about their future gender identity (Pyne, 2017). Castañeda (2014) argues that hormone blockers offer a way for medical providers to return trans children to a normative linear narrative of gender development and the trans child "becomes a recuperable transgender body in a way that the adult transgender body cannot, because the latter is already fully formed" (p. 60). Medical discourses often prop up normative ideas about gender, sexuality, and development, ignoring the way these issues are complicated for everyone. For trans children and youth, narratives of gender and sexual development become heightened in the push to create a progress narrative. Unlike gay youth, young trans people often feel like they "miss out" on being a young boy or girl, and their linear narratives struggle to account for these gaps in their gendered stories.

[1] In 2016, an external review of the Centre for Addiction and Mental Health Gender-Identity Clinic of the Child, Youth, & Family Services in Ontario, Canada was conducted and one of the key recommendations was that "gender variance versus gender dysphoria should be distinguished and explained" (p. 3).

The medicalization and measurement of sexuality and gender detracts from the complexity of trans youths' sexuality, often forcing them to describe themselves within a fixed or narrow understanding of sexuality and gender, when, in fact, some trans youth describe their sexuality as fluid and dependent on relational factors (Galupo, Henise et al., 2016). These heteronormative and cisgender conceptualizations of sexuality and gender limit how we conceptualize sexuality and the lives of trans youth. In this next section, I explore how developmental theorists influence how we understand the sexual development of trans youth.

Sexuality and Intelligibility in Trans Identity Development

Youth, and particularly trans youth, are uniquely situated in narratives about time and development. Trans youths' development is marked by time; they are waiting to be approved for hormones, hoping that over time people will use their new name, scheduling their next estrogen or testosterone shot, celebrating how long they have had their name, delaying puberty with hormone blockers, and waiting for a body that cannot change soon enough. Trans youth are not yet adults but are constrained by the pressure to narrate their identity development into adulthood and out of their youth so that they are intelligible within a normative trajectory of development. Normative trans narratives adhere to cisgender heteronormative progress narratives and have failed to conceive of young trans people (Aizura, 2012; Castañeda, 2014). In my review of sexuality and gender-identity development models, I find that heteronormative and cisgender frameworks influence how researchers conceptualize identity developmental models because of the way they position sexuality and gender as two separate aspects of one's identity, rather than taking an intersectional approach to thinking about identity development in relation to sexuality, gender, age, class, race, (dis)ability, and citizenship.

Numerous models of sexual- and gender-identity development have been proposed and modified over the past 30 years, and, yet, they rarely consider the ways gender and sexuality identity development are interconnected. In contrast to heterosexual and cisgender youth who are thought to develop their sexual and gender identities with ease, LGBTQ youth are often characterized by various stages that might include confusion, struggle, ambivalence, integration, and synthesis (Russell et al., 2014). A common developmental model used to describe lesbian, gay, and bisexual people is the CASS Homosexual Identity Development Model developed by Vivienne Cass in 1979. Following in the wake of the removal of homosexuality from the DSM, the CASS model was one of the first to account for a theory of development that did not pathologize lesbian and gay people. This model includes six stages: Identity Confusion, Identity Comparison, Identity Tolerance, Identity Acceptance, Identity Pride, and Identity Synthesis. Although these stages are sequential, Cass argued that individuals might revisit stages at different points in their lives, influencing our understanding that sexuality is a lifelong process. In line with this understanding of sexual identity development, the first study to explore the development of adolescent lesbian and gay identity in depth also concluded that sexual identity development should be viewed as an ongoing process rather than as a series of stages or phases (Herdt & Boxer, 1993).

Critiques of the CASS model argue that it is too rigid in its linear progression (Akerlund & Cheung, 2000), do not capture the full range of LGBTQ identity-development experiences (Russell et al., 2014), and is outdated and not applicable to lesbian identity development (Nichols, 1999). In response to stage models of LGB identity, D'Augelli (1994) created a "life span" model of sexual orientation development that takes social contexts into account. Working with D'Augelli's model, Bilodeau and Renn (2005) found that transgender identity development, as described by trans college students, narrate gender identity in the same processes D'Augelli outlines. Mallon (1999) warns social service practitioners against the use of traditional models of human development with trans youth because they are based on biological constructions of gender.

Based on the CASS model, trans theorist Aaron Devor (2004) developed a Fourteen Stage Model of Transsexual Identity Formation that includes stages about gender discomfort and identity confusion, which leads to an acceptance of one's transsexual or transgender identity and transition, and concludes with the development of integration and pride (p. 41). In contrast to the linear progression of the CASS model, Devor explains how some trans people may not go through each stage, may go through a stage more than once, may go backwards or forwards through stages, may go through some stages faster or slower or "may conclude that the best way for them to live their lives is to go no further than any particular stage" (p. 44). The flexibility and fluidity offered in this model attempts to account for the messiness of gender and the unique lives of every trans person. This model also includes a stage in which one accepts their post-transition gender and sex identities. This stage is constructed as happening after an individual transitions, and yet many trans youth may not have access to the ways they want to transition. Future models of trans identity development need to account for how young people's navigation of and agency in their transition process might influence their sexuality.

In one of the first large studies about trans youth, Grossman and D'Augelli (2006) found that they varied widely in the timing of their awareness of the incongruence between the sex they were assigned at birth and their gender identity. They report that this awareness occurs between 6 and 15 years of age and that youth identified with the label of transgender between 7 and 18 years of age. The study also found that trans youth often expressed initial confusion about the relationship between their sexual attractions and their gender identity, but over time came to understand these as separate aspects of their identity. In contrast to previous assumptions about the relationship between one's biological sex as a determinate for one's sexual and gender identity, young people's gender identity is often more likely to influence their sexual identity (Galupo, Davis, et al., 2014; Galupo, Henise et al., 2016). Models of trans youth identity development and sexual development must consider their unique relationship to gender and sexuality. In this next section, I examine how trans youths' desire for belonging and recognition is of great importance in social contexts like their family and at school.

Sexuality in the Social Context of School and Family

A new direction within research about trans youth attempts to think differently about trans youth, to consider them not as either at-risk or resilient, but rather, focuses on understanding the ways in which trans youth negotiate their development within various social contexts and the ways that individual characteristics influence how they engage with and experience their social world. This new paradigm in trans youth literature recognizes the importance of continuing to examine the risks and challenges faced by trans youth in addition to the ways these youth are resilient and thriving. This research explores the complex ways young people construct an understanding of their identities and experiences, the complicated relationship that individuals have both to the particularities of their lives and to the social categories we use to make sense of the world, the social contexts in which they are engaged, and the varied ways that context matters in the health and development of trans youth. Recent studies have looked to trans youths' experiences in their family and at school as a way to explore how they navigate these social contexts. I draw on this research to consider how family and school influences trans youths' sexualities.

Trans youth, like all youth, narrate the self in relation to their family. Materially, as well as emotionally, trans youth are reliant upon their family even as they are developing an identity that separates themselves from their family. Family acceptance is often described as one of the factors effecting the mental health and well-being of trans youth.[2] Trans youth need support from family, friends, and peers during their coming-out process and familial support can be essential to the transgender person's identity development (Ryan, 2001, 2009). Young trans people are often still financially dependent on and live with their parents at the time of their coming-out process (D'Augelli et al., 2010; Grossman et al., 2006). Most youth come out to a friend or other person close to them before coming out to their parents and family (e.g., D'Augelli et al., 1998; Ryan, 2009). Trans youth often conceal their trans status because they fear that by disclosing their trans identity to their family they risk parental rejection, withdrawal of financial support, social restrictions, forced counseling, violence, and homelessness (Johnston & Valentine, 1995; Kawale, 2004; Kirby & Hay, 1997; Ryan, 2009). Research has explored how some young trans people withdraw from their family as a way to cope (Greene, 1994),

[2] Very little research has been conducted on the relationship trans youth have with their family and much of the research I draw on in this section only explores the experiences of LGB people. I am aware that transgender identities and issues often get grouped together with those of LGB people and yet I find this research helpful for thinking about the experiences of young trans people (Blumer et al., 2012). Like trans youth, LGB youth often have complex relationships with their family because of their gender identity and expression. Additionally, these two groups share many of the same challenges, including financial dependence and the need for emotional support from their family.

while others may cope by using substances (Valentine & Skelton, 2003), engage in risky sexual behaviors, or attempt suicide (Savin-Williams, 1998). Trans youth might also keep their trans identity a secret from their family because they worry that something is "wrong" with them. Family reactions are not stagnant or simply binary, but change and are negotiated over time and in different contexts, and influences how trans youth navigate their sexuality (Gorman-Murray, 2008). Home is often the site in which family relationships are negotiated and is a dynamic space for young LGBTQ people (de Montigny, 2013).

When home feels like a site of exclusion, peer groups offer important sites for new identities to be explored and recognized (de Montigny, 2013). For trans youth, family can take new forms and may include friends, the LGBTQ community, or those that have acted as mentors or role models (Beam, 2007). In a case study with two trans youth, Rosario et al. (2009) explores the fluid and complex ways trans youth describe their gender identities, gender expression, and sexuality. For Robert/Taisha/TJ, one of the trans youth Rosario discusses, family is a place where they are accepted as a transwoman but are met with confusion and anger when they go back to being a boy. Robert/Taisha/TJ's friends also express confusion when they identify as a boy, and assume that they are now a female-to-male transsexual, however, it is unclear whether they are treated any differently because of this change. For Starr, the other trans youth Rosario describes, the drag ball scene[3] is a site in which the authentic presentation and expression of gender are judged by other trans people and she is awarded for the "realness" of her gender expression. The approval, respect, and power offered in these awards travels beyond the site of the ballroom and suggests to Starr that she is intelligible as a real woman, a marker of her mobility in public spaces and her desirability to heterosexual men. Starr's narrative pushes against the typical story researchers tell about trans youth and Rosario's analysis offers a more complex understanding of the everyday lives of trans youth. Over the 7 years Rosario met with Starr, she was moved from residential placements and group homes, often running away for a period of a few days and then returning with new clothes and accessories. These various housing arrangements never became sites where Starr felt at home or had a sense of family. Starr found her home in the "house" scene and expressed a great desire to be recognized as a "real" woman in the scene. In this example, family and home are important sites in which trans youth are seeking acceptance and approval of their gender and identity.

Rosario's study points to the complex ways trans youth are exploring their gender and sexuality in the social spaces that influence their lives. This complexity is exposed in the changing ways trans youth want to be addressed, the various

[3] The drag ball scene, also known as ball culture, is explored in Jennie Livingston's 1990 documentary, *Paris is Burning*. Within ball culture there are "houses," often made up of queer and trans youth (who are often homeless) and led by a "mother" (an older transgender woman or queer man who has won a lot of competitions), that compete against other "houses." Rosario describes the drag balls as places where youth can find support and explore expressions of race, gender, sexuality, and class through dance competitions and "walk" to "compete for 'realness' in a variety of categories, not only female drag but also male drag – usually mimicking and subtly mocking white, upper-class styles (e.g., tennis club, suburban male, Wall Street banker)" (Rosario, 2009, p. 301).

spaces and situations trans youth find themselves in everyday, and the desire trans youth have to belong and feel in relation to others. For the young trans people in the study, becoming intelligible to others and avoiding abuse, often meant changing their appearance, behavior, body, and name. In this sense, trans youths' gender and sexual identities are negotiated in multiple contexts and in relation to others, complicating the story that sexuality is fixed and stable.

Although young trans people spend much of their young lives with their family, children's gender-variant behavior often first arises as a problem when they enter school and is sometimes first understood as a sign of a child's future sexuality (Pleak, 2009). In response to LGBT bullying at schools and the suicide prevalence among trans youth, there has been a push to document the campus climate for LGBT students through surveys. In a national study of high school-age LGBT experiences, 65 percent of trans youth reported feeling unsafe, 87 percent had been verbally harassed or threatened, and 53 percent had been physically harassed in school due to their gender expression (Greytak et al., 2009). In a national study of the campus climate for LGBT students, faculty, and staff, Rankin (2003) reported that nearly three-quarters of the respondents believed that transgender people were more likely than other population groups to be harassed at their colleges and universities. Studies have also documented how 70 percent of transgender students said they have gone out of their way to not use campus bathrooms (Kosciw et al., 2016). Conservative groups fear that cisgender youth will be put at risk if trans youth are allowed to use their preferred bathroom and cite unfounded concerns about the greater potential for sexual assault and decreased safety. Recent debates about the accessibility of bathrooms for trans students highlight the need to address the ways trans youth negotiate their sexuality at school. These studies also tell us about the potential harm and threats trans youth face when expressing and navigating their gender and sexuality at school.

Lydia Sausa (2003) began working with trans youth in a doctoral program at the University of Pennsylvania, exploring the HIV prevention and educational needs of trans youth. Building on his previous work with trans youth, Sausa used focus groups to explore the school experiences of 24 trans youth in Philadelphia and presented his recommendations for school administrators and educators (Sausa, 2005). Sausa argues that to effectively provide a safe learning environment for all students, it is imperative that the voices and experiences of trans youth are heard by education professionals and reflected in their policies and practices. These studies point to some of the issues trans youth encounter in school and continue to be at the forefront of discussions about trans youth. Trans youth are trying out new identities and expressions of their sexuality at school, despite how these are not always safe spaces. Future research might look to explore how trans youth are negotiating their sexuality at school and how the social context of school influences how trans youth express and understand their sexuality.

Conclusion

Although many of the recent studies about trans youth emphasize the complexity of trans youths' lives, there remains a large gap in the literature about how they negotiate and understand their sexuality. There are a number of possible reasons as to why this is the case. In the past 10 years there has been an increase in the number of trans youth coming out (Staley, 2011) and it may be that because this is such a new phenomenon that researchers are only recently considering the sexual lives of trans youth. The desexualization of youth and the sole attention to gender in the lives of trans youth has also lead researchers to ignore the sexual lives of trans youth. The attention that has been given to their gender identity and gender discrimination has set the grounds for future research about their sexual lives and, yet, because this research has tended to focus on their resilience and vulnerability, there has been a failure to conceive of trans youth as sexual beings. The sexuality of trans youth has also possibly received little attention because of the ways trans people are pathologized by the medical community and their bodies are seen as undesirable by society. For example, the high numbers of trans women that are murdered each year speak of the way trans bodies are treated in society (Betcher, 2007, 2013). Research about trans youth needs to think more broadly about sexuality and models of trans youth identity development and sexual development must consider their unique relationship to gender and sexuality. Queer and trans youth scholars continue to open up our conceptualization of sexuality to consider the ways race, class, (dis)ability, nationhood, and citizenship influence how young people navigate their sexuality in their daily lives. Researchers need to keep in mind how young people's multiple identities influence how they narrate and negotiate their sexuality in social spaces like school, family, peer groups, and social media.

In order to further understand and support trans youth, we need to find ways to increase the knowledge we have about their sexual health and sexual development. Research about trans youths' sexuality can help them get more resources they want and need, rather than limiting the narrative they have to tell to get those resources. Future research must build on how we understand the lives of trans youth by exploring their sexual subjectivity and sexuality.

References

Aizura, A. Z. (2006). Of Borders and Homes: The Imaginary Community of (Trans)sexual Citizenship. *Inter-Asia Cultural Studies 7*(2), 289–309.

Akerlund, M. & Cheung, M. (2000). Teaching beyond the Deficit Model: Gay and Lesbian Issues among African Americans, Latinos, and Asian Americans. *Journal of Social Work Education*, *36*, 279–292.

American Psychological Association. (2013). "Fact sheet: Gender diversity and transgender identity in children", July 20, 2016, www.apadivisions.org/division-44/resources/advocacy/transgender-children.pdf.

American Psychiatric Association. (2013). *Diagnostic and Statistical Manual of Mental Disorders, 5th edn*. Washington, DC: American Psychiatric Association.

Bailey, J. M. & Zucker, K. J. (1995). Childhood Sex-Typed Behavior and Sexual Orientation: A Conceptual Analysis and Quantitative Review. *Developmental Psychology, 31*, 43–55.

Bauer, G. R., Hammond, R., Travers, R., Kaay, M., Hohenadel, K. M., & Boyce, M. (2009), "I Don't Think This Is Theoretical; This Is Our Lives": How Erasure Impacts Health Care for Transgender People. Journal *of the Association of Nurses in AIDS Care*, *20*(5), 348–361.

Beam, C. (2007). *Transparent: Love, Family, and Living the T with Transgender Teenagers*. Toronto, ON: Harcourt.

Bell, A. P., Weinberg, M. S., & Hammersmith, S. K. (1988). *Sexual Preference: Its Development in Men and Women*. Bloomington, IN: Indiana University Press.

Bettcher, T. M. (2007). Evil Deceivers and Make-Believers: On Transphobic Violence and the Politics of Illusion *Hypatia*, *22*(3), 43–65.

(2013). Trans Women and "Interpretive Intimacy": Some Initial Reflections. In Castañeda, D. (Ed.), *The Essential Handbook of Women's Sexuality: Diversity, Health, and Violence*, Vol. 1. Meanings, Development, and Worldwide Views (51–68). Santa Barbara: Praeger.

Bilodeau, B. & Renn, K. A. (2005). Analysis of LGBT Identity Development Models and Implications for Practice. In Sanlo, R. L. (Ed.), *Sexual Orientation and Gender Identity: New Directions for Student Services* (vol. 111, 25–40). San Francisco: Josey-Bass.

Blumer, M. L. C., Green, M. S., Knowles, S. J., & Williams, A. (2012). Shedding Light on Thirteen Years of Darkness: Content Analysis of Articles Pertaining to Transgender Issues in Marriage/Couple and Family Therapy Journals. *Journal of Marital and Family Therapy 38*, 244–256.

Bockting, W. O., Benner, A., & Coleman, E. (2009). Gay and Bisexual Identity Development among Female-to-Male Transsexuals in North America: Emergence of a Transgender Sexuality. *Archives of Sexual Behavior*, *38*, 688–701.

Bockting, W. O. & Coleman, E. (1991). A Comment on the Concept of Transhomosexuality, or the Dissociation of the Meaning. *Archives of Sexual Behavior*, *20*(4), 419–421.

Bullough, V. & Bullough, B. (1993). *Cross dressing, Sex, and Gender*. Philadelphia: University of Pennsylvania Press.

Bungener, S. L., Steensma, T. D., Cohen-Kettenis, P. T., & de Vries, A. L. C. (2017). Sexual and Romantic Experiences of Transgender Youth before Gender-Affirmative Treatment. *Pediatrics 139* (3), e20162283.

Castañeda, C. (2014). Childhood. *Transgender Studies Quarterly*, *1*(1–2), 59–61.

Clements-Nolle, K., Marx, R., Guzman, R., & Katz, M. (2001). HIV Prevalence, Risk Behaviors, Health Care Use, and Mental Health Status of Transgender Persons: Implications for Public Health Intervention. *American Journal of Public Health*, *91*, 915–921.

Cohen-Kettenis, P. T. & Pfäfflin, F. (2003). *Transgenderism and Intersexuality in Childhood and Adolescence: Making Choices*. Thousand Oaks, CA: Sage Publications.

Coogan, K. (2006). Fleshy Specificity: (Re)considering Transsexual Subjects in Lesbian Communities. *Journal of Lesbian Studies*, *10*(1/2), 17–41.

Cromwell, J. (2001). Skin Memories. In Ahmed, S. & Stacey, J. (Eds.), *Thinking through the Skin* (52–68). London: Routledge.

Dargie, E., Blair, K., Pukall, C., & Coyle, S. (2014). Somewhere under the Rainbow: Exploring the Identities and Experiences of Trans Persons. *Canadian Journal of Human Sexuality, 23* (2), 69–74.

D'Augelli, A. R. (1994). Identity Development and Sexual Orientation: Toward a Model of Lesbian, Gay, and Bisexual Development. In Trickett, E. J., Watts, R. J., & Birman, D. (Eds.), *Human Diversity: Perspectives on People in Context* (312–333). San Francisco: Jossey-Bass.

D'Augelli, A. R., Grossman, A. H., Starks, M. T., & Sinclair, K. O. (2010). Factors Associated with Parents' Knowledge of Lesbian, Gay, and Bisexual Youths' Sexual Orientation. *Journal of GLBT Family Studies 6*(2), 1–21.

D'Augelli, A. R., Hershberger, S. L., Pilkington, N. W. (1998). Lesbian, Gay, and Bisexual Youth and Their Families: Disclosure of Sexual Orientation and Its Consequences. *American Journal of Orthopsychiatry, 68*(3):361–371.

D'Augelli, A. R. & Patterson, C. J. (2001). *Lesbian, Gay, and Bisexual Identities and Youth: Psychological Perspectives*. New York: Oxford University Press.

de Montigny, J. (2013). Negotiating everyday spaces, making places: Queer & trans* youth in Montréal. Master's thesis. Concordia University, Montréal.

Devor, H. (1993). Sexual Orientation Identities, Attractions, and Practices of Female-to-Male Transsexuals. *Journal of Sex Research, 30*(4), 303–315.

(2004). Witnessing and Mirroring: A Fourteen Stage Model of Transsexual Identity Formation. *Journal of Gay & Lesbian Psychotherapy, 8*(1–2), 41–67.

Diamond, L. M. (2008). *Sexual Fluidity: Understanding Women's Love and Desire*. Cambridge, MA: Harvard University Press.

Diamond, L., Pardo, S. T., & Butterworth, M. R. (2011). Transgender Experience and Identity. In Schwartz, S. J., Luyckx, K., & Vignoles, V. L. (Eds.), *Handbook of Identity Theory and Research*, Vol. 2 (pp. 629–647). New York: Springer.

Doorn, C. D., Poortinga, J., & Verschoor, A. M. (1994). Cross-Gender Identity in Transvestites and Male Transsexuals. *Archives of Sexual Behavior, 23*(2), 185–201.

Dozier, R. (2005). Beards, Breasts, and Bodies: Doing Sex in a Gendered World. *Gender and Society, 19*, 297–316.

Driver, S. (Ed.). (2008). *Queer Youth Cultures*. Albany: State University of New York Press.

Ekins, R. & King, D. (1999). Toward a Sociology of Transgendered Bodies. *The Sociological Review, 47*(3), 580–602.

(2006). *The Transgender Phenomenon*. London: SAGE.

Feinberg, L. (1996). *Transgender Warriors: Making History from Joan of Arc to Rupaul*. Boston: Beacon Press.

Galupo, M. P., Henise, S. B., & Mercer, N. L. (2016) "The Labels Don't Work Very Well": Transgender Individuals' Conceptualizations of Sexual Orientation and Sexual Identity, *International Journal of Transgenderism, 17*(2), 93–104

Galupo, M. P., Davis, K. S., Grynkiewicz, A. L., & Mitchell, R. C. (2014). Conceptualization of Sexual Orientation Identity among Sexual Minorities: Patterns across Sexual and Gender Identity. *Journal of Bisexuality, 14*, 433–456.

Galupo, M. P., Lomash, E., & Mitchell, R. C. (2016). "All of My Lovers Fit into This Scale": Sexual Minority Individuals' Responses to Two Novel Measures of Sexual Orientation. *Journal of Homosexuality, 64*(2), 145–165.

Galupo, M. P., Mitchell, R. C., Grynkiewicz, A. L., & Davis, K. S. (2014). Sexual Minority Reflections on the Kinsey Scale and the Klein Sexual Orientation Grid: Conceptualization and Measurement. *Journal of Bisexuality, 14*, 404–432.

Gorman-Murray, A. (2008). Queering the Family Home: Narratives from Gay, Lesbian and Bisexual Youth Coming Out in Supportive Family Homes in Australia. *Gender, Place and Culture 15*(1), 31–44.

Grant, J. M., Mottet, L. A., Tanis, J., Harrison, J., Herman, J. L., & Keisling, M. (2011). *Injustice at Every Turn: A Report of the National Transgender Discrimination Survey*. Washington, DC: National Center for Transgender Equality and National Gay and Lesbian Task Force.

Green, J. N. (1999). Beyond Carnival: Male Homosexuality in Twentieth-Century Brazil. Chicago: University of Chicago Press.

Greene, B. (1994). Lesbian and Gay Sexual Orientations: Implications for Clinical Training, Practice, and Research. In Greene, B. & Herek, G. M. (Eds.), *Psychological Perspectives on Lesbian and Gay Issues, Vol. 1. Lesbian and Gay Psychology: Theory, Research, and Clinical Applications* (1–24). Thousand Oaks, CA: Sage Publications.

Greytak, E., Kosciw, J., & Diaz, E. (2009). *Harsh Realities: The Experiences of Transgender Youth in Our Nation's Schools*. New York: Gay, Lesbian, Straight Education Network.

Grossman, A. & D'Augelli, A. (2006). Transgender Youth: Invisible and Vulnerable. *Journal of Homosexuality, 51*(1), 111–128.

Grossman, A. H., D'Augelli, A. R., & Salter, N. P. (2006). Male-to-Female Transgender Youth: Gender Expression Milestones, Gender Atypicality, Victimization, and Parents' Responses. *Journal of GLBT Family Studies, 2*, 71–92.

Herdt, G & Boxer, A. (1993). *Children of Horizons: How Gay and Lesbian Teens Are Leading a New Way Out of the Closet*. Boston: Beacon Press.

Heyes, C. J. (2000). Reading Transgender, Rethinking Women's Studies. *NWSA, 9*(2), 170–180.

Hines, S. (2007). *Transforming Gender: Transgender Practices of Identity, Intimacy, and Care*. Bristol: Policy Press.

Johnston, L., & Valentine, G. (1995). "Wherever I Lay My Girlfriend, That's My Home": The Performance and Surveillance of Lesbian Identities in Domestic Environments. In Bell, D. & Valentine, G. (Eds.), *Mapping Desire: Geographies of Sexualities* (99–113). London: Routledge.

Katz-Wise, S. L., Reisner, S. L., White, J. M., & Keo-Meier, C. L. (2016). Differences in Sexual Orientation Diversity and Sexual Fluidity in Attractions among Gender Minority Adults in Massachusetts. *Journal of Sex Research, 53*(1), 74–84.

Katz-Wise, S. L. (2015). Sexual Fluidity in Young Adult Women and Men: Associations with Sexual Orientation and Sexual Identity Development. *Psychology & Sexuality, 6*, 189–208.

Kawale, R. (2004). Inequalities of the Heart: The Performance of Emotion Work by Lesbian and Bisexual Women in London, England. *Social and Cultural Geography 5*(6), 565–581.

Kinnish, K. K., Strassberg, D. S., & Turner, C. W. (2005). Sex Differences in the Flexibility of Sexual Orientation: A Multidimensional Retrospective Assessment. *Archives of Sexual Behavior*, *34*(2), 10. doi:10.1007/s10508-005-1795-9.

Kirby, S. & Hay, I. (1997). (Hetero)sexing Space: Gay Men and 'Straight' Space in Adelaide, South Australia. *Professional Geographer 49*(3), 295–305.

Kosciw, J. G. & Cullen, M. K. (2001). *The GLSEN 2001 National School Climate Survey: The School-Related Experiences of Our Nation's Lesbian, Gay, Bisexual and Transgender Youth*. New York: Gay, Lesbian, and Straight Education Network.

Kosciw, J. G., Gretak, E. A., Giga, N. M., Villenas, C., & Danischewski, D. J. (2016). *The 2015 National School Climate Survey: The Experiences of Lesbian, Gay, Bisexual, Transgender, and Queer Youth in Our Nation's Schools*. Boston: GLSEN.

Kuklin, S. (2014). *Beyond Magenta: Transgender Teens Speak Out*. Somerville: Candlewick Press

Kuper, L. E., Nussbaum, R., & Mustanski, B. (2012). Exploring the Diversity of Gender and Sexual Orientation Identities in an Online Sample of Transgender Individuals. *Journal of Sex Research*, *49*, 244–254.

Lev, A. (2004). *Transgender Emergence: Therapeutic Guidelines for Working with Gender-variant People and Their Families*. New York: Haworth Clinical Practice Press.

(2013). Gender Dysphoria: Two Steps Forward, One Step Back. *Clinical Social Work Journal*, *41* (3), 288–296.

Lewins, F. (1995). *Transsexualism in Society: A Sociology of Male-to-Female Transsexuals*. South Melbourne: Macmillan Education Australia.

Mallon, G. P. (1998). *We Don't Exactly Get the Welcome Wagon: The Experiences of Gay and Lesbian Adolescents in Child Welfare Systems*. New York: Columbia University Press.

(1999). Knowledge for Practice with Transgendered Persons. *Journal of Gay & Lesbian Social Services*, *10*(3/4), 1–18.

Menvielle, E. J. & Tuerk, M. A. (2002). A Support Group for Parents of Gender Nonconforming Boys. *Journal of the American Academy of Child and Adolescent Psychiatry*, *41*(8), 1010–1013.

Meyer-Bahlburg, H. F. L. (2002). Gender Identity Disorder in Young Boys: A Parent- and Peer-Based Treatment Protocol. *Clinical Child Psychology and Psychiatry*, *7*(3), 360–376.

Meier, S. C., Pardo, S. T., Labuski, C., & Babcock, J. (2013). Measures of Clinical Health among Female-to-Male Transgender Persons as a Function of Sexual Orientation. *Archives of Sexual Behavior*, *42*, 463–474.

Money, J. (1988). *Gay, Straight, and In-Between: The Sexology of Erotic Orientation*. New York: Oxford University Press.

National Association of School Psychologists (2014), "Safe schools for transgender and gender diverse students [Position statement]," Communique´, 13 July 2016.

Nichols, S. L. (1999). Gay, Lesbian, and Bisexual Youth: Understanding Diversity and Promoting Tolerance in Schools. *The Elementary School Journal*, *99*, 505–519.

Noble, J. B. (2006). *Sons of the Movement: FtMs Risking Incoherence on a Post-Queer Cultural Landscape*. Toronto: Women's Press.

Ontario Human Rights Commission (2014), "Policy on preventing discrimination because of gender identity and gender expression," July 13, 2014.

O'Shaughnessy, M., Russell, S., Heck, K., Calhoun, C., & Laub, C. (2004). *Consequences of Harassment Based on Actual or Perceived Sexual Orientation and Gender Nonconformity and Steps for Making Schools Safer.* Davis: California Safe School Coalition and 4-H Center for Youth Development, University of California, Davis.

Ott, M. Q, Corliss, H. L, Wypij, D., Rosario, M., & Austin, S. B. (2011). Stability and Change in Self-Reported Sexual Orientation Identity in Young People: Application of Mobility Metrics. *Archives of Sexual Behavior*, *40*, 519–532.

Pearson, G. S. (2013), Editorial. *Perspectives in Psychiatric Care*, *49*, 219–220. doi:10.1111/ppc.12041

Pleak, R. R. (1999). Ethical Issues in Diagnosing and Treating Gender-Dysphoric Children and Adolescents. In Rottnek, M. (Ed.), *Sissies and Tomboys: Gender Nonconformity and Homosexual Childhood*. New York: New York University Press.

(2009). Transgender People. In Ruiz, P. & Primm, A. (Eds.), *Disparities in Psychiatric Care: Clinical and Cross-cultural Perspectives*. Philadelphia: Lippincott Williams & Wilkins.

Prieur, A. (1998). *Mema's House, Mexico City: On Transvestites, Queens, and Machos*. Chicago: University of Chicago Press.

Prosser, J. (1998). *Second Skins: The Body Narratives of Transsexuality*. New York: Columbia University Press.

Pyne, J. (2017). "Arresting Ashley X: Trans Youth." Puberty Blockers and the Question of Whether Time is on Your Side. *Somatechnics* *7*(1), 95–123.

Rainess, S. J. (2015). *Real Talk for Teens: Jump-Start Guide to Gender Transitioning and Beyond*. Oakland: Transgress Press.

Rankin, S. R. (2003). *Campus Climate for Gay, Lesbian, Bisexual, and Transgender People: A National Perspective*. New York: National Gay and Lesbian Task Force Policy Institute.

Rosario, M., Schrimshaw, E. W., & Hunter, J. (2009). Disclosure of Sexual Orientation and Subsequent Substance Use and Abuse among Lesbian, Gay, and Bisexual Youths: Critical Role of Disclosure Reactions. *Psychology of Addictive Behaviors*, *23*, 175–184.

Rowniak, S. & Chesla, C. (2013). Coming Out for a Third Time: Transmen, Sexual Orientation, and Identity. *Archives of Sexual Behavior*, *42*, 449–461.

Russell, S. T., Toomey, R. B., Ryan, C., & Diaz, R. M. (2014). Being Out at School: The Implications for School Victimization and Young Adult Adjustment. *American Journal of Orthopsychiatry*, *84*, 635–643.

Ryan, C. (2001). Counseling Lesbian, Gay and Bisexual Youths. In D'Augelli, A. & Patterson, C. (Eds.), *Lesbian, Gay and Bisexual Identities and Youth* (224–250). New York: Oxford University Press.

(2009). *A Practitioner's Resource Guide: Helping Families to Support Their LGBT Children*. Rockville: Substance Abuse and Mental Health Services Administration.

Sausa, L. A. (2003). The HIV prevention and educational needs of trans youth: A qualitative study. University of Pennsylvania, Philadelphia. Retrieved from http://repository.upenn.edu/dissertations/AAI3087465

(2005). Translating Research into Practice: Trans Youth Recommendations for Improving School Systems. *Journal of Gay & Lesbian Issues in Education*, *3*, 1.

Savin-Williams, R. (1998). Lesbian, Gay and Bisexual Youths' Relationship with Their Parents. In Patterson, C. & D'Augelli, A. (Eds.), *Lesbian, Gay and Bisexual Identities in Families* (75–98). New York: Oxford University Press.

Savin-Williams, R. C. & Cohen, K. M. (1996). *The Lives of Lesbians, Gays, and Bisexuals: Children to Adults*. Fort Worth: Harcourt Brace College Publishing.

Sember, R., Lawrence, A. A., & Xavier, J. (2000). Transgender Health Concerns. *Journal of the Gay & Lesbian Medical Association*, *4*, 125–134.

Spack, N. P., Edwards-Leeper, L., Feldman, H. A., et al. (2012). Children and Adolescents with Gender Identity Disorder Referred to a Pediatric Medical Center. *Pediatrics*, *178*(3), 418–425.

Spade, D. (2004). Fighting to Win. In Sycamore, M. B. (Ed.). *That's Revolting! Queer Strategies for Resisting Assimilation* (47–53). Berkeley, CA: Soft Skull.

Staley, R. (August 12, 2011). When boys would rather not be boys: Kids are being diagnosed – and identifying themselves – as transgendered younger than ever before. *Macleans*.

Stryker, S. (2008). Transgender History, Homonormativity, and Disciplinarity. *Radical History Review*, *100*, 145–157.

Testa, R. J., Coolhart, D., & Peta, J. (2015). *The Gender Quest Workbook: A Guide for Teens and Young Adults Exploring Gender Identity*. Oakland: Instant Help.

Tsoi, W. F. (1990). Developmental Profile of 200 Male and 100 Female Transsexuals in Singapore. *Archives of Sexual Behavior*, *19*(6), 595–605.

Ulrichs, K. H. (1994). *The Riddle of 'Man-Manly' Love, 2 vols*, translated by Michael A. Lombardi-Nash, foreword by Vern L. Bullough. Buffalo, New York: Prometheus Books.

Valentine, G. & Skelton, T. (2003). Finding Oneself, Losing Oneself: The Lesbian and Gay "Scene" as a Paradoxical Space. *International Journal of Urban and Regional Research 27*(4): 849–866.

Valentine, D. (2007). *Imagining Transgender: An Ethnography of a Category*. Durham, NC: Duke University Press.

van Anders, S. M. (2015). Beyond Sexual Orientation: Integrating Gender/Sex and Diverse Sexualities in Sexual Configurations Theory. *Archives of Sexual Behavior*, *44*(5), 1177–1213.

Veale, J., Saewyc, E. M., Frohard-Dourlent, H., Dobson, S., Clark, B., & The Canadian Trans Youth Health Survey Research Group. (2015). *Being Safe, Being Me: Results of the Canadian Trans Youth Health Survey*. Vancouver: University of British Columbia.

Winter, S. J. (2002). Transgender and Society: An Asian Perspective. *Newsletter of the Comparative and Historical Section of the American Sociological Society*, *14*(3), 16–18.

WPATH. (2011). *Standards of Care: For the Health of Transsexual, Transgender and Gender Non-Conforming People, 7th edition*. www.wpath.org.

Zucker, K. J. (2004). Gender Identity Development and Issues. *Child and Adolescent Psychiatric Clinics of North America*, *13*(3), 551–568.

Zucker, K. J., Green, R., Coates, S., et al. (1997). Sibling Sex Ratio of Boys with Gender Identity Disorder. *Journal of Child Psychology and Psychiatry*, *38*(5), 543–551.

PART II

How Do We Study Sexual Development?

14 Critical Methods for Studying Adolescent Sexuality

Sara I. McClelland

Those who work with "critical methods" often turn their gaze to examining how power runs through the process of knowledge production. Or as Michelle Fine argues, critical researchers work to trace the "biography of our questions" (Fine, 2017, p. 5). As social scientists studying adolescences and young adulthood are increasingly drawn to critical perspectives in their research, many still wonder how to proceed and what methods are available. The modifier of "critical," as I use it here, signals a researcher's commitment to accounting for and examining the role of inequality, even when it might be difficult to observe, has become normalized, or is disavowed by participants. Critical methods work to dislodge assumptions, make clearer what is hidden or difficult to hear. It is a practice of drawing attention to power, including how concepts are defined, how data are collected and analyzed, and the history of the theories that guide our work (Fahs & McClelland, 2016; Fox et al., 2009; Kurtiş & Adams, 2015; Teo, 2015).

This perspective is especially important when it comes to child and adolescent sexuality development research. It is here, early in life, that we can see how norms, for example, "health" and "safety," have restricted the questions researchers ask, limited the information gathered, and produced policies that wrap around young bodies in an effort to contain thoughts, ideas, and desires deemed unhealthy and dangerous (Garcia & Fields, 2017; McClelland & Fine, 2014). A range of methodological practices is necessary, especially methods that press a researcher to ask more, ask why, wonder about what is unsaid or unsayable, and what cannot be heard or is un-imaginable. In line with Fine's (2016) call for "just methods in revolting times," I urge researchers to carefully consider what one cannot see (what appears to be shared, but is not) when designing research on, with, and about oppression. My aim in this chapter is to advocate for several critical methods that bring these questions to the foreground in one's research design.

Background

Sexuality and Young People

Because sexuality is often used as a dividing line between adulthood and childhood, discourses of innocence and protection are used to reinforce barriers to sexual information (Fields, 2005). Conversations about sex education, both in the United States and abroad, often hold within them enormous urgency and are consistently sites of moral panics about what children will learn (Garcia & Fields, 2017). Part of the panic around children's sexuality is that this development is imagined to inevitably go wrong; if children gain access to the "wrong" kind of sexual knowledge or experience, they may not become the "good" kind of sexual citizen (Robinson, 2012). This unbounded fear of how children encounter sexuality has made any talk of young people and sex inherently suspect. More than 25 years ago, Rex Stainton Rogers and Wendy Stainton Rogers (1992) noted the dangers associated with asking young people about sexuality:

> These days about the only situation in which it is legitimate to even talk to children about sex is within sex education or investigation for alleged abuse. Anything else risks the accusation of being sexually abusive or the stigma of being erotically involved (p. 176).

This fragile constellation of ideas about when it is "appropriate" to talk with young people about sex has severely limited what researchers have investigated, leaving questions unasked and outcomes unexamined (see Collins, 2003). This history deeply informs contemporary research on child and adolescent sexuality and requires that researchers contend with how methods in the field have grown up and around these barriers and worries about appropriateness and risk.

Critical Approaches to Research

Critical approaches to methods have been developing for several decades, across many disciplines (e.g., Barad, 2007; Bennett, 2009; Traub, 2015). In psychology, critical methods have often involved engaging with the history of the field, aiming to disrupt the colonial, racist, and homophobic structures that have determined what norms and procedures gain epistemic authority (Adams, 2014; Martín-Baró, 1994; Teo, 2015). In other words, which voices, theories, and methods have been institutionalized and which have been marginalized or delegitimized? There is a long tradition of critiquing these histories in psychology, especially from feminist psychologists who have called attention to how disciplinary norms have kept marginalized voices systematically silenced (Warner et al., 2016; Weisstein, 1968; Wilkinson, 1991). With this history in mind, critical researchers continue, today, to develop practices that bring consistent and close attention to how concepts are theorized, assessed, and observed.

Describing methods as "critical" is a way to mark that research is not a clear window into a phenomenon. Critical methods work to make the methodological process more evident rather than less evident. While research is typically designed to reduce bias and know something with more certainty, critical methods focus on collecting more information about differences, variations, and imperfections in the research process itself. This, in turn, foregrounds the research process alongside representing complex individual and social phenomena. When reflecting on the complicated relationship between empirical work and critical work, Lisa Jean Moore (2016) argues that one could consider this move toward critical work as "[e]mpirical research methods created and refined through serious engagements with queer, post-structural, feminist, social justice, and other politically sophisticated theorizing [to] facilitate useful research" (p. 33). This space of mixing (epistemologies, theories, and histories) requires that critical methods develop the flexibility that is needed to produce a research design – and – deeply critique the limitations and assumptions built into this design.

A Question of Methods

Critical methods can occur at any point or throughout a research design. Examples include critical perspectives that researchers might take to expand notions about who is sampled (Hitchens et al., 2018), who is imagined as expert (Torre et al., 2012), how concepts are defined (Smith et al., 1999), or how epistemologies influence the production of knowledge (Bowleg et al., 2017). In addition to these, I argue that inequality and disparities potentially hide in and among participants' imaginations and expectations (McClelland, 2010, 2014, 2017). In other words, aspects of inequality might shape data with an invisible hand that cannot be "controlled for" or predicted and that most methods enable these expectations to hide in plain sight. Participants may normalize their experiences with violence, aggression, insults, and discrimination, and they may, at times, lose the ability to label such experiences as "weird" and "abnormal," making them all the more insidious and difficult to document or analyze. Accommodation to these conditions must be documented – especially for those who experience the constant "drip feed" of discrimination (Fine & Ruglis, 2009). As participants are often unwilling to label discriminatory actions, researchers must pursue questions in this field using a wide variety of critical designs. Critical methods, for example, might attend to the ways that a participant's responses reflect not only their individual experiences, but also histories of how institutions, schools, neighborhoods, families, and peer groups have set up young people to imagine their lives, or how political, economic, and personal vulnerability operates for some more than others in any data collection process.

Cellophane

Ten years ago, Michelle Fine and I (McClelland & Fine, 2008) wrote about concerns we had surrounding how young women talked to researchers (us) about their sexuality. After several young women told us about how they didn't know and didn't need to know more about sex education, we wondered about the political and cultural brakes that pressed on young women and on those of us listening. In that essay, we developed the metaphor of "cellophane" in order to symbolize the mixture of public policies, commercialization, and feminist desires that wrapped young women and those who do research with them in a "collective discursive cellophane." We argued that cellophane was being produced by:

> . . . a market economy that rushes to commodify young female bodies; sociopolitical, moral, and hetero-normative panics that obsess over young women's sexualities; racist imagery and institutional practices that vilify the sexualities of women of color; and by schools increasingly kidnapped by the policy of teaching Abstinence-Only-Until-Marriage curricula in place of serious sexuality education. (McClelland & Fine, 2008, p. 232)

These layers of cellophane, we worried, made it difficult for young women to speak about their desires, since their tongues might be weighed down with dominant assumptions and panics. Similarly, we worried, our ears might be clogged with our own dominant feminist discourses for their desires.

Facing the reality of cellophane in a researcher's work, we made a series of suggestions for what we called "methodological release points" as a way to craft research methods that acknowledge these political and discursive contexts and still manage to understand something about what it means to be a young woman living and developing sexually in the early decades of the twenty-first century. In the spirit of "expanding the methodological imagination" (Fine, 2007), I dive into these questions again and make additional suggestions for how one might integrate these release points into their research practices.

Methodological release points offer analytical wedges that invite new questions about "opacity, obscurity, obstruction" that are inevitably a part of any research about issues related to sex and sexuality (Traub, 2015, p. 3). Rather than trying to surmount these obstacles, methodological release points invite researchers to work within the liminal (Morawski, 1994) and the noninnocent (Lather, 2007) spaces feminist researchers have long invited us to imagine. As Patti Lather (1993) argues, "better research" is not a matter of looking harder or more closely at our objects of study. But rather, we must see "what frames our seeing-spaces of constructed visibility and incitements to see which constitute power/knowledge" (p. 675). In other words, critical methods press us to understand the process and politics of knowledge production, while also continuing to be knowledge producers. It is this somewhat paradoxical space that animates critical methods.

Moving Forward

At stake in any discussion of research methods is the potential for profound misunderstanding and misinterpretation about what researchers see and hear when we study a phenomenon. Those who do research often have a hard time imagining life in the shadows; as a result, "our affective responses to police shootings, school closings, evictions, and varied enactments of precarity differ wildly from those who live under the boot of oppression" (Fine, 2016, p. 348). With this and the many other arguments made about the racist and colonial implications of knowledge production (see Kurtiş & Adams, 2015; Teo, 2011), social scientists are increasingly drawn to developing and using critical research methods. But many still wonder, what might this look like? How should I proceed? And, what can critical methods help me see or hear that I would have otherwise missed?

Four Examples

In order to encourage readers to use critical methods in their work, I draw on four examples from my own research. I start with a discussion of the *self-anchored ladder*, a method that invests in meanings that participants bring to research and how these affect the scores they provide. Second, I discuss *survey marginalia* methods that invite participants into the research dynamic, thickening the already complicated definitions of "inside" and "outside" a survey design. Third, I discuss *Q methods* as a way to ask participants to show us their thoughts, creating a mosaic of associations that can be analyzed empirically as well as used as a way to invite complicated and messy lives into research. Finally, I discuss interview analysis strategies, which focus on *adaptation to injustice* within the interview dynamic and present potential analytic frameworks to contend with cellophane as it appears in qualitative interviews.

The Self-Anchored Ladder

The self-anchored ladder item, adapted from Cantril's ladder (1965), is an item where the participant is asked a question and provided a Likert-like response scale. However, unlike most Likert items, no textual anchors are provided (e.g., the scale does not provide terms such as *mostly agree* to *mostly disagree*). Instead, the participant is instructed to place a mark anywhere on a 10-point ladder to indicate their level of response and also asked to describe the low, middle, and high ends of this scale (see Figure 14.1). As a result, the participant responds to the question, but also provides their interpretation of the concepts in the question. This provides an extremely important level of data for a researcher to consider. While interviews might be helpful in gaining access to these details, the ladder opens up a small but powerful way for participants to demonstrate how they imagine concepts and the wide range of ways they imagine what is possible. In other words, the ladder vividly illustrates how they envision "a little" and "a lot" of something in their lives.

Researchers have consistently found that individuals rely on different interpretations and experiences when responding to survey items, but these differences are rarely captured in survey designs (Landrine et al., 1992). This can result, for example, in participants responding with "highly agree" to a survey item, but using very different criteria than other participants in the same study. This produces data that appear to be consistent, but can easily lead to misinterpretation.

In a study with young adults, aged 18–28 years, I used the self-anchored ladder in a study that examined the relationship between sexual satisfaction scores and

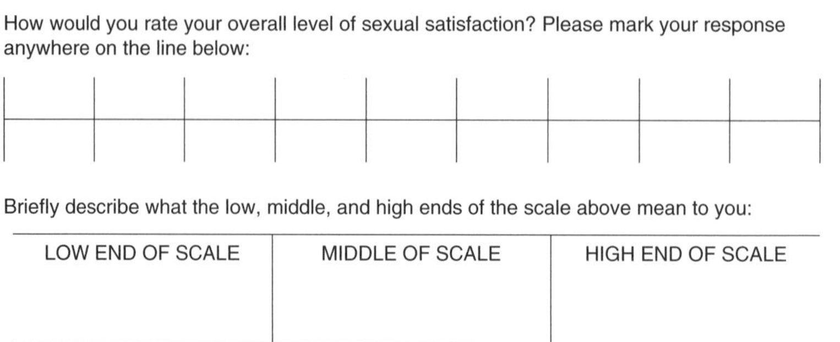

How would you rate your overall level of sexual satisfaction? Please mark your response anywhere on the line below:

Briefly describe what the low, middle, and high ends of the scale above mean to you:

LOW END OF SCALE	MIDDLE OF SCALE	HIGH END OF SCALE

Figure 14.1 *Example of self-anchored ladder item (McClelland, 2017)*

participants' definitions of sexual satisfaction (McClelland, 2017). I developed four analytic strategies for working with the data provided by the self-anchored ladder. In my own study, each analysis told a different story. When I compared sexual satisfaction scores across demographic groups (e.g., race or sexual identity), they did not appear to significantly differ from one another, signaling that racial-minority and White, as well as sexual-minority and heterosexual participants, did not differ from one another in their sexual satisfaction. In addition to this quantitative analysis, when I examined how participants organized "sexual satisfaction" on the unanchored ladders, I found several different organizational strategies for ranking low to high. For example, some relied on how often they felt satisfied (e.g., 50 percent of the time), while others used the presence/absence of emotional closeness as measures of sexual satisfaction. I also examined how often participants used specific terms when describing sexual satisfaction and found a wide range of terms that were used by some, but no term stood out as consistently used when participants defined sexual satisfaction in this format. Lastly, I examined the role of what individuals imagined as "worst" and "best" in their appraisals and how these evaluations informed numerical scores. Across these findings, I argue for how researchers might make knowledge claims about young adults' sexual satisfaction, but also develop greater insight into the limitations of making these kinds of claims without the full picture that the self-anchored ladder can offer. As a self-report procedure, the self-anchored ladder provides researchers with the kinds of data to do this necessary investigative work.

For example, I found that there were important group differences in how participants drew on experiences with gender, race, pain, violence, and expectations about future pleasures when answering the self-anchored ladder item. Female participants defined the low end of their ladders using terms related to pain, fear, and depression. Of note, their sexual satisfaction scores on the ladder were consistently higher than their male counterparts. Male participants relied on the absence of sex as their low point. As a result, a very different definition of sexual satisfaction emerged across these two groups. The ratings, I argue, cannot necessarily be compared between these two groups (McClelland, 2017). The self-anchored ladder does not dispense with making comparisons across groups but, rather, insists on making comparisons with a great deal of attention to conceptual analysis as a function of any research endeavor.

The ladder is best suited for researchers who are interested in the possibilities and limitations of measurement, especially those who either already have, or wish to develop, critical awareness of how measures obscure diverse perspectives and are interested in bringing this critique to the practice of measurement. Critical social scientists might most benefit from using the self-anchored ladder to bring greater attention to issues of social inequality and develop commitments to disrupt colonial, racist, and homophobic structures that undergird psychology's theories and methods (Teo, 2015). This would include studying how terms that are used to sort groups and people may actually obscure the ways that some have learned to expect less or more. For example, researchers might examine concepts that have been well developed and have a long history of use in psychological research (e.g., subjective well-being), as well as those that are less well developed and require further analysis, perhaps due to emergent theoretical or empirical work (e.g., empowerment).

Researchers working with children might use the self-anchored ladder in verbal or written forms to understand how young participants are imagining a concept, perhaps by asking children to describe images or words they associate with the "best" and "worst" of something. This method might prove very useful in research about early childhood or young adult sexuality where there often a lot of discomfort talking about these ideas. A researcher might use a ladder within an interview to bring more attention to possible comparisons with others (i.e., "how do you think your friend would answer this question?") or with younger selves (i.e., "how would you have answered this question last year?").

Survey Marginalia

If you've taken a paper and pencil survey, have you ever left a note in the margin? Perhaps you wanted to explain your answer or reword the question to better fit your experience. Maybe you wrote "sometimes" next to a question since the only response options were "all the time" or "never" and neither of those felt right to you. These are all examples of survey marginalia (i.e., the notes, marks, or comments left by participants in the margins of self-administered surveys). Unfortunately, marginalia are nearly always disregarded and often seen as unimportant by survey researchers. I argue, instead, that marginalia are an invaluable tool for any researcher who wants to understand more about the phenomenon, person, or group they are studying (McClelland, 2016). Marginalia offer an opportunity for participants to "speak back" to the researcher and enable several types of feedback, including: (1) ideas that are thought to be unpopular or undesired; (2) disagreements with the imagined (and real) researcher; (3) viewpoints that are more extreme than a survey allows; (4) questions and indications of what is not clear in survey items; (5) ideas that are important to a person but not asked about; and (6) ideas that are asked about but not interesting or relevant to the participant (McClelland, 2016). In short, this critical method involves paying attention to the ways that participants resist being misunderstood by a researcher. When thinking about research with young people, honoring this resistance is especially important; research is potentially a place for young people to have a voice, to express, and be heard. Studies of survey marginalia offer a powerful way for participants to be present in research and interrupt researchers' assumptions and misunderstandings.

In my own study of survey marginalia, I examined the comments and marks that participants left in a survey about sexual health (McClelland & Holland, 2016). Rather than ignore the marginalia, I used them to develop new information and new analysis procedures for the survey analysis portion of the study. For example, guided by the survey marginalia, I could see that participants were not able to indicate when a question was not applicable to them and skipped over several items when they were not sexually active. Rather than code these data as missing (and eliminating these participants from the analysis), I developed a modified scoring procedure which kept these participants in the analysis sample. When we used these new procedures, several key findings changed. In other words, the comments people made in the margins were critical to making more accurate observations about their sexual health. When survey items do not adequately capture elements of a person's experience, the consequences can be extreme, yet often remain unexamined. With this in mind, we developed a set of guidelines for researchers to use when pursuing studies of survey marginalia. Three categories stand out as relevant for researchers who are interested in developing analysis of survey marginalia: (1) marginalia that aim to clarify or explain survey responses, (2) marginalia that aim to correct the survey, and (3) marginalia that communicate a survey item is not applicable (see McClelland & Holland, 2016 for more detail).

In a study about adolescent girls, Valerie Hey (1997) studied marginalia in another form; she collected the notes that girls wrote to one another during the school day. While the girls in her study called these "bits of silliness," Hey studied these notes for their "invisible communication activities" and found that these notes captured aspects of female friendship, emotional labor, and the high stakes of femininity that would have been missed if these notes were ignored. In fact, Hey (1997) described the notes as a form of marginalia: "The girls' notes were intentionally 'marginal;' for example, they were written on the margins of more official writing" (p. 51). Much like my argument for researchers to recuperate the notes left in surveys, Hey (1997) described the ways that she had to work to position her analysis of the girls' notes since these data are in a form that is "at odds with the notion of research as a serious scientific endeavor" (p. 51).

Leaving comments in the margins of a survey, crossing out words, and changing the text of the survey are all ways that participants can make their voices heard, even if a researcher did not ask for their input (or asked for input only in a specific format, as in "check all that apply"). Marginalia is often a way for a participant to say, "You won't know the answer by asking like this," or "I can't make my experience fit here," or "This is what you need to know" (Smith, 2008).

Marginalia, therefore, offer an important way for researcher and participant to communicate with one another during a study, even if they are not physically in the same place. When participants are faced with survey questions that do not match their experience, the person may reject the survey, accommodate their experience to fit the questions, or reformulate the questions to accommodate their experience (in other words, provide inaccurate data). Without greater attention to the feedback that participants leave (when researchers provide the opportunity), those asking the questions risk not knowing what we have missed in the process of trying to learn something.

As researchers increasingly turn to administering surveys online, these issues of marginalia, I argue, are just as important, but more difficult to address. This is one reason to consider keeping surveys in a paper format when possible. The interaction with participants may be valuable enough to outweigh any time or cost savings that online administration offers. In addition to this suggestion, I have several others for those looking to consider collecting and analyzing survey marginalia in online survey formats. Comment boxes that ask for "any additional thoughts on the survey" should not be confused or conflated with the opportunity to offer marginalia. A comment box at the end of a survey asks for summative thoughts and impressions; this differs greatly from the comments and markings that can be spontaneously offered while answering items. A researcher might consider adding comment boxes to individual items and asking participants about their impression of an item, for example, who they thought about while answering a question, or asking for additional comments about their response. In addition, a researcher might ask for feedback on the survey itself (the structure, the pace, or the content) at intervals throughout the survey. It should be noted that this is asking for a lot of labor on the part of the participant and should not be asked lightly. Researchers must honor the time and labor that is involved with answering survey questions; my advice is to ask only for feedback that you are willing and able to analyze.

Marginalia challenge researchers' assumptions (about the world, about those they are studying, and about the research process) and bring heighted attention to the ethical dimensions of research. Studies of marginalia extend calls from feminist scholars of color who argue that margins of all kinds should be recognized as locations of political knowledge and power. Writers such as bell hooks (1984), Gayatri Spivak (1990), and Linda Tuhiwai Smith (2006) call for attention to the power of "speaking back from the margins" of a group, society, or nation as an essential way to bring greater attention to those who are routinely ignored in political decision making, and indeed, marginalized. This perspective is also part of a long tradition in psychology, including feminist psychology (Unger, 1998) and critical participatory action research (Torre et al., 2012). These writers and scholars all encourage us as researchers to listen more carefully to participants' demands to be heard. Analysis of marginalia provides one of the many available methodological tools to see this promise through.

Q Methodology

Another kind of critical approach to methods can be seen in the body of work using Q methodology (Stephenson, 1953; Watts & Stenner, 2005). While quantitative researchers often focus on "how frequently" or "how much" something happened, Q methods focus attention on the subjectivity of participants and foreground meaning-making within quantitative designs. Q methodology has been used by feminist researchers to challenge assumptions in research designs by turning to participants' definitions as a primary source of interest (Brownlie, 2006; Kitzinger, 1986). In a study of young adults (McClelland, 2014), I examined how participants prioritized and defined dimensions of sexual satisfaction using a Q methods. Rather than predict sexual satisfaction as an outcome or examine correlated variables, I examined interpretations of sexual satisfaction and the priorities that individuals ascribed to "feeling satisfied."

Studies using Q methodology ask participants to sort a set of statements (or other stimuli) from low to high endorsement (e.g., agreement or importance). In my study with young adults, I developed 63 statements concerning a wide range of descriptions concerning possible behaviors, feelings, and experiences associated with sexual satisfaction (for more detail, see McClelland, 2014). Example statements included, "After sexual activity is over, I know I am sexually satisfied when my genitals feel relaxed" and "The emotional closeness I feel to a partner is what makes sex satisfying for me." The first step in this process is called a "Q sort." In my case, this involved me handing participants the 63 statements, each printed on an individual card, and asking participants to sort the cards along a nine-point scale, ranging from *most disagree* to *most agree*, with a mid-point of *neutral*. They were given a prompt that asked: "What is important to you in determining your own sexual satisfaction? Distribute the statements from those that you most agree with to those you most disagree with." Participants were instructed to sort the cards using a quasi-normal distribution, which restricted how many cards they could place in each of the nine categories. This decision was made in order to create an iterative ranking process: each card was evaluated in relationship to the other 62 cards. For all steps of the procedure, I was present, although at a distance from the participant during the sorting procedure, which allowed for privacy since the researcher could not see how the cards were sorted.

The second step in this process is analyzing the Q sorts, which requires a "Q factor analysis." Q factor analysis examines correlations (much like a traditional factor analysis), however, instead of correlating items, this method correlates individuals. That is, Q factor analysis examines correlations between the Q sorts produced by participants and combines individuals who displayed similar sorting patterns into a factor (i.e., they consistently agreed and disagreed with the same statements). These factors are understood to represent a shared subjective interpretation that differs from the other factors in the study. In my study, this allowed me to analyze "groups of participants who make sense of (and who hence Q 'sort') a pool of items in comparable ways" (Watts and Stenner, 2005, p. 68) and, thus, represents a powerful way to examine interpretations of psychological constructs such as sexual satisfaction. I used these and other procedures to determine groups of individuals who placed statements in similar positions during the sorting procedure.

Because Q methodology looks for patterns of interpretation in addition to demographic differences, feminist researchers using this method have been able to explore variability within groups rather than treating demographically similar groups as stable and homogenous (Brownlie, 2006; Darwin & Campbell, 2009). I found that this diverse sample of young adults relied on four distinct ways of defining satisfaction, each related to sexual orientation and/or gender: emotional and masculine; relational and feminine; partner focused; and orgasm focused (McClelland, 2014). Findings such as these require researchers to move beyond simply examining the frequency with which individuals report sexual outcomes, but *how* individuals develop expectations for satisfying sex and how these expectations differ for groups who have less access to power and fewer rights in the sexual domain (e.g., Bay-Cheng & Eliseo-Arras, 2008).

Researchers working with children and young adults could use Q methods in a variety of ways when studying development. For example, sorts can be done with pictures rather than words, allowing children and/or those with lower reading skills to present a mosaic of images that might represent complex ideas about what feels important to them right now (e.g., Allgood & Svennungsen, 2008; Taylor et al., 1994). In addition, with an eye toward examining the development of expectations over time, researchers working with children and adolescents could ask participants to sort stimuli (images, text, and sounds) using a longitudinal design (i.e., multiple times over the course of a year or several years). These sorts could be analyzed for the changes to specific factors, emergence of new factors, and the development of (or restriction) concerning ideas about oneself.

In studies of sexuality, researchers might ask young people to reflect on how they make decisions about sexual experiences and within the sort might be cards related to parents, peers, messages learned at school, among others. In cross-sectional designs, young people can also be asked to reflect on how they sort the cards in the present moment and then also sort the cards as they would have 5 years ago or 5 years in the future. This design allows a participant to demonstrate how they see ideas developing and changing in the moment and could enable a researcher to better understand those aspects of sexuality development that might be difficult to talk about or that might be confusing to think about when asked about in an interview situation. Q methods allow for a kind of privacy-in-public that allows a participant to "sort their thoughts" while also being able to communicate complex ideas to a researcher.

Interview Data: Examining Adaptation to Injustice

Lastly, I draw our attention to critical methods when analyzing qualitative data. I return here to the image of cellophane that I discussed earlier in this chapter

(McClelland & Fine, 2008). We developed the metaphor of cellophane as one way to talk about dilemma that faces researchers when participants discount or downplay their experiences of trauma or discrimination, and, instead, say that everything is "fine" or that their experiences are "no big deal."

In a study of young bisexual women, my colleagues and I (McClelland et al., 2016) studied how young bisexual women described experiences of discrimination. In that study, we focused on those moments when participants told us that they were "fine," "used to it," or when negative interactions were "not that bad." The interviews held important insights into the messages young queer women had heard about themselves, which we argued created an environment in which discrimination became normalized. As a result, discriminatory messages were perceived as part of the normal social landscape and truly something that is "not a big deal" (Baker, 2008, 2010; Calder-Dawe & Gavey, 2016). For example, when a participant says, "Everything is fine," this comment might be recorded as an endorsement of a positive attitude (i.e., everything is actually fine). However, additional questions of when, why, and how this particular statement was used and what else it might stand in for, contribute insight into the person and what they feel "fine" about. In our analysis, we focused on developing an analytical strategy that moved beyond participants' surface-level descriptions to explore language choices, silences, and gaps in communication in participants' accounts. Using a critical methods perspective, we aimed to represent individuals' experiences, as well as focus on how they represented (or did not represent) their experience.

Linda Alcoff (1991) reminds researchers to attend to the "discursive context" in which words are spoken and to not forget that we cannot always see or hear the relevant environments of those who are speaking. Celia Kitzinger and Sue Wilkinson (1997) argue, too, that, "part of being a feminist means not validating, but directly *challenging* women's taken-for-granted experience" (1997, p. 572, emphasis in original). Hollway and Jefferson (2000) and Josselson (2004) also argue that qualitative approaches have been useful in exploring the meanings and layers of phenomena, but may be limited when we commit to "telling it like it is" (Midgley, 2006). As a result, critical researchers face a difficult task: balance the desire to recognize the specific perspective of individuals and their accounts, with the task of documenting and critiquing the conditions in which they live and survive, even when the participant disagrees (e.g., Josselson, 2011).

Feminists have argued that unequal status due to gender, race/ethnicity, and colonial histories are especially important to consider when examining language (Lather, 1993; Spivak, 1988, 1993). As this work has moved into feminist psychology, researchers have analyzed aspects of power, status, and socialization in what participants talk about and how they talk (Boonzaier, 2008; Owen, 2012; Ussher, 2004; see also Wilkinson & Kitzinger, 2000). This perspective demands not only attention to "context," but also how language is used (or not used) to communicate. Participants' communications (in surveys, experiments, or interviews) may be motivated by, and may be constrained by, several social forces that are not clearly visible (e.g., not feeling safe or being in a low status position) and, in addition, may be outside the participant's or the researcher's awareness. In other words, a critical methods perspective demands researchers ask a set of questions about the situation, the person, and participants' many social roles.

When asked about whether they had ever faced discrimination as a result of their bisexuality, the young women in my study consistently said "no." In our analysis, however, we examined how participants came to see negative experiences surrounding their bisexuality as normal and expected. Participants filled our ears with examples of negative interactions with peers, disrespectful comments from family members, or slurs heard from strangers. Nearly all participants described hearing derogatory remarks regularly, but they did not see this as a form of sexuality-based discrimination. Typical responses from participants included: "Ye – um . . . not – I mean, not personally, somebody has never, like, come up to me and been, like, telling me straight up, discriminating me." This young woman's statement that she had not faced discrimination, followed by retreat ("Ye – um . . . not – I mean, not personally"), exemplifies responses concerning what "counted" as discrimination. This is not surprising if one considers the term "discrimination" as signaling a prototypical standard, such as being refused a job or housing, which these young women may have not yet encountered. However, we heard story after story of young women being called "dyke," being ridiculed in public, getting "weird looks," and a slew of negative experiences concerning their sexuality.

Why do participants acknowledge negative experiences but minimize reporting the discrimination they face? While sexism and heterosexism are important political tools to aid individuals in recognizing discrimination, these tools also position the individual as damaged as a result of being discriminated against. As a result, it becomes more difficult when these experiences become so normal as to be invisible and/or they become associated with being damaged (Fine, 2012). Laina Bay-Cheng (2015) argues that the neoliberal discourse of choices and the capitalist discourse of "empowerment" have made it impossible for young women to acknowledge feeling out of control of their sexuality and have imposed extremely stiff fines (in the form of negative self-concept) if one is to imagine oneself as disempowered. These and other cultural discourse norms are too infrequently acknowledged as shaping what can and cannot be imagined, much less spoken, in research contexts. This presents psychologists with a set of methodological dilemmas when studying unjust circumstances.

The findings from my study of bisexual young women builds on previous research concerning individuals with marginalized identities who also frequently minimized their experience of discrimination (Crosby, 1984; Major et al., 2002). Individuals internalize negative messages about bisexuality and this, in turn, affects their ability to perceive future events as discriminatory. The use of a critical perspectives in the analysis of the interview data was key. While participants disavowed or minimized their experiences of discrimination, we did not. Participants also described negative comments they heard as "not a big a deal," but, in our analysis, we called attention to these comments as requiring psychological labor, even if the person did not themselves tell us about this labor or see it as difficult. Critical methodological approaches require that researchers attend to moments when individuals do not insist on better treatment or more resources, but, instead, report being satisfied with the *status quo* (Crocker & Major, 1989; Crosby, 1984; McClelland, 2010).

When individuals downplay or trivialize injustices, the question remains: How can one ask people to report on what, to them, has become normal? This presents a methodological dilemma to those who are interested in documenting discriminatory experiences or individuals' responses to discrimination. When individuals stop recognizing situations, experiences, or people as injurious, researchers face a set of potential silences that can too easily be misinterpreted. When turning to adolescents and considering these questions of adaptation, one might also wonder how much time it takes for adaptation to injustice to occur? In my own research with young people aged 16–24 years old, I have seen the ways that young people come to think of negative experiences as normal. But this should live alongside the other examples of young people being incredibly angry and mobilizing their anger toward social change. Examples such as the SPARK Movement (sparkmovement.org) and the Everyday Sexism Project (Bates, 2016) highlight how anger is not absent, adaptation is not complete, and young people are a force to be reckoned with.

Conclusion

Critical methods contribute to the project of developing empirical procedures that simultaneously prioritize developing knowledge claims (*What do we know?*) and developing skepticism about this very knowledge (*Who is missing? What have we missed?*). Rather than just addressing these important questions within a limitations section, or in pilot-testing measures, or while recruiting a "diverse sample," critical methods – and the skepticism they bring – can and should be employed throughout every step of the research process. The four examples I present here demonstrate that without attention to social norms and silences at several steps in a study, researchers risk overlooking many aspects of young people's lives, particularly the ways that inequality shapes development and the expectations that young people develop for their sexual futures.

Critical methods are crucial to study the sexual development of children and adolescence. This kind of approach enables a researcher to be in relationship with participants and take young people's role in the research process seriously and treat them as interlocutors. Critical research methods can help teach young people that their perspectives are important and valued. In addition, studying children and adolescents' sexuality requires that the researcher attend to uncertainty and messiness in people's lives. Research with people at this early developmental stage should build in flexibility and to the methodological approaches that allow young people to share the contradictions and messiness that is part of being a person and often a part of being a young person. Sexuality research with young people also often lives in the realm of the imagination and fantasy, which inevitably requires that researchers develop methods that can attend to this kind of unruly material.

The four methods I discuss in this chapter are just a few of the possibilities for critical researchers looking to attend to uncertainty and multiplicity in their studies of sexual development of children and youth. Other methods include critical participatory research (Torre et al., 2012), critical mixed methods (Shammas, 2017), and the long history of feminist ethnographic practices (Behar & Gordon, 1995), just to name a few. My hope is that researchers are inspired by this body of work on critical methods. With these tools in mind, researchers are encouraged to set off to understand and also feel humbled by the enormity of what it means to understand the experience of another.

References

Adams, G. (2014). Decolonizing Methods: African Studies and Qualitative Research. *Journal of Social and Personal Relationships*, *31*(4), 467–474.

Alcoff, L. M. (1991). The Problem of Speaking For Others. *Cultural Critique*, 20, 5–32.

Allgood, E. & Svennungsen, H. O. (2008). Toward an Articulation of Trauma Using the Creative Arts and Q-methodology: A Single Case Study. *Journal of Human Subjectivity*, *6*(1), 5–24.

Baker, J. (2008). The Ideology of Choice: Overstating Progress and Hiding Injustice in the Lives of Young Women: Findings from a Study in North Queensland, Australia. *Women's Studies International Forum*, *31*, 53–64.

(2010). Claiming Volition and Evading Victimhood: Post-Feminist Obligations for Young Women. *Feminism & Psychology*, *20*, 186–204.

Barad, K. (2007). *Meeting the Universe Half-way: Quantum Physics and the Entanglement of Matter and Meaning*. Durham, NC: Duke University Press.

Bates, L. (2016). *Everyday Sexism: The Project that Inspired a Worldwide Movement*. New York: Macmillan.

Bay-Cheng, L. Y. (2015). The Agency Line: A Neoliberal Metric for Appraising Young Women's Sexuality. *Sex Roles*, *73*, 279–291. doi:10.1007/s11199-015-0452-6.

Bay-Cheng, L. Y. & Eliseo-Arras, R. K. (2008). The Making of Unwanted Sex: Gendered and Neoliberal Norms in College Women's Unwanted Sexual Experiences. *Journal of Sex Research*, *45*, 386–397.

Behar, R. & Gordon, D. A. (Eds.). (1995). *Women Writing Culture*. Berkeley: University of California Press.

Bennett, J. (2009). *Vibrant Matter: A Political Ecology of Things*. Durham, NC: Duke University Press.

Boonzaier, F. (2008). If the Man Says You Must Sit, Then You Must Sit: The Relational Construction of Woman Abuse: Gender, Subjectivity and Violence. *Feminism & Psychology*, *18*, 183–206.

Bowleg, L., del Río-González, A. M., Holt, S. L. et al. (2017). Intersectional Epistemologies of Ignorance: How Behavioral and Social Science Research Shapes What We Know, Think We Know, and Don't Know about Us Black Men's Sexualities. *The Journal of Sex Research*, *54*(4–5), 577–603.

Brownlie, E. B. (2006). Young Adults' Constructions of Gender Conformity and Nonconformity: A Q Methodological Study. *Feminism & Psychology, 16*(3), 289–306.

Calder-Dawe, O. & Gavey, N. (2016). Making Sense of Everyday Sexism: Young People and the Gendered Contours of Sexism. *Women's Studies International Forum*, 55, 1–9.

Cantril, H. (1965). *The Pattern of Human Concern*. New Brunswick: Rutgers University Press.

Collins, W. A. (2003). More than Myth: The Developmental Significance of Romantic Relationships in Adolescence. *Journal of Research on Adolescence*, *13*, 1–24.

Crocker, J. & Major, B. (1989). Social Stigma and Self-Esteem: The Self-Protective Properties of Stigma. *Psychological Review*, *96*, 608–630.

Crosby, F. J. (1984). The Denial of Personal Discrimination. *American Behavioral Scientist*, *27*, 371–386.

Darwin, Z. & Campbell, C. (2009). Understandings of Cervical Screening in Sexual Minority Women: A Q-methodological Study. *Feminism & Psychology, 19*(4), 534–554.

Fahs, B. & McClelland, S. I. (2016). When Sex and Power Collide: An Argument for Critical Sexuality Studies. *The Journal of Sex Research*, *53*(4–5), 392–416.

Fields, J. (2005). Children Having Children: Race, Innocence, and Sexuality Education. *Social Problems*, *52*(4), 549–571.

Fine, M. (2007). Expanding the Methodological Imagination. *The Counseling Psychologist*, *35*(3), 459–473.

(2012). Troubling Calls for Evidence: A Critical Race, Class and Gender Analysis of Whose Evidence Counts. *Feminism & Psychology*, *22*, 3–19.

(2016). Just Methods in Revolting Times. *Qualitative Research in Psychology*, *13*, 347–365.

(2017). *Just Research in Contentious Times*. New York: Teachers College Press.

Fine, M. & Ruglis, J. (2009). Circuits and Consequences of Dispossession: The Racialized Realignment of the Public Sphere for U.S. Youth. *Transforming Anthropology*, *17*, 20–33.

Fox, D., Prilleltensky, I., & Austin, S. (Eds.). (2009). *Critical Psychology: An Introduction*. Los Angeles: Sage.

Garcia, L. & Fields, J. (2017). Renewed Commitments in a Time of Vigilance: Sexuality Education in the USA. *Sex Education*, *17*(4), 471–481.

Hey, V. (1997). *The Company She Keeps: An Ethnography of Girls' Friendships*. Bristol, PA: McGraw-Hill Education (UK).

Hitchens, B. K., Carr, P. J., & Clampet-Lundquist, S. (2018). The Context for Legal Cynicism: Urban Young Women's Experiences with Policing in Low-Income, High-Crime Neighborhoods. *Race and Justice* 8(1), 27–50. doi:10.1177/2153368717724506.

Hollway, W. & Jefferson, T. (2000). *Doing Qualitative Research Differently: Free Association, Narrative and the Interview Method*. Thousand Oaks: Sage.

hooks, b. (1984). *From Margin to Center*. Boston: South End Press.

Josselson, R.E. (2004). The Hermeneutics of Faith and the Hermeneutics of Suspicion. *Narrative Inquiry*, *14*(1), 1–28.

(2011). "Bet You Think This Song Is about You": Whose Narrative Is It in Narrative Research? *Narrative Works*, *1*, 33–51.

Kitzinger, C. (1986). Introducing and Developing Q as a Feminist Methodology: A Study of Accounts of Lesbianism. In S. Wilkinson (Ed.) *Feminist Social Psychology: Developing Theory and Practice* (151–172). Stony Stratford: Keynes.

Kitzinger, C. & Wilkinson, S. (1997). Validating Women's Experience? Dilemmas in Feminist Research. *Feminism & Psychology*, *7*(4), 566–574.

Kurtiş, T. & Adams, G. (2015). Decolonizing Liberation: Toward a Transnational Feminist Psychology. *Journal of Social and Political Psychology*, *3*(1), 388–413.

Landrine, H., Klonoff, E.A., & Brown-Collins, A. (1992). Cultural Diversity and Methodology in Feminist Psychology: Critique, Proposal, Empirical Example. *Psychology of Women Quarterly*, *16*, 145–163.

Lather, P. (1993). Fertile Obsession: Validity after Poststructuralism. *The Sociological Quarterly*, *34*, 673–693.

(2007). Getting Lost. *Feminist Efforts towards a Double(d) Science*. New York: SUNY Press.

Major, B., Quinton, W. J., & McCoy, S. K. (2002). Antecedents and Consequences of Attributions to Discrimination: Theoretical and Empirical Advances. *Advances in Experimental Social Psychology*, *34*, 251–330.

Martín-Baró, I. (1994). *Writings for a Liberation Psychology*. Cambridge, MA: Harvard University Press.

McClelland, S. I. (2010). Intimate Justice: A Critical Analysis of Sexual Satisfaction. *Social and Personality Psychology Compass*, *4*(9), 663–680.

(2014). "What Do You Mean When You Say That You're Sexually Satisfied?" A Mixed Methods Study. *Feminism & Psychology*, *24*(1), 74–96.

(2016). Speaking Back from the Margins: Participant Marginalia in Survey and Interview Research. *Qualitative Psychology*, *3*(2), 159–165.

(2017). Conceptual Disruption: The Self-Anchored Ladder in Critical Feminist Research. *Psychology of Women Quarterly*, 41(4), 451–464. doi:10.1177/0361684317725985

McClelland, S. I. & Fine, M. (2008). Writing *on* Cellophane: Studying Teen Women's Sexual Desires; Inventing Methodological Release Points. In Gallagher, K. (Ed.), *The Methodological Dilemma: Creative, Critical and Collaborative Approaches to Qualitative Research* (232–260). London: Routledge.

(2014). Over-Sexed and Under Surveillance: Adolescent Sexualities, Cultural Anxieties, and Thick Desire. In Rasmussen, M. L., Quinlivan, K., & Allen, L. (Eds.), *Interrogating the Politics of Pleasure in Sexuality Education* (12–34). New York: Routledge.

McClelland, S. I. & Holland, K. J. (2016). Toward Better Measurement: The Role of Survey Marginalia in Critical Sexuality Research. *Qualitative Psychology*, *3*(2), 166–185.

McClelland, S. I., Rubin, J. D., & Bauermeister, J. A. (2016). Adapting to Injustice: Young Bisexual Women's Interpretations of Microaggressions. *Psychology of Women Quarterly*, *40*(4), 532–550.

Midgley, N. (2006). Psychoanalysis and Qualitative Psychology: Complementary or Contradictory Paradigms? *Qualitative Research in Psychology*, 3, 213–231.

Moore, L. J. (2016). When Is a Clitoris Like a Lesbian? A "Sociologist" Considers Thinking Sex. *WSQ: Women's Studies Quarterly*, *44*(3), 328–331.

Morawski, J. G. (1994). *Practicing Feminisms, Reconstructing Psychology: Notes on a Liminal Science*. Ann Arbor: University of Michigan Press.

Owen, L. (2012). Living Fat in a Thin-Centric World: Effects of Spatial Discrimination on Fat Bodies and Selves. *Feminism & Psychology*, *22*, 290–306.

Robinson, K. H. (2012). 'Difficult Citizenship': The Precarious Relationships between Childhood, Sexuality and Access to Knowledge. *Sexualities*, *15*(3–4), 257–276.

Shammas, D. (2017). Underreporting Discrimination among Arab American and Muslim American Community College Students: Using Focus Groups to Unravel the Ambiguities within the Survey Data. *Journal of Mixed Methods Research*, *11* (1), 99–123.

Smith, L. T. (2006). Colonizing Knowledges. In *The Indigenous Experience: Global Perspectives*. Toronto: Canadian Scholars' Press Inc.

Smith, M. V. (2008). Pain Experience and the Imagined Researcher. *Sociology of Health & Illness*, *30*(7), 992–1006.

Smith, P. H., Smith, J. B., & Earp, J. A. L. (1999). Beyond the Measurement Trap: A Reconstructed Conceptualization and Measurement of Woman Battering. *Psychology of Women Quarterly*, 23(1), 177–193.

Spivak, G. C. (1990). Poststructuralism, Marginality, Postcoloniality and Value. In Collier, P. & Geyer-Ryan, H. (Eds.), *Literary Theory Today* (219–244). Ithaca: Cornell University Press.

(1988). Can the Subaltern Speak? In Nelson, C. & Grossberg, L. (Eds.), *Marxism and the Interpretation of Culture* (271–313). Champaign: University of Illinois Press.

(1993). *Outside in the Teaching Machine*. New York: Routledge.

Stainton Rogers, R. & Stainton Rogers, W. (1992). *Stories of Childhood: Shifting Agendas of Child Concern*. Buffalo: University of Toronto Press.

Stephenson, W. (1953). *The Study of Behavior: Q Technique and its Methodology*. Chicago: University of Chicago Press.

Taylor, P., Delprato, D.J., & Knapp, J.R. (1994). Q-methodology in the Study of Child Phenomenology. *Psychological Record*, *44*, 171–183.

Teo, T. (2011). Radical Philosophical Critique and Critical Thinking in Psychology. *Journal of Theoretical and Philosophical Psychology*, *31*(3), 193–199.

(2015). Critical Psychology: A Geography of Intellectual Engagement and Resistance. *American Psychologist*, *70*(3), 243–254.

Torre, M. E., Fine, M., Stoudt, B. G., & Fox, M. (2012). Critical Participatory Action Research as Public Science. In Cooper, H. & Camic, P. (Eds.), *APA Handbook of Research Methods in Psychology* (Vol. 2.). Washington, DC: American Psychological Association.

Traub, V. (2015). *Thinking Sex with the Early Moderns*. Philadelphia: University of Pennsylvania Press.

Unger, R. K. (1998). *Resisting Gender: Twenty-Five Years of Feminist Psychology*. Thousand Oaks: Sage Publications

Ussher, J. M. (2004). Biological Politics Revisited: Reclaiming the Body and the Intra-Psychic within Discursive Feminist Psychology. *Feminism & Psychology*, *14*, 425–430.

Warner, L. R., Settles, I. H., & Shields, S. A. (2016). Intersectionality as an Epistemological Challenge to Psychology. *Psychology of Women Quarterly*, *40*(2), 171–176.

Watts, S. & Stenner, P. (2005). Doing Q Methodology: Theory, Method and Interpretation. *Qualitative Research in Psychology*, *2*(1), 67–91.

Weisstein, N. (1968). *Kinder, Kuche, Kirche as Scientific Law: Psychology Constructs the Female*. Boston: New England Free Press.

Wilkinson, S. (1991). Why Psychology (Badly) Needs Feminism. In Aaron, J. & Walby, S. (Eds.), *Out of the Margins: Women's Studies in the Nineties* (191–203). London: Falmer Press.

Wilkinson, S. & Kitzinger, C. (2000). Thinking Differently about Thinking Positive: A Discursive Approach to Cancer Patients' Talk. *Social Science & Medicine*, *50*, 797–811.

15 Loving Possibilities in Studies of Sexuality Education and Youth

Jessica Fields and Lorena Garcia

To study youth, sexuality, and development is to enter an emotionally fraught terrain. For many, questions about sexual behaviors, desires, intimacies, and identities invoke notions of vulnerability, danger, and risk; in doing so, they excite worry, fear, and concern (Irvine, 2008). Adults may feel indignant about the social inequalities that riddle young people's pursuit of sexual health and well-being or dismissive of sexual identities and explorations that seem like the fleeting preoccupations of youth. While strong emotions can be a resource in contentious debate about sexual norms and policies (Irvine, 2002), feelings can seem like obstacles to clear understanding and insight in most substantive areas of inquiry. Researchers may decide to interrogate their feelings, but also resolve to stand outside the emotional fray. In studies of youth and sexuality, the impulse is often to defend against the challenges and opportunities even ostensibly "good" feelings present. In this chapter, we explore the possibility of research that pursues another option and allows methodology to be touched by love for the young people and the sexual experiences and meanings we hope to understand. How can love recast the scene of research – our approach, our questions, and our conclusions – about youth sexuality?

Drawing on the work of bell hooks, we understand love to be a "mix[ture of] various ingredients: care, affection, recognition, respect, commitment, and trust, as well as honest communication" (2000, p. 5). This mixture is created, reproduced, and challenged through interactions, institutions, and ideologies. Cultural frames "name and define the emotion, set the limits of its intensity, specify the norms and values attached to it, and provide symbols and cultural scenarios that make it socially communicative" (Illouz, 1997, pp. 4–5). Cultural understandings and symbols structure people's experiences of love (often framed as romance), which are also shaped by the connection between culture and capitalism. According to Illouz, "cultural entrepreneurs of capitalism," informed by middle-class culture, integrated romance and love into new markets for leisure and personal commodities in the early twentieth century. Across classes, genders, racialized groups, and sexualities, culture is a "tool kit" from which people draw to give meanings to and act on love (Swidler, 2013). As social actors, we all have the capacity to pull from and develop cultural "repertoires" to negotiate what love and its practice mean in our social worlds.

The notion of bringing love to the social world of scholarship – particularly social science research, particularly studies of youth, and particularly studies of sexuality – may be startling, but we find precedent in our discipline of sociology and in feminist, queer, and anti-racist scholarship. Sociological theories have cast emotions as tools of analysis, allowing researchers to ask what their own experiences of data collection suggest about a setting's emotional culture (Kleinman and Copp, 1993). New insights emerge in this sort of analysis: for example, a researcher's own discomfort in a sex education classroom can shed light on the emotional and social risks teachers take in associating themselves with female sexuality as students mock and disparage images of women's bodies (Fields, 2008).

Emotions offer visceral experiences of social difference, inequality, and affinity and thus promise substantive insight into normalized and oppressive conditions. The feelings Alison Jaggar describes as "outlaw emotions" can help qualitative researchers notice and learn from moments at which we bristle against the ordinary, oppressive demands of a setting or identity (1989). Outlaw emotions are "distinguished by their incompatibility with the dominant perceptions and values" – thus their outlaw status. Indeed, these feelings are outlawed and valuable because they are "politically [and] epistemologically subversive" (Jaggar, 1989, p. 166). Rather than mute such feelings as violations of social and scientific norms, feminist and queer scholars rely on those feelings to discern the disciplining lines and normative orientations that help to shape the racialized, gendered, and sexualized bodies, lives, and groups we observe (Ahmed, 2006).

In the following chapter, we bring sociological theories of emotion and intersectional analyses of race, gender, and sexuality to bear on studies of youth and development. Our discussion focuses on sexuality education – our shared area of expertise – but our argument reaches across studies of youth, sexuality, and development. We explore feelings as methodological signals – flashes that mark or even incite a break down in conventional research practices. As fantasies of smoothly unfolding designs and practices fade and falter, researchers can no longer rely on method "to drain anxiety from situations in which we feel complicitous with structures of power, or helpless to release another from suffering, or at a loss as to whether to act or to observe" (Behar, 1996, p. 6). And, in that moment of vulnerability, a methodological opportunity emerges.

We aim to build on the specific methodological opportunity love affords. Rather than mute verboten feelings as violations of social and scientific norms, feminist and queer scholars can find in love the affective grounds for a methodology that accounts for the here and now (the troubled history with which we contend) and, simultaneously, looks toward a there and then (some grander set of possibilities) in which we might, as José Esteban Muñoz (2009) describes, "feel differently" (both feeling different things and experiencing those feelings in alternative ways). In studies of sexuality, youth, and development, a loving, pragmatic, and utopian vision allows adults, people of color, queer people, women, and other members of marginalized communities not only to understand rationally what is possible given the material reality of the worlds we study and disciplines we navigate but also to risk feeling that the usual possibilities are "not enough, that indeed something is missing." (p. 1). Once researchers allow ourselves to feel our interest in youth, sexuality, and development differently, a new methodology may become possible. Love – an emotion often forbidden in research and in adult/youth relationships – may become newly, thrillingly, and delicately possible as an orienting emotion in the work conducted by adults, researchers, educators, and advocates.

Relinquishing Fear

A move toward love requires first a move away from fear. Much research about youth and sexuality education is rooted in this affective state related to but distinct from love. While fear may arise out of love – for example, we often fear for the well-being of those we love – it is not an inevitable expression of love. Nevertheless, fears for children navigating a dangerous world dominate adults' understandings of young people's sexual lives and obscure more caring and respectful expressions of concern for the well-being of children and youth.

Researchers, educators, health care providers, policy makers, and families routinely begin with the assumption that young people's sexual desires and expressions are bad news not only for young people – particularly youth of color – but also for the communities and institutions young people inhabit. For decades, public, private, formal, and informal sexuality education has promoted sexual abstinence as the most (perhaps the only) reasonable and safe choice for young people, affirming a picture of students' sexual lives as filled with risk, danger, and compromise: violent and immoral at their worst, rudderless and confusing at their best (Levine, 2002). Sexuality educators' role has been to introduce some sort of clarity into a confusing and difficult experience of growing up, becoming sexual, and managing one's own and others' desires (Fields, 2008; Gilbert, 2014). For some students, even this ideal seems out of reach. Sexuality education promises these young people a greater intervention: one of few means available to prevent them from traveling down a thorny path of poor sexual decisions that will lead inevitably to unintended and undesirable consequences like sexually transmitted infections, unwanted pregnancies, too-early sexual activity, and heartbreak (Garcia, 2012; Kendall, 2013).

This narrative of risk has fostered a particular emotional world for sex education debates and practice (Irvine, 2002, 2008). Here we mainly refer to how these debates and practices are carried out in the United States. The notions of risk, prevention, and harm in both abstinence-only or comprehensive instruction have fostered a fearful climate that constrains teachers' and administrators' efforts to proffer innovative and transformative classroom work (Fields, 2008; Kendall, 2013). Sara I. McClelland and Michelle Fine argue that, although the Right may lose local and federal battles over abstinence-only education, they have prevailed in the debate over sexuality education: the idea that young people should not be sexually active enjoys undue sway in sexuality education practice, policy, and evaluation research (2008).

In the drive to determine the risks young people face and how best to minimize or even eliminate their exposure to risk, adults aggravate another risk: that of casting young people as "in crisis" and in "need of rescue" (see Gilbert et al., 2018 on a similar risk in approaches to LGBTQ sexuality and youth). Educators, researchers, and policy makers run the risk of dismissing young people's capacity to make choices and respond to the racialized, gendered, sexual, classed, and other institutional inequalities they inhabit, confront, and navigate as they explore and claim sexual lives and, more broadly, move toward adulthood. As the roles of youth-as-victim and adults-as-protector become more ossified, the recognition, respect, trust, and honesty that define love may be more difficult to achieve. The role adults play in constituting and maintaining the inequalities and injustices young people encounter in schools, in their intimate lives, and in public conversation becomes more difficult to perceive (Schaffner, 2005). What other emotional and affective responses might there be to risk and vulnerability in young people's lives – loving, insistent responses that offer care, invite self-scrutiny, and commit to creating new institutional, relational, and intimate possibilities in the face of developmental, structural, and systemic vulnerability?

Reaching across Rifts

Many who study youth, sexuality, and development have aimed to be young people's advocates and allies (Shanahan, 2007; see, for example, Kimmel et al., 2013; Lamb et al., 2016; Santelli et al. 2006). Similarly, many researchers have tried to reimagine the relationships adult educators, researchers, and parents build with young people in the overlapping categories of queer youth, girls, and youth of color (for examples, see Best, 2007; Bettie, 2003; Leadbetter & Way, 1996; Morris 2016; Pérez, 2015; Rios, 2011; Taft, 2010).

Amy Best's 2007 edited volume, *Representing Youth: Methodological Issues in Critical Youth Studies*, offers one important methodological model. In her introduction to the essay collection, Best reflects on her own school-based ethnographies of race, gender, and sexuality in young people's lives: *Prom Night: Youth, Schools, and Popular Culture* (2000) and *Fast Cars, Cool Rides: The Accelerating World of Youth and Their Cars* (2005). Best discusses the "conceptual rift between my everyday world and the youth worlds I studied" (2007, p. 3). Committed to examining this rift, Best "interrogates the very construction of 'American youth culture'" (2007, p. 3). She recognizes how everyday lay and scholarly understandings of that culture are inflected with not only race, class, gender, and sexuality, but also "differences of citizenship, immigrant status, and nationality" (2007, p. 4). Among this constellation of categories and experiences, age emerges as not only a marker of development and difference but also an axis of "power and difference" that inflects research practice. Best calls on scholars of children and youth to attend to the implications of age for "how we see, understand, and interact with youth, and for the knowledge we produce and disseminate" (2007, p. 4). Age contributes to the conceptual rifts that Best interrogates: as adults struggle with method and conceptualization, ideas break down and researchers are compelled to try to do things – perhaps even feel things – differently.

The rifts with which Best contends reflect developmental differences between young people and adults and structural differences in the advantages afforded people at different stages of their lives. In their review of twenty-first-century research on adolescence, sociologists Robert Crosnoe and Monica Kirkpatrick Johnson describe lives as "a tapestry of three threads – developmental trajectories (physical and psychological growth), social pathways (sequences of institutional roles and activities), and social convoys (continuity and change in interpersonal relations) – situated in settings of daily life, larger structures of society, and the broader sweep of history" (2011, p. 440). These threads and settings extend across the life course, rendering development a lifelong and intricate process. Shifting roles and responsibilities in school, employment, and other institutions and pathways give shape to developmental trajectories, as do shifting, significant, and sometimes contentious relationships with family, friends, and peers. Always, young people's experiences of these processes, roles, and relationships are situated in the broader and quotidian social and historical contexts of young people's sexual lives, ranging from access to condoms to emerging gender and sexual identity categories, from punishing responses to the sexual lives of youth of color to the persistent racialization of school-based sexuality education.

Bridging rifts between adults and youth requires more than seeing past, through, or despite differences in age, development, and generation. The divide is often oppressive, as evident in the familiar and oppressive premise that adults categorically know better than young people about their safety, intimacy, and well-being – a premise some call "adultism" (Gong and Wright, 2007). Adultist thinking masks the structural and categorical inequalities that disadvantage the young people whose development interests and occupies us; adultist inequalities riddle responses to young people's sexuality and development. Adults strain against and even unwittingly affirm structures and ideas that prevent them from providing young people with information and skills necessary to their sexual rights and well-being; through sexuality education that affirms heteronormative intimacy and focuses on the dangers of sexual expression, adults obscure a discourse of desire in favor of warnings that assume adults always know better (Fine, 1988; Fine and McClelland, 2006; Garcia, 2009).

As adults, researchers cannot help but be similarly implicated in the adultist conditions with which youth contend, including hierarchical ideas about youth, status, and morality. In their consideration of participant observation with children and youth, Gary Fine and Kent L. Sandstrom find a parallel for such entrenched stratification in research that reaches across racialized, gendered, and cultural difference:

> Like the white researcher in black society, the male researcher studying women, or the ethnologist observing a distant tribal culture, the adult participant observer who attempts to understand a children's culture cannot pass unnoticed as a member of that group. (1988, p. 13)

In a gesture reminiscent of calls for white people and men to act as allies to people of color and women, Fine and Sandstrom urge researchers to be "friends" to the children and youth they study, because the role will allow adult researchers to "interact with [children and youth] in the most trusted way possible – without having any explicit authority role." By minimizing one's authority as an adult and winning young people's trust, Fine and Sandstrom argue, adults are better able to move easily in young people's worlds and achieve the insight that comes with in-depth qualitative analysis.

But friendship cannot undo the methodological implications of adultism any more than alliance can undo the methodological implications of racism and sexism. The rift adult researchers confront is marked not simply by difference but also by disparity and disadvantage. To heed Best's call to recognize age as an axis of power is to raise more fundamental questions about adults' interest in young people and our capacity to understand and faithfully and fairly represent them. Again, the extensive sociological literature on the position and responsibilities of white people about race, including when teaching about the experiences of people of color is instructive (Best, 2003; DeVault, 1995; Omi & Winant, 1994; Picower, 2009). Sociologists have wondered what to do with an outsider's curiosity about a group. Is that curiosity objectifying, is it well placed? Is the outsider an appropriate authority on the group being studied? Sociologists, ethnographers, and feminists have called on people with structural advantages to approach their work with humility, sometimes suggesting that people with privilege should not do the work or, at least, should make room for members of the communities being studied to play a central role in defining the field and producing knowledge.

Like other activist scholarship (e.g., anti-racist, feminist, or queer), anti-adultist research makes sense of young people's experiences of sexuality, adolescence, and education by remaining attentive to the institutional contexts young people navigate and the broader material and ideological conditions they encounter, resist, and sustain – contexts and conditions that shape the developmental threads Crosnoe and Fitzpatrick identify. Such attention engages actively with the politics of knowledge production: the axes of racialized, gendered, sexual, and generational inequalities that subjugate some understandings and knowers to the immediate benefit of others. With that attention, anti-adultist researchers enter the realm of "salvage," "rescue," or "corrective" projects (Clifford, 1988; Domínguez, 1994). According to Virginia Domínguez, these projects include "the push to 'diversify' the academy, to create room for other or different 'voices' in the written scholarly record (as well as on our course syllabi and our conference panels), and to 'open up" our scholarly and educational institutions" (2000, p. 363). In scholarship on sexuality and youth, rescue projects include conducting participatory research with young people or highlighting the experiences and accounts of marginalized youth (e.g., see, Akom et al., 2008; Cammarota and Fine, 2010; Davis, 2015; Ray, 2017).

Domínguez warns that even well-intentioned efforts to respond to institutionalized exclusions frequently lead to only "cosmetic change" and reinforce "the institutionalized system of difference and value that it purports to challenge" (Domínguez, 2000, p. 363). Gendered, racialized, and other hierarchical norms continue to govern decision making and knowing in the academy, despite the increasing visibility of women, people of color, and queers. One remedy has been to insist that members of the subjugated group conduct the corrective research themselves: women studying women, people of color studying people of color, queers studying queers. This option is unavailable to youth studies: participatory and emancipatory research methods can place young people at the center of data collection and analysis, but academia is an insistently adult space. Credential requirements, norms of social exchange, and demands of development make change in academia difficult to achieve, particularly if we seek change on academia's terms.

Here, feelings emerge as a site of opportunity and potential transformation. Recognizing emotion's capacity to incite a break in conventional research practices allows anti-adultist researchers to reject fantasies of seamless research designs and practices. The vulnerability achieved as researchers relinquish worry and certainty signals a methodological opportunity. The affective and intimate possibility of love in studies of sexuality, youth, and development becomes a new ground for understanding.

Affective Responses to Adultism

The measure of a project's worth cannot be whether its author shares the perspectives and experience being corrected. That logic asserts another bifurcating logic – insiders and outsiders, rescuers and victims. Domínguez argues instead that a "'politics of love – and not 'identity politics' – should be the criterion used for distinguishing between good and bad 'rescue projects'" (2000, p. 365): "I want us to consider validating rescue projects as worthwhile projects[,] but doing so based on a different criterion of value – namely, genuine love, respect, and affection" (2000, p. 365). She continues,

> The kind of love, respect, and affection I have in mind is the kind of love we feel for family members, tough love at times but never disengagement or hagiography. Love, yes, love – the thing most of us are not open about in our scholarly writing, the kind most of us have been professionally socialized into excising from our scholarly writing. (2000, p. 365)

Domínguez calls on researchers to risk flouting professional and intellectual convention in the name of a politics of love.

Others have invoked intimate emotion when advocating methodological shifts in studies of children and youth. While Fine and Sandstrom advocate friendship primarily for its instrumental value to the ethnographer hoping to move freely through the worlds of children and youth, the relational nature of friendship also introduces feeling into the researcher/researched relationship. As Fine and Sandstrom note, affect distinguishes friendship from other roles – for example, "leader" or "observer" – that adult researchers might assume in their relationships with the children they study:

> The key to the role of friend is the explicit expression of *positive affect* combined with both a relative lack of authority and a lack of sanctioning of the behavior of those being studied. In turn, adopting the friend role suggests that the participant observer treats his or her informants with *respect* and that he or she *desires* to acquire competency in their social worlds. (1988, p. 7, emphasis added)

Orienting feelings – positive affect, respect, and desire, in this case – toward and about others are central to the relationships that Fine and Sandstrom suggest adult researchers form with young people across conceptual and generational divides.

Michelle Fine and Sara I. McClelland more explicitly invoke affect in their approaches to youth, sexuality, and sexuality education in their 2006 revisiting of Fine's 1988 foundational article, "Sexuality, Schooling, and Adolescent Females: The Missing Discourse of Desire." Fine and McClelland introduce the notion of "thick desire" to call for more than attention to the missing discourse of sexual desire in the sexuality education available to young people. They urge adults – researchers and educators – themselves to become more desiring. As they explain in the article's concluding paragraphs,

> Thick desire is offered as a framework to move us away from mourning the "missing discourse of desire" and on to demanding more publicly subsidized educational, social, legal, economic, and health care supports for young people as they develop complex social and sexual biographies in adolescence and beyond. Thick desire is meant to be a tool to see what is missing and to say what needs to be done. (Fine and McClelland 2006, p. 328)

In the framework, Fine and McClelland propose adults will foster and deploy thick desire as an orienting emotion, allowing themselves to feel differently while thinking about youth and imagining the lives they might pursue. Desire here is not simply romantic or sexual; nor is it located outside of inquiry, in the intimate and sexual lives educators and researchers expect and hope young people will pursue with partners. Instead, desire is a wide-ranging and foundational feeling for adult researchers and educators pursuing sexual and social justice for youth.

While the affects that friendship and thick desire bring to studies of youth and sexuality hold promise, we remain committed to the possibility of love. Writing and theorizing about love, hooks quotes M. Scott Peck (1978) when she describes love as "the will to nurture our own and other's spiritual growth" (hooks, 2000, p.6). This is not a love that romanticizes adults' relationships with young people. Instead, it is a behavior – a methodological tool – that orients adults toward youth and the world. hooks advocates for the use of love as verb, writing that, "We would all love better if we used [the term] as a verb . . . Since the choice must be made to nurture growth, this definition counters the more widely accepted assumption that we love instinctually" (2000, pp. 4–5). Researchers might imagine we tend, or do not tend, toward caring, respectful, trusting, and honest sentiments toward the youth we study. However, hooks' definition of love calls on us to pursue both the feeling and the collection of behaviors intentionally, actively, and overtly. A methodological practice emerges – one to which researchers can aspire, one they can learn, and one that insists on vulnerability, care, and mutuality in studies of youth and sexuality and in relationships between adults and young people.

As a guiding practice and emotion in researchers' interactions with children and youth, love highlights that, in our work as researchers, educators, and advocates, adults also benefit from the social change we seek for them because, ultimately, we all inhabit the larger social world together. Friendship encourages researchers to establish non-hierarchical relationships with young people. Thick desire helps the researcher, first, identify what is missing in young people's sexual lives and sexuality education and, second, articulate a vision of how else things might be for young people. Love helps the researcher ensure that the pursuit and vision are marked by a relationship with youth marked by vulnerability, intimacy, and mutuality.

Loving Young People Loving

What analytic shifts and insights will accompany a turning away from the stance of protection and a turning toward a stance and practice of love and mutuality? In 2008, Jessica published a book about abstinence-only and comprehensive sex education, at the core of which stood concerns about sexual justice in relationships between teachers and students. In *Risky Lessons* (2008), she examined the reproduction of gender, racial, and other social inequalities; varying possibilities for boys and girls to claim and recognize sexual subjectivity; and the potential for schools to become a site for something other than the rehearsal of restrictive understandings of sexuality and intimacy. Jessica aimed to take sexuality seriously, imagining a world in which young people might explore a range of intimate possibilities, including sexual pleasure, same-sex attractions and behaviors, and agentic decision making. In *Risky Lessons*, Jessica argued that fear, worry, and contempt were fundamental to the debate over abstinence-only and comprehensive sex education and that the affective life of the sex education classroom was restrictive, even oppressive. And, in the midst of all of this attention to sexual justice, pleasure, agency, subjectivity, and emotion, Jessica paid little attention to love.

Indeed, it comes up so infrequently in *Risky Lessons* that we can list the instances here, in a brief paragraph. Love appears first in a discussion of private school teachers' successful efforts to have their school host an exhibit on LGBTQ families, entitled "Love Makes a Family"; second, in the description of a teacher (working at that same private school) describing for her students the physiology of orgasm during what she called "lovemaking"; and, third, in an exploration of the invoking of love and marriage in conservative Christian discussions of abstinence and virginity. Jessica argued that conservative Christian discussions of sexual abstinence present love as what young people risk compromising if they become sexually active before they marry. Finally, in *Risky Lessons*, Jessica asserted critically that conventional understandings of youth and sexuality routinely dismiss young people's feelings of love, passion, and intimacy as "puppy love." For all of its impatience with the dismissal of young people's love, *Risky Lessons* offered little on how else researchers, educators, young people, and adults might otherwise understand it. Like other feminist, social science studies sex education, *Risky Lessons* comfortably explored agency, subjectivity, pleasure, and social inequality. But love remained elusive.

The absence of love in *Risky Lessons* reflects a general neglect of love in the research about sex education. Love is among the emotions routinely excised from sexuality when instruction, policy, and debate focus on health, well-being, and risk. Concern prevails – concern that young people will contract an infection or disease, get pregnant, or become sexually active before they are ready (however defined). Worry governs the instruction – worry that teachers will cross some invisible but definite line in their teaching, undermine parents' rights, or somehow compromise students' innocence with inappropriate sexual knowledge. It is a worried teaching, a concerned teaching.

In sexuality education classrooms and scholarships, students' lives often appear as if loveless; their intimate relationships with one another are often dismissed as immature; and their families are often imagined as sites of corruption and inadequacy. Mothers and fathers are implicated in the fantasy of students' home lives as poor role models, as inadequately loving, as immoral. The teacher then steps in with a certain sort of love to repair students' lives, to offer them an affection and guidance that is otherwise unavailable. An adultist lack of trust has particular consequences for young people's *sexual* subjectivity. Their relationships become no more than puppy love, their desires and emotions merely a function of raging hormones. When adults do take young people's sexuality seriously, they too often cast it as only-and-always dangerous to young people as individuals and to society as a whole.

Yet, youth are not simply trapped in their own bodies and minds; they also move about the world and encounter broader cultural frames on love, especially romantic love, that they may experience as intensified because of the various developmental shifts they experience at their age. One key component of these shifts is identity development, that is, young people's exploration of who they are and would like to be as they move toward adulthood. This identity formation often entails "trying on" various identities that can include, although are not limited to, clothing choices, hairstyles, and listening to particular musical genres, as well as participation in activities ranging from sports to social movement marches and rallies. Swidler

(2013, p. 90) points out that "trying out" of "possible selves" makes youth "voracious cultural consumers . . . They are in the process of forming and reforming strategies of action, developing the repertoire of cultural capacities out which they will construct the patterns of their adult lives." According to Swidler, such practices and their associated meanings reveal how culture operates in "unsettled lives." Appreciating the importance of culture in young people's lives and what they do with it as they craft identities and experiences for themselves facilitates our ability to recognize their agency in making sense of love and its role in their lives.

Second-generation Latina girls, for instance, spoke of love in their interviews with Lorena (Garcia, 2009) when they shared their experiences and understandings of what they considered to be their first sexual experiences, which they all connected to notions of virginity and virginity loss. Some of them did identify the idea of "being in love" as central to these experiences, but there were some girls who questioned the weight placed on romantic love to decide on first sexual experiences. Seventeen-year-old Olivia states, "I think girls sometimes put too much importance on love and romance as a reason to lose their virginity and that is why they regret it sometimes because they had this romantic illusion of what it would be like and how the other person will love them forever. I didn't want it to be about that at all!" (pp. 609–610). Olivia and other young Latinas who shared this critique of romantic love discourses point to the significance of a "caring" relationship with their sexual partner, in which mutual respect allowed them to better negotiate sexual safety and explore their sexuality.

Conclusions

In his consideration of teaching and love, Muñoz reminds readers that "the production of knowledge and, more specifically, the production of desire for knowledge, is a two-way street" (2005, p. 119). Inquiry – in the classroom, field site, or laboratory – represents an opportunity for people to come to know facts, texts, strategies, histories, *and one another* as individuals, members of groups, and historically located subjects. While the ordinary conditions of knowledge production may work against such engagements and lessons, "the possibility of such recognition is always present" (hooks, 1994, p. 13). The potential for such recognition can also be fostered by how we carry out our research.

Young people, like adults, have the ability to challenge and develop alternative ways of approaching love. Martin Luther King, Jr.'s (1981) writings and speeches exemplify an alternative engagement with love – one embedded in the analysis of and struggle for social justice. According to King, love can be mobilized to advocate for social change, sometimes requiring people to disrupt the *status quo*. In one of his sermons, he writes, "The hope of a secure and livable world lies with disciplined nonconformists, who are dedicated to justice, peace, and brotherhood. The trailblazers in human, academic, scientific and religious freedom have always been nonconformists" (p. 22). bell hooks (2000) similarly connects love to social justice projects, stressing the importance of being clear about what we mean by love and not relying on definitions generated and disseminated to us by mass media. Informed by the work of Martin Luther King, Jr. and others, hooks explains, "An individual does not need to be a believer in a religion to embrace the idea that there is an animating principle in the self – a life force (some of us call it a soul) that when nurtured enhances our capacity to be more fully self-actualized and able to engage in communion with the world around us" (p. 13). Love, as conceptualized by such influential visionaries, is about the love we have for our individual selves, the love we share with others in our relationships with them, and a love oriented toward and responsible to the communities and world here we inhabit.

Many of us carry out research on sexuality education because we are invested in transforming sexuality education practice so that is relevant, meaningful, and respectful of young people and their realities, including what they desire from their sexuality education. Scholars in this area have made significant contributions to how we think about and study sexuality education, but our exploration of the potentiality of love, as discussed by scholars and activists in other areas, suggests that sexuality education research can be immensely enriched by a deeper engagement with questions about love. It seems that it is easier for researchers to talk about sexual risk and to live in fear than it is to recognize and acknowledge love. How might this limit our ability to discern other questions we need to be asking in our sexuality education research, such as that perhaps it is love rather than pleasure that is the unspeakable subject in sexuality education? This question, in turn, might lead us to further investigation into how and why pedagogy based in love, for the most remains absent. We might also consider how Love can be integrated into the practice of sexuality education. Such integration may challenge the tendency for adults to remain adult-centered in our work for and with youth. Instead of meeting young people where they are, in their social worlds and where they are in their developmental trajectories, we tend to dismiss them by claiming that it is just growing pains or an inevitable part of adolescent struggles. We do not readily listen to their perspectives or their questions. Although young people live in a youth-obsessed culture in which concerns with profits and markets train our attention on desirable and validated young femininities and masculinities, they cannot count on adults to be curious about the everyday lives of young people – what they want and envision for themselves, including their comprehension and enactment of love.

Risks remain, of course. Attending to love as an orienting emotion in our scholarship can be the basis for some to judge it as less rigorous and, therefore, less deserving of serious engagement with it (Domínguez, 2000; hooks, 1994; Muñoz, 2005). And there is also risk in loving people, including young people we come to know through our work, because it means we open ourselves up to the possibility of failing and disappointing them and *vice versa*. And, yet, love can be an enabling feeling, as Muńoz asserts when he considers how love can shape teaching by one's willingness to reveal the "seams of one's pedagogy . . . which has everything to do with promise, possibility and potentiality (not inevitably) of failure" (2005, p. 12). Identifying love as possibly the most closeted and yet enabling feeling, Domínguez writes, "It is about time that we recognize it when it is there, value it rather than denigrate it, and flaunt it because we are proud (for good reasons, i.e., not blindly) of the persons we love and of the quality of the work that love (and those people) enable us to produce" (2000, p. 388).

Love as an emotion and as a practice opens up a methodological opportunity in our research about youth sexuality. The incorporation of love as central to our work requires that we acknowledge young people's engagements with love as valid and deeply meaningful to them; recognize and value the role of love in animating our commitment to their sexual development and education; and see how it connects to other issues relevant to them and to their communities. Love also demands that we appreciate this emotional state as a practice we adopt in our work on and with young people. The approach requires researchers to take responsibility for making sure that young people are included in conversations, particularly those aimed at developing knowledge or programming to provide them with skills, tools, and knowledge to not just survive in our society, but also thrive. We can aim for collaborations with them that recognize that neither they nor we have all the answers – to assume otherwise is to pretend that our interactions with one another are irrelevant for social change. Adults have privilege *vis-à-vis* children and youth because of age; and based on their social location as young people, children and youth have critical insights and expertise on their lives. An appreciation of this allows us to formulate collaborations that draw on our respective strengths from a loving stance.

References

Ahmed, S. (2006). *Queer Phenomenology: Orientations, Objects, Others*. Durham, NC: Duke University Press.

Akom, A. A., Cammarota, J., & Ginwright, S. (2008). Youthtopias: Towards a New Paradigm of Critical Youth Studies. *Youth Media Reporter*, *2*(4), 1–30.

Behar, R. (1996). *The Vulnerable Observer: Anthropology That Breaks Your Heart*. Boston: Beacon Press.

Best, A. L. (2000). *Prom Night: Youth, Schools, and Popular Culture*. Abingdon: Routledge.

(2003). Doing Race in the Context of Feminist Interviewing: Constructing Whiteness through Talk. *Qualitative Inquiry*, *9*(6), 895–914.

(2005). *Fast Cars, Cool Rides: The Accelerating World of Youth and Their Cars*. New York: New York University Press.

(Ed.) (2007). *Representing Youth: Methodological Issues in Critical Youth Studies*. New York: New York University Press.

Bettie, J. (2003). *Women without Class: Girls, Race, and Identity*. Berkeley: University of California Press.

Cammarota, J. & Fine, M. (Eds.) (2010). *Revolutionizing Education: Youth Participatory Action Research in Motion*. New York: Routledge.

Clifford, J. (1988). *The Predicament of Culture: Twentieth-Century Ethnography, Literature, and Art*. Cambridge, MA: Harvard University Press.

Crosnoe, R. & Kirkpatrick Johnson, M. (2011). Research on Adolescence in the Twenty-First Century. *Annual Review of Sociology*, *37*, 439–460.

Davis, G. (2015). *Contesting Intersex: The Dubious Diagnosis*. New York: New York University Press.

DeVault, M. L. (1995). Ethnicity and Expertise: Racial-Ethnic Knowledge in Sociological Research. *Gender & Society*, *9*(5), 612–631.

Domínguez, V. (1994). A Taste for "the Other": Intellectual Complicity in Racializing Practices. *Current Anthropology*, *35*(4), 333–348.

(2000). For a Politics of Love and Rescue. *Cultural Anthropology*, *15*(3), 361–393.

Fields, J. (2008). *Risky Lessons: Sex Education and Social Inequality*. New Brunswick, NJ: Rutgers University Press.

Fine, G. & Sandstrom, K. (1988). *Knowing Children: Participant Observation with Minors*. Newbury Park, CA: Sage Publications.

Fine, M. (1988). Sexuality, Schooling, and Adolescent Females: The Missing Discourse of Desire. *Harvard Educational Review*, *58*(1), 29–54.

Fine, M. & McClelland, S.I. (2006). Sexuality Education and Desire: Still Missing after All These Years. *Harvard Educational Review*, *76*(3), 297–338.

Garcia, L. (2009) "Now Why Do You Want to Know about That?" Heteronormativity, Sexism, and Racism in the Sexual (Mis)Education of Latina Youth. *Gender & Society*, *23*(4), 520–541.

(2012). *Respect Yourself, Protect Yourself: Latina Girls and Sexual Identity*. New York: New York University Press.

Gilbert, J. (2014). *Sexuality in School: The Limits of Education*. Minneapolis: University of Minnesota Press.

Gilbert, J., Fields, J., Mamo, L., & Lesko, N. (2018). Intimate Possibilities: The Beyond Bullying Project and Stories of LGBTQ Sexuality and Gender in U.S. Schools. *Harvard Educational Review*, *88*(2), 163–183.

Gong, J. & Wright D. (2007). Context of Power: Young People as Evaluators. *American Journal of Evaluation*, *28*(3), 327–333.

hooks, b. (1994). *Teaching to Transgress: Education as the Practice of Freedom*. New York: Routledge.

(2000). *All about Love: New Visions*. New York: William Morrow.

Illouz, E. (1997). *Consuming the Romantic Utopia: Love and the Cultural Contradictions of Capitalism*. Berkeley: University of California Press.

Irvine, J. M. (2002). *Talk about Sex: The Battles over Sex Education in the United States*. Berkeley: University of California Press.

(2008). Transient Feelings: Sex Panics and the Politics of Emotions. *GLQ: A Journal of Lesbian and Gay Studies*, *14*(1), 1–40.

Jaggar, A. M. (1989). Love and Knowledge: Emotion in Feminist Epistemology. *Inquiry*, *32* (2), 151–176.

Kendall, N. (2013). *The Sex Education Debates*. Chicago: University of Chicago Press.

Kimmel, A., Williams, T. T., Veinot, T. C., et al. (2013). "I Make Sure I Am Safe and I Make Sure I Have Myself in Every Way Possible": African-American Youth Perspectives on Sexuality Education. *Sex Education*, *13*(2), 172–185.

King, M. L., Jr. (1981). *Strength to Love, 1963*. Philadelphia: Fortress.

Kleinman, S. & Copp, M. A. (1993). *Emotions and Fieldwork*. Newbury Park, CA: Sage Publications.

Lamb, S., Roberts, T., & Plocha, A. (2016). *Girls of Color, Sexuality, and Sex Education*. New York: Springer Nature.

Leadbeater, B. J. R., & Way, N. (Eds.). (1996). *Urban Girls: Resisting Stereotypes, Creating Identities*. New York: New York University Press.

Levine, J. (2002). *Harmful to Minors: The Perils of Protecting Children from Sex*. Minneapolis: University of Minnesota Press.

McClelland, S. I. & Fine, M. (2008). Embedded Science: Critical Analysis of Abstinence-Only Evaluation Research. *Cultural Studies Critical Methodologies*, *8*(5), 50–81.

Morris, M. W. (2016). *Pushout: The Criminalization of Black Girls in Schools*. New York: New Press.

Muñoz, J. E. (2005). Teaching Minoritarian Knowledge, and Love. *Women & Performance: A Journal of Feminist Theory*, *14*(2), 117–121.

(2009). *Cruising Utopia: The Then and There of Queer Futurity*. New York: New York University Press.

Omi, M. & Winant, H. (1994). *Racial Formation in the United States: From the 1960s to the 1990s*. New York: Routledge.

Peck, M. S. (1978). *The Road Less Traveled: A New Psychology of Love, Traditional Values and Spiritual Growth*. New York: Simon & Schuster.

Pérez, G. M. (2015). *Citizen, Student, Soldier: Latina/o Youth, JROTC, and the American Dream*. New York: New York University Press.

Picower, B. (2009). The Unexamined Whiteness of Teaching: How White Teachers Maintain and Enact Dominant Racial Ideologies. *Race Ethnicity and Education*, *12*(2), 197–215.

Ray, R. (2017). *The Making of a Teenage Service Class: Poverty and Mobility in an American City*. Berkeley: University of California Press.

Rios, V. M. (2011). *Punished: Policing the Lives of Black and Latino Boys*. New York: New York University Press.

Santelli, J., Ott, M.A., Lyon, M., Rogers, J, Summers, D., & Schleifer, R. (2006). Abstinence and Abstinence-Only Education: A Review of U.S. Policies and Programs. *Journal of Adolescent Health*, *38*(1), 72–81.

Schaffner, L. (2005). So-Called Girl-on-Girl Violence Is Actually Adult-on-Girl Violence. *Great Cities Institute Working Paper No. GCP-05–03*.

Shanahan, S. (2007). Lost and Found: The Sociological Ambivalence toward Childhood. *Annual Review of Sociology*, *33*, 407–428.

Swidler, A. (2013). *Talk of Love: How Culture Matters*. Chicago: University of Chicago Press.

Taft, J. K. (2010). *Rebel Girls: Youth Activism and Social Change across the Americas*. New York: New York University Press.

16 Difficulties in the Study, Research, and Pedagogy of Sexuality

Deborah P. Britzman

This chapter presents psychoanalytic approaches to thinking about child and adolescent sexuality with emphasis on the difficulties and obstacles made from its study, research, and pedagogy. Psychoanalysis treats sexuality as the erotic ecology of human relationality, affect, fantasy, belief, and thought (Green, 2000; Laplanche, 2011). With this primary focus on learning more from the makeup of the sensate life of the human condition, this chapter proposes that the emotional logic of developing expressions of sexuality challenges the adequacy of language and meaning. While notoriously difficult to educate and symbolize, sexuality serves as the psychic scenery for the human's on-going learning revolution, much of it driven by fantasy. From a psychoanalytic view, sexuality is not an acquired trait, a consequence of normality or maturity, a sudden eruption of too many hormones in adolescence, or, simply a culmination of object choice and identity. Rather, as backdrop for perceptions, fantasy, thinking, and desires, sexuality derives its stirring expressions and uneven development from bodily drives that have pressure, an internal source, an aim, and object. Each of these drive functions is at odds with one another (Freud, 1915a). My working suppositions are that from the beginning of life the mutability and proclivities of human sexuality involve its dispersal across wide-ranging human activity and interest, including areas not typically associated with sexuality. On these views, the origin, reach, and valences of sexuality constitute the primal difficulties in its symbolization with the added element of the vexing functions of sexuality itself (Freud, 1905).

Difficulties in Translating Sexuality

Sexuality can refer to sensate thoughts and the capacity for bodily excitement and pleasure. It can present as curiosity, interest, and the desire to master knowledge. Sexuality also references fantasies that excite imagination with scenarios of erotic ties, wishes, and gratification. Then too, sexuality incites passionate attachments to knowledge and love of beauty. Affectively, sexuality stretches into feelings of shame, disgust, and guilt. While associated with love and intimacy, sexuality may manifest as aggression, violence, and hatred (Glocer Fiorini, 2017; Stoller, 1986). As aggression, sexuality is also expressed through attachments to ideologies of desire "that call into being fantasies" of group origin, political anger, and a future without enemies (Young-Bruehl, 1996, pp. 185–187). As bodily excitement, sexuality is beholden to the sexual drives. Sexuality is the means by which the human translates their unique qualities of the otherness of psychical life that includes the transpositions of their libidinal history.

Freud (1905, 1915a) emphasizes variability with the argument that human sexuality begins with infantile life and its budding precociousness, as originally bisexual and polymorphously perverse. The sexual drives seek release from internal pressure and gratification is oriented by the pleasure principle. Any object, including the self, can be erotically charged. The element of perversity in the sexual drive refers to pleasure without social utility and Freud (1905) considers perversity a fundamental human characteristic (p. 191). In this light, while sexuality is seemingly related to an automatic and even careless urge for discharge, its expressions must be taken through psychical processes, affect, and fantasy. For these reasons, Freud separates the biological function of reproduction from sexuality *writ large* (Freud, 1905). He proposes the paradox that the aim of sexual excitement is the release of tension; yet, sexuality is that tension and thus resists satisfaction.

At the border between culture and biology and finding expression in nature and nurture, the reach and destiny of sexuality in the life worlds of childhood and adolescence are typically unacknowledged by the adult world. This supposed absence of meaning leads to adult failure to interpret and engage the sexual logic of childhood and adolescent longings, wishes, fantasies, theories, beliefs, and disappointments. Why this is the case is best explained with Freud's (1905) view on matters he terms "infantile sexuality" (p. 173) and "infantile amnesia" (p. 137). Both are qualities of sexuality and a challenge to their symbolization.

To grasp the meanings of infantile sexuality and infantile amnesia, the reader is advised to keep in mind three central psychoanalytic ideas. First, sexuality has an unconscious dimension. Second, Freud's theories center infantile sexuality inside family relations and as affecting child and adolescent anticipations for love, separation, and loss expressed through emotions such as jealousy, anger, grief, anxiety, and joy. Freud (1905, 1930) includes these affects as expressions of sexuality. His idea is that infancy and early childhood, subject as they are to dependency, helplessness, care, and erotic excitement, stand as life's most impressionable, unconscious, and repressed events. And third, due to "infantile amnesia," adults forget their earliest years and repress their childhood fantasies and wishes with the significant consequence that adults cannot understand their own childhood as the basis for their current experiences in love and loss (Freud, 1913, 1920, 1937). Forgetting is fuel for the cultural mythology that children are asexual and innocent and adolescents are plagued by hormones.

In referring to sexuality as a problem of the translation of otherness (e.g., polymorphous perversity, bisexuality, fantasy, infantile sexuality, the drives, and the unconscious), this chapter moves beyond a behavioral psychology of stimulus, response, and conditioning and those cognitive behavioral theories that privilege mind over matter. Readers are requested to keep an open mind and entertain the idea that sexuality, as ongoing learning revolution, is tied to fantasy and infantile wishes and, in this sense, the emotional logic of sexuality contains a failure for knowledge along with an intersubjective gap in trying to communicate this failure to others (Kristeva, 2000; Laplanche, 1989, 2011).

To specify the idea of the failure of translation, this chapter leans on the psychoanalytic view that sexuality, as an expression of bodily drives, seeks satisfaction through release of tension and serves as the means for and disturbance of symbolization (Freud, 1905; Klein, 1959). Yet, when the meanings of sexuality become symbolically equated with narrow conventions, laws, and prohibitions, when sexuality is considered only through the strictures of normality and pathology, and when sexuality is reduced to mature genital relations, sexuality can only be thought of as a split between freedom and subjection (Foucault, 1980). However, for children and adolescents, their emotional logic of desire trumps theories of social processes. Fantasies and wishes, due to their investments in the pleasure principle, are more persuasive and this holds for adults. Their mind too is rooted in infantile life (Klein, 1959). The fantasies and theories of sexuality created by children and adolescents involve all human emotions with the added elements of an unknown future, a revival of the past, and an uncertainty over bodily boundaries, while tasked with constructing a self and getting to know the world of others (Meltzer & Harris, 2011; Waddell, 2005). In order for adults to understand the sexuality of children and adolescents, they must sensitize their attention to the meanings behavior conveys or disguises and listen for the child and adolescent's emotional logic that fuses theories of infantile sexuality with ideality and anxiety over the fate of love (Britzman, 2006, 2016; Perret-Catipovic & Ladame, 1998; Phillips, 1998). Freud (1905) puts the adult dilemma in the form of advice: "The behavior of children at school, which confronts a teacher with plenty of puzzles, deserves in general to be brought into relation with their budding sexuality" (p. 203).

So, imagine sexuality. Imagine sexuality from its nomadic, infantile beginnings: the drive, the cry, the touch, and the breath dedicated to the skin, the voice, the gaze, the breast, the milk, the suck, the coo, and the hands of the other. Imagine then the erotic sensitivities of the mouth, the anus, the genitals, and the mind. Imagine, as Freud (1911) imagined, the infantile mind as swaying between the poles of the pleasure principle, or the wish for immediate gratification, and the reality principle as the experience of frustration, delay, and thinking. Imagine sexuality as the stirrings made from wanting, waiting, wishing, seeing, finding, losing, and desiring. Imagine sexuality as being and having and as active and passive. In this oceanic realm of affect, the symbolization of bodily activity is precarious. There is the bodily mix up of pain and pleasure experienced as tension in the theater of the mind (McDougall, 1995). From looking, overhearing, touching, and smelling, from being held and then holding, imagine sexuality. From the capture of the transitional object and the creation of the fetish, to the anguish made when objects are lost, imagine sexuality (Winnicott, 2001). Imagine sexuality as both affected and constituting. These impressive movements propose sexuality as registration, impression, disruption, and desire (Aulagnier, 2001).

Sexuality gives to us our desire for separation and union and for fantasy and recognition. Thinking of sexuality through its psychodynamics gives a clue as to what is most vulnerable in symbolizing human desire. Feelings are oceanic and deflated, and loved and hated. Both danger and safety and pleasure and pain seem to revolve around anticipation of losing and finding again the object of satisfaction (Green, 2000). But which object is thought to be sufficient? The right one, the wrong one, the accidental one, the no one, and the one unknown: who can really tell for sure? The human's porous erotic ecology may be its most radical proposal to the other and to transformations within the self. Yet, in trying to communicate the depth of this radical proposal, sexuality dissolves language into affect. With the problem of translation, sexuality can be thought of as an enigmatic message tied to the question, what does the other want from me? (Laplanche, 2011). Putting Eros to words may be the child's first difficulty and invention and one that persists in arguments over the place of sexuality in social theory, education, and political life (Britzman, 1998, 2015; Young-Bruehl, 1996).

With these free-ranging difficulties in the formulation of sexuality, Jean Laplanche's (1989) insistence that the human is a self-theorizing creature can now be joined with Julia Kristeva's (2000) formulation that thoughts, however nascent, are co-present with sexuality (p. 82). Kristeva's theories further develop Freud's (1915b, 1923) assumption of the dynamic unconscious dedicated to psychical reality that disrupts ordinary modes of conscious thoughts. An original discord or agitation then motivates the movements of thought. Freud's (1915a) term is "instinct," irreducible to need and in contemporary psychoanalytic discussions is referred to as "drives." He defines instinct from a dynamical psychological view: "An instinct appears to us as a concept on the frontier between the mental and the somatic, as the psychical representative of the stimuli originating from within the organism and reaching the mind, as a measure of the demand made upon the mind for work in connection with the body" (1915a, pp. 121–122). Of note in Freud's speculation is that body and mind are inseparable but not without conflict as to the meaning of bodily stimulations and its translation into thought, affect, fantasy, and activity. Despite Freud's abstract portrayal, his frame of the drives as an internal demand for sensate thought remains key for understanding the nature of child and adolescent urgency for action often accompanied by confusion when adults question their reasons. Their only reply is, "Because I felt like it."

Key Themes in the Study of Sexuality

The previous section introduced this chapter's theoretical frame for conceptualizing Freudian views on the origin of sexuality. The second section engages Freud's (1905) orientation to psychical development with the history of sexuality in the human sciences as proposed by Michel Foucault (1980, 1985, 1988). Both approaches have been central to debates over the logic and purpose of sex education for children and adolescents and are scaffolds for discussions in the fields of queer theory, feminism, and cultural studies (de Lauretis, 2010). Often, Freud and Foucault are treated as opposed to one another (Butler, 1993; Pinar, 1998; Warner, 1993), just as childhood sexuality has been considered as separate from that of adolescence and adulthood (Britzman, 2016). In the late twentieth century, the nature, course, and restrictions of sexuality revolved around debates of constructivism versus essentialism. The choice was put starkly: sexuality is either a mode of power/knowledge/pleasure, as Foucault (1980, 1985, 1988) claimed; or, sexuality is the root of cultural and individual proclivities to neurosis and perversion, as Freud (1905, 1930) stressed. While Freud and Foucault both utilize the archeological method for their theories of sexuality, each seemed to find its relics in different ruins. Freud begins with the relics of infancy, childhood, and adolescence as the buried past of human life, whereas Foucault finds in discourses of human science the discursive means for the subject to speak of the history of knowledge of sexuality.

Debates on essentialism and constructivism flounder on the vicissitudes of the course of human susceptibility to fantasy, beliefs, and narratives (Glocer Fiorini, 2017; Gozlan, 2015; Rose, 1986, 1992). The third section of this chapter extends the views of Freud and Foucault with the exemplary theories of Julia Kristeva, Jacqueline Rose, and Eve Kosofsky Sedgwick. These women emphasize the subject of language and focus sexuality with scenes of vulnerability, uncertainty, and transformation. They highlight the work of symbolization through its difficulties, gaps, and pleasures. Kristeva's (2000) literary psychoanalytic orientation presents sexuality as co-present with thought (p. 82). She argues that sexuality inaugurates the desire for narrative revolts, particularly for the adolescent and the artist. Rose (1986) invites feminists to think with the psychoanalytic theories of Jacques Lacan who focused on three registers of psychical and social life: the real, the imaginary, and the symbolic. Rose's question is whether an understanding of the depth, conflicts, and narratives of gender and sexuality would affect the ways in which sexual relations are understood. Sedgwick (1990) opens the homosexual/heterosexual divide, treating not ontology but epistemology as a strategy to deconstruct pernicious binary operations.

I think it is important to note that all of these feminist theorists stretch their concerns with the literary fictions of life and language play. Rose (1984, 1986, 2014) and Kristeva (2001a, 2001b) find in the lives of women and children a means to analyze world affairs. Sedgwick (1990, 1994, 1999, 2003) authored memoirs, studied the homoeroticism of canonical literature, wrote on the body and its illness, discussed fatness, and elaborated on Buddhist thought. Her (1990) theories in defense of gayness introduced antihomophobic inquiry into the study of sexuality (p. 4). Taken together, these three theorists bring into consideration the interrelations and breakdowns within sexual difference, otherness, and intersubjectivity. Childhood and adolescence, along with problems of love, are ever present in their work.

This chapter concludes with some challenges to research and pedagogy. Of special interest is how the fields of psychoanalysis, feminism, and queer theory open creative ways to learn from the affective tensions between sexuality and culture, biology and meaning, and sexuality and intersubjectivity. Here are my questions: Why has sexuality been such a problem for imagining the relationship between social change and transformations of knowledge? What does the little child as subject have to do with these conflicts? Can research and pedagogy move beyond the entrenched binary conflict of nature versus culture on the one hand, and the individual versus discourse on the other hand? Must we choose between biology and meaning? Or, can a focus on studies of childhood and adolescent sexuality serve as pathway for a deeper understanding of the vulnerabilities and pleasures of symbolization?

Problems of Origins

Freud and Foucault are known for their interest in analyzing obstacles to thinking. More generally, their concern is with places where we are not thinking. For Freud, the place where we are not thinking begins with the body: the drives, the unconscious, and the displacements of bodily impressions onto the wider world. Freud turns to psychical reality and its claims on perception, fantasy, wish, and the ego's mechanisms of defense against anxiety.

Foucault (1983) stresses the specificities of technologies of power in tandem with the functions of regimes of discourse and treated both as regulating and producing the subject. He analyzed institutional practices that seem to think for us: education, medicine, and government, and hospitals, prisons, and schools. These practices subject us to the actions of others, form the scaffolds of and desire for self-knowledge and identity, and affect the ways we imagine the normal, the pathological, and care of the self.

So how have Freud and Foucault approached the difficulties in symbolizing sexuality? Foucault (1980) asks how practices of sexuality became tied to the social mechanisms of power, discourse, pleasure, identity, and knowledge. For Freud (1927) social mechanisms have a psychical life and, indeed, given their human origins, they too carry out psychological functions. In his studies on culture and group psychology, for example, Freud turns to the problem of unhappiness and discontentedness. He (1930) treats culture through its restrictions on drives and as social prohibitions and includes the rule to love thy neighbor as containing unreasonable demands that lead to neurotic, psychotic, and perverse trends. But Freud (1905) also suggests an unsolvable internal demand with his view that sexuality resists satisfaction even as the drives seek release from tension.

Discourse and Research

Foucault

Foucault (1980, 1985, 1988) wrote three volumes on the histories of sexuality. He questions the ways researchers and social theorists present a history of the subject and in so doing, they too become subject to the workings of power, knowledge, and pleasure. His first volume, *The History of Sexuality*, introduces a plan of study that surveys three hundred years of mechanisms, techniques, and institutions in the human sciences and Western Christianity whereby sexuality becomes a discourse of differentiating, categorizing, and problematizing bodies. Foucault gives Freud his due with the pointed comment that, while from a contemporary vantage it may be easy to denounce Freud for normalizing sexuality, "the fact remains that in the great family of technologies of sex ... of all the institutions that set out in the ninetieth century to medicalize sex, [psychoanalysis] was the one, up to the decade of the nineteen forties, that rigorously opposed the political and institutional effects of the perversion-heredity-degenerescence system" (1980, p. 119).

Foucault asks the modern question: who have we become? Or, what has happened to us that we think and act in a particular way? "For a long time, the story goes, we supported a Victorian regime, and we continue to be dominated by it even today. Thus the image of the imperial prude is emblazoned on our restrained, muted and hypocritical sexuality" (Foucault, 1980, p. 3). With two short sentences Foucault introduces the myths of passive history – "the story goes" – and, what he thinks of as problems with the belief in "the repressive hypothesis." Briefly, the repressive hypothesis promotes the view that power, like a King, bears down on the docile body of the subject. Foucault considers power not as repressive but as circulating. As actions upon actions, power incites sexuality rather than limits it. Two of Foucault's (1980) examples concern: (1) the simultaneous occurrence of psychiatric pathologicalization of homosexuality as degenerate identity with homosexual claims for the right to an identity, and (2) in terms of the figure of the child, the moral panic over masturbation that leads to an incitement to pedagogy, school psychology, and the new field of social hygiene in school curriculum (p. 40). Once actions became sutured to identity, Foucault argues, sexuality is no longer merely one kind of practice among others but instead is taken as constituting the truth of the self. Indeed, Foucault's (1980) archeology of sexuality in medical, governmental, and pedagogical discourse relates the late nineteenth and twentieth century human science's investment in tying sexuality to identity as the incitement to narrate, examine, confess, and teach. Elizabeth Young-Bruehl (1996) finds a comparable dynamic in her study of prejudices. She proposes these procedures as incitements for structures of adolescent education: "the greater the felt danger of puberty the more education is called to the rescue – specifically, the education for self control ... [By] reinforcing the idea that puberty is explosive, education ... promoted hysteria and then got progressively better at promoting obsessionality" (p. 333).

Foucault's second volume, *The Use of Pleasure*, notes again his three axes of inquiry into sexuality: "(1) the formation of sciences *(saviors)* that refer to it, (2) the systems of power that regulate its practice, (3) the forms within which individuals are able, are obliged, to recognize themselves as subjects of this sexuality" (1985, p. 4). From there, however, his second volume focuses not on science but its antecedents: the antiquity of fear, morality, and conduct, along with the study of ethics and the development of the idea of true love. His history of sexuality links the problem of telling the truth to the self-reflective practices this required. In this second volume, Foucault analyzes practices of the self with the problem of transformation: "The object was to learn to what extent the effort to think one's own history can free thought from what it silently thinks, and so enable it to think differently" (1985, p. 9). Knowledge of self is thus tied to a notion of critical self-reflection that no longer accepts "the order of things" as Foucault (2001) puts it in his genealogy of the human sciences.

His (1988) third volume, *The Care of the Self*, stands as a careful reading of fourth century Roman ancient texts written to instruct on matters of everyday life. Foucault traces the subtle means by which thinking sexuality became associated with illness and health, body and soul, austerity and constraint, and self-examination and morality. Care refers to the activities that prescribed ways in which free men of antiquity cultivated their knowledge of self through such practices as gymnastics, daily exercise, journal writing, mediation, control of diet, recording daily bodily practices and activities, and so on. The major principle or demand was "take care of oneself" (p. 43). The volume begins with the activity of how to interpret dreams as forecast for values and in relation to proper and improper social conduct. The austerity of rules for sexual conduct instructed ethical relations to others. This last volume focuses on the discourse regimes of the body and the arts of living. He concludes with descriptions of ancient texts that instructed on matters of the rules for social intercourse, marital relations, and man–boy love. Eros would then be linked to a rigorous discipline, rationalizations for the practices of the self, and anxiety over the health of the soul.

Freud

In the beginning of the twentieth century and just a few years into his discovery of the unconscious, Freud (1905) wrote "Three Essays on Sexuality." His topics were sexual aberrations, infantile sexuality, and transitions in puberty. The groundwork for this study was laid out in his three earlier books on dream interpretation, jokes, and everyday mistakes. Sleep, laughter, and errors are both estranging and familiar to us all and, for Freud, opened studies of unconscious life and an analysis of its eruptions of pleasure and wishes that go against the conventions of morality and reason. His purpose in "Three Essays on Sexuality" is to specify human variability of love, happiness, and unhappiness as rooted in impressive early life. In privileging the erotic body as the object of psychoanalytic thought, studies of sexuality would have to grapple with unconscious motives and fantasies in conflict with a history of social and family attitudes and demands.

Freud (1905) returned to his "Three Essays on Sexuality" over a 20-year period. He added more footnotes, drew upon the young field of child psychoanalysis, and, from there, reformulated his early speculations. These essays are worth revisiting as they form the backdrop, not only of Freudian theory, but also may give contemporary readers insight into what we inherit as we try to sketch the relation between difficulties in understanding our own sexuality and that of others.

Freud's views radically transformed what counts as sexual, when masculinity and femininity count, and what counts as normality and pathology. He treats sexuality as a psychical constellation, developed from an idea that is not founded in reproach: "In the sphere of sexual life we are brought up against particular and, indeed, insoluble difficulties as soon as we try to draw a sharp line to distinguish mere variations within the range of what is physiological from pathological symptoms" (Freud, 1905, pp. 160–161). These essays of the early Freud (1905) propose the interweaving of three counter-arguments. The first argument dated the advent of sexuality to the beginning of life and infantile life was depicted through its polymorphous perversity (meaning we can make any object a sexual object, including ourselves) and bisexuality (meaning the capacity for both homosexual and heterosexual choice of object). The second argument is that sexuality does not have a natural course and, indeed, there is no such thing as a normal sexuality. The third argument is that sexuality, originally infantile, creates the child's desire for knowledge and mastery, and so between the third and fifth year of life, the child experiences the urge for sexual research. When Freud (1905) calls the child a sexual researcher, he proposes the child's desire to know its origin as both a step toward autonomy in thinking and a step back to infantile life. Then, and now, the most disputed debates concern Freud's view that the child's curiosity is tied to erotic pleasure and the creation of wishful fantasies rather than as a consequence of external trauma. His other insistence is that very young children are astute observers of the circulation of love in family life and will create some sort of mashed-up meaning from what they see and hear but do not yet understand.

His (1905) first essay, "The Sexual Aberrations," is inclusive: the cause or origin of the choice of the object is variable. Neither homosexuality nor heterosexuality can be caused or explained away. Freud supposes that the choice of the object is due to a mix up of constitution, accidents, experience, and desire (pp. 170–171). In this opening essay, aberrations are the model for understanding sexuality and by beginning there Freud denaturalizes the course of sexuality.

Freud's second essay "Infantile Sexuality," provides the foundation for his claims of sexuality in childhood and its infantile roots: "We have good reason to believe that there is no period at which the greater capacity for receiving and reproducing impressions is greater than precisely during the years of childhood" (1905, p. 175). Infantile sexuality, Freud admits, is difficult to imagine, unless one looks carefully at what the child is doing during thumb-sucking or even earlier, when taking the breast into the mouth. Freud then considers this earliest enjoyment with the breast as the template for adult sexuality: "No one who has seen a baby sinking back satiated from the breast and falling asleep with flushed cheeks and a blissful smile can escape the reflection that this picture persists as a prototype of the expression of sexual satisfaction in later life" (1905, p. 182). And, in this bliss the sexual drive becomes detached from need and hunger and, even when satisfied, aims for more pleasure. Thumb-sucking, Freud believes, creates new pleasures beyond the breast: a preference for one's own skin that is more readily available, an experience of both sucking and touching oneself, a feeling of independence from the world of others, and the self-stimulation of an erotic zone. He sums up the qualities of infantile sexuality: "At its origin it attaches itself to one of the vital somatic functions; it has as yet no sexual object, and thus is auto-erotic; and its sexual aim is dominated by an erotogenic zone" (1905, pp. 182–183). Most important is that experiences of pleasure seek to repeat an early and lost satisfaction. The object, in Freud's formulation, is retroactive and comes after the aim.

Freud's (1905) third essay, "Transformations of Puberty," focuses on the problems of adolescent sexual excitation as the build-up of tension and release with a fulsome mental constellation founded by the drives. It is here that the idea of adolescence enters psychoanalytic discussion. In adolescence, the capacity to act upon bodily excitations, Freud argues, brought a different consideration to the meanings of the genitals and a new awareness and attitude toward sexual difference. The third essay is the most conservative on distinguishing developments in female sexuality and is well criticized within contemporary psychoanalysis (e.g., see Abrevaya & Thomson-Salo, 2015; Glocer Fiorini, 2017; Gozlan, 2015; Kristeva, 2001b; Rose, 1986). Of most value, however, is Freud's observation that, for adolescents, fantasies of sexuality dominate mental life and retain echoes of infantile sexuality.

When Freud (1905) wrote "Three Essays on Sexuality," the child's natality and its susceptibility to and dependence upon parental love and family life were not thought of as the germs for the child's sexuality. Nor was the child seen as subject to sexual drives or even curious about her/his own origin, the mysteries of grown-up love, or the question of sexual difference. Neglected sexuality, Freud supposed, signifies more than cultural repression. Adult forgetting of her/his own sexual research in early life is due to the psychological factor of infantile amnesia discussed earlier in this chapter. Adults forget their earliest jealousy, hatreds, and passionate, although impossible, desires. But they remain subject to the derivatives of sexuality through feelings of shame, guilt, and moral anxiety. The affective element of sexuality leads to its own repression in the form of the separation of affect from ideation. Yet the accords of sexuality carry memory disturbances, calmed, or repressed in latency. Freud's argument is that something within the sexual drive causes it to awaken, sleep, and sublimate; the roots of latency and sublimation are in infantile sexuality.

Freud's theories of the infancy of sexuality propose the problem of symbolization. He supposes the child's sexual researches and the theories made are doomed to fail. Nonetheless, these erotic efforts, just as with the sucking of the thumb, remain, for Freud, quite important: "They constitute a first step towards taking an independent attitude in the world, and imply a high degree of alienation of the child from the people in his environment who formerly enjoyed his confidence" (1905, p. 197). Freud's argument, based on his clinical and autobiographical work, is that the child's research and desire to master knowledge gives way to separateness and singularity, and then, specifically after the period of latency, creates new lifelong problems such as alienation, loss of mastery, and uncertainty over what the other wants (Britzman, 2011, 2016).

Freudianism is accused of being a theory of pansexualism. Today, psychoanalysis continues to be disparaged as interpreting everything as sexual. Freud was quite aware of this reception. He took great pains to give the reach of sexuality new definitions: sexuality as a bodily mental constellation, as in excess of reproductive functions and, due to infantile sexuality, notoriously difficult to educate. How do such unworldly drives incite research, politics, pedagogy, and social change? In any relation with children and adolescence, when addressing sexuality, adults face a riddle and paradox that they too have experienced once before. The riddle concerns, what counts as sexuality? The paradox belongs to the human problem of the drive for knowledge, itself a quality of sexuality: the more anxious and uncertain we are about the development of sexuality and its basis in fantasy life, the more we create harsh procedures dedicated to certainty and control.

Claims for Sexuality

The Foucauldian view that human practices of knowledge create the subject and object of inquiry serves as pressure points for relating the history of sexuality in contiguity with discursive forms of power. Foucault specifies two meanings of the subject: "subject to someone else by control and dependence, and tied to his own identity by a conscious or self-knowledge. Both meanings suggest a form of power which subjugates and makes subject to" (1983, p. 212). While keeping intact the relations among the drive to knowledge, identity, and subjection, Foucault's conception of discourse turns away from the receptivity and impressions of psychical life and instead focuses the practices that form the subject. Some indicators for guiding research and critique follow from Foucault's inquiries.

First, as an effect of power/knowledge/pleasure sexuality is given a history formed through technologies of regulation and subjection to self-knowledge. The meanings of sexuality are neither a natural phenomena nor a floating boat tossed on the stream of discourse. Discourses of the human sciences give the subject names, identities, purposes, and investments in the circulation of power. Second, it is difficult to think of sexuality without the twin problems of the repressive hypothesis and the accompanying promise for liberation, enlightenment, truth, and identity. Third, sexuality becomes tied to and regulated by self and cultural practices. Sexuality is then an incitement to discourse urging the subject to speak, to confess, to read, to write, and to translate bodily erotic practices into a sexual identity. Foucault's view developed the idea that the human sciences and its knowledge both incite and produce sexuality. Consequently, even activities that seem neutral such as school examinations, can have an erotic basis. And fourth, discourses of sexuality subject the individual to relations of power, pleasure, identity, and self-knowledge. The tension is that due to its circulating power, discourse is unstable and made so by the subject's procedures of interpretation, transgression, and resistance.

Freud can be read as articulating five interrelated claims for thinking with sexuality in mind. It should be evident by now that the Freudian frame emerges from the study of the natality and its psychical and social transformations animated by family life and being with others. In this sense, the consequences of development, as an emotional situation, are uneven and best approached as admixture of accidents, circumstances, history, and the proclivities of character.

First, sexuality is diverse, variable, and multilayered in expression. While object choice is one facet, humans have the capacity to sexualize any activity. Second, children are not empty vessels waiting to be filled with knowledge and fantasies are more persuasive than are the facts of life. Third, sexuality leans on a forgotten history of lost objects and enigmatic messages. Fourth, sexuality develops unevenly and is subject to regression, fixations, and repression. The child's early precocity lays the grounds for her/his infantile theories of sexuality. Such exciting theories are then subject to latency or an amnesiac period of deferral; and the return of sexuality in adolescence opens into adolescent preoccupation with fantasy, belief, and ideality. And, fifth, precocious sexuality creates a failure of theory due to its infantile beginnings. The failure also resides within the sexual drive's tendency to resist satisfaction.

While the key debates between Freud and Foucault have revolved around whether sexuality is essentially innate or formed through discursive structures, a close reading of these theorists can bring readers into a different understanding, precisely due to the fact that the destiny of knowledge, whether it be that of psychical life or organizations of the human science, must lean on the impossible human desire for mastery, thought here as a quality of infantile sexuality.

Vulnerability and Symbolization: Three Exemplary Thinkers

In her study of the history and use of children's literature, Jacqueline Rose proposes a stunning claim for reading Freud to children:

> We have been reading the wrong Freud to children.
>
> We do not realize that Freud was first brought up against the unconscious when asking how we remember ourselves as a child. . . . The most crucial aspect of psychoanalysis for discussing children's fiction is its insistence that childhood is something in which we continue to be implicated and which is never simply left behind.

> We have been reading the wrong Freud to children, because this is the most reductive, even if it is the most prevalent, reading of Freud. It is reductive to the extent that it holds off the challenge, which is present in Freud's own work, to the very notion of identity, development and subjective cohesion, which this conception of childhood is so often used to sustain.
>
> (1986, p. 13)

Contemporary psychoanalysis, feminism, and queer theory have taken the challenge of new readings of Freud in order to engage the uneven, discordant relations within the individual and the social, and do so as affected, given that the object of inquiry is the subject of human life.

Teresa de Lauretis, for example, argues that sexuality proposes a question of translation due to "the stubborn drive . . . [And] the queer space of the drive or what Freud means when he says that the drive is a frontier concept."(2010, p. 13). Indeed, Freud (1920) thought of the life and death drives as residing between the psyche and the soma. He named the drives as his great mythology and needed a conceptual invention to articulate the psychical vicissitudes of internal bodily pressures and to speculate on human development as subject to regression, repetition, and aggression. De Lauretis (1991) coined the term "queer theory" as a provocation to deconstruct normality and to construct a means for analyzing the relation between binary thinking and moral panics provoked when sexuality is linked to fantasies of normality. And queer theory, much of it relying on psychoanalytic and Foucauldian formulations, has provided children, adolescents, early childhood educators, high school teachers, teacher educators, and social theorists with strategies of critiques of normalization, new reading practices, and a surprising vocabulary for welcoming the complex desires of children and adolescents (e.g., see, Barber & Clark, 2002; Bolt & Salvio, 2006; Facundo, 2016; Gilbert, 2014; Kincaid, 1992; Meiners & Quinn, 2012; and Stockton, 2009). The three exemplary theorists discussed later provide new frames for thinking beyond binary splitting with a view toward an interest in symbolization that can accommodate elements of human incoherence.

Julia Kristeva

Kristeva's early work focused on abjection and horror and then to creativity, civil rights, art, and literature. She is known for her work in semiotics, although just as pertinent is her contemporary psychoanalytic discussions of Freud and Melanie Klein along with her work as a psychoanalyst (2000, 2001b, 2010). Kristeva's (1995) psychoanalytic writing introduced the term "new maladies of the soul," by which she means that modern life and the social and internal demands to be a well-formed, normal person effectuate new forms of depression, obsessionality, the syndrome of adolescent ideality, the need to believe, and inhibitions in creativity. How does Kristeva link these preoccupations to sexuality?

Kristeva proposes psychoanalysis as ". . . a theory not of sexuality exclusively but of the development of thought co-present to sexuality" (2000, p. 82). No doubt, she adds, this insistence is disturbing since thought is more readily linked to rationality, consciousness, and reason. She continues, "Psychoanalysis neither biologizes nor sexualizes the essence of man but emphasizes the copresence of sexuality and thought" (p. 82). While language links sexuality to thought "what the human says does not subsume sexuality" (2000, p. 3). Given the constitutive gap proposed by infantile sexuality, Kristeva further argues that intellection and language are small features of sexual desire (2000, p. 33). Her third term, the unconscious, borders sexuality and thought. Kristeva's approach is based on the tension between sexuality and language, discussed earlier in this chapter as a failure of translation.

Kristeva's (1995, 2000, 2010) inquiries into the problem of the desire to become a speaking subject propose that individuals are not caught in lack but in vulnerability due to intersubjectivity. Where does the disappointed patrilineal subject turn? She identifies new maladies of the soul to include addictions to: consumerism, self-help guides, the remote control, the universe of television, and the information highway. She also argued that the disappointed subject might turn to words, art, creativity, and, perhaps, even to the analyst.

Kristeva centers then the excitable drive-ridden emotional world: its ups and downs, affect storms, dissociative closures, and vulnerabilities. The emotional world, she argues, is a requirement for and effect of the "co-presence of thought and sexuality" (2000, p. 82). This combination subjects us to overstimulation: obsessive thoughts, addiction to sex, cutting, anxiety, and depression. The balance, or copresence, is precarious. Must one overrule the other? Is it thought or sexuality that is swayed by consumer culture and the desire to belong to an ideology? Is it culture, drives, or infantile theories that invest in bad romance and exciting fads doomed to go out of date? As for today, Kristeva maintains that the conflict between universality and difference has a new flavor:

> It is no longer a matter of conforming to the universal (in the best cases, everyone aspiring to the same values, human rights, for example) or asserting one's difference (ethnic, religious, sexual) as untouchable and sacred; still less of fighting one of these tendencies with the other or simply and skillfully combining them. It is a matter of pushing the need for the universal *and* the need for singularity to the limit in each individual, making this simultaneous movement the source of both thought and language. "There is meaning": this will be my universal. And "I" use words of the tribe to inscribe my singularity. *Je est un autre* ("I is another"): this will be my difference, and "I" will express my specificity by distorting the nevertheless necessary clichés of the codes of communication and by constantly deconstructing ideas/concepts/ideologies/philosophies that "I" have inherited . . .
>
> Other eras have had this experience. Its radicalness, however, is unique in our century, one of education and information.
>
> (2000, p. 19)

If, as Kristeva argues, our century is "one of education and information," it is also characterized by brainwashing, ideality, virtual reality, and miscommunication.

And, we are left to wonder, how then to have a mind of one's own and want to invest in the idea that "there is meaning"? This question is particularly urgent for adolescents who, as discussed earlier by Freud (1905), are mesmerized, against all odds, by their sexual fantasies.

Kristeva analyzes the dominance of fantasy as indicating "the adolescent syndrome of ideality" (2007, p. 714). Her argument is that, while the child was once a researcher motived by a drive for curiosity, the adolescent has given up research and seeks instead perfection with certainty that it must exist. The form this certainty takes is a belief in paradise and the adolescent defenses involve the ego mechanisms of isolation of meaning from affect and the splitting of the object into only good or bad. The force of belief tends to obliterate ambiguity and ambivalence and seems to serve what Young-Bruehl (1996, pp. 184–185) identifies as "ideologies of desire" that underscore fundamentalist politics. In one way, the syndrome of ideality is a more forceful version of infantile theories of sexuality. The ideality of perfection – whether it takes the form of desire for a perfect body, a world without conflict, a perfect romance, flawless beauty, utopian politics, and so on – is a defense against imperfection and vulnerability. Inevitably, both the defense and fantasy fail, leaving the adolescent to withdraw in disappointment and depression (Tamaki, 2013). In Kristeva's terms: "a new type of speaking subject who *believes in the existence of the erotic object* (the object of desire and/or love). He only seeks because he is convinced it must exist. The *adolescent is not a researcher in a laboratory, he's a believer*. We are all adolescents when we are enthralled by the absolute" (2007, p. 717, italics original).

Perhaps Kristeva's greatest contribution to an understanding of adolescence belongs to her views on the syndrome of ideality and that adolescence persists in the life world of the adult mind. To break open this claustrum of belief, certainty, and a turn away from ambivalence in meaning, and to begin again to translate and research, adults must privilege modes of desire dependent on questioning, thinking, and analyzing. The adult must say to the adolescent, "I want you to think with me, even if thinking also involves your mental pain and the challenge of its translation."

Jacqueline Rose

Rose introduced to British feminism the psychoanalytic writing of Jacques Lacan, first by translating into English Lacan's seminar *Feminine Sexuality* (Mitchell & Rose, 1985) and, then, with her analysis of sexuality and vision (Rose, 1986). Rose presented Lacan's twin claims that (1) the woman does not exist and (2) there is no such thing as a sexual relation (1986, p. 70). These formulations do require mental gymnastics and a capacity to think against the mythologies of a unified self and sexual cohesion by paying close attention to the operations of language. The problem engaged in Lacan's first claim was that "the woman" is not an absolute category. "The woman, therefore, is *not*, because she is defined purely against the man (she is the negative of that definition – 'man *is* not woman') and because this very definition is designated by fantasy, a set which may well be empty" (Rose, 1986, p. 74).

In opposition to Lacan's view, de Beauvoir (2011), for instance, places the question of woman into the immediacy of psychosocial existence and lack of social status. She argued that the woman is not born but made. Rose (1986) troubles this social construction since it cannot settle the vexing signifiers of femininity and masculinity. For this reason, Rose introduced Lacan into conversation with feminists.

Rose points out that Lacan was interested in the workings of the symbolic law and its demand that two genders line up with biology. Psychoanalysis encounters this biology and must move, Rose argues, "towards a recognition of the fully social constitution of identity and norms, and then back again to that point of tension between ego and unconscious where they are endlessly remodeled and endlessly break" (1986, p. 7). While we are constrained by the world, constraint is also an element of our inner world due to the fact the ego is divided and subject to the unconscious. There is no absolute position that can guarantee the separateness and stability of masculinity and femininity (Gherovici, 2017; Gozlan, 2015).

The other problem Rose (1986) proposes for feminism belongs to Lacan's insistence that there is no sexual relation. Lacan considers sexuality as resistance to identity and communication. His view follows from Freud's (1905) theory that something within the sexual drives resists satisfaction. At the heart of ego, life is both incoherence or non-unity and the defense against the real. The ego's solution is to idealize sexual relations within the realm of the imaginary. In the earliest years idealization plays out through the child's love of the parent and the fantasy that a better family awaits the child. For adolescence, as discussed earlier in this chapter, the idealization of love leads to the wish for a perfect relation and the "incredible need to believe" (Kristeva, 2009, p. 3). Lacan was pointing to a tension between need and demand, between recognition and misrecognition, between knowledge and ignorance, and between the position of man or woman. This is one way to conceive of Lacan's view that there is no sexual relation. "For Lacan," Rose writes, "that break is always within language, it is the break of the subject in language" (1986, p. 76). Rose's important concern to this chapter's discussion turns on specifying the object of sexuality. Must the object of sexuality be objectified? Or, is the object made unreal in order to be phantasized and enjoyed? The new problem is where to locate this alienation: in the sexual relation, in the non-relation that is sexuality, or within the sexual drives that carry a resistance to satisfaction?

Eve Kosofsky Sedgwick

Sedgwick's, *Epistemology of the Closet*, proposes that Western culture is affected and split by the "crisis of homo/heterosexual definition, indicatively male" (1990, p. 1). She argues for a critical reappraisal of this binary logic through a theory she named "antihomophobic inquiry" (p. 4). The difficulty, Sedgwick supposes, begins with defining sexuality without the closet. Her important question remains whether homosexuality can matter to how heterosexuality becomes elaborated. But, rather than reversing the binary, Sedgwick proposes a universalizing view of sexuality that could account for human variation as its feature. Are there words we can claim for sexuality that does not disavow otherness?

Sedgwick's orientation expands Foucault's approach through semiotic distinctions: "that modern Western culture has placed what it calls sexuality in a more and more distinctively privileged relation to our most prized constructs of individual identity, truth, knowledge . . . that the language of sexuality not only intersects with but transforms the other languages and relations by which we know" (1990, p. 3). So, on the one hand, Sedgwick situates thoughts of sexuality as immersed in a problem of language. On the other hand, to grasp the language of sexuality, one must study what is not said. Her model then involves opening the closet with its epistemology.

Sedgwick's epistemological rule for the closet is worth quoting: "In dealing with an open-secret structure, it's only by being shameless about risking the obvious that we happen into the vicinity of the transformative" (1990, p. 22). This measure then led to her formulation of a number of axioms dedicated to the open frame of uneven development. I quote just of few of Sedgwick's axioms:

> *Axiom 1: People are different from each other* (italics original, p. 22).
>
> *Axiom 2: The study of sexuality is not coextensive with the study of gender; correspondingly, antihomophobic inquiry is not coextensive with feminist inquiry. But we can't know in advance how they will be different* (italics original, p. 27).
>
> *Axiom 3: The immemorial, seemingly ritualized debates on nature versus nurture take place against a very unstable background of tacit assumptions and fantasies about both nurture and nature* (italics original, p. 41).
>
> *Axiom 7: The paths of allo-identification are likely to be strange and recalcitrant. So are the paths of auto-identification* (italics original, p. 59).

If people are different from each other and if this difference plays through sexuality – in debates over its definition and propriety, in its slides into infantile fantasy and ideality, and, in the conflicts among structure, experience, and language – if all these tensions are true in that they affect our imagination, then it may be best to treat sexuality as a soft, pliable, and impressible and subject to affect, fantasy, and defense as well as to narrative revolt.

Taken together, Rose, Kristeva, and Sedgwick highlight sexuality in tandem with thought and as such constitute emotional logic to be translated and engaged. Their work brings into awareness novel styles for listening needed to the fate of ideality, the splitting off of affect from ideas, and the centrality of fantasy. In emphasizing a symbolic relational turn, and in considering aspects of vulnerability founded by self/other love, these theorists argue that understanding sexuality begins with an open-ended capacity to listen to a far more complex sense of development. Their approaches to sexuality lead to some listening guidelines for adults to think with children and adolescents:

- Stay close to uncertainty, incompleteness, and vulnerability
- Follow emotional oscillations and the eruption of affect and fantasy
- Become interested in where and why words evoke anxiety
- Attend to failure of translation as an indication of desire
- Study emotional logic and the need to believe
- Listen for fantasies involving ideality and rigidity of belief

Research Urgencies

De Certeau's definition of historiographical research suggests that it is obstacles, the things we do not know, that set the researcher to work. "Research," he argues, "no longer merely seeks successful comprehension. It returns to things it cannot understand. It measures by fortifying its needs and methods" (1988, p. 39). While de Certeau was advising adult researchers, it is not a big leap to recall precocious research, namely that of the child's earliest sexual researches composed from infantile theories and magical thinking. And too, recall that the adolescent protest carries forward a fossilized infantile sexuality but now as a fortification for fantasy, ideality, and ideologies of desire. In this sense, adolescents cannot leave what they think they already know and are compelled to exchange research with ideality and fantasies of belief. There is also a buried research belonging to infantile amnesia that has as its consequence adult failure to translate the reach of sexuality in the life world of the mind.

Adults, who work with children and adolescence as they are affected by these competing styles of research, may still develop a capacious view of the reach and startles in imagining what seems unimaginable in sexuality. The idea that sexuality provokes a theory of knowledge means one must ask what kind of theory is made, what role fantasy plays in the desire for knowledge, and what echoes of infantile sexuality resonate with the need to believe. In asking these questions, researchers, teachers, and those charged with the well-being of children and adolescents can be more inventive with linking sexuality to the problem of developing minds. Enlightenment models that provide information and that propose transcendence from ignorance into knowledge do not transfer to proper behavior. Pedagogy will have to open studies of love in its variability within life's passions and fantasies, and consider the push for and against intersubjectivity (Britzman, 2015). This chapter, then, has argued that, if sexuality can serve as an index to affect, drive, fantasy, and desire, adults, children, and adolescents are already involved in fascinating difficulties of symbolization. In freely associating with the problem of thinking sexuality as the slow work of animating the desire for a mind, we can pay close attention to the copresence of sexuality and thought. Surely these learning urgencies – those made from origin, vulnerability, discourse, and symbolization – may be treated as pathways for listening to the emotional logic of children and adolescents. These urgencies of learning may also be the means for adults to encourage an opening to symbolization dedicated to respect for speaking subjects, courage with words, a curiosity toward the twists and surprises of desire and, an audacity for conceptualizing the ongoing challenges of developing life, love, and sexuality.

References

Abrevaya, E. & Thomson-Salo, F. (Eds.) (2015). *Homosexualities: Psychogenesis, Polymorphism, and Countertransference*. London: Karnac Books.

Aulagnier, P. (2001). *The Violence of Interpretation: From Pictogram to Statement*. Trans. A. Sheridan. London: Routledge Press.

Barber, S. & Clark, D. (Eds.) (2002). *Regarding Sedgwick: Essays on Queer Culture and Critical Theory*. New York: Routledge Press.

Bolt, G. & Salvio, P. (Eds.) (2006). *Love's Return: Psychoanalytic Essays on Childhood, Teaching, and Learning*. New York: Routledge Press.

Britzman, D. (1998). *Lost Subjects, Contested Objects: Toward a Psychoanalytic Theory of Learning*. Albany: State University of New York Press.

(2006). Little Hans, Fritz and Ludo: On the Curious History of Gender in the Psychoanalytic Archive. *Studies in Gender and Sexuality* 7(2), 113–140.

(2011). *Freud and Education*. New York: Routledge Press.

(2015). *A Psychoanalyst in the Classroom: On the Human Condition of Education*. Albany: State University of New York Press.

(2016). *Melanie Klein: Early Analysis, Play and the Question of Freedom*. London: Springer Press.

Butler, J. (1993). *Bodies That Matter: On the Discursive Limits of "Sex."* New York: Routledge.

de Beauvoir, S. (2011). *The Second Sex*. Trans. C. Borde and S. Malovany-Chevallier. New York: Knopf.

de Certeau, M. (1988). *The Writing of History*. Trans. T. Conley. New York: Columbia University Press.

de Lauretis, T. (1991). Queer Theory: Lesbian and Gay Sexualities, an Introduction. *Differences* 3 (2), iii–xviii.

(2010). *Freud's Drive: Psychoanalysis, Literature and Film*. New York: Palgrave Macmillan.

Facundo, A.C. (2016). *Oscillations of Literary Theory: The Paranoid Imperative and Queer Reparative*. Albany: State University of New York Press.

Foucault, M. (1980). *The History of Sexuality, Vol. 1: An Introduction*. Trans. R. Hurley. New York: Vintage Press.

(1983). Afterword: The Subject and Power. In H. Dreyfus & P. Rabinow (Eds.), *Michel Foucault: Beyond Structuralism and Hermeneutics, Second Edition* (208–226). Chicago: University of Chicago Press.

(1985). *The Use of Pleasure, Vol. 2*. Trans. Robert Hurley. New York: Pantheon books.

(1988). *The Care of the Self, Vol. 3*. Trans. Robert Hurley. New York: Vintage Books.

(2001). *The Order of Things: An Archeology of the Human Sciences*. London: Routledge Press.

Freud, S. (1953–1974). *The Standard Edition of the Complete Psychological Works of Sigmund Freud*. Strachey, J. (Ed. and trans.), in collaboration with Freud, A., 24 vols. London: Hogarth Press and the Institute for Psychoanalysis.

(1905). Three Essays on Sexuality. *SE* 7, 135–244.

(1911). Formulations on the Two Principles of Mental Functioning. *SE* 12, 218–226.

(1913). The Claims of Psycho-Analysis to Scientific Interest. *SE* 13, 165–190.

(1915a). Instincts and Their Vicissitudes. *SE* 14, 117–140.

(1915b). The Unconscious. *SE* 14, 166–215.

(1920). Beyond the Pleasure Principle. *SE* 18, 7–64.

(1923). The Ego and the Id. *SE* 19, 12–66.

(1927). The Future of an Illusion. *SE* 21, 5–58.

(1930). Civilization and Its Discontents. *SE* 21, 64–157.

(1937). Analysis Terminable and Interminable. *SE* 23, 216–253.

Gherovici, P. (2017). *Transgender Psychoanalysis: A Lacanian Perspective on Sexual Difference*. New York: Routledge.

Gilbert, J. (2014). *Sexuality in School*. Minnesota: University of Minnesota Press.

Glocer Fiorini, L. (2017). *Sexual Difference in Debate: Bodies, Desires, and Fictions*. London: Karnac Books.

Gozlan, O. (2015). *Transsexuality and the Art of Transitioning: a Lacanian Approach*. New York: Routledge.

Green, A. (2000). *Chains of Eros: The Sexual in Psychoanalysis*. Trans. L. Thurston. London: Rebus Press.

Kincaid, J. (1992). *Child-Loving: The Erotic Child and Victorian Culture*. New York: Routledge Press.

Klein, M. (1959). Our Adult World and Its Roots in Infancy. In *Envy and Gratitude & Other Works, 1946–1963, Vol. 4*, (247–263). London: Hogarth Press.

Kristeva, J. (1995). *New Maladies of the Soul*. Trans. R. Guberman. New York: Columbia University Press.

(2000). *The Sense and Non-Sense of Revolt. The Powers and Limits of Psychoanalysis, Vol. 1*. Trans. J. Herman. New York: Columbia University Press.

(2001a). *Hannah Arendt*. Trans. R. Guberman. Vol. 1 of Female Genius: Life, Madness, Words. New York: Columbia University Press.

(2001b). *Melanie Klein*. Trans. R. Guberman, Vol. 2 of Female Genius. New York: Columbia University Press.

(2007). Adolescence, Syndrome of Ideality. *Psychoanalytic Review* 94(5): 714–725.

(2009). *This Incredible Need to Believe*. Trans. B. Bie Brahic. New York: Columbia University Press.

(2010). *Hatred and Forgiveness*. Trans. J. Herman. New York: Columbia University Press.

Laplanche, J. (1989). *New Foundations for Psychoanalysis*. Trans. D. Macey. London: Basil Blackwell.

(2011). *Freud and the Sexual: Essays 2000–2006*. Fletcher, J. (Ed.). Trans. J. Fletcher, J. House and N. Ray. London: International Psychoanalytic Books.

McDougall, J. (1995). *The Many Faces of Eros: A Psychoanalytic Exploration of Human Sexuality*. New York: W. W. Norton & Company.

Meltzer, D. & Harris, M. (2011). *Adolescence: Talks and Papers*. Harris Williams M. (Ed.). London: Karnac Books.

Meiners, E & Quinn, T. (Eds.) (2012). *Sexualities in Education: A Reader*. New York: Peter Lang.

Mitchell J. & Rose, J. (Eds.) (1985). *Feminine Sexuality: Jacques Lacan and the École Freudienne*. Trans. J. Rose. New York: WW Norton.

Perret-Catipovic, M. & Ladame, F. (Eds.) (1998). *Adolescence and Psychoanalysis: The Story and the History*. London: Karnac Books.

Phillips, A. (1998). *The Beast in the Nursery: On Curiosity and Other Appetites*. New York: Pantheon Books.

Pinar, W. (Ed.) (1998). *Queer Theory in Education*. Mahwah: Lawrence Erlbaum Associates, Inc. Publishers.

Rose, J. (1984). *The Strange Case of Peter Pan: or the Impossibility of Children's Fiction*. London: Macmillan Press Ltd.

(1986). *Sexuality in the Field of Vision*. London: Verso Books.

(1992). *The Haunting of Sylvia Plath*. Cambridge: Harvard University Press.

(2014). *Women in Dark Times*. London: Bloomsbury.

Sedgwick, E. K. (1990). *Epistemology of the Closet*. Berkeley: University of California Press.

(1994). *Fat Art, Thin Art*. Durham: Duke University Press.

(1999). *A Dialogue on Love*. Boston: Beacon Press.

(2003). *Touching Feeling: Affect, Pedagogy, and Performativity*. Durham: Duke University Press.

Stoller, R. (1986). *Sexual Excitement: Dynamics of Erotic Life*. London: Maresfield.

Stockton, K. (2009). *The Queer Child, or Growing Up Sideways*. Durham: Duke University Press.

Tamaki, S. (2013). *Hikikomori: Adolescence without End*. Trans. J. Angles. Minneapolis: University of Minnesota Press.

Waddell, M. (2005). *Inside Lives: Psychoanalysis and the Growth of the Personality*. London: Karnac Books.

Warner, M. (Ed.) (1993). *Fear of Queer Planet*. Minneapolis: University of Minnesota Press.

Winnicott, D. W. (2001). *Playing and Reality*. Philadelphia: Brunner-Routledge.

Young-Bruehl. E. (1996). *The Anatomy of Prejudices*. Cambridge: Harvard University Press.

17 Numbers and Stories

Bridging Methods to Advance Social Change

Stephen T. Russell

Across the world, debates about social policy for adolescent sexual and reproductive health and education rage. Policy approaches for addressing adolescent sexuality are embedded in politics, and policy approaches shift – sometimes dramatically – with changing political administrations or leadership, and with evolving ideologies and social movements. In the realm of adolescent sexuality, there is consistent, strong research from a range of disciplines and perspectives that documents the efficacy of comprehensive adolescent sexuality and reproductive health education for addressing the complex medical, psychological, interpersonal, and social needs of adolescent development (Haberland & Rogow, 2015). At the same time, there have been longstanding debates about social and educational policies and programs to support adolescent sexual and reproductive education and health in many countries around the world, debates that are rooted in deeply held feelings and beliefs regarding sexuality, adolescence, and adolescent sexuality (Russell, 2005). Policy debates often involve scientific research, yet knowledge from research is often over-shadowed by powerful, long-established values and beliefs (including myths and stereotypes) regarding sexuality. If we take the position that knowledge informed by research should play a role in public decision making, we should ask: How can research better inform policies, programs, and practices that promote adolescent sexual and reproductive health?

What is clear is that research is often not central to policy-making decisions regarding adolescent sexuality. Perhaps the clearest example is the decades-old debate regarding whether sexuality education should be "comprehensive" or whether it should focus only on "abstinence." This debate has been central to shifting policy in the United States for several decades (Santelli et al., 2006, 2017), and the "abstinence-only-until-marriage" (AOUM) policy approach for US adolescent sexual health education was exported to other countries during the G. W. Bush presidency (Lo et al., 2016). A more recent global example is the notion of "gender ideology," which has emerged around the world, especially in Europe and South America (Grzebalska & Soós, 2016; Wilkinson, 2017), as a movement

The author received support from grant R24HD042849 awarded to the Population Research Center at the University of Texas at Austin by the Eunice Kennedy Shriver National Institute of Child Health and Human Development, and the Priscilla Pond Flawn Endowment at the University of Texas at Austin. The content is solely the responsibility of the author and does not necessarily represent the official views of the National Institutes of Health.

opposing comprehensive sexuality education as well as gender equality, abortion, same-sex marriage, and transgender rights. Both AOUM and gender ideology are important examples of opposition to well-established, research-based adolescent sexuality education policy and programs.

There are multiple forms of knowledge, and multiple scientific approaches to generating information and evidence about the world. A premise of this *Handbook* is that some forms of research – in particular, empirical quantitative sciences – have historically been more prominent, had more status, or have been more valued; these forms of research have historically had more influence on public discourse and policy (Russell, 2016). Despite the relative status of some forms of (empirical, quantitative) science, there is growing awareness and appreciation of the contributions to knowledge of multiple forms of inquiry – that is, bringing together, triangulating, or bridging multiple epistemological or scholarly approaches. Yet, when scientific conclusions or consensus is inconsistent with politically dominant values or opinions, they may be rejected in favor of ideology (Tolman et al., 2005, p. 4).

In this chapter, I consider methods or approaches relevant for research on sexualities in adolescence. My focus is not on methods of scientific design and inquiry but on methods of application and utility – that is, methods for designing, conducting, and applying research in ways that are useful as well as usable for social change (Nutley et al., 2007). A focus on application and utility refers not to whether research, when completed, is used, but to the methods involved in designing research that is community informed and designed with application in mind (Russell, 2016). I narrate a case example of an integrated approach to research/policy /practice focused on the issue of LGBT-inclusive curriculum in secondary schools. Drawing from that story, I highlight several interrelated principles that inform methods for approaching research in ways that maximize the degree to which a variety of forms of research is responsive to contemporary issues or needs for adolescent sexualities, and the degree to which research is useful for policies, programs, or practices to support healthy adolescent sexuality. These principles include: (1) conducting research in the context of researcher–advocate partnerships; (2) designing and communicating research results in ways that situate the issues as responsive to their local and broader contexts; (3) centering scholarship in the voices of participants; and (4) translation, interpretation, and dissemination of the findings from research for community use.

Research and Advocacy for LGBT-Inclusive Curricula

I present the story of research/policy/practice for LGBT-inclusive curriculum in public schools in California as a case example of methods that were guided by the goals of application and utility. This work grew out of a coordinated, multi-year effort to improve the experiences of LGBT students in California schools. The California Safe Schools Coalition (CSSC) had formed in the late 1990s as a coalition of organizations and individuals dedicated to improving school climate and eliminating harassment and discrimination based on actual or perceived sexual orientation and gender identity (Laub & Burdge, 2016). The CSSC formed following successful advocacy and passage of the California Student Safety and Violence Prevention Act of 2000 (AB 537), one of the first state laws in the United States to include "actual or perceived sexual orientation and gender identity" as part of the nondiscrimination policy for public instruction. The CSSC mission was to focus on coalition building; evaluation (to understand the climate of California schools and efforts to prevent discrimination); accountability (to hold the state accountable for implementing the new law to provide a safe school climate for all students); and local change (through training and education).

I served as an individual member of the CSSC and led evaluation efforts to document school climate and safety for LGBT students, and identify policies, programs, and practices that could reduce discrimination and improve school climate. In our first report – *Safe Place to Learn* – we identified a number of strategies in schools that were associated with students' perceptions of safety at school, including the critical role of inclusive curricula for creating safe and supportive learning environments for LGBT and all students (O'Shaughnessy et al., 2004). Based on analyses of school-based surveys of high school students, in 2006 the CSSC published a research brief (*Lessons that Matter;* Burdge et al., 2012) and subsequent academic publications that showed that LGBT, as well as heterosexual ("straight"), students reported feeling safer at school if they reported "education about LGBT issues at school" (Russell et al., 2006; Russell & McGuire, 2008). Importantly, these findings held in analyses that aggregated more than 1,200 student surveys across 154 schools; not only was there a positive effect of LGBT-inclusive curriculum for individual students but in schools where a higher proportion of students reported learning about LGBT issues, students reported higher average levels of safety and lower rates of bullying (Snapp, McGuire et al., 2015).

Those initial findings were compelling: no other school strategy that we had studied – including the presence of inclusive policies, gay–straight alliance clubs, or proactive intervention of teachers – demonstrated consistent and strong associations with students' perceptions of safety at school, and measurable differences across schools. Yet, we realized that we had a limited understanding of what those associations meant in the day-to-day lives of students, teachers, and classrooms. Members of the CSSC pointed to varied and diverse ways that "education about LGBT issues" might take place in school, including in a wide range of contexts (classroom lessons, school assemblies, informal interactions with teachers) and content (lessons might focus on tolerance and respect for diversity, the contributions of LGBT people in history, or anti-bullying policies in schools). We realized that qualitative research on students' and teachers' experiences with LGBT-inclusive curriculum was critical for understanding the statistical results. The collaborative team began a program of research/advocacy to better understand what was meant by having "education about LGBT issues" at school: What were the *contexts* of that learning? And what was the *content*? These questions would help address the ultimate concern: Given the strong associations with positive student well-being and school climate, what could school teachers, administrators, and policy makers actually do to promote inclusive curricula?

Informed by principles of applied developmental science, community-based participatory research, and critical race and sexualities studies, a collection of research and advocacy efforts were designed to address these questions. A series of mixed/multiple method studies included:

- An extended 2008 *statewide survey* of more than 1,200 California high school students, which included more detailed questions about the content and context of learning about LGBT issues in schools.
- Seven *focus groups* with twenty-six youth, asking about their perceptions of school safety, students' experience of LGBT curricula in schools, and the impact of LGBT-inclusive curricula on school climate, well-being, and achievement.
- Intensive *case studies* of four schools in which education professionals from a CSSC partner organization (the Gay–Straight Alliance (GSA) Network, now called the Genders and Sexualities Alliance Network) conducted professional development and capacity building for implementation of known promising approaches to inclusive curriculum.
- Student *school climate surveys* conducted before and after the capacity building and curricular implementation at each of the case study schools.
- Fifteen *key informant interviews* with adults who were school board members, school administrators, teachers, and advocates from community-based organizations to explore barriers and support for ethnic studies and LGBT-inclusive curriculum within their school or district.

These multiple methods, together, offered a more comprehensive portrait of the role of LGBT-inclusive curricula than could the initial student survey data alone. For example, the revised survey results identified that inclusive curricula efforts are most effective in promoting a positive school climate when they reach a critical mass in schools, and when those efforts are perceived by students to be supportive (rather than neutral or unsupportive) of LGBT topics (Snapp, McGuire et al., 2015). Focus group and interview data (Snapp, Burdge et al., 2015) documented that LGBT-inclusive curricula – most often taught in social studies, humanities, or health-education classes – rarely met standards of social justice education (Miller & Kirkland, 2010). These studies provide both descriptive information about students' and professionals' experiences related to LGBT-inclusive curricula, as well as recommendations for action by multiple stakeholders, including students, parents, teachers, school personnel, and education policy makers.

Results from these diverse data sources were used in multiple community and academic presentations and publications (described further later in the chapter). Funding for this set of studies came from multiple collaborative grants to both community-based organization and university-based partner participants in the CSSC (these research projects were funded by the California Endowment, The Ford Foundation, Indiana University/Research-to-Practice Collaborative, the State Equality Fund, and anonymous donors). During the course of this collaborative process to learn more about LGBT-inclusive curricula, members of the CSSC began legislative advocacy for inclusive curriculum. The 2006 research brief and subsequent research findings were used by youth and organizational advocates in legislative advocacy that led to the passage of the *Fair, Accurate, Inclusive, and Respectful (FAIR) Education Act* in California in 2011, a law that compels the inclusion of the political, economic, and social contributions of persons with disabilities and LGBT people into educational textbooks and the social studies curricula in California public schools.

Methods to Maximize Research Use

This example of research and advocacy for LGBT-inclusive curriculum offers a case to examine several interrelated principles for maximizing the utility of research on adolescent sexualities. First, the development of partnerships between researcher, community organizations and advocates can facilitate research that asks and answers authentic questions – questions that are useful, useable, and urgent. Second, translation and interpretation of research and theory is essential for communicating increasingly complex results of empirical research into formats and messages that can be easily (and often quickly) communicated to advocates and policy makers. Third, research can be designed and communicated in ways that situate it with respect to the local (both micro and macro) contexts. Fourth, centering scholarship and its translation on the voices or experiences of youth (or, more generally, the subjects that are the focus of inquiry) both makes the scholarship authentic and legitimate to research participants, and also assists in translation and interpretation of whatever forms research may take. I argue later in this chapter that these are methods for maximizing the utility of research (Weiss, 1979). With the word "utility," I refer not only to the use and application of research results (although that is the important outcome or goal) but also to the development of research questions and associated methods that are informed by community needs (especially those which are urgent, see Russell, 2016) and designed with use or application in mind.

Researcher–Community–Advocate Partnerships

A principle that I believe is core to the utility of research is partnerships between professionals or experts with deep knowledge of community (individual, family, organizational, and institutional) needs and researchers who have interest and ability to apply the tools of research to community-based questions and needs. Much has been written about partnerships between researchers, universities, and community organizations (Lerner & Simon, 1998). Central to such partnerships is a reframing of "expert," which requires conscious efforts to identify (and at times invert) culturally presumed (and thus typical and expected) power dynamics based on education credential and employment position, status, and experience (Russell

& Horn, 2016). The CSSC included experts from multiple realms, and one of our goals was to be conscious of what we had to offer to the group, but also what we could learn from other stakeholders or constituents for informing our contribution to the group. The challenge as a researcher was to have expertise about how research could be conducted and used but to interpret needs and analyze how research methods could contribute to the evolving dialogue about school policies, programs, and practices (Russell, 2016). Clearly there may be many examples of highly relevant, useful, and influential research related to adolescent sexualities that has been designed and carried out by researchers independent of community collaboration; the point I make is that researcher – community – advocate partnerships are particularly strategic for research utility. For example, on the topic of LGBT inclusion in state-level nondiscrimination and anti-bullying laws, a study of policy advocates identified that coalitions made up of diverse constituents were instrumental for successful legislative action to pass enumerated state laws (Russell et al., 2016).

The CSSC became a coalitional partnership that, at its best, was remarkably successful in effecting legislative and institutional policy changes, including the passage of the *FAIR Education Act*. Because it included representatives of multiple stakeholder groups – students, parents, teachers, education administrators, policy makers, and communications experts – these experts from diverse perspectives were able to play three crucial roles: (1) strategically identifying needs among students and within schools; (2) refining those needs into questions for research and evaluation that could generate relevant answers; and (3) communicating the findings in ways that spoke relevant messages to key (and often distinct) audiences.

First, the CSSC represented multiple vantage points and points of view that allowed it to identify needs and action strategies (including the role of LGBT-inclusive curriculum) from among students and within schools. There had been no history of research on the role of LGBT-inclusive curriculum on reducing harassment and promoting student safety and achievement. However, students and teachers spoke of the invisibility of LGBT issues at school, and pointed out that integrating attention into the formal curriculum would be a significant step in raising awareness, affirming individual LGBT students, and shifting the culture of schools to be inclusive. This perspective in the coalition made the issue of curricular inclusion a priority for coalition goals, not only for research and evaluation but also for practice and policy.

Second, the need for curricular inclusion was first refined as a single research question for the state-wide survey of high school students – the *Preventing School Harassment Survey*: "Have you had education about LGBT issues at school?" It was analysis of that question that yielded such strong results for school safety and lower harassment (Russell et al, 2006). Those findings led to a detailed elaboration through the subsequent survey effort to identify the contexts (e.g., in school subject courses, school assemblies, or student handbooks) and content (e.g., LGBT contributions to history or literature, LGBT inclusion in health education, or school policies to prevent LGBT bullying) related to the simple question about "education about LGBT issues." Results identified that inclusive curricula were effective for promoting positive school climate when they reached a critical mass within a school, and that the presence *and* effectiveness of LGBT-inclusive curricula varied across subject areas (Snapp, Burdge et al., 2015). These finding prompted additional new questions: Why does LGBT-inclusive curricula seem to matter more in some contexts (i.e., courses) than others? Does the difference have to do with the substantive content, or the tone of support or affirmation? Those new questions prompted a qualitative approach using focus groups to hear directly from students about their experiences with LGBT-inclusive curriculum in schools (Snapp, McGuire et al., 2015). The multi-method, peer-reviewed academic research that resulted was fundamentally shaped by the CSSC dialogue about what was needed (and what was working but needed to be documented) in schools.

Third, as a coalition of diverse stakeholders, the CSSC was positioned to communicate the findings of the research and evaluation efforts in ways that spoke relevant messages to key (and often distinct) audiences. Youth and education advocacy organizations as well as education professional organizations were able to quickly share news from the CSSC with their constituent groups through Listservs, newsletters, and organizations meetings and conferences. The presence of communications and marketing professionals aided in identifying key audiences, messages, and strategies for communication. Finally, the presence of senior state legislative staff was essential for applying the research findings for legislative efforts (a subject to which I return later).

This example of the CSSC illustrates ways that, through an intentional partnership, research may not only be applied or used but might be conceptualized and designed from the beginning to have utility for addressing the identified need. Thus, having identified the crucial link between LGBT-inclusive curricula and students' perceptions of safety at school, the partnership set out to design, study, and apply new insights that might inform policy and practice to improve school safety.

Translation, Interpretation, and Dissemination

Typically, research is communicated to other researchers (indeed this is a principle aspect of the scientific endeavor – academic publication through peer review). Some research findings make their way into public or policy discourse, either through the efforts of researchers or because the findings have been sought out by policy makers or policy advocates. Ultimately, for research to be most useful for social problems, findings need to reach beyond the bounds of the scientific community. Although there is growing support for community-engaged and applied research, historically there has been stigma associated with popular or public attention to the work of individual researchers: public or media attention were an indicator that research was not "serious" or "academic" (Guerra et al., 2011). That sentiment has changed and is changing. Many policy makers and advocates for adolescent sexual health and education seek research-based knowledge to inform policies, programs, and practices. Likewise, a growing number of researchers want their research to be useful and to contribute to positive social change by informing policies, programs, and practices (Russell, 2015). Further, a growing number of scholars are challenging what they believe is a false dichotomy between producing research and applying it: research *versus* practice. That is, many scholars understand themselves and their roles as researcher/advocates, and many community practitioners or advocates are actively engaged in research (see Russell & Horn, 2016).

For research to be useful, it must be understood in relation to the social questions or problems that it might address. Thus, the communication of research is central to research utility, and there are multiple approaches for translation, interpretation, and dissemination of research with the goal of utility. Research is legitimated (and thus most scientifically credible) when communicated through scientific peer review; thus, when it is published in scientific outlets (articles in research journals or books). The dilemma is that those publications are designed for, and typically only reach, an audience of researchers, or in some cases specialized practitioner audiences who seek high-quality (and often highly technical) scientific reports. There are multiple other formats for communicating research results, presented briefly in Table 17.1. There is an established tradition of research or policy briefs geared for policy makers and practitioners, as well as longer research reports issued sometimes by academic institutions but more often by "think tank" or community/nongovernmental organizations. Both research briefs and longer reports are typically designed for policy-maker and practitioner audiences, but may also appeal to the general public. In the last decades with the advent of new forms of media and communications, especially the advent of social media, visuals and graphic representations of data and results are increasingly important.

In addition to these forms of publishing research results, there are typical methods for presenting research that align with the audiences and goals of those formats – academic and practitioner conferences, workshops, and webinars. Beyond these publications and presentations, there are multiple forms of press or media and social media communication strategies that are increasingly important for translating research findings to various audiences. Table 17.1 presents information about audiences and formats for press briefings (presentations), as well as for op-eds, blogs, and infographics. Increasingly, strategic communications may involve a number of coordinated efforts: When an article is published in an academic journal, the scholar may coordinate a press release, op-ed, and/or blog posts to ensure dissemination of the results beyond the academic journal readership. Thus, there are multiple methods for strategically translating research questions into practical key take-home messages, and interpreting results through creative description and graphics.

Returning to the case study of LGBT-inclusive curriculum, the first findings that focused specifically on LGBT-inclusive curriculum were presented in the *Lessons that Matter* research brief (Russell et al., 2006), which followed a format developed

Table 17.1 *Methods of translation, interpretation, and dissemination of research for public use*

Form	Primary audience	Typical format
Publications		
Academic publication	Researchers; practitioners	Peer-reviewed journal articles; book chapters; edited and authored books
Research/policy brief	Policy makers; practitioners	1–4-page summaries of key findings; selected visuals; recommendations
Community/ policy report	Practitioners; policy makers; general public	Extended detailed report of research and/or organizational advocacy
Presentations		
Academic conferences	Researchers; practitioners	Academic posters; brief presentations (10–15 minutes); featured presentations (1 hour)
Practitioner conferences	Researchers; practitioners	Posters; brief and featured presentations; skills-building workshops
Workshops	Practitioners	1-hour to multi-day trainings
Webinars	Practitioners in different locations	1–3-hour online presentations/skills-building trainings
Media/Press materials		
Press briefings	Policy makers; practitioners	Expert presentations or panels made up of brief presentations
Press release	General public	300–800 words outlining newsworthy content of research findings
Op-ed	General (or outlet-focused) public	300–750-word focused, persuasive opinion statement based on research findings
Blog	General (or outlet-focused) public	300–600-word personal/diary-style statement integrating research findings
Social media	General (or focused) public	Twitter: 140 characters; single images, videos Facebook: custom-length text, image, video posts
Infographics	General public	Clear, visual representation of concepts or data

by the CSSC for a research brief series (for an example see Russell et al., 2006). That standard format included a very brief statement of the issue or question, two to four key findings stated in practical language (each with several brief paragraphs of explanation), and graphic representations of each finding. Each research brief ended with a series of recommended action steps for multiple constituent groups: state and local education policy makers (from legislators to school board members), school administrators, and teachers, parents, and students. The briefs were designed to be visually appealing, graphically consistent, and to fit a 2- or 4-page format (for hard-copy printing, front and back, on standard or folded letter-sized paper).

In the early discussions of the research findings on LGBT-inclusive curriculum, it was difficult for me to explain in simple terms the importance of the results of multi-level analyses (statistical analyses that simultaneously test differences between students as well as differences across schools, because students are clustered within schools). Those results indicated that there were statistically significant effects of learning about LGBT issues at both the individual student level *and* at the school level. At first, CSSC colleagues' reaction was that the results were "too scientific" or too technical and not practical. However, when I suggested that we disregard the multi-level results, one CSSC member (the leader of a state-wide community-based LGBT advocacy organization) said: "it seems important that individual students feel safer, and that also schools overall are safer. The question is: how do we explain that?"

That question prompted me to consider different ways of explaining the data and results. I needed to shift my thinking away from the multi-level regression model and think more concretely about what the results meant practically. I realized that at the school level there was a wide range of the proportion of students in any given school that reported learning about LGBT issues (from a low of 23 percent in some schools to a high of 90 percent in others). That basic information helped us identify a method to present the results graphically: rather than try to present results from a multi-level statistical model, we simply split the sample into schools in which less than 50 percent of students reported learning about LGBT issues compared with schools in which more than 50 percent did. We then graphically displayed the proportion of students who felt safe in each type of school: 24 percent of students reported LGBT bullying in schools in which less than half of the students reported learning about LGBT issues; in school where more than half learned about LGBT issues, only 11 percent reported LGBT bullying (Russell et al., 2006). That simple graphic offered a new interpretation of the more complex statistical analyses in a way that was visually appealing and easy to interpret.

These findings prompted discussion and advocacy that ultimately led to the passage of the *FAIR Education Act*. Yet, once the law was passed, advocates quickly realized that there were few curricular resources specific to LGBT people and experiences, and there was a need for educational tools for how to implement the *Act*. The GSA Network began several efforts to pilot curriculum inclusion tools in four schools, and collaborated with me to analyze and evaluate what worked. A follow-up report, *Implementing Lessons that Matter*, was the culmination of this implementation and evaluation project. Based on case studies of four schools (which included in-depth interviews with teachers and school administrators and pre-/post-surveys of students), the report was written for audiences that included students, parents, teachers, school administrators, and policy makers, as well as academics interested in translational research (Burdge et al., 2013). The report was designed to look like a composition notebook, directly suggesting that it was a learning tool, visually making the connection to school curriculum.

A key theme in this case example is the interactive relationship between research, practice, and advocacy. New results prompted new policy and practice advocacy, which led to further and more refined questions for research, evaluation, and implementation, questions which were best answered by methods that included not only the "numbers" from large-scale surveys but also the stories that were collected through observations, interviews, and focus groups with a broad range of constituents. Researcherpractitioner/advocate partnership in the curriculum design and implementation phase allowed for additional process learning (i.e., what works and how), which provided new tools for educators, and new academic and practical scholarship. To date there have been more than one thousand unique page views of the webpages associated with the *Implementing Lessons that Matter* report on the GSA Network website (notably, the average time that readers spend on the report webpage is 10.01 minutes, far greater than on other pages on the organization's website). Data from the project has been published (Snapp & Russell, 2016) and presented at multiple research and professional development conferences. In addition, workshops based on the reports have been requested by and conducted for multiple non-profit organizations and school districts in California and around the country.

Situating Research Results in Context

A third principle for maximizing the utility of research is that research must be situated in the context of its intended use. This is a key barrier to research application in the social and behavioral sciences. High-quality research on key questions of public importance may not have been conducted in the immediate community where the concern is urgent. Further, broad population-based research may be perceived as impersonal or not specific to a local need: for example, individuals may be skeptical that state-wide survey results truly apply to the schools and students in their own city or town. Scholars and advocates may either directly use local data to augment and complement the results of research or they may situate, translate, or interpret the results in ways that are directly responsive to local data, needs, or discourse.

One challenge for the GSA Network when beginning the implementation and evaluation project that culminated in the *Implementing Lessons that Matter* report was simple geographic access: based in the San Francisco Bay Area, the organization had the logistical challenge of proximity to schools in which they could conduct the intensive capacity-building and LGBT-inclusive curricular implementation. To address this challenge, they strategically partnered with schools that had distinct demographic profiles, including: urban and suburban; large public and small magnet; majority low-income and majority high-income; and schools with some history as well as some with no history of LGBT-inclusive curriculum (Burdge et al., 2013). That strategy was intended to disrupt criticism that all of the schools were from San Francisco (a city with a reputation for LGBT inclusion), but also to enable the results to speak to the incorporation of sexuality-related and -inclusive curriculum in different profiles of schools in different kinds of communities. The report treated schools as case studies, a strategy that allowed key findings to be identified based on characteristics of schools, while also enabling summative conclusions across schools. The approach also offered the opportunity to describe population profiles combined with qualitative data on the LGBT- and sexuality-related culture in schools that emerged from the in-depth implementation project. In this way, the report maximized the possibility that it could be useful to schools beyond the implementation schools.

Situating the results of research in context is a principle that can apply not only to the local context of implementing curriculum in schools but also to the context of systems of influence. For example, participation in the CSSC of senior state legislative staffers was essential because it brought expert knowledge of the legislative context, which aided in applying the research findings to legislative action. When the first research results showed strong associations between LGBT-inclusive curricula and student and school safety, many in the CSSC assumed the results were important knowledge for teachers and advocates but that there was little that could be done in terms of education policy *per se* (much less state policy or law). Yet, legislative professionals were familiar with state education codes and laws and recognized an opportunity.

In the early 2000s, the rhetoric of "the gay agenda" was still strong, especially with respect to schooling (Whatley, 1999); many in the CSSC could not imagine a formal policy agenda for LGBT-inclusive curriculum given that strong rhetoric. At that time, the California Education Code included provisions to assure that the roles and contributions of members of under-represented racial, ethnic, and cultural groups to the economic, political, and social development of California and the United States were included in history and social studies lessons. Thus, state law provided a provision for inclusive curriculum with respect to race, ethnicity, and cultural groups but there were no references to sexual orientation and gender identity or disability in such laws. Given the passage of AB 537 (pertaining to nondiscrimination), legislative staff saw an opportunity to argue to extend the existing Education Code to include the contributions of LGBT people and people with disabilities in history and social studies lessons. In this way, the discourse around the proposed legislation focused on the idea that the law was not new: sponsoring legislators pointed out that the existing code simply needed to be amended to be consistent with the nondiscrimination law that had already been passed. Further, the approach largely avoided the criticism that the legislation was a "gay" issue because the *Act* included reference to both the contributions of LGBT people and people with disabilities. This strategy – to amend an existing statute in reference to the existing nondiscrimination law and include other groups that had been historically omitted – was unthinkable to those who were unfamiliar with the legislative process and context. Thus, advocacy for LGBT-inclusive curriculum in California was made possible by rich context-specific understandings of not only students' needs and the realities of schools and classrooms, but also policy and legislative contexts.

Centering Participants' Voices

Finally, maximizing the utility of research may be aided by centering the discourse or advocacy efforts in the voices or stories of participants. This principle is related to each phase of the research – for identifying and specifying the questions, designs, and approaches to research. Regarding application and utility, the persuasive power of individuals' voices and stories can be especially effective. Here, I do not mean that personal anecdote should stand alone (see Tolman et al., 2005), rather, stories from directly impacted individuals can often be useful and strategic complements to other forms of summative or statistical data. Narratives personalize complex or abstract information, bringing it to life.

The initial CSSC research brief on LGBT-inclusive curriculum became used as a tool for advocacy for the *FAIR Education Act*, and was particularly effective as a tool when coupled with personal stories. In particular, the GSA Network used the research brief during Queer Youth Advocacy Day, an event during which high school GSA members gathered at the California state capitol to meet with legislators and lobby for bills relevant to LGBT youth (for further discussion of Queer Youth Advocacy Day, see Russell et al., 2010). Youth participated in a day of training, followed by a day of lobbying their local state legislators. The lobbying training included learning about state-wide research, including the data presented in the *Lessons that Matter* research brief, as well as training to outline and practice sharing personal stories about why LGBT-inclusive curriculum was important for creating a safe and supportive school climate. Youth were trained to bridge their personal stories with numbers (or the results from the state-wide research) in making the case for the *FAIR Education Act*. This direct policy advocacy is yet another form of research translation and dissemination. It was a particularly persuasive strategy in that it combined the "authority" of large-scale, state-wide survey data with the rhetorical power of personal stories told by youth.

Queer Youth Advocacy Day was a clear example of an advocacy process that centered youth's voices as a method of bridging stories and research results to make a compelling advocacy case for legislation. This is often the approach taken in policy advocacy: matching research or other data or numbers with compelling personal narratives. Further, Tolman and colleagues (2005) point out that the results of qualitative research may serve this same purpose – that is, to systematically study, summarize, and thematically present youths' stories in advocating for adolescent sexual health and rights.

Conclusions

I have argued that in research on sexualities in adolescence we might broaden understandings of "research methods" to include not only the methods of design and execution of research but also the methods of application and use of the results. I suggest that through drawing from and bringing together multiple methodological approaches we may be better able to design, conduct, and use adolescent sexuality research from multiple perspectives, vantage points, and disciplines in ways that promote positive social change for social justice (Russell, 2015). Using the case study of LGBT-inclusive curriculum advocacy in secondary schools in the state of California, I illustrate ways that coalitions that bridge research, practice, and policy might be employed to promote proactive and positive adolescent sexuality policy and practice. I highlight multiple forms of translation, interpretation, and dissemination of research findings to make them useful for community application and advocacy for social and policy change. Finally, I suggest that situating research results in local or policy contexts and centering the voices of participants are important strategies for promoting the application and use of research.

Adolescence and sexuality remain topics rooted in cultural tensions and anxieties. There is a notable gap between the knowledge grounded in contemporary research understandings of adolescent sexual health and current adolescent sexual health and education policy and practice. And social changes and debates continue, shifting with political changes locally and around the world. I have suggested strategies for engaging research with practice and policy in meaningful and authentic collaboration, and for "putting the results to work" in communities for youth. These strategies were illustrated through an example from an earlier time. The critical question for researchers and advocates will be to imagine ways that these strategies may be adapted for shifting political and sociocultural realities moving forward.

References

Burdge, H., Sinclair, K., Laub, C., & Russell, S. T. (2012). *Lessons that Matter: LGBT Inclusivity and School Safety* (Gay-Straight Alliance Network and California Safe Schools Coalition Research Brief No. 14). San Francisco: Gay–Straight Alliance Network. www.gsanetwork.org/files/aboutus/PSH%20Report%206_2012.pdf.

Burdge, H., Snapp, S., Laub, C., Russell, S. T., & Moody, R. (2013). *Implementing Lessons that Matter: The Impact of LGBT-Inclusive Curriculum on Student Safety, Well-Being, and Achievement*. San Francisco: Gay–Straight Alliance Network and Tucson, AZ: Frances McClelland Institute for Children, Youth, and Families at the University of Arizona.

Grzebalska, W. & Soós, E. (2016, March 1). Conservatives vs. the "Culture of Death": How Progressives Handled the War on "Gender"? Retrieved from www.feps-europe.eu/

resources/publications/364-conservatives-vs-the-culture-of-death-how-progressives-handled-the-war-on-gender.html.

Guerra, N. G., Graham, S., & Tolan, P. H. (2011). Raising Healthy Children: Translating Child Development Research into Practice. *Child Development*, *82*(1), 7–16.

Haberland, N. & Rogow, D. (2015). Sexuality Education: Emerging Trends in Evidence and Practice. *Journal of adolescent health*, *56*(1), S15–S21.

Laub, C. & Burdge, H. (2016). The Use of Research in Policy and Advocacy for Creating Safe Schools for LGBT Students. In Russell, S. T. & Horn, S. S. (Eds.), *Sexual Orientation, Gender Identity, and Schooling: The Nexus of Research, Practice, and Policy* (310–329). New York: Oxford University Press.

Lerner, R. M. & Simon, L. A. K. (1998). The New American Outreach University. In Lerner, R. M. & Simon, L. A. K. (Eds.), *University-Community Collaborations for the Twenty-First Century: Outreach Scholarship for Youth and Families* (3–23). New York: Garland Publishing, Inc.

Lo, N. C., Lowe, A., & Bendavid, E. (2016). Abstinence Funding Was Not Associated with Reductions in HIV Risk Behavior in Sub-Saharan Africa. *Health Affairs*, *35*(5), 856–863.

Miller, S. J. & Kirkland, D. E. (Ed.). (2010). *Change Matters: Critical Essays on Moving Social Justice Research from Theory to Policy (Vol. 1)*. New York: Peter Lang.

Nutley, S. M., Walter, I., & Davies, H. T. (2007). *Using Evidence: How Research Can Inform Public Services*. Bristol: Policy Press.

O'Shaughnessy, M., Russell, S. T., Heck, K., Calhoun, C., & Laub, C. (2004). *Safe Place to Learn: Consequences of Harassment Based on Actual or Perceived Sexual Orientation and Gender Non-Conformity and Steps for Making Schools Safer.* San Francisco: California Safe Schools Coalition. www.casafeschools.org/SafePlacetoLearnLow.pdf

Russell, S. T. (2005). Conceptualizing Positive Adolescent Sexuality Development. *Sexuality Research and Social Policy*, *2*(3), 4–12.

(2015). Human Developmental Science for Social Justice. *Research in Human Development*, *12*(3–4), 274–279. doi:10.1080/15427609.2015.1068049.

(2016). Social Justice, Research, and Adolescence. *Journal of Research on Adolescence*, *26*(1), 4–15. doi:10.1111/jora.12249.

Russell, S. T. & Horn, S. S. (Eds.). (2016). *Sexual Orientation and Gender Identity in Schooling: The Nexus of Research, Practice, and Policy.* New York: Oxford University Press.

Russell, S. T., Horn, S. S., Moody, R. L., Fields, A., & Tilley, E. (2016). Enumerated US State Laws. In Russell, S. T. & Horn, S. S. (Eds.), *Sexual Orientation, Gender Identity, and Schooling: The Nexus of Research, Practice, and Policy* (255–271). New York: Oxford University Press.

Russell, S. T., Kostroski, O., McGuire, J. K., Laub, C., & Manke, E. (2006). *LGBT Issues in the Curriculum Promotes School Safety* (California Safe Schools Coalition Research Brief No. 4). San Francisco: California Safe Schools Coalition.

Russell, S. T., & McGuire, J. K. (2008). The School Climate for Lesbian, Gay, Bisexual, and Transgender (LGBT) Students. In Shinn, M. & Yoshikawa, H. (Eds.), *Changing Schools and Community Organizations to Foster Positive Youth Development* (133–158). Oxford: Oxford University Press.

Russell, S. T., Toomey, R., Crockett, J., & Laub, C. (2010). LGBT Politics, Youth Activism, and Civic Engagement. In Sherrod, L., Flanagan, C., & Torney-Purta, J. (Eds.), *Handbook of Research on Civic Engagement in Youth* (471–494). Hoboken: John Wiley & Sons, Inc.

Santelli, J. S., Kantor, L. M., Grilo, S. A., et al. (2017). Abstinence-Only-Until-Marriage: An Updated Review of US Policies and Programs and their Impact. *Journal of Adolescent Health, 61*(3), 273–280.

Santelli, J., Ott, M. A., Lyon, M., Rogers, J., Summers, D., & Schleifer, R. (2006). Abstinence and Abstinence-Only Education: A Review of US Policies and Programs. *Journal of Adolescent Health, 38*(1), 72–81.

Snapp, S. D., Burdge, H., Licona, A. C., Moody, R. L., & Russell, S. T. (2015). Students' Perspectives on LGBT-Inclusive Curriculum. *Equity & Excellence in Education, 48*(2), 249–265.

Snapp, S. D., McGuire, J. K., Sinclair, K. O., Gabrion, K., & Russell, S. T. (2015). LGBT-Inclusive Curricula: Why Supportive Curricula Matter. *Sex Education, 15*(6), 580–596.

Snapp, S., & Russell, S. T. (2016). Inextricably Linked: The Shared Story of Ethnic Studies and LGBT-Inclusive Curriculum. In Russell, S. T. & Horn, S. S. (Eds.), *Sexual Orientation, Gender Identity, and Schooling: The Nexus of Research, Practice, and Policy* (143–164). New York: Oxford University Press.

Tolman, D. L., Hirschman, C., & Impett, E. A. (2005). There Is More to the Story: The Place of Qualitative Research on Female Adolescent Sexuality in Policy Making. *Sexuality Research & Social Policy, 2*(4), 4–17.

Weiss, C. H. (1979). The Many Meanings of Research Utilization. *Public Administration Review, 39*(5), 426–431.

Whatley, M. H. (1999). The "Homosexual Agenda." In Epstein, D. & Sears, J. T. (Eds.), *A Dangerous Knowing: Sexuality, Pedagogy and Popular Culture* (229–241). New York: Cassell.

Wilkinson, A. (2017). Latin America's Gender Ideology Explosion. *Anthropology News, 58*, e233–e237. doi:10.1111/AN.379.

18 *Doing It*: Participatory Visual Methodologies and Youth Sexuality Research

Katie MacEntee and Sarah Flicker

Introduction

In this chapter, we explore the contributions of participatory visual methodologies (PVMs) to the study of youth sexuality. PVMs are a series of methods that actively engage participants in creating and analyzing visual media (e.g., photographs, video, or drawings) as part of the research process. PVM scholarship is situated at the intersection of diverse disciplines, including anthropology, geography, education, visual sociology, and public health. Mitchell and Sommer (2016) defined PVM in relation to public health as:

> *Modes of inquiry* that can engage participants and communities, eliciting evidence about their own health and well-being. At the same time, they are also *modes of representation* and *modes of production* in the co-creation of knowledge, as well as *modes of dissemination* in relation to knowledge translation and mobilization (p. 521).

Images invite an expansion of ideas and evoke new questions (Eisner, 1997). The production of images can be a way for participants to represent abstract ideas that are poorly expressed in more referential forms, such as the written word (Pauwels, 2010). This may be particularly important when working with youth on sexuality research, as many young people often have difficulty finding and using vocabulary to talk about sex, feelings, and desire.

With theoretical foundations in feminist theory, critical pedagogy, and community-based research, there is strong evidence that supports the emancipatory potential of these methods when used to engage marginalized groups democratically in research activities (Ball, 2008; Brandt, 2008; Chalfen, 2011; Garcia et al., 2013; Lapenta, 2011; Mitchell, 2011; Mitchell & De Lange, 2011; Prosser & Burke, 2008; Sinding et al., 2008; Springgay et al., 2008). The emphasis on participant-led production and analysis of visual data can disrupt and flatten traditional hierarchies of power between researchers and participants (Flicker et al., 2014; Flicker et al., 2008). Youth are especially drawn to these methods because they are fun, can be more accessible and engaging than other research methods, and draw on their everyday uses of technologies. However, research teams can have difficulty knowing which visual method will best answer their questions about youth sexuality. Engaging young people in visual production and dissemination in sexuality research also raises particular ethical questions that will also shape a project's methodological approach. Therefore, in this chapter we:

(1) provide a brief overview of PVMs and their potential application to the study of youth sexuality;
(2) discuss and offer illustrative case studies of three digital PVMs in the context of youth sexuality research:
   (a) photovoice – taking pictures and discussing them in a group
   (b) digital storytelling – creating short narrative audiovisual productions
   (c) cellphilms – using *cell ph*ones to make f*ilms*
(3) explore some of the ongoing methodological and ethical considerations related to integrating PVMs into youth sexuality research and interventions.

Where Do PVMs Come From?

Images are ubiquitous in our lives. Visual methodologies involve an inquiry into how visual texts (or images), in all their various forms and functions, are culturally infused representations of subjective experiences (Pink, 2001). Visual methodologies emerged as a distinct interdisciplinary and multidisciplinary field in the 1980s (Pink, 2003). However, visual methods, such as drawing and documentary filmmaking, have a much longer history across many scholarly disciplines. Methodologists often distinguish between different types of visual data, including found images, public media, and pictures or video produced by researchers and participants during a research study (Weber, 2008).

Visual research is part of visual culture (Rose, 2014). It encompasses an analysis of both the practice of looking (how do we look at pictures?) and the symbolic representations of meaning in images (what do these pictures tell us?) (Rose, 2016). The constructed nature of images and their multiple interpretive possibilities are generally understood to be strengths of the approach. Therefore, while there is never a fundamental meaning to be uncovered within an image that will be true across contexts and people, the representational possibilities afforded by visual methods allow for rich, diverse, and interpretive expressions of meaning to be elucidated (Eisner, 2003). This makes the method particularly compelling for sexuality research; it celebrates and makes space for the diversity of ways in which sexual development occurs and may be understood.

Due to their commitment to participatory processes and principles, PVMs demand that researchers relinquish control, share power, and meaningfully engage participants as research partners. PVMs have been influenced by several other theories and areas of academic inquiry. We focus here on the contributions of community-based research, critical pedagogy, feminist theory, and media scholarship.

Specifically, PVMs draw from community-based research's focus on collaborative, participant-driven research approaches that are committed to having an action component (Israel et al., 1998). This means that the work undertaken often has an explicit social justice mandate and is used to mobilize for progressive advocacy efforts. Freire's (1984) work on critical pedagogy (or conscienzation through dialogue) has also informed the focus on collaborative knowledge production. Feminist theory has shared useful frameworks for thinking about representation (Alcoff, 1991) and research reflexivity (Pillow, 2003). All three of these traditions understand research participants to be experts on their own lives. These theories also support democratic modes of research engagement that recognize the diverse needs of different community members. Consequently, using PVMs should challenge and disrupt hierarchical power relations that regularly occur in more conventional research processes. PVM projects often follow a 'research as intervention' approach: for many participants, engaging in collective documentation and reflection can be a very empowering process. Sharing their finished products can also be a source of pride, particularly when dissemination contributes to social change efforts.

Furthermore, while not all PVMs involve digital technology, those that do often draw on critical media scholarship to articulate the significance of the digital in media production. Jenkins (2006) describes digital technology as a central tool for modern-day convergent culture that facilitates the transfer of information across different media platforms. Rejecting a technologically determinist view of technologies (or the idea that technology, in and of itself, is emancipatory or oppressive), Jenkins (2013) observes that young people are at the centre of a "profound and prolonged" change in how media is produced and consumed (p. 110). He argues that we are now in an era of participatory culture – when everyone with access to technology has the capacity to manipulate cultural production. While not universally accessible, many young people are creating media that are reaching broad audiences. PVMs capitalize on this trend but encourage adopting a critical lens. Questions such as: 'Who is making the media?,' 'What is the media telling us?,' 'Who is consuming the media?,' and 'What does it mean to them?' become central sites of analysis.

PVMs with Youth

PVMs are particularly well suited for work with young people. The visual process can be fun and engaging for young people who may be less interested in sitting to complete surveys or answering interview questions (Drew et al., 2010). The visual component can present more accessible entry points for young people who may lack literacy skills or who are verbally shy. The approach supports cognitive understandings to be expressed and interlaced with sensual and emotive ways of understanding. Furthermore, involving young participants collaboratively in the analysis of their visual texts leads to rich and diverse research findings (Luttrell, 2010).

Including young people as agents in the research process can introduce new perspectives and insights that may be overlooked by adult researchers, and will likely benefit the youth participants by exposing them to new skills (Flicker, 2008). Participant-driven methods may present an opportunity for unexpected findings to emerge in ways that researcher-driven questions may sometimes miss. In her arts-based work with Indigenous youth, Flicker and colleagues (2014) report that youth identified that both the process (fun, participatory, empowering) and products (communicate information, raise awareness) of visual methods were important for decolonizing the research process. In many ways, as we will go on to articulate, the process and products are inextricably linked and mutually constitutive in this work.

As early as preschool, young people are asked to draw, paint, and represent their lives visually. As they mature, many become proactive archivists and curators of their experiences on various social media platforms (e.g., Instagram, Facebook, Snapchat). Because they are often encouraged to visually depict their lives, many become very skilled in the medium. As such, young people's visual texts can be read as agentic representations of knowledge (Buckingham & Sefton-Green, 1994). This is perhaps more so now then ever before. With increased access to the means of media production, people everywhere are using cell phones to produce and share digital media.

Among all cell-phone users globally, people under the age of 30 use their phones the most diversely, taking photographs and video as well as accessing social media and the Internet (Pew Research Center, 2012). Teenage girls are especially involved in visually based social media applications, posting pictures and comments prolifically (Lenhart & Pew Research Center, 2015). Jenkins typified young people's engagement in this participatory culture as collaborative, inclusive, and capable of disrupting dominant discourses in more mainstream (corporate) media practices (Jenkins et al., 2009). The visual products that young people create during PVM projects similarly echo and diverge from the types of visual media that young people create and interact with daily. The emphasis on collaboration and reflexivity during PVM research are therefore familiar patterns of engagement for young people already involved in the participatory culture of youth-based media consumption and production.

Youth come from many different social locations: the idea of one homogeneous, or 'real,' youth voice makes no sense. In contrast to essentialist understanding of a singular youth voice, Gubrium, Hill, et al. (2014) explore the idea of 'strategically authentic voice' that emerges out of the collaborative, intersubjective participatory visual workshop. They argue that PVMs contribute to centering the perspective of young people, while recognizing that these viewpoints are informed by workshop facilitators, other participants, the research team, imagined (and real) audience members, and the circulating discourses on the research topic. The images that young people create during PVMs should not be read as neutral. Images are socially mediated constructions that are designed to replicate or disrupt dominant representations.

Joanou (2009) argues that it is essential for researchers to discuss images with the young person who created them in order to gain an understanding of its intended message. Recognizing the transformative potential of articulating one's life or community experience, Holtby et al. (2015) contend that PVMs, and the focus on the visual, may cause young people to acutely experience a "burden of representation" (p. 319) to speak on behalf of a diverse community of people that may or may not identify in a similar fashion. Therefore, while these methodologies are well suited to bring forward the perspectives and experiences of young people, it is wise to remember this work is dependent on mitigating research factors (e.g., facilitation and context) that help ensure the methods are used critically and (as we will discuss) with careful consideration of the ethical implications of this work (Switzer, 2017).

Application of PVMs in Sexuality Research with Youth

There are several factors that support integrating PVMs with youth when considering research around sexuality. Sex and the body, in many cultures and contexts, can be taboo subjects or sources of embarrassment and discomfort. PVMs can relieve some of the embarrassment associated with discussing these subjects in public, or make it easier to "talk about the hard things" (Flicker et al., 2014, p. 26). For instance, in Wilson and Flicker's photovoice project exploring sexual agency in Toronto youth communities, young women were able to flag and explore the practice of transactional sex without disclosing their own engagements in the practice (Wilson & Flicker, 2015). Creating and then discussing their visual texts can take the attention away from individual behavior that may be stigmatizing or socially unacceptable to talk about in public. The distance afforded by documenting trends through imagery rather than having to 'confess' your own behavior can help make space for difficult conversations.

The topics of sex and sexuality are complex and uncomfortable for some individuals to discuss. This may be particularly true for young people who are in the process of exploring, discovering, and testing who they are as sexual beings in the world. People do not always know the appropriate terminology or exactly how to express in words the complex and sometimes contradictory feelings associated with, for example, love, desire, pleasure, and loss. The visual medium offers a means to communicate these layered and abstract topics.

The production and discussion of participants' visual texts is especially well suited for unpacking how social systems and cultural practices can influence young people's decisions and actions around sex. For example, MacEntee (2016a) reports on how young women in a rural area of South Africa made digital stories that reveal some of the different ways that culture, tradition, normative gender roles, and youth agency interplay to affect young women's ambiguity around whether (or not) young people should have access to condoms. Youth's visual texts allow for the expression of complexities and the juxtaposition of sometimes contradictory social messages about what is appropriate/inappropriate and how they might negotiate these messages during sexual encounters.

Sexual relationships are increasingly moving fluidly between online and offline spaces. Online dating and social media applications such as Tinder and Instagram are increasingly mainstream and normalized means of finding sexual partners. Sexting (sending sexually explicit material across cell phones) is a criminalized activity for young people in many countries and is fraught with possibilities for future sexual shaming and coercion. Nevertheless, the practice has proliferated and can also allow youth to engage in frank sexual conversations on their own terms (Dobson & Ringrose, 2016). PVMs are an interesting way for young people to tease apart the influence of digital technology on sexual relationships. For example, MacEntee and Mandrona (2015) report on a PVM project with teachers. The teachers created cellphilms that raised concerns over their students' uncritical and possibly dangerous use of cell phones and social media. These educators were particularly worried about learners' access to pornography and online dating. The teachers screened these cellphilms to their students to engage them in discussions regarding their concerns. The teachers were surprised at how articulately the young people expressed their ideas about cellphone use and sexuality. This led the teachers to reconsider their view of students' use of digital technology and their ability to make informed decisions about their sexual practices. This project illustrates how mobile technology might be integrated into research to develop more nuanced understanding of the ways in which media and technology are influencing young people's sexuality and development.

Three Examples of Digital PVMs

We will now provide a brief overview of photovoice, digital storytelling, and cellphilming as three examples of PVMs. There are several other PVMs, including drawing (Theron et al., 2011) and collage (Allen & Ingram, 2015), that have also been used to explore and study youth sexuality. Here, we focus on these three examples to attend to the ways that digital technologies are transforming the landscape of possibilities for the fields of sexuality and youth studies. There is considerable overlap between these methods: they each involve a process of participant-driven visual production and analysis. Still, there are also distinct features that are worth considering, which we introduce in this section alongside a summary of commonly used procedures. We also provide a case study application for each.

Photovoice

Photovoice is most often attributed to the work of Wang and Burris (1997), who developed the photography-based method while working with female farmers in rural China. Lykes (2001) used a similar photographic approach with women in post-conflict Guatemala. The method typically begins by researchers asking participants to take photographs that relate to a particular theme or topic. Project organizers normally facilitate an introduction to photo technique (e.g., how to use a camera, composition, framing), as well as some training on the ethical implications of taking photographs in a research context.

Once the photographs have been taken, participants engage in participatory analysis activities in order to discuss what their photographs mean and why they are significant. Wang (2008) recommends using the following questions to spark reflection and discussion (often described as the SHOWED method):

What is **S**een here?
What is really **H**appening?
How does this relate to **O**ur lives?
Why are things this **W**ay?
How could this image be used to **E**ducate people?
What else can we **D**o about it?

Other researchers have asked participants to work with their photographs to make posters (Stuart, 2006), or photonovellas. These processes all facilitate participants identifying issues, themes, and theories of relevance across and between their photos. After discussing their pictures, participants often title and write short captions about their images to help explain their intended meaning and relevance to the issues under investigation. Subsequently, photographs and captions can be displayed in community venues or online and exhibited to peers and policy makers as a stimulus for change. The photos, captions, and discussion recordings become the data set for analysis.

Case Study: Picturing Queer and Trans Teen Lives in Small-Town Ontario

Holtby and colleagues (2015) worked with a small group of LGBTQ teens to visually depict their experiences living in small-town Ontario as sexual and gender minorities. Fifteen youth participated in a series of four photovoice sessions. The first meeting consisted of a review of the project, discussing consent procedures, distributing cameras, and providing some basic training on how to take photographs. Participants had four days to take five to ten photographs that represented their experiences as queer and/or trans youth. The second meeting focused on group discussions framed by the SHOWED technique. The third meeting was a chance for further discussion and to provide feedback on the research process. The fourth brought together key participants and members of a youth advisory committee to discuss how they would like to exhibit selected photographs at community events. Youth were provided with cameras, transit tokens, and honoraria for volunteering for the research. Sessions were audio recorded and copies of participants' pictures and narratives were retained for analysis.

Key themes that emerged from the data were both the invisibility and hypervisibility of LGTBQ youth. Some youth photographed empty benches to portray the ways in which they felt images of people 'like them' or role models were missing from public spaces and discourse. In one image, a participant purposely situated herself to be barely visible in the frame as a way of showing her feelings of absence or erasure. By contrast, other youth felt hyper-visible. This was expressed through photographs of 'gay things' like rainbow paraphernalia, and led to a discussion on the ways that young people can purposefully mark themselves for others to see. In these ways, the youth used the photovoice process to visually document complex ideas around representation. The pictures became tangible and concrete openings for abstract discussions. A community exhibit of the photovoice was held and two papers emerging from the project were written by a team of researchers, including a former participant who joined the research lab as a student (Holtby et al., 2015; Klein et al., 2015).

Digital Stories

Digital storytelling is often associated with Lambert (2012) and the StoryCenter in Berkeley, California.[1] The process was adapted as a research method by Gubrium (2009). Digital stories are usually short (3–5-minute) first-person narrative, multimedia productions. A research prompt is used to inspire participants to develop scripted stories that share personal experiences or perspectives. Participants work collaboratively to peer review and refine their scripts. Storyboards can be used to help participants plan how their scripted story can be paired with visual media. Participants then find or produce these visuals and use editing software to digitally stitch them together sequentially. A voiceover of participants reading their script and music is added to complete the media production. The final products can be shared virtually or screened in public venues.

Documentation of the process, as well as the final products, become data for understanding how particular groups make meaning out of a given phenomenon. Gubrium and Turner (2011) offer an intertextual transcribing method to decipher how participants use the multimodal method to express their perspectives and experiences. This strategy is particularly interesting for its equal consideration of the verbal, textual, and visual components of digital stories. This highlights the method's emphasis on multimodality that reflects a current media trend (e.g., memes and mash-ups) of mixing, playing with, and reconstituting digital media to make political statements and current events.

Case Study: Storying Indigenous Youth HIV-Prevention Activism in Canada

The Native Youth Sexual Health Network (NYSHN) uses a peer-to-peer model to work across issues of sexual and reproductive health, rights, and justice throughout North America. NYSHN is very concerned about the pervasive deficit model that dominates public health discourse surrounding Indigenous youth. NYSHN partnered with several researchers across Canada on the *Taking Action* research project to explore the potential for using the arts to reimagine HIV-prevention possibilities that

[1] www.storycenter.org

adopt a strengths-based perspective (Flicker et al., 2013; Flicker et al., 2014). In the second phase of the project, the team gathered a group of Indigenous youth leaders from across Canada to create digital stories about their HIV-prevention activism (Danforth & Flicker, 2014; Flicker et al., 2013). Participants received flip cameras in the mail and participated in a series of planning conference calls to help them think about digital storytelling and the prompt: "What does Indigenous HIV activism mean to you?" They then participated in a week-long retreat to create their stories.

The resultant stories situated HIV in the context of Indigenous youth's lives and communities; they made connections between HIV and structural violence, loss of culture, and abusive relationships. For example, in one story, a youth describes how her parents' home became a space of violence because of intergenerational trauma that was connected to her grandparents' experiences of residential schooling. She discusses how she fell into a path of drugs and sex to numb the pain. This led her on a journey of self-discovery where she met many others who faced similar hardships. Through connecting with other women, this youth began to heal. Over videos and photographs of Indigenous women gathering supportively in song and dance, she narrates: "I will start my own fire. For my fuel I will forgive, first myself. Secondly, I will forgive my parents, and their parents for the continuation of this vicious cycle . . . No matter who you are, or what you've been through, we're all worthy of love."

In contrast to conventional public health messaging on HIV and AIDS that promote behavior change and biomedical treatment, the youth-produced stories rejected individual prevention models. They foregrounded Indigenous ways of knowing that highlight the relationality between physical, spiritual, and mental health, as well as individual, family, and communal health (Flicker et al., 2017). They also emphasize the importance of reclaiming ceremonies, traditional knowledge, and culture for intergenerational healing.

The youth were reunited the following summer to engage in a series of participatory analysis activities to identify commonalities across the stories. For instance, after screening each story, participants were asked to use sticky notes to document key ideas arising. They then put all the sticky notes up on a wall and clustered them into larger themes. The youth then named and wrote paragraph to describe each theme (e.g., "Addiction has Spoken for Us: Let's Break the Silence" or "Stay Strong, Stay Sexy, Stay Native"). To validate these, each storyteller was asked to identify the themes that they felt were most salient in their own stories. In the final exercise, youth discussed how these clusters might be used to curate movie nights. They developed a suggested playlist of stories and discussion guides for each theme. This youth-developed curriculum was then used in screenings across the country to prompt dialogue, educate, and challenge stigma.

Cellphilms

A cellphilm is a participant-produced video made with a cell phone or another type of accessible mobile technology. MacEntee et al. (2016) explain the method to have emerged from the increased availability of cell phones, which in turn has increased people's everyday production of visual media. Increased cell phone access also offers a means to overcome some of the unequal power dynamics presented by participatory video (Milne et al., 2012) techniques that rely on more expensive and specialized video technology. The cellphilm method begins with participants exploring a research prompt or theme. The participants can then work individually or in small groups to decide on a topic for their story. A storyboard is used to flesh out the cellphilm visually and narratively. After reviewing the ethics of filming with the group, the participants proceed to shoot their video. Depending on the amount of time, as well as participants' (and researchers') technical skills and access to video editing applications, the cellphilms may or may not involve post-filming editing. A cellphilm workshop can be completed in as few as 3 hours; more in-depth workshops can last several days.

Participants screen and discuss their cellphilms. This may lead to another round of filming and editing, as participants may be inspired to re-represent their original cellphilm (Mitchell et al., 2014), or it may lead to the production of completely new cellphilms (Mitchell et al., 2016). The videos can be shared in screenings, from phone to phone, or archived online for wider audience viewing. The digital nature of the videos means that they may be presented multiple times and to different audiences as a teaching tool (MacEntee & Mandrona, 2015). Creating online participatory archives of cellphilms (and photovoice or digital stories) allow the visual media to evolve over time with participant and public engagement (Burkholder, 2016; Burkholder & MacEntee, 2016).

Case Study: Telling Stories about Cell Phones and Sex, in and around Schools in Rural South Africa

In a rural area of KwaZulu Natal, South Africa, the cellphilm workshop *Telling stories about cellphones and sex*, took place over four meetings and involved nine girls and three boys between 14 and 21 years old (MacEntee, 2015). The cellphilm method was chosen because young people had relatively high access to cell phones in a school that had limited infrastructure, electricity, and few computers. The participants worked collaboratively to brainstorm the researcher-generated prompt, which was the same as the project title. In this region, sexual activity is the leading cause of HIV transmission. Consequently, youth sexual activity and living with HIV are both highly stigmatized. The prompt's emphasis on 'telling stories' was meant to present participants with an opportunity to share their knowledge about these topics without having to disclose personal information and risk social stigmatization or punishment.

The participants worked individually to complete a storyboard. They then worked collaboratively, using cell phones that the researcher provided for this task, to shoot their cellphilms. The person whose story was being shot was the director. While they negotiated the acting of different scenes, the ultimate decisions of how the cellphilm was to be filmed (the location, angle of the camera, etc.) was decided on by the director. Participants used a no-editing-required technique

(Mitchell & De Lange, 2011), that used the 'pause' feature on the phone's video recorder to film the scenes sequentially. This avoids the need for any video editing post-filming. The cellphilms were then screened and discussed as a group.

All the cellphilms that the youth created during this workshop (fourteen in total) were of a dramatic genre. Each story covers a range of issues and themes, however, the majority of them touched on transactional sex – the practice of exchanging sex, often with an older man, for high-end commodities such as cell phones. Their productions also depict young women using their phones to explore and express their sexuality, especially over social media, in ways that transgress normative gender roles. Discussing these cellphilms, the participants explained how young women choose a transactional partner. Along with having money and being willing to pay for cell phones and other high-end commodities, a potential partner must also be physically attractive. The girls recognized that these relationships come with great risk to young women. Their cellphilms depict girls who engage in transactional sex to obtain a cell phone experiencing sexual violence, sexual coercion, unplanned pregnancy, social stigma and bullying, HIV and AIDS, and death.

There were ethical concerns over how to frame the cellphilms to engage wider audiences in a generative discussion over the complex and sensitive issues raised by the female participants. Despite being fictionalized composite stories, some of the cellphilms closely imitated actual events at the school. There was a risk that showing the cellphilms in the community might have prompted (further) stigmatization of the people on which the stories may have been based. There was also a concern that the stories would be construed as depicting the direct experiences of the research participants. This might lead to negative feedback or punishment. Thus, the participants decided against screening their cellphilms at their school or at an organized community event.

The cellphilms have been screened with permission, however, in other ways. One of the participants took a copy of her cellphilm on her phone and showed it privately to her mother. This led to them discussing the cellphilm and the practice of transactional sex at schools. The participants were also keen that the cellphilms be screened outside their community, for example, in international academic settings. As a result, they have been shown in Canada, Sweden, and the United States. However, these screenings have raised their own set of ethical concerns. Screeners need to frame the cellphilms carefully, for example, by asking audiences to reflect on their position in relation to the cellphilms that they are watching. Information about the research process can help diverse audiences to engage in a constructive interpretation of the data and avoid reinforcing dominant racialized discourses of African girls as victims and in need of saving (MacEntee, 2016b).

Choosing among Methods for the Study of Youth Sexuality

As the case studies illustrate, photovoice, digital storytelling, and cellphilming, can produce copious data for researchers interested in learning more about youth perspectives on sexuality. In addition to an analysis of the visual texts produced by participants, data such as audio or video recordings of the process, photo documentation of participant engagement in the doing of this work, field notes, focus groups, one-on-one interviews, and audience interviews can be collected as supplementary data that 'captures' the dynamic ways that young people make sense of the visual process and the photographs/stories/videos that they created. Lapenta (2011) argued that "grounding of the images in a shared interpretation of their real and personal experience" can "empower marginalized groups to articulate and 'voice' their opinions to researchers or policymakers" (p. 208). It quickly becomes evident to practitioners that the PVM process is highly generative. Furthermore, empirical data and resources are effective knowledge engagement tools.

There is considerable variation within each of the methods already discussed. For instance, when photovoice was popularized in the 1990s, participants were usually given disposable cameras to take their pictures. Rolls of film were printed to facilitate discussion. As access to digital photography has proliferated, increasingly projects are using digital cameras or cell phones with young people. Nowadays, there is the option of printing photos or working with them in their digital format.

Likewise, different projects give participants more or less time to produce the visual texts (Catalani & Minkler, 2010). For photovoice, for example, Dakin and colleagues (2015) describe meeting with participants twice a week for seven weeks, and participants taking photographs between each meeting. In contrast, Gervais and Rivard (2013) describe participants taking and working with photographs within a few hours.

A digital storytelling workshop typically takes participants several meetings, or approximately 24 hours of group time, to complete. It is a highly facilitated process. The process requires a degree of computer literacy on the part of the researcher and participants. As editing software becomes more and more intuitive and integrated, this time frame may be shorter, especially among youth with high media literacy skills.

The case studies also draw attention to the overlap and fluidity between the methods. Depending on how a project evolves 'on the ground,' participants may work, for example, with photovoice photographs and captions on the computer so that they begin to resemble the sequential narrative of a digital story (e.g., see Gubrium and Harper's (2016) discussion of Claudia Mitchell's photovoice work on sexual health in sub-Saharan Africa). Alternatively, a digital story might be made on a cell phone in a way that makes the final product indistinguishable from a cellphilm. Table 18.1 summarizes key similarities and differences across the three methods.

Given this variation and fluidity, research teams need to think about how the different PVMs might contribute to the particular study of youth sexuality. When making decisions about project methodology, the scope of the research will be limited by budget, equipment access, and the technological fluency of participants and facilitators. While all PVMs described herein require a significant investment of time and resources to effectively accomplish, with modifications all three

Table 18.1 *Comparing three methods*

Method	Photovoice	Digital storytelling	Cellphilms
Time	2+ hours	3+ days	3+ hours
Type of research question	Exploratory and looking for scoping responses (i.e., identifying range of issues)	Exploratory and looking for personal, experiential responses	Exploratory and looking for contextual analysis
Access to technology	Low tech	High tech	Low tech
Facilitation skills	High	High	Moderate
Technology fluency (of participants)	Low	Medium	Low
Visual fluency (of participants)	Low	Medium	Low
Types of visual data produced	Photographs	Multimedia visual stories	Videos
Display/curation	Photography exhibit Projections Online	Screenings Online	Screenings Phone to phone Online
Archiving	Permanent/ travelling exhibit Private computer Online	Private computer Online	On the phone Private computer Online

methods can be adapted for relatively modest research budgets. The investment of time and energy by the participant and research group is perhaps the biggest barrier to deep and critical PVMs. In our work, we have observed several times that the visual production process is best repeated two or three times to really allow participants and researchers to produce and reflect on the visual media and the research questions. Alongside pragmatic questions about project budgets, time, and infrastructure, we present a series of theoretically driven questions that research teams and communities should consider before engaging with participatory visual research on youth sexuality:

(1) How might a visual method productively coincide or diverge from existing community practices of talking about issues related to sexuality and sex?
(2) Do the participants favor a particular visual method, especially as it relates to the study of sexuality? Why?
(3) How might the visual methods that young people already use to engage in matters regarding sex and sexuality be integrated as research method?

(4) How ready are participants, facilitators, and communities to literally see youth representations of sex and sexuality? What guidelines are necessary to put in place to address issues of, for example, nudity or violence?
(5) Are there local experts/artists who can act as (co-)facilitators for this work on youth sexuality? Do members of the research team have technical training as artist facilitators?
(6) What types of research questions are being asked? Are you looking to identify a wide scope of issues (photovoice)? Or is the focus to explore more up-close and particularized understandings of a specific topic (digital storytelling or cellphilms)?
(7) How will the visual products be disseminated? Does the community have the means to disseminate in this way? Will decision makers be open to this visual medium as a form of knowledge representation for youth sexuality?
(8) What are the risks (and to whom) of sharing youth generated material? What parameters can be put into place upfront to mitigate these risks?

These questions are meant to help researchers think through project planning and administration issues. The questions also point toward the socially contentious issues underlying the study of youth sexuality (e.g., social discomfort of recognizing young people's rights to sexuality; and the capacity of young people to lead decision making on matters relating to their sexuality). On the one hand, the questions might raise awareness of the ways introducing PVMs can heighten these existing challenges. On the other hand, reflecting carefully on the answers to these questions may help project teams to see the potential benefit in using photovoice, digital storytelling, or cellphilming. Teams may come to find that PVMs often encourage nuanced, productive, and engaged analyses of these contentions in order to ultimately stimulate community-based change.

Ethical Issues

When conducting research on youth sexuality there are numerous ethical concerns. Likewise, PVMs, like all methodologies, also have ethical challenges and limitations. Publications like Warr et al.'s (2016) *Ethics and Visual Research Methods* offer significant insights into the unique complexities of consent, confidentiality, anonymity, representation, and ownership when working with visual data. When considering a stigmatized and contested issues, such as youth sexuality, there is the added concern for participants' comfort and safety. Current best-practice guidelines in PVMs (Gubrium et al., 2014) suggest that consent needs to be negotiated in an ongoing, multistep fashion that considers the self-determination of participant/content creators. We outline the following list of (by no means exhaustive) questions to point toward the complexities of negotiating ongoing consent when using PVMs to study youth sexuality:

(1) *Consent to participate:* Do we want to participate in this research project that involves taking pictures/making cellphilms? Are we comfortable looking at and working closely with images that will take up issues of sexuality?
(2) *Consent to photography*: Is it okay for us to take your picture and include it in our research project? Are we comfortable potentially taking videos or pictures that depict aspects of our own sexuality or the sexuality of youth generally?
(3) *Consent to group agreements/guidelines*: Can we all agree about the parameters for the kinds of pictures/videos that are acceptable to gather for this project (e.g., nudity, violence, illegal activity)?
(4) *Third-party consent*: Do we have written or verbal permission from everyone who is featured in our work? Do we feel prepared to safely negotiate obtaining the informed consent to take someone's picture/video in relation to youth sexuality with someone outside the research project?
(5) *Consent to sharing the work:* Is it okay for us to share our work publicly? In what contexts and forms? Are there particular images/files that you want to include/exclude from dissemination?
(6) *How do you want to be represented:* would you prefer to be named as the artist who took this picture or to remain anonymous?

When working with youth on issues regarding consent in any of these contexts, parental/guardian consent may also be required. For some youth, accessing parental consent for involvement in research on sexual matters may be tricky; their desire to participate may be (mis)interpreted as admitting to being sexually active (Flicker & Guta, 2008). This may inadvertently cause harm from guardians who are not supportive of youth expressing their sexuality. Care needs to be taken to ensure that youth are supported in navigating this process and that consent forms do not 'out' sexual identities of behaviors.

While participants may be excited and eager to be pictured and share visual art at the beginning or when they first create it, they may feel differently when some time has passed after the workshop. For example, in the digital story case study referred to earlier, one of the youth decided to create a digital story about her experience of sexual violence. During the workshop, she found creating her story in a supportive environment to be extremely liberating and healing. In the moment, she provided consent for the research team to publicly share her story. However, when the research team recontacted her to double check several months later (before publicly sharing the work), the youth decided that the story was too personal to share. She was happy for it to be used internally as data, but uncomfortable with the idea of it being screened for an audience. Maintaining contact and checking in with young participants, whose lives and beliefs can change dramatically in a short time, is critical.

Another option is for participants to post their visuals online over social media themselves. This allows them to maintain control over their work and remove it on their own terms should they ever feel the need (Burkholder & MacEntee, 2016). In the cellphilm case study there was an example of a participant keeping a copy on her phone, which opens up the possibility of her sharing the video online at a later date. Regardless of who is posting content online, it is extremely important to engage young people in critical discussions regarding the permanence of digital footprints. Once content is publicly posted (particularly in digital form), it is very difficult to retract.

Anonymity is increasingly difficult to maintain when integrating digital technology. Risks associated with disclosure may be heightened when considering the stigmatization of youth and sexuality and/or when issues of violence and coercion are being raised (e.g., the cellphilm case study). There is an imperative to respect young people's right to privacy and self-disclosure as it relates to their sexualities. However, doctoring images or obscuring faces through pixilation, for example, may not be totally possible or a welcome solution for participants (Jordan, 2014). Many digital cameras and other mobile technology have the capacity to document location; this makes ensuring participant confidentiality during and after the research process more complex (Warr et al., 2016). Strategies such as avoiding faces or taking more metaphorical or abstract images are other options that visual researchers have employed to avoid the immediate recognition of young participants (Ruiz-Casares & Thompson, 2016). Strategies such as using pseudonyms or assigning numbers can also be adapted to the visual process to help ensure that participants' identities remain anonymous. However, the visual production process and its capacity to represent individuals in a recognizable manner, means that keeping participants identities confidential is more challenging or undesirable.

Sometimes PVM participants want to be recognized for their work and have their identities linked to their art. The rigor of maintaining participant confidentiality in research can be interpreted as being in opposition to the emancipatory and empowerment components of the participatory process. In these circumstances, it may be important to give youth a choice as to whether and how they want their contributions publicly recognized or credited.

When dealing with sexual issues, there are further challenges when considering the possibility of participants disclosing abuse. There are clear legal regulations on a researchers' responsibility to report disclosed abuse of a minor, and this limitation in confidentiality must be made clear to participants at the onset of the project. Appropriate and accessible resources and support should also be identified and made available to participants. However, beyond these standards of practice, PVMs can also elicit the (re)enactment of sexual encounters and violence. The acting and viewing of such situations can bring about difficult emotions for participants (and researchers). On the one hand, the process can be a moment to destigmatize these experiences. On the other hand, people may feel uncomfortable or re-traumatized. This may also be the case if/when the images are distributed to the public. Balancing the needs of the individual and the group likely entails ongoing, participant-centered, reflexive discussion on the ethics of visual production and representation.

Conclusion

In this chapter, we have reviewed three digital PVMs as they relate to the study of youth sexuality, with a careful attention to how research teams might begin to choose between methods. We have also provided a brief overview of the unique ethical concerns related to using PVMs to study youth sexuality. However, we want to conclude by noting that technological innovations will likely continue to change the parameters for how we do our work. Technological innovation continues to present new opportunities for rethinking the ways in which we gather, collect, collate, archive, synthesize, and share new media. The possibilities are limited only by our own imaginations.

Youth culture is synonymous with digital and mobile technologies in many parts of the world. PVMs offer new opportunities to engage youth in sexual research that reflects the ways they are already navigating the world and their sexual lives. By leveraging their interests and expertise as early adopters of mobile participatory cultures, PVMs provide youth and researchers with an opportunity to literally *see* and *experience* their world in new ways. As illustrated in our case studies, PVMs have been instrumental in amplifying unique youth perspectives on sexuality. Using photovoice literarily showed us the ways that LGBTQ experience erasure. Digital storytelling helped us indigenize HIV-prevention messages. Creating cellphilms gave us a window into understanding the ubiquitous nature of transactional sex in some young women's lives. These methods help us to see the multiple, messy, juxtaposing, and often contradictory ways in which youth understand themselves as sexual beings. The engaging products developed become unique advocacy tools and dissemination products. Most importantly, we are all transformed by the process.

References

Alcoff, L. (1991). The Problem of Speaking for Others. *Cultural Critique*, *20*, 5–32.

Allen, L. & Ingram, T. (2015). "Bieber Fever": Girls, Desire and the Negotiation of Girlhood Sexualities. In Renold, E., Ringrose, J., & Egan, R. D. (Eds.), *Children, Sexuality and Sexualization* (141–158). New York: Palgrave Macmillan.

Ball, H. (2008). Quilts. In Knowles, J. G. & Cole, A. L. (Eds.), *Handbook of the Arts in Qualitative Research: Perspectives, Methodologies, Examples, and Issues* (363–368). Thousand Oaks, CA: Sage.

Brandt, D. (2008). Touching Minds and Hearts: Community Arts as Collaborative Research. In Knowles, J. G. & Cole, A. L. (Eds.), *Handbook of the Arts in Qualitative Research: Perspectives, Methodologies, Examples, and Issues* (351–362). Thousand Oaks, CA: Sage.

Buckingham, D. & Sefton-Green, J. (1994). *Cultural Studies Goes to School: Reading and Teaching Popular Media*. London: Taylor & Francis.

Burkholder, C. (2016). We Are HK too! Disseminating Cellphilms in a Participatory Archive. In MacEntee, K., Burkholder, C., & Schwab-Cartas, J. (Eds.), *What's a Cellphim?: Integrating Mobile Phone Technology into Participatory Arts-Based Research and Activism*. Rotterdam: Sense.

Burkholder, C. & MacEntee, K. (2016). Exploring the Ethics of a Participant-Produced Cellphilm Archive: The Complexities of Dissemination. In Warr, D., Guillemin, M., Cox, S. M., & Waycott, J. (Eds.), *Visual Research Ethics: Learning from Practice*. London: Palgrave MacMillan.

Catalani, C. & Minkler, M. (2010). Photovoice: A Review of the Literature in Health and Public Health. *Health Education & Behavior*, *37*(3), 424–451.

Chalfen, R. (2011). Differentiating Practices of Participatory Visual Media Production. In Margolis, E. & Pauwels, L. (Eds.), *The SAGE Handbook of Visual Research Methods* (186–200). Los Angeles: Sage.

Dakin, E. K., Parker, S. N., Amell, J. W., & Rogers, B. S. (2015). Seeing with Our Own Eyes: Youth in Mathare, Kenya Use Photovoice to Examine Individual and Community Strengths. *Qualitative Social Work*, *14*(2), 170–192. doi:10.1177/1473325014526085.

Danforth, J. & Flicker, S. (2014). *Taking Action!!: Art and Aboriginal Youth Leadership for HIV Prevention*. Toronto, ON: Taking Action. www.takingaction4youth.org/wp-content/uploads/2009/11/1455_TakingAction2_Booklet_LowRes.pdf.

Dobson, A. S. & Ringrose, J. (2016). Sext Education: Pedagogies of Sex, Gender and Shame in the Schoolyards of Tagged and Exposed. *Sex Education*, *16*(1), 8–21. doi:10.1080/14681811.2015.1050486.

Drew, S. E., Duncan, R. E., & Sawyer, S. M. (2010). Visual Storytelling: A Beneficial But Challenging Method for Health Research with Young People. *Qualitative Health Research*, *20*(12), 1677–1688. doi:10.1177/1049732310377455.

Eisner, E. W. (1997). The Promise and Perils of Alternative Forms of Data Representation. *Educational Researcher*, *26*(6), 4–10.

(2003). On the Differences between Scientific and Artistic Approaches to Qualitative Research. *Visual Arts Research*, *29*(57), 5–11.

Flicker, S. (2008). Who Benefits from Community-Based Participatory Research? A Case Study of the Positive Youth Project. *Health Education & Behavior*, *35*(1), 70–86.

Flicker, S., Danforth, J., Konsmo, E., et al. (2013). "Because We Are Natives and We Stand Strong to Our Pride": Decolonizing HIV Prevention with Aboriginal Youth in Canada Using the Arts. *Canadian Journal of Aboriginal Community-Based HIV/AIDS Research*, *5*, 4–24.

Flicker, S., Danforth, J. Y., Wilson, C., et al. (2014). "Because We Have Really Unique Art": Decolonizing Research with Indigenous Youth Using the Arts. *International Journal of Indigenous Health*, *10*(1), 16.

Flicker, S., & Guta, A. (2008). Ethical Approaches to Adolescent Participation in Sexual Health Research. *Journal of Adolescent Health*, *42*(1), 3–10. doi:10.1016/j.jadohealth.2007.07.017.>

Flicker, S., Maley, O., Ridgley, A., et al. (2008). e-PAR: Using Technology and Participatory Action Research to Engage Youth in Health Promotion. *Action Research*, *6*(3), 285–303. doi:10.1177/1476750307083711.

Flicker, S., Native Youth Sexual Health Network, Wilson, C., et al. (2017). "Stay Strong, Stay Sexy, Stay Native": Storying Indigenous Youth HIV Prevention Activism. *Action Research*. doi:10.1177/1476750317721302.

Freire, P. (1984). *Pedagogy of the Oppressed*. Translated by M. Bergman Ramos. New York: The Continuum Publishing Corporation.

Garcia, A. P., Minkler, M., Cardenas, Z., Grills, C., & Porter, C. (2013). Engaging Homeless Youth in Community-Based Participatory Research: A Case Study from Skid Row, Los Angeles. *Health Promotion Practice*, 15(1), 18–27.

Gervais, M., & Rivard, L. (2013). "SMART" Photovoice Agricultural Consultation: Increasing Rwandan Women Farmers' Active Participation in Development. *Development in Practice*, *23*(4), 496–510. doi:10.1080/09614524.2013.790942.

Gubrium, A. (2009). Digital Storytelling: An Emergent Method for Health Promotion Research and Practice. *Health Promotion Practice*, *10*(2), 186.

Gubrium, A., & Harper, K. (2016). *Participatory Visual and Digital Methods*. London: Routledge.

Gubrium, A., Hill, A., & Flicker, S. (2014). A Situated Practice of Ethics for Participatory Visual and Digital Methods in Public Health Research and Practice: A Focus on Digital Storytelling. *American Journal of Public Health*, *104*(9), 1606–1614.

Gubrium, A., Krause, E., & Jernigan, K. (2014). Strategic Authenticity and Voice: New Ways of Seeing and Being Seen as Young Mothers through Digital Storytelling. *Sexuality research & social policy : journal of NSRC : SR & SP*, *11*(4), 337–347. doi:10.1007/s13178-014-0161-x.

Gubrium, A., & Turner, K. C. N. (2011). Digital Storytelling as an Emergent Method for Social Research and Practice. In Hesse-Biber, S. N. (Ed.), *The Handbook of Emergent Technologies in Social Research* (469–491). New York: Oxford University Press.

Holtby, A., Klein, K., Cook, K., & Travers, R. (2015). To Be Seen or Not to Be Seen: Photovoice, Queer and Trans Youth, and the Dilemma of Representation. *Action Research*, *13*(4), 317–335. doi:10.1177/1476750314566414.

Israel, B. A., Schulz, A. J., Parker, E. A., & Becker, A. B. (1998). Review of Community-Based Research: Assessing Partnership Approaches to Improve Public Health. *Annual Review of Public Health*, *19*(1), 173–202.

Jenkins, H. (2006). *Convergence Culture: Where Old and New Media Collide*. New York: New York University Press.

(2013). From New Media Literacies to New Media Expertise. In Fraser, P. & Wardle, J. (Eds.), *Current Perspectives in Media Education: Beyond the Manifesto* (110–127). Basingstoke: Palgrave Macmillan.

Jenkins, H., Purushotma, R., Weigel, M., Clinton, K., & Robison, A. (2009). *Confronting the Challenges of Participatory Culture: Media Education for the 21st Century*. Cambridge, MA: MIT Press.

Joanou, J. P. (2009). The Bad and the Ugly: Ethical Concerns in Participatory Photographic Methods with Children Living and Working on the Streets of Lima, Peru. *Visual Studies*, *24*(3), 214–223. doi:10.1080/14725860903309120.

Jordan, S. R. (2014). Research Integrity, Image Manipulation, and Anonymizing Photographs in Visual Social Science Research. *International Journal of Social Research Methodology*, *17*(4), 441–454. doi:10.1080/13645579.2012.759333.

Klein, K., Holtby, A., Cook, K., & Travers, R. (2015). Complicating the Coming Out Narrative: Becoming Oneself in a Heterosexist and Cissexist World. *Journal of homosexuality*, *62*(3), 297–326.

Lambert, J. (2012). *Digital Storytelling: Capturing Lives, Creating Community.* New York: Routledge.

Lapenta, F. (2011). Some Theoretical and Methodological Views on Photo-Elicitation. In Margolis, E. & Pauweles, L. (Eds.), *The Sage Handbook of Visual Research Methods* (201–213). Thousand Oaks, CA: Sage.

Lenhart, A., & Pew Research Center. (2015). Teens, Social Media & Technology Overview 2015: Smarphones Facilitate Shifts in Communication Landscape for Teens. Retrieved from www.pewinternet.org/2015/04/09/teens-social-media-technology-2015/.

Luttrell, W. (2010). 'A Camera Is a Big Responsibility': A Lens for Analysing Children's Visual Voices. *Visual Studies*, *25*(3), 224–237. doi:10.1080/1472586X.2010.523274.

Lykes, B. (2001). Creative Arts and Photography in Participatory Action Research in Guatemala. In Reason, P. & Bradbury, H. (Eds.), *Handbook of Action Research: Participative Inquiry and Practice* (363–371). London: Sage.

MacEntee, K. (2015). Using Cellphones to Discuss Cellphones: Gender-Based Violence and Girls' Sexual Agency in and around Schools in Rural South Africa in the Age of AIDS. In Gillander Gådin, K. & Mitchell, C. (Eds.), *Being Young in a Neoliberal Time: Transnational Perspectives on Challenges and Possibilities for Resistance and Social Change* (31–52). Sundsvall: Forum for Gender Studies at Mid Sweden University.

(2016a). Girls, Condoms, Tradition, and Abstinence: Making Sense of HIV Prevention Discourses in Rural South Africa. In Mitchell, C. & Rentschler, C. (Eds.), *Girlhood and the Politics of Place* (315–332). New York: Berghahn.

(2016b). Facing Constructions of African Girlhood: Reflections on Screening Participant's Cellphilms in Academic Contexts. In MacEntee, K., Burkholder, C., & Schwab-Cartas, J. (Eds.), *What's a Cellphilm? Mobile Digital Technology for Research and Activism* (137–152). Rotterdam: Sense.

MacEntee, K., Burkholder, C., & Schwab-Cartas, J. (2016). *What's a Cellphilm? Integrating Mobile Technology into Visual Research and Activism.* Rotterdam: Sense.

MacEntee, K., & Mandrona, A. (2015). From Discomfort to Collaboration: Teachers Screening Cellphilms in a Rural South African School. *Perspectives in Education*, *33*(4), 43–56.

Milne, E.-J., Mitchell, C., & De Lange, N. (2012). *Handbook of Participatory Video.* Plymouth: AltaMira.

Mitchell, C. (2011). *Doing Visual Research.* Los Angeles, London: Sage.

Mitchell, C., & De Lange, N. (2011). Community-Based Participatory Video and Social Action in Rural South Africa. In Margolis, E. & Pauwels, L. (Eds.), *The SAGE Handbook of Visual Research Methods* (171–185). Los Angeles: Sage.

Mitchell, C., De Lange, N., & Moletsane, R. (2014). Me and My Cellphone: Constructing Change from the Inside through Cellphilms and Participatory Video in a Rural Community. *Area*, *48*(4), 1–7. doi:10.1111/area.12142.

(2016). Poetry in a Pocket: The Cellphilms of South African Rural Women Teachers and the Poetics of the Everyday. In MacEntee, K., Burkholder, C., & Schwab-Cartas, J. (Eds.), *What's a Cellphilm? Integrating Mobile Technology into Visual Research and Activism* (19–34). Rotterdam: Sense.

Mitchell, C. & Sommer, M. (2016). Participatory Visual Methodologies in Global Public Health. *Global Public Health*, *11*(5–6), 521–527. doi:10.1080/17441692.2016.1170184.

Pauwels, L. (2010). Visual Sociology Reframed: An Analytical Synthesis and Discussion of Visual Methods in Social and Cultural Research. *Sociological Methods & Research*, *38*(4), 545–581.

Pew Research Center. (2012). Global Digital Communication: Texting, Social Networking Popular Worldwide. Retrieved from www.pewglobal.org/2011/12/20/global-digital-communication-texting-social-networking-popular-worldwide/.

Pillow, W. (2003). Confession, Catharsis, or Cure? Rethinking the Uses of Reflexivity as Methodological Power in Qualitative Research. *International Journal of Qualitative Studies in Education*, *16*(2), 175–196. doi:10.1080/0951839032000060635.

Pink, S. (2001). *Doing Visual Ethnography: Images, Media, and Representation in Research*. Thousand Oaks: Sage.

(2003). Interdisciplinary Agendas in Visual Research: Re-Situating Visual Anthropology. *Visual Studies*, *18*(2), 179–192.

Rose, G. (2014). On the Relation between 'Visual Research Methods' and Contemporary Visual Culture. *The Sociological Review*, *62*(1), 24–46. doi:10.1111/1467-954X.12109.

(2016). *Visual Methodologies: An Introduction to the Interpretation of Visual Materials*. London: Sage.

Ruiz-Casares, M., & Thompson, J. (2016). Obtaining Meaningful Informed Consent: Preliminary Results of a Study to Develop Visual Informed Consent Forms with Children. *Children's Geographies*, *14*(1), 35–45.

Stuart, J. (2006). 'From Our Frames': Exploring with Teachers the Pedagogic Possibilities of a Visual Arts-Based Approach to HIV and AIDS. *Journal of Education*, *38*, 67–88.

Switzer, S. (2017). What's in an Image? Towards a Critical Reading of Participatory Visual Methods. In Capous-Desyllas, M. & Morgaine, K. (Eds.), *Creating Social Change through Creativity: Anti-Oppressive Arts-Based Research Methodologies*. Cham, CH: Palgrave MacMillan.

Theron, L., Mitchell, C., Smith, A. L., & Stuart, J. (2011). *Picturing Research*. Rotterdam: Springer.

Wang, C. (2008). Using Photovoice as a Participatory Assessment and Issue Selection Tool. In Minkler, M. & Wallerstein, N. (Eds.), *Community Based Participatory Research for Health: From Process to Outcomes*, 2nd edn. (179–196). San Francisco: Jossey-Bass.

Wang, C. & Burris, M. A. (1997). Photovoice: Concept, Methodology, and Use for Participatory Needs Assessment. *Health Education & Behavior*, *24*(3), 369–387. doi:10.1177/109019819702400309.

Warr, D., Waycott, J., & Guillemin, M. (2016). Ethical Issues in Visual Research and the Value of Stories from the Field. In Warr, D., Cox, S., Guillemin, M., & Waycott, J. (Eds.), *Ethics and Visual Research Methods: Theory, Methodology, and Practice* (1–16). New York: Palgrave MacMillan.

Weber, S. (2008). Visual Images in Research. In Knowles, J. G. & Cole, A. L. (Eds.), *Handbook of the Arts in Qualitative Research* (41–54). Los Angeles: Sage.

Wilson, C., & Flicker, S. (2015). Picturing Transactional $ex: Ethics, Challenges and Possibilities. In Gubrium, A., Harper, K., Otañez, M., & Vannini, P. (Eds.), *Participatory Visual and Digital Research in Action*. Walnut Creek: Left Coast Press.

19 Research under Surveillance

Sexuality and Gender-Based Research with Children in South Africa

Deevia Bhana

> One of the key sites of contemporary tensions around sexuality is the state and status of childhood: although sex is now widely thought of as fulfilling and life-enhancing activity, this applies only to adults. Just as sexuality is defined as a special area of life, so children are constructed as a special category of being; sexuality is seen as particularly problematic and, in some respects, as inimical to childhood itself
>
> (Jackson & Scott, 2010: p. 101).

The image of childhood as a "special category" shapes ideas around sexual innocence. Sexual innocence works to reinforce the special category of children. It is an enduring categorization of children (Robinson, 2013; Jackson & Scott, 2010) and represents a hegemonic pattern even in South Africa (Bhana, 2016a, 2016b). This discursive strategy of childhood operates to position a near-exclusive focus on sexuality as dangerous to children and assumes that sexual risk and protection from sex and sexuality is the only way to reduce harm to children's development. This chapter draws attention to the perils of doing school-based sexuality research when the assumption of the research runs contrary to dominant views about childhood sexual innocence. The chapter focuses on different stages of the research process to demonstrate how several discourses cohere in defense of childhood sexual innocence to limit what is possible to know, research, and examine about children's sexual and cultural worlds. I argue that these discourses and practices based on childhood sexual protection constrain school-based sexuality research and are a hindrance to children's right to discuss, contest, and represent themselves on issues about sexuality that matter to them. The special category of childhood produces an environment of surveillance, suspicion, and fear generated by a motif that normalizes sexual innocence by producing an exclusive focus on the child as vulnerable, needing to be rescued from sexuality (Egan, 2013). This produces an environment of fear and anxiety and makes such research risky for researchers.

One important mechanism of the risky regulatory environment is the university ethics committee or institutional review boards (IRBs). Other regulatory mechanisms that produce the special category of childhood include access to school sites that remain difficult to navigate when the research is antithetical to the dominant view of childhood sexual innocence. While institutional obstacles hinder the research process, public homophobic vitriol around school-based sexuality research is also an important regulatory mechanism, especially under heteronormative conditions. The stages of the research process that are highlighted in this chapter include the difficult process of negotiating with a university ethics committee, negotiating access with the provincial Department of Education, and bearing moral indignation during the conclusion of the project.

The obstacles faced in the process of conducting research that associated children with sexuality (and heteronormativity), is embedded within the normalization of childhood innocence that casts children as ignorant of sex and sexuality.

To understand the hegemonic and normalized construction of childhood as innocence, scholars have suggested that Foucault's (1977) understanding of disciplinary power remains relevant (Graham et al., 2017). Foucault (1977) has used Bentham's notion of the panopticon to theorize the disciplinary effect of power. By drawing attention to the metaphor of the panopticon prison design, Foucault shows how the design of the prison or its architecture allows a guard to monitor the prisoners although the prisoners are unable to see the guard. This produces the effect of uninterrupted surveillance that coerces individuals to submit to power. Under constant surveillance, the prisoners become their own guard and normalize their own conduct. A sense of permanent surveillance is induced so that obedience is confirmed as an automatic response and a function of power (Foucault, 1977). This kind of surveillance and self-surveillance can be applied to the research process involving children and sexuality (Graham et al., 2017).

A discourse of danger, risk, and fear maintains the normalization of children as innocents. Another discourse of presumed heterosexuality is present although this can be seen as a contradiction to the discourse of childhood innocence (Allen & Rasmussen, 2017; Clark, 2013; Renold et al., 2016; Robinson, 2013; Sundaram & Sauntson, 2016). A range of social apparatuses are put to work in governing and regulating these discourses in which the researcher is also implicated. The panopticon as noted by Foucault (1977) ensures the functioning and visibility of power without power being verifiable. Doing sexuality research with children operates in a similar way where all subjects, including the researcher, are caught up in the surveillance of childhood sexual innocence, but they cannot verify from where they are being observed.

To demonstrate the obstacles in the course of doing research in South Africa, I draw from the experiences of three research projects that sought to foreground children and young people's *own* perspectives around gender and sexuality. In the first research project described later in this chapter, titled "Stop the violence: boys and girls in and around schools," the study sought to examine the experiences of children from the age of 6 years old. In applying for ethics approval the university ethics committee asked, "Does the study need to include children of such a very young age?" Sikes (2008, p. ix) suggests that "researching topics that focus, or even touch on young people and sex can be contaminated by . . . moral panic spread in society." When children at age 6 are deemed capable of participating in research the panic is exacerbated resulting in "risk management" (see Allen et al., 2014).

The second, "Learning sex: how high school students consume pornography and give meaning to gender and sexualities" was the original title of a project with my graduate student (Carboni & Bhana, 2017) emerging out of a larger study titled, "Learning from the learners." The studies sought to examine how young people make meaning of their sexuality, and in the age of increasing access to the Internet, which in turn increases access to explicit material and pornography, we wanted to know from young people how and what they learnt about gender and sexuality. Access to public schools was denied and a letter of regret was received from a provincial Department of Education boldly written "NOT SUITABLE."

The third project, "A climate study of homosexuality and homophobia in South African secondary schools" examined how schools managed, gave meaning to, and experienced homosexuality (Bhana, 2014a). Against the broader context in South Africa, where corrective rape of lesbians has become widespread (Msibi, 2012) and homophobic stances are taken publicly by political leaders, despite a rights-based context in the country, the study sought to examine from race- and class-specific school contexts how non-normative sexuality was experienced. This research advocating equality on the basis of sexual orientation in South African schools received public challenge on social network sites and was undermined. The attack framed the research as a "gay mafia" brigade, working toward destroying the very fabric of heterosexuality in South Africa. I elaborate how this censure operates to produce and reinforce heterosexual domination and marginalize the integrity of both the research and the researcher. In this case, I argue the panopticon operates on a hetero-ethical basis. It produces a contradictory "ethical" position that makes researching childhood sexuality a difficult exercise while contradictorily also confirming heterosexuality as the only way to research express sexuality. Of concern here is the vitriol directed at the research that undoubtedly emerged because of the visibility given to non-normative sexualities at school.

In summary, the aggregate effect of this kind of treatment, exemplified by the response to these three projects, prevents any challenge to a discourse about childhood innocence and preserves the heteronormative assumption. This hetero-ethical stance squeezes out and limits the opportunities to do research with children around what is both contentious and problematic (Allen et al., 2014). Like Allen et al. (2014), I argue further that if we are to address children as sexual agents, we must "refuse to contribute to the perpetuation" of a research environment that seeks to close off the opportunities for researching sexuality and schooling. Indeed, while the panopticon is powerful enough to ensure obedience to the dominant discursive construct of childhood sexual innocence, it is not without resistance and is constantly open to resistance (Allen, 2008; Flanagan, 2012; Graham et al., 2017). There are opportunities for resistance, albeit with repercussions.

Contextualizing Childhood Sexuality

There is a contextual basis for understanding the surveillance of children and sexuality in South Africa. Sex and sexuality occupy an important place, especially in the context of the country's major social and economic problems. Gendered poverty, structural inequalities, the historical legacies of apartheid, girls' subordinate position within gendered society, male power, and economic and social upheavals create patterns of vulnerability to and experience of violence in South Africa (Shefer, 2014). One report suggests that more than 27 percent of men in South Africa admitted to raping and sexually coercing women and girls (Jewkes et al., 2011). In the crucible of structural inequalities, unemployment has reached 27.5 percent (Statistics South Africa, 2015), chronic disease in the face of HIV is rampant, violence against women and girls has increased, and all contribute to social turmoil. Girls, in particular, are harmed. Leading figures in the study of masculinity and violence have argued that men's emasculation, particularly those who are on the fringes of and marginalized in the economic base, has led to catastrophic effects for women and girls (Ratele, 2016).

Boys and girls at school are not immune from the broader social landscape. Documenting the complex processes through which young South Africans navigate gender, sexuality, and schooling, scholars have pointed to a multiplicity of factors, including ideological, social, cultural and economic factors, that produce a context that girls have been described as being 'scared at school' (Bhana, 2012; Human Rights Watch, 2001). Children in these circumstances often find themselves in what the overdeveloped world would consider "unchildlike contexts" (Bhana & Epstein, 2007, p. 123). There remain real concerns about children's vulnerability in relation to sexuality as well as their need for protection from sexual violence, harassment, and abuse. In order to address how these forms of violence and inequalities play out and how to challenge these the voices of children and young people need to be heard in order to develop appropriate interventions to address sexual and gender violence against children. As such, research that addresses children's active agency and gives attention to controversial issues is necessary both to address inequalities through which gender and sexuality are experienced and through which it is hidden by a discourse of childhood innocence.

Indeed, in the context where children are rendered vulnerable to sexual abuse and violence, it is important to prevent the construction of research with children as "difficult" as this reinforces the assumption that sexuality and childhood are "inimical" (Jackson & Scott, 2010) to each other. It is precisely this problem that needs investigation. With insight, scholars might be in a better place to understand what is dangerous about childhood sexuality that puts it under surveillance as a "no-go" arena of academic work. Working with children as sexual subjects means also that we have better knowledge of how meanings are shaped by gendered ideologies and what puts boys and girls at risk to violence and risk.

What Can Children Teach Us?

In these projects, the views and voices of children, even at age 6, were taken seriously by the researchers (Bhana, 2016a). A focus on children's own meaning of sexuality can tell us more about how sexuality is shaped by and the effects of the broader social order, and, in particular, to the ways in which gender and heterosexuality are key ordering principles through which they actively negotiate, challenge, and reproduce meanings. Such a focus situates sexuality not as a blank slate upon which children operate but as involving material, social, ideological, and cultural practices through which children themselves give meaning to social relations in tandem with their everyday lives. Researching childhood sexuality from children's standpoint can raise questions, increase debate, develop interventions, and change policy in ways that tell us about their agency, desires, and passions while also illuminating their pains, suffering, inequalities, violence, relations of domination, and subordination (Bay-Cheng, 2013; Bhana, 2016a; Carmody & Ovenden, 2013; Egan, 2013; Lamb, 2010; Renold et al., 2016).

Wood et al. (1998), in their study of sexual violence and coercion in South Africa, note that legal definitions of sexual harassment is not the same as how young women interpret it. For instance, when women in their study talked about 'forced love' they did not see force as violent. Instead, the young women interpreted men's force as a masculine expectation where being forceful was important to prove love. Instead of viewing children as innocent, research from the vantage point of boys' and girls' own points of view may offer insight into how and why sexual harassment continues and is tolerated, especially by women and girls.

Hlavka (2014), in her study of young people in the United States, argues that girls' experience of sexual abuse was normalized under gendered ideologies, where male sexual demands were assumed to be routine and expected based on male heterosexual prowess and female docility. Girls, therefore, did not see sexual abuse and violence but normalized it as what men and boys do. By listening to and giving children an opportunity to talk about their own experiences, researchers can have better insight into the underlying gendered and cultural ideologies through which sexual harassment and violence is normalized, as well as develop context specific interventions that appraise children's own understanding of sex, sexuality, pleasure, harassment, and violence.

Thus, it is important to conceptualize childhood sexuality as both productive and dangerous (Bay-Cheng, 2013; Carmody & Ovenden, 2013; Lamb, 2010; Tolman & McClelland, 2011). Both sexual agency and sexual protection need to be integrated in this conceptualization of sexuality. Ascribing children the role of active social agents who are invested in sexuality as both desirable and dangerous is thus particularly important. However, the dominant discourse of sexual innocence works to disrupt attempts to learn from children's own voices what they consider to be both pleasurable and dangerous. By viewing research that seeks to demonstrate children's agency to express their own views about sexual matters within sexual danger alone, rather than a continuum, our ability to develop appropriate skills for boys and girls to discern pleasure from danger are limited.

"Does the Study Need to Include Children of Such a Very Young Age?"

In the North, a tradition of working with children, gender, and sexuality is long established (Mac An Ghail, 1994; Thorne, 1993). While my own research is rooted in the current conjuncture in South Africa, my students and I engage with the broader debates around the ways in which childhood has been constructed. Allen (2008), writing in New Zealand, suggests that the climate of risk anxiety mobilizes a risk-management response from university ethics committees. The gaze upon research about sexuality and children often squeezes out the possibility to work with children's own standpoint and own perspectives around sexuality (Allen, 2008, 2014; Clark, 2013; Flanagan, 2012; Renold, 2005).

As noted earlier, "Does the study need to include children of such a very young age?" was the question posed to me in a letter from the University of KwaZulu-Natal's Humanities and Social Science Ethics Committee in 2013. The question from the university ethics committee sparked an interest in how to understand the surveillance and regulation of research when it comes to children, gender, and sexuality. The question arose in response to my application for ethical approval and clearance for the project "Stop the violence: boys and girls in and around schools." The study sought to examine the ways in which gender, sexuality, and violent schooling cultures were produced in a range of primary and high schools in South Africa. The study involved a range of social actors in diverse race- and class-specific school settings and included a focus on the actual experiences, words, and lives of children from the age of 6–18 years old.

The premise of the case study was to understand from the vantage point of boys and girls in South Africa, in various social settings, across different age groups, how they negotiated gender and sexuality in the context of violent relations at school. Schools in South Africa are not regarded as safe spaces, with girls, especially, vulnerable to violence enacted by male peers and teachers (Human Rights Watch, 2001). The research sought to understand how boys and girls engaged with each other as gendered and sexual beings, how they mediated such relations, and the ways in which heterosexuality, in particular, suffused such relations. As heterosexuality operates under conditions that support gender-oppressive relations (Butler 1990), the research was interested in how such unequal relations of power manifest as children engage with each other in schools, with particular attention to how violence coheres around such relations. Such research is valuable to develop appropriate interventions that could make schools more sensitive to the complex operation of gender relations of power, and to understand the ways in which sexuality foregrounds children's gendered cultures. It has implications for addressing violent gender and sexual relations. "Does the study need to include children of such a very young age?" functioned to articulate concerns around the dominant position of children and sexuality as a dangerous liaison.

The question was not surprising. Addressing gender and sexuality at the age of 6 years, is one that typically falls outside of the usual focus on older children and young people (Bhana, 2016a; Robinson, 2013). The question about researching children of 'such a very young age' constructed children at age 6 years of incapable of making sense of sexuality. I focus on this point because putting children (especially those under 10 years old), sex, and sexuality together has been established problematic throughout the globe (Renold, 2005). These assumptions are based on outdated theoretical notions on age and stage development underpinned by developmental psychology (MacNaughton, 2000). The assumption was also that questions asked would focus on aspects of adult sexuality in unseemly ways. They may also have believed that talking about sex with children makes children prematurely sexual.

While the question and concern about doing sexuality research with children is expected, the fact that the ethics committee had little knowledge about new theories and policy about children's sexual and gendered capability, agency, and rights was frustrating. My frustrations drew chiefly from the conservative one-sided model of children as victims of sexuality and researchers, such as myself, as "guilty" and potentially guilty of violating ethics when doing sexuality research with children.

As Graham et al. (2017) note, the panopticon subordinates but it does so in ways that increases the utility of power. I was under the panopticon as we all were. I felt that my position as sexuality researcher was brought under the spotlight for potentially being open to violating the rights of children. And I began to feel guilty and imbricated in the disciplinary mechanisms that regulate childhood sexuality. Simply put, power operates more efficiently when surveillance becomes self-surveillance. I had to convince the committee in my written response about the need to do research drawing on the South African policy context, which accords children the right to be heard and the right to participate in research as experts in their own right as safeguarded by the Children's Act 2005 (Act No. 38, and the Children's Amendment Act 2007, Act No. 41). I also had to bring the committee's attention to theories about children and child development. Theories derived from the sociology of childhood (James & Prout, 1997) and health-related research with young children (Alderson, 2008) were drawn from to convince the committee that children are indeed capable of making sense of sexuality and of abstract health-related issues. In the North (Blaise, 2005), I argued that even at age 6 years, sexuality and gender power relationships are being produced, and if we are to develop a way of understanding gender power inequalities and constructions of masculinities and femininities based on unequal relations then researching even younger children is necessary. I also had to convince the committee that children's safety and welfare were paramount and doing no harm was a key principle underlying the research. Indeed, a key question posed by the ethics committee was founded on concerns about sexual abuse and sexual harassment. The ethics committee's concerns about sexual abuse are especially significant considering the fact that boys and girls at school have been found to be victims of sexual harassment (Human Rights Watch, 2001).

Part of the problem in South Africa, especially, is that feminist work often highlights only the issues around younger girls and sexual violence, and, while this is a scourge to be eradicated, there are multiple ways in which children express their sexuality and gender about which we have very little evidence. If we take children seriously, as we should, and as promulgated by the Children's Act 2005, which supports the rights of children to equality and dignity, then we need to recognize them as agents with rights and accord them the status that is often eroded by concerns framed only by a focus on their vulnerability, their immaturity, and their incapacity (because of dominant theories advocating their immature development) rather than their agency.

Questioning the ethics of the university ethics committee, I put it to the committee that part of the reason for their rejection might be the fear and discomfort that adults feel about children's competency as both victims and agents and perpetrators of violence. The fact that there was so little work with children in South Africa was testimony to our preoccupation with protection as the only way of understanding children's worlds as vulnerable and victims rather than as capable agents and strategists. To view children as experts in their own right, able to think, know, and feel (and which encourages them to chat, talk, and reflect) is key to permitting the expression of rights and supporting the assertion of their autonomy.

The principle that children are indeed actors with rights is key to the Children's Act 2005, which in South Africa suggests that every "child that is of such an age, maturity and stage of development as to be able to participate in any matter concerning that child has the right to participate in an appropriate way and views expressed by the child must be given due consideration." In advancing the argument that children have agency as prescribed by policy advancements in South Africa, I showed that opposition to a project that included 6-year-olds was actually a problem of the regulatory environment of the ethics committee and its surveillance of sexuality that included children as young as 6 years. In South Africa, children under the age of 18 years are regarded as minors and all research conducted with them requires special attention and is vigilantly monitored for due diligent processes. This remains an important part of the work of ethics committees; however, by restricting research that seeks to understand how gender and sexuality are shaped through children's own voices ethics committees inadvertently reduce the possibilities of engaging with children's agency. In South Africa, children can consent to medical treatment from the age of 14 years, they can consent to an HIV test from 12 years without parental approval, and they are also able to terminate pregnancy at any age (Strode, 2015). Children are also permitted to engage in consensual sex from the age of 12 years as long as the partner is not more than 2 years older.

Ethical approval was granted in 2013 based on careful arguments from policy (Children's Act 2005) that sanctioned children's right to participate in research and evidence from research that documented how children enact gender and sexuality

(Bhana & Epstein, 2007; Blaise, 2005; Keddie, 2003). The resistance to the dominant position of the ethics committee opened up new possibilities for researching childhood sexuality in South Africa. However, the question and the lengthy response of and to the ethics committee is an indication of the ways in which ethics committees are themselves caught up in discourses about what counts as legitimate research with children.

The attempt by the ethics committee to regulate and change the course of the project by focusing on the age of participants is of concern, especially as it requires the laborious process of engaging with and convincing members of the ethics committee that such research is indeed ethical – almost positioning the researcher as someone interested in doing harm to children. It questions the integrity of researchers working in the field. The over cautious response by the ethics committee surrounding the question of the age of the children suggests that the ways in which the disciplinary mechanism of childhood sexual innocence operates incites ethics committees to do the regulatory work of the panopticon, reinstating imaginary boundaries between childhood and adulthood, and keeping invisible the sexual agency, knowledge, and behaviors of children, especially children in schools.

Warning, Danger Ahead: Porn Research NOT SUITABLE for Learners

In this chapter, I argue that research that addresses childhood sexuality is posed as risky, especially when an idealized notion of sexual innocence is invoked, a notion that is separate from the idea of innocence connected to the age of the participants (as was discussed in the last section). In this section, I focus on the next project that sought to examine young people's use of online sexually explicit materials (SEMs). In 2016, I submitted an application with my postgraduate student (Carboni & Bhana, 2017) to conduct research in several high schools in South Africa to the provincial Department of Education. The aim of the project, "Learning sex: how high school students consume pornography and give meaning to gender and sexualities," was to understand how young people come to learn about sexuality through online SEMs, including porn. An understanding of children as active agents in experiencing and exploring sexuality was a key theoretical principle of this research, combined with the identification of sexuality as a pleasurable domain of life.

When young people seek pleasure, their sexuality is often framed as a problem rather as a normative growth process of desiring and curious sexual beings. SEMs and online access to pornography is a significant vehicle through which young people learn about gender and sexuality. In the absence of comprehensive sexuality education that recognizes pleasure and desire as motivations in young people's sexual lives, accessing online SEMs has become an important way to access information and to find sexual pleasure (Ollis, 2016). There are contentious views about porn – whether or not it contributes to healthy sexual development

(Ollis, 2016) or is potentially damaging to sexual development (Dines, 2010), and whether the information or images are accurate or distorted. South Africa ranks in the top 20 of users on Pornhub, an international online porn site (Zwane, 2017). Research in the country suggests that SEMs are a vital source of sexual and reproductive health information, especially for adult men (Stern et al., 2015). Concerns about what young people are learning through online SEMs focus on misogynistic portrayals of women in porn and gender-role expectations dependent on male sexual prowess. Critics argue these can get in the way of gender equitable relations.

Concern about the use of social media in light of young people's consumption of SEMs was recently in the media with the headline, "Are our children overexposed to social media?" (Desai, 2016). Condemning the loss of childhood (perhaps invoking the norm of childhood innocence) and overexposure to sex through online SEMs, Desai says, "The echo of children gleefully playing in streets is quickly disappearing – today, the interaction between children is restricted to a screen ... that has resulted in them maturing at an alarming rate." Desai's concerns reflect back on the disciplinary mechanisms through which children and childhood are problematized, as noted in the previous section. These interconnections show the powerful elements in the social system through which childhood is regulated. Exploring sexuality through online resources without supervision, information, and critical reflection about SEMs can be problematic, especially when young people learn about sex through representations of women subjected to degrading sexual practices, but there was little South African research to support this view.

The research project was designed to address the gap in South Africa by addressing young people as gendered beings, while they were actively engaging with online SEMs. However, the provincial Department of Education declined the request to conduct the research. In its letter, the department acknowledged that there was merit in the research but after "deep consideration and wide consultation of the proposed topic the research could not be permitted." The Department of Education reasoned that the research focus was not in line with the national curriculum and, therefore, could not add value to the curriculum. The department anticipated negative reactions from schooling communities and suggested that the study be scaled up to young people at tertiary institutions in South Africa, "who were older and able to deal with the SEM issues." We appealed the decision by changing the title of the project to remove the word porn, especially as it could be offensive, and replacing it with SEMs, but that did not work in the appeal to the department against the decision.

Adults, parents, and educational stakeholders play a significant role in protecting children and young people from harm (Bay-Cheng, 2013; Koepsel, 2016; Lamb, 2015; Robinson, 2013). In South Africa, this has not been uniformly the case, with girls, in particular, raising concerns about male peers and male teachers as they confront sexual harassment and objectification (Bhana, 2012; Human Rights Watch, 2011). The Department of Education's concerns were numerous: about the nature of the study, the focus on an area that was formally excluded from schools, and the potential responses from school communities and parents. The department has an obligation to protect children from sexual abuse and violence and manage responses from parents and community stakeholders, especially when SEMs and pornography are viewed as dangerous for young people's development, as it is embedded within a system that supports gender inequalities and violence (Dines, 2010; Lamb, 2010).

Research is not innocent. Doing research about SEMs with young people would have an effect. It would affect young participants by the way particular points of view and values are conveyed, and can shape young people's view of sexuality in ways that are unpredictable. Such research also has the potential to engage with young people as they critically evaluate SEMs.

The decision to reject access to schools was potentially situated within additional efforts to preserve the sacredness of schools. Allen (2007) calls this playing safe, which can operate as a moralizing mechanism to echo the religious and cultural beliefs of the community and in schools. In South Africa, as in all schools, gender and sexuality is deeply embedded in everyday practices and approaches, whether adults like this or not (Epstein & Johnson, 1998) – a view that sees the school day as sacred does not make room for the study of sexuality in it.

The fact that the Department of Education declined the course of study does not mean that the potential to explore young people and SEMs at school is lost. Indeed, private schools who did not require the provincial Department of Education's rubber stamp agreed to participate (Carboni & Bhana, 2017). In light of this, the Department of Education officials opened up the possibility of presenting the findings to them and if "necessary they would then pursue such a topic in Life Orientation (LO) curriculum." Doing research in private schools functioned as a strategic tactic to divert panic and parental uproar from public schools under the governance of the Department of Education. Preventing research in schools that seeks to understand better how young people are giving meaning to sexuality, how might these meanings be important for their sexual health, and why these meanings could work against gender equality does not serve the interests of young people.

"Gay Mafia's Weapons of Heterosexual Destruction"

This section draws from the third project titled a "Climate study on homosexuality and homophobia in secondary schools in South Africa." Motivated by the ways in which heterosexuality is normalized in school settings, the study addressed a major gap in research in South Africa and the continent about the experiences and approach to same-sex relations at school (Bhana, 2014a, 2014b). Unlike the previous two studies, we were permitted to research this topic, especially as it did not focus on younger children but secondary schooling. South Africa also has a firm human rights policy environment. In the broader African context, thirty-eight countries have banned same-sex relations. Unlike the rest of the continent, South Africa's constitutional democracy secures equality on the basis of sexual orientation. However, a dominant view is to construct same-sex relations as un-African, although ample evidence has critiqued this view (Epprecht, 2012; Msibi, 2012). In South Africa, the Human Rights Watch (2011) identified thirty-one murders of lesbians and hate crimes against lesbian women. The homophobic violence, especially against lesbian women in working-class contexts, has resulted in 'corrective rape' or heterosexual men's desire to correct women who do not subscribe to heterosexual norms through acts of rape (Altman et al., 2012). The violence against lesbian women must be understood, as I have described in earlier parts of this chapter, as a complex combination of structural inequalities, male disempowerment in the economic sphere, and hetero-patriarchal cultural norms, where men have historically been seen as providers of heterosexual families. The virulent crusading against homosexuality in the country (Msibi, 2012) is a blight on South Africa's democracy and ethically problematic. As Msibi (2012) suggests, progressive laws in South Africa and the violence against lesbians and gays must be understood against the context of male power, heterosexual domination, and the context of major economic fault lines where men are unable to express power. Male heterosexual weakness is thus expressed in and through violence against gays and lesbians.

Unlike the North, where research in schools about non-normative sexualities is ascendant, in South Africa we know very little about the practices and approaches to heterosexist discourses (Reygan, 2016). Of importance here is attention to understanding and addressing young people at school against the broader context of rights as well as attending to heterosexual domination. The project involved an investigation into the views and perspectives of teachers, parents, and young people and the implications for gender and sexual justice. Working within an understanding of Foucauldian notions of disciplinary power and queer theorizing (Butler, 1990), the project involved an interrogation of the silences around sexuality at school and the policing of non-normative sexualities. For example, a 19 year old in the study stated, "Gay people should be killed so that we don't have any more gay people in our country." Indeed, doing research in an environment where gays and lesbians have been murdered (Human Rights Watch, 2011) does increase the danger associated with conducting research that seeks to excavate the silences in relation to heterosexual domination.

Under pressure to perform sexuality within dominant gender norms, the study illustrated the state of heterosexual domination at schools and the problematic construction of sexuality and homosexuality as perverse to childhood (Bhana, 2014a). Sexual innocence was positioned through the construction of the innocent child (Robinson, 2013; Jackson & Scott, 2010), while contradictorily positioning all children as heterosexual. For instance, David, a teenage learner, stated that "There's only two genders ... I prefer to stay away from [homosexuals] because I know what they are doing is wrong" (Bhana, 2014a, p. 53). The study showed that the normalization of heterosexuality and of the gender binary was key to the function of schooling in its current form. Several areas of intervention were suggested to produce the climate of justice and respect for same-sex relations at school (Bhana, 2014a). One of the major conclusions made in this project was the need to "develop a critically reflective and transformative approach to challenge and readjust narrow constructions of sexuality" (Bhana, 2014b, p. 365)

The institutional response to the study was positive – university ethics approval was granted with no concerns about the focus of the study. A rights-based approach contributed to the research being viewed in the context of policy discussions about young people and same-sex sexualities is increasing in South Africa (Francis, 2017; Msibi, 2012). The project included interviews with parents, school managers, learners, and teachers. The findings of the study pointed to a heteronormative environment that made the school climate difficult for same-sex relations and the teaching of sexuality beyond heterosexuality (Bhana, 2014a).

Doing sexuality work around non-normative sexualities, however, can be risky for the researcher. In March 2017, 3 years after the project was published (Bhana, 2014a), I received correspondence that accused me and others working in the field of homosexuality and schooling to be part of the "gay mafia" brigade turning "straight people gay":

> Below is a link to my blog post Gay Agenda Part 2: The Gay Mafia's Weapons of Heterosexual Destruction, How They're Turning Straight People Gay.
>
> You appeared on the post due to your research on homosexuality in South African schools and your book Under Pressure: The Regulation of Sexualities in South African Secondary Schools. So i think its fair and honorable I make you aware I mentioned your role or your plans along with X and Y on introducing pro-gay attitudes into local schools. http://spydawrita.blogspot.co.za/2017/02/gay-agenda-part-2-gay-mafias-weapons-of.html [see Nthithe, 2017]
>
> You are more than welcome to share this with your colleagues . . . and . . . others + your friends in the gay community. (March 2017, email correspondence)

In the online site listed was an attempt to regulate, attack, and bring down the work around sexual justice:

> In part 1 of my Gay Agenda series, I explained how there is a secret gay agenda funded by wealthy and powerful homosexuals popularly referred to as the velvet mafia or gay mafia in positions of global influence who want to aggressively effeminize straight men by using bullying tactics (HOW IRONIC); thus turning us into moist, sissy, manginas the same way a zombie bite turns its unfortunate victim into a member of the undead hoards.

Specifically, my own work was castigated:

> don't know about you, but I see people like Professor Bhana setting up South Africa for compulsory gay school curriculums and gay programming under the guise of "fighting bullying"

This blog must be situated against the context in South Africa, the attack on gays and lesbians, corrective rape, and violence, as well as the evidence from the initial research project condemning gays and lesbians to death. My response to the blog is thus careful, and I needed to be vigilant, given the overall environment and the policing of sexuality. Working within the understanding of the panopticon, it is clear that heteronormative discourses circulate widely and shape how research about sexual justice in schools is viewed. However, I understand that, by selecting same-sex relations in schools as an important area of investigation, I broke silences and challenged normative assumptions around childhood as heterosexual.

Even when doing social justice work, one might conclude that one's research has little impact, or only has an impact on the people and schools studied. This research had larger reach, however, to have this larger reach, it also became criticized by blogs, such as the one described earlier, that are an attempt to regulate, reject, and shame its existence. As Allen et al. (2014, p. 35) argue, "Not only is sexuality research constituted by its very nature as 'risky' but sexuality research which attempts to unsettle particular sexual tropes (Rasmussen, 2004) is considered especially dangerous." The attack on this research is a result of questioning heterosexual norms within childhood where both innocence and heterosexuality are presumed markers of children's sexuality. As a woman in South Africa during a time of unrest, I felt particularly vulnerable. The blog has the potential to regulate such research and could prevent future work. I was drawn further into the pantoptican whirlpool as I wondered about the effects of this research on my work as a sexuality researcher. I was particularly concerned as my academic profile is public and could not predict what the outcome of this blog and attack would mean for my personal safety. Moreover, I was concerned about the extent to which these attacks based on dominant heterosexual assumptions and linked to the mythical, though powerful, conceptualization of homosexuality being un-African could affect my research in the community and in South Africa. If communities were mobilized against the work to promote sexual justice in schools then it would be difficult to access schools in the future. Mainly, it would be difficult to ensure my safety and the safety of my students and researchers connected to my research projects. Significantly, the censure noted earlier has the potential to marginalize and negate the claims made in the research by its appeal to common sense and simplistic understandings of sexuality. It also challenged me as a researcher with regard to my expertise and methods. As Allen et al. (2014, p. 37) suggest:

> When discourses of risk intersect with sexuality research they exercise a regulating effect over the study and may have negative repercussions for researchers beyond the project/academia (e.g. damage to moral integrity . . .)

Unlike the first two research projects, which addressed institutional obstacles, in this section, I have focused on what Allen has referred to as risk beyond the project and beyond the university ethics committees, and gatekeepers intimidating and frightening researchers out of the field and damaging moral integrity. While, in this case, we had no trouble with the IRB, given the participants were over 10 years, the general public, upon hearing about the findings, crossed the boundary between the lives of researchers and the life of a research study to unsettle and threaten me and my work.

Conclusion

By focusing on my experiences in three research projects, the chapter has examined some of the discourses and practices through which school-based sexuality research is constrained. Childhood sexuality is under surveillance and regulated. When research involves children, sex and sexuality a hyper-regulatory environment is invoked (Strode, 2015). In this regard, the panoptic technological power and its apparatuses regulate what is admissible research while perpetuating the ideal of childhood sexual innocence. When the logic of childhood innocence is defied, a spectacle is produced bringing to light a system of regulatory mechanisms that expects nothing more than sexual innocence confounded and complicated by heterosexual assumptions. As Allen et al. (2014, p. 42) note: "School-based sexualities research faces a set of material and discursive regulations that can serve to inhibit methodological possibilities and subsequently the knowledge such research can produce."

Doing research with children and sexuality one is constantly under surveillance at different stages of the research process. In response to these three studies, the registries of truth operates to produce and reinforce childhood as a stage of innocence. In doing so, it sets out the limits of what can be done in researching childhood sexualities. The writing of this chapter was inspired by the question raised by the university ethics committee, "Do you have to research children of such a young age?," by the concerted efforts to gain access to schools to understand online SEMs, and by the homophobic public attack against "queer" research in schools.

My aim in this chapter was to draw attention to the problems of doing sexuality research with children and open up the dialogue to engage with the regulatory research environment that at times forbids research that puts children at the center of the investigation or brings to light silences in schools. In South Africa, this remains an important ethical issue. There is an urgent need to refuse to collaborate with the institutional forces that circumscribe such research. I have shown how resistance to the ethics committee, for example, can yield positive results, especially if adult members are better equipped with knowledge about children's sexual agency away from normalized discourses. I have also shown how attacks from outside the research environment have the potential to undermine the choice a researcher makes to pursue research. In refusing to submit to the ethical panopticon, I have shown how it might be possible, albeit with constraints, to work toward making childhood sexuality research a legitimate area of investigation.

Finally, the chapter has sought to make a place for transforming the current cul-de-sac when it comes to childhood sexuality research into a road forward. Ethical research demands that we confront the exercise of power and surveillance over children in South Africa to ensure that children are heard and their needs addressed. Research can be used to address the need to protect children, but if it is only permitted if it protects children from their developing sexuality, we have few chances of intervening to enhance and transform the conditions of their lives.

References

Alderson, P. (2008) Competent Children? Minors' Consent to Health Care Treatment and Research. *Social Science & Medicine 65*(11), 2272–2283.

Allen, L. (2007). Denying the Sexual Subject: Schools' Regulation of Student Sexuality. *British Educational Research Journal*, *3*(2), 221–234.

(2008). Young People's Agency in Sexuality Research Using Visual Methods. *Journal of Youth Studies*, *11*, 565–577.

Allen, L. & Rasmussen, M. L. (Eds.). (2017). *The Palgrave Handbook of Sexuality Education*. London: Palgrave MacMillan.

Allen, L., Rasmussen, M. L., Quinlivan, K., et al. (2014). "Who's Afraid of Sex at School?" The Politics of Researching Culture, Religion and Sexuality at School. *International Journal of Research and Method in Education*, *37*(1), 31–43.

Altman, D., Aggleton, P., Williams, M., et al. (2012). Men Who Have Sex with Men: Stigma and Discrimination. *Lancet*, *380*, 439–454.

Bay-Cheng, L. Y. (2013). Ethical Parenting of Sexually Active Youth: Ensuring Safety While Enabling Development. *Sex Education*, *13*(2), 133–145

Bhana, D. (2012). Girls Are Not Free – In and Out of the South African School. *International Journal of Educational Development*, *32*, 352–358.

(2014a). *Under Pressure: The Regulation of Sexualities in South African Secondary Schools*. Braamfontein: Mathoko's Books.

(2014b). Ruled by Hetero-norms? Raising Some Moral Questions for Teachers in South Africa. *Journal of Moral Education*, *43*(3), 362–376.

(2016a). *Childhood Sexuality and AIDS Education: The Price of Innocence*. Abingdon: Routledge.

(2016b). *Gender and Childhood Sexuality in Primary School*. Singapore: Springer.

Bhana, D. & Epstein, D. (2007). "I Don't Want to Catch It" Boys, Girls and Sexualities in an HIV Environment. *Gender and Education*, *19*(1), 109–125.

Blaise, M. (2005). *Playing It Straight Uncovering Gender Discourses in the Early Childhood Classroom*. London and New York: Routledge.

Butler, J. (1990). *Gender Trouble: Feminism and the Subversion of Identity*. New York: Routledge.

Carboni, N. & Bhana, D. (2017). Forbidden Fruit: the Politics of Researching Young People's Use of Online Sexually-Explicit Material in South African Schools. *Sex Education*, 17(6), 635–646.

Carmody, M. & Ovenden, G. (2013). Putting Ethical Sex into Practice: Sexual Negotiation, Gender and Citizenship in the Lives of Young Women and Men. *Journal of Youth Studies*, *16*(6), 792–807.

Clark, J. (2013). Passive, Heterosexual and Female: Constructing Appropriate Childhoods in the "Sexualisation of Childhood" Debate. *Sociological Research Online*, *18*(2) doi:10.5153/sro.3079.

Desai, T. (2016). Are Our Children Overexposed to Social Media? Retrieved from www.vocfm.co.za/are-our-children-overexposed-to-social-media/.

Dines, G. (2010). *Pornland: How Pornography Has Hijacked Our Sexuality*. Boston: Beacon Press.

Egan, R. D. (2013) *Becoming Sexual: A Critical Appraisal of the Sexualisation of Girls*. Oxford: Polity Press.

Epprecht, M. (2012). Sexual Minorities, Human Rights and Public Health Strategies in Africa. *African Affairs*, *111*, 223–243.

Epstein, D. & Johnson, R. (1998). *Schooling Sexualities*. Buckingham: Open University Press.

Flanagan, P. (2012). Ethical Review and Reflexivity in Research of Children's Sexuality. *Sex Education*, *12*(5), 535–544.

Foucault, M. (1977). *Discipline and Punish: The Birth of the Prison*. New York: Pantheon.

Francis, D. (2017). *Troubling the Teaching and Learning of Gender and Sexuality Diversity in South African Education*. New York: Palgrave

Graham, K., Treharne, G. J., & Nairn, K. (2017). Using Foucault's Theory of Disciplinary Power to Critically Examine the Construction of Gender in Secondary Schools. *Social and Personality Psychology Compass*, *11*(2), e12302.

Hlavka, H. R. (2014). Normalizing Sexual Violence: Young Women Account for Harassment and Abuse. *Gender & Society*, *28*(3), 337–358.

Human Rights Watch. (2001). *Scared at School: Sexual Violence against Girls in South African Schools*. New York: Human Rights Watch.

(2011) We'll Show You You're a Women: Violence and Discrimination against Black Lesbians and Transgender Men. Available at: www.hrw.org/reports/2011/12/05/we-ll-show-youyou-re-woman.

Jackson, S. & Scott, S. (2010) *Theorizing Sexuality*. Maidenhead: McGraw-Hill-Open University Press.

James, A. & Prout, A. (1997). *Constructing and Reconstructing Childhood: New Directions in the Sociological Study of Childhood*. Oxford: Routledge.

Jewkes, R., Sikweyiya, Y., Morrell, R., & Dunkle, K. (2011). Gender Inequitable Masculinity and Sexual Entitlement in Rape Perpetration in South Africa: Findings of a Cross Sectional Study. *PloS One*, *6*(12), e29590.

Keddie, A. (2003). Little Boys: Tomorrow's Macho Lads. *Discourse: Studies in the Cultural Politics of Education*, *24*(3), 289–306.

Koepsel, E. R. (2016). The Power in Pleasure: Practical Implementation of Pleasure in Sex Education Classrooms. *American Journal of Sexuality Education*, *11*(3), 205–265.

Lamb, S. (2010). Porn as a Pathway to Empowerment? A Response to Peterson's Commentary. *Sex Roles*, *62*(5–6), 314–317.

(2015). Revisiting Choice and Victimization: A Commentary on Bay-Cheng's Agency Matrix. *Sex Roles*, *73*(7–8), 292–297.

Mac An Ghail, M. (1994). *The Making of Men: Masculinities, Sexualities and Schooling*. Buckingham: Open University Press.

MacNaughton, G. (2000). *Rethinking Gender in Early Childhood Education*. London: Paul Chapman Publishing.

Msibi, T. (2012). "I'm Used to It Now": Experiences of Homophobia among Queer Youth in South African Township School. *Gender and Education*, *24*(5), 515–533.

Nthite, M. (2017). Gay Agenda Part 2: The Gay Mafia's Weapon of Heterosexual Destruction; How They're Turning Straight People Gay. Retrieved from http://spydawrita.blogspot.co.za/2017/02/gay-agenda-part-2-mafias-weapons-of.html?=1.

Ollis, D. (2016). "I Felt Like I Was Watching Porn": The Reality of Preparing Pre-Service Teachers to Teach about Sexual Pleasure. *Sex Education*, *16*(3), 308–323.

Rasmussen, M. L. (2004). "That's So Gay!" A Study of the Deployment of Signifiers of Sexual and Gender Identity in Secondary School Settings in Australia and the United States. *Social Semiotics*, *14*(3), 289–308.

Ratele, K. (2016). *Liberating Masculinities*. Cape Town: HSRC Press.

Renold, E. (2005). *Girls, Boys, and Junior Sexualities: Exploring Children's Gender and Sexual Relations in the Primary School*. London: Routledge Falmer.

Renold, E., Ringrose, J., & Egan, D. (2016). *Children Sexuality and Sexualisation*. Basingstoke: Palgrave MacMillan.

Reygan, F. (2016). Making Schools Safer in South Africa: An Antihomophobic Bullying Educational Resource. *Journal of LGBT Youth*, *13*(1), 173–191.

Robinson, K. (2013) *Innocence, Knowledge and the Construction of Childhood: The Contradictory Nature of Sexuality and Censorship in Children's Contemporary Lives Contemporary Lives*. New York: Routledge.

Shefer, T. (2014). Pathways to Gender Equitable Men: Reflections on Findings from the International Man and Gender Equality Survey in the Light of Twenty Years of Gender Change in South Africa. *Men and Masculinities*, *17*(5), 502–509.

Sikes, P. (2008). *From Teacher to Lover: Sex Scandals in the Classroom*, In Johnson, T. S. (Ed.), (vii-xii). New York: Peter Lang.

Statistics South Africa. (2015). *General Household Survey (Revised)*. Pretoria: Statistics South Africa.

Stern, E., Cooper, D., & Gibbs, A. (2015). Gender Differences in South African Men and Women's Access to an Evaluation of Informal Sources of Sexual And Reproductive Health (SRH) Information. *Sex Education*, *15*(1), 48–63.

Strode, A. (2015). A Critical Review of the Regulation of Research Involving Children in South Africa: From Self-Regulation to Hyper-Regulation. *South African Journal of Medicine*, *2*, 334–346.

Sundaram, V. & Sauntson, H. (2016). *Global Perspectives and Key Debates in Sex and Relationships Education: Addressing Issues of Gender, Sexuality, Plurality and Power*. Basingstoke: Palgrave MacMillan.

Thorne, B. (1993). *Gender Play, Girls and Boys in School*. Buckingham: Open University Press.

Tolman, D. L. & McClelland, S. I. (2011). Normative Sexuality Development in Adolescence: A Decade in Review, 2000–2009. *Journal of Research on Adolescence*, *21*(1), 242–255.

Wood, K., Maforah, F., & Jewkes, R. (1998). "He Forced Me to Love Him": Putting Violence on Adolescent Sexual Health Agendas. *Social Science & Medicine*, *47*, 233–242.

Zwane, J. (2017). SA Beats Rest of Continent in Porn-Watching. *News 24*, January 7.

PART III

Media, Family, Education

What Roles Might Adults Play?

Media

20 Entertainment Media's Role in the Sexual Socialization of Western Youth

A Review of Research from 2000–2017

L. Monique Ward, Jessica D. Moorman, and Petal Grower

Learning about the sexual norms and scripts in one's culture is a complex developmental process that takes place over many years and involves many informants. Although parents and family members are usually our initial sexual educators, they are not the only ones. Instead, there are several indications that the mainstream media serve as important sources of sexual models, scripts, and messages for youth in Western nations. First, sexual content is prevalent in the media, with analyses estimating that sexual content appears in 85 percent of major motion pictures (Jamieson et al., 2008) and 82 percent of television programs (Fisher et al., 2004). Second, levels of media consumption are high. US children and teens aged 8–18 years reported spending 7.5 hours with media per day in one study (Rideout et al., 2010), and 9 hours a day in a study of teens aged 13–18 years (Common Sense Media, 2015). Such high consumption likely means regular and frequent exposure to the sexual themes presented. Third, adolescents acknowledge using media content for sexual learning. In one survey of 458 adolescents aged 14–16 years, 57 percent named the media as an important source of sexual learning; this level was higher for girls (61.4 percent), White youth (64 percent), and 16-year-olds (66 percent) (Bleakley et al., 2009).

Several theories support a potential role of media exposure as a sexual educator. One prominent theory is cultivation theory (Gerbner et al., 2002), which argues that repeated, long-term exposure to commonly portrayed media messages fosters analogous beliefs in media users, most likely by making relevant schemas chronically accessible (Shrum, 1996). A second theoretical framework supporting research in this area is social cognitive theory (Bandura, 2002), which examines the influence of observational learning on the adoption of specific behaviors. The expectation is that viewers' own sexual decisions can be shaped by observing, identifying with, and following the rewarded actions of media models.

To investigate the media's role in modern sexual socialization, this chapter reviews major findings concerning the nature of sexual portrayals in mainstream entertainment media and their effects on the sexual development of children and adolescents. In selecting material to review, we set several parameters. We focus on analyses of the following mainstream entertainment media: television, films, music, music videos, and video games. We do not focus heavily on print media (magazines, newspapers, or books), news media, or social media; however, we do include some studies that assessed magazine use in their media measures. We also do not include analyses of pornography/sexually explicit media (for reviews of this domain, see Chapter 22; Koletic, 2017; Owens et al., 2012; Peter & Valkenburg, 2016). Because most studies focused on heterosexual youth and heterosexual relationships, our analyses center on these themes; however, there is an emerging literature that examines media portrayals of same-sex relationships (e.g., Bond, 2015; Dennis, 2009; Netzley, 2010), and effects of this content on beliefs about homosexuality (e.g., Bond & Compton, 2015; Calzo & Ward, 2009; for review, see Ward, Reed, et al., 2013).

For source material we draw on peer-reviewed publications, and do not include unpublished dissertations or conference papers. We focus on research testing children or adolescents (not college students), and on studies conducted in industrialized Western nations, who often share media (i.e., North America, Europe, Australia). To keep the review current, we focus on empirical studies and content analyses published in the new millennium, from 2000 to 2017. We begin with a summary of content analyses documenting the nature and prevalence of sexual content in mainstream media. We continue with a review of studies examining how media exposure contributes to young people's sexual attitudes, cognitions, and perceptions (ACP). We conclude with an analysis of studies examining links between media use and sexual behavior.

What Is Sexual Content Like in Mainstream Media?

Television Programs

Findings about Overall Programming

A first step in studying television's sexual content has often been to document its prevalence: How often are verbal sexual references or physical sexual behaviors depicted? A common strategy, here, has been the content analysis, in which a sample of television programming is recorded and then systematically coded by a team of scholars who document the number and nature of sexual references. The most recent large-scale efforts to assess the prevalence of sexual content on television were conducted at the start of the new millennium and published from 2004 to 2007. As part of this effort, Fisher et al. (2004) coded 1,276 television programs representing a composite 3-week sample (recorded in 2001) from 11 major networks. In total, 82.1 percent of the episodes studied contained at least one instance of sexual talk or behavior. In their series of *Sex on TV* studies, Kunkel and colleagues documented the presence of sexual talk and behavior every other year from 1997 to 2005 (Kunkel et al., 1999, 2001, 2003, 2005, 2007). In their final analysis of 1,154 programs from the 2004–2005 television season, Kunkel and colleagues (2005) found sexual content in 77 percent of prime time programs. Findings across their studies indicate slight changes from year to year in these rates, but the general trends have persisted.

In addition to documenting the prevalence of sexual content, analyses continue to validate four common features of this content that were noted in earlier reviews of the field (e.g., Ward, 2003). First, findings continue to indicate that on mainstream television, sexual talk is more prevalent than sexual behavior. For example, Kunkel and colleagues (2005) reported that talk about sex was present in 68 percent of programs and sexual behaviors were shown in 35 percent of programs. Second, findings indicate that when sexual behavior is depicted, it tends to be mainly kissing and flirting (e.g., Carpentier et al., 2017; Flynn et al., 2015). For example, of the eight sexual behaviors coded by Fisher et al. (2004), physical flirting was found in 49.5 percent of programs, kissing or touching in 48.6 percent, but implied intercourse only in 10.5 percent. Indeed, in their analysis of sexual content on reality dating programs, Kim and Wells (2015) found that physical flirting accounted for more than 86 percent of all sexual behavior. Third, data continue to demonstrate that the prevalence of this content varies by genre. For example, Kunkel et al. (2005) found that movies (92 percent), sitcoms (87 percent), and dramas (87 percent) contained sexual content most frequently, and reality shows contained it least often (28 percent). Fourth, findings indicate that references to the risks and responsibilities of sex, such as discussions of safe sex practices or disease prevention, are minimally present. Fisher and colleagues (2004) reported that of programs noted to feature sexual content, 2.9 percent contained messages of sexual patience, and 5.2 percent mentioned sexual precautions. Similarly, in a recent study of 75 episodes of 25 programs popular among emerging adults, only 7 percent of all coded scenes contained any mention of sexual health, risk, or responsibility (Carpentier et al., 2017).

Although each of these studies focused on US programming, similar patterns have emerged in analyses of the television content from other Western countries. For example, in their analysis of 139 episodes of seven British drama serials (e.g., *Coronation Street, EastEnders*), Al-Sayed and Gunter (2012) found that 78 percent of the episodes contained sexual content. In addition, sexual talk was more prevalent than sexual behavior (62 percent of scenes vs. 38 percent of scenes), and the leading type of sexual behavior was passionate kissing. However, the authors did note that the second most common sexual behavior was implied intercourse. In their analysis of a 2-week sample of TV programming in Israel, Eyal et al. (2014) found that 80.5 percent of the programs contained at least one instance of sexual content, and more so for foreign programs (93.3 percent) than domestic content (69.52 percent). Both foreign and domestic programs portrayed more sexual talk (76 percent of programs) than sexual behavior (56.7 percent), and again the most common sexual behavior was passionate kissing. One standout was that 18.9 percent of episodes with sexual content addressed risks and responsibilities.

Findings about Youth-Oriented Programming

Other analyses have focused more specifically on television programs that are especially popular with young people. One relatively consistent pattern emerging is the continued dominance of "light" sexual behavior (i.e., flirting, sexual innuendo), over more explicit behaviors (Malacane & Martins, 2017; Ortiz & Brooks, 2014; Signorielli & Bievenour, 2015). Unfortunately, it is difficult to draw strong conclusions beyond this because different approaches to sampling have been used, and the results are therefore somewhat mixed. For example, one study (Kunkel et al., 2005) reported that top teen-rated programs contain *more* sex-related scenes per hour (M=6.7) than prime time programing (M=5.9) or programming overall (M=5.0); another study found that levels of sexual content were *quite similar* on popular programming oriented to adolescents versus adults (Malacane & Martins, 2017); and a third study (Signorielli & Bievenour, 2015) found that tween programs had fewer sexual behaviors (M=5.1) than young adolescent programs (M=12.8).

Mixed results are also seen concerning the presence of risk and responsibility messages and of consequences of sexual experiences. Signorielli and Bievenour (2015) examined the amount and types of sexual content appearing in 39 programs that are popular with tweens (8–11 years) and young adolescents (12–15 years). Although dating/flirting/romance appeared as a significant thematic element in 51.2 percent of these programs, only one episode of the 39 coded contained a risk and responsibility message. These results match the patterns reported by Malacane and Martins (2017), who reported that 27.8 percent of the *adult-oriented* episodes coded contained a risk and responsibility message, whereas none of the *youth-oriented* programs did. However, others who focus more specifically on the consequences of sexual talk and behavior report that such consequences are present, and tend to be more negative than positive. Aubrey (2004) examined sexual consequences appearing in 84 episodes of 16 prime-time dramas that featured characters aged 12–22 years (e.g., *7th Heaven, Dawson's Creek, Gilmore Girls*). She found that 90.5 percent of episodes contained at least one verbal or visual sexual reference. Of the 676 scenes with a sexual reference, 220 featured a negative consequence (32.5 percent), whereas only 28 (4.1 percent) featured a positive consequence. Consequences, both negative and positive, were much more likely to be social (e.g., humiliation) and emotional (e.g., disappointment) than physical (e.g., sexually transmitted infection [STI]). In their analysis of the sexual portrayals of teen and young adult characters from five popular teen dramas, Ortiz and Brooks (2014) found that characters received negative consequences for sexual behavior 3.69 times on average, and positive consequences 2.98 times on average. The most common consequence, positive or negative, was social/emotional. Finally, there is evidence that these levels vary by genre. In their analysis of 40 programs commonly viewed by teens, Gottfried et al. (2013) found that dramas were most explicit but had more risk and responsibility messages than cartoons, comedies, and reality programs.

A final pattern that has emerged both in broad analyses of television programming and in youth-oriented programming is the prominence of gendered sexual scripts that outline different sexual roles for women and men. This script has been labeled the heterosexual script, and it describes the courtship strategies, commitment orientations, and sexual goals considered appropriate for women and men in heterosexual relationships (Kim et al., 2007). According to this script, men are expected to actively pursue sexual relationships, to objectify women, and to prioritize sex over emotion; conversely, women are expected to be sexually passive, to use their looks and bodies to attract men, to set sexual limits, and to prioritize emotions over sex (Kim et al., 2007). References to this script have been documented to occur 15.5 times per hour in prime-time television programs preferred by teens (Kim et al., 2007), and to appear in 11.45 percent of the interactions between characters on "tween"-oriented programming (Kirsch & Murnen, 2015). Analyses of reality dating programs indicate that references to men as always looking for sex occur 3.6 times per hour, and references to women as sex objects occur 5.9 times per hour (Ferris et al., 2007).

Motion Pictures

Although motion pictures are a prominent medium that regularly features sexual content, few studies have investigated the nature and prevalence of the sexual themes conveyed. One of the most comprehensive projects to investigate this medium was led by Bleakley et al. (2012), who analyzed 855 films, which included 15 of the 30 top-grossing movies for *each* year from 1950 to 2006. Each film was coded for the presence or absence of sexual content in 5-minute segments, and sexual content was defined to include kissing on the lips, nudity, sexual behavior, or sexual intercourse, implicitly or explicitly shown. Several studies have emerged from this dataset, with analyses finding differences in movie sexual content by gender, year, and movie rating. Of the 855 films studied, 84.6 percent contained sexual content in at least one 5-minute segment, with lower levels in G-rated films (68.2 percent) than in R-rated films (88.3 percent) (Nalkur et al., 2010). In addition, gender differences have emerged, whereby 57 percent of the female characters were involved in sexual content compared to 30 percent of male characters (Bleakley et al., 2012).

Other studies have focused on films of a particular genre, such as romantic comedies, or on films directed at a particular audience, such as adolescents. In their analysis of 90 films directed at teens that were released from 1980 to 2007, Callister et al. (2011) found that 28 percent of films contained adult sexual activity, and 80 percent contained teen sexual activity, with an average of 6.5 teen sexual acts per film. The most common sexual activity depicted was passionate kissing. No differences were found over time in the overall prevalence of sexual acts, nor in the presence of sexual dialogue. However, as observed with television content, there was little depiction of safe sex practices, risks, or consequences.

Music Videos

A third medium studied for its sexual content is the music video, with analyses focusing on the visual presence of sexual behaviors and sexualized appearance. Findings indicate that sexual imagery is prevalent in music videos, appearing in 58.5 percent of music videos in one study (Turner, 2011) and in 84 percent of videos in another (Ward, Rivadeneyra, et al., 2013). The sexual acts reported to occur most frequently are sexual or suggestive dance, sexual objectification, and self-touching. For example, King et al. (2006) examined the presence of 19 sexual behaviors for women and 16 sexual behaviors for men in 411 music videos appearing on four networks. The most frequent sexual behaviors for women were sexual dance, flirting, and caressing/stroking of the self. For men it was hugging/embracing, sexual dance, and groping one's own genital area.

Analyses also indicate that the presence of sexual imagery varies by artist gender and music genre. One strong finding is that in music videos, female characters and artists are shown in sexual ways more often than male characters and artists. Across several studies, analyses indicate that female artists and characters display more body parts, are more provocatively dressed, are more often sexually objectified, engage in more sexually suggestive dance, and engage in more sexual behavior than do their male counterparts (Aubrey & Frisby, 2011; Frisby & Aubrey, 2012; King et al., 2006; Wallis, 2011; Ward, Rivadeneyra, et al., 2013). A second significant finding is that music genre matters, such that rhythm and blues (R&B), rap, and pop music videos are noted to contain more sexual content than rock or country music videos (Frisby & Aubrey, 2012; Turner, 2011).

Music Lyrics

A fourth medium studied for its sexual content has been the lyrics of popular music. Indeed, Pardun et al. (2005) found that of the six teen-oriented media formats they examined, sexual content was *most* prevalent in popular music, with sexual content appearing in 40 percent of the units coded (each line of lyrics). This rate compares to 12 percent of units for movies and 11 percent of units for TV programs. Within their music data, the most common sexual content was references to relationships (52 percent), sexual innuendo (19 percent), and references to sexual intercourse (15 percent). A few studies have conducted systematic analyses of the nature of sexual references in music. In their analysis of 279 top songs from 2005, Primack et al. (2008) found that 37 percent of songs contained references to sexual intercourse. Of these references, 65 percent were classified as references to degrading sex, in which one partner (nearly always women) was objectified, the other had a voracious sexual appetite, and a heavy emphasis was placed on physical characteristics. Focusing on themes about masculinity and femininity in the top songs by Black artists across 20 years, Avery et al. (2017) found that references to men as sex focused appeared in 22 percent of songs, and references to women as sex objects appeared in 15 percent of songs. These rates varied by genre, and were particularly high in rap/hip-hop music; here, 39 percent of songs referenced men as sex focused, and 36 percent of songs referenced women as sexual objects. In a recent study, Smiler et al. (2017) analyzed 1,250 songs from 1960 to 2008, taking the top 50 songs from even-numbered years. They found that 71 percent of songs addressed a dating relationship, 22 percent featured sexual references, and 13 percent objectified the female body. These patterns differed somewhat by decade and genre. References to sexual activity increased four-fold over time, with rates hitting 27 percent of songs in the 1990s and 35 percent of the songs in the 2000s. Rates of sexual objectification increased four-fold over time, as well, going from 6 percent of songs in the 1970s to 31 percent of songs in the 2000s. Genre differences were quite strong, whereby references to sexual activity appeared in 14 percent of rock songs, 32 percent of R&B songs, and 70 percent of rap songs from 1990 to 2008. Sexual explicitness and objectification of women were also highest in rap songs, matching findings of Avery et al. (2017).

Is There Any Evidence That Media Use Is Associated with Adolescents' Sexual Attitudes, Cognitions, and Perceptions?

Overview of the Diverse Studies in This Field

Given the frequency of sexual references, as reported, scholars have questioned whether regular exposure to this content could be shaping adolescents' sexual beliefs and assumptions. Although the content is not highly explicit, it could still be influential in establishing sexual norms, both by which portrayals are present and which are not (e.g., references to risks and responsibilities). Accordingly, one prominent domain of research in this area examines relations between media use and adolescents' ACP concerning sex, sexual roles, and sexual relationships. This section reviews the work of 48 studies addressing this question. Most of these studies (N=40) are quantitative, explore multiple media, and cover a range of methodologies, including correlational, experimental, and longitudinal designs. Common approaches examine adolescents' media consumption based on overall hours of exposure, frequency of exposure to sexual content, or frequency of exposure to specific genres (e.g., reality programs, music videos) or media products (e.g., a listing of 50 TV programs).

Within this quantitative research, viewer ACP commonly focus on a narrow set of beliefs, such as recreational attitudes toward sex (e.g., Ward & Friedman, 2006); sexual outcome expectancies, which are the types of social and emotional outcomes adolescents expect of their sexual encounters (e.g., Martino et al, 2009); beliefs about traditional gender roles in relationships (e.g., Rouner et al., 2003); or perceptions of peers' sexual activities (e.g., Bleakley et al., 2017). ACP measures are examined both as factors moderating and mediating relations between entertainment media consumption and adolescent sexual behavior (e.g., Bleakley et al., 2017), and as outcomes in their own right (e.g., Aubrey et al., 2014). Results find that relations between media use and adolescents' sexual ACP sometimes depend on demographic factors such as pubertal timing (e.g., Brown et al., 2005), gender (e.g., Gottfried et al., 2011), and prior sexual experience (e.g., Frison et al., 2015); on media use behaviors, such as seeking out sexual content (e.g., Bleakley et al., 2010) and parental regulation of media content (Fisher et al., 2009); and viewers' personal connections with media characters (Aubrey et al., 2014; Driesmans et al., 2016; Rivadeneyra & Lebo, 2008).

The remaining eight studies rely on qualitative approaches to assess how adolescents perceive specific sexual content, and include methods such as focus group interviews, in-depth interviews, and thematic analyses of open-ended survey responses. Analyses have focused on perceptions such as adolescents' understandings of the objectification of women (Stephens & Few, 2007); attitudes toward relationships (e.g., Hartley et al., 2014; Len-Ríos et al., 2016); and knowledge of safe sex practices (e.g., Jones et al., 2011; Watson & McKee, 2013; Werner-Wilson et al., 2004). This group of studies showcases how adolescents process media content and navigate messages about sex, gender, and relationships presented in the media. These studies also illuminate the types of conclusions youth draw about themselves, their peers, and the values of the world around them (e.g., Hartely et al., 2014). No singular conclusion can be drawn across this qualitative work, but what becomes clear is that adolescents actively engage with the media they consume, think critically about the content, and are nevertheless influenced by media messages.

Contributions of Television Use to Sexual ACP

Twenty-eight of the 48 studies included in this portion of our review focus on television and identify TV consumption and its sexual messages as robust correlates of adolescents' sexual ACP. One common assessment of television use is overall quantity of consumption. For example, correlational work by Eggermont (2004) revealed that greater overall television consumption is associated with a greater investment in the physical appearance of a romantic partner. This study, conducted with 428 Belgian 15–16 year olds, revealed that this association was moderated by gender, with boys exhibiting greater investment in the physical appearance of a potential partner compared with girls.

Examining content by genre, Gottfried et al. (2011) conducted a two-wave longitudinal study with a sample of 474, 12–17-year-old respondents (63.1 percent female). Researchers explored the contributions of differing quantities and representations of sex in 13 comedies, 7 cartoons, 9 dramas, and 11 reality programs. Through content analysis, researchers first determined the overall sexual content and sexual risk messages of these programs. Researchers then assessed the quantity of consumption of the programs listed for each genre and their relations to adolescents' intentions to have sex, positive attitudes toward sex, perceptions of peers' sexual activity, and self-efficacy (confidence they could do what it takes) to have sex. Gottfried and his team found that greater consumption of comedies and less consumption of dramas was associated with an assumption of more sexual experience among one's peers and a more positive attitude toward sex. In turn, these beliefs predicted greater intention to have sex and greater likelihood of having had sex over the past year. The authors also reported that participants' consumption of cartoons and reality programs did *not* predict any of the sexual beliefs or behavior, and attribute the latter finding to the type of reality programs included in their sample (e.g., *Extreme Home Makeover*).

Aubrey et al. (2014) conducted one of the few experimental studies among teens, investigating whether exposure to teen pregnancy reality programs affects adolescent girls' perceptions of the risks of becoming pregnant. They found that viewing *16 & Pregnant*, compared to the control reality TV program *Made*, lowered participants' perceived risk of getting pregnant and increased the perceived benefits. The authors also found that these effects depended on participants' levels of parasocial interaction, a perceived personal friendship with a media personality (Horton & Wohl, 1956; Rubin & Rubin, 2001), and homophily, the degree to which viewers perceive themselves to be similar to a media persona in terms of background, traits, and abilities (Hoffner & Cantor, 1991). Among girls who had viewed the *16 & Pregnant* episode, expressing greater homophily and parasocial interaction predicted even lower pregnancy risk perceptions, greater perceived benefit of teen pregnancy, more favorable attitudes toward teen pregnancy, and greater acceptance of pregnancy myths such as "most teenage fathers stay involved with the young woman they have made pregnant." Other research has reached similar conclusions, reinforcing relations between the consumption of sexually charged TV programming and negative ACP outcomes for adolescents (e.g., Ward & Friedman, 2006). Findings from these studies also indicate that aspects of the media content, such as explicitness and genre, and aspects of the media viewer, such as homophily, may shape the nature and strength of media effects on viewer sexual attitudes.

Contributions of Movie Viewing to Sexual ACP

Six studies examined movies' role in shaping adolescents' ACP concerning sexuality, sexual roles, and sexual relationships (Bleakley et al., 2009, 2011, 2017; Brown et al., 2005; Driesmans et al., 2016; Harris et al., 2004). Brown et al. (2005) examined how pubertal timing influenced the consumption and interpretation of sexual media content among adolescent girls. For media content, they focused on R-rated movie viewing (in the article, R-rated movies are not intended to be viewed by anyone under the age of 16 without an accompanying parent or guardian), as well as girls' exposure to television, music, and magazines featuring content about sexually transmitted diseases, birth control, and dating. The authors report that the effects of

R-rated movies depended on the timing of girls' pubertal transitions. More specifically, early-maturing girls consumed more R-rated movies and were more likely than their later-blooming peers to interpret the content as endorsing teen sexual activity. In an experimental study, Driesmans et al. (2016) showed some participants a romantic teen movie (*High School Musical*) and others a non-romantic movie (*Over the Hedge*), and then surveyed everyone on their idealistic beliefs about romantic relationships (e.g., agreeing that "There will only be one true love for me"). Researchers found that the relation between movie exposure and romantic beliefs depended on participant age and level of parasocial interaction. Younger participants exposed to *High School Musical* and those who reported higher levels of parasocial interaction exhibited greater endorsement of idealistic beliefs about relationships.

Together, these findings indicate that the sexual and romantic content of movies is indeed associated with adolescents' ideas about sex and relationships, and that these effects depend on maturation, age, and teens' parasocial engagement with the characters. These findings also speak to the important role that developmental life-stage plays in shaping the media's role as a sexual socializer. It cannot be assumed that sexual content affects 11-year-old girls in the midst of puberty the same way it affects 16- or 17-year-old girls who may already have had some romantic or sexual experience. Future studies need to be more mindful of attributes such as pubertal timing, and also need to assess participants' personal connections with media characters.

Contributions of Music and Music Videos to Sexual ACP

Music and music videos were the subjects of nine studies included in this review (Brown et al., 2005; Bryant, 2008; Frison et al., 2015; Kistler et al., 2010; Robillard, 2012; Stephens & Few, 2007; ter Bogt et al., 2010; van Oosten et al., 2015; Ward et al., 2005). For the most part, these studies focus on rap, R&B, and sexually suggestive music videos. For example, Stephens and Few (2007) conducted focus groups among 15 pre-adolescent girls and boys aged 11–13 years, exploring how music videos featuring sexualized images of Black women influenced their attitudes about Black women's attractiveness and decision making in establishing relationships. The young people they talked with did indeed support the importance of physical attractiveness in attracting a potential mate, naming skin color, hair, body size, and traditional gender roles as important determinants of what makes a Black woman a worthy partner. Music videos, Stephens and Few (2007) found, provided a salient set of examples for who and how Black women should be in relationships.

Correlational research demonstrates connections between regular, everyday exposure to sexually suggestive music videos and teens' beliefs about sex and sexual roles. Consumption of rap, R&B, and sexually suggestive music videos is associated with a greater endorsement of stereotypical beliefs about gender (Robillard, 2012; Ward et al., 2005), adversarial attitudes about male–female relationships (Bryant, 2008), and lower self-efficacy for condom use (Robillard,

2012). Longitudinal work like that of van Oosten et al. (2015) suggests that music video consumption predicts an increased acceptance of female token resistance, which is defined as the notion that women say 'no' to sex when they actually mean 'yes.' This finding was significant only for young women watching male artists.

As a group, these studies make clear that highly sexualized content like that commonly found in rap and R&B music videos is linked to stereotypical and potentially harmful beliefs about sex and sexual roles, and that these relations differ based on the gender of the adolescent and the artist. It is perhaps not surprising that gender plays a role here, because music videos are replete with messages about gendered sexual roles. As noted earlier, the female body and female performers are often highly sexualized, whereas similar portrayals of men are significantly less common (Aubrey & Frisby, 2011; Frisby & Aubrey, 2012; King et al., 2006; Wallis, 2011).

Strengths and Limitations

As a group, these 48 studies represent a range of approaches to the study of media sexual socialization. One of the strengths of this work is the breadth of methods used to assess adolescents' sexual ACP. Via correlational, experimental, and longitudinal studies, and via qualitative focus groups and interviews, these studies make a clear case for media's role in the sexual socialization of adolescents' in Western nations. Short- and long-term effects of the media on adolescents' sexual ACP have been observed (e.g., Frison et al., 2015; van Oosten et al., 2015), and these relations appear to be underpinned by the quantity, explicitness, and vividness of the sexual content portrayed (Bleakley et al., 2011; ter Bogt, et al., 2010). Qualitative work reminds us that, although adolescents are not passive consumers of these media, their beliefs about sex are indeed shaped by consumption of them (e.g., Eyal & Ben-Ami, 2017; Harris, 2015; Hartley et al., 2014; Len-Ríos et al., 2016).

The range of sexual ACP measures included in this work is another strength of these studies. Assessments that captured teens' perceived norms about peer sexual behavior (e.g., Eggermont, 2005), attitudes about teen parenthood (Aubrey et al., 2014), sexually objectifying beliefs about women (e.g., ter Bogt et al., 2010), recreational attitudes toward sex (e.g., Ward & Friedman, 2006), and self-efficacy and behavioral intentions toward sex (e.g., Bleakley et al., 2017), demonstrate the wide-ranging influence that entertainment media have on adolescents' sexual ACP. However, despite this apparent breadth, this selection of attitudes and beliefs are still somewhat constrained in that they all center on sexual risk, with few assessments of sexual self-concept, sexual satisfaction, and sexual pleasure. In what ways is adolescents' media use linked to empowering views of one's own sexuality, sexual assertiveness, sexual confidence, or sexual agency? These questions have yet to be fully addressed.

At the same time, the wide array of measures employed thus far is both a blessing and a curse; this diversity makes comparing across samples more challenging. Research conducted by Bleakley and her colleagues offer one possible solution. By relying on a reasoned action approach, which explores how attitudes, norms, self-efficacy, and behavioral intentions are influenced by the media, Bleakley and her collaborators offer consistent categories of measures to assess adolescents' sexual ACP. By consistently and repeatedly measuring injunctive and descriptive norms, attitudes toward sex or relationships, self-efficacy, and behavioral intentions, a clearer picture emerges about relations between media and this set of adolescents' ACP.

A second limitation of this literature is its lack of diversity concerning the race, ethnicity, religion, language, and social class of the populations studied (Henrich et al., 2010; Ward, 2003). This critique of media sexual socialization studies has implications for the types of conclusions researchers can draw about media contributions in diverse populations. By no means do all studies contribute to this absence. For example, Len-Ríos et al. (2016) focused on Latino adolescents' experiences of media and romantic relationships. Gottfried et al.'s (2011) study included a diverse sample composed mostly of African-American and Latino youth. Yet, participants of color are frequently overlooked, especially those of Asian or Middle Eastern descent living in Western nations. Whether we focus on new immigrants or members of families living in Western contexts for generations, further work is needed to explore how race, religion, language, and ethnicity shape media sexual socialization outcomes for this segment of society.

Is There Any Evidence that Media Use Is Associated with Adolescents' Sexual Behavior?

Parents, educators, and policy makers have been concerned for decades with adolescents' decisions to engage in sexual activity, and of the potential role of the media in hastening, facilitating, or promoting these decisions. This concern is warranted given that media content is highly sexualized and tends to depict sexual relationships as casual, fun, and risk free. Given that adolescents are still developing in terms of their cognitive, social, and emotional skill sets, especially concerning planning and future-oriented thinking, they may not be adequately prepared to enact scripts and behaviors modeled from the media in a way that is safe and healthy (Collins et al., 2017). In the forthcoming pages, we review much of the work published in the last 17 years that tests contributions of media use to sexual behavior among adolescents. Our analysis is organized by research design, focused first on longitudinal surveys and then cross-sectional surveys; we did not find experiments that examined sexual behavior as an outcome. Within each type of design, we first review the work that examines adolescents' decisions to engage in penile–vaginal intercourse (PVI), and then review literature that looks at sexual behaviors beyond PVI, including kissing, breast or genital touching, and oral sex. Finally, we close this section by offering insights for future directions and a critique of the field at large.

Findings from Longitudinal Studies

One of the core tools that developmental researchers use to demonstrate the potential influence of early life experiences or beliefs is to conduct longitudinal research. Here, scholars measure attitudes or experiences at multiple time points, and use advanced statistics to determine whether *earlier* beliefs or experiences affect subsequent beliefs or experiences. These beliefs and experiences may be assessed at different time intervals, such as 6 months or a year apart. Such approaches are often perceived as "the gold standard" of developmental research because they provide insight into the nature of change within an individual. To better understand how media might influence teens' sexual behavior, several longitudinal studies have been conducted investigating whether teens who consume more media, in general, or more sexual media, in particular, initiate PVI earlier than teens who consume less.

Longitudinal studies linking the initiation of PVI to sexualized media exposure generally do support this association. In studies examining PVI as the lone outcome variable, exposure to sexual content in movies, sexual talk and behavior on television, and even general assessments of TV exposure and computer use (dichotomized to more or less than 2 hours per day) predicted increased likelihood of engaging in PVI a year or two later (Ashby et al., 2006; Avelar e Silva et al., 2016; Brown et al., 2006; Collins et al., 2004; O'Hara et al., 2012). Adolescents' expectations about and regret regarding the consequences of engaging in PVI are also affected. Studies show that teens who consume more sexualized media express lower expectations of contracting an STI or getting pregnant than do teens who consume less sexualized media. However, although high-media-consuming teens anticipate fewer negative health consequences, they seem to also experience more regret following the initiation of PVI (Martino et al., 2009; Ragsdale et al., 2014).

Work with more diverse samples has demonstrated an interesting pattern of results and promising areas for future research. For example, Martino et al. (2005) examined the effect of sexualized television exposure on the safe sex efficacy (how comfortable adolescents feel discussing sexually sensitive topics with a potential partner), perceived peer norms, and negative outcome expectancies among an ethnically diverse sample of 12–17 year olds. Sexual television exposure predicted safe sex efficacy for African Americans and Whites, but not for Hispanics. Interestingly, this same sexualized television exposure predicted adolescents' belief that more of their friends had engaged in PVI and fewer negative consequences of engaging in PVI for all three groups. These three mediators in turn predicted initiation of intercourse for all three groups. A study by Jackson et al. (2008) showed different patterns of results for Black and White adolescents who all had a television in their bedroom (providing an increased opportunity for viewing sexualized media content without adult supervision). Although significantly more Black adolescents than White adolescents had a television in their bedroom, having a television in the bedroom was unrelated to Black adolescents' sexual risk taking and media practices. This finding regarding media use and sexual risk taking among Black teens stands in contrast to the findings of White teens, who reported less parental oversight of adolescent media use, regular viewing of mature content television programs, and greater likelihood of having seen R-rated movies at home. Together, these studies highlight how media may influence adolescents' sexual behavior differently and through different mechanisms for different groups. Future research should examine these mechanisms more closely and also investigate how other contextual factors may explain these differences.

Research also suggests that exposure to sexual media content influences adolescents' tendency to engage in sexual behaviors other than PVI. Typically, researchers have examined a hierarchy of sexual behaviors, including kissing/deep kissing, fondling of the breasts, touching of genitals, and oral sex, as well as PVI. In general, longitudinal studies have supported the contribution of media exposure to progression through this hierarchy of sexual behavior (Bleakley et al., 2008; Pardun et al., 2005; Jeong et al., 2010). It is important to note that, as with PVI, research suggests that these patterns may differ for girls and boys and for different racial/ethnic groups. For example, Hennessy et al. (2009) found that Hispanic and African-American adolescents actually consumed less sexualized media content over time compared to their same age White peers, and that, unlike for White teens, there was little to no association between changes in media exposure and the sexual behaviors assessed. Similarly, Frison et al. (2015) examined associations between music television exposure, perceived peer norms, and four different sexual behaviors, and found complex and unexpected bidirectional associations between these variables. Given the strengths of longitudinal work, this body of literature would support the notion that exposure to media content, in general, and exposure to sexualized media content, in particular, each has an impact on adolescents' decisions to engage in a variety of sexual behaviors, including PVI.

Findings from Cross-Sectional Survey Studies

There have also been several cross-sectional studies that examined associations between adolescents' current levels of sexualized media exposure and their decisions to engage in sexual behavior. Although the use of cross-sectional methods means that researchers cannot infer causality, studies using this design do offer insights into how everyday consumption of several types of media is associated with adolescents' sexual behavior. Much of this work has examined associations between sexualized media content on television and adolescents' sexual behaviors; however, studies have also examined online activity, music lyrics, video games, movies, magazines, and newspapers. As with much of the longitudinal work, consumption of sexual content on television, in movies, and in magazines has been associated with increased likelihood of PVI, increased likelihood of engaging in oral sex, greater intention to engage in sexual intercourse, and more sexual partners (Barr et al., 2014; L'Engle et al., 2006; Pardun et al., 2005; Parkes et al., 2013). However, there are some important caveats to note: these effects do not always hold when controlling for relevant demographic variables (e.g., age, race, socioeconomic status) or for all groups. For example, Hispanic and African-

American adolescents sometimes seem to be buffered against these effects and other times seem to be more susceptible to them (Bleakley et al., 2008; Somers & Tynan, 2006). As with the longitudinal work in this area, researchers need to be mindful as to the more complex associations between these variables and the potential mechanisms at play among different racial/ethnic groups.

Other studies have examined associations between exposure to mature-rated video games, music videos, or sexually degrading music lyrics and adolescents' tendencies to engage in a variety of sexual behaviors. In the case of video games, results indicate that frequent playing of mature-rated video games is associated with higher levels of rebelliousness, sensation seeking, favorable views of deviant behavior in oneself and others, and affiliation with deviant peers (Hull et al., 2014). Rebelliousness, sensation seeking, attitudes toward deviant behavior, and affiliation with deviant peers in turn were associated with a tendency to use alcohol, particularly to reduce nervousness regarding sexual activity. Studies exploring associations between music videos or sexually degrading music lyrics and sexual behavior show that increased music media exposure is associated with increased likelihood of requesting a sexting message (for boys); inconsistent condom use and decreased condom use self-efficacy; and increased likelihood of engaging in sexual intercourse and other non-coital sexual behaviors (Primack et al., 2009; Robilliard, 2012; Van Ouytsel et al., 2014).

A Critique of the Recent Studies

Strengths of the Work

One of the major strengths of this body of research is its emphasis and strong foundation of longitudinal studies. Of the 39 studies reviewed for this review, 19 were longitudinal. This aspect deserves special mention because longitudinal work allows researchers to make stronger claims about the directionality of the links between variables than is possible with cross-sectional work. Another major strength of research utilizing this design is the fact that longitudinal work allows us to study intra-individual change and make claims about trajectories of change, rather than making inter-individual comparisons that may or may not reflect the process of development for individuals. From a developmental perspective, the ability to make strong claims about intra-individual change is invaluable, and is particularly important given the unique influence of sexualized media content as a socialization agent.

The way in which some researchers have attempted to capture the nature of sexualized media also deserves special mention. Several studies undertook extensive content analyses to provide insight into the content of the media adolescents are regularly consuming (Collins et al., 2004; Fisher et al., 2009; Pardun et al., 2005; Tolman et al., 2007). Because of how time- and labor-intensive content analyses are to conduct, they are not feasible to complete in many media studies. Even so, small-scale content analyses can supplement other methods (e.g., surveys) and add depth to our understanding of media content. Continued use of these intensive content analytic methods will be vital to the field's moving forward because the media and what they present to our youth are constantly changing. To better study the variety of ways that media may socialize adolescents, we must first have a strong understanding of what the media landscape contains.

Limitations of the Media Measures

Despite these strengths, there are several potential areas for improvement in future research. One limitation of the existing work concerns how researchers measure media use. Their assessments of media use are often quantified in terms of the number of minutes or hours per day a certain medium is consumed. The problem with this type of measurement is that the sheer amount of time an individual is exposed to a certain medium may not be the most meaningful way to understand how and why they are affected by it. In other words, considering media effects purely in terms of time of media exposure is an overly simplistic way of assessing how media may influence perceptions of social reality. By including more nuanced assessments of media use (e.g., by presenting program exemplars for participants to report their familiarity), researchers can potentially develop more accurate models examining these media effects. Accordingly, we encourage broader and deeper measures of media use in future studies.

Even though this use of exemplars may in part allow for more complex and accurate models of media effects, this approach is not without weaknesses. A major limitation of conducting content analyses on media is that it is difficult to know how generalizable the results may be, particularly in the case of small-scale content analyses. One concern is that these exemplars may not accurately capture participants' exposure. Some participants may actually consume a great deal of the type of media under study (e.g., reality TV), but may not heavily consume the particular exemplars assessed in the survey. A second problem with this method is the extent to which different exemplars typify the media of interest. For example, in a survey that asks respondents to rate how often they watch 30 different television programs, these 30 programs may not actually be representative. Although content analyses allow us to have more confidence in understanding what exactly is shown in different media, there may be significant variation in the programs' actual content.

A final important issue for researchers in this field to address is the over-emphasis on sexual risk. Engagement in sexual behavior is a normal part of healthy sexuality development. Although there are certainly safe and unsafe ways to engage in these sexual behaviors, it is important for researchers to move past solely risk-oriented conceptualizations of sexuality to emphasize the agency and pleasures involved (Tolman & McClelland, 2011). Although some media content does present sexual relationships in a problematic way, it is likely that other content could provide models of age-appropriate desire, courtship, safe sex practices, and romance that could validate, educate, and inspire young viewers (Ward et al., 2006). We therefore argue that future researchers should work to integrate a more holistic and normative view of sexuality into their work on understanding how exposure to sexualized media influences adolescents' sexual behavior. It may be that exposure to this content may help empower adolescents to pursue rewarding and healthy sexual relationships, but we must first include measures in our research that can assess this possibility.

References

Al-Sayed, R. & Gunter, B. (2012). How Much Sex Is There in Soap Operas on British TV? *Communications*, *37*, 329–344. doi:10.1515/commun-2012–0019.

Ashby, S., Arcari, C., & Edmonson, M. (2006). Television Viewing and Risk of Sexual Initiation by Young Adolescents. *Archives of Pediatrics and Adolescent Medicine*, *160*, 375–380.

Aubrey, J. S. (2004). Sex and Punishment: An Examination of Sexual Consequences and the Sexual Double Standard in Teen Programming. *Sex Roles*, *50*, 505–514.

Aubrey, J. S., Behm-Morawitz, E., & Kim, K. (2014). Understanding the Effects of MTV's 16 and Pregnant on Adolescent Girls' Beliefs, Attitudes, and Behavioral Intentions toward Teen Pregnancy. *Journal of Health Communication*, *19*, 1145–1160. doi:10.1080/10810730.2013.872721.

Aubrey, J. S. & Frisby, C. M. (2011). Sexual Objectification in Music Videos: A Content Analysis Comparing Gender and Genre. *Mass Communication & Society*, *14*, 475–501.

Avelar e Silva, R. N. A., Wijtzes, A., van de Bongardt, D., van de Looij-Jansen, P., Bannink R., & Raat, H. (2016). Early Sexual Intercourse: Prospective Associations with Adolescents' Physical Activity and Screen Time. *PloS One*, *11*, e0158648.

Avery, L. R., Ward, L. M., Moss, L., & Uskup, D. (2017). Tuning Gender: Representations of Femininity and Masculinity in Popular Music by Black Artists. *Journal of Black Psychology*, *43*, 159–161. doi:10.1177/0095798415627917.

Bandura, A. (2002). Social Cognitive Theory of Mass Communication. In Bryant, J. & Zillmann, D. (Eds.), *Media effects: Advances in Theory and Research* (121–153). Mahwah: Erlbaum.

Barr, E., Moore, M., Johnson, T., Merten, J., & Stewart, W. (2014). The Relationship between Screen Time and Sexual Behaviors among Middle School Students. *Health Educator*, *46*, 6–13.

Bleakley, A., Ellithorpe, M. E., Hennessy, M., Khurana, A., Jamieson, P., & Weitz, I. (2017). Alcohol, Sex, and Screens: Modeling Media Influence on Adolescent Alcohol and Sex Co-Occurrence. *Journal of Sex Research*, 1026–1037. doi:10.1080/00224499.2017.1279585.

Bleakley, A., Hennessy, M., Fishbein, M., Coles, H., & Jordan, A. (2009). How Sources of Sexual Information Relate to Adolescents' Beliefs about Sex. *American Journal of Health Behavior*, *33*, 37–48. doi:10.5993/AJHB.33.1.4.

Bleakley, A., Hennessy, M., & Fishbein, M. (2010). A Model of Adolescents' Seeking of Sexual Content in Their Media Choices. *Journal of Sex Research*, *48*, 309–315. doi:10.1080/00224499.2010.497985.

Bleakley, A., Hennessy, M., Fishbein, M., & Jordan, A. (2008). It Works Both Ways: The Relationship between Exposure to Sexual Content in the Media and Adolescent Sexual Behavior. *Media Psychology*, *11*, 443–461.

(2011). Using the Integrative Model to Explain How Exposure to Sexual Media Content Influences Adolescent Sexual Behavior. *Health Education & Behavior*, *38*, 530–540. doi:10.1177/1090198110385775.

Bleakley, A., Jamieson, P., & Romer, D. (2012). Trends of Sexual and Violent Content by Gender in Top-Grossing U.S. Films, 1950–2006. *Journal of Adolescent Health*, *51*, 73–79. doi:10.1016/j.jadohealth.2012.02.006.

Bond, B. (2015). Portrayals of Sex and Sexuality in Gay- and Lesbian-Oriented Media: A Quantitative Content Analysis. *Sexuality & Culture*, *19*, 37–56. doi:10.1007/s12119-014-9241-6.

Bond, B. & Compton, B. (2015). Gay On-Screen: The Relationship between Exposure to Gay Characters on Television and Heterosexual Audiences' Endorsement of Gay Equality. *Journal of Broadcasting & Electronic Media*, *59*, 717–732. doi:10.1080/08838151.2015.1093485.

Brown, J. D., Halpern, C., & L'Engle, K. (2005). Mass Media as a Sexual Super Peer for Early Maturing Girls. *Journal of Adolescent Health*, *36*, 420–427. doi:10.1016/j.jadohealth.2004.06.003.

Brown, J. D., L'Engle, K., Pardun, C., Guo, G., Kenneavy, K., & Jackson, C. (2006). Sexy Media Matter: Exposure to Sexual Content in Music, Movies, Television, and Magazines Predicts Black and White Adolescents' Sexual Behavior. *Pediatrics*, *117*, 1018–1027. doi:10.1542/peds.2005-1406.

Bryant, Y. (2008). Relationships between Exposure to Rap Music Videos and Attitudes toward Relationships among African American Youth. *Journal of Black Psychology*, *34*, 356–380. doi:10.1177/0095798408314141.

Callister, M., Stern, L. A., Coyne, S. M., Robinson, T., & Bennion, E. (2011). Evaluation of Sexual Content in Teen-Centered Films from 1980 to 2007. *Mass Communication and Society*, *14*, 454–474. doi:10.1080/15205436.2010.500446.

Calzo, J. & Ward, L. M. (2009). Media Exposure and Viewers' Attitudes towards Homosexuality: Evidence for Mainstreaming or Resonance? *Journal of Broadcasting & Electronic Media*, *53*, 280–299. doi:10.1080/08838150902908049.

Carpentier, F., Stevens, E., Wu, L. & Seely, N. (2017). Sex, Love, and Risk-n-Responsibility: A Content Analysis of Entertainment Television. *Mass Communication and Society*, *20*(5), 686–709. doi:10.1080/15205436.2017.1298807.

Collins, R. L., Elliott, M. N., Berry, S. H., et al. (2004). Watching Sex on Television Predicts Adolescent Initiation of Sexual Behavior. *Pediatrics*, *114*(3), e280-e289. doi:10.1542/peds.2003-1065-L.

Collins, R., Strasburger, V., Brown, J. D., Donnerstein, E., Lenhart, A., & Ward, L. M. (2017). Sexual Media and Childhood Well-Being and Health. *Pediatrics*, 140, s162–s166. doi:10.1542/peds.2016-1758X.

Common Sense Media. (2015). *The CommonSense Census: Media Use by Tweens and Teens*. San Francisco: Common Sense Media.

Dennis, J. (2009). The Boy Who Would Be Queen: Hints and Closets on Children's Television. *Journal of Homosexuality*, *56*, 738–756. doi:10.1080/00918360903054210.

Driesmans, K., Vandenbosch, L., & Eggermont, S. (2016). True Love Lasts Forever: The Influence of a Popular Teenage Movie on Belgian Girls' Romantic Beliefs. *Journal of Children and Media, 10*, 304–320. doi:10.1080/17482798.2016.1157501.

Eggermont, S. (2004). Television Viewing, Perceived Similarity, and Adolescents' Expectations of a Romantic Partner. *Journal of Broadcasting & Electronic Media, 48*, 244–265. doi:10.1207/s15506878jobem4802_5.

(2005). Young Adolescents' Perceptions of Peer Sexual Behaviours: The Role of Television Viewing. *Child: Care, Health and Development, 31*, 459–468. doi:10.1111/j.1365-2214.2005.00525.x.

Eyal, K. & Ben-Ami, Y. (2017). It Only Happens Once: Adolescents' Interpretations of Mediated Messages about Sexual Initiation. *Mass Communication and Society, 20*, 68–91. doi:10.1080/15205436.2016.1187754.

Eyal, R., Raz, Y., & Levi, M. (2014). Messages about Sex on Israeli Television: Comparing Local and Foreign Programming. *Journal of Broadcasting & Electronic Media, 58*, 42–58. doi:10.1080/08838151.2013.875021.

Fisher, D. A., Hill, D. L., Grube, J. W., Bersamin, M. M., Walker, S., & Gruber, E. L. (2009). Televised Sexual Content and Parental Mediation: Influences on Adolescent Sexuality. *Media Psychology, 12*, 121–147. doi:10.1080/15213260902849901.

Fisher, D., Hill, D., Grube, J., & Gruber, E. (2004). Sex on American Television: An Analysis across Program Genres and Network Types. *Journal of Broadcasting & Electronic Media, 48*, 529–553.

Flynn, M., Park, S-Y., Morin, D., & Stana, A. (2015). Anything but Real: Body Idealization and Objectification of MTV Docusoap Characters. *Sex Roles, 72*, 173–182. doi:10.1007/s11199-015-0464-2.

Frisby, C. M. & Aubrey, J. S. (2012). Race and Genre in the Use of Sexual Objectification in Female Artists' Music Videos. *Howard Journal of Communications, 23*, 66–87. doi:10.1080/10646175.2012.641880.

Frison, E., Vandenbosch, L., Trekels, J., & Eggermont, S. (2015). Reciprocal Relationships between Music Television Exposure and Adolescents' Sexual Behaviors: The Role of Perceived Peer Norms. *Sex Roles, 72*, 183–197. doi:10.1007/s11199-015-0454-4.

Gerbner, G., Gross, L., Morgan, M., Signorielli, N., & Shanahan, J. (2002). Growing Up with Television: Cultivation Processes. In Bryant, J. & Zillmann, D. (Eds.), *Media Effects: Advances in Theory and Research, 2nd edn.* (43–67). Mahwah: Lawrence Erlbaum.

Gottfried, J. A., Vaala, S. E., Bleakley, A., Hennessy, M., & Jordan, A. (2013). Does the Effect of Exposure to TV Sex on Adolescent Sexual Behavior Vary by Genre? *Communication Research, 40*, 73–95. doi:10.1177/0093650211415399.

Harris, A. L. (2015). Urban Lit and Sexual Risk Behavior: A Survey of African-American Adolescent Girls. *Journal of National Black Nurses' Association: JNBNA, 26*, 58–63. https://mgetit.lib.umich.edu/go/1668292.

Harris, R., Hoekstra, S., Scott, C., Sanborn, F., Dodds, L., & Brandenburg, J. (2004). Auto-Biographical Memories for Seeing Romantic Movies on a Date: Romance Is Not Just for Women. *Media Psychology, 6*, 257–284. doi:10.1207/s1532785xmep0603_2.

Hartley, J. E., Wight, D., & Hunt, K. (2014). Presuming the Influence of the Media: Teenagers' Constructions of Gender Identity through Sexual/Romantic

Relationships and Alcohol Consumption. *Sociology of Health & Illness*, *36*, 772–786. doi:10.1111/1467-9566.12107.

Hennessy, M., Bleakley, A., Fishbein, M., & Jordan, A. (2009). Estimating the Longitudinal Association between Adolescent Sexual Behavior and Exposure to Sexual Media Content. *Journal of Sex Research*, *46*, 586–596. doi:10.1080/00224490902898736.

Henrich, J., Heine, S. J., & Norenzayan, A. (2010). The Weirdest People in the World? *Behavioral and Brain Sciences*, 33(2–3), 61–83.

Hoffner, C. & Cantor, J. (1991). Perceiving and Responding to Mass Media Characters. In Bryant, J. & Zillmann, D. (Eds.), *Responding to the Screen: Reception and Reaction Processes* (63–103). Hillsdale: Erlbaum.

Horton, D. & Wohl, R. (1956). Mass Communication and Para-Social Interaction: Observation on Intimacy at a Distance. *Psychiatry*, *19*, 188–211. doi:10.1080/00332747.1956.11023049.

Hull, J. G., Brunelle, T. J., Prescott, A. T., & Sargent, J. D. (2014). A Longitudinal Study of Risk-Glorifying Video Games and Behavioral Deviance. *Journal of Personality and Social Psychology*, *107*, 300–325. doi:10.1037/a0036058.

Jackson, C., Brown, J. D., & Pardun, C. J. (2008). A TV in the Bedroom: Implications for Viewing Habits and Risk Behaviors during Early Adolescence. *Journal of Broadcasting & Electronic Media*, *52*, 349–367.

Jamieson, P., More, E., Lee, S., Busse, P., & Romer, D. (2008). It Matters What People Watch: Health Risk Behaviors Portrayed in Top-Grossing Movies Since 1950. In Jamieson, P. & Romer, D. (Eds.), *The Changing Portrayal of Adolescents in the Media Since 1950* (105–131). Oxford: Oxford University Press.

Jeong, S. H., Hwang, Y., & Fishbein, M. (2010). Effects of Exposure to Sexual Content in the Media on Adolescent Sexual Behaviors: The Moderating Role of Multitasking with Media. *Media Psychology*, *13*, 222–242. doi:10.1080/15213269.2010.502872.

Jones, R. K., Biddlecom, A. E., Hebert, L., & Mellor, R. (2011). Teens Reflect on Their Sources of Contraceptive Information. *Journal of Adolescent Research*, *26*, 423–446. doi:10.1177/0743558411400908.

Kim, J. L., Sorsoli, C. L., Collins, K., Zylbergold, B. A., Schooler, D., & Tolman, D. A. (2007). From Sex to Sexuality: Exposing the Heterosexual Script on Primetime Television Network. *Journal of Sex Research*, *44*, 145–157.

Kim, J. & Wells, B. (2015). Assessing Alcohol and Sexual Content on Reality Dating Programs. *Psychology of Popular Media Culture*, *6*, 237–254. doi:10.1037/ppm0000098.

King, K. A., Laake, R. A., & Bernard, A. L. (2006). Do the Depictions of Sexual Attire and Sexual Behavior in Music Videos Differ Based on Video Network and Character Gender? *American Journal of Health Education*, *37*, 146–153.

Kirsch, A. C. & Murnen, S. K. (2015). "Hot" Girls and "Cool Dudes": Examining the Prevalence of the Heterosexual Script in American Children's Television Media. *Psychology of Popular Media Culture*, *4*, 18.

Kistler, M., Rodgers, K. B., Power, T., Austin, E. W., & Hill, L. G. (2010). Adolescents and Music Media: Toward an Involvement-Mediational Model of Consumption and Self-concept. *Journal of Research on Adolescence*, *20*, 616–630. doi:10.1111/j.1532-7795.2010.00651.x.

Koletic, G. (2017). Longitudinal Associations between the Use of Sexually Explicit Material and Adolescents' Attitudes and Behaviors: A Narrative Review of Studies. *Journal of Adolescence, 57,* 119–133. doi:10.1016/j.adolescence.2017.04.006.

Kunkel, D., Biely, E., Eyal, K., Cope-Farrar, K., Donnerstein, E., & Fandrich, R. (2003). *Sex on TV 3: A Biennial Report of the Kaiser Family Foundation.* Menlo Park: Henry J. Kaiser Family Foundation.

Kunkel, D., Cope, K., Farinola, W., Biely, E., Rollin, E., & Donnerstein, E. (1999). *Sex on TV: A Biennial Report to the Kaiser Family Foundation.* Menlo Park: Kaiser Family Foundation.

Kunkel, D., Cope-Farrar, K., Biely, E., Farinola, W., & Donnerstein, E. (2001). *Sex on TV 2: A Biennial Report to the Kaiser Family Foundation.* Menlo Park: Kaiser Family Foundation.

Kunkel, D., Eyal, K., Finnerty, K., Biely, E., & Donnerstein, E. (2005). *Sex on TV 4: A Biennial Report of the Kaiser Family Foundation.* Menlo Park: Henry J. Kaiser Family Foundation.

Kunkel, D., Farrar, K. M., Eyal, K., Biely, E., Donnerstein, E., & Rideout, V. (2007). Sexual Socialization Messages on Entertainment Television: Comparing Content Trends 1997–2002. *Media Psychology, 9,* 595–622. doi:10.1080/15213260701283210.

L'Engle, K., Brown, J. D., & Kenneavy, K. (2006). The Mass Media Are an Important Context for Adolescents' Sexual Behavior. *Journal of Adolescent Health, 38,* 186–192.

Len-Ríos, M., Streit, C., Killoren, S., Deutsch, A., Cooper, M., & Carlo, G. (2016). U.S. Latino Adolescents' Use of Mass Media and Mediated Communication in Romantic Relationships. *Journal of Children and Media, 10,* 395–410. doi:10.1080/17482798.2016.1144214.

Malacane, M. & Martins, N. (2017). Sexual Socialization Messages in Television Programming Produced by Adolescents. *Mass Communication and Society, 20,* 23–46. doi:10.1080/15205436.2016.1203436.

Martino, S. C., Collins, R. L., Elliott, M. N., Kanouse, D. E., & Berry, S. H. (2009). It's Better on TV: Does Television Set Teenagers Up for Regret Following Sexual Initiation? *Perspectives on Sexual and Reproductive Health, 41,* 92–100. doi:10.1363/4109209.

Martino, S. C., Collins, R. L., Kanouse, D. E., Elliott, M., & Berry, S. H. (2005). Social Cognitive Processes Mediating the Relationship between Exposure to Television's Sexual Content and Adolescents' Sexual Behavior. *Journal of Personality and Social Psychology, 89,* 914–924. doi:10.1037/0022-3514.89.6.914.

Nalkur, P. G., Jamieson, P. E., & Romer, D. (2010). The Effectiveness of the Motion Picture Association of America's Rating System in Screening Explicit Violence and Sex in Top-Ranked Movies from 1950 to 2006. *Journal of Adolescent Health, 47,* 440–447.

Netzley, S. (2010). Visibility that Demystifies: Gays, Gender, and Sex on Television. *Journal of Homosexuality, 57,* 968–986. doi:10.1080/00918369.2010.503505.

O'Hara, R. E., Gibbons, F. X., Gerrard, M., Li, Z., & Sargent, J. D. (2012). Greater Exposure to Sexual Content in Popular Movies Predicts Earlier Sexual Debut and Increased Sexual Risk Taking. *Psychological Science, 23,* 984–993. doi:10.1177/0956797611435529.

Ortiz, R. & Brooks, M. (2014). Getting What They Deserve? Consequences of Sexual Expression by Central Characters in Five Popular Television Teen Dramas in the United States. *Journal of Children and Media*, *8*, 40–52. doi:10.1080/17482798.2014.863477.

Owens, E., Behun, R., Manning, J., & Reid, R. (2012). The Impact of Internet Pornography on Adolescents: A Review of the Research. *Sexual Addiction & Compulsivity*, *19*, 99–122. doi:10.1080/10720162.2012.660431.

Pardun, C., L'Engle, K., & Brown, J. (2005). Linking Exposure to Outcomes: Early Adolescents' Consumption of Sexual Content in Six Media. *Mass Communication & Society*, *8*, 75–91. doi:10.1207/s15327825mcs0802_1.

Parkes, A., Wight, D., Hunt, K., Henderson, M., & Sargent, J. (2013). Are Sexual Media Exposure, Parental Restrictions on Media Use and Co-Viewing TV and DVDs with Parents and Friends Associated with Teenagers' Early Sexual Behaviour? *Journal of Adolescence*, *36*, 1121–1133. doi:10.1016/j.adolescence.2013.08.019.

Peter, J. & Valkenburg, P. (2016). Adolescents and Pornography: A Review of 20 years of Research. *Journal of Sex Research*, *54*, 509–531. doi:10.1080/00224499.2016.1143441.

Primack, B. A., Douglas, E. L., Fine, M. J., & Dalton, M. A. (2009). Exposure to Sexual Lyrics and Sexual Experience among Urban Adolescents. *American Journal of Preventive Medicine*, *36*, 317–323. doi:10.1016/j.amepre.2008.11.011.

Primack, B.A., Gold, M.A., Schwarz, E.B., & Dalton, M.A. (2008). Degrading and Non-Degrading Sex in Popular Music: A Content Analysis. *Public Health Reports*, *123*, 593–600.

Ragsdale, K., Bersamin, M., Schwartz, S., Zamboanga, B., Kerrick, M., & Grube, J. (2014). Development of Sexual Expectancies among Adolescents: Contributions by Parents, Peers and the Media. *Journal of Sex Research*, *51*, 551–560. doi:10.1080/00224499.2012.753025.

Rideout, V. J., Foehr, U. G., & Roberts, D. F. (2010). *Generation M2. Media in the Lives of 8–18 Year Olds*. Menlo Park: Kaiser Family Foundation. http://eric.ed.gov/?id=ED527859.

Rivadeneyra, R. & Lebo, M. J. (2008). The Association between Television-Viewing Behaviors and Adolescent Dating Role Attitudes and Behaviors. *Journal of Adolescence*, *31*, 291–305. doi:10.1016/j.adolescence.2007.06.001.

Robillard, A. (2012). Music Videos and Sexual Risk in African American Adolescent Girls: Gender, Power and the Need for Media Literacy. *American Journal of Health Education*, *43*, 93-103. doi:10.1080/19325037.2012.10599224.

Rouner, D., Slater, M. D., & Domenech-Rodriguez, M. (2003). Adolescent Evaluation of Gender Role and Sexual Imagery in Television Advertisements. *Journal of Broadcasting & Electronic Media*, *47*, 435–454. doi:10.1207/s15506878jobem4703_7.

Rubin, R. B. & Rubin, A. M. (2001). Attribution in Social and Parasocial Relationships. In Manusov, V. & Harvey, J. H. (Eds.), *Attribution, Communication Behavior, and Close Relationships* (320–337). Cambridge: Cambridge University Press.

Shrum, L. J. (1996). Psychological Processes Underlying Cultivation Effects: Further Tests of Construct Accessibility. *Human Communication Research*, *22*, 482–509.

Signorielli, N. & Bievenour, A. (2015). Sex in Adolescent Programming: A Content Analysis. *Communication Research Reports*, *32*, 304–313. doi:10.1080/08824096.2015.1089856.

Smiler, A., Shewmaker, J., & Hearon, B. (2017). From "I Want to Hold Your Hand" to "Promiscuous": Sexual Stereotypes in Popular Music Lyrics, 1960–2008. *Sexuality & Culture*, 21(4), 1083–1105. doi:10.1007/s12119-017-9437-7.

Somers, C. L. & Tynan, J. J. (2006). Consumption of Sexual Dialogue and Content on Television and Adolescent Sexual Outcomes: Multiethnic Findings. *Adolescence*, *41*, 15–38.

Stephens, D. P. & Few, A. L. (2007). The Effects of Images of African American Women in Hip Hop on Early Adolescents' Attitudes toward Physical Attractiveness and Interpersonal Relationships. *Sex Roles*, *56*, 251–264. doi:10.1007/s11199-006-9145-5.

ter Bogt, T. F., Engels, R. C., Bogers, S., & Kloosterman, M. (2010). "Shake It Baby, Shake It": Media Preferences, Sexual Attitudes and Gender Stereotypes among Adolescents. *Sex Roles*, *63*, 844–859. doi:10.1007/s11199-010-9815-1.

Tolman, D. L., Kim, J. L., Schooler, D., & Sorsoli, C. L. (2007). Rethinking the Associations between Television Viewing and Adolescent Sexuality Development: Bringing Gender into Focus. *Journal of Adolescent Health*, 40(1), 84.e9–84.e16.

Tolman, D. L. & McClelland, S. I. (2011). Normative Sexuality Development in Adolescence: A Decade in Review, 2000–2009. *Journal of Research on Adolescence*, *21*, 242–255.

Turner, J. S. (2011). Sex and the Spectacle of Music Videos: An Examination of the Portrayal of Race and Sexuality in Music Videos. *Sex Roles*, *64*, 173–191.

van Oosten, J. M., Peter, J., & Valkenburg, P. M. (2015). The Influence of Sexual Music Videos on Adolescents' Misogynistic Beliefs: The Role of Video Content, Gender, and Affective Engagement. *Communication Research*, *42*, 986–1008. doi:10.1177/0093650214565893.

Van Ouytsel, J., Van Gool, E., Ponnet, K., & Walrave, M. (2014). The Association between Adolescents' Characteristics and Engagement in Sexting. *Journal of Adolescence*, *37*, 1387–1391.

Wallis, C. (2011). Performing Gender: A Content Analysis of Gender Display in Music Videos. *Sex Roles*, *64*, 160–172.

Ward, L. M. (2003). Understanding the Role of Entertainment Media in the Sexual Socialization of American Youth: A Review of Empirical Research. *Developmental Review*, *23*, 347–388.

Ward, L. M., Day, K., & Epstein, M. (2006). Uncommonly Good: Exploring How Mass Media May Be a Positive Influence on Young Women's Sexual Health and Development. In Diamond, L. (Ed.), *Rethinking Positive Adolescent Female Sexual Development: New Directions in Child and Adolescent Development* (57–70). San Francisco: Jossey Bass.

Ward, L. M. & Friedman, K. (2006). Using TV as a Guide: Associations between Television Viewing and Adolescents' Sexual Attitudes and Behavior. *Journal of Research on Adolescence*, *16*, 133–156. doi:10.1111/j.1532-7795.2006.00125.x.

Ward, L. M., Hansbrough, E., & Walker, E. (2005). Contributions of Music Video Exposure to Black Adolescents' Gender and Sexual Schemas. *Journal of Adolescent Research*, *20*, 143-166. doi:10.1177/0743558404271135.

Ward, L. M., Reed, L., Trinh, S., & Foust, M. (2013). Sexuality and Entertainment Media. In Tolman, D., Diamond, L. M., Bauermeister, J., William, G., Pfaus, J., & Ward, L.

M. (Eds.), *APA Handbook of Sexuality and Psychology, Volume 2: Contextual Approaches* (373–423). Washington, DC: American Psychological Association.

Ward, L. M., Rivadeneyra, R., Thomas, K., Day, K., & Epstein, M. (2013). A Woman's Worth: Analyzing the Sexual Objectification of Black Women in Music Videos. In Zurbriggen, E. & Roberts, T-A. (Eds.), *The Sexualization of Girls and Girlhood: Causes, Consequences, and Resistance* (39–62). New York: Oxford University Press.

Watson, A. F. & McKee, A. (2013). Masturbation and the Media. *Sexuality & Culture*, *17*, 449-475. doi:10.1007/s12119-013-9186-1.

Werner-Wilson, R. J., Fitzharris, J. L., & Morrissey, K. M. (2004). Adolescent and Parent Perceptions of Media Influence on Adolescent Sexuality. *Family Therapy*, *31*, 303–313.

21 Adventure, Intimacy, Identity, and Knowledge

Exploring How Social Media Are Shaping and Transforming Youth Sexuality

Marijke Naezer and Jessica Ringrose

Introduction: Sexual Risks, Harm, and Panic

> Does porn hurt children? (New York Times, 2014)
>
> Swapping nude images spells danger for teens (USA Today, 2017)
>
> Selfies "can fuel" body image worries says ChildLine (BBC, 2014)
>
> The Dangers of Teen Sexting: Sexting a problem with major consequences (Psychology Today, 2012)[1]

News headlines over the past few years show that public debates about young people's online sexual practices have tended to focus on the dangers posed by technology (Döring, 2009; Hasinoff, 2015; Livingstone, 2011). Practices related to consuming, producing, and exchanging sexually explicit material, such as watching porn and 'sexting,' are constructed as inherently harmful practices that damage young people, especially White, middle-class girls (for a critique, see Egan, 2013; Mulholland, 2017).

A risk and harm paradigm has prevailed through the dominance of high-profile psychological research on youth, sexuality, and technology. For example, researchers have investigated correlations between young people's consumption of 'sexually explicit material' or 'pornography' and negative developmental outcomes such as a view of girls and women as objects (e.g., Peter & Valkenburg, 2007, 2009), sexual dissatisfaction, sexual dysfunction (e.g., Peter & Valkenburg, 2008) and sex addiction (e.g., Cooper, 2000; Delmonico & Griffin, 2012). The phenomenon of youth 'sexting' (exchanging sexual text messages, pictures, or videos, and having sexual conversations via webcams) has likewise been constructed largely as a technological risk, with research findings highlighting reputational damage,

[1] Respectively, www.nytimes.com/2014/03/29/sunday-review/does-porn-hurt-children.html?mcubz=3, www.usatoday.com/story/news/nation/2015/02/21/swapping-nude-images-spells-trouble-teens/23824495/, www.bbc.com/news/uk-scotland-27909281, www.psychologytoday.com/blog/teen-angst/201207/the-dangers-teen-sexting.

bullying, harassment, blackmailing, sexual violence including child pornography and forced prostitution, and even suicide (for overviews, see Karaian & Van Meyl, 2015; Salter et al., 2013). In addition, the practice of sharing (sexy) selfies has been constructed as the cause and/or evidence of psychological problems, such as narcissism and body dysmorphia (for overviews, see Burns, 2015; Senft & Baym, 2015).

The dominance of this risk and harm approach to technology, (social) media, and youth sexuality has fuelled a discourse of youth sexualization, both public and academic, that finds 'the media,' in general, and social media, in particular, responsible for making young people engage with 'too much too young' (Bragg & Buckingham, 2009), set in contrast to a pre-technology childhood innocence (Fischer, 2006; Robinson, 2013). The overwhelming focus on risk and harm is problematic: it severely limits our view, not only in terms of which practices are considered relevant (watching porn, sexting and sharing sexy selfies) but also in terms of which outcomes become known and imaginable (negative outcomes) (see also Hasinoff, 2015; Karaian & Van Meyl, 2015; Naezer, 2017; Tiidenberg, 2018).

Moreover, the current dominant approach to technology, (social) media, and youth sexuality we have outlined is often stereotypically gendered and heteronormative: the majority of analyses are focused on girls, who are portrayed as victims of technology and/or boys and men who perpetrate harm via technology. In much of the research, boys and masculinity are naturalized as sexist and predatory and ignored as objects of study (Bragg, 2015). These limited, gendered, and heteronormative 'moral panics' (Hasinoff, 2015; Renold & Ringrose, 2011; Robinson, 2013; Waskul, 2006), or the 'scary futurology' (Smith, 2010) of youth sexuality, has resulted in the condemnation, policing, and pathologizing of young people (Renold et al., 2015, p. 4).

In this chapter, we argue that this dominant anti-technology narrative in psychological research that informs many popular ideas about technological risk does not reflect the complexities of young people's experiences with sexuality and social media. We will use research from the fields of gender studies, queer studies, sociology, anthropology, pedagogy, and media studies, as well as our own empirical data to argue for a more nuanced and complex understanding of social media's impact on youth sexuality. First, we will explore further the dichotomous thinking represented in present-day discourses about youth, sexuality, and social media. After that, we will go into the small, but growing, number of critical, empirical studies that interrogate and challenge these dichotomies by focusing on young people's own experiences and perspectives, which are much more varied. Building on these studies, we explore our own research findings attempting to broaden the scope of public and academic debates by introducing four different dimensions of online sexuality. For each of these dimensions, we will discuss how young people's practices and ideas complicate stereotypical, gendered, and heteronormative narratives and dichotomies.

Deconstructing Dichotomies about Youth, Digital Technology and Sexuality

In the introduction, we indicated how social media have been constructed as 'dangerous' (as opposed to safe) and 'bad' (as opposed to 'good'). In this section, we explore further two underlying dichotomies that seem to play a role in these debates: those of 'online' versus 'offline' and 'public' versus 'private.'

The idea of cyberspace as existing only in the interaction between machines and users has led many researchers (and policy makers, journalists, and other professionals) to conceptualize virtual space as separated from 'offline life' (also referred to as 'real life') (Hillis, 1999, p. xiii). Over the last years, this dichotomy has been dramatically challenged through concepts like digital mediation (e.g., Van Doorn, 2009). As danah boyd's extensive research points out, for teens, online and offline worlds are indeed tightly entwined: "The performances that take place online are not isolated acts, disconnected from embodied settings, but rather conscious acts that rely on a context that spans mediated and unmediated environments and involves people who are known in both settings" (2008a, p. 128). This troubling of the online–offline dichotomy is reinforced by Warfield's analysis of young women's selfie-taking practices (2016). Her analysis reveals how selfies materialize through the image, but also through online and offline interactions with (including viewing and discussion of) images, challenging the online–offline (as well as the material–discursive) dichotomy.

Another dichotomy that seems to underlie debates about young people, sexuality, and social media is that of 'private' versus 'public,' where the perceived 'private' nature of intimacy and sexuality (Chambers, 2013; Plummer, 2003; Reynolds, 2010) is contrasted to the perceived 'public' nature of social media (e.g., boyd, 2008b). In her theory of 'networked publics,' boyd (2008b, pp. 125–126, 2014) describes four properties that she considers fundamental to social media environments: persistence (communications are recorded 'for posterity'), searchability (search and discovery tools make it easy to find people and content), replicability/spreadability (content can be copied from one place to another), and scalability/visibility (the audience can potentially consist of all people across space and time). Although newer applications such as Tumblr (unclear authorship, 'disorienting' architecture) and Snapchat (disappearing content) trouble this analysis (Cho, 2015; Handyside & Ringrose, 2017), the four properties distinguished by boyd are still dominant in our perceptions of social media and contribute to concerns about 'the end of privacy.' They also contribute to warnings for youth, especially girls, not to perform 'private' or 'intimate' activities such as sexting in online spaces (Hasinoff, 2015).

These privacy warnings for girls not only have a strong 'abstinence' character, they also seem to promote victim-blaming when things go wrong, and they deny the complex entanglements of 'the public' and 'the private' with regard to intimacy. For example, Pascoe (2010, pp. 130–132) has pointed out that by 'publicly' sharing relationship information, partners signal to their networked publics, but also to their partner, that they are dedicated to the relationship. Moreover, Pascoe (2010, pp. 119–120) argues, sexual and romantic relationships are, "for all their emphasis on privacy and exclusivity, profoundly social." Friends and peers play an important role in meeting and interacting with potential partners, in initiating, developing, and recovering from romantic relationships; and in learning from those experiences (see also Krebbekx, 2018). 'The public' is thus not absent from 'the private,' and public norms, practices, and institutions influence which 'private,' intimate practices and feelings are legitimate and rewarding. What is important for our arguments about youth sexuality is that the public and the private are thus not two separate entities, and intimacy is not necessarily confined to the private sphere (see also Attwood et al., 2017).

Critical Studies of Youth Sexuality and Social Media

Critical studies about youth sexuality and social media are seeking to disrupt and move beyond 'moral panics' about digital technology (Hasinoff, 2015) and a prime way to do so is to study experiences of sexuality and social media from the perspective of young people themselves (Renold et al., 2015). In this highly interdisciplinary field of research at the intersections of media studies, sociology, anthropology, and pedagogy, two main approaches may be distinguished: one that approaches the topic from a gender perspective, and one that approaches it from a queer perspective.

Gender researchers focusing on youth, sexuality, and social media have analyzed how young people, mainly girls, construct gendered sexual identities or subjectivities through practices such as creating profiles, using applications, sharing pictures, tagging, and commenting on peers' pictures (e.g., Albury, 2015; Renold & Ringrose, 2017; De Ridder & Van Bauwel, 2013; Ringrose et al., 2013; Warfield, 2016). These studies pointed out how boys and, especially, girls navigate double sexual standards and slut shaming in a 'postfeminist' context (Gill, 2007a, 2009; McRobbie, 2009), where it is assumed that gender equality has been met, and where women and girls are increasingly encouraged to use their 'sexual freedom' to pursue sexual pleasure. Such a discourse of sexual liberation obscures how girls and women are called upon to produce themselves in a particular way, namely as desirable heterosexual subjects (Evans et al., 2010; Gill, 2007b, 2009). Moreover, the postfeminist ideal of sexual freedom coexists with more conservative notions about women's and girls' sexuality, which holds girls and women responsible for upholding their sexual 'reputation' as modest, pure, innocent, and careful (e.g., Ringrose, 2011). Boys, on the other hand, are pressured to present a heterosexualized, 'hard' masculinity through certain types of self-performance, as well as via technological affordances such as the 'phallic' collecting, posting, tagging, and rating of girls' and women's digital bodies (e.g., Harvey & Ringrose, 2015; Renold & Ringrose, 2017).

Gender research about youth (hetero)sexuality and social media demonstrates how, in some respects, young people's navigations of sexual norms are similar to older processes of identity performance, while at the same time they are also different. Slut-shaming practices, for instance, have been well documented historically, even if sometimes labeled differently, and are repeated in young people's online communication, but young people can also use social media affordances to challenge the norms underlying slut-shaming behaviors (e.g., by performing 'slutty' femininity as a positive, empowering subject position in online profiles) (Dobson, 2015; Ringrose, 2011). Moreover, social media enable young people to access a wide variety of knowledge, providing them with new techniques for the performance of gendered subjectivities. Examples of these techniques include the citation of 'porno scripts' and 'sexualized' online imagery and symbolism, which can be employed for the performance of 'sexy' femininity (Ringrose, 2011). The affordances described by boyd (2008b, 2014) (persistence, searchability, replicability/spreadability, and scalability/visibility) make a difference, in that they add extra temporal, spatial, affective, and performative dimensions to young people's online/offline practices. For example, sexy images of girls and women can be collected, saved, and used by boys in their performances of macho, heterosexual masculinity (Ringrose & Harvey, 2015a).

While the vast majority of gender research about youth sexuality and social media has focused on the user's performance of (gendered, heterosexual) subjectivities/identities, some research has been done on the role of social media in the performance of sexual and romantic relationships (most notably, Handyside & Ringrose, 2017; Pascoe, 2010). Pascoe (2010), for instance, notes how social media mediate young people's courtship practices such as meeting, flirting, going out, and breaking up. She analyzes how technology impacts young people's courtship practices in terms of privacy, monitoring, and vulnerability (2010, pp. 138–145). Social media provide young people with a sphere of privacy, in which they can communicate with their significant others often beyond the gaze of adults. This allows them a certain freedom and permits them to have intensely emotional, vulnerable conversations, while at the same time rendering them potentially susceptible to the forwarding of personal information. Moreover, freedom is compromised by practices through which partners monitor each other in order to manage anxieties about betrayal, for example, by checking a partner's digital communication with other people (see also Handyside & Ringrose, 2017), which contributes to a structure of surveillance and control.

The ways that LGBTQ youth experience sexuality online have not been researched to nearly the same extent as (assumed) heterosexual youth, although we are seeing a welcome increase in studies recently (e.g., Albury & Byron, 2016; Cho, 2015; Hillier & Harrison, 2007; Maliepaard, 2017; Pullen, 2014; Szulc & Dhoest, 2013). One of the most pertinent findings of this research is that for some queer young people who experience isolation, loneliness, and rejection by their family or peers at home or in school, the Internet can be a 'haven' (Tropiano, 2014, p. 57) where they can become part of a larger LGBT community, although Szulc and Dhoest (2013) found that among their research participants (both young people and adults), sexuality-related issues became less salient in their Internet use after their 'coming out.' Hillier and Harrison (2007) describe how many of their research participants met queer peers for the first time online, which helped them to combat feelings of loneliness and build a social network, through which they found not only recognition, friendship, and love, but also relevant information about sexuality that they could not access offline. Cho (2015) shows how young people's investment in online networks can be highly political. Focusing specifically on queer young people of color on Tumblr, his research makes clear that "users connect based on shared passion to formulate a robust anti-statist, anti-heteronormative, anti-white-supremacist politics" (2015, p. 189), thereby challenging traditional notions of race, gender, and sexuality.

The Research Study and Focus

Building on these important studies of youth, sexuality, and social media, and drawing on ethnographic data, we aim to offer a nuanced and complex understanding of how young people navigate both social and technological structures in their online/offline sexual practices. The ethnographic data were collected during one and a half years of fieldwork among young people aged 12–18 years in the Netherlands in 2013–2014. Research methods included online and offline (participant) observation, six focus group meetings, 29 in-depth interviews, and a survey.[2] Research participants were diverse in terms of age, gender, sexual experiences/identifications, ethnicity, educational level, and class.

A case study of Kyra (15 years) and Mark's (17 years)[3] heterosexual relationship offers a thread for exploring four different dimensions of mediated sexuality via social media use: sexuality as (1) adventure, (2) intimacy, (3) identity, and (4) knowledge building. Kyra and Mark's relationship case study is not meant to be representative of how all young people navigate social norms and technological affordances in their online/offline sexual practices. Indeed, conceptually we use this case as a reference point for a discussion of digitally mediated sexuality, but, in each section, we will also compare Kyra and Mark to other research participants, whose experiences were sometimes similar and sometimes rather different. A central point of focus is how all these experiences reproduce, but also challenge and disrupt, heteronormative formations, including stereotypically gendered, heteronormative, dominant discourses about youth sexuality and social media.

[2] For more discussion of the methodology of this study see (Naezer, 2017).
[3] This case study was previously discussed in (Naezer, 2015). All names are pseudonyms.

Mediated Experiments and Sexual Adventures

The first dimension of digitally mediated sexual experience we explore is that of sexual experimentation and adventure made possible through online networks. In an interview that happened to fall on their 6-month dating anniversary, Kyra and Mark elaborated on the role played by social media in their relationship. The couple first met on *Chatlokaal* (which translates as Chatroom), a Dutch chatbox that is comparable to the international Chatroulette, where people can anonymously chat with others with whom they are randomly connected by the application. If conversation partners do not want to continue the conversation, they can simply click a button in order to be connected to somebody else. It is impossible to look people up, since users don't make profiles, so meeting a person two times is only possible through coincidence. An important difference between Chatlokaal and Chatroulette is that Chatroulette allows the use of webcams, which is not possible on Chatlokaal.

On a boring evening during the summer holidays, Kyra and Mark both decided to take a look on Chatlokaal. Kyra: "It was 12 PM and I couldn't sleep because of the heat, I got bored, so I decided to go do something on my phone. I went to Twitter, and Twitter gave me a link to Chatlokaal." Just like Kyra, many other young people described websites such as Chatlokaal and Chatroulette as a place to go to if you are bored and want to have some fun. For example, a boy explained in an interview: "We always did Chatroulette with a group of boys. We talked to girls, from Poland for example. Nothing serious, just to have some fun." Online chatting with unknown people can thus be a way of countering boredom.

Social media like Chatlokaal and Chatroulette have a reputation for attracting adult men looking for sexual interactions with girls. Research participants were well aware of this reputation and it never took long before it was brought up in conversations. Kyra for instance said: "Normal conversations are exceptional [on websites like Chatlokaal]. More often people are like: 'I'm horny, looking for a girl . . . If that happens, I'm always like: ok, click, gone, bye! I don't like that." Kyra characterized such sexualized encounters on Chatlokaal as unpleasant, and tried to avoid them as much as possible by ending the conversation when a conversation partner was much older, or when a conversation partner made a sexual remark.

Other research participants experienced the sexual aspect of these websites differently, however. During a focus group meeting with girls, one of the participants brought up Chatroulette, causing hilarity as the girls started recounting stories about their encounters with 'dirty men' who exposed naked body parts, masturbated in front of their webcam, asked sexual questions, and made sexual requests. The girls talked about their encounters with these men with obvious heightened affect in the form of excitement, thrill, pleasure, and what we interpret as a sense of power. They laughed approvingly at each other's stories about how they reacted to the 'dirty men' (usually by calling them names and/or ending the conversation), showing that both their participation in Chatroulette as well as their offline discussions about those adventures can be interpreted as forms of 'affective' friendship and solidarity mediated through digital technologies (Cho, 2015).

Adult professionals (academics, teachers, health workers, police officers) with whom we discussed this often expressed concerns, and searched for ways to protect young people, especially girls, against this sexual contact with adult men. While this may be helpful in some instances, like in Kyra's case, it could prove problematic in the cases of research participants experimenting with fun and humor when visiting chat rooms such as Chatlokaal and Chatroulette with the expectation of engaging in sexual interactions. Finding and laughing at 'dirty men' was for them a way of having fun, experiencing an 'adventure' (Naezer, 2017), alone or together with friends. The anonymity in this case, and the fact that conversations can be ended with just one mouse click, gave participants a feeling of safety and control.

Albury and Byron (2016) found in relation to feelings of safety that LGBTQ youth feel more protected initiating intimacy via hookup apps on their mobile phone than interacting in offline spaces like school. In this case, the anonymity and random connections of platforms like Chatlokaal are counter to boyd's notions of persistence (communications are not necessarily recorded for posterity), searchability (finding specific people and content is nearly impossible) and scalability/visibility (unless someone records and shares the conversation, it is not visible for others). It offers a place of adventure, experimentation, friendship, and fun for participants in ways that counter dominant narratives of social media harm. That is, a practice that is generally regarded as 'dangerous,' might not necessarily or exclusively lead to harm (see also Naezer, 2017).

Another finding that troubles present-day discourse about youths' use of social media is that risk is a subjective concept (Naezer, 2017). Different researchers and research participants disagree about what is risky and what is the most relevant and/or most threatening risk. For instance, receiving sexual questions, remarks, or images may be experienced as a very relevant and threatening risk of online chatting by some youth like Kyra, but not by others, like the girls who participated in our focus group meeting. Moreover, several queer research participants pointed out other risks that were much more relevant and threatening to them, namely the possibility of other people 'finding out' about their sexual identification, desires, or activities, and the possibility of (digital) violence. For these research participants, online adventures such as the one described by Kyra and Mark often involved distress and anxiety along with excitement and adventure, which sometimes lead them to avoid these spaces altogether, thus limiting their opportunities for engagement online. Thus we need to account for the diversity with regard to how sexual risk is experienced online and to question when risk actually leads to harm or not (Livingstone, 2008).

Developing Digital Intimacy

A second dimension of digitally mediated sexuality is the development of relational intimacy. For Kyra and Mark, at some point in their first conversation, the anonymous and volatile character of Chatlokaal started to become a barrier. They felt like they were 'connecting,' and needed a more stable medium: "Because [on Chatlokaal], if your mobile crashes, you lose him, and I did not want that to happen" (Kyra). Even though the couple wanted to 'move' to another medium, they were very careful about exchanging 'personal' information (even though they had already had a rather 'personal' conversation). Kyra reproduced the well-known trope of the catfish[4]: "If you give that person your phone number, and he turns out to be somebody else ... " Therefore, they decided to use Kik first, which is comparable to MSN and affords chatting without exchanging phone numbers but with the use of a personal 'identification code' so that people are traceable. As mutual trust built up, Kyra and Mark moved again to Viber, a service that affords making phone calls (and, since 2014, also video calls) for free, using the Internet. Only after that, they exchanged phone numbers and 'talked' via WhatsApp. Moreover, they had conversations on Skype, with a webcam. With each 'step,' Kyra checked whether Mark was really Mark: she analyzed his online profiles and asked him to send her pictures via WhatsApp, which she checked using Google. For Kyra, their Skype conversation was the definite confirmation that Mark was indeed the 17-year-old boy he claimed to be. Mark did not conduct any research about Kyra, which reflects contemporary discourse that mostly focuses on girls as the vulnerable population in online intimacy, and that encourages girls more than boys to take safety measures.

Kyra and Mark's case complicates easy assumptions about online behavior and risk. Kyra's advanced strategies to check on Mark contradict the stereotypical notion of girls as foolish or thoughtless, and incapable of 'protecting themselves,' while Mark's lack of such strategies contradicts the notion of boys as 'in control.' Their choices also reproduce a gendered danger discourse, however, which constructs girls as vulnerable (and responsible for protecting themselves) and boys as predatory. While, to some extent, and for some young people, the checking up may be a pleasant aspect of online romance, the emphasis on girls as vulnerable and responsible for protecting themselves also limits their freedom to 'carelessly' enjoy their romantic adventures.

Kyra and Mark became increasingly attracted to each other and wanted to meet each other offline. Unfortunately, they lived far apart: he lived in a big city in the west of the Netherlands; she in a small village in the east of the country. To some extent, social media offered a solution. Mark explained: "She sent me pictures of Nando, the dog, and of her house and the surroundings. And that all becomes real at that moment. It becomes reality." About their Skype conversations Kyra said: "If there is a good Internet connection, you really feel like: I'm talking to him." Mark added: "You're talking for fifteen minutes and you hardly notice that there is a distance." Geographical distance almost 'dissolved' as Mark and Kyra exchanged

[4] A catfish is somebody who pretends to be someone else online, in order to pursue romantic and/or sexual relationships and/or sexual abuse.

love, attention, and commitment in their highly affective, digitally mediated interactions, thus creating their own intimate space or 'mobile intimacy' (Hjorth & Lim, 2012).

Several research participants indicated that such conversations could also become more sexual, and talking about sex or doing 'sexual things' was often considered easier via social media such as WhatsApp than offline. One girl described such conversations as potential turn ons: "You're not together, but you can be aroused. And then it's fun to tease the other. That one of you says 'I miss you', or 'I think about you', or 'I get turned on', and that you send something like: 'I can't be with you right now, but here's a picture of me; that's all I can do for you at this moment'." In cases such as these, media serve not to bridge geographical distance, but to emphasize or use it in order to extend and remediate sexual interactions.

Intimacy is not limited to 'private' online spaces, however. Kyra and Mark, for instance, also included each other in their online profiles on Twitter and Facebook, after a few months of online dating and meeting several times in person offline, thereby creating a public intimacy that defied their physical separation and distance. For instance, Mark's profile picture was a picture of him and Kyra and his Twittername was her name with a heart next to it. His biography read, in a mix of English and Dutch: "I'll love you forever @[Kyra], she means the world to me ♥♥ 18'07'13 ♥," the latter being the date on which they officially started dating. It's interesting that in the first part of this quote he addresses Kyra ("I'll love you forever"), while in the second part, he talks *about* her, to a more general audience ("she means the world to me"). This makes clear that he also addresses a larger audience in expressing how much he loves her. Apparently, the (semi-)public character of the pictures and messages is important, as he confirmed during the interview: "Otherwise it is as if the other is not important to you." For Mark, publicly performing the relationship online was a way of showing his love and his commitment to Kyra. Social media such as Twitter, on which you can make a profile, afford this public performance of intimacy and the construction of a normative relationship via digital imagery. While to some extent this is comparable to offline public performances of intimacy, such as wearing a pendant with a partner's initials, or kissing and cuddling in public spaces such as the school, it is also different, both in terms of the techniques that are available and in terms of persistence, searchability, replicability/spreadability, and scalability/visibility of the information (boyd, 2008b, 2014).

We also want to point out that not all groups are able to harness the affective opportunities of social media for building intimate, romantic relationships in the same ways. Young people who are in non-normative relationships such as same-sex and socially mixed (e.g., ethnically mixed, interreligious, mixed-age, mixed-class, and mixed-popularity) relationships, and relationships that started or largely take place via social media, often do not dare to show-off this relationship online, afraid of negative reactions (see also Ringrose, 2011). Lana explained about her present relationship with a girl: "When we started dating, I had already had my coming out[5] in school, but she hadn't. At one moment, I changed my relationship status on Facebook, and I changed my profile picture into a picture of us together. And she did the same. For her, this was her coming out." This demonstrates how for young people in queer relationships, every (semi-)public statement about that relationship automatically feels like a highly political and potentially dangerous revelation.

As has been illustrated in other research, depending on the school context, claiming a non-normative gender or sexual identity makes young people vulnerable to targeting and negative comments (e.g., Payne & Smith, 2013). Couples in non-normative romantic involvements are less likely to receive support from their social network and society in general, and more likely to encounter negative reactions when appearing in public (Lehmiller & Agnew, 2006, p. 41; McGlotten, 2013). For several research participants who were in a non-normative relationship, fear of such negative reactions was a reason not to make their relationship public online: "I was not 'out', so I had to hide my relationship, also on social media" (Connor, 18 years old). Els, who was 16 and in a relationship with a 30-year-old man when she was first interviewed, reflected on this 3 years later: "I did not post anything about our relationship on social media. It was all much too complicated, with my parents who didn't agree ... Other people at some point change their status, 'in a relationship with ... ', but I didn't. I was afraid of other people's reactions. [...] I did find it a shame that I wasn't able to do that. I would have loved to show the rest of the world that he was mine!" Only a few research participants in non-normative romantic relationships did publicly perform their relationship online, resulting in both positive and negative reactions. For Bob (14 years old), the latter was the case: "They [pupils at his school] yell at me: 'hey, out of the closet', or 'hey, gay'. [...] Most of the time I can deal with it, but sometimes [...] I call in sick, otherwise I'd explode." Thus, where Kyra and Mark could publicly perform their relationships on social media without fear or risk of harm, young people in non-normative romantic relationships feel like they have to keep their relationship secret as they are concerned about the possibility of negative reactions, which limits their opportunities to use social media for building intimacy through public performances of their romantic relationships.

Performing Smart and Mature Sexual Identities

A third dimension of sexuality that came to the fore through the case study data is that of youth performing 'smart' and 'mature' sexual identities in ways that can simultaneously reproduce and challenge moral panic discourses. During

[5] The 'coming out' trope is highly popular in the Netherlands, although it has been severely criticized for presupposing an essentialist and static idea of sexuality and subjectivity, and for creating false dichotomies of living 'in the closet' versus living 'out of the closet' and of homo- versus hetero-sexuality (Butler, 1991; Sedgwick, 2008 [1990]).

a discussion of whether Kyra and Mark exchanged 'intimate' pictures of themselves, Kyra explained:

KYRA: I never have stupid pictures . . . Never made stupid pictures of myself.

INTERVIEWER: What are stupid pictures?

KYRA: Undressing for a picture, I don't do that. Do I look like a fool to you?

Kyra explicitly linked the making of nude images to 'stupidity,' vehemently rejecting the possibility of making such an image. This echoes and reproduces familiar slut-shaming and victim-blaming tropes surrounding girls who engage in the practice of making but, more importantly, sharing sexy pictures, of which girls are keenly aware (Henry & Powell, 2018; Kofoed & Ringrose, 2012; Richards, 2017; Ringrose & Harvey, 2015b). Girls' fear of being called a slut has often translated into a negative attitude toward displaying sexiness online (Duits & Zoonen, 2011; Jackson & Vares, 2015; Ringrose, 2011). By so strongly associating undressing for a picture with being stupid, and by distancing herself from such pictures in the interview, Kyra performed a specific feminine 'self' that was not only sexually *modest*, but also *smart* (not foolish).

Mark likewise mentioned that he too never undressed for a picture or in front of a webcam, because: "that will only cause trouble." Even though Mark joined Kyra in rejecting the online exchange of sexy pictures, he did not connect this to his own personality or identification as something that would make him a 'fool' as emphasized so strongly by Kyra. While they both responsibilized themselves as having to make 'good' decisions online, which was probably reinforced by the fact that they were interviewed by an adult, highly educated researcher, the implications of 'trouble' for Kyra were stated with much greater affective intensity, because of the perceived link between 'trouble' and being sexually adventurous for girls, as well as the perceived link between 'trouble' and reprehensible personality traits ('stupidity').

Another aspect of identity was highlighted by Mark when we discussed the couple's future:

INTERVIEWER: Do you talk about the future with each other?

KYRA: Mark does, but I don't.

MARK: She doesn't. I'm the one wondering: how about our future? Kyra doesn't. But she's still young [. . .] If she wants to date other boys first, I can understand that.

Both during the interview and in his online displays of love, Mark repeatedly emphasized that he is serious about the relationship, and dreams of a future together with Kyra. By attributing Kyra's lack of interest in building a future together to her 'being young,' and contrasting this to his own commitment to the relationship, he positions himself as more mature. Contrary to dominant conceptions of boys as invested in performing sexual prowess online, Mark performed commitment and (sexual) maturity by emphasizing the 'serious' and lasting nature of his relationship with Kyra, both online and offline.

Thus we see here how young people use social media for claiming 'smartness' and 'adultness' through performances of specific types of responsible, serious, and mature sexual practices and relationships, in contrast to the types of gendered public discourses about young people (girls) perpetually at risk because of naivety and inexperience as they navigate intimacy online.

These processes of identity performance are even more complicated for queer youth, whose experiences are practically invisible in dominant, heteronormative discourses about sexuality. This invisibility makes it much harder to perform 'selves' that are recognizable for others. They are less likely to receive support from their social network and society in general, and more likely to encounter negative reactions when appearing in public (Lehmiller & Agnew 2006, p. 41; McGlotten 2013; Payne & Smith 2013). For many queer youth, especially those who were not 'out,' performing maturity through public (online) performances of serious relationships was therefore complicated or even impossible.

A more common way for these young people to perform maturity was to emphasize their 'acceptance of' and 'openness about' their own queer identity or desires, and/or knowledge about sexual diversity, which is quite different from heterosexual youth performing idealized forms of heterosexual relationships. For example, during a national meeting of Gay–Straight Alliance members, Leroy (15 years) gave a presentation and recounted: "I told a friend that I was gay, and that friend told it to somebody else, who posted it on Twitter. At first, I was devastated, but now I post about it myself. I'm not ashamed anymore." This narrative of 'coming of age through the acceptance of and openness about one's queer identity' was common both offline and online. Even though the narrative itself is familiar, what is significant is that social media's affordances of sharing can magnify exposure; negotiating this visibility and overcoming shame and stigma is therefore understood as a sign of queer maturity.

Sexual Decision Making, Knowledge Building, and Sharing

In this final section, we discuss a fourth dimension of digitally mediated sexuality, namely that of sexual knowledge building/sharing and decision making. In negotiating the physical aspects of their relationship, Kyra and Mark explored various forms of contraception including the pill. As is common in the Netherlands, Kyra first went to her general practitioner (GP), together with her mother: "He did not really explain much. Well, he explained things, but it was very short." She found it 'awkward' to ask for more information, because her mother and a doctor's assistant were also present at the conversation. Back home she consulted with Mark and both visited Sense.info, a Dutch website funded by the Dutch government and hosted by two nongovernmental organizations (SOA Aids Nederland and Rutgers), the communal health centers (GGD), and the National Institute for Public Health and the Environment (RIVM). On this website, young people can chat online with health professionals about sexuality. This worked much better for Kyra than the offline appointment with her GP: "Online, you're anonymous, whereas in real life [offline], everybody knows who you are." Mark noted that, not only the anonymity, but also the lack of face-to-face contact is key: "You don't see each other, you don't hear each other, you can be completely yourself." The affordances to remain (partly) anonymous and to 'talk' without face-to-face contact makes the Internet and social media and chat services particularly suitable for sexual knowledge building.

According to Kyra and Mark, another advantage of the Internet and social media in terms of sexual knowledge building is that a vast amount of information about sexuality from a multitude of perspectives and sources is available online that may be missing from people's offline worlds at school or in the family. In particular, the opportunity to learn and get information from peers through media such as forums and chats is highly valued:

KYRA: The GP gives you information, but if a young person provides it, you get an opinion. And I liked that better: what do you think about that particular pill, those kinds of things.

MARK: Peers are the people you hang out with; you don't hang out with your GP.

KYRA: [. . .] Young people [. . .] are like yourself.

According to Kyra and Mark, peers feel 'closer,' more 'alike' and can therefore be a more trusted or relatable source of information than adults. In their search for information about contraception, the Internet and social media enabled them to get into contact with peers in a way not possible in their offline communities. What is significant about these complex knowledge building practices is that, faced with the limitations of an (awkward) physical encounter with her GP (alongside her parent), and a perceived lack of knowledgeable peers in her offline network, Kyra works alone and together with Mark digitally to build sexual knowledge and perform sexual decision making (see also Naezer et al., 2017).

We would like to note further that young people are not only consuming knowledge about sex and sexuality via websites and social media but also developing and spreading knowledge (Cho, 2015; Naezer et al., 2017; Ringrose & Mendes, 2018). This means that digital knowledge building goes further than just 'seeking information' online: it also involves young people creating textual and visual digital materials that they share online. Indeed, one queer participant, Lana, made a 'coming out' video about her own process of 'accepting' her attraction to girls, uploaded it to YouTube and posted a link to the video on her Tumblr page. In its first 4.5 months on YouTube, the video was watched more than 600 times. Through such activities, young people contribute to the development and mainstreaming of knowledge about sexual diversity (see also Byron & Hunt, 2017). This empirically substantiates the notion of young people as 'produsers' (Bruns, 2013), that is, curators who simultaneously produce and use ('produse') digital knowledge that may be missing from not only dominant discourses but the spaces and places conventionally understood to be where young people can learn about sexuality (see also Naezer et al., 2017).

Conclusion

In this chapter, we have explored Kyra and Mark's heterosexual relationship together with a range of other participants' normative and non-normative experiences and identifications of negotiating sexuality online. We aimed to show how a risk-centered approach is one sided, failing to grasp much of the complexity of how young people are navigating social media and how digital mediation is transforming youth sexuality. Through our analysis, a more nuanced picture arises that illustrates different dimensions of how social media is offering (1) new routes for sexual adventure and experimentation (e.g., chatting randomly with unknown people), (2) new digital ways of building romantic intimacy (e.g., through online 'private' conversations or 'public' declarations of love), (3) new themes and venues for performing sexual identities (e.g., performing 'smart femininity' through the rejection of digital 'stupid pictures,' or performing 'maturity' through online displays of a romantic relationship or online openness about queer desires), as well as (4) new routes for sexual decision making and knowledge building (e.g., conducting real time, anonymous conversations that require no face-to-face contact, with people who may not be accessible offline).

Social media transform youth sexuality, enabling forms of communication that are not as accessible or even impossible offline, such as (anonymous) conversations with people who are not physically near, which may be 'dirty men' exposing their genitals for a webcam, (potential) romantic partners sending romantic or sexual messages, health care professionals providing advice about topics like contraception, or (non-normative) role models providing knowledge, support, and inspiration. Social media also afford public displays of romantic relationships, which can work in performative ways to establish relationships, and/or to enact specific (e.g., 'queer,' 'smart,' 'mature') sexual identities. We have expanded boyd's characterization of digitally mediated interaction as more persistent, searchable, replicable/spreadable, and visible by showing how in some digital contexts, such as WhatsApp, Chatlokaal, and Sense.info, it is in fact the (semi-)privacy, (semi-)anonymity, and the non-persistent, non-searchable, non-replicable/spreadable, and/or non-visible nature of the communication that facilitates new forms of communication such as knowledge building.

Our analysis has shown that the dichotomies that are so pervasive in present-day dominant discourse are not a reflection of how social media work for young people nor how they use these digital contexts in performing their sexuality. These digital platforms are not simply 'good' or 'bad,' 'dangerous' or safe'; therefore, they are dynamic, complex, subjective, and sometimes contradictory constellations of risk, safety, and pleasure. Neither do sexual practices take place simply 'offline' or 'online': these worlds are entangled confirming previous research disrupting this false dichotomy. Analyses of young people, sexuality, and social media should therefore take these complexities into account and avoid simplistic, binary conclusions about youth, sexuality, and/or social media.

Finally, our analysis shows how young people's online/offline sexual practices are profoundly social, and young people are constantly navigating dominant discourses that are ageist, sexist, and heteronormative. We have demonstrated how young people are active agents, negotiating these discourses in highly complex ways. Sometimes they reproduce sexist and heteronormative narratives (recall for instance Kyra's equation of girls who undress for images as fools). On the other hand, they refute assumptions about them being immature and unable to sustain meaningful intimate relationships. Some young people were highly critical of heteronormative narratives and structures, as was exemplified by young people using social media to 'queer' their identities and digital social spaces. These complexities directly challenge present-day stereotypical, gendered, and heteronormative moral panic over social media's impact on youth sexuality, while confirming the need for contextualized studies of how young people navigate technological affordances and dominant discourses in their online/offline performances of sexuality.

References

Albury, K. (2015). Selfies, Sexts, and Sneaky Hats: Young People's Understandings of Gendered Practices of Self-representation. *International Journal of Communication*, *9*, 1734–1745.

Albury, K. & Byron, P. (2016). Safe on My Phone? Same-Sex Attracted Young People's Negotiations of Intimacy, Visibility, and Risk on Digital Hook-Up Apps. *Social Media + Society*, *2*(4), 1–10.

Attwood, F., Hakim, J., & Winch, A. (2017). Mediated Intimacies: Bodies, Technologies and Relationships. *Journal of Gender Studies*, *26*(3), 249–253.

boyd, d. (2008a). Taken out of context: American teen sociality in networked publics. (Doctoral dissertation). Berkeley: University of California.

(2008b). Why Youth Love Social Network Sites: The Role of Networked Publics in Teenage Social Life. In Buckingham, D. (Ed.), *Youth, Identity, and Digital Media* (119–142). Cambridge, MA: MIT Press.

(2014). *It's Complicated: The Social Lives of Networked Teens*. New Haven: Yale University Press.

Bragg, S. (2015). What about the Boys?: Sexualization, Media and Masculinities. In Renold, E., Ringrose, J., & Egan, D. R. (Eds.), *Children, Sexuality and Sexualization* (89–104). Houndmills: Palgrave Macmillan.

Bragg, S. & Buckingham, D. (2009). Too Much too Young? Young People, Sexual Media and Learning. In Attwood, F. (Ed.), *Mainstreaming Sex: The Sexualization of Western Culture* (129–146). London: I.B. Taris.

Bruns, A. (2013). Produsage: Towards a Broader Framework for User-Led Content Creation. In Du Gay, P., Hall, S., Janes, L., Madsen, A. K., Mackay, H., & Negus, K. (Eds.), *Doing Cultural Studies: The Story of the Sony Walkman* (117–121). London: Sage.

Burns, A. (2015). Self(ie)-Discipline: Social Regulation as Enacted through the Discussion of Photographic Practice. *International Journal of Communication*, *9*, 1716–1733.

Butler, J. (1991). Imitation and Gender Subordination. In Fuss, D. (Ed.), *Inside Out: Lesbian Theories, Gay Theories* (13–32). New York: Routledge.

Byron, P. & Hunt, J. (2017). "That Happened to Me Too": Young People's Informal Knowledge of Diverse Genders and Sexualities. *Sex Education*, *17*(3), 319–332.

Chambers, D. (2013). *Social Media and Personal Relationships: Online Intimacies and Networked Friendship*. Houndsmills: Palgrave Macmillan.

Cho, A. (2015). Sensuous participation: Queer youth of color, affect, and social media. (Doctoral dissertation). Austin: University of Texas.

Cooper, A. (Ed.) (2000). *Cybersex: The Dark Side of the Force: A Special Issue of the Journal Sexual Addiction and Compulsion*. Philadelphia: Brunner-Routledge.

Delmonico, D. L. & Griffin, E. J. (Eds.). (2012). *Revisiting the Dark Side of the Force: Cybersex Twelve Years Later: A Special Issue of the Journal of Sexual Addiction and Compulsivity*. Philadelphia: Brunner-Routledge.

De Ridder, S. & Van Bauwel, S. (2013). Commenting on Pictures: Teens Negotiating Gender and Sexualities on Social Networking Sites. *Sexualities*, *16*(5–6), 565–586.

Dobson, A. S. (2015). *Postfeminist Digital Cultures: Femininity, Social Media, and Self-representation*. New York: Palgrave Macmillan.

Döring, N. M. (2009). The Internet's Impact on Sexuality: A Critical Review of 15 Years of Research. *Computers in Human Behavior*, *25*(5), 1089–1101.

Duits, L. & Zoonen, L. V. (2011). Coming to Terms with Sexualization. *European Journal of Cultural Studies*, *14*(5), 491–506.

Egan, D. R. (2013). *Becoming Sexual: A Critical Appraisal of the Sexualisation of Girls*. Cambridge: Polity Press.

Evans, A., Riley, S., & Shankar, A. (2010). Technologies of Sexiness: Theorizing Women's Engagement in the Sexualization of Culture. *Feminism & Psychology*, *20*(1), 114–131.

Fischer, N. (2006). Purity and Pollution: Sex as a Moral Discourse. In Seidman, S., Fischer, N., & Meeks, C. (Eds.), *Handbook of the New Sexuality Studies* (56–64). London: Routledge.

Gill, R. (2007a). Critical Respect: The Difficulties and Dilemmas of Agency and 'Choice' for Feminism. *European Journal of Women's Studies*, *14*(1), 69–80.

(2007b). Postfeminist Media Culture: Elements of a Sensibility. *European Journal of Cultural Studies*, *10*(2), 147–166.

(2009). Beyond the 'Sexualization of Culture' Thesis: An Intersectional Analysis of 'Sixpacks', 'Midriffs' and 'Hot Lesbians' in Advertising. *Sexualities*, *12*(2), 137–160.

Handyside, S. & Ringrose, J. (2017). Snapchat Memory and Youth Digital Sexual Cultures: Mediated Temporality, Duration and Affect. *Journal of Gender Studies*, *26*(3), 347–360.

Harvey, L. & Ringrose, J. (2015). Sexting, Ratings and (Mis)Recognition: Teen Boys Performing Classed and Racialized Masculinities in Digitally Networked Publics. In Renold, E., Ringrose, J., & Egan, R. D. (Eds.), *Children, Sexuality and Sexualization* (352–368). Houndmills: Palgrave Macmillan.

Hasinoff, A. A. (2015). *Sexting Panic: Rethinking Criminalization, Privacy, and Consent.* Urbana: University of Illinois Press.

Henry, N. & Powell, A. (2018). Technology-Facilitated Sexual Violence: A Literature Review of Empirical Research. *Trauma, Violence & Abuse*, *19*(2), 195–208. doi:10.1177/1524838016650189.

Hillier, L. & Harrison, L. (2007). Building Realities Less Limited than Their Own: Young People Practising Same-Sex Attraction on the Internet. *Sexualities*, *10*(1), 82–100.

Hillis, K. (1999). *Digital Sensations: Space, Identity, and Embodiment in Virtual Reality.* Minneapolis: University of Minnesota Press.

Hjorth, L. & Lim, S. S. (2012). Mobile Intimacy in an Age of Affective Mobile Media. *Feminist Media Studies*, *12*(4), 477–484.

Jackson, S. & Vares, T. (2015). New Visibilities? "Using Video Diaries to Explore Girls" Experiences of Sexualized Culture. In Renold, E., Ringrose, J., & Egan, D. R. (Eds.), *Children, Sexuality and Sexualization* (307–321). Houndmills: Palgrave Macmillan.

Karaian, L. & Van Meyl, K. (2015). Reframing Risqué/Risky: Queer Temporalities, Teenage Sexting, and Freedom of Expression. *Laws*, *4*(1), 18–36.

Kofoed, J. & Ringrose, J. (2012). Travelling and Sticky Affects: Exploring Teens and Sexualized Cyberbullying through a Butlerian-Deleuzian-Guattarian Lens. *Discourse: Studies in the Cultural Politics of Education*, *33*(1), 5–20.

Krebbekx, W. (2018). Making sex, moving difference: An ethnography of sexuality and diversity in Dutch schools. Doctoral dissertation. University of Amsterdam.

Lehmiller, J. J. & Agnew, C. R. (2006). Marginalized Relationships: The Impact of Social Disapproval on Romantic Relationship Commitment. *Personality and Social Psychology Bulletin*, *32*(1), 40–51.

Livingstone, S. (2008). Taking Risky Opportunities in Youthful Content Creation: Teenagers' Use of Social Networking Sites for Intimacy, Privacy and Self-Expression. *New Media & Society*, *10*(3), 393–411.

(2011). Internet, Children, and Youth. In Consalvo, M. & Ess, C. (Eds.), *The Handbook of Internet Studies* (348-368). Oxford: Wiley-Blackwell.

Maliepaard, E. (2017). Bisexual Safe Space(s) on the Internet: Analysis of an Online Forum for Bisexuals. *Tijdschrift voor economische en sociale geografie*, *108*(3), 318–330.

McGlotten, S. (2013). *Virtual Intimacies: Media, Affect, and Queer Sociality.* Albany: State University of New York Press.

McRobbie, A. (2009). *The Aftermath of Feminism: Gender, Culture and Social Change.* London: Sage.

Mulholland, M. (2017). "When Difference Gets in the Way": Young People, Whiteness and Sexualisation. *Sexuality & Culture: An Interdisciplinary Quarterly*, *21*(2), 593–612.

Naezer, M. (2015). Love, Lust and Learning: Youth, Sexuality and Social Media [Liefde, Lust & Leren: Jongeren en Seksualiteit op Social Media]. *Raffia*, *27*(1), 3–6.

(2017). From Risky Behaviour to Sexy Adventures: Reconceptualising Young People's Online Sexual Activities. *Culture, Health & Sexuality*, *20*(6):715–729. doi:10.1080/13691058.2017.1372632.

Naezer, M., Rommes, E., & Jansen, W. (2017). Empowerment through Sex Education? Rethinking Paradoxical Policies. *Sex Education*, *17*(6), 712–728.

Pascoe, C. J. (2010). Intimacy. In Ito, M., Baumer, S., Bittanti, M., et al. (Eds.), *Hanging Out, Messing Around, and Geeking Out: Kids Living and Learning with New Media* (117–148). Cambridge, MA: MIT Press.

Payne, E. & Smith, M. (2013). LGBTQ Kids, School Safety, and Missing the Big Picture: How the Dominant Bullying Discourse Prevents School Professionals from Thinking about Systemic Marginalization or ... Why We Need to Rethink LGBTQ Bullying. *QED: A Journal in GLBTQ Worldmaking*, *1*(1), 1–36.

Peter, J. & Valkenburg, P. M. (2007). Adolescents' Exposure to a Sexualized Media Environment and Their Notions of Women as Sex Objects. *Sex Roles*, *56*(5), 381–395.

(2008). Adolescents' Exposure to Sexually Explicit Internet Material and Sexual Preoccupancy: A Three-Wave Panel Study. *Media Psychology*, *11*(2), 207–234.

(2009). Adolescents' Exposure to Sexually Explicit Internet Material and Notions of Women as Sex Objects: Assessing Causality and Underlying Processes. *The Journal of Communication: A Publication of the National Society for the Study of Communication*, *59*(3), 407–433.

Plummer, K. (2003). *Intimate Citizenship: Private Decisions and Public Dialogues*. Seattle: University of Washington Press.

Pullen, C. (Ed.) (2014). *Queer Youth and Media Cultures*. Houndmills: Palgrave Macmillan.

Renold, E., Egan, R. D., & Ringrose, J. (2015). Introduction. In Renold, E., Ringrose, J., & Egan, R. D. (Eds.), *Children, Sexuality and Sexualization* (1–21). Houndmills: Palgrave Macmillan.

Renold, E. & Ringrose, J. (2011). Schizoid Subjectivities? Re-Theorizing Teen Girls' Sexual Cultures in an Era of 'Sexualization'. *Journal of Sociology*, *47*(4), 389–409.

(2017). Selfies, Relfies and Phallic Tagging: Posthuman Part-icipations in Teen Digital Sexuality Assemblages. *Educational Philosophy and Theory*, *49*(11), 1066–1079.

Renold, E., Ringrose, J., & Egan, R. D. (2015). *Children, Sexuality and Sexualization*. Houndmills: Palgrave Macmillan.

Reynolds, P. (2010). Disentangling Privacy and Intimacy: Intimate Citizenship, Private Boundaries and Public Transgressions. *Human Affairs*, *20*(1), 33–42.

Richards, G. (2017). Cybersexism: Digital Sociability and Gendered Identities at Play. Paper presented at the World Anti-Bullying Forum, Stockholm, Sweden.

Ringrose, J. (2011). Are You Sexy, Flirty, or a Slut? Exploring 'Sexualization' and How Teen Girls Perform/Negotiate Digital Sexual Identity on Social Networking Sites. In Gill, R. & Scharff, C. (Eds.), *New Femininities: Postfeminism, Neoliberalism and Subjectivity* (99–117). Houndmills: Palgrave Macmillan.

Ringrose, J. & Harvey, L. (2015a). BBM is Like Match.com: Social Networking and the Digital Mediation of Teens' Sexual Cultures. In Bailey, J. & Steeves, V. (Eds.), *eGirls, eCitizens* (199–226). Ottawa: University of Ottawa Press.

(2015b). Boobs, Back-off, Six Packs and Bits: Mediated Body Parts, Gendered Reward, and Sexual Shame in Teens' Sexting Images. *Continuum*, *29*(2), 205–217.

Ringrose, J., Harvey, L., Gill, R., & Livingstone, S. (2013). Teen Girls, Sexual Double Standards and 'Sexting': Gendered Value in Digital Image Exchange. *Feminist Theory*, *14*(3), 305–323.

Ringrose, J. & Mendes, K . (2018). Mediated Affect & Feminist Solidarity: Teens Using Twitter to Challenge 'Rape Culture' in and Around School. In Sampson, T., Ellis, D., & Maddison, S. (Eds.), *Affect and Social Media*. London: Rowman and Littlefield.

Robinson, K. H. (2013). *Innocence, Knowledge and the Construction of Childhood: The Contradictory Nature of Sexuality and Censorship in Children's Contemporary Lives*. London: Routledge.

Salter, M., Crofts, T., & Lee, M. (2013). Beyond Criminalisation and Responsibilisation: Sexting, Gender and Young People. *Current Issues in Criminal Justice*, *24*(3), 301–316.

Sedgwick, E. K. (2008 [1990]). *Epistemology of the Closet*. Berkeley: University of California Press.

Senft, T. M. & Baym, N. K. (2015). What Does the Selfie Say? Investigating a Global Phenomenon. *International Journal of Communication*, *9*(2015), 1588–1606.

Smith, C. (2010). Review: Papadopoulos, Linda: Sexualisation of young people. *Participations*, *7*(1), 175–179.

Szulc, Ł. & Dhoest, A. (2013). The Internet and Sexual Identity Formation: Comparing Internet Use before and after Coming Out. *Communications – The European Journal of Communication Research*, *38*(4), 347–365.

Tiidenberg, K. (2018). "Nude Selfies til I Die" – Making of 'Sexy' in Selfies. In Nixon, P. G. & Düsterhöft, I. K. (Eds.), *Sex in the Digital Age*. Oxford: Routledge.

Tropiano, S. (2014). "A Safe and Supportive Environment": LGBTQ Youth and Social Media. In Pullen, C. (Ed.), *Queer Youth and Media Cultures* (46–62). Houndmills: Palgrave Macmillan.

Van Doorn, N. A. J. M. (2009). Digital spaces, material traces: Investigating the performance of gender, sexuality, and embodiment on internet platforms that feature user-generated content. (Doctoral dissertation). Amsterdam: University of Amsterdam.

Warfield, K. (2016). Making the Cut: An Agential Realist Examination of Selfies and Touch. *Social Media + Society*, *2*(2), 1–10.

Waskul, D. D. (2006). Internet Sex: The Seductive 'Freedom To'. In Seidman, S., Fischer, N., & Meeks, C. (Eds.), *Handbook of the New Sexuality Studies* (281–289). London: Routledge.

22 A Sociological/Psychological Model for Understanding Pornography and Adolescent Sexual Behavior

Jennifer A. Johnson and Ana J. Bridges

Introduction

Pornography is now a ubiquitous experience for adolescents, with 90+% of boys and 60+% of girls being exposed to it at some point in their teenage lives (Häggström-Nordin et al., 2005; Sabina et al., 2008). It is a normative form of sexual education for adolescents (Häggström-Nordin et al., 2009; Hunter et al., 2010; Morgan, 2011; Ward, 2003) and provides a framework for how adolescents begin their understanding of sexuality and sexual interactions (Peter & Valkenburg, 2010 & 2011). First contacts with pornography tend to be unwanted or accidental (Wolak et al., 2007) and occur during elementary school years without adult supervision on media readily available in the home (Allen & Lavender-Stott, 2015). Adolescent responses to first exposure tend to be complex and often times contradictory, especially for girls (Allen & Lavender-Stott, 2015; Attwood, 2005). Boys report feelings of excitement, curiosity, or shock upon seeing pornography for the first time (Allen & Lavender-Stott, 2015), while about a quarter of boys and girls demonstrate emotional distress (Grubbs et al., 2015; Mitchell et al., 2003).

Compared to exposure, fewer adolescents intentionally use pornography for the purpose of sexual pleasure, with rates ranging from 38 percent of boys and 2 percent of girls (Flood, 2007) over a decade ago to 40 percent of boys and 13 percent of girls more recently (Bleakley, Hennessy, & Fishbein, 2011). Chen et al. (2013) recently reported that 59 percent of Taiwanese high schoolers had intentionally used pornography in the past year. Reasons for using or searching for pornography differ for boys and girls. For boys, pornography is motivated by sexual interest and masturbation, whereas, for girls, it is more out of curiosity (Doornwaard et al., 2017; Wallmyr & Welin, 2006). It is important to note that measures of exposure and intentionality can vary significantly depending on how the measures are operationalized. More restrictive measures (in terms of duration, frequency, and recency) will produce lower numbers. Similarly, the cultural context of the study affects prevalence estimates, with studies done in more conservative cultures showing lower rates of use (Peter & Valkenburg, 2016). Overall, data indicate that a majority of male and female adolescents have been exposed to pornography and that a "sizeable minority of males" use it intentionally for sexual purposes (Peter & Valkenburg, 2016, p. 515).

Research on pornography as a form of sexual education for adolescents remains under-theorized, largely due to the social and political debates surrounding the role of pornography in the lives of adults. Pornography is most often discussed as a form of speech or a form of sexual behavior. This dichotomy largely frames the 'porn wars,' which began in the late 1970s and early 1980s with attempts to illegalize pornography as a form of sexual behavior that constitutes violence against women. These attempts were met with resistance as others argued that pornography represents a form of personal expression particularly important to marginalized and stigmatized sexualities. This historical debate continues to split feminist scholars into two camps – those who frame pornography as a form sexual violence against women and those who approach it as a path toward appreciating sexual diversity and sexual empowerment for women (Bridges & Jensen, 2010; Juffer, 1998; Paasonen, 2010; Weitzer, 2000). But this historical debate has largely centered on the role of pornography in the sexual lives of adult men and women.

The Internet has transformed pornography into a mainstream commercial product easily accessible to teens at any given time. To date, little theoretical work has been done specifically to understand the impact of modern pornography on the lives of adolescents. Instead, much of the literature over the past 25 years on adolescent sexuality and pornography has focused on asking empirical questions related to behavioral and attitudinal associations (Wright, 2013). How many adolescents watch pornography? At what age do they begin? Are the sexual behaviors and attitudes of adolescents who watch pornography different from those who don't? Research has produced some relatively robust answers to some of these questions (for reviews, see Owens et al., 2012 and Peter & Valkenburg, 2016), but the data are almost always cross-sectional and can only speak to associations rather than causality. Rarely do researchers follow adolescents over time. Furthermore, these questions are almost always asked as empirical rather than theoretical questions (Wright, 2011). There is little in the way of theory that speaks directly to adolescent engagement with pornography; thus, our understanding of the complex pathways and mediators of pornography's impact is minimal.

There has been some recent theoretical work focused on understanding motivations for and mediators of pornography use that ask increasingly complex questions such as how do race, sexuality, and parental involvement come together to shape adults' choices with regard to pornography? How does pornography impact the sexual health and well-being of users? Does it impact all people in the same way? Under what conditions might it impact their lives differently? Who looks at what under what personal, social, and historical circumstances with what type of outcomes? For example, Grubbs et al. (2017) propose a "Hedonic Reinforcement Model" of pornography consumption to better understand what motivates people to watch pornography, while Wright's (2011) 3AM model seeks to explain the complex pathways users navigate to find, use, and act on pornography.

The pathways and motivations for adolescents, however, are unique and require theoretical models specific to their location in the life course (Wright, 2014). In order to develop a more comprehensive understanding of the role of pornography in the sexual behaviors and sexual health of adolescents, scholars need to deepen their understanding of pornography as a commercial media product and complicate their questions with regard to adolescents interactions with pornographic materials as well as the larger public health questions related to education, disease, and violence.

Thus, our goals in this chapter are threefold. First, we define pornography and describe its content. Second, we present a comprehensive sociological–psychological model of pornography use and adolescent sexual behavior that integrates findings from the past 15 years of research. Drawing on new work focused on life course and mediators, our model synthesizes this area to organize and understand the differential impacts of pornography on the lives of individual teens. Third, we emphasize the sociological context of adolescent pornography use and outline how the Internet has given rise to the online commercial pornography industry, transforming the content of pornography and its accessibility. Any new theoretical work on pornography and adolescent sexuality must take into account the ways in which new technologies have created a deluge of readily accessible pornography that is radically different from the type of material with which most parents are familiar. We conclude with suggestions for moving this research area forward, in the hopes of helping teens, schools, policy makers, and public health agencies better understand the risk and protective factors associated with adolescent pornography use.

Pornography: Definition and Content

Although historically scholars, legislators, and others have debated the definition of pornography, focusing at times on the nature of what is portrayed (e.g., Lott, 1994; Russell, 1993), who has access to it (Barron & Kimmel, 2000), or how it differs from erotica or other forms of sexual media (Senn & Radtke, 1990; Steinem, 1978), perhaps the clearest definition of pornography is provided by Hardy (2008). Hardy defines pornography as a "commercial genre concerned with the explicit representation of human sexuality" (p. 60). In this simple definition, pornography is clearly situated as (1) a commercial business, one that is primarily concerned with economic viability and profit; (2) a genre, or type of medium with its own unique set of conventions and stylistic features (Bridges, 2010); and (3) portraying or representing human sexuality explicitly, meaning in detail, clearly, or straightforwardly (versus implied or suggested).

The foundation of the modern pornography industry can be traced to the launch of Playboy in 1953 with the first publication of its iconic magazine featuring Marilyn Monroe. Billed primarily as a men's lifestyle magazine, Playboy pioneered the monetization of women's bodies via advertising and intersecting commercial interests. In 1969 and then in 1974, Penthouse and Hustler launched subsequent publications, each trying to carve out space in the market by increasing the amount of nudity, vulgarity, and aggression portrayed in the images (Dines, 2010a). This escalation in the level of vulgarity and aggression culminated in the use of 'gonzo' pornography, which was pioneered in the 1990s and came to dominate the industry circa 2008 (Hardy, 2008). According to Merriam-Webster (2017), gonzo means either (a) a style of journalism that involves journalist participation and lack of objectivity; or (b) exaggerated, bizarre, outlandish, or extreme. Gonzo pornography includes extreme forms of sexual behavior filmed from the vantage point of the viewer. The angle of the camera is directly on the act of penetration and there is little in the way of story line or context (Hardy, 2008). The term gonzo pornography has come to be synonymous with the concept of hardcore, which is defined by how much damage is done to a woman's body (Dines, 2006; Purcell, 2012).

How representative gonzo pornography is among the 15 billion terabytes of pornography in existence is near impossible to measure. While it is clear the content of pornography has radically changed since Playboy was delivered in a brown paper bag many decades ago, attempts to systematically characterize the content of modern pornography have produced mixed results. These inconsistencies are not only due to methodological challenges associated with cataloging such a large population of material but also because of the differing ways in which sexual behaviors are interpreted, particularly related to what constitutes violence (Paasonen, 2010). For example, McKee (2005) defines violence as "any form of behavior directed toward the goal of harm; or injuring another living being who is motivated to avoid such treatment" (p. 282). His focus is on the intent of the perpetrator (to injure or harm) and the response of the target (who is motivated to avoid the harm). If the target appears to consent, does not resist, or expresses enjoyment in response to the intent to injure or harm, then McKee argues the behavior in question is not considered violent. Using a sample of the 50 most popular pornography videos containing 838 scenes, McKee found a total of 16 scenes (1.9 percent) featured some form of violence, measuring violence as any form of behavior directed toward the goal of harm, including verbal harm, with 81 percent of those scenes (13 out of 16) containing violence against women by men and 31 percent (4 out of 13) containing violence perpetrated by women against men.

Bridges et al. (2010) took issue with this definition, arguing that pornography is a performance where pleasure is expected as an element of the script. Thus, how a performer responds to any given behavior is a dubious measure of actual violence. Instead, they focused on the behaviors of perpetrators, rather than defining violence by the target's responses. Defining violence "as any purposeful action causing physical or psychological harm to oneself or another person, whereby psychological harm is understood as assaulting another verbally or nonverbally" (p. 1072), they coded a sample of 304 scenes from 50 of the most popular pornographic videos over a 7-month period. The coders tallied 3,376 unique instances of aggression, finding nearly 90 percent of scenes contained some element of aggression. Of these, 70.3 percent of aggressive acts were perpetrated by men and 94.4 percent of violent acts were targeted at women. Clearly, how one chooses to define aggression or violence makes all the difference in what conclusions one draws about the nature of modern pornography.

Klaassen and Peter (2015) attempted to find a middle ground by coding for both the behaviors and intent. Violence was operationalized through the same categorization of 14 aggressive behaviors used by Bridges and colleagues (2010) as well as through measures of coercion including intoxication, manipulation, and overt nonconsensual behavior similar to that of McKee (2005). The sample included the first scene in 100 of the most popular videos from each of the four of the most popular websites (Pornhub, RedTube, YouPorn, and xHamster) for a total of 400 scenes. Results show that 40 percent of scenes contain acts of physical violence, with 93 percent of those containing violence against women.

The lack of standardization of measures of violence and the wide range of levels of violence found using various definitions makes it difficult to generalize about the content of modern pornography (McKee, 2005; Paasonen, 2010). However, there are two consistent outcomes. First, when violence is measured as present, it is almost always perpetrated by men against women. Second, a common set of behaviors that are potential forms of violence (including choking, gagging, slapping, biting, pinching, bondage, and spanking) are hallmarks of gonzo pornography (Dines, 2006, 2010b). Bridges and colleagues (2010) found that 75 percent of all video scenes coded contained spanking, 41 percent included open hand slapping, 53.9 percent contained gagging, and 27.6 percent contained choking. Klaassen and Peter (2015) found 27 percent of scenes contained spanking and 18.8 percent contained gagging. McKee (2005) did not report on rates of specific types of behaviors.

Viewing pornography, especially pornography that includes violent content such as gonzo pornography, is associated with a host of negative attitudes toward women. Much research with adults indicates increased exposure to pornography is associated with less egalitarian attitudes among men and more hostile sexism (Hald, Malamuth, et al., 2013), more positive attitudes toward violence against women (Hald et al., 2010), more opposition to affirmative action policies for women (Wright & Funk, 2014), a decreased likelihood to intervene as a bystander in a potential sexual assault situation (Foubert et al., 2011), and an increased belief in rape myths among both men (Foubert et al., 2011) and women (Brosi et al., 2011).

The impact of this type of content on actual behaviors is a contentious question. Recently, a meta-analysis of 22 studies (N=20,820) measuring both pornography use and actual acts of sexual aggression found a positive association between consumption of pornography and self-reported history of committing acts of verbal and physical sexual aggression (Wright et al., 2016). A second meta-analysis found similar associations between frequent pornography use and sexually aggressive behaviors, particularly for violent pornography and/or for men at high risk for sexual aggression (Malamuth et al., 2012). While the causal relationship between pornography viewing and aggressive behaviors remains unclear, pornography is clearly associated with aggressive sexual behavior and, at minimum, can be interpreted as an indicator of interest in such behavior.

Sociological–Psychological Model of Adolescent Pornography Use

In Figure 22.1 we present a sociological–psychological model of adolescent pornography use. This represents an integration of empirical research covered in approximately 60 articles published over the past 15 years (since 2000). The model is divided into five major components: (a) predisposing factors for pornography use; (b) sexual behavioral outcomes of pornography use; (c) moderators that affect the associations between pornography use and sexual behaviors; (d) mechanisms or mediators for the link between pornography use and sexual behaviors; and (e) the sociological context in which all of these factors operate. We review each in turn below.

Before we begin, however, a caveat is in order. Much of the research on pornography use in adolescents is cross-sectional instead of longitudinal, so it is often not possible to determine with certainty what variables should be considered risk factors and what variables might be better considered outcomes of use. In some

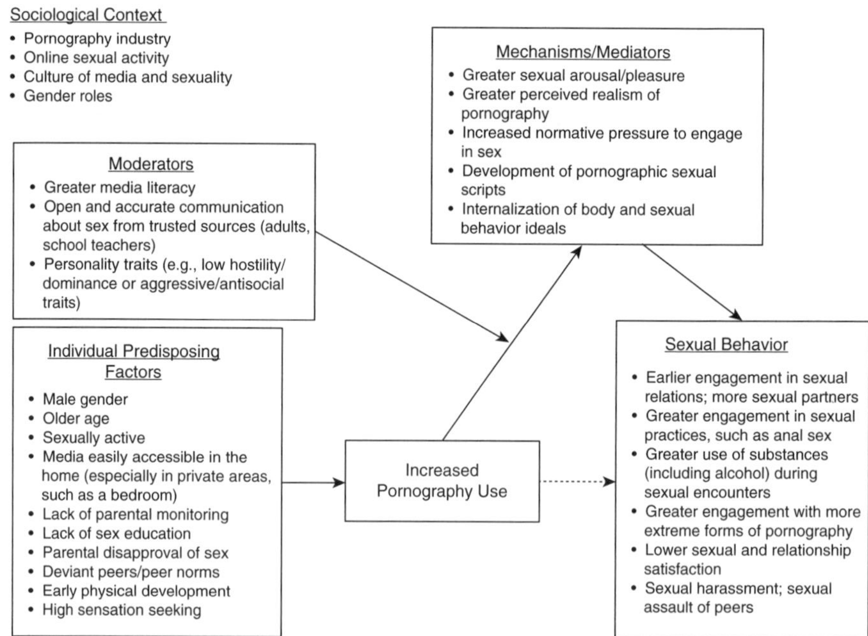

Figure 22.1 *Sociological–psychological model of pornography use and adolescent sexual behavior*

cases, the decisions were easy (e.g., gender as a risk factor). In other cases, however, the decisions were not obvious (e.g., is lower sexual satisfaction something that drives teens to use pornography, perhaps to learn more about how to have more satisfying sex, or is it an outcome of expectations about what sex ought to look, sound, and feel like, learned from watching pornography?). When possible, we have relied on longitudinal and experimental studies to categorize variables according to whether they appear to be risk factors for or consequences of pornography use. However, when that was not possible, we used our collective professional judgment, relying on the 20+ years' experience we have in researching this topic.

Predisposing Factors

A number of studies have explored what variables are associated with increased frequency of pornography use in adolescents. Across cultures and samples, male gender consistently emerges as one of the strongest predictors of pornography use (Peter & Valkenberg, 2016). However, other demographic variables also seem to increase the likelihood that adolescents will use pornography, including older age (Brown & L'Engle, 2009; Vandenbosch et al., 2015; Ybarra & Mitchell, 2005), already being sexually active (Bleakley et al., 2008; Bleakley, Hennessy, Fishbein, & Jordan, 2011; Ševčíková & Daneback, 2014), and early physical development of secondary sex characteristics (Luder et al., 2011; Peter & Valkenburg, 2006, 2016). In terms of personality characteristics, research strongly indicates that adolescents who are 'sensation seeking' (defined as eager to experience new, intense, or novel experiences or take heightened risks in search of new sensations) are more likely to use pornography and use it more often than non-sensation seeking peers (Beyens et al., 2015; Luder et al., 2011; Peter & Valkenburg, 2006, 2011; Ševčíková & Daneback., 2014).

These predisposing factors are largely unchangeable. However, there are other factors that are readily modifiable or at least present as potential targets of prevention and intervention efforts. These include peer and family factors, educational factors, and environmental factors. In the peer domain, having friends or peer groups who are delinquent or share perceptions of peer norms that embrace delinquency is linked to increased pornography use in adolescents (Hasking et al., 2011; Holt et al., 2012). In terms of family factors, adolescents are less likely to use pornography when they have stronger bonds with their family (Mesch, 2009; Mesch & Maman, 2009) or a primary caregiver (Ybarra & Mitchell, 2005), more positive patterns of communication (Ma & Shek, 2013), greater mutuality in parent/child relationships (Shek & Ma, 2012), and stronger overall family functioning (Shek & Ma, 2012). A lack of sex education, or inadequate sex education, is also associated with increased use of pornography, likely because teens are turning to pornography to fill in gaps in their knowledge (Doornwaard et al., 2017; Tanton et al., 2015). Finally, when pornography or the ability to access pornography is easy for adolescents, and especially if computers or other electronic devices are in private and largely unmonitored areas of the home, such as bedrooms, then pornography use increases (Ševčíková & Daneback, 2014; Wolak et al., 2007).

Although these areas are the most robustly studied predisposing factors associated with pornography use, a few others are emerging and many others are understudied. For instance, in one article, having a non-heterosexual orientation was associated with increased use of pornography in teens (Peter & Valkenburg, 2011), and at least one article found perceived benefits to pornography use for sexual minorities who may lack other sources of information about sex and/or who may see pornography as an avenue to explore questions about their developing sexuality (Arrington-Sanders et al., 2015). However, it may be that this would not present as a risk factor if sexual education was comprehensive and included discussions of gay, lesbian, bisexual, and other forms of sexuality. Race and economic status are also understudied. Ybarra & Mitchell (2005) found no differences in pornography-use rates across race and socioeconomic class, while Brown and L'Engle (2009) found African-American boys to have higher rates of use. Buzzell (2005) found use rates higher in urban compared to rural areas. Furthermore, there is no clear research on how race and class intersect with sexuality and gender to shape adolescent experience with pornography.

Another possible predisposing factor for pornography use is the view of women as sexual objects, or having more permissive views of sex (Peter & Valkenburg, 2007, 2008, 2010). However, studies that have explored pornography use and these types of attitudes longitudinally generally find pornography use is a stronger predictor of subsequent attitudes rather than *vice versa* (Peter & Valkenburg, 2010). Therefore, we see attitudes about the instrumentality of sex, women as sex objects, and permissive sexual attitudes as being downstream in our model, following pornography use rather than preceding it (see later for a discussion of mediators/mechanisms).

Sexual Behaviors/Outcomes

The bulk of studies examining possible sexual behavioral outcomes of pornography use have followed a four-decade-long tradition of examining associations between pornography use and sexual violence perpetration (for a review, see Malamuth et al., 2012). More recently, studies have focused on other outcomes, including satisfaction in relationships, sexual behaviors, and use of substances or alcohol during sex. In general, the findings suggest greater use of pornography in adolescents is associated with numerous sexual outcomes. Outcomes can be grouped as being related to sexual experiences, intimacy or satisfaction, sexual violence perpetration, and sexual appetite.

Regarding sexual experiences, researchers find adolescents, especially girls, who view pornography begin having sex at an earlier age (Brown & L'Engle, 2009; Cheng et al., 2014; Häggström-Nordin et.al., 2005), report a greater number of past sexual partners (Braun-Courville & Rojas, 2009), and engage in a greater variety of sexual behaviors, including anal sex (Braun-Courville & Rojas, 2009;

Mattebo et al., 2016). While each of these outcomes is not problematic in and of itself, research shows that earlier sexual initiation, more partners, and greater sexual exploration put adolescents at greater risk of unintended pregnancy, sexually transmitted infections, and sexual assault (Epstein et al., 2014). More recent research is showing adolescent pornography use to be associated with reduced relationship and sexual satisfaction with real-life partners (Morgan, 2011), and greater likelihood of using substances during sexual encounters (Braun-Courville & Rojas, 2009; Morelli et al., 2017), both of which suggest a lower sense of intimacy during sexual activity.

In terms of sexual violence perpetration, studies across cultures and ages find male teens who use more pornography, especially violent or degrading pornography, are more likely to engage in sexual harassment or even sexual assault (Bonino et al., 2006; Stanley et al., 2016; Wright et al., 2016; Ybarra et al., 2014). Furthermore, pornography use appears to lead to habituation in teens – the more pornography use an adolescent views, the more he or she seeks out more extreme (i.e., violent, degrading, or fetish) forms of pornography. Simply put, the adolescent appears to become bored with "typical" pornographic content and seeks novelty (Zillmann, 2000). Since these more extreme forms of pornography are also those most closely associated with and predictive of future sexual violence perpetration, this is indeed troubling.

Moderators

The link between pornography use and sexual behavioral outcomes is not identical for all adolescents. Some studies have examined variables that may shift that link. Variables that change the nature of the relationship between pornography use and sexual behavioral outcomes are called moderators. In general, relatively few studies have explored moderator variables in adolescents; however, those that have find personality and education are important. In terms of personality, adolescents who are hostile, dominant, aggressive, or antisocial show stronger links between the use of pornography and sexual outcomes, especially sexual violence perpetration (for reviews, see Malamuth & Huppin, 2005, and Owens et al., 2012). It appears that adolescents who are more agreeable or cooperative are less likely to be negatively impacted by pornography use. In addition, good relationships with trusted adults that can be vehicles for accurate and honest information about sex and increased media literacy (i.e., the ability to analyze and evaluate critically messages in media), dampen the link between pornography use and negative sexual outcomes. These are likely to be important because trusted adults and greater media literacy provide alternative narratives about pornography (i.e., as telling one particular story about sex, and not a particularly honest one).

Gender is an especially salient moderator, given, as discussed earlier, the level and direction of violence found in most easily available pornography. For both boys and girls, pornography exposure is consistently associated with earlier and/or quicker onset of sexual activity, a greater number of partners, and a higher likelihood of engaging in risky sexual behaviors such as anal sex, sex with multiple partners, using drugs or alcohol during sex, and engaging in paid sex (Braun-Courville & Rojas, 2009; Brown & L'Engle, 2009; Hald, Kuyper, et al., 2013; Wright, et al, 2013). For girls, the earlier the exposure, the more pronounced the risk (Sinković et al., 2013), suggesting gender moderates the relation between pornography use and sexual outcomes. Pornography increases female users' physical insecurities related to sexual performance (Löfgren-Mårtenson & Månsson, 2010; Stewart & Szymanski, 2012). However, when asked about the impact of pornography on their lives, women report feeling more sexually empowered and open to more diverse sexual experiences (Weinberg et al., 2010) as well as increased feelings of sexual competence, liberalization, and decreased sexual shame (Johansson & Hammarén, 2007). More research is needed to explore the contradictions between self-perceptions of pornography use, which are generally positive, and the empirical evidence linking pornography to more negative sexual behavioral outcomes.

Mechanisms/Mediators

To understand what mechanisms may be responsible for the link between pornography use and behavioral outcomes, cognitive behavioral theory and learning theories, especially classical conditioning and operant condition theories, are instructive. These theories emphasize the role that rewards, punishment, and thoughts (including attitudes and expectations) play in shaping our behavior (Bandura, 1978; Pavlov, 1927; Skinner, 1950). Learning is a "relatively enduring change in behavior, resulting from experience" (Gazzaniga et al., 2011, p. 225). Our experiences are shaped by learning how two things are associated, such as the sound of a dentist's drill and subsequent oral pain. However, later refinement of learning theories emphasized the role of cognitive processes such as expectations, predictions, beliefs, and interpretations (Hollis, 1997), observation (versus direct experience; Bandura, 1978), and culture (Gazzaniga et al., 2011). For instance, there is relatively good consensus among researchers that a link between media violence exposure and aggression exists (Gentile et al., 2007), possibly because higher exposure to media violence may promote a belief that violence is a common and inevitable part of life or because violence is normalized as a way to resolve problems. Humans readily learn by observing and then imitating others, especially others who are seen as admirable, attractive, or high status (Gazzaniga et al., 2011), so viewing material that includes violence perpetration by desirable models, especially in the absence of negative consequences for committing the violent act, may be learned and then imitated (Bridges, 2010).

In terms of learning principles, most pornography use is accompanied by masturbation or other sexual stimulation (Bridges et al., 2016). There are few things as pleasurable as an orgasm, which functions as a primary reward for humans (Schultz, 2015). According to operant conditioning theory of learning, when pornography use is repeatedly paired with such a highly stimulating and pleasurable activity and outcome, then this increases the likelihood of future use. Furthermore, consistent with classical conditioning theory of learning, the pleasure of orgasm is repeatedly paired with the presentation of sex that is so prevalent in popular pornography (which, as we reviewed earlier, tends to tell a sexual story about people that is devoid of intimacy and that is oftentimes demeaning to women). As a consequence, adolescents may come to associate pleasure with a lack of intimacy and with being demeaning to women (or even come to believe that women enjoy being treated in this way, since such treatment is nearly universally met with demonstrations of pleasure; Bridges et al., 2010). If this association, or learning, occurs, then it is not surprising that viewing sex in an instrumental way or even sexually harassing or assaulting peers may follow. Indeed, in a three-wave longitudinal study of Dutch teens, Peter and Valkenburg (2007) found pornography use increased later views of women as sex objects, and Bonino and colleagues (2006) found viewing women as sex objects predicted future sexual violence perpetration. To the extent that adolescents perceive pornographic media as real, they are more likely to endorse views of women as sex objects and to imitate behaviors in pornography in their own lives (Peter & Valkenburg, 2006). They may also experience a greater sense of pressure to engage in sex, particularly if they believe their peers are also doing this (Bleakley, Hennessy, Fishbein, & Jordan, 2011; Weber et al., 2012).

Some theorists have explained that pornography use, like all media, teaches viewers what to expect in sexual encounters. There are very few other sources to set such expectations since most sexual encounters in real life occur in private; in many other types of media, sexual encounters are implied but not shown (Bleakley et al., 2012). Therefore, one of the few methods teens have of learning what sex actually looks like is through pornography (Morgan, 2011; Ward, 2003). Because pornography presents a distorted view of sex, but oftentimes adolescents lack alternative narratives about sex, the singular narrative in much of popular pornography becomes a template for how one ought to behave in sexual encounters (Bandura, 1967; Simon & Gagnon, 1986; Wright, 2011). This template is called a sexual script. In fact, Peter and Valkenburg (2006) found teens who perceived pornography as more realistic were more likely to be influenced by it than teens who saw it as less realistic. As Wright (2011) articulates, adolescents acquire this sexual script by viewing pornography, and this script is then activated and applied in sexual encounters with real-life partners. When real life fails to imitate art, is it any wonder adolescents may end up dissatisfied?

Finally, pornography also tells a unique story about who is eligible for sex and sets conventional standards of physical beauty (as do most other types of media) and sexual performance that are often impossible for viewers to achieve in real life. The greater the use of these media, the more these body and sexual behavioral ideals are internalized, and the less likely it is that adolescents will be comfortable with their own bodies and behaviors during sex with a real partner. Trying to "numb out" during sex, such as by using substances, and being dissatisfied with sex are all likely outcomes from this internalization of body ideals (Calogero & Thompson, 2009; Tylka, 2015).

Sociological Context and the Pornography Industry

Pornography has come to dominate and define the sexual landscape of adolescents through technological innovation, competitive marketing strategies, and the intentional use of gender stereotypes to capture attention. Pornography is, at its core, a commercial artifact. It is not a reflection of innate sexual desires, personal choice, or the politics of free speech. Instead, it is a product that is produced, distributed, and marketed by a profit-seeking industry that resides at the center of the modern digital economy (Johnson, 2011; Ogas & Gaddam, 2011; Tarrant, 2016). The most systematic measurement conservatively estimates pornography as comprising about 4 percent of Internet content, which translates to about 40 million pornographic websites (Ogas & Gaddam, 2011). The largest distributor of pornography on the web is MindGeek.com, a multi-national, privately held technology company that bills itself as a leader in web design, information technology, web development, and search engine optimization. With headquarters in Luxembourg, MindGeek.com controls 8 of the top 10 pornographic websites including PornHub.com, YouPorn.com, and RedTube.com, as well as large production companies including Playboy Plus Entertainment, Vivid, and Brazzers (Pinsker, 2016). On its website, the company reports approximately 115 million daily visitors to its various sites, exposing them to three billion advertising impressions as they browse 15 terabytes of pornographic material. MindGeek.com did not arrive at such prominence in the industry through the production of pornographic material. Rather, it came to dominate the industry through software development and a mastery of algorithms and online analytics (Auerback, 2014; Wikipedia.com, 2017).

The story of MindGeek's rise to prominence illuminates how adolescents come to find and experience modern pornography. MindGeek's origins, circa late 1990s, can be traced to the development and testing of software to build and manage affiliate programs. Affiliate programs centralize the distribution and monetization of online content across numerous websites, while at the same time tracking consumer choices and preferences as they browse those various websites (Auerback, 2014; Forrester, 2016; Tarrant, 2016). MindGeek used pornographic material found on early websites to test and monetize the software. The affiliate business model creates competition between and among the affiliate websites as each competes to attract potential paying consumers. It is this competition for profit that drives the sexual practices found in modern pornography. Affiliate websites sell and market what is most likely to attract attention in a crowded field, most likely to hold users' attention, and most likely compel them to spend money. Overwhelming, the most profitable type of material is gonzo/hard-core pornography (Dines, 2006; Johnson, 2011). Consequently, gonzo/hard-core, defined by the high level of violence against women, is the most prolific and widely dispersed among the 15 terabytes of pornography currently on the web. And now, with the development of 'tube sites' (defined later), gonzo porn is free and easily available to anyone regardless of age.

In the early 2000s, in an effort to stand out among the increasingly crowded field of online pornography, affiliate programs began to move bits of content out from behind the paywall to offer free teasers of the unique content available to paid users. MindGeek developed an algorithm to pirate and aggregate this free content on 'tube sites' such as YouPorn.com or PornHub.com, which present thumbnails for easy browsing surrounded by advertising banners. Upon clicking on any 'free' content, MindGeek begins collecting user data to feed its complex algorithm, which subtly customizes the presentation of genres of pornographic material to direct site visitors toward material that is most likely to convert the casual user into a paying customer. MindGeek then uses search engine optimization to ensure these sites dominate the first page of any search results for pornography. Thus, the material that is found most easily on the Internet is that which is most profitable. In other words, gonzo is presented first and often to maximize the chances that the casual user will spend money. All of this is invisible to the user. For the user, tube sites feel like a cornucopia of free choice. Yet, behind the scenes, technological and commercial practices shape and direct the user's experience, with the goal of extracting profit.

This corporate landscape of online pornography shapes adolescent sexual behavior in multiple ways. First, because online pornography is fundamentally a commercial enterprise, the sexual behaviors and interactions depicted in pornography are those that are most profitable. Because MindGeek uses sophisticated algorithms to control search results, any search for pornography or free porn will bring to the forefront material that promotes spending and maximizes profits. Thus, the content that is presented first and most easily found is that which is preferred by sophisticated adult (mostly) male users who spend money on pornography. In other words, adolescents do not view content that is consistent with the beginning of their sexual growth and development, they start at advanced stages.

Second, the sophisticated use of algorithms to direct traffic and influence choice has implications for how adolescents understand their own sexual interests and choices. When adolescents start their sexual journey with 'tube sites,' instead of the adolescents' innate or naturalistic sexual desires, the pornography industry establishes their baseline of sexual behavior. Curiosity may bring them to the pornography industry but algorithms will control their journey throughout. This is an important new line of research created by the political economy of the online pornography industry, which bases its algorithms for presenting content based on the appetite of more mature males; how does sexual maturation occur when initiation into sexual behavior begins, not with pictures of breasts but with hard-core, gonzo pornography? How do adolescents differentiate their own sexual interests from that of content oriented toward adult sexual behaviors, most likely containing hard-core content and male aggression against women? How do they come to understand themselves as sexual beings when they begin with sexual behaviors requiring mature judgment and confidence? What are the implications of this distortion of sexual development for the sexual health of adolescent boys and girls? Are the implications the same for sexual minority youth compared to heterosexual youth?

Third, since the goal of the pornography industry is to convert users into paying subscribers, it collects metadata on users as they explore content on the website. The pornography industry will have early access to individualized data on adolescent boys and girls, and will use these data to customize their online experiences to suit commercial interests. Much like other online retailers, the tentacles of marketing can reach into the adolescent's computer to send notifications and display advertisements into his or her view. This is called push marketing. For the adolescent, who has little experience with sexuality, the marketing techniques of the pornography industry may be overwhelming and particularly persuasive.

Finally, the use of algorithms to aggregate content puts adolescents at security risk in several ways. First, because algorithms scoop up material from across the web automatically, it is highly probable illegal material such as child pornography is present among the free pornography thumbnail clips. It is a federal offense to view and distribute such material; even inadvertent contact can result in a criminal investigation. Second, the highly gendered and racialized content found in online pornography (Dines, 2006, 2010b; Ward, 2003) is associated with less egalitarian attitudes among males and more hostile sexism (Hald, Malamuth, et al., 2013) as well as more positive attitudes toward violence against women (Hald, et al., 2010). More traditional and less egalitarian views on gender increase the likelihood of interpersonal violence (Reyes et al., 2016) and are considered risk factors for interpersonal violence (Centers for Disease Control and Prevention, 2017). Therefore, pornography use may put sexual partners of users at risk for violence. Lastly, the next frontiers for profit include directing traffic toward webcams, private sessions (where the user can pay to interact directly with pornography performers), applications (apps) such as SnapChat or Instagram, and virtual reality technologies, thus giving the industry more direct access to the social and sexual lives of adolescents.

For the adolescent, who most likely enters the world of pornography through commercial tube sites around middle school (Allen & Lavender-Stott, 2015), prior to their first romantic relationship (Cheng et al., 2014), the hidden undercurrents of the pornography industry can carry them in directions of which they may not be aware. There is a misconceptualization that online pornography is a panoply of equally accessible types of sexuality such that anyone can find whatever type of content in which they are interested, thus creating the illusion that users are in control of their choices. This 'illusion of choice' may be true, theoretically, but in practice the industry has a vested interest in shaping choices and directing traffic. The consequences of the onslaught of free pornography on the sexual behaviors of adolescents are just coming into view as the first cohorts to experience modern corporate pornography are reaching adulthood.

Concluding Comments

In this chapter, we have articulated a sociological–psychological model, based on the past 15 years of research into adolescents and pornography use. We describe the numerous predisposing factors associated with greater engagement in pornography use by teens, how this use might exert its influence on sexual behavior, and what variables may moderate these relations. To date, much of the research on adolescent pornography use is strictly empirical or use theories that are quite broad, lacking specificity or precision, which muddies the research waters (Wright, 2014). Little attention has been paid to the ways in which intersecting identities of race, class, gender, ability, and sexuality differentially shape an adolescent's relationship to pornographic material, and even less attention has been paid to the technological and economic mechanisms through which adolescents discover and then use pornography. We seek to bridge these gaps through a sociological–psychological model of adolescent pornography use that encourages the mapping and discovery of differential pathways of adolescent pornography use and various outcomes. Our model proposes a framework that integrates the individual and relational factors shaping adolescents' pornography use and associated outcomes within larger sociological questions related to the social, economic, and technological context of modern digital pornography. We conceptualize pornography as a commercial product that is active at multiple levels in the life of an adolescent. We recognize that pornography is built into the technological infrastructure of their cell phones, computers, and Internet search engines; it resides in their families, relationships, and sociocultural environments; and it permeates their identities, values, and attitudes toward themselves, their bodies, and their sexual identities. These systemic pathways are not experienced in the same way for all adolescents: race, class, gender, and sexuality differentially structure these potential pathways. Lastly, given the strong relationship between pornography and risky sexual behaviors, up to and including engagement in sexual aggression or violence, our model assumes a goal of harm reduction through intervention and education.

Research to date provides some suggestions for ways to help adolescents understand and navigate their own sexualities within the context of pornography messages about sex. For instance, recognizing risk factors that increase likelihood of engagement with pornography can help fiduciary adults plan carefully to minimize exposure, especially for young teens. Having Internet-connected devices in public areas of the home, limiting accessibility, installing Internet filters, or increasing monitoring of teens may help reduce use. Providing greater access to more comprehensive sex education, from a variety of trusted sources, can reduce the need for teens to search for pornography in order to learn what to do after saying "yes" to having sex, a place where most school-based sex education stops (Coy et al., 2016). Sex education and informal opportunities for discussion about sex can and should also include increased literacy about pornography (Klein, 2016). Since most teens will see pornography at some point during their adolescence (Mitchell et al., 2003), equipping them with information to contextualize such media (including counter-acting narrow messages about sex that are part of the pornographic script) will be crucial to reducing its potential negative impact.

Pornography is a commercial product that has filled a void many sexual minority teens have, providing one of the only avenues for them to understand, explore, or even see their identities represented. For instance, Arrington-Sanders and colleagues (2015) found young Black men who were attracted to other men felt pornography played a positive role in their self-understanding. However, since there is rarely negotiation of safe sex practices (e.g., condom use) or consent, additional opportunities to enhance protective factors (e.g., by including discussions of sexual orientation, disease prevention, and consent negotiation in sexual-education communication in the home and at school) are critical.

All of these efforts, however, will be in vain so long as there are profits to be made by producing and marketing pornography. Given that gonzo/hard-core pornography is the most profitable and prolific on the web, reluctance on the part of parents, educators, and policy makers to directly confront what adolescents see in pornography is highly problematic and puts the sexual health of adolescents in the hands of a manipulative and suspect industry (akin to putting a fast food corporation in charge of a teen's diet). For adolescents who typically will first encounter pornography in middle school, before their first romance and well before their first sexual encounter, the industry plays a more fundamental role in the development of their sexual identity than among many of today's parents who came of age prior to the online revolution. Given the historical trajectory of the industry culminating in a flood of easily accessible, extremely explicit, and largely aggressive pornography, adolescents' initiation into sex is unlike any other generation prior. As such, traditional notions of sexual education and longstanding debates about pornography no longer apply and, in fact, may put adolescents at risk. Conceptualizing pornography as a commercial product rather than a form of sexual expression or of speech opens the door to other means of approaching the discussion. Like other commercial products with health implications, such as alcohol, tobacco, or sugar, educators and public health agencies need to develop educational campaigns to help adolescents and parents build skills that facilitate the identification of the true nature of pornography and the sexual behavior it promotes.

References

Allen, K. R. & Lavender-Stott, E. S. (2015). Family Contexts of Informal Sex Education: Young Men's Perceptions of First Sexual Images. *Family Relations*, *64*, 393–406. doi:10.1111/fare.12128.

Arrington-Sanders, R., Harper, G. W., Morgan, A., Ogunbajo, A., Trent, M., & Fortenberry, J. D. (2015). The Role of Sexually Explicit Material in the Sexual Development of Same-Sex-Attracted Black Adolescent Males. *Archives of Sexual Behavior*, *44*, 597–608. doi:10.1007/s10508-014-0416-x.

Attwood, F. (2005). What Do People Do with Porn? Qualitative Research into Consumption, Use and Experience of Pornography and Other Sexually Explicit Media. *Sexuality & Culture*, *9*, 65–86.

Auerback, D. (2014, October 23). Vampire porn: MindGeek is a cautionary tale of consolidating production and distribution in a single, monopolistic owner. *Slate Magazine*. www.slate.com/articles/technology/technology/2014/10/mindgeek_porn_monopoly_its_dominance_is_a_cautionary_tale_for_other_industries.html

Bandura, A. (1967). Behavioral Psychotherapy. *Scientific American*, *216*, 78–86.

(1978). Social Learning Theory of Aggression. *Journal of Communication*, *28*, 12–29.

Barron, M. & Kimmel, M. (2000). Sexual Violence in Three Pornographic Media: Toward a Sociological Explanation. *Journal of Sex Research*, *8*, 161–168.

Beyens, I., Vandenbosch, L., & Eggermont, S. (2015). Early Adolescent Boys' Exposure to Internet Pornography: Relationships to Pubertal Timing, Sensation Seeking, and Academic Performance. *The Journal of Early Adolescence*, *35*, 1045–1068.

Bleakley, A., Hennessy, M., & Fishbein, M. (2011). A Model of Adolescents' Seeking of Sexual Content in Their Media Choices. *Journal of Sex Research*, *48*, 309–315. doi:10.1080/00224499.2010.497985,

Bleakley, A., Hennessy, M., Fishbein, M., & Jordan, A. (2008). It Works Both Ways: The Relationship between Exposure to Sexual Content in the Media and Adolescent Sexual Behavior. *Media Psychology*, *11*, 443–461. doi:10.1080/15213260802491986.

(2011). Using the Integrative Model to Explain How Exposure to Sexual Media Content Influences Adolescent Sexual Behavior. *Health Education & Behavior*, *38*, 530–540. doi:10.1177/1090198110385775,

Bleakley, A., Jamieson, P., & Romer, D. (2012). Trends of Sexual and Violent Content by Gender in Top-Grossing U.S. Films, 1950–2006. *Journal of Adolescent Health*, *51*, 73–79. doi: 10.1016/j.jadohealth.2012.02.006.

Bonino, S., Ciairano, S., Rabaglietti, E., & Cattelino, E. (2006). Use of Pornography and Self-Reported Engagement in Sexual Violence among Adolescents. *European Journal of Developmental Psychology*, *3*, 265–288. doi:10.1080/17405620600562359.

Braun-Courville, D. K. & Rojas, M. (2009). Exposure to Sexually Explicit Web Sites and Adolescent Sexual Attitudes and Behaviors. *Journal of Adolescent Health*, *45*, 156–162. doi:10.1016/j.jadohealth.2008.12.004.

Bridges, A. J. (2010). Methodological Considerations in Mapping Pornography Content. In Boyle, K. (Ed.), *Everyday Pornography* (34–48). New York: Routledge.

Bridges, A.J. & Jensen, R. (2010). Pornography. In Edleson, J., Bergen, R., & Renzetti, C. (Eds.), *Sourcebook on Violence against Women, 2nd edn.* (133–149). Thousand Oaks: Sage.

Bridges, A. J., Sun, C. F., Ezzell, M. B., & Johnson, J. (2016). Sexual Scripts and the Sexual Behavior of Men and Women Who Use Pornography. *Sexualization, Media, & Society*, *2*, 1–14. doi:10.1177/2374623816668275.

Bridges, A. J., Wosnitzer, R., Scharrer, E., Sun, C., & Liberman, R. (2010). Aggression and Sexual Behavior in Best-Selling Pornography Videos: A Content Analysis Update. *Violence Against Women*, *16*, 1065–1085.

Brosi, M. W., Foubert, J. D., Bannon, R. S., & Yandell, G. (2011). Effects of Women's Pornography Use on Bystander Intervention in a Sexual Assault Situation and

Rape Myth Acceptance. *Oracle: The Research Journal of the Association of Fraternity/Sorority Advisors*, *6*, 26–35.

Brown, J. D. & L'Engle, K. L. (2009). X-rated: Sexual Attitudes and Behaviors Associated with Us Early Adolescents' Exposure to Sexually Explicit Media. *Communication Research*, *36*, 129–151.

Buzzell, T. (2005). Demographic Characteristics of Persons Using Pornography in Three Technological Contexts. *Sexuality & Culture*, *9*, 28–48.

Calogero, R. M. & Thompson, J. K. (2009). Potential Implications of the Objectification of Women's Bodies for Women's Sexual Satisfaction. *Body Image*, *6*, 145–148.

Chen, A.-S., Leung, M., Chen, C.-H., & Yang, S. C. (2013). Exposure to Internet Pornography among Taiwanese Adolescents. *Social Behavior and Personality*, *41*, 157–164. doi:10.2224/sbp.2013.41.1.157.

Centers for Disease Control and Prevention (CDC). (2017). Sexual violence: Risk and protective factors. www.cdc.gov/violenceprevention/sexualviolence/riskprotectivefactors.html.

Cheng, S., Ma, J., & Missari, S. (2014). The Effects of Internet Use on Adolescents' First Romantic and Sexual Relationships in Taiwan. *International Sociology*, *29*, 324–347.

Coy, M., Kelly, L., Vera-Gray, F., Garner, M., & Kanyeredzi, A. (2016). From 'No Means No' to 'an Enthusiastic Yes': Changing the Discourse on Sexual Consent through Sex and Relationships Education. In *Global Perspectives and Key Debates in Sex and Relationships Education: Addressing Issues of Gender, Sexuality, Plurality and Power* (84–99). New York: Palgrave Macmillan.

Dines, G. (2006). The White Man's Burden: Gonzo Pornography and the Construction of Black Masculinity. *Yale Journal of Law & Feminism*, *18*, 283–297.

(2010a, May 17). Not your father's Playboy. *CounterPunch*. www.counterpunch.org/2010/05/17/not-your-father-s-playboy/.

(2010b). *Pornland: How Pornography Has Hijacked Our Sexuality*. New York: Beacon.

Doornwaard, S. M., de Boer, F., Vanwesenbeech, I., van Nijnatten, C. H. C. J., ter Bogt, T. F. M., & van den Eijnden, R. J. J. M. (2017). Dutch Adolescents' Motives, Perceptions, and Reflections toward Sex-Related Internet Use: Results of a Web-Based Focus-Group Study. *Journal of Sex Research*, *54*, 1038–1050. doi:10.1080/00224499.2016.1255873.

Epstein, M., Bailey, J. A., Manhart, L. E., Hill, K. G., & Hawkins, J. D. (2014). Sexual Risk Behavior in Young Adulthood: Broadening the Scope beyond Early Sexual Initiation. *The Journal of Sex Research*, *51*, 721–730.

Flood, M. (2007). Exposure to Pornography among Youth in Australia. *Journal of Sociology*, *43*, 45–60. doi:10.1177/1440783307073934.

Forrester, K. (2016, September 26) Making sense of modern pornography: While the Internet has made porn ubiquitous, it has also thrown the industry into severe decline. *The New Yorker*. www.newyorker.com/magazine/2016/09/26/making-sense-of-modern-pornography.

Foubert, J. D., Brosi, M. W., & Bannon, R. S. (2011). Pornography Viewing among Fraternity Men: Effects on Bystander Intervention, Rape Myth Acceptance and Behavioral Intent to Commit Sexual Assault. *Sexual Addiction & Compulsivity*, *18*, 212–231.

Gazzaniga, M. S., Heatherton, T. F., & Halpern, D. F. (2011). *Psychological Science, 4th edn*. New York: W. W. Norton & Co.

Gentile, D. A., Saleem, M., & Anderson, C. A. (2007). Public Policy and the Effects of Media Violence on Children. *Social Issues and Policy Review, 1*, 15–51.

Grubbs, J., Braden, A., Kraus, S. W., Wilt, J., & Wright, P. (2017, September 25). Pornography and pleasure-seeking: Toward a hedonic reinforcement model. Open Science Framework. https://psyarxiv.com/jevb7.

Grubbs, J. B., Stauner, N., Exline, J. J., Pargament, K. I., & Lindberg, M. J. (2015). Perceived Addiction to Internet Pornography and Psychological Distress: Examining Relationships Concurrently and over Time. *Psychology of Addictive Behaviors*, *29*, 1056–1067.

Häggström-Nordin, E., Hanson, U., & Tydén, T. (2005). Associations between Pornography Consumption and Sexual Practices among Adolescents in Sweden. *International Journal of STD and AIDS*, *16*, 102–107. doi:10.1007/s10508-010-9714-0.

Häggström-Nordin, E., Tydén, T., Hanson, U., & Larsson, M. (2009). Experiences of and Attitudes towards Pornography among a Group of Swedish High School Students. *The European Journal of Contraception & Reproductive Health Care*, *14*, 277–284.

Hald, G. M., Kuyper, L., Adam, P. C., & Wit, J. B. (2013). Does Viewing Explain Doing? Assessing the Association between Sexually Explicit Materials Use and Sexual Behaviors in a Large Sample of Dutch Adolescents and Young Adults. *Journal Of Sexual Medicine*, *10*, 2986–2995.

Hald, G. M., Malamuth, N. M., & Lange, T. (2013). Pornography and Sexist Attitudes among Heterosexuals. *Journal of Communication*, *63*, 638–660.

Hald, G. M., Malamuth, N. M., & Yuen, C. (2010). Pornography and Attitudes Supporting Violence against Women: Revisiting the Relationship in Nonexperimental Studies. *Aggressive Behavior*, *36*, 14–20.

Hardy, S. (2008). The Pornography of Reality. *Sexualities*, *11*, 60–64. doi:10.1177/13634607080110010209.

Hasking, P. A., Scheier, L. M., & Abdallah, A. B. (2011). The Three Latent Classes of Adolescent Delinquency and the Risk Factors for Membership In Each Class. *Aggressive Behavior*, *37*, 19–35.

Hollis, K. L. (1997). Contemporary Research on Pavlovian Conditioning: A "New" Functional Analysis. *American Psychologist*, *52*, 956–965.

Holt, T. J., Bossler, A. M., & May, D. C. (2012). Low Self-Control, Deviant Peer Associations, and Juvenile Cyberdeviance. *American Journal of Criminal Justice*, *37*, 378–395.

Hunter, J. A., Figueredo, A. J., & Malamuth, N. M. (2010). Developmental Pathways into Social and Sexual Deviance. *Journal of Family Violence*, *25*, 141–148.

Johansson, T. & Hammarén, N. (2007). Hegemonic Masculinity and Pornography: Young People's Attitudes toward and Relations to Pornography. *Journal of Men's Studies*, *15*, 57–70.

Johnson, J. A. (2011). Mapping the Feminist Political Economy of the Online Commercial Pornography Industry: A Network Approach. *International Journal of Media & Cultural Politics*, *7*, 189–208.

Juffer, J. (1998). *At Home with Pornography: Women, Sex, and Everyday Life*. New York: New York University Press.

Klaassen, M. J. & Peter, J. (2015). Gender (in) Equality in Internet Pornography: A Content Analysis of Popular Pornographic Internet Videos. *Journal of Sex Research*, *52*, 721–735.

Klein, M. (2016, October 30). Kids need porn literacy. *Psychology Today*. www.psychologytoday.com/blog/sexual-intelligence/201610/kids-need-porn-literacy.

Löfgren-Mårtenson, L. & Månsson, S. A. (2010). Lust, Love, and Life: A Qualitative Study of Swedish Adolescents' Perceptions and Experiences with Pornography. *Journal of Sex Research*, *47*, 568–579.

Lott, B. (1994). *Women's Lives: Themes and Variations in Gender Learning*. Belmont: Brooks/Cole.

Luder, M. T., Pittet, I., Berchtold, A., Akré, C., Michaud, P. A., & Surís, J. C. (2011). Associations between Online Pornography and Sexual Behavior among Adolescents: Myth or Reality?. *Archives of Sexual Behavior*, *40*, 1027–1035.

Ma, C. M. S. & Shek, D. T. L. (2013). Consumption of Pornographic Materials in Early Adolescents in Hong Kong. *Journal of Pediatric and Adolescent Gynecology*, *26*, S18–25. doi:10.1016/j.jpag.2013.03.011,

Malamuth, N. M., Hald, G. M., & Koss, M. (2012). Pornography, Individual Differences in Risk and Men's Acceptance of Violence against Women in a Representative Sample. *Sex Roles*, *66*, 427–439. doi:10.1007/s11199-011-0082-6.

Malamuth, N. & Huppin, M. (2005). Pornography and Teenagers: The Importance of Individual Differences. *Adolescent Medicine Clinics*, *16*, 315–326. doi:10.1016/j.admecli.2005.02.004.

Mattebo, M., Tydén, T., Häggström-Nordin, E., Nilsson, K. W., & Larsson, M. (2016). Pornography Consumption among Adolescent Girls in Sweden. *The European Journal of Contraception & Reproductive Health Care*, *21*, 295–302.

McKee, A. (2005). The Objectification of Women in Mainstream Pornographic Videos in Australia. *Journal of Sex Research*, *42*, 277–290. doi:10.1080/00224490509552283.

Merriam-Webster. (2017). Gonzo. www.merriam-webster.com/dictionary/gonzo.

Mesch, G. S. (2009). Social Bonds and Internet Pornographic Exposure among Adolescents. *Journal of Adolescence*, *32*, 601–618.

Mesch, G. S. & Maman, T. L. (2009). Intentional Online Pornographic Exposure among Adolescents: Is the Internet to Blame? *Verhaltenstherapie & Verhaltensmedizin*, *30*, 352–367. doi:10.1037/t01038-000.

Mitchell, K., Finklehor, D., & Wolak, J. (2003). The Exposure of Youth to Unwanted Sexual Material on the Internet: A National Survey of Risk, Impact, and Prevention. *Youth & Society*, *34*, 330–358. doi:10.1177/0044118X02250123.

Morelli, M., Bianchi, D., Baiocco, R., Pezzuti, L., & Chirumbolo, A. (2017). Sexting Behaviors and Cyber Pornography Addiction among Adolescents: The Moderating Role of Alcohol Consumption. *Sexuality Research and Social Policy*, *14*, 113–121.

Morgan, E. M. (2011). Associations between Young Adults' Use of Sexually Explicit Materials and Their Sexual Preferences, Behaviors, and Satisfaction. *Journal of Sex Research*, *48*, 520–530. doi:10.080/00224499.2010.543960.

Ogas, O. & Gaddam, S. (2011). *A Billion Wicked Thoughts: What the World's Largest Experiment Reveals about Human Desire*. New York: Penguin Group.

Owens, E. W., Behun, R. J., Manning, J. C., & Reid, R. C. (2012). The Impact of Internet Pornography on Adolescents: A Review of the Research. *Sexual Addiction & Compulsivity*, *19*, 99–122. doi:10.1080/10720162.2012.660431.

Paasonen, S. (2010). Online Pornography: Ubiquitous and Effaced. In Burnett, R., Consalvo, M., & Ess, C. (Eds.) *The Handbook of Internet Studies*. West Sussex: Wiley Blackwell.

Pavlov, I. P. (1927). *Conditioned Reflexes*. London: Oxford University Press.

Peter, J. & Valkenburg, P. M. (2006). Adolescents' Exposure to Sexually Explicit Online Material and Recreational Attitudes toward Sex. *Journal of Communication*, *56*, 639–660. doi:10.1111/j.1460–2466.2006.00313.x.

(2007). Adolescents' Exposure to a Sexualized Media Environment and Their Notions of Women as Sex Objects. *Sex Roles*, *56*, 381–395. doi:10.1007/s11199-006-9176-y.

(2008). Adolescents' Exposure to Sexually Explicit Internet Material, Sexual Uncertainty, and Attitudes toward Uncommitted Sexual Exploration: Is There a Link? *Communication Research*, *35*, 579–601. doi:10.1177/0093650208321754.

(2010). Processes Underlying the Effects of Adolescents' Use of Sexually Explicit Internet Material: The Role of Perceived Realism. *Communication Research*, *37*, 375–399. doi:10.1177/0093650210362464.

(2011). The Use of Sexually Explicit Internet Material and Its Antecedents: A Longitudinal Comparison of Adolescents and Adults. *Archives of Sexual Behavior*, *40*, 1015–1025. doi:10.1007/s10508-010-9644-x.

(2016). Adolescents and Pornography: A Review of 20 years of Research. *Journal of Sex Research*, *53*, 509–531. doi:10.1080/00224499.2016.1143441.

Pinsker, J. (2016) The hidden economics of porn. *The Atlantic*. www.theatlantic.com/business/archive/2016/04/pornography-industry-economics-tarrant/476580/.

Purcell, N. J. (2012). *Violence and the Pornographic Imaginary: The Politics of Sex, Gender, and Aggression in Hardcore Pornography* (Vol. 42). New York: Routledge.

Reyes, H. L. M., Foshee, V. A., Niolon, P. H., Reidy, D. E., & Hall, J. E. (2016). Gender Role Attitudes and Male Adolescent Dating Violence Perpetration: Normative Beliefs as Moderators. *Journal of Youth and Adolescence*, *45*, 350–360. doi:10.1007/s10964-015–0278-0.

Russell, D. E. H. (1993). *Against Pornography: The Evidence of Harm*. Berkeley: Russell Publications.

Sabina, C., Wolak, J., & Finkelhor, D. (2008). The Nature and Dynamics of Internet Pornography Exposure for Youth. *CyberPsychology & Behavior*, *11*, 691–693. doi:10.1089/cpb.2007.0179.

Schultz, W. (2015). Neuronal Reward and Decision Signals: From Theories to Data. *Physiological Reviews*, *95*, 853–951. doi:10.1152/physrev.00023.2014.

Senn, C. Y. & Radtke, H. L. (1990). Women's Evaluations of and Affective Reactions to Mainstream Violent Pornography, Nonviolent Pornography, and Erotica. *Violence and Victims*, *5*, 143–155.

Ševčíková, A. & Daneback, K. (2014). Online Pornography Use in Adolescence: Age and Gender Differences. *European Journal of Developmental Psychology*, *11*, 674–686.

Shek, D. T. L. & Ma, C. M. S. (2012). Consumption of Pornographic Materials among Early Adolescents in Hong Kong: Profiles and Psychosocial Correlates. *International Journal on Disability and Human Development*, *11*, 143–150. doi:10.1515/ijdhd-2012-0024.

Simon, W. & Gagnon, J. H. (1986). Sexual Scripts: Permanence and Change. *Archives of Sexual Behavior*, *15*, 97–120. doi:10.1007/BF01542219.

Sinković, M., Štulhofer, A., & Božić, J. (2013). Revisiting the Association between Pornography Use and Risky Sexual Behaviors: The Role of Early Exposure to Pornography and Sexual Sensation Seeking. *Journal of Sex Research*, *50*, 633–641.

Skinner, B. F. (1950). Are Theories of Learning Necessary? *Psychological Review*, *57*, 193–216.

Stanley, N., Barter, C., Wood, M., et al. (2016). Pornography, Sexual Coercion and Abuse and Sexting in Young People's Intimate Relationships: A European Study. *Journal of Interpersonal Violence*, doi:10.1177/0886260516633204.

Steinem, G. (November 1978). Erotica and pornography: A clear and present sifference. Ms Magazine, 53–54 & 75–76.

Stewart, D. N. & Szymanski, D. M. (2012). Young Adult Women's Reports of Their Male Romantic Partner's Pornography Use as a Correlate of Their Self-Esteem, Relationship Quality, and Sexual Satisfaction. *Sex Roles*, *67*, 257–271.

Tanton, C., Jones, K. G., Macdowall, W., et al. (2015). Patterns and Trends in Sources of Information about Sex among Young People in Britain: Evidence from Three National Surveys of Sexual Attitudes and Lifestyles. *BMJ Open*, *5*, e007834. doi:10.1136/bmjopen-2015-007834.

Tarrant, S. (2016). *The Pornography Industry: What Everyone Needs to Know*. New York: Oxford University Press.

Tylka, T. L. (2015). No Harm in Looking, Right? Men's Pornography Consumption, Body Image, and Well-Being. *Psychology of Men & Masculinity*, *16*, 97–107.

Vandenbosch, L., van Oosten, J. M. F., & Jochen, P. (2015). The Relationship between Sexual Content on Mass Media and Social Media: A Longitudinal Study. *Cyberpsychology, Behavior, and Social Networking*, *18*(12). doi:10.1089/cyber.2015.0197

Wallmyr, G. & Welin, C. (2006). Young People, Pornography, and Sexuality: Sources and Attitudes. *Journal of School Nursing*, *22*, 290–295.

Ward, L. M. (2003). Understanding the Role of Entertainment Media in the Sexual Socialization of American Youth. *Developmental Review*, *23*, 347–388. doi:10.1016/S0273-2297(03)00013-3.

Weber, M., Quiring, O. & Daschmann, G. (2012). Peers, Parents and Pornography: Exploring Adolescents' Exposure to Sexually Explicit Material and Its Developmental Correlates. *Sexuality & Culture*, *16*, 408–427. doi:10.1007/s12119-012-9132-7.

Weinberg, M. S., Williams, C. J., Kleiner, S., & Irizarry, Y. (2010). Pornography, Normalization, and Empowerment. *Archives of Sexual Behavior*, *39*, 1389–1401.

Weitzer, R. J. (2000). *Sex for Sale: Prostitution, Pornography, and the Sex Industry*. New York: Routledge.

Wikipedia.com. (2017) MindGeek. https://en.wikipedia.org/wiki/MindGeek.

Williams, L. (2004). *Porn Studies*. North Carolina: Duke University Press.

Wolak, J., Mitchell, K., & Finkelhor, D. (2007). Unwanted and Wanted Exposure to Online Pornography in a National Sample of Youth Internet Users. *Pediatrics*, *119*, 247–257. doi:10.1542/peds.2006-1891.

Wright, P.J. (2011). Mass Media Effects on Youth Sexual Behavior: Assessing the Claim for Causality. *Communication Yearbook*, *35*, 343–386.

(2013). A Three-Wave Longitudinal Analysis of Preexisting Beliefs, Exposure to Pornography, and Attitude Change. *Communication Reports*, *26*, 13–25.

(2014). Pornography and the Sexual Socialization of Children: Current Knowledge and a Theoretical Future. *Journal of Children and Media*, *8*, 305–312.

Wright, P. J., Bae, S., & Funk, M. (2013). United States Women and Pornography through Four Decades: Exposure, Attitudes, Behaviors, Individual Differences. *Archives of Sexual Behavior*, *42*, 1131–1144. doi:10.1007/s10508-013-0116-y.

Wright, P. J. & Funk, M. (2014). Pornography Consumption and Opposition to Affirmative Action for Women: A Prospective Study. *Psychology of Women Quarterly*, *38*, 208–221. doi:10.1177/0361684313498853.

Wright, P. J., Tokunaga, R. S., & Kraus, A. (2016). A Meta-analysis of Pornography Consumption and Actual Acts of Sexual Aggression in General Population Studies. *Journal of Communication*, *66*, 183–205. doi:10.1111/jcom.12201.

Ybarra, M. L. & Mitchell, K. J. (2005). Exposure to Internet Pornography among Children and Adolescents: A National Survey. *Cyberpsychology & Behavior*, *8*, 473–486.

Ybarra, M. L., Strasburger, V. C., & Mitchell, K. J. (2014). Sexual Media Exposure, Sexual Behavior, and Sexual Violence Victimization in Adolescence. *Clinical pediatrics*, *53*, 1239–1247.

Zillmann, D. (2000). Influence of Unrestrained Access to Erotica on Adolescents' and Young Adults' Dispositions toward Sexuality. *Journal of Adolescent Health*, *275*, 41–44.

23 Young People, Pornography, and Gendered Sexual Practices

Maddy Coy and Miranda A. H. Horvath

Introduction

Attention to how young people navigate sexual relationships and encounters is growing from several directions. On both sides of the Atlantic and Pacific, there has been a push for sex education to include emotional and relational dimensions and concern over the impact of pornography and sexualized popular culture. Policy makers have scrambled to respond to parental anxiety and evidence that access to pornography shapes young people's attitudes and behaviors. This has created momentum around the need for educators to address young people's sexual norms (Department for Culture, Media and Sport, 2016; Wolak et al., 2007; Women and Equalities Committee, 2016). Practitioners in the United Kingdom that work directly with young people in schools, youth settings, and sexual violence support services have spearheaded campaigns for sex and relationships education that goes beyond 'plumbing and prevention' to the messiness of negotiating when and how sex is mutually desired (End Violence Against Women, 2017). In response, the Westminster government recently announced the introduction of compulsory sex education (Department for Education, 2017), with a proposal that it is renamed 'relationships and sex education.'

Angst about the sexualization of childhood in advertising, toys, music videos/ lyrics, and fashion runs in parallel to these debates and campaigns, often somewhat hypocritically ignited by the tabloid media (Coy, 2013). Rosalind Gill usefully defines "sexualisation" as the "the extraordinary proliferation of discourses about sex and sexuality across all media forms as well the increasingly frequent erotic presentation of girls," women's and (to a lesser extent) men's bodies in public spaces' (Gill, 2007, p. 151). Increases in the volume and changes of tone in sexualized imagery – equating sexual objectification of women with empowerment, for example (Gill, 2007) – are amplified through their ubiquity in advertising, music videos, and other forms of media, which are in turn constantly accessible in the palms of our hands through smartphones and tablets (Coy, 2013; Horvath et al., 2013). These rapid advances in technology have fuelled fears about the influences of sexualized media including pornography, because of the ways in which young people live as digital natives, with little distinction between online and offline communications (Livingstone & Smith, 2014). The sexual and digital 'revolutions' have transformed *what* it is possible to represent about sex in popular culture and public space, and *how* these representations are created and disseminated.

Researchers from multiple disciplines are driven to hear directly from young people about how they make sense of this cacophony and explore their views on pornography, popular culture, and sexual relationships. For several years, we have been part of this investigative and analytic tradition, commenting on how sexualized popular culture shapes social norms and examining young people's perspectives (see, e.g., Coy, 2009; Coy et al., 2013; Horvath et al., 2013; Martellozzo et al., 2017). Despite our different disciplinary locations – Maddy as a sociologist and Miranda as a psychologist – our shared concern is the investigation of gendered dynamics in the production of sexual norms; that is, how young people develop their sexual beliefs and behaviors and how norms about sex and gender influence these. In this chapter, we draw together analysis from the United Kingdom and internationally about sexualized popular culture, young people's access and exposure to pornography, and, finally, links between pornography and sexual coercion. We also include data from an unpublished survey of young people in the United Kingdom about their views on the impact of pornography on sexual expectations that we conducted together in 2013.

Young People and Sexualized Sexism in Popular Culture and Pornography

In the Anglophone West, where there are social, economic, cultural, and linguistic similarities (Bay-Cheng, 2015), public policy and academic arenas have addressed how sexualized popular culture is experienced by and influences young people (Coy & Garner, 2012). The American Psychological Association Task Force report (2007), the Australian Senate inquiry into the sexualization of children in contemporary media (2008), and reviews commissioned by the Westminster government in the United Kingdom (Bailey, 2011; Papadopoulos, 2010) have thrust the influences of pornography on young people into popular and policy spotlights. Discourse in these arenas focuses on the ways in which popular culture is saturated with sexualized motifs: ideas and 'ideals' about women's bodies in advertising, music videos (and lyrics), and computer/video games; in the presence and expansion of sexualized dance clubs (lap/pole/strip dancing) in city high streets, including billboards for clubs. Academic engagement with the concept and meaning of 'sexualization' is also proliferating (Coy & Garner, 2012; Gill, 2011). Problematically, pornography is often considered as a distinct, unrelated entity to sexualized popular culture, despite the clear crossovers (e.g., Coy, 2014). Indeed, the mainstreaming of pornography has led to the argument that the term 'pornographification' captures how conventions of pornography have become embedded in entertainment, advertising, and fashion (Tyler & Quek, 2016).

The most apparent crossover is that in both pornography and wider sexualized popular culture, the dominant motif is of the (hetero)sexualization of women and girls' bodies for the gratification of men and boys. Cultural studies scholar Angela McRobbie (2009) has argued that popular culture has become a conduit for instilling gendered codes of behavior, as the influence of social institutions such as schools and church diminished.

Much concern in the sexualization debates is about the impact on the developing sexuality of children and young people. The developmental stage of adolescence is a crucial window in which these stories are absorbed. A recent study with 125 young people aged 10–12 years in Wales (Renold, 2013) explored the pervasive pressures of sexualization in popular culture and sexism. Girls recounted awareness of heteronormative double standards: of their bodies and appearance being scrutinized; being viewed as property of boys with girlfriend status as a 'defining feature'; and sexual harassment as an inevitable playground practice. These were reinforced by peer norms, parents, teachers, and through the media and popular culture. In this study, girls talked about unwanted and unsolicited sexualized adverts online (pop-ups) differently than boys, finding them 'harmful and offensive' and linking them to other forms of sexual harassment they experienced (Renold, 2013, p. 115).

This sexualization of girls and women is one way in which their 'space for action' (Jeffner, 2000) is limited (Coy, 2009). For example, in the United Kingdom, a recent annual survey of young women by Girlguiding (2016) found almost half of girls (47 per cent) reported that anxiety about their body being judged held them back from doing things they would like to do, including taking part in sport and speaking in class. Eighty percent of young women aged 17–21 years and 70 percent of those aged 11–16 years agreed that women are too often shown as sex objects in the media and popular culture (Girlguiding, 2016).

In light of this, we advocate that the term 'sexualized sexism' (Coy, 2014) might be clarifying, for two reasons: first, it makes clear that sexualization and pornographification are deeply gendered, and that these limited and reductive portrayals of women and girls reinforce gender as a social hierarchy (Coy, 2014). As Gill (2011) notes, the term 'sexualization' is unclear. She asked if 'sexism' would be more fitting to capture how popular culture reflects and reproduces inequalities between women and men. The term sexualized sexism clarifies that mostly, when we talk about sexualization of popular culture, we are talking about the (hetero) sexualization of women and girls' bodies. How sexualized sexism is racialized is also critically important: there are race and class distinctions in *how* women are portrayed as sexually available. bell hooks (2004) also talks of 'racialized sexism,' where race and gender intersect to perpetuate stereotypes that become archetypes – for example, the strong Black woman or submissive Asian woman. These remain underexplored in much research and commentary, despite Black feminist writers long highlighting the enmeshment of racism, sexualization, and sexism in popular culture and pornography (c.f., Crenshaw, 1991; Hill Collins, 1990; Larasi, 2013;

Rose, 2008). Marai Larasi, a Black feminist activist based in the United Kingdom gave evidence to an inquiry into sexual violence and harassment and highlights this as an overlooked concern.

> The other thing about pornography is that it is incredibly racist. It constructs groups of young men as thugs and monsters, and constructs all women as sluts, as filth, basically. It also constructs particular groups of women as exotic, as asking for it, as beasts, as animals, et cetera. What does that mean to a young black woman in [London] who is seeing herself represented in that way? What does it do to the young black man who sees himself represented as a thug? (Women and Equalities Committee, 2016, p. 48).

Academic analyses of constructions of femininity, and conceptual interpretations of how women and girls may relate to them, are often more cautious about linking sexualized sexism to harmful impacts. In part, this appears to stem from avoidance of what might be seen as theoretical T-junctions of false empowerment/victimhood (e.g., Lamb, 2015; Renold & Ringrose 2011). In many analyses, young women's sense of agency has become a dominant discourse and framing for exploring their experiences/views of sexualization, although often applied to notions of identity/self rather than sexual practices (Coy & Garner, 2012). Laina Bay-Cheng (2015) develops this argument, suggesting that shifts in gendered norms of contemporary popular culture require new conceptual frameworks. She presents a model that seeks to account for an equation of sexiness with empowerment (Gill, 2007) that she terms the "agency line," a neoliberal norm for young women to measure themselves and others against that jostles uncomfortably with constructions of the virgin/slut.

> Agency has not erased or eclipsed the Virgin-Slut Continuum or the sexism that results in pervasive sexual assault, harassment and shaming of young women. Girls must still ward off accusations of promiscuity, but they now do so while also compelled to play the parts of sexual libertines. (Bay-Cheng, 2015, p. 286).

While this continuum of virgin/slut, bisected by an "agency line" (Bay-Cheng, 2015) appears as a common reference point, not all young women, especially those from minority communities, are positioned equally in relation to it (Tolman et al., 2015). Developmental contours and age-appropriate sexual expectations may also vary its salience (Tolman, et al., 2015). Nevertheless, a 'postfeminist media sensibility' where personal power is associated with a sexualized self and individual choices are venerated is the contemporary context in which young women must negotiate these possibilities (Gill, 2007). Young women's ambivalent engagement with the available representations of womanhood in popular culture also indicates the limits of an agency discourse: they understand the artifice of airbrushing and photoshopping, yet, nevertheless, absorb these images as a normative benchmark for their own embodied selves (Baker, 2008; Renold, 2013). Persistent and ongoing inequalities between women and men are obscured in these contemporary narratives of self-sexualization (Coy & Garner, 2010; Gavey, 2012; Gill, 2012). These themes are significant when exploring young people's perspectives on pornography, as they signal the need for critical interrogation of connections between young women's sense of agency, embodied autonomy, and the unequal conventions of heterosexuality (Holland et al., 1998; Lamb & Peterson, 2012).

So, when Bay-Cheng (2015) makes a trenchant call to shift our attention from scrutinizing young women to examining the contexts in which they negotiate a sense of self and sexual encounters, examining pornography is one means to extend enquiry toward these contexts and influences. However, despite the exploration of young women's engagement with sexualized sexism, many silences about young men's perspectives on sexualization, pornography, and masculinities remain (Garner, 2012). Given the gendered asymmetry of victimization and perpetration in sexual violence, we suggest that it is critical to focus on how young women's 'space for action' (Jeffner, 2000) is limited by young men's behaviors, constructions of masculinities, and the influences of pornography.

Young People's Engagement with Pornography: The Gendered Contours

Surveys suggest that significant proportions of adolescents access, or are exposed to, online pornography, with estimates ranging from 42 percent in the United States in one older study (Wolak et al., 2007 reporting on a national survey of 1,422 young people aged 10–17 years from 2005) to 48 percent in the United Kingdom (Martellozzo et al., 2017, survey of 1,001 young people aged 11–16 years conducted in 2015). A difficulty in drawing comparative conclusions from the evidence base is that definitions of pornography (and 'young people') vary (Horvath et al., 2013). Very little research exists about young people from minoritised communities, LGBT adolescents, or those with impaired physical or intellectual capacity (Horvath et al., 2013). Much attention does not move beyond debates about an emphasis on how shockingly high the proportion of young people who have seen pornography is and how best to restrict access (e.g., through age restrictions and filters by Internet service providers). This overshadows the more subtle, nuanced considerations of how pornography influences young people's perspectives about women, men, and sex that we explore in this chapter.

In the United Kingdom, there has been increased concern from policy makers and politicians about the impacts that increased accessibility to pornography may be having on young people (Department for Culture, Media and Sport, 2016; Nash et al., 2015; Papadopolous, 2010). Ease of access to the Internet and online pornography has been a key catalyst for this anxiety. The Australian Senate also initiated an inquiry in 2016 into "Harm Being Done to Australian Children Through Access to Pornography on the Internet" that invited submissions on the extent of young people's consumption of pornography and its impact on healthy relationships. The final report accepted a correlation between exposure to pornography and harm, based on the evidence submitted by a range of experts from differing positions and disciplines (Commonwealth of Australia, 2016). Yet, as

Livingstone and Smith (2014, p.643) note, "research often stops at measuring children's exposure, apparently presuming that exposure to pornography or 'sexting' is inevitably harmful (or that children cannot report on any harm that results)." Peter and Valkenburg (2016) make a similar argument, perhaps more implicitly, when they note that research has rarely separated use of pornography from implications. Deeper exploration that integrates the differing dimensions of exposure to and engagement with pornography among female and male adolescents is a way to shed light on how use and implications might be linked.

A first step is to identify whether young women's and young men's engagement with pornography differs, and in what ways. Here the evidence base has built steadily over the last two decades and is unequivocal: young men and boys are more likely than girls and young women to be exposed to pornography; they are also more likely to access, seek, or use pornography; and they are exposed to or access pornography more frequently (e.g., Flood, 2009; Horvath et al., 2013; Martellozzo et al, 2017; Wolak et al., 2007). Boys and young men generally view pornography more positively and state that they view it primarily out of curiosity, while girls and young women generally report that it is unwelcome, socially distasteful, and that they feel much more uncomfortable than boys and young men when viewing pornography (Horvath et al., 2013). Young people's emotional responses to pornography are also revealing: surveys and focus groups consistently show that young women report shock and disgust, and young men sexual excitement (Flood, 2009; Martellozzo et al., 2017).

It is possible that these responses are rooted in social norms about sexuality that deny young women the possibility to be interested in sex, summarized by Bay-Cheng (2015, p. 281) as "be desirable, but not desiring." Young men report sexual excitement, for instance, in line with social gendered norms that equate masculinity with sexual prowess and conquest, although this connection is rarely expressed explicitly. For instance, in one study involving focus groups and interviews with 110 young people aged 13–19 years, participants reported that it was taken for granted that young men will use pornography – although a few were critical – and reported that it would be 'weird' for young women to do so (Coy et al., 2013). Gendered differences in use of pornography can, therefore, be understood as an expression of heteronormative codes of sexual behavior (see Holland et al., 1998). What is less often commented on is that young women's distress may be because of identification with how the women and girls in pornography are depicted (Flood, 2009; Kelly, 1988). In other words, the reason why young women report more negative reactions to pornography than young men may not simply be because of social codes that deny girls and women space to actively desire sex. Rather, and as we will explore through our own survey data in this chapter, young women recognize how women's bodies are subordinated and violated in pornography, and this worries and angers them.

The deeply heteronormative dynamic of contemporary pornography means that little research exists with LBGT young people about their views and experiences. There is evidence that young gay men turn to pornography to learn about sex since even where sex education exists it focuses on heterosex (Kubicek et al., 2010). Some have questioned what this might mean for how young men learn about masculinity and sexual expectations (Kendall, 2004). In a recent project in Scotland involving young people aged 14–20 years, LGBT participants perceived that pornography targets heterosexual men and were more critical of the sexism in it than heterosexual participants (Zero Tolerance, 2014).

So, with clearly gendered differences in deliberate use of pornography (Peter & Valkenburg, 2016), the next step to explore is motivation. Here, again, there is a consistent theme – in general, young people are seeking information about sex, in the absence of adequate sex education. Curiosity about naked bodies and sexual positions are often underneath this broader search for information (e.g., Martellozzo et al., 2017). As one young person reported in one of our research projects, pornography is "where most people learn about sex," even where this had not been their motivation in seeking or accessing pornography (Coy et al., 2013, p. 40). Some young people frame pornography as entertainment, again, a further reminder of the mainstreaming of pornography into popular culture.

Differences between young women and young men in reasons for seeking pornography remain stark. Our own survey of 1,002 young people (527 female, 472 male, three transgender) aged 16–21 years for the 2014 BBC documentary *'Porn: What's the Harm?'* identified clearly different reasons why young women and young men watch online pornography (Horvath & Coy, 2014). Almost one in five (17%, n=98/570) described the difference as "women for education, men for arousal"; in other words, women look for tips, men for sexual pleasure.

> I think men watch it to pleasure themselves, young women watch it because they think they can better themselves at sex if they do it like a female porn star on the screen. (Young man, 16 years)[1]

> I think girls generally look because they want to know what/how rather than guys who want to watch for enjoyment. Of course this is a gender stereotype but society's attitude does hold true for most of my friends. (Young woman, 17 years)

Tracing a relationship between how young people interpret what Meagan Tyler (2011) terms the 'sex of pornography' and their own sexual practices is not straightforward. Research that explores the impact of pornography must grapple with the perennial conundrums of measurement and attribution. It is extremely difficult to obtain accurate accounts of exactly when, what type, and how much pornography a young person accesses and whether any direct impact can be discerned and/or measured. Nevertheless, a strong imperative for such research has been the well-documented role of pornography as a "manual for sex education" (Flood, 2009; Hilton, 2007; Peter & Valkenburg, 2016; Rothman et al., 2015).

[1] Unattributed quotes in this chapter are from the, as yet unpublished, survey data. The survey was commissioned by the BBC, designed by us, and administered by ICM. Data was weighted to be nationally representative of all young people in the United Kingdom. The project received ethical approval from Middlesex University's Department of Psychology Ethics Committee.

Pornography and Young People's Sexual Norms

One dominant model for investigating the influence of pornography is sexual script theory, developed by Gagnon and Simon (1974). In this framework, an innate human sexuality is rejected in favor of a framework where sociocultural influences (e.g., the mass media) interact with interpersonal and intrapsychic adaptations (individual circumstances and cognition) to create a template for behavior. Adolescence is a key developmental stage for the creation of sexual scripts, as is their explicitly gendered nature (Wiederman, 2015; see Jackson, 1999 for a more detailed discussion). Feminists researching sexual violence have used this model to highlight how the dominant sexual script is highly gendered and prescribes heteronormative positions for men and women, focusing on privileging men's sexual interests over women's (Frith, 2009; Gavey, 2005; Hyde et al., 2008; Jackson, 1999; Jackson & Cram, 2003;). Studies about pornography that have used a sexual script model find a similar reinforcing of gender as a hierarchy (Bridges et al., 2016; Sun et al., 2016). Yet, sexual script theory is not without critique. Originating in symbolic interactionism, it has limited scope to incorporate social structures, power, and inequalities in the analysis of how sexual scripts are generated (Jackson, 1999). Others have suggested that sexual script theory lacks explanatory power since it does not account for the "mechanisms through which individuals acquire and maintain their respective sets of sexual scripts" (Wiederman, 2015, p. 17; see also Jackson, 1999). This is perhaps why it has gained such traction in research that seeks to establish the impact of pornography, where the aim has often been to identify a correlation between pornographic sexual scripts – so pornography as a mechanism – and sexual practices. How production of pornography draws on sexual scripts (Escoffier, 2007) has therefore been extended to explore how the enactment of such scripts in pornography might then influence viewers and users (e.g., Bridges et al., 2016; Sun et al., 2016). It is also the case that the concept of sexual scripts is used more widely. As Wiederman (2015) notes that sexual script is often used as a synonym for attitudes and norms, a much looser sense than its original formulation.

This broader conceptualization is a more helpful way of exploring the complexity of influences on sexualized beliefs and behaviors, while also allowing for how pornography reflects and reproduces wider social gendered norms. Few researchers claim any causal relationship between pornography and attitudes/behavior, noting instead the strength of correlations/associations. Most studies are also cross-sectional, although a small number are longitudinal and able to comment on change over time (Peter & Valkenburg, 2016). The content of pornography viewed by adolescents also requires further investigation and updating, as Peter and Valkenburg (2016) suggest, although inferences can be drawn from one analysis that reveals violence and aggression was present in 88 percent of scenes, and directed at women in 95 percent of these (Bridges, 2010).

This is the context in which several reviews of the impact of pornography on young people's attitudes and behaviors have been completed (e.g., Flood, 2009,

2016; Horvath et al., 2013; Peter & Valkenburg, 2016). These draw on studies conducted in the West with adolescents, and, despite their slightly different scopes, they reach strikingly similar conclusions. Michael Flood (2009) – a prominent scholar on pornography and young people – reviewed international research and divided evidence into emotional and psychological harms and those that affect sexual practices. His core thesis is that the differential patterns of deliberate consumption of pornography between young women and young men are reflected in its impact, leading to sexist and sexually objectifying attitudes and behavior. For young men, he contends, these may lead to greater likelihood of perpetrating sexual violence.

Horvath et al.'s (2013) rapid evidence assessment for the Children's Commissioner in England reviewed 276 papers published over a 30-year period from 1983 to 2013. Their conclusions reflected and expanded those by Flood (2009): pornography is linked to more sexually permissive attitudes, including greater acceptance of casual sex and unrealistic expectations of sex. These findings can be used to make a reactionary moralistic argument about pornography as a contaminant of childhood. But this analysis often obscures the impacts of sexualized sexism on attitudes toward women's bodies and constructions of femininities and masculinities, focusing instead on how pornography is inappropriately invading childhood (leaving implications for adults unacknowledged). As we have previously argued, critiques of sexualization in much popular and policy discourse often center on preservation of childhood innocence (Coy & Garner, 2012). However, also like Flood (2009), Horvath et al. (2013) support the necessity of a feminist analysis, reporting that "gender differences have emerged as a continuous and highly pertinent theme" of the studies they synthesized (p. 6). A core finding was that evidence shows pornography is associated with a belief that women are sex objects and less progressive gender role attitudes (e.g., male dominance and female submission).

Finally, Peter and Valkenburg's (2016) review of research on adolescents and pornography focuses on 1995–2015 to account for the mainstreaming of the Internet since the mid-1990s. Their 'tentative' conclusion is that the typical adolescent user of pornography is male, with a tendency for sensation seeking, and from a troubled family background. Emphasis is thus shifted toward the individual characteristics of young men rather than on social norms and expectations associated with masculinities. Most of the studies they reviewed were quantitative (66 of 75), and confirmed relationships between use of pornography and "less progressive" sexual beliefs. Findings from the nine qualitative studies further echo this, with more frequent use weakening progressive beliefs about women's equality.

In sum, each of these literature reviews on the impact of pornography on young people highlights gendered patterns in exposure to pornography and motivations for seeking or viewing it, and correlations with sexist attitudes, with less evidence about influences on sexual practices. The role of individual characteristics – mediators – is weighted differently. This further complicates relationships between use and implications. Peter and Valkenburg (2016) note that much public discourse about how adolescents navigate and are affected by pornography is based on a "simplistic notion" that young people just copy the sexual practices that they have seen (p. 526). They crystallize here the interpretative dilemma for those researching the impact of pornography: the impossibility of determining causation. Some studies do suggest that young people mimic what they see in pornography, and use it as a template for their sexual encounters. A greater proportion of boys seek to emulate it than of girls (Martellozzo et al., 2017). This chimes with the frequent observation that young people turn to pornography for sex education.

In Rothman et al.'s (2015) study of Black and Hispanic youth aged 16–17 years in the United States, just over half (54 percent) had tried out a sexual act that they had seen in pornography, and almost half (44 percent) had been asked to do something sexual that their partner had seen in pornography. Marston and Lewis (2014) found that young people aged 16–18 years in the United Kingdom offered pornography as a vocabulary of motive for engaging in anal sex, based on young men's desire to copy pornography, although the researchers argue this is only a "partial" explanation. Another adolescent in a recent UK study articulated a connection more explicitly.

> Yes and can learn bad things like watching anal sex and then some boys might expect anal sex with their partner. (Young woman, 13 years, cited in Martellozzo et al., 2017, p. 37)

Again, this represents a difference between young women and young men – "some boys might expect" – that is mirrored in our own BBC survey findings. Our questions explored whether young people perceived that online pornography affected what young women and young men expect from sex. We defined 'online pornography' as "images and/or films of people doing sexual acts online. This includes images and/or films that have been downloaded from the internet or sent electronically." Just over half of respondents (54%, n=536) reported that pornography affects what young women expect from sex. Common themes were that young women to be expected to be treated as a sex object, or would not expect sexual pleasure.

> Because they're seen to be an object and have to act or look in a certain way when sex should be much more than this. (Young woman, 16 years)

> A lot of the time pornography shows women being dominated by men, so women tend to expect that's how they should be treated. (Young woman, 19 years)

The question this must lead us to is: What do young women learn about sexual pleasure in relation to their subordination? Evidence of this can be discerned in the linguistic fields of the young people that participated in our survey. They described pornography in terms including "slaves," "degrading," "objects," that young women might feel "frightened" or "scared" by the treatment of women they saw. One in eight responses identified objectification as a theme in relation to young women's expectations (n=66/541, 45 young women and 21 young men) and one in six for those of young men (n=91/611, 62 young women and 29 young men).

> Women seem degraded and purely there for men's enjoyment. (Young woman, 20 years)
>
> You see yourself as an object to satisfy men and you start to view men and sex as rough and you expect it to be role play and so on. (Young woman, 18 years)

While Peter and Valkenburg (2016) note an evidence gap on the content of pornography viewed by adolescents, the discursive language that young people use to describe it gives strong clues about both what they see in pornography and how they make sense of pornographic representations of women, men, and sex.

Pornography and Sexual Coercion

The final theme from studies about pornography is the consistent correlation with attitudes and behaviors that support and/or condone sexual coercion (Flood, 2009; Horvath et al., 2013). Meta-analyses of research on adults' use and experience of pornography, using experimental data and samples of college students and the general public, suggest correlations between pornography, attitudes supporting sexual violence (e.g., Hald et al., 2010; Malamuth et al., 2012), and committing sexual aggression (e.g., Wright et al., 2016). Individual studies with young adults, typically samples of undergraduate college students, confirm these connections (e.g., Bridges et al., 2016).

The evidence base for adolescents is more limited (Rothman et al., 2015), but the extant findings are persuasive. Brown and L'Engle's (2009) longitudinal study (n=967 US high school students) found adolescent males (but not females) that used sexually explicit media were more likely to have perpetrated sexual harassment. Ybarra et al.'s (2011) later longitudinal study of 10–15 year olds in the United States (n=1588 at first wave, dropping to 1159 by the third) reported a correlation between sexual aggression and exposure to "X-rated" material. Unusually, in variance with other studies, they found that boys and girls were equally likely to perpetrate sexual aggression.

Flood's (2016) updating of his overview in a submission to the Australian Senate inquiry, situates his argument in a rapidly evolving context of "violent, hostile, sexist" online pornography. He describes pornography as "rape training," arguing that "exposure increases the risk of children and young people's perpetration of sexual assault" (Flood, 2016, p. 19). A recent European study of 4,564 young people aged 14–17 years in five countries (Bulgaria, Cyprus, Italy, England, Norway) supports this. The authors found a number of correlations between attitudes, behavior, and pornography (Stanley et al., 2016). Boys who watched pornography (using a self-defined concept) were more likely to have negative attitudes toward equality between women and men, and agree with the statement "women lead men on sexually and then complain about the attention they get." The perpetration of sexual coercion and abuse by boys was significantly associated with viewing online pornography.

In one recent UK study, one boy who participated in the focus groups also made an explicit link, telling the research team that:

> One of my friends has started treating women like he sees on the videos – not major – just a slap here or there. (Young man, 13 years, cited in Martellozzo et al., 2017, p. 37)

This young man draws attention to significant issues, not least the minimization of violence against young women. He also 'others' abusive behaviors, a distancing strategy deployed by men that Maria Garner (2016) terms "I'm not 'that' guy." This is another finding reflected in our BBC survey, where young men did not acknowledge their own role or that of their peers in making young women feel like objects; those who "force," call young women "sluts," or "treat in a degrading manner" were first of all ungendered "people," and cast in the classic perpetrator-as-other mold. In this way, young men claimed that their practices would not be influenced by pornography but others would.

More directly, three-quarters of respondents (74%, n=737) said that online pornography affects what young men expect from sex. The most common responses were that young men expect young women to behave like women in pornography, specifically as sex objects, and for women's bodies to look and act like those of women that perform in pornography.

> They assume that pornography is like real sex, they don't expect to have to actually pleasure women. (Young woman, 18 years)

> Guys will expect the chance for rougher sex, or for a girl to be very flexible etc. (Young man, 17 years)

What this demonstrates is how pornography creates and disseminates representations of women, men, and sex that are rooted in notions of masculine dominance and sexual objectification of women. Young people were very clear about this when reflecting on how they expect pornography to influence sexual norms, expectations, and practices.

> I think it could make a girl think they have to do more for guys, a lot of porn is male directed and so involves a lot of male satisfaction i.e. blowjobs. It also often puts women in degrading positions. Girls might then think they have to do these sorts of things to please guys. (Young woman, 21 years)[2]

> It can make a boy not look for love just look for sex and it can pressure us girls to act and look and behave in a certain way before we might be ready for it. (Young woman, 13 years, cited in Martellozzo et al., 2017, p. 37)

The way that young people describe other youths as using pornography as an aspirational template for sex is significant, as interventions with young people often focus on a version of media literacy that enables them to critically analyze pornography as unreflective of 'real' sexual intercourse, particularly in the absence

[2] Unattributed quotes in this section are also from the, as yet unpublished, survey data.

of emotional connection. Yet, young people are able to recognize the performative nature of online pornography, and many are keenly aware of how sexual pleasure and gender roles are exaggerated. Nevertheless, they perceive that it influences their peers (but as we have noted, not their own) expectations and practices. This suggests that interventions that aim to disrupt how pornography influences young people will need to extend beyond contrasts with 'real' sexual intimacy.

For example, research demonstrates that female and male adolescents exonerate young men's sexual coercion because of a belief in the inevitable male sexual drive (Hyde et al., 2008): often expressed as "boys will be boys." This evidence makes visible "the power of heterosexuality-as-masculinity" (Holland et al., 1998, p. 13) that young people so eloquently describe as the essence of pornography. Hence, young people's accounts of encountering online pornography illustrate that pornography reflects and reproduces an unequal gender order: men as sexually dominant, women as sexually available and always willing; men as 'doing,' women as 'being' (Holland et al., 1998).

Pornography, Coercion, and Sexual Consent: Joining the Dots

What does this body of evidence on sexualized sexism in popular culture and pornography mean for young people's negotiations of sex and sexual consent?

Perhaps another, linked, question is "what does 'freedom' to consent[3] mean in the wider contexts of heteronormativity and the sexist, racist sex of pornography?" If, as Emma Renold (2013) argues, consent is a social process negotiated in peer group cultures, then how do the messages of popular culture and pornography influence these social understandings of consent? Existing research suggests that the answer is strongly.

For example, at the level of *demonstrating* consent, the study of young people's views of pornography (Martellozzo et al., 2017) asked young people whether watching pornography has "led me to believe that sexual activities should be agreed to by everyone involved," where respondents had to rate how much they agreed or disagreed. Young people who did think that pornography taught them about consent and safe sex were more likely to be male than female. A quarter of young men (23%, n=55/241) who answered the question agreed, and only one in six young women (13%, n=25/195). The majority of young people did not think that pornography had shown them about mutual, respectful consent. This was also discussed in the focus groups.

> Consent is not shown [in online pornography] the man just does as he pleases without gaining consent. (Young woman, 13 years, cited in Martellozzo et al., 2017, p. 56)

[3] The Sexual Offences Act (2003) that applies to England and Wales defines consent in terms of both "freedom" and "capacity" to make the choice to agree to sex.

> It's not usually [shown] – they just have sex or the man usually dominates the woman. (Young man, 15 years, cited in Martellozzo et al., 2017, p. 56)

Some have framed sexualized sexism as a "conducive context"[4] for violence against women and girls (Coy et al., 2008, End Violence Against Women, 2011). A "conducive context" means building foundations that are necessary for violence to be possible; influencing attitudes and expectations and normalizing certain practices (Kelly, 2007). This is not to claim a causal relationship between sexualized popular culture and violence against women and girls: men and boys who perpetrate violence exercise agency. Rather, it is to draw attention to the links between representations of women's bodies as sexualized commodities, and gendered practices where men sexually violate women's bodies. Pervasive depictions of young women's bodies as objects and commodities in sexualized popular culture have been discursively linked to sexual exploitation of girls (Melrose, 2013). This is also one way of moving beyond an individualized framework of sexual script theory to conceptualizing how social, gendered inequalities that are embedded in sexualized sexism and pornography inform everyday relations between women and men (Connell, 2009).

There is limited data on the prevalence of sexual violence experienced by young people. A UK study involving 1,353 young people found that a third of girls (31 percent) had experienced sexual violence in the context of intimate partner relationships, with pressure used more frequently by abusive partners than physical force (Barter et al., 2009). The 2013 US Youth Risk Behavior Survey of 9,900 high school students indicated that around one in seven young women had experienced sexual violence from an intimate partner in the last 12 months (Vagi et al., 2015).

As Holland and colleagues (1998) argue, when young people's views about sexual practices are examined, they reveal both the gendered asymmetry of violence and coercion, and the meanings associated with masculinity, femininity, and heterosexuality that sit underneath: young men's instrumental sexuality and young women's "active engagement in the construction of their femininity" (p. 9). In Hyde et al.'s (2008) qualitative study involving focus groups with 102 young women and 129 young men aged 15–19 years in Ireland, they concluded that "references to sexual pressure emerged as an aside that were treated as almost unremarkable" (p. 486). While young women viewed coercion from young men as mundane and inevitable, young men did not report coercion by young women. They conclude that while young men might be under "social coercion" to perform hegemonic masculinity through sexual prowess, young women are subject to coercion by individual young men as well as the wider group pressures and expectations of appropriate femininity.

This finding was replicated in our research with young people in England about their understandings of sexual consent (Coy et al., 2013). Consent as a legal delineator of sexual violence varies by jurisdiction, since in some countries/states

[4] This concept was developed by Liz Kelly (2007) in relation to trafficking, and has since been applied to various forms of violence.

rape and sexual assault are defined by use of force. It is the lynchpin of the Sexual Offences Act 2003 in the United Kingdom for determining wanted sex from violence. While there is research with young adults – typically college students – about their understandings of consent (e.g., Muehlenhard et al., 2016), few studies focus on adolescents. The Office for the Children's Commissioner in England commissioned a study of how young people understood sexual consent and what influenced these understandings as part of a wider inquiry into sexual exploitation of children in group and gang contexts.[5] The core finding was that, while young people understand the concept of consent when applied to real life situations that contain contextual elements, a raft of assumptions about gendered sexual norms come into play. Young women who initiated sexual interaction (e.g., through sexting), wore sexualized clothing, or danced with strangers in clubs were held at least partially culpable for sexual violence. No such scrutiny was applied to young men's sexual activity (Coy et al., 2013).

The discussions with young people about sexual consent also included pornography (see Coy et al., 2013). Here it becomes apparent that the gendered messages in, and of, pornography are reflected in young people's understandings of sexual consent. These include the notion that men are seekers of sex, and entitled to sexual access to women's bodies. When men are thus cast as in control of when and how sex takes place, this justifies coercion, particularly of the "verbal cajolery" that "stretches boundaries" (Hyde et al., 2008). Alongside these constructions of appropriate masculine sexual behavior, sexual desire remains a missing discourse for young women (Holland et al., 1998). How this operates with respect to the "agency line" reference point (Bay-Cheng, 2015) that demands young women to appear sexually empowered and interested in and excited by pornography despite their awareness of its sexism needs further exploration (see also Vera-Gray, 2017).

Conclusion

A consistent finding from the existing evidence base exploring young people's perspectives is an association between boys engaging with pornography and sexually objectifying girls and women.

Young people are clear about the impact and influence of the gendered norms they are navigating and express that influences of online pornography reinforce gendered hierarchies where young women are expected to behave as sex objects for young men's pleasure. There is no one story, of course, as there are pockets of resistance and rejection, and indications that some young people do not identify, or disavow, these impacts. Young people also critically engage with the performative sexism of pornography. Yet, there is a *dominant* story that emerges when we make connections with their understandings of sexual consent, and data on gendered

[5] Horvath and colleagues' (2013) Rapid Evidence Assessment of the impact of pornography on young people was also commissioned as part of the same inquiry.

patterns of pornography use and impact. This is particularly important, given the consistent acknowledgment by young people themselves that online pornography is a poor model for consent or safe sex (Martellozzo et al, 2017). The different positioning of young men and young women in relation to sex, long documented in studies of young people's heterosexual relationships (e.g., Holland et al., 1998), appears to be strongly reinforced by engagement with online pornography. Young women and young men are not, when it comes to making sense of pornography and sexualized sexism, 'in the same boat' (Holland et al., 1998).

This underscores the relevance and importance of an analytic lens on gendered expectations when exploring young people's sexual norms and relationships. Current debates about the impact of pornography on young people have (re)opened a window for critical feminist perspectives to be heard. However, the policy focus – and much of the research – is on the dangers to corrupting childhood innocence. Generation is an important factor in addressing how young women and men's views, beliefs, and values are formed, but as the overarching theme of sexualized sexism is the perpetuation of stereotypes about women and men, an analysis of gender is absolutely critical. The seeming entrenchment of gender norms by adolescence is the driver for calls for compulsory sex and relationships education that addresses equality, consent, and pornography. Here the focus has to be not further shaming of young women but changing boys' behavior as a platform to ending sexual coercion and violence.

There is still so much about the intersections of social inequalities that we need to explore in the context of pornography: how LGBT young people negotiate the deeply heteronormative discourses of much popular culture and sexualized sexism; how race, ethnicity, colonialism, and minority community contexts shape perspectives and practices. We need to ask more searching questions about the role of pornography in sustaining dominant discourses and expectations, and about how young women and young men resist and reject them.

References

American Psychological Association (2007). *Report of the APA Task Force on the Sexualisation of Girls*. Washington, DC: American Psychological Association.

Australian Senate Committee (2008). *Sexualisation of Children in the Contemporary Media*. Canberra: Parliament House.

Baker, J. (2008). The Ideology of Choice: Overstating Progress and Hiding Injustice in the Lives of Young Women: Findings from a Study in North Queensland, Australia. *Women's Studies International Forum*, *31*, 53–64.

Bailey, R. (2011). *Letting Children be Children – Report of an Independent Review of the Commercialisation and Sexualisation of Childhood*. London: Department of Education.

Barter, C., McCarry, M., Berridge, D, & Evans, K. (2009). *Partner Exploitation and Violence in Teenage Intimate Relationships*. London: NSPCC.

Bay-Cheng, L. (2015). The Agency Line: A Neoliberal Metric for Appraising Young Women's Sexuality, *Sex Roles*, *73*(7–8), 279–291.

Bridges, A., (2010) Methodological Considerations in Mapping Pornography Content. In Boyle, K. (Ed.), *Everyday Pornography.* (34–49). London: Routledge.

Bridges, A., Sun, C. F., Ezzell, M., & Johnson, J. A. (2016). Sexual Scripts and the Sexual Behavior of Men and Women Who Use Pornography, *Sexualization, Media and Society.* doi:10.1177/2374623816668275.

Brown, J. D. & L'Engle, K. (2009). X-rated Sexual Attitudes and Behaviors Associated with U.S. Early Adolescents' Exposure to Sexually Explicit Media. *Communication Research*, *36*(1), 129, 151.

Commonwealth of Australia (2016). *Harm Being Done to Australian Children through Access to Pornography on the Internet.* Canberra: Environment and Communications References Committee.

Connell, R. W. (2009). *Gender*, *2nd edn*. Cambridge: Polity Press.

Coy, M. (2009). Milkshakes, Lady Lumps and Growing Up to Want Boobies: How the Sexualisation of Popular Culture Limits Girls' Horizons. *Child Abuse Review*, *18*(6), 372–383.

(2013). Children, Childhood and Sexualised Popular Culture. In Wild, J. (Ed.), *Exploiting Childhood.* London: Jessica Kingsley.

(2014). *'Pornographic Performances': A Review of Research on Sexualisation and Racism in Music Videos* London: End Violence Against Women.

Coy, M. & Garner, M (2010). Glamour Modelling and the Marketing of Self-Sexualisation: Critical Reflections *International Journal of Cultural Studies*, *13*(6), 657–675.

(2012). Definitions, Discourses and Dilemmas: Policy and Academic Engagement with the Sexualisation of Popular Culture *Gender & Education*, *24*(3), 285–301.

Coy, M., Kelly, L., Elvines, F., Garner, M., & Kanyeredzi, A. (2013). *Sex without Consent, I Suppose That Is Rape: How Young People in England Understand Sexual Consent.* London: Office of the Children's Commissioner.

Coy, M., Lovett, J., & Kelly, L. (2008). *Realising Rights, Fulfilling Obligations: A Template Integrated Strategy on Violence against Women for the UK.* London: EVAW.

Crenshaw, K. (1991). Mapping the Margins: Intersectionality, Identity Politics, and Violence against Women of Colour. *Stanford Law Review*, *43*(6), 1241–1299.

Department for Culture, Media and Sport (2016). *Child Safety Online: Age Verification for Pornography Consultation Response*. London: Department for Culture, Media and Sport. www.gov.uk/government/uploads/system/uploads/attachment_data/file/534965/20160705_AVConsultationResponseFINAL__2_.pdf.

Department for Education (2017). Schools to teach 21st century relationships and sex education. Press release www.gov.uk/government/news/schools-to-teach-21st-century-relationships-and-sex-education.

End Violence Against Women (2011). *A Different World Is Possible: A Call for Long-Term and Targeted Action to Prevent Violence against Women and Girls*. London: End Violence Against Women.

(2017). Government announces compulsory relationships & sex education in all schools. www.endviolenceagainstwomen.org.uk/451–2/.

Escoffier, J. (2007). Scripting the Sex: Fantasy, Narrative and Sexual Scripts in Pornographic Films. In Kimmel, M (Ed.), *The Sexual Self: The Construction of Sexual Scripts* (61–79). Nashville: Vanderbilt University Press.

Flood, M. (2009). The Harms of Pornography Exposure among Children and Young People. *Child Abuse Review*, *18*(6), 384–400.

(2016). Submission to the Inquiry into the harm being done to Australian children through access to pornography on the internet. www.aph.gov.au/DocumentStore.ashx?id=1966f277-6267-4398-a8a6-7be9f97358a8&subId=410413.

Frith, H. (2009). Sexual Scripts, Sexual Refusals and Rape. In Horvath, M. A. H. & Brown, J. (Eds.), *Rape: Challenging Contemporary Thinking* (99–122). Cullompton: Willan Publishing.

Gagnon, J. H. & Simon, W. (1974). *Sexual Conduct: The Social Sources of Human Sexuality*. Chicago: Aldine Press.

Garner, M. (2012). The Missing Link: The Sexualisation of Culture and Men, *Gender and Education*, *24*(3), 325–331.

(2016). Conflicts, Contradictions and Commitments: Men Speak about Sexualisation of Culture. (PhD thesis). London: London Metropolitan University.

Gavey, N. (2005). *Just Sex? The Cultural Scaffolding of Rape*. New York: Routledge.

(2012). Beyond "Empowerment"? Sexuality in a Sexist World, *Sex Roles*, *66*(11–12), 718–724.

Gill, R. (2007). Postfeminist Media Culture: Elements of a Sensibility, *European Journal of Cultural Studies 10*(2), 147–166.

(2011). Sexism Reloaded, or, It's Time to Get Angry Again! *Feminist Media Studies 11* (1), 61–71.

(2012). Media, Empowerment and the "Sexualization of Culture" Debates, *Sex Roles*, *66* (11–12), 736–745.

Girlguiding (2016). *Girls' Attitudes Survey*. London: Girlguiding UK.

Hald, G. M., Malamuth, N. M., & Yuen, C. (2010). Pornography and Attitudes Supporting Violence against Women, *Aggressive Behavior*, 36, 14–20.

Hill Collins, P. (1990). *Black Feminist Thought: Knowledge, Consciousness and the Politics of Empowerment*. New York: Routledge.

Hilton, G. L. S. (2007). Listening to the Boys Again: An Exploration of What Boys Want to Learn in Sex Education Classes and How They Want to Be Taught. *Sex Education*, *7*, 161–174.

hooks, b. (2004). *We Real Cool: Black Men and Masculinity*. London: Routledge.

Holland, J., Ramazanolgu, C., & Thomson, R. (1998). *The Male in the Head: Young People, Heterosexuality and Power*. London: The Tufnell Press.

Horvath, M. A. H., Alys, K., Massey, K., Pina, A., Scally, M., & Adler, J. R. (2013). *'Basically, Porn Is Everywhere . . . ': A Rapid Evidence Assessment on the Effects that Access and Exposure to Pornography Has on Children and Young People*. London: Office for the Children's Commissioner.

Horvath, M. A. H. & Coy, M. (2014). *Young People and Online Pornography Survey Findings*. Unpublished internal report for BBC3 Programme 'Porn: What's the harm?' London: Middlesex University and London Metropolitan University.

Hyde, A., Drennan, J., Howlett, E., & Brady, D. (2008). Heterosexual Experiences of Secondary School Pupils in Ireland: Sexual Coercion in Context. *Culture, Health & Sexuality*, *10*(5), 479–493.

Jackson, S. (1999). *Heterosexuality in Question*. London: Sage.

Jackson, S. M. & Cram, F. (2003). Disrupting the Sexual Double Standard: Young Women's Talk about Heterosexuality. *British Journal of Social Psychology*, *42*(1), 113–127.

Jeffner, S. (2000). Different Space for Action: The Everyday Meaning of Young People's Perception of Rape, Paper at ESS Faculty Seminar, University of North London, May 2000.

Kelly, L. (1988). *Surviving Sexual Violence*. Cambridge: Polity Press.

(2007). A Conducive Context: Trafficking of Persons in Central Asia. In Lee, M. (Ed.), *Human Trafficking* (73–91). Cullompton: Willan Publishing.

Kendall, C. N. (2004). Educating Gay Male Youth: Since When Is Pornography a Path towards Self Respect? *Journal of Homosexuality*, *47*, 83–128.

Kubicek, K., Beyer, W. J., Weiss, G., Iverson, E. & Kipke, M. D. (2010). In the Dark: Young Men's Stories of Sexual Initiation in the Absence of Relevant Sexual Health Information. *Health Education & Behavior*, *37*, 243–263.

Lamb, S. & Peterson, Z. (2012). Adolescent Girls' Sexual Empowerment: Two Feminists Explore the Concept. *Sex Roles*, *66*(11–12), 703–712.

Lamb, S. (2015). Revisiting Choice and Victimization: A Commentary on Bay-Cheng's Agency Matrix. *Sex Roles*, *73*(7–8), 292–297

Larasi, I. (2013, November 10). Why must we accept the casual racism in pop videos? *The Observer*. www.theguardian.com/commentisfree/2013/nov/10/black-women-music-industry-sex.

Livingstone, S. & Smith, P. (2014). Annual Research Review: Harms Experienced by Child Users of Online and Mobile Technologies: The Nature, Prevalence and Management of Sexual and Aggressive Risks in the Digital Age. *Journal of Child Psychology and Psychiatry*, *55*(6), 635–654.

Malamuth, N. M., Hald, G. M., & Koss, M. (2012). Pornography, Individual Differences in Risk and Men's Acceptance of Violence against Women in a Representative Sample. *Sex Roles*, 66, 427–439.

Marston, C. & Lewis, R. (2014). Anal Heterosex among Young People and Implications for Health Promotion: A Qualitative Study in the UK. *BMJ Open*, *4*, e004996.

Martellozzo, E., Monaghan, A., Adler, J. R., Davidson, J., Leyva, R., & Horvath, M. A. H. (2017). *"I Wasn't Sure It Was Normal to Watch it . . . "A Quantitative and Qualitative Examination of the Impact of Online Pornography on the Values, Attitudes, Beliefs and Behaviours of Children and Young People*. London: Middlesex University, NSPCC, OCC. (Revised version, May 2017).

McRobbie, A. (2009). *The Aftermath of Feminism: Gender, Culture and Social Change*. London: Sage.

Melrose, M. (2013). Twenty-First Century Party People: Young People and Sexual Exploitation in the New Millennium. *Child Abuse Review*, *22*(3), 155–168.

Muehlenhard, C. L., Humphreys, T. P., Jozkowski, K. N., & Peterson, Z. D. (2016). The Complexities of Sexual Consent among College Students: A Conceptual and Empirical Review, *Journal of Sex Research*, *53*(4–5), 457–487.

Nash, V., Adler, J. R., Horvath, M. A.H., et al. (2015). *Identifying the Routes by which Children View Pornography Online: Implications for Future Policy-Makers Seeking to Limit Viewing*. London: Department of Media, Culture and Sport.

Papadopoulos, L. (2010). *Sexualisation of Young People Review*. London: Home Office.

Peter. J. & Valkenburg, P. (2016). Adolescents and Pornography: A Review of 20 Years of Research. *Journal of Sex Research*, *53*(4–5), 509–531.

Renold, E. (2013). *Boys and Girls Speak Out: A Qualitative Study of Children's Gender and Sexual Cultures*. Cardiff: Cardiff University.

Renold, E. & Ringrose, J. (2011). Schizoid Subjectivities? Re-Theorizing Teen Girls' Sexual Cultures in an Era of 'Sexualization', *Journal of Sociology 47*(4), 389–409.

Rose, T. (2008). *The Hip Hop Wars: What We Talk about When We Talk about Hip Hop-and Why It Matters*. New York: Basic Books.

Rothman, E. F., Kaczmarsky, C., Burke, N., Jansen, E., & Baughman, A. (2015). "Without Porn . . . I Wouldn't Know Half the Things I Know Now": A Qualitative Study of Pornography Use among a Sample of Urban, Low-Income, Black and Hispanic Youth. *Journal of Sex Research*, *52*(7), 736–746.

Stanley, N., Barter, C., Wood, M., et al. (2016). Pornography, Sexual Coercion and Abuse and Sexting in Young People's Intimate Relationships: A European Study. *Journal of Interpersonal Violence*. doi:10.1177/0886260516633204.

Sun, C., Bridges, A., Johnson, J. A., & Ezzell, M. (2016). Pornography and the Male Sexual Script: An Analysis of Consumption and Sexual Relations. *Archives of Sexual Behavior*, *45*(4), 983–994.

Tolman, D., Anderson, S. M., & Belmonte, K. (2015). Mobilizing Metaphor: Considering Complexities, Contradictions, and Contexts in Adolescent Girls' and Young Women's Sexual Agency. *Sex Roles*, *73*(7–8), 298–310.

Tyler, M. (2011). *Selling Sex Short: The Pornographic and Sexological Construction of Women's Sexuality in the West*. Newcastle upon Tyne: Cambridge Scholars Press

Tyler, M. & Quek, K. (2016). Conceptualizing Pornographication: A Lack of Clarity and Problems for Feminist Analysis. *Sexualization, Media and Society*. doi:10.1177/2374623816643281.

Vagi, K., Olsen, E. O. M., Basile, K., & Vivolo-Kantor, A. (2015). Teen Dating Violence (Physical and Sexual) among US High School Students: Findings from the 2013 National Youth Risk Behavior Survey. *JAMA Pediatrics*, *169*(5), 474–482.

Vera-Gray, F. (2017) www.womenonporn.org/.

Wiederman, M. W. (2015). Sexual Script Theory: Past, Present, and Future. In DeLamater, J. & Plante, R. F. (Eds.), *Handbook of the Sociology of Sexualities, Handbooks of Sociology and Social Research*. New York: Springer.

Wolak, J., Mitchell, K., & Finkelhor, D. (2007). Unwanted and Wanted Exposure to Online Pornography in a National Sample of Youth Internet Users *Pediatrics 119*(2), 247–257.

Women and Equalities Committee (2016). *Sexual Harassment and Sexual Violence in Schools*. London: House of Commons.

Wright. P. J., Tokunaga, R. S., & Kraus, A. (2016). A Meta-Analysis of Pornography Consumption and Actual Acts of Sexual Aggression in General Population Studies. *Journal of Communication*, *66*(1), 183–205.

Ybarra, M., Mitchell, K. J., Hamburger, M., Diener-West, M., & Leaf, P. J. (2011). X-Rated Material and Perpetration of Sexually Aggressive Behavior among Children and Adolescents: Is There a Link? *Aggressive Behavior 37*, 1–18.

Zero Tolerance (2014). *"He's the Stud and She's the Slut" Young People's Attitudes to Pornography, Sex and Relationships*. Edinburgh: Zero Tolerance.

Family

24 Puberty as Biopsychosocial Enfolding

Mothers' Accounts of their Early-Developing Daughters

Celia Roberts

Understood as the physical process of sexual development, puberty has traditionally been separated from the psychosocial processes of maturation studied by social scientists and humanities scholars. The rich feminist sociological literature on girlhood, for example, has had little to say about pubertal processes, despite an intense interest in sexuality and bodies (see, e.g., Attwood & Smith, 2011; Harris, 2004; Renold & Ringrose, 2013). Medical researchers have also adhered to this division of labor, offering research on the physical elements of puberty without addressing psychological experience or socio-material environments (see, e.g., Bouvattier & Pienkowski, 2016). Developmental psychologists have made some headway into bridging these gaps, with recent work studying the connections between early life trauma, hormonal activity, pubertal timing, and psychosocial outcomes for individuals, but such studies tend to reproduce distinctions between biological, psychological, and social processes in their design and reporting. Negriff et al., for example, produce diagrams of connection in which early trauma, cortisol levels, and delinquency are boxes joined by arrows in structural equation models (Negriff et al., 2015). Working within the interdisciplinary field of Feminist Technoscience Studies (FTS), in contrast, I want to argue for a very different mode of thinking about puberty: one that troubles conventional distinctions between the biological, psychological, and the social.

The need for a new approach, in my view, intensifies amid recent scientific and public debates about the changing nature of contemporary puberty. As described in *Puberty in Crisis: The Sociology of Early Sexual Development* (Roberts, 2015), many scientists and clinicians claim that the timing of female puberty is shifting. While in the 1960s only 1 percent of girls would sexually develop before their ninth birthday, now up to 40 percent of some populations in both rich and poor countries have this experience (Aksglaede et al., 2009; Herman-Giddens et al., 1997; Parent, 2003; Rubin et al., 2009). While such claims have been contested, the majority scientific and medical view is that population-level changes in female pubertal timing are apparent. The findings for boys are much less clear. Although some authors argue that a related, less dramatic trend is becoming evident in boys, early-onset puberty is 10–15 times more prevalent in girls (Bouvattier, 2016, p. 67).

To date, there is no consensus on the causes of these widespread, population-level changes; whether they are the result of environmental toxins, adiposity (fatness), childhood stress, or other, as yet unknown, factors. The consequences of early sexual development also remain contested: Does early onset puberty cause long-term physical harm? What are the shorter-term physical effects? And are there worrying short- and/or long-term psychosocial outcomes? While the idea of girls starting to develop at 6, 7, or 8 might fill many of us with anxiety, is there really anything to worry about? And why has boys' puberty not (yet?) changed in the same way?

In *Puberty in Crisis*, I explored medical and scientific articulations of early developing girls, historicizing the ways in which early puberty is measured, analyzing claims about its epidemiological spread, and critically engaging with research on its causes and effects (Roberts, 2015). I also examined clinical research on the use of hormonal treatments (so-called puberty blockers) in early developing girls. This work is a contribution to the field of FTS. Although ethnographic in orientation, the research was largely text-based: my 'objects' were published scientific papers and books, pharmaceutical advertising, policy literatures, and popular culture, public policy, and environmentalist representations. Working through and with this diverse set of texts, I argued that puberty is a form of biopsychosocial enfolding – an experience or phenomenon that exemplifies the impossibility of disarticulating the biological, social, or psychological as distinct 'factors' contributing to sexual development. Using feminist corporeality theory (Butler, 1993; Grosz, 1994; Wilson, 2004), this argument deliberately troubles both traditional understandings of bodies and conventional disciplinary boundaries of knowledge production. This trouble is intended to be productive – theorizing puberty as biopsychosocial enfolding should build a richer understanding of contemporary changes in sexual development and help girls and those who care about them to get on better with this sometimes challenging experience.

FTS' Accounts of Bodies

FTS is a 'branch' of Science and Technology Studies (STS), an interdisciplinary field that engages with scientific knowledge and practices as its object, asking "How does science get done?" Scientific research, for STS scholars, does not simply provide facts and arguments but tells stories that literally articulate bodies. Borrowed from Donna Haraway, 'articulate' here carries a double meaning: that relating to speech (to bring something into language) and that pertaining to connection (as in an articulated mechanical joint) (Haraway, 1997). Bodies (human and non-human) in this way of thinking are articulated with and through science, technology, and medicine, as well as other powerful cultural discourses. In contemporary worlds, bodies neither preexist encounters with science, technology, and medicine, nor constitute 'blank slates' on which cultural meanings are straightforwardly inscribed. Rather, they are the dynamic outcomes of ongoing relations between a wide range of actors and forces, and, thus, as Haraway writes,

> syntactically and materially ... always a verb, or at least a gerund. Always in formation, embodiment is ongoing, dynamic, situated, and historical. No matter what the chemical score for the dance – carbon, silicon, or something else – the partners in infoldings of the flesh are heterogeneous. That is, the infolding of others to one another is what makes up the knots we call beings or, perhaps better, following Bruno Latour, things. Things are material, specific, non-self-identical, and semiotically active. (Haraway, 2008, pp. 249–250)

Various FTS scholars trace the "infoldings of the flesh" that constitute particular health conditions. Analyzing scientific claims that Black Americans are more likely to suffer from hypertension than their White counterparts, for example, Anne Fausto-Sterling argues that an individual's experience of racism and structural inequality may cause hypervigilance, a way of being in the world that is connected to forms of biological stress (including raised cortisol) that increase the likelihood of hypertension (Fausto-Sterling, 2004, p. 9). Writing with colleagues Coll and Lamarre in two papers on the development of human sex differences through early childhood, Fausto-Sterling argues that "experience changes the body and is not merely driven by events internal to the individual" (Fausto-Sterling et al., 2012a, 2012b, p. 1770). Echoing Haraway, these arguments trouble distinctions between 'biological' and 'social' forces, suggesting (rather controversially for some feminist scholars and social scientists for whom reference to biological forces are possibly essentialist) physiological pathways between social experience and health outcomes mediated by hormonal and neural signaling.

Exploring the history of genetic science, Evelyn Fox Keller makes a related, but more strongly stated, claim that it makes no sense to attempt to separate the role of "genes" and "the environment" in articulating bodies: "It makes useless to proceed by trying to separate nature from nurture and looking at how they interact. The causal effects of nature and nurture on development are simply not separable" (Keller, 2010, p. 81). For Keller this is as much a question of research practice – what questions get asked, and how are they answered – as of intrinsic logic. Research that asks 'how much' of a particular bodily condition (e.g., early-onset puberty) is determined by genes and how much by the environment are both "unanswerable" and "meaningless" (Keller, 2010, p. 5). Similarly to Haraway, Keller uses "unfolding" to describe the complex relations of forces that produce bodies:

> A cell's DNA is always and necessarily embedded in an immensely complex and entangled system of interacting resources, that are, collectively, what give rise to the development of traits. Not surprisingly, the causal dynamics of the process by which development unfolds are also complex and entangled, involving causal influences that extend upward, downward and sideways. (Keller, 2010, p. 51)

Exploring related territory, but using examples from physics rather than biology, Karen Barad uses the term "intra-action" to describe processes of physical becoming (Barad, 2007). For Barad, bodies emerge in intra-actions of a wide range of forces and actors, none of which, in her view, precede the intra-action (hence her refusal to use the more typical 'interaction,' which implies the mingling of preexisting entities). For Barad, bodies, as active, changing and complex entities, continually intra-act with the practices, objects, and discourses that measure, define, diagnose, and treat them. Scientific and biomedical measuring practices, then, are part of what Barad would call the "apparatus" of contemporary puberty; radically, the apparatus is understood here to be ontologically performative. Rather than describing or intervening into already existing entities, these practices literally bring phenomena such as bodies and worlds into being.

For me, taking these approaches into the field of early sexual development means trying to come to grips with scientific and medical articulations – through reading scientific and medical texts, listening to expert discourse, and/or observing relevant practices (e.g., of treating early developing children or conducting lab experiments) – and attempting to understand how these fold in with other forces to produce certain kinds of bodies. It may also mean talking to those living with early-onset puberty to learn how these medical and scientific formulations are articulated with personal lives and broader cultural concerns.

Focusing on scientific, medical, environmentalist, and popular media discourses, however, *Puberty in Crisis* has little to say about the lived experience of early-onset puberty. Worried that such attention might add too much additional burden to children who were perhaps already feeling self-consciously 'different' from their peers, I had not at that point conducted interviews with, or observations of, families where a child was developing early. (Interestingly, the existing psychological and medical literatures also have had little to say about girls' or parents' qualitative experiences of early onset puberty with one notable important exception (Pinto, 2007).) After completing the book, however, I became increasingly curious about how girls and their families were living with early-onset puberty. Wanting also to intervene in a more direct way in public and policy debates, in 2016, then, I initiated a consultative study, collaborating with the Sex Education Forum (a UK umbrella organization for relevant charities, government entities, schools, and individuals) in order to develop better information for sex educators, teachers, and school nurses about early sexual development. We surveyed 127 school nurses and sex educators, interviewed eight of these in depth, and also tried to find parents of early developers who were happy to speak about their experiences. This work is ongoing: to date I have interviewed six mothers (tellingly, my attempts to recruit 'parents' has so far led to mothers), and a policy briefing for educators, nurses, and parents is in preparation. This chapter focuses on the interviews with mothers, exploring if and how an understanding of sexual development as biopsychosocial enfolding plays out in their accounts of their early-developing daughters. What do mothers' stories tell us about early-onset puberty and how we might best address it?

Methods

This consultative study about the impact of early sexual development on families and schools was funded by Lancaster University's 'Impact and Knowledge

Exchange Fund' and ethical approval for the empirical work was granted by Lancaster University's Research Ethics Committee. The core aim of the interviews with parents was to elicit accounts of living with and caring for early-developing girls. Interviews followed a loose structure and were undertaken face-to-face or on the telephone. They were audio recorded and fully transcribed. I use pseudonyms and have changed identifying details to protect anonymity in the following.

The analysis undertaken here is diffractive: it resists the formal coding of transcripts that springs from grounded theory's suggestion that theorization should be lead solely from data (Davies, 2014; Jackson & Mazzei, 2012; Mazzei, 2014; Taguchi, 2012). Rather than trying to accurately reflect the interviewee's world or worldview or to find similarities across groups of transcripts, diffractive analysis 'plugs concepts in' (Deleuze, 1995; Mazzei, 2014) in order to elaborate possible, diverse accounts, fully aware that any particular articulation or narrative is an interested, situated, and partial one. This style of analysis is informed by FTS, particularly the work of Haraway and Barad, which suggests that all scientific accounts (including social scientific ones) are actually diffractive, even when they aspire to be reflective of truth or reality.

Practically, the diffractive approach entails careful listening to recordings and reading of transcripts and theoretical texts with an eye for the intra-action of words (semiotics) and human and non-human things (materialities). Lisa Mazzei describes this as "reading-the-data-while-thinking-the-theory" (Mazzei, 2014, p. 743). In this chapter I discuss four case studies, highlighting the details of different stories rather than looking for cross-cutting themes. My analysis is informed by my theoretical orientation toward understanding puberty as biopsychosocial: in (re)writing the mothers' stories I am looking for materials with which to theorize the situated material semiotics and actions constituting contemporary pubertal embodiment. The case study method is well suited to this approach because it openly acknowledges the situated story re/writing elements of qualitative research. The stories told here are selected and rephrased by me.

Diffractive analysis of interview data with parents provides us with important routes into the material semiotic enfoldings constituting early sexual development; routes that are different to those I have explored elsewhere. Mothers' accounts of their daughters' bodies, their joint encounters with medicine and their ways of living together through early-onset puberty and its associated materialities (blood, sweat, clothing, swimming pools, injections, toilets, and sweets among other things) help us to understand this experience better and to notice where and how scientific and biomedical figurations become entangled with cultural and personal narratives of growth and development, sexuality, sex, and gender. As Mazzei argues,

> Such an analysis offers a way to consider the entanglement of bodies, texts, relationships, data, language and theory that we are just beginning to understand and that presents the possibility of much productive potential for qualitative researchers. (Mazzei, 2014, p. 745)

Case Study 1: "It's Hard to Know Where the Child Ends and the Hormones Start"

"We're just a normal family," explains Tina, White British mother of four young children. One experience that makes their lives different, however, is that at age two her daughter Maddy started to develop a breast bud. At first, Tina was told by her general practitioner (GP) that this was "puppy fat." Retrospectively, Tina argues that she knew that something more serious was happening to her daughter: "It was mother's instinct – I knew it wasn't right for her to look like that on top." After Maddy developed a second breast bud when she was three, Tina secured an appointment at a specialist unit in a teaching hospital in a local city. Here, much to her shock, a diagnosis of precocious puberty was delivered and a decision made to immediately inject Maddy with "puberty-blocking" medication (gonadotropin-releasing hormone analogs or GnRHa). Despite her preexisting concerns about her daughter, Tina recalls this as a "horrible day": she had never heard of precocious puberty and was not given any time to process the diagnosis before being asked to agree to Maddy receiving an intramuscular injection:

> I was completely in shock, I didn't – I was just, 'You've got to do what you've got to do haven't you?' And Maddy – we didn't have to prepare Maddy for it. It was just like ten minutes later she'd had the injection. Even when they'd given the diagnosis, I phoned my partner (because my partner couldn't get a day off to come along) .., and I was just in pieces because I'd never even heard of it before until they said that they were doing blood tests for this precocious puberty. I obviously went home and researched it and I'd never even heard of it until that day.

Since this appointment, Maddy has received monthly injections at the hospital. Her breast development has stopped, but the buds have not disappeared. She is 4 and will be starting school soon. Her mother worries that she will be teased, and hopes that the buds will disappear.

Tina's ignorance of precocious puberty is not unusual: this is a rare and little-discussed condition. Tina told me that none of her family had heard of it, and that the teachers at her child's school were also "all . . . completely shocked" to hear about Maddy's sexual development. This shock is certainly understandable – most of us do not expect 3- or 4-year-olds to be entering puberty – but does seem to carry a particular cultural freight and deep ambivalence relating to childhood sexuality (Roberts, 2015). Despite her attempt to educate herself and getting involved in relevant parents' organizations, Tina still feels ill-informed. No one has given her guidance on how to talk to her daughter about her condition or how to manage her early physical development. Tina also feels that Maddy's behavior has become more challenging since the development started but cannot clearly articulate why. As she succinctly puts it, "it's hard to know where the child ends and the hormones begin."

Maddy, in the meantime (according to her mother) is not so concerned about her breast buds. She is, however, profoundly concerned about the hormonal injections. Indeed, she has developed a serious needle phobia that interferes with treatment.

At her most recent hospital visit, despite receiving a sedative, she had to be held down to receive the injection in her buttocks. Tina reports: "... they had to pin her down again. It's horrible to watch her but I know she has to have it done if she wants a normal childhood." A "normal" childhood, for Tina, is one without sexual development. She assumes that Maddy will, as the doctors plan, continue to receive the injections until she is at a "normal" age to go through puberty (11 years) (see Bouvattier, 2016, p. 71). Coming off the medication at that point, for Tina, will mean "Maddy's just going to be a normal teenager going through it with her friends, I'm hoping."

In Tina's narrative, hormones – both endogenous and pharmaceutical – are key actors in early-onset puberty. Anxiety, needles, and physical restraint dominate clinical encounters, despite medical intervention being figured as necessary to ensuring a present and future normality. Conventional accounts of hormonal action in puberty – that hormones lead to moodiness – are also at play here, although Tina has difficulties making these stick to her 4-year-old child. Her partner, in contrast, she reports, thinks that Maddy is difficult because her mother is "too lenient" because she "has an illness": he does not blame the hormones.

Multiple materialities also figure in Tina's attempts to explain her daughter's condition to me and to others. In a tabloid newspaper article she read a list of possible causes of early-onset puberty, including excessive junk food consumption, coming from a single-parent family and not having older brothers. Reading this list was, she states, "really horrible": her daughter did not fit into any of these categories, which were, in any case, guilt inducing. In the end, with support from Maddy's clinicians, Tina has accepted a position of somewhat fatalist non-knowing: "It's one of them things that she's unlucky to be one of them children that's got it. ... It's one of those questions you can't answer. ... I don't actually know the reason why she's got it." Having spent a lot of time with the scientific literature, I feel this position is quite realistic. Beyond specific brain tumors, there are few clear answers as to why any particular child experiences early-onset puberty. Although part of known story about early development, junk food, paternal absence, and (over)weight are not materialities that articulate Maddy's experience for Tina.

Case Study 2: "I Just Had These Moments of Deep Sadness that She Was Going to Accelerate Out of Childhood"

White, middle-class Kate lives in a large English city with her two daughters and husband. At seven her oldest daughter, Lara, started to complain that her vulva was wet. Her parents did not take this seriously until she started developing hips and breasts at eight. When I interviewed her mother, Lara was well into puberty:

> It's not like precocious puberty, like she hasn't started her period or anything like that, but she's now nine and a half and she has pronounced swelling breasts, pubic

> hair, body odour, traditional like puberty body odour and vaginal discharge and it feels very hormonal, mood swings and things . . . She's in Year Four [ages eight to nine]. . . . [I]t just took me completely by surprise.

Looking for information online and discussing with family and friends (some of whom were medical professionals), Kate realized quite quickly that Lara was going through early-onset puberty. "Luckily," Kate says, they had already shared some puberty books, so Lara could quickly come to an understanding of what was happening too.

In the interview, Kate discussed the differences between her own and her daughter's emotional responses to this surprising situation. Kate describes feeling upset, anxious, and uncertain about what the immediate and longer-term outcomes might be. Having read some scientific research on the Internet, she became particularly worried about whether Lara's height might be "stunted" and that she might end up as "a short woman in our family of tall people."[1] She wondered whether her daughter would start menstruating early and how this might be managed at primary school and was highly concerned how Lara might be treated in public spaces. Kate felt distressed that she might have to arm her daughter against catcalling and other sexual behavior in the street.

In articulating her concerns to me, Kate referred to her own experience of going through puberty in high school, noting a disjuncture between Lara's physical development and still-to-develop interest in sexuality, which was not part of her own experience:

> . . . sexuality has not really entered the way she thinks about things yet. . . . that hasn't blossomed at all, so it's the out-of-synch-ness in terms of our traditional understanding and definitely my traditional understanding. I feel looking back that my body development was in synch with that bit of my identity coming to the fore and being important to me. . . . I can't quite get my head round those two things differently, 'cause for me they were inextricably linked.

Here, 'traditional' conceptualizations of puberty as the dawn of teenage sexuality clash with Kate's understanding of her daughter as not yet sexual. Early-onset puberty is articulated as an "out-of-synch" material-semiotic experience; a mismatch between bodies, identities, and cultural understandings.

Kate reports that Lara is strong in her resistance of her mother's expressions of concern. Pubertal development is common among Lara's year-four (ages eight to nine) friends: four other girls in the class and some boys seem to have started puberty. When her mother told her about our interview and asked if there was anything she wanted her to say, Lara replied "Oh it's just normal mum!" Telling this story, Kate continued, "[So] I just didn't ask anything more. I was just like 'Ok, this is not fucking normal for me.., but for her [it is]." Although her fears "that it would become a point of upset or social anguish for her in some way," have not come true, Kate notes that Lara has developed techniques to hide her body while getting

[1] Height loss is the most frequently studied physical outcome of early development (for a critical discussion see Roberts, 2015, pp. 175–178).

changed into sports or swimming gear. Lara has also adjusted her clothing – now favoring looser clothes, in part, perhaps, to hide her breasts and hips. Her mother attends to these new desires:

> She doesn't like to wear really skimpy swimming costumes and the way she deals with it is to be really firm and clear and she says, 'I don't want that one, I want one with arms,' and then I just get that one for her.

As these strategies indicate, clothes can articulate puberty in undesired ways: Lara burst into angry tears when Kate purchased her a bra, an unwanted step too far into teen age. Here, mother and daughter struggle to define what is 'normal' and to negotiate the boundaries of non-sexual child/sexual(ized) young person that are often contested at puberty. Lara uses clothes and body practices of un/dressing to hide her changing body, but yet resists her mother's figuration of her development as "not normal" and rejects some of her attempts to be helpful.

Like Tina, Kate notices emotional changes in her early-developing daughter: "wild kind of emotional cadences" can leave Lara "rolling around on the floor in a state of utter [distress]." She describes Lara as "stroppy," as having sleeping difficulties, and not wanting to play with her younger sister in the way she used to. Like Tina, Kate finds it impossible to disentangle the effects of pubertal processes from the possible psychosocial effects of early development in thinking through these shifts. Is Lara behaving in these ways because she is worrying about her development, or does puberty directly cause distress? In Tina's terms, where does the child end and the hormones start in all this?

Cultural narratives or 'traditional understandings' of puberty haunt Kate's narrative in other ways. Although Lara insists she is "normal," Kate feels upset about a loss of a version of family life, remembered from her own experience of middle childhood as a time of pleasurable play and family time, free from teenage or adult concerns about sexuality:

> I just had these moments of deep sadness that she was going to accelerate out of the bit of childhood that I'd really been looking forward to being a parent of . . . [I was also worried about] the impact on Olivia, my youngest one, of having this kind of histrionic teenage kind of developing older sister that isn't like the eight year old she could play with when she was six . . .. I don't think Olivia's going to have the same journey through at all, so that's strange. And so, yes, it's a mourning of a version of our family which I had imagined I think.

Kate is consoled by other materialities, however. Although breasts, bras, and pubic hair might disrupt visions of in-sync family life, roller skates and Harry Potter indicate appropriate childhood pleasures:

> I think a lot of the turmoil has been in me and [husband] and not for her really. I mean obviously she's coping with stuff . . . Occasionally [we're] feeling like . . . she's lost a version of childhood. But it's probably quite interesting because she's definitely still a kid now, so the dust is settling a bit you know? She still wants to read *Harry Potter* and she wants to roller skate and she wants to do all these things.

Concerned about "stunted growth" and menstruation, Kate sought medical advice early on. She knew that puberty-blocking medication could be prescribed for precocious puberty, and was worried that this might also be necessary for Lara:

> I guess when it first happened . . . I was like, 'Oh God, so within a year there'll be periods! And . . . so maybe we should take drugs to stop it!' . . . I'd heard that that can happen and in fact I've got a colleague whose daughter started her period at maybe six and did go to the Children's Hospital and got it stopped and then started again . . . [M]y initial instinct was 'Let's go to the doctor and get this sorted out because this is wrong,' even though I knew that that was wrong. And then the doctor was really dismissive. . . . [O]ur GP . . . said 'This is normal, this is happening more and more, there's nothing to be done.' She was eight.

The GP's response helped Kate to manage her anxiety but did not fully allay her fears, particularly about sexual objectification. Resonating with popular feminist discourses about 'everyday sexism,' these concerns were fuelled by others' reminiscences of objectification at puberty:

> [A] couple of my friends, early developers themselves . . . had very strong reactions ('Oh my God, it was awful! The objectification from older men, from my dad's friends, from people in the street! It was just awful, it changed my life, it changed what I felt about my body, who I was in society!') and it really, really affected me. And they were talking about developing at kind of nine, ten! And I was [talking about an even younger age] – so you know, that was super hard.

Kate's response to this concern was to strongly affirm positive female embodiment and sexuality, providing her children with as positive a model of female and (hetero)sexual desire as she could by being naked at home, "proud" of her own pubic hair, and encouraging her daughters' athletic interests.

When we met, Kate was, like Tina, struggling to understand why her daughter was going through early puberty. After reading material on the Internet and thinking and debating the issue with family and friends, she surmised that the increase in early-onset puberty was a mixture of positive evolutionary change and increased environmental toxicity:

> So I do feel like the majority cause must be that we are healthier, larger, bigger and that the old evolutionary trigger is still kicking when kids are viable; you know, when the body becomes strong and ready to reproduce. I do feel like that. But that then doesn't totally answer for me why there are lots of tall skinny girls in Lara's life and in our lives who aren't going through it. . . . I do have moments when I feel like there are a lot of chemicals in the world that we don't understand what they do. . . . I think it's a combination of those kind of long swathes of evolution but also some short term environmental stimulus that must be having some kind of impact . . . That's the best I've come up with.

Although it cannot explain why her healthy, slim, and athletic daughter should be going through puberty earlier than her "tall, skinny peers," this theory gives Kate something positive to hang on to. Lara has always been well: perhaps her early development is a sign of this, rather than of pathology. Here, Kate escapes the more mother-blaming implications of some public discourses that Tina had felt hurt by –

that early puberty was a result of family formation, or excessive junk food consumption. Without wanting to leap to simplistic explanations, it seems that class position may play a role in women's differing abilities to sidestep the troubling implications of these discourses. While Tina was reading an article about early-onset puberty in the tabloid press, Kate was wading through scientific publications and critical sociological accounts (including an article of mine) online. While Tina's supportive family had never heard of early-onset puberty, some of Kate's close family were medical professionals and could engage in anxiety-reducing, informed conversation about the likelihood of particular outcomes. Kate also has a high-status job in which she is used to being treated as a competent professional. She expects to make decisions about her daughter's health care and is highly critical of what she calls "big pharma." Tina, on the other hand, felt totally excluded from the hospital's decision to medicate her child, and had unquestioning faith in the safety of the medication, even over the long term.

Of course, the significant difference in the girls' ages also plays a huge part in these two women's accounts. Taking a 3-year-old with developing breasts to a specialist clinic is a very different experience from taking an 8-year-old to a GP. As these stories show, a 3-year-old with breasts is likely to be diagnosed with "precocious puberty," understood as a worrying medical condition that must be treated (and immediately). An 8-year-old with notably greater development is, in contrast, more likely to be articulated as medically "normal" (Roberts, 2015).

Case Study 3: "Breda Is Full on"

White, British Rebecca is the single mother of Breda, who started to sexually develop when she was "six or seven," growing breasts at eight and menstruating by her tenth birthday. In year five (ages nine to ten) now, her mother reports that

> [S]he's pretty much the tallest in her class . . . for quite a while she's really curvy and she's got a very, she's got a young woman's body . . . Breda is full on . . . She's got a round waist, . . . her boobs have really grown, and so she's got the body of a 13 year old at least.

Even though her mother was keeping an eye on Breda's physical development and educating her about menstruation, it was still a bit of a shock when she got her first period. Rebecca has had to negotiate special material arrangements around, *inter alia*, sanitary provision in school toilets, swimming lessons, and dancing outfits. Breda has problems getting to sleep and experiences menstrual pain. Her periods are very heavy – her mother has to get her up in the night to change her pad because otherwise "there is blood everywhere." This can also lead to problems at school, as Breda does not like changing her pad there. Her mother would like also her to wear deodorant – “she stinks” – but Breda is not interested and will only do so sometimes.

Breda’s father died when she was a baby, which, her mother reports, has “definitely had an impact on her. … [S]he’s been quite shy really, she’s really sensitive, she cries loads.” Breda is creative and emotionally expressive – she knows her own mind – and she loves to dress up, to dance, and to experiment with makeup and fashion. Now that she is so developed physically, however, this can, Rebecca reports, cause problems between the two of them:

> she likes sequins and sparkly things and that’s fine, … she’s very confident in wearing what she wants, but she looks much older than she is and I’m guessing she’ll continue to do that and … so that is a concern for me … .. Now she’s got boobs she wants to wear like crop tops and really short shorts. So that’s the discussion I’m starting to have and we argue like hell sometimes … [S]he wants to go in inappropriate things for school [non-uniform days] like summer dresses but little, you know? So she grows really quickly and suddenly her dress is up her arse and I’m like, ‘No you’ve got to wear leggings or something.’ And so she’ll come down and say, ‘No I’m just wearing this!’ So now I have to get her to plan what she wears the night before and we have to agree on it ‘cause it’s just not worth the arguing, ‘cause she’s really fiery!

Due to her professional background, Rebecca has heightened awareness of sexual abuse risk. While reporting that Breda currently has no interest in boys, Rebecca is concerned that Breda might be an object of desire for older boys and men. This had sometimes come out in everyday conversations, where men had commented on Breda’s body:

> [P]eople don’t always think about the way they talk, so some men have said to me ‘Oh she’s got beautiful – Oh what a … ’ in a way that they’d talk about an adult or a woman they liked. But it’s Breda! And I know they’re not talking about her like that, but there’s not that much differentiation and so I’m just like, ‘Ok, so I’m not going to put anything on that person [i.e., I am not going to think they might sexually abuse a child] but I’m like, “Oh what do I do with that? … This is my daughter and how this person has talked about her.”’ And then some people realise and say, ‘Oh no, sorry,’ ‘cause they’re just not thinking. ‘Cause she *is* very gorgeous! … And when you say ‘She’s ten,’ they’re like, ‘Oh God!’ [LAUGHS].

Rebecca’s laugh here is rueful, even bitter: she understands the risks her daughter faces. Breda is also of mixed-race heritage, and Rebecca worries that this may be an added attractive quality for some men. Her attempts to control her daughter’s clothing choices, then, are but one part of a larger strategy to protect her from sexual abuse.

Rebecca’s reference to her daughter’s fiery temper is repeated throughout the interview. While Breda has always been a strong-willed person, her mother reports that she has become more rebellious and difficult to live with during puberty. The materialities of this are articulated in a complex way: her sleeping difficulties mean she can be cranky in the mornings; and she needs to eat more and can be bad-tempered if she gets hungry. For Rebecca, this constitutes the core difficulty of the early sexual development. Breda is not upset about her body, even though menstruating means she misses out on swimming lessons, which is "really boring." She was happy about starting to menstruate and "really likes her pubic hair." Rebecca admires her daughter's "gorgeous" body but is stressed about how to live with the poor sleep and irritability:

> So I think she's ok with it. My concerns are more around the behaviour stuff because that's much harder for me to handle and that will have quite lasting implications potentially, and the sleeping ... How can I get her to sleep more and to understand that actually that's really important?

Like Kate, Rebecca was at pains to point out to me that her daughter is "still very much a little girl as well." She plays with dolls and engages in imaginary games with her mother and her friends. Overall, then, Rebecca is quite positive about her daughter's development. Despite her worries about sexual abuse, she remarks that it might be easier for her daughter when she goes to high school because she will have already experienced puberty. Like Kate, Rebecca has worked hard to instill a positive attitude toward women's bodies and sexuality in her daughter, treading a fine line between facilitating her daughter's enjoyment of fashion and her body and protecting her from sexist objectification.

Rebecca does not have a clear view of why Breda might have developed early; indeed she did not seem particularly interested to pursue this topic in our conversation. Although she had rung her doctor's surgery to discuss Breda's development, she had no concerns about the physical effects of early-onset puberty. Her daughter is tall, healthy, and beautiful and Rebecca articulates her development as a form of "natural" (i.e., non-pathological) change. The medical response to her request for information may have played into this: although the GP surgery nurse said she had never heard of a girl menstruating at 10, she confirmed the next day that "No, the doctor says that's completely normal these days and it's only if they start before eight that we need to worry about them stopping growing and so on ... Ten shouldn't be an issue." Here, expert discourse supports Rebecca's desire to articulate her daughter's development as "natural" and "normal," but leaves her to get on with the new parenting challenges on her own.

Case Study 4: "She Needs Her Injections"

Michaela and her husband are Northern European; their two daughters are locally adopted children from an ethnic minority. Their daughter, Bethany, entered puberty when she was six, developing breasts and pubic hair, and having her first period just before her eighth birthday. Her periods quickly became regular, during which time her parents sought formal medical advice. Tests proved that Bethany did not have a brain tumor (which in some cases causes early puberty) but that her growth was likely to stop soon. One of the tallest girls in year five (ages nine to ten), she was 138 cm. Like Kate, Michaela has medical professionals in her family from whom she sought advice. Together with supportive pediatric endocrinologists, then, Michaela and her husband decided that Bethany should take GNRHa injections to stop her periods and halt her early-onset puberty. Their biggest worry was her height – they are both from tall families and were concerned that Bethany should have every chance to keep growing. They also felt that although Bethany had found periods "interesting" at first (her mother's choice of word), being the only girl menstruating in her class would soon become difficult. Bethany's school had not handled this situation well – two teaching assistants had accompanied her into the adult toilet to assist with changing her sanitary pad, which was, as her mother firmly said "unnecessary." More importantly, perhaps, some school staff and parents were "totally shocked" that Bethany was developing so fast: Michaela described this as "really not helping."

Although concerned about the health risks of putting "loads and loads of hormones" into her daughter's body, Michaela was very positive about the effects of GnRHa on Bethany's body and life. After six weeks of some particularly worrying medication (taken in tablet form), Bethany had moved on to monthly injections and had not had any side effects. (Michaela's concerns about the tablets arose from the patient information sheet that stated that the drugs were designed to reduce sex offenders' sex drive and should not be used on children. GnRH analogs are indeed also used for this purpose as well as in some *in vitro* fertilization treatments and to treat endometriosis and prostate cancer, as their function is to interfere with hormonal signaling between the brain and the gonads.) In the interview, Michaela was full of praise for the medical team treating her daughter, who had been reassuring, kind, and optimistic. She had also prepared Bethany thoroughly for the tests and felt that she approached the injections bravely:

> I think generally she feels all right about it. She's had them for a year now and the nurse is very, very nice . . . and every time after an injection I buy her a big sweetie [both laugh], so, that sweetens the deal! . . . [S]he's very, very brave. . . . It's really no big deal. She's very calm. She thinks it's important, she needs her injections.

Bethany lives separately from an older birth sister who has also gone through early-onset puberty and is ahead of her in treatment terms. This helped Bethany and her mother a lot: it meant they had more knowledge about what to expect and also – importantly – that they were able to frame Bethany's development as "something that runs in the [birth] family." Indeed, when I asked Michaela about her views on what might have caused Bethany's early development, she gave a detailed and knowledgeable summary of all the possible explanations, including being overweight and a high-fat diet (neither apply in this case), early childhood trauma and/or living with a non-biologically related father (which do apply), more general population changes, and genetic factors. Ultimately, Michaela guesses that Bethany's development is some kind of mixture of genetic factors and trauma-related neurological changes: as an adoptive parent, Michaela knows that "trauma changes brains" and that this may well impact on sexual development.[2] Michaela frames early sexual development as "fine" and yet something to be "brave" about, but also that will end quite soon (they are planning that Bethany will only take the medication for one year, that is, until she is in year six, ages ten to eleven).

As a survivor of early childhood trauma, Bethany already faces significant emotional and social challenges (Hughes & Baylin, 2012; Schofield et al., 2006). Her mother, however, describes her as "incredibly resilient" and notes that she has managed her early sexual development well. In her mother's view, this is largely because Bethany has a very positive sense of her body – the family spends a lot of time in Northern Europe where nudity is normalized, and her parents are very open about sexuality and sexual development. Bethany's relative ease in the face of her early-onset puberty resonates with the only existing qualitative study of girls' experiences of early development (mentioned in my introduction). Undertaken by US-based scholar Kristina Pinto, this interview-based study found that girls who had experienced serious life challenges (death of a parent, abuse or neglect, poverty, or racism) seemed to take early-onset puberty in their stride, with some even being pleased that their bodies were somehow demonstrating that they were psychosocially older than their years (Pinto, 2007).

Interestingly, all the girls in my study – no matter what their life circumstances – (according to their mothers at least) find early-onset puberty less worrying than their parents might have imagined. Their previous life experiences, however, shape the stories their mothers tell. In contrast to Kate's account of Lara's innocent (now lost) childhood, for example, Michaela's story about Bethany figures early-onset puberty as just one of a series of major life challenges. Unlike 4-year-old Maddy who has to be held down at the hospital, Bethany is described as "resilient" and able, with the help of sweets, to cope with the GNRHa injections and to understand that they are "important."

The difference between starting periods at eight and at ten, noted by Rebecca's GP surgery nurse, is evident in the mothers' accounts. Unlike Breda's, Bethany's bleeding body is articulated as a problem requiring medication. Although menstruation might be "interesting" for her, it is too difficult – her mother claims – to manage both materially and emotionally until the later primary years. Such concerns about how early-onset puberty will be managed at English schools are, I suggest, realistic. Our wider consultation found school nurses and teachers ill prepared to support early developers at primary school. Indeed, schools often appear as sites of friction and concern in mothers' accounts. Kate was very critical of her daughter's primary school's failure to educate her daughter about puberty or to provide a supportive environment for the year five (ages nine to ten) children who were experiencing a wide range of sexual development stages. Indeed, she accused the school of "passing the buck" on the responsibility to educate pupils about sexual development at an appropriate time for their developmental stage. Kate felt strongly that children should not only to be taught about puberty but

[2] For a discussion of this argument (Roberts, 2016).

discuss how to deal with the wide range in developmental timing they encounter among their peers, which is, she noted, "a significant social thing to guide them through." Michaela similarly felt that school sex education was provided too late for her child.

The Sex Education Forum takes a similar view, arguing that children have a right to know about puberty before it happens (Sex Education Forum, 2016). Most current information on sexual development, however, is aimed at 10- and 11-year -olds. Although two guides for parents, both called *The New Puberty*, have recently been published (Dunn, 2017; Greenspan & Deardorff, 2014), there is a paucity of information for girls starting puberty at six or seven. As the mothers in my study note, puberty at this age is articulated rather differently with discourses of sexuality. Rather than a welcomed initiation into early teen age, early-onset puberty is described by teachers, parents, family, and friends as "shocking" and risky. New educational materials, in my view, need to be written to provide alternative, more positive accounts for younger children.

Puberty as Biopsychosocial Enfolding

Mothers' accounts of their early-developing daughters move freely over topics and experiences that would elsewhere be classified as "social," "psychological," or "biological." Breda's menstrual bleeding, for example, would in medical contexts be framed in predominantly physiological terms. For Rebecca and Breda, however, this flow is also a psychosocial problem: How can it be managed at night? What needs to be done to excuse Breda from swimming? How can the social difficulties of needing to change sanitary pads at primary school be managed? Is she allowed to wear underwear and a pad under her leotard during dance class? Mothers frequently grapple with feelings – their own and their daughters' – in their accounts. The girls seem more volatile and distressed, and these changes vibrate with cultural understandings of teenagers' (and women's) moods as hormonally driven (Roberts, 2007). None of them seem sure, however, that these changing moods can be directly attributed to hormones. Puberty reduces sleep, causes embarrassment, and can lead to arguments and/or painful medical interventions. Girls and mothers can become anxious and irritable when faced with such experiences. How could one ever disentangle these from physical changes? Adult height is similarly acknowledged as a mixed physiological and a psychosocial issue. Both Michaela and Kate worry that their early-developing daughters may end up as short people in tall families, but articulate this as a biopsychosocial problem, not simply a physical or medical one.

These enfoldings can produce intense feelings of responsibility, creating minefields for mothers trying to care for their children: the girls and mothers in my case studies struggle to co-articulate sometimes competing versions of "the new puberty." Such struggles seem to centre on clothing, body management, and sexuality. As noted earlier, Kate reported that Lara became very angry when her mother purchased a bra "just in case" she wanted it. Arguably, this response indicates that Lara is willing to accept her own development as "normal" only on terms that she perceives as age appropriate. Wearing a bra (or in Breda's case, using deodorant) is going too far. Aware of discourses of risk, blame, and maternal responsibility (arguably agreeing to be interviewed by me is just another form of taking such responsibility) mothers develop strategies both to contain their own anxieties and to mind the gaps between physical and psychosocial stages. GnRH analogs may be one way to do this when the difficulties are too strong – for Bethany, stopping menstruating allowed her to fit in better with her peers and for her parents to feel positive about her future height – or when a child is, like Maddy, very young.

Questions around the causes of early-onset puberty also indicate the enfolding of biological, social, and psychological forces in mothers' accounts. Each of these mothers had made some attempts to engage with existing medical and scientific discourses on the causes of early-onset puberty (although Rebecca's interest in this was minimal). As I show in *Puberty in Crisis*, the current scientific explanations of changes in pubertal timing are indeed confusing and compartmentalized: some focus on (over)weight (or 'adiposity'); others on early childhood trauma and/or 'absent fathers'; others on exposure to environmental toxins; others on genetics. Interestingly, none of the mothers spoke of being early developers themselves. For those living with birth children, genetic inheritance did not come into play as an actor in their accounts. For Michaela, in contrast, genetics played an important role because of the similar experience of her daughter's birth sister and her own lack of genetic connection to her child. Explanations pertaining to (over)weight had no purchase in these mothers' accounts. None of these girls were heavy; indeed, their mothers described them as "normal," "slim," and/or "athletic." (Given the stigma attached to childhood obesity, however, we would have to query whether mothers of overweight children be willing to participate in my study.) The possible contributing role of environmental toxins was raised by two of the mothers, but they remained justifiably puzzled as to why their daughters would be more affected than their peers if these were the main cause or trigger of early development. Childhood trauma and loss appeared to be relevant in two cases, but only Michaela seemed to have an awareness of the literature on this (knowledge of the neuroscience of trauma is typical of contemporary UK adopters) (Mackenzie & Roberts, 2017). The other two mothers also did not mention any early psychosocial challenges in their daughters' lives and both had lived with biologically related, caring fathers.

In the absence of clear scientific explanations, however, each mother had developed some kind of narrative about why their daughter was an early developer. Tina was fatalistic, while Kate grappled with a rather uncertain evolutionary explanation, mixing physical environmental changes (more food, more toxins) with contemporary girls' improved health and nutrition. Rebecca was content to remain undecided; while Michaela turned to genetics and early trauma. However they came to it, these mothers all understood that early-onset puberty is, as yet, a poorly understood condition and one that is most likely to mix a wide range of factors across a diverse population of girls. We can take from this, I suggest, both that population-level explanations (e.g., increasing obesity levels or exposure to toxins) are unlikely to provide explanatory power and reassurance to mothers of early-developing girls, at least in the foreseeable future; and that mothers can tolerate quite high levels of uncertainty about cause if they are confident in their ability to support their child through this experience.

Conclusion

Learning from this diffractive analysis of mothers' accounts, I want to suggest that rather than attempting to isolate causal factors or to delineate and classify the troubles ensuing from early-onset puberty as either biological, psychological, or social, we can understand sexual development better if we shift toward a model of embodiment as the inevitable and inextricable enfolding of these forces. FTS helps us to value and comprehend such intra-actions in their inherent complexity, rather than trying to isolate and describe discrete causal factors. Taking this FTS sensibility into a diffractive analysis of parents' accounts illuminates the ways in which stories of lived experience readily articulate these enfoldings, moving across and through categories that social and medical scientists conventionally keep separate. There is much to learn, I suggest, from mothers' accounts of their early-developing daughters – not just about the difficulties and joys involved in parenting such girls, but also in how to think differently about the complex nature of sexual development and sexed embodiment *per se*. Early-onset puberty is a scientific and biomedical conundrum, but also something parents and children have to get on with. Diffractively conceptualizing sexual development through FTS helps us find new ways to approach both challenges.

References

Aksglaede, L., Sorensen, K., Petersen, J. H., Skakkebaek, N. E., & Juul, A. (2009). Recent Decline in Age at Breast Development: The Copenhagen Puberty Study. *Pediatrics*, *123*(5), e932–939.

Attwood, F. & Smith, C. (2011). Investigating Young People's Sexual Cultures: An Introduction. *Sex Education*, *11*(3), 235–242.

Barad, K. M. (2007). *Meeting the Universe Halfway: Quantum Physics and the Entanglement of Matter and Meaning*. Durham, NC: Duke University Press Books.

Bouvattier, C. (2016). Precocious Puberty Therapeutic Management: GnRH Analogs Treatment. In Bouvattier, C. & Pienkowski, C. (Eds.), *Early Puberty: Latest Findings, Diagnosis, Treatment, Long-Term Outcome* (67–73). Switzerland: Springer.

Bouvattier, C. & Pienkowski, C. (Eds.). (2016). *Early Puberty: Latest Findings, Diagnosis, Treatment, Long-Term Outcomes*. Switzerland: Springer.

Butler, J. (1993). *Bodies That Matter: On the Discursive Limits of Sex*. Abingdon: Routledge.

Davies, B. (2014). Reading Anger in Early Childhood Intra-Actions: A Diffractive Analysis. *Qualitative Inquiry*, *20*(6), 734–741.

Deleuze, G. (1995). *Negotiations*. New York: Columbia University Press.

Dunn, A. (2017). *The New Puberty*. Melbourne: Melbourne University Publishing.

Fausto-Sterling, A. (2004). Refashioning Race: DNA and the Politics of Health Care. *Differences: A Journal of Feminist Cultural Studies*, *15*(3), 1–37.

Fausto-Sterling, A., Coll, C. G., & Lamarre, M. (2012a). Sexing the Baby: Part 1 – What Do We Really Know about Sex Differentiation in the First Three Years of Life? *Social Science & Medicine*, *74*(11), 1684–1692.

(2012b). Sexing the Baby: Part 2 Applying Dynamic Systems Theory to the Emergences of Sex-Related Differences in Infants and Toddlers. *Social Science & Medicine*, *74*(11), 1693–1702.

Greenspan, L. & Deardorff, J. (2014). *The New Puberty: How to Navigate Early Development in Today's Girls*. Emmaus: Rodale Books.

Grosz, E. A. (1994). *Volatile Bodies: Toward a Corporeal Feminism*. Indianapolis, IN: Indiana University Press.

Haraway, D. J. (1997). *Modest–Witness@Second–Millennium.FemaleMan–Meets–OncoMouse: Feminism and Technoscience*. New York: Routledge.

(2008). *When Species Meet*. Minneapolis: University of Minnesota Press.

Harris, A. (2004). *Future Girl: Young Women in the Twenty-first Century*. London: Psychology Press.

Herman-Giddens, M., Slora, E., Wasserman, R., et al. (1997). Secondary Sexual Characteristics and Menses in Young Girls Seen in Office Practice: A Study from the Pediatric Research in Office Settings Network. *Pediatrics*, *99*(4), 505–512.

Hughes, D. A. & Baylin, J. F. (2012). *Brain-Based Parenting: The Neuroscience of Caregiving for Healthy Attachment*. New York: W.W. Norton & Co.

Jackson, A. Y. & Mazzei, L. (2012). *Thinking with Theory in Qualitative Research: Viewing Data across Multiple Perspectives*. London: Routledge.

Keller, E. F. (2010). *The Mirage of a Space between Nature and Nurture*. Durham, NC: Duke University Press.

Mackenzie, A. & Roberts, C. (2017). Adopting Neuroscience: Parenting and Affective Indeterminancy. *Body & Society*, 23(3), 130–155. doi:10.1177/1357034X17716521.

Mazzei, L. A. (2014). Beyond an Easy Sense: A Diffractive Analysis. *Qualitative Inquiry*, *20*(6), 742–746.

Negriff, S., Saxbe, D. E., & Trickett, P. K. (2015). Childhood Maltreatment, Pubertal Development, HPA Axis Functioning, and Psychosocial Outcomes: An Integrative Biopsychosocial Model. *Developmental Psychobiology*, *57*(8), 984–993.

Parent, A.-S. (2003). The Timing of Normal Puberty and the Age Limits of Sexual Precocity: Variations Around the World, Secular Trends, and Changes after Migration. *Endocrine Reviews*, *24*(5), 668–693.

Pinto, K. (2007). Growing Up Young the Relationship between Childhood Stress and Coping with Early Puberty. *The Journal of Early Adolescence*, *27*(4), 509–544.

Renold, E. & Ringrose, J. (Eds.). (2013). *Feminist Theory: Special Issue on Feminisms, Sexualisation and Contemporary Childhoods*, *14*(3).

Roberts, C. (2007). *Messengers of Sex: Hormones, Biomedicine, and Feminism*. Cambridge: Cambridge University Press.

(2015). *Puberty in Crisis: The Sociology of Early Sexual Development*. Cambridge: Cambridge University Press.

(2016). Psychology, Evolution and the Traumatised Child: Exploring the Neurophysiology of Early Sexual Development. *Australian Feminist Studies*, *30*(86), 377–3885.

Rubin, C., Maisonet, M., Kieszak, S., et al. (2009). Timing of Maturation and Predictors of Menarche in Girls Enrolled in a Contemporary British Cohort. *Paediatric and Perinatal Epidemiology*, *23*(5), 492–504.

Schofield, G., Beek, M., & British Association for Adoption & Fostering. (2006). *Attachment Handbook for Foster Care and Adoption*. London: BAAF.

Sex Education Forum. (2016). *The Sex Educational Supplement: The Puberty Issue*, *20*(2).

Taguchi, H. L. (2012). A Diffractive and Deleuzian Approach to Analysing Interview Data. *Feminist Theory*, *13*(3), 265–281.

Wilson, E. A. (2004). *Psychosomatic: Feminism and the Neurological Body*. Durham, NC: Duke University Press.

25 Stolen Childhood

Understanding Sexualization of Young Girls through "Child Marriage" in Zimbabwe

Sandra Bhatasara, Manase Kudzai Chiweshe, and Nelson Muparamoto

Introduction

In this chapter, we examine how female children are forced into sexual relationships with older men under the guise of marriage. We analyze how this sexualization of girls is underpinned by patriarchal values that promote a myriad of harmful cultural practices, and the consequences of this on girls' growth and development. Houseknecht and Lewis (2005) note that child marriages were common throughout history for a variety of reasons, including financial and other forms of insecurity, as well as for political and financial reasons. Today, child marriage is still practiced in developing countries. Several studies acknowledge that accurate data on the true extent of child marriage is difficult to obtain because many marriages go unregistered and girls' ages are often falsified (IPPF, 2006, p. 11). However, the United Nations Children's Fund (UNICEF; 2013) estimates that, globally, some 64 million young women (aged 20–24 years) were married before the age of 18. In this chapter, we argue against defining these unions as marriage and we understand them as the criminal abuse of girls. As Cullen (2017) concludes, child "marriage is a front, a cultural arrangement made by men to have their way and pleasure by sexually abusing children without the penalty of the law. To save children from such grave sexual abuse, we have to campaign against child brides and expose it for what it is – legalized, economic, socio-cultural paedophilia" (par. 17).

Child marriage is common in Zimbabwe, and 21 percent of children, mostly girls, are married before the age of 18. Research has shown that it is mostly the female child, as opposed to the male child, who ends up in a "child union" (Sibanda 2011; United Nations Population Fund, 2012). According to the Girl Child Network (GCN), an estimated 8,000 girls have been forced into early marriages or were held as sex slaves since 2008 in Zimbabwe (Anon, 2014).

The practice of child marriages reflects society's negative attitude toward women, revealing the fact that important decisions such as when to marry, choice of partner, and sexuality are controlled by patriarchy from an early age until old age. At the core of the problem in Zimbabwe is the continued recognition of customary law alongside general law (Section 111B of the Constitution). Perceptions of masculinity and acceptable sexuality for men and women, girls' and women's lower worth compared to boys and men, poverty, and the power imbalance between the sexes create a situation in which families and communities feel obliged to marry their daughters very young (Greene et al., 2015). Child marriage is a business transaction, an agreement between families that regulates girls' and women's sexuality and reproduction, while men's sexuality remains unrestrained and, in some cases, encouraged, both within and outside of marriage. In a blog entry, Liepert (2011) described child marriages as something akin to culturally sanctioned pedophilia. Yet, Cullen (2017, para. 10) argues:

> Some say it is not paedophilia if the man has sex with a nine year old provided it is approved by socio-cultural or religious custom. They say the child marriage phenomenon is driven by socio-cultural forces and economic considerations. One international NGO says, "One aspect that clearly distinguishes child marriage from pedophilia is that the socio-cultural milieu, where child marriage is practiced, condones, and in many cases, perpetuates the practice . . . This is the reason, unlike pedophilia, child marriage is practiced and defended by not only the parents, but also their community and leaders.

Child Marriage or Child Rape: A Conceptual Debate

Conceptual debates on defining child marriage are key to legal responses to the issue. In this section, we outline the social and legal debates, noting how various contexts across the world have attempted to deal with the legal ramifications of lawful child marriage and illegal rape and sexual abuse of children. An expert in women's law, Hodzi (2014, p. 7) defines a child marriage as: "Any marriage carried out below the age of 18 years, before the girl [or boy] is physically, physiologically, and psychologically ready to shoulder the responsibilities of marriage and childbearing." There are, however, contestations around using the concept of marriage, because, in many countries across the world, marriage requires consent of an individual who is of legal age. For example, in October 2017 India's Supreme Court ruled that sex with an underage wife constitutes rape. The decision by the court in India was made on the basis that a child cannot consent to sex or marriage. In Zimbabwe, Hodzi (2014, pp. 8–9) summarizes this contestation by arguing:

> If a marriage is supposed to take place with consent and between adults (i.e., persons of 18 years and over), then how is it that society has come to define a child living in the guise of a union as a married child? What is a marriage? Can society continue to claim that a marriage has occurred because a bride price has been paid? What then really legitimises a marriage? Is it the fact that a girl's virginity has been broken and she is now pregnant?

Hodzi raises pertinent questions around the framing of child marriages. These questions require further interrogation, which, according to her, should see us moving toward defining instances where an adult is living with and having children with a person under 18 as sexual exploitation and pedophilia.

According to UNICEF (2014), the legally prescribed marriageable age in some jurisdictions is below 18 years, especially in the case of girls; and even when the age is set at 18 years, many jurisdictions permit earlier marriage with parental consent or in special circumstances, such as teenage pregnancy. In the Zimbabwean Constitution, a child is defined as any person below 18 years, yet, when it comes to criminalizing sex with a young person, the Criminal Law Code defines a young person as anyone below the age of 16 years. The constitution as the supreme law of the country thus trumps all other definitions of what a child is in Zimbabwe. This means that calling unions where one person is over 18 and the other under 18 years of age "marriages" is an anomaly. This is further supported by human rights lawyer and African Union Goodwill Ambassador for Ending Child Marriage Nyaradzayi Gumbonzvanda who argues that "with child marriage we are sanctioning rape, we are sanctioning abduction, we are sanctioning a modern form of slavery, it's trafficking, it's forced labour . . . It's a huge bundle of violations, and the moment we just call it 'marriage', it is like we are giving it a blessing and acceptability" (NewsDay, 2015).

The starting point of eradicating child marriages should then be on contesting whether these unions should ever be called marriages in the first instance. The 1948 Universal Declaration of Human Rights states that marriage should be entered only with the free and full consent of the intending spouses. But, in the majority of child marriages, there is often an element of coercion involved; parents, guardians, or families pressurize, collude, or force children into marriage. Today, many girls are still raised by their parents to accept child marriage as the norm, a 'given,' and many give their consent as a duty and sign of respect. Although an adolescent girl may attain sexual maturity early, she will often not be physically mature enough to conceive a child (UNICEF, 2013), nor will she be cognitively or psychologically mature enough for marriage and the related responsibilities of being a wife or a mother (Research and Advocacy Unit, 2014).

Rhetoric around cultural relativism has been used to justify harmful practices. Ataman (2013) argues that in some cases culture has been used as an excuse for practicing child and women abuse. Ataman (2013, p. 65) notes:

> Cultural defense is based on the idea that persons socialized in a minority or foreign culture, who regularly conduct themselves in accordance with their own cultural norms, should not be held fully accountable for conduct that violates officials' law, if that conduct conforms to the prescriptions of their own culture.

In these cases, rape of young girls who, based on their ages, cannot consent to sex, becomes a cultural practice even where the law expressly prohibits it. It is this cultural relativism that has seen inaction from many institutions in positions of authority to address the tragedy of child marriage. Many civil society organizations working across the world have steered away from issues such as child marriage. One example is how Margaret Capelazo of Care Canada refutes the link between child/forced marriage and pedophilia because, for her, marriage "is caused by social rules and biases that devalue girls, and related social and economic pressure. [While] Paedophilia is a psychiatric phenomenon and a diagnosed mental disorder" (Cullen, 2017, para. 15). In this argument, we should thus separate child marriages from pedophilia. It is thus important to go beyond the marriage rhetoric and speak of child abuse in appropriate terms. Sanitizing this criminal and cruel practice through cultural and religious excuses exacerbates the problem.

History of 'Child Marriage' in Zimbabwe

There is no doubt that 'child marriage' as a social construct in Zimbabwe is historically patterned. Precolonial traditions and cultures endorsed child marriages through various practices. It was part of the culture of Zimbabweans, be it Ndebele or Shona (Zimbabwe's two largest tribes), to have a female child married (Hodzi, 2014). One widely practiced custom that fueled child marriages in the precolonial period was *kuzvarira* (wife pledging). Jeater (1992) noted that the practice of *kuzvarira* occurred when young girls were pledged to 'big men' who were rich in exchange for grain during food shortages. The child was given away at any age when the family felt she was capable of performing her duties as a wife, usually when she reached puberty. Among the BaKalanga, some families pledged their daughters even before they were born – the unborn child bride called *nlongo buta* (the sleeping bride). Bride price (*malobolo*) would be paid well in advance, while her marital position was already recognized at her husband's residence for years before the marriage was solemnized (Ndlovu, 2016).

The practice of *chimutsa mapfihwa* was also a flourishing cultural practice through which young girls substituted a sister's or aunt's marital position (Chinyoka, 2011). Girls were given off to their living sister's or aunt's husband when a sister or an aunt failed to conceive or satisfy her husband sexually, had consistent miscarriages, or failed to conceive a boy child. In extreme but prevalent cases, the sister or aunt would actually invite the child to be part of the polygamous arrangement as a way of preserving the marriage from other external women or lineages. If the husband was rich, the wife wanted to protect the wealth by letting her younger sister join her so that the man does not marry elsewhere. A related practice was when a girl was also given as *bondwe* to her sister's or aunt's husband in the event that the sister or aunt died. Another practice that supported child marriage was *chiramu* (sexual play), a practice whereby the husband of the child's sister had sexual rights over the child. This often led to pregnancy and ultimately polygamy (Chinyoka, 2011).

Another form of child marriage that was persistently practiced in Zimbabwe was *kuripa ngozi* (the pledging into marriage of a girl to appease the spirit of a dead person). In this case, if a man was murdered, a young girl or 'homicide bride' was given by the family of the accused to the family of the deceased to compensate for the loss of their relative. It was believed among the Shona people that failure to appease the spirit of the dead would bring misfortune to the accused and his clan (Hanzi, 2006). In many precolonial societies in Zimbabwe, child marriages were also used to build or strengthen alliances between families. This included the betrothals of young children or babies.

Polygamous marriages also gave rise to child marriages. In the traditional Shona custom and philosophy of the family, a man could have as many wives as possible, particularly if the man was able to provide for the needs of the family (Machingura, 2011). The philosophy behind polygamy was that the more wives a man had, the more children he was likely to have. Having a large group of descendants also had something to do with a large labor force who would work in the fields of the family head (Bourdillon, 1976). The idea of a polygamous marriage usually came at the suggestion of the wife's relatives, who feared that the son in law would demand back the dowry paid as *roora* or *lobola* (bride wealth) in the event of conflict or failure of their daughter to conceive.

Prevalence of Child Marriage

Zimbabwe is one of the countries where the prevalence of 'child marriage' has been declining over the last few years (Pazvakavambwa & Wanjau, 2015). The rate has declined from 34 percent in 2006 to 31 percent in 2011 (ibid). However, although 'child marriages' still continue in Zimbabwe, data on this phenomenon is not readily available. Currently, the rate of child marriages in Zimbabwe stands at 30 percent against the global rate of 29 percent. From the few research studies conducted, for instance, by UNICEF (2016), one in three women aged 20–49 surveyed reported that they married before the age of 18 and an estimated 4 percent marry before the age 15. The Multiple Indicator Cluster Survey[1] revealed that 25 percent of adolescent girls aged 15–19 were married or in union (UNICEF, 2016), and thus experience challenges of early marriage. The Zimbabwe Demographic Health Survey, conducted in 2010–2011, estimated that 31 percent of girls in Zimbabwe marry before they reach the age of 18 years and about 15 percent of these are married before they reach 15 years.

'Child marriages' are also prevalent among particular social groups in the country, such as certain religious groups. For example, it was noted that 'child marriage' is most common among the Johanne Marange Apostolic sect, which is believed to constitute 1.2 million of the country's population and which believes in polygamy (Sibanda, 2011). Human Rights Watch (2015) echoes similar sentiments that 'child marriage' is common in indigenous apostolic churches, charismatic evangelical groupings that mix Christian beliefs with traditional cultures and have approximately 1.2 million followers across the country.

[1] Developed by UNICEF, it is an international survey program to support countries to collect internationally comparable data on a wide range of indicators on the situation of women and children.

Social Drivers and Causes of Child Marriages

A coalescence of cultural, economic, religious, and social factors underpins the prevalence and continued practice of 'child marriages' in Zimbabwe. Along the same lines, Pazvakavambwa and Wanjau (2015) argued that causes of child marriage are complex, interrelated, and dependent. Poverty has been largely implicated in perpetuating 'child marriages' in the country (Human Rights Bulletin, 2014). The UNICEF (2016) survey showed that children in households in the poorest wealth quintiles and rural areas are at greater risk of being child mothers and being in teenage marriage. In poverty circumstances, poor families marry their female children as an economic coping strategy to improve the economic situation of the family. Young girls are also married early to escape the costs associated with raising them. For many families in chronic poverty, marriage often seems like the best way to safeguard girls' futures and lighten their economic burden (Pazvakavambwa & Wanjau, 2015). In other instances, young girls drop out of school because their poor parents or guardians cannot meet the costs of their education; hence, they end up in child marriages with the hope to escape poverty. It is estimated that an average of 7 out of 10 girls in Zimbabwe live in dire poverty, and drop out of school because of poverty-related factors (Mawere, 2012).

Hassan (2014), however, dismisses the poverty argument and avers that child marriage is fueled by negative attitudes toward women and girls where there is no tradition of educating them, allowing them to exercise choice about their future, or expecting that they will work outside the home and contribute to family resources. In Zimbabwe, women and girls are subject to the effects of deep-rooted norms, attitudes, and behaviors that assign them a second-class citizen status compared to men and boys within the household, the community, and in society at large (Sibanda, 2011). According to this view, girls are expected to marry young because they are not seen to be of much value until they are married. Society attaches a high value to marriage, which means young, unmarried girls are disempowered. Hence, marrying young means transitioning into a new social status in which young women and girls are treated with respect. Being able to find a husband is also seen as a sign that they have been raised well, which earns their mother more respect. Related to this is the notion of child bearing, in a context were women gain status through motherhood. Having children young accords young girls status that they would not otherwise get in a context that regard women as having less value.

Harmful traditional, religious, and cultural practices legitimize and perpetuate child marriages. Harmful practices emanate from the deeply entrenched discriminatory views and beliefs about the role and position of women and girls in society (Wadesango et al., 2011). There are religious doctrines that promote and encourage 'child marriages' in some churches such as Johane Marange and Johane Masowe sects. The Johane Marange and Johane Masowe sects (including other apostolic sects) are known for 'marrying' off young girls, particularly into polygamous marriages, under the guise of religion. Their doctrine requires girls to marry between ages 12 and 16 to prevent sexual relations outside marriage. Hence, as soon as a girl reaches puberty, any man in the church can claim her for his wife. Most girls drop out of school in July when the Johane Marange Apostolic sect celebrates Passover, a religious festivity during which marriage ceremonies take place. Most of the older men who 'marry' young girls hide behind prophecies. Moyo (2010) observed that most of the men usually abuse their position as prophets to hand-pick girls for the elderly men in the church who already have other wives. The men argue that the 'marriages' are approved by the 'holy spirit,' therefore, they cannot be disputed by anyone, especially the young girls themselves.

The Holy Spirit is used as a tool or intimidation, instilling fear in girls and other church members not to reject child marriages as they are threatened with curses (Sibanda, 2011). The same Holy Spirit is used to validate child marriages as the prophets would have been "*directed*" by the Holy Spirit to marry young girls (ibid). Women and girls in these sects are powerless, viewed as minors, and this is biblically justified. In that regard, most infamous marriages in the Johane Marange and Johane Masowe sects are still arranged between adult men and underage girls, mostly without the consent of the girls. Consequently, girls as young as eight are married as fifth or sixth wives to old men (Machingura, 2011). Such women and girls who are forced into such unions are religiously made to feel guilty and that it is irreligious to opt out or run away. It is common to find that the Johane Marange men defend the sect's practices of marrying off young girls by arguing that it has been their tradition for years and there is nothing wrong with the practice. Marriage is also strictly between members of the aforementioned sects and any marriage outside that setting is radically sanctioned against or censured (Machingura, 2011). Hence, 'marrying' off young girls, often into polygamous marriages, safeguards these girls from finding spouses outside the church.

Long-established practices such as virginity testing expose young girls to 'child marriages' when conducted within certain contexts. Human Rights Watch (2015) reported that Archbishop Johannes Ndanga, president of the Apostolic Churches Council of Zimbabwe, admitted that 'virginity testing' (which includes the insertion of fingers into the vagina) of girls as young as 12, was widely practiced in the apostolic churches. If found to be virgins they would get marks on their foreheads and older men in the church will then choose these 'fresh girls' to become their wives, often joining polygamous unions. In the event that a man marries a woman who is not a virgin, she is required to find a virgin girl for her husband to marry as compensation, hence fueling 'child marriages.' In the same context, it is common to hear about stories of girls who are found to be non-virgins being influenced into polygamous marriages with older men (already with wives) in the Johanne Marange Apostolic sect, whereas virgins are encouraged to become head wives with men who had not been married before (Machingura, 2011).

Child marriages are also a result of practices that devalue women and girls and discriminate against them (Human Rights Bulletin, 2014). Among them are deeply entrenched patriarchal practices that commoditize women such as payment of bride wealth (*roora/lobola* in Zimbabwe). Discriminatory patriarchal norms that link a girl's perceived sexual 'purity' to upholding family's honor

(Human Rights Watch, 2015) and payment of bride wealth force many young girls into 'early marriages.' Hence, for some families, it is honorable to marry their female children while they are still virgins so that they can benefit from bride wealth, rather than to wait until the girls are 'defiled,' hence limiting their chances of getting bride wealth. In situations where girls become pregnant through consensual sex or rape, to avoid stigma, families may view the girls' rights and well-being as secondary to the preservation of family 'honor' (Pazvakavambwa & Wanjau, 2015), hence the girls are coerced into 'marriages.' Related to this commodification is the supposed need to protect girls' sexuality, hence 'child marriage' is ill conceived as a protective mechanism against premarital sex, unplanned pregnancies, and sexually transmitted infections (STIs). This is becoming more common in Southern Africa (including Zimbabwe) with the high level of defilement and rape, and studies have found that parents may prefer to marry off their children early to ensure they are married as virgins (Pazvkavambwa & Wanjau, 2015).

Even outside of religious practice, deep-rooted gender inequalities ensure that women and girls are accorded lower status than men and boys. Sociocultural traditions, attitudes, and beliefs interact to disadvantage women and girls, for instance, denying them access to education and confining them to the domestic sphere. In many patriarchal customary laws and traditions, women and girls are given less negotiating power around issues of marriage, sexual and reproductive health, and rights issues compared to men of the same age (Pazvakavambwa & Wanjau, 2015). In that regard, young girls are often married off young without their consent. The fact that they are girls and also young (young people's voices in many cultures in Zimbabwe are muted) puts them in a precarious position *vis-à-vis* child marriage.

The definitions of a child, which are also contested, also promote 'child marriages' (Wadesango et al., 2011). In most societies in Southern Africa (including Zimbabwe), the onset of puberty is seen as a cutoff point between childhood and womanhood. Girls who have reached puberty are recognized and treated as adults although they have not attained the age of maturity. Once a girl reaches puberty all teachings are directed toward pleasing one's future husband as well as being a gentle and obedient wife (Kambarami, 2006). The fate of young girls is aggravated by high levels of school dropout and high levels of teenage pregnancies in the country. Many adolescents, especially those not attending school are likely to engage in sex, for various reasons such as the economic benefit, experimenting, or just plain promiscuity (Pazvakavambwa & Wanjau, 2015), and this often results in unplanned teenage pregnancies that may force the young girls to get married. Paradoxes and legal contradictions are also rife regarding child marriages in Zimbabwe. Others think feeble laws and inadequate implementation of the laws result in child marriages being conducted with impunity (Sibanda, 2011). The government is often either unable to enforce existing laws, or rectify discrepancies between national laws on marriage age and entrenched customary and religious laws.

Interrupted Childhood and Stolen Futures: Impacts of Child Marriages

The consequences of child marriage for young girls are multiple and devastating to their growth and development, in the present and future. Here we can refer to intersectionalities or interlocking experiences, oppressions, and deprivations that girls face in child marriages. The impact is not only catastrophic for the girls but it also has wider societal implications as it limits girls' empowerment, rights, and choices, which, in turn, negatively impacts their social and economic participation (Progressio, 2016). Human Rights Bulletin (2014) outlines the general effects of child marriage in Zimbabwe as poverty (child brides, uneducated, have no access to employment, thus, are trapped in poverty); maternal mortality (girls younger than 15 years are five times more likely to die during childbirth); illiteracy (child brides are pulled out of schooling); infant mortality (mortality of babies born to women under 20 years is higher than those born to older women); HIV and AIDS and other STIs (because of low status, young married girls cannot negotiate sex in marriages); and abuse and violence (wife battery is rampant, leading to posttraumatic stress and depression).

Child marriage is now widely recognized as a violation of children's rights and a direct form of discrimination against girls who are often deprived of their basic rights to health, education, development, and equality. According to Sibanda (2011), child marriage is a human rights violation that robs children of their childhood and prevents them from obtaining education, enjoying optimal health, bonding with others of their own age, maturing, and, ultimately, choosing their own life partners. Child marriage is one of the most prevalent forms of sexual exploitation of girls (Pazvakavambwa & Wanjau, 2015; Sibanda, 2011). Their childhoods are effectively shortchanged, their education ended, their emotional and social development interrupted. Other harmful consequences include separation from family and friends and lack of freedom to interact with peers and participate in community activities (Juru, 2003).

Child marriages deprive girls of the opportunity to obtain education that would be helping them live an economically rewarding life in future (Wadesango et al., 2011). Their education is disrupted because they have to take care of their husbands, do household chores, and, in some cases, farm work (ibid.). Child marriage forces the child wives into a cycle of intergenerational poverty because they tend to have more children, be more dependent on a husband who may be more abusive, and thus have fewer independent income options (Pazvakavambwa & Wanjau, 2015). At the same time, divorce is also high among child wives, and they are usually left to fend for their families on their own, thus, getting condemned to a life of financial and social insecurity, which, in turn, perpetuates the feminization of poverty (ibid.). More so, many young girls get into polygamous marriages as second or third wives where they face disempowerment, competition, and related strain and stress at very young ages. Ultimately "the hardship of dealing with a polygamous marriage and parenting is often beyond the capacity of an under-age wife" (UNICEF, 2003, p. 12)

The negative health consequences of girls' limited access to reproductive health information and services can be life threatening, for example, early childbearing contributes to maternal mortality and is a leading cause of death among girls aged 15–19 globally (Human Rights Watch, 2015). In the Zimbabwean context, girls are expected to give birth early after marriage because this is an opportunity to prove their fertility in a society that values family and children highly. Indeed, there is tremendous pressure from their husbands and in-laws to conceive, resulting in them getting pregnant when they are not physically, mentally, and emotionally prepared for childbirth (Pazvakavambwa & Wanjau, 2015). Yearly childbearing can have multiple detrimental effects on a girl's life and health. For example, girls aged 10–14 years old are five times more likely to die in pregnancy or childbirth than those aged between 20 and 24 years (Progressio, 2016). Research has also confirmed that girls who fall pregnant before the age of 18 risk getting complications such as prolonged or obstructed labor because of an underdeveloped pelvis, which may lead to loss of life or maternal complications (UNICEF, 2003). Among the disabilities associated with early childbirth is obstetric fistula, an injury that leaves girls in constant pain, vulnerable to infection, incontinent, and often shunned by their husbands, families, and communities (United Nations Population Fund, 2012). Child marriage and social expectations such as submissiveness or subordination toward their often older and more sexually experienced husbands, limit girls' access to their sexual reproductive health rights. Because culturally they cannot deny their husbands sex or insist on condom use, child brides are often exposed to such serious health risks as premature pregnancy, STIs, and, increasingly, HIV and AIDS (Wadesango et al., 2011). As minors, child brides are rarely able to assert their wishes, such as whether to use family-planning methods or practice safe sexual relations (Pazvakavambwa & Wanjau, 2015). Their powerlessness also makes child brides highly susceptible to marital rape, often without capacity to seek social or legal recourse. Such rape can cause permanent, serious physical damage to the child, and one can only imagine the accompanying mental agony (Sibanda, 2011). In addition, in many African cultures, pregnant women are forbidden consumption of certain food (as taboo), and for pregnant young girls this means deprivation of nutrients from certain foods and results in impairment of physical and mental development of both the young mother and her baby (Wadesango et al., 2016).

Child marriage can also result in bonded labor or enslavement, commercial sexual exploitation, and violence against the victim (Stormorken et al., 2007). Similarly, girls married early are more likely to experience violence, abuse, and forced sexual relations (Pazvakavambwa & Wanjau, 2015). Child brides are frequently susceptible to domestic violence because the age difference emphasizes the powerlessness of the girl child (Nkomo, 2014). Social isolation, with little or no education, poor vocational training, and a responsibility to run families at a young age increases the female child's vulnerability to domestic violence (ibid.). Based on interviews with some child brides in Zimbabwe, Human Rights Watch (2015) described that the girls had experienced violence such as beatings or verbal abuse from their in-laws or other relatives. Nearly all the child brides said their husbands had abandoned them, leaving them to care for children without financial support, and many described mental distress and suicidal feelings as a result of their situation. The impact of violence on child brides cannot be easily quantified and often persists throughout their entire lives. They are often marginalized from society with few support systems, contributing to a lack of confidence and low self-esteem, which, in turn, increases their powerlessness and vulnerability to poverty, resulting in them being less likely to leave the abusive husbands (Pazvakavambwa and Wanjau, 2015).

In the Zimbabwean context, the voices of married girls are predominantly missing from both research and policy discourses. Because of the legal implications of marrying a child, husbands of child brides keep them isolated and hidden from society, in general, law enforcers, researchers and human rights activists. Their lack of autonomy, coupled with lack of education, inhibit child brides from participating in public spheres, hence their voices are rarely heard.

All this supports the notion of interrupted childhood and stolen futures. Evidently, child marriage effectively brings a girl's childhood and adolescence to a premature and unnatural end by imposing adult roles and responsibilities before she is physically, psychologically, and emotionally prepared (United Nations Population Fund, 2012). Child marriage contributes to intergenerational poverty, ill health, illiteracy, and powerlessness. In these circumstances, the married girls experience violence, abuse, reduced levels of sexual and reproductive health, and lower levels of education with corresponding high rates of illiteracy (Pazvakavambwa & Wanjau, 2015)

Conclusion

Child marriages are steeped in a system of harmful practices, which are justified using custom and religion under a patriarchal worldview that has no place in any democratic spaces. Culture and religion continue to be used within a cultural relativism paradigm to defend acts of pedophilia and child molestation. It is all too apparent that the world is no longer short of declarations and treaties that recognize rights of young girls. What the world, and not least the African region, is woefully short of, though, is the implementation of these rights. The law remains inadequate in the face of cultural arguments.

The law also tends to be divorced from the lived realities of girls across Zimbabwe. Notwithstanding the urgency of alignment of subsidiary laws to the current Constitution of Zimbabwe Amendment (No. 20) Act 2013, the country has various mechanisms of protecting girls from child marriage and sexualization within the society. Apart from the domestic statutes that are in place to abolish child marriage and protect children from sexual abuse, Zimbabwe is party to the key international instruments that seek to protect children from harmful practices and sexual abuse (Research and Advocacy Unit, 2014). Some of these instruments include the African Charter on the Rights and Welfare of the Child (the African Children's Rights Charter), the Protocol to the African Charter on Human and Peoples Rights on the Rights of Women in Africa (the Maputo Protocol), Convention on the Elimination of all Forms of Discrimination Against Women, and Convention on the Rights of the Child (Research and Advocacy Unit, 2014).

The current supreme law of the land prioritizes children's rights through section 19 of the constitution and mandates the state to adopt policies and measures to ensure that in matters relating to children, the best interests of the children are paramount[2]. Section 81 further elaborates the rights of children and defines a child as every boy and girl under the age of 18 years[3]. Section 78 on marriage rights outlines that persons aged 18 and above can voluntarily start a family[4]. Section 26, besides unequivocally stating that marriage is entered into with free and full consent, also outlaws pledging of children into marriage.

Apart from the constitutional provisions, there is subsidiary legislation, which does to some extent protect girls from child marriage and sexualization. However, there is need to align the subsidiary acts and legislation to the supreme law of the land. Significant acts that need to be harmonized to have a common position on child marriage and sexualization include the Children's Act [Chapter 5:02] (Act 14 of 2002), Marriage Act [Chapter 5:11] (Act 22/2001), Customary Marriages Act, [Chapter 5:07] (Act 23/2004), and the Criminal Law (Codification and Reform) Act [Chapter 9:23] Act 23/2004. The aforementioned acts have sections that conflict with constitutional provisions of children as they define a child differently from the supreme law. For instance, the Children's Act [Chapter 5:02] (Act 14 of 2002) states that 'child' means a person under the age of 16 years and includes an infant. Consequently, this means the Children's Act is reducing the legally acceptable age at which individuals are considered as girls and boys from the constitutional provision of 18 to 16 years (Research and Advocacy Unit, 2014). Similarly, the Marriage Act [Chapter 5:11] lowers the age for girls as they can marry at the age of 16 but boys cannot. Whereas the marriage act lowers minimum age at which girls can marry the Customary Marriages Act, [Chapter 5:07] does not set a minimum age at which one can marry.

References

Anon. (2014, August 6). Chiefs join fight to end child marriage. *The Zimbabwean*. www.thezimbabwean.co/2014/08/chiefs-join-fight-to-end/.

Ataman, G. G. (2013). Uses of Culture and 'Cultural Relativism' in Gender Violence Discussions, *Kadın Araştırmaları Dergisi*, *13*(2), 61–80.

Bourdillon, M. F. C. (1976). *The Shona Peoples: An Ethnography of the Contemporary Shona, with Special Reference to Their Religion*, Gweru: Mambo Press.

[2] Constitution of Zimbabwe (No 20) of 2013: Section 19

[3] Constitution of Zimbabwe (No 20) of 2013: Section 81

[4] Constitution of Zimbabwe (No 20) of 2013: Section 78

Chinyoka, K. (2011). *Effects of Streaming on Academic Performance in Zimbabwe: A Critical Reflection*. Deutschland: Lambert Academic Publishing.

Cullen, S. (2017). Child Brides – A Cover for Cultural Pedophilia? Preda Foundation. www.preda.org/fr-shays-articles/child-brides-a-cover-for-cultural-pedophilia/.

Greene, M. E., Perlson, S., Taylor, A., & Lauro, G. (2015). *Engaging Men and Boys to Address the Practice of Child Marriage*. Washington, DC: GreeneWorks.

Hanzi, R. (2006). Sexual abuse and exploitation of the girl child through cultural practices in Zimbabwe: A human rights perspective. (Masters dissertation). Pretoria: University of Pretoria.

Hassan, Y. (2014). *Protecting the Girl Child: Using the Law to End Child, Early and Forced Marriage and Related Human Rights Violations*. London: Equality Now.

Hodzi, R. (2014). Paedophilia not 'child marriage': A critical analysis of 'child marriages' in apostolic sects in Zimbabwe. (Masters dissertation). Harare: University of Zimbabwe.

Houseknecht, S. K. & Lewis, S. K. (2005). Explaining Teen Childbearing and Cohabitation: Community Embeddedness and Primary Ties. *Family Relations*, *54*(5), 607–620.

Human Rights Bulletin (2014). *Child Marriages*. Harare: Zimbabwe Human Rights NGO Forum.

Human Rights Watch (2015). Zimbabwe: Scourge of Child Marriage. www.refworld.org/docid/5656c1ff4.html.

IPPF (2006). *Ending Child Marriage: A Guide for Global Policy Action*, London: International Planned Parenthood Federation (IPPF).

Jeater, D. (1992). *Marriage, Perversion and Power: The Construction of Moral Discourse in Southern Rhodesia, 1894–1930*, Oxford: Clarendon Press.

Juru, P. C. (2003). *Research Report towards Equity: Boy/ Girl Child Preference*. Gweru: Zimbabwe.

Kambarami, M. (2006). *Femininity, Sexuality and Culture: Patriarchy and Female Subordination in Zimbabwe*. Alice, South Africa: Africa Regional Sexuality Resource Centre, University of Fort Hare.

Liepert, D. (2011, January 29). Rejecting the Myth of Sanctioned Child Marriage in Islam. *Huffington Post*. www.huffingtonpost.com/dr-david-liepert/islamic-pedophelia_b_814332.html.

Machingura, F. (2011). A Diet of Wives as the Lifestyle of the Vapostori Sects: The Polygamy Debate in the Face of HIV and AIDS in Zimbabwe. *Africa 5*(2), 186–210.

Mawere, M. (2012). Girl Child Dropouts in Zimbabwean Secondary Schools: A Case Study of Chadzamira Secondary School in Gutu. *International Journal of Politics and Good Governance 3*(3), 1–18.

Moyo, L. (2010). Girl Child Network (GCN) in Drive to Stop Child Marriages, The Standard, September 26, 2010.

Ndlovu, S.G. (2016, June 22). Child marriage: Prohibited socio-cultural practice. *Chronicle*. www.chronicle.co.zw/child-marriages-prohibited-socio-cultural-practice.

NewsDay (2015, June 19). To end child marriage is to break cycle of poverty. *NewsDay*. www.newsday.co.zw/2015/06/19/to-end-child-marriage-is-to-break-cycle-of-poverty.

Nkomo, S.N. (2014). A Critical Analysis of Zimbabwe's Legal Response to Traditional Cultural Practices and Gender-Based Violence. (Masters of Laws thesis). Cape Town: University of the Western Cape.

Pazvakavambwa, B & Wanjau, C. (2015). *Preliminary Research into the Extent, Factors and Effects of Child Marriage Research in Zambia, Zimbabwe and Malawi*. Pretoria: VSO Rhaisa.

Progressio (Catholic Institute for International Relations). (2016). *The Price of Womanhood: Young women's Sexual and Reproductive Health and Rights in Zimbabwe*. London: Progressio.

Research and Advocacy Unit (2014). *Let Them Grow First: Early Marriage in Goromonzi, Zimbabwe*, Harare: Research and Advocacy Unit.

Sibanda, M. (2011). *Married too Soon: Child Marriage in Zimbabwe*, Harare: Research and Advocacy Unit.

Stormorken, S. L., Vincent, K., & Santisteban R. (2007). *No More Excuses: Ending all Harmful Traditional Practices against Girls and Young Women*. Oslo: Plan.

UNICEF. (2003). *Child Protection: An Analysis and Achievements in 2003*. New York: UNICEF.

2013. *Ending Child Marriage: Progress and Prospects*. New York: UNICEF.

2014. Child marriage. www.unicef.org/protection/57929_58008.html.

2015. *State of the World's Children Report: Reimagine the Future*. New York: UNICEF.

2016. *Extended Analysis of Multiple Indicator Cluster Survey (MICS) 2014: Child Protection, Child Marriage and Attitudes towards Violence*. Harare: UNICEF.

United Nations Population Fund, 2012. *Marrying too Young: End Child Marriage*. New York: United Nations Population Fund.

Wadesango, N., Rembe, S., & Chabaya, O. (2011). Violation of Women's Rights by Harmful Traditional Practices. *Anthropologist 13*(2), 121–129.

Education

26 The Fertile, Thorny, and Enduring Role of Desire and Pleasure in Sexuality Education

Sarah Garland-Levett and Louisa Allen

In this chapter we trace how desire and pleasure intersect with the field of school-based sexuality education. Our aim is to trace the trajectory of desire and pleasure in sexuality education research and practice and the forms this has taken. We begin with the seminal work of Michelle Fine (1988) whose identification of a missing discourse of desire in sex education in the United States, galvanized a generation of feminist researchers to explore its absence in other global locations. Since this work, researchers have also sought to explore the potential and problematics of desire and pleasure's inclusion in programs. This chapter traces and explores their effects on thinking about the content and delivery of sexuality education. The ways in which a concentration on a missing discourse of desire has contributed to reconfiguration of notions of sexual health and offered critiques of gendered and sexual identities is explored.

Some feminists held high hopes for the inclusion of desire and pleasure in sexuality education, particularity its perceived potential for opening possibilities for young women's sexual subjectivity and agency. The realities of implementing this discourse in practice, however, have been tempering. Not only has the uptake of pleasure within sexuality education been piecemeal internationally but the politics of such a move are complex and challenging. Debates around the sexualization of young women in media and popular culture have burdened notions of young women's pleasure and desire, rendering them once again 'victims' of powerful others. Desire and pleasure have also been recognized as having regulating and normalizing effects that can 'other' particular sexual identities, cultures, and religious beliefs. In interrogating these politics and challenges, we attempt to sketch the school-based landscape of sexuality education as simultaneously fertile, thorny, and enduring.

The Missing Discourse of Female Sexual Desire in Schools

In 1988 Michelle Fine's article 'Sexuality, Schooling, and Adolescent Females: The Missing Discourse of Desire' was published in the *Harvard Educational Review*. This article ignited discussion around the inclusion of desire and pleasure in sexuality education, which continues 30 years later. Fine provocatively suggested desire was missing from sex education in US schools and this was of detriment to young people, particularly young women. In this article she claimed that anti-sex rhetoric in US sex education was inhibiting the sexual subjectivities and responsibilities of high school students. Drawing on four dominant discourses that framed national debates over sex education, Fine traced these in the context of a New York public high school in the 1980s. Through these discourses, she demonstrated the way female sexuality is constructed as vulnerable to male predators, highlighting that women are taught to protect themselves from pregnancy, disease, and being used.

Fine's feminist critique of school sex education argued that female sexual desire is suppressed in school classrooms, and, instead, girls are offered a dominant discourse of female sexual victimization in which marital heterosexuality is privileged. She argued that female sexuality framed as "a risk" and "vulnerability" denies young women a sexual subjectivity informed by desire and their own sexual meanings. Instead, it reduces girls to sexual gatekeepers who are incapable of being active and agentic initiators and negotiators in their sexual relationships. This critique held implications for young women's experience of themselves as sexual subjects and how they might successfully navigate sexual situations in order to enjoy positive sexual outcomes.

Although absent from curricula and formal lessons, Fine argued that the fourth discourse, a discourse of desire, was present in the informal spaces of schooling and the lives and imaginations of those she conducted her research with (Fine, 1992). The young women in her study demonstrated that issues of violence and victimization are inextricably entangled with their experience of sexuality, yet, the presence of sexual pleasures, lusts, and desires also have a vital role in shaping their sexual subjectivities. Fine (1988) called for schools to offer young women "a language and experience of empowerment," so that they might experience "entitlement rather than victimization, autonomy rather than terror" (p. 50). These ideas stimulated a discussion about desire's inclusion in sexuality education, which remains an issue for contemporary program policy, design, and delivery (McGeeney & Kehily, 2016).

Feminists Accept the Desire Gauntlet

Debate around desire in sexuality education sparked by Fine's work has predominately been taken up by feminist researchers. What was appealing to feminists about Fine's ideas were that they highlighted the "gender-based power inequities [that] shape, define and construct experiences of sexuality" (p. 41) in schooling contexts. As such, this work inspired an abundance of feminist research that sought to both evidence the missing discourse of desire and pleasure in school in various international contexts, and attempt to argue for its inclusion (e.g., Alldred and David, 2007; Allen, 2004; Beasley, 2008; Carmody, 2009; Hirst,

2004, 2013; Ingham, 2005; Jackson & Weatherall, 2010; Kiely, 2005; Lenskyi, 1990; Rasmussen et al.; 2004; Sundaram & Sauntson, 2016; Tolman, 2002). Researchers in predominately Western contexts similarly identified desire and pleasure as missing from curricula in countries like England, Ireland, Canada, Australia, and New Zealand. Many harbored the idea that creating a place for desire and pleasure in sexuality education might offer a strategy to combat dominant discourses of female sexuality as passive, objectified, and victimized (Lamb, 2010).

An influential group of researchers to further Fine's insights during the 1990s were the Women, Risk and AIDS Project (WRAP). Their British-based work generated gendered insights into contextual complexities around women's access to practicing safer sex and exercising agency in their heterosexual relationships (Thomson & Holland, 1994). This study qualitatively analyzed 75 young women's narratives about their heterosexual experiences and relationships. It demonstrated that when young women are informed about reproduction and the 'dangers' of sexuality, without an understanding of sexual pleasure, girls lack "verbal and conceptual ammunition with which to make informed and meaningful choices" (Thomson & Holland, 1994, p. 19). Other feminists (Tolman, 1994, 2002) have also contributed to these findings by theorizing the way young women's negotiation of sexual safety is mired in gendered sexual scripts in which female sexuality is passive and male sexuality active (Tolman et al., 2010). Tolman and her colleagues' work furthered the claim that sexuality education that serves only to teach the risks and dangers of sexuality is unlikely to be relevant to young people's lives (Alldred & David, 2007; Measor et al., 2000).

Research advocating for the inclusion of desire and pleasure in sexuality education offers a range of reasons why this might be important. These span the promotion of safer sex and the importance of equality in sexual relationships to practice this (Beasley, 2008; Holland et al., 1992). The WRAP researchers found, for instance, that while some young women wanted their boyfriends to use condoms, they often felt powerless, embarrassed, or awkward about insisting on this. Often, they worried boyfriends would be offended by such a suggestion that might imply distrust, or that condoms would reduce pleasurable sensation. Other reasons for including desire in sexuality education entail increasing awareness of a wider range of sexual practices beyond penetrative heterosex (Tolman, 1994, 2002) and promotion of safe alternatives (Ingham, 2005). Discussions of desire that transcend heterosexual intercourse might also engender recognition of diverse sexual identities (Hirst, 2004) and more empowering forms of gendered sexual subjectivity (Allen, 2012; Tolman, 2002).

Calls for the inclusion of pleasure in sexuality education are premised not only on claims of making learning more relevant and meaningful to young people but that addressing pleasure legitimates young people's sexuality (Allen, 2007). This legitimization is understood as essential for the creation of discursive spaces to foster sexual responsibility (Schalet, 2010). Tolman (2002) argues it is unsafe and unhealthy to deny female adolescent sexual desire that recognizes a young woman's sexual subjectivity and decision-making power. Without a sense of sexual entitlement or knowledge about what they find sexually pleasurable, young women are ill positioned to make informed decisions about what sexual activity they engage in. This recognition of young people as sexual subjects is extended by Carmody (2009), who suggests they have the potential to become *ethical* sexual subjects who can build mutually respectful and pleasurable sexual experiences with others. Building on Foucault's ideas around ethics, Carmody's ethical sexual subjectivity is one that reflects the impact of desire on both the self and those they affect through our sexual relations. In this way, ethical sexual subjectivity, in its emphasis on care for the self and other, provides the basis for mutually safe and equal sexual relations with new possibilities for intimate pleasures.

Calls for pleasure's inclusion are seen to not only have relevance for enabling a more active and positive female sexual subjectivity, but also for expanding notions of male sexuality that are experienced negatively or as restrictive. Allen (2004) contends that the invisibility of pleasure and desire in the curriculum affects young women and young men differently. As well as legitimating and making space for female pleasure and sexual entitlement, there may also be benefits of offering up a narrative of male sexuality that is not expressed through hegemonic male (hetero)sexuality (Connell & Messerschmidt, 2005). These include enabling young men to express and experience their sexuality in diverse and alternative ways that do not involve exercise of gendered power over others. Beasley (2008) argues the integration of pleasure into teaching about sexual health might promote more egalitarian (hetero)sexual practices that have the potential to mitigate rates of sexual violence. Her research suggests that recognizing pleasure in sexuality education may result in women having a greater role in sexual negotiations and increased use of condoms by men (Beasley, 2008).

Heteronormativity and the Missing Discourse of Desire

Fine's ideas about the missing discourse of desire in sex education were initially conceptualized in relation to cis-gendered[1] and heterosexual relationships. This orientation was apparent in subsequent work around desire and pleasure undertaken by the Women Risk and AIDS and Men Risk and AIDs projects in Britain, which focused on unequal gendered power in heterosexual relationships. In projects such as this, lack of gay, lesbian, and bisexual participants was not a failure to acknowledge or include these sexual identities but inability to attract them. The activism of the LGBT movement was just gaining momentum in the academy, and its work in recognizing and attempting to disrupt heteronormativity[2]

[1] Cis-gender refers to a person whose gender identity aligns with the sex they were assigned at birth.

[2] Heteronormativity refers to a set of naturalized practices and assumptions in which is it assumed that heterosexuality is natural and preferred, and any sexuality beyond this is marked as 'other' and abnormal. Heteronormativity depends on and reproduces binary gender, where only female and male gender identities are recognized, and these are assumed to be complementary opposites.

in nascent form. For many who identified as LGBT during this era, previous experience of research 'inclusion' had amounted to studies that rendered their sexuality 'abnormal,' 'deviant,' 'other.' It is hardly surprising then that many were reluctant to participate in studies of sexuality until such heteronormative practices had been exposed and critiqued.

This important work began to occur from the 1990s when a number of researchers drew attention to heterosexuality's dominant and naturalized status in diverse institutional spaces, including sexuality education (Epstein & Johnston, 1998; Harrison et al., 1996; Lenskyj, 1990; Letts & Sears, 1999). Thought in sexuality research was influenced by Judith Butler's (1999) popular notion of the "heterosexual matrix" as the "grid of cultural intelligibility through which bodies, genders, and desires are naturalized" (p. 194). The heterosexual matrix offered a tool for thinking about the bodies and desires that are nullified in the sexuality curriculum's implicit assumption that sexuality is *hetero*sexuality. Although reluctantly sexualized spaces in any form, researchers began to document the ways schools are institutions that have historically and implicitly naturalized heterosexuality as preferred and natural (Epstein et al., 2003; Ferfolja, 2007; Hillier et al., 1999).

This critique was extended to the sexuality curriculum where content was recognized as heteronormative by default (Allen, 2004; Elia & Eliason, 2010; Lamb, 2013; Thorogood, 2000). Capitalizing on the queer theoretical work of Butler (1999) such heteronormativity was evident in the way sexuality education was founded upon the construction of gender in uncontested binary terms (Harrison & Ollis, 2015). Repeated pregnancy prevention messages and the linking of 'sexual and reproductive health' were identified as erasing possibilities for non-procreative sexualities. As Allen (2004) wrote, "equating sexual activity with reproduction is a construction of sexuality that is fundamentally (hetero)sexual and ultimately defined in terms of men's' penetration of women" (p. 154). Contraceptive methods, often taught heavily in sexuality programs, were seen to carry associated meanings about what constitutes 'sex' and the context in which it occurs (Holland et al., 1992). And, in terms of a missing discourse of desire in sexuality education, while it might only be an unofficial whisper at school for heterosexual-identified youth, it constituted a resounding silence for those who were lesbian, gay, or bisexual.

Recognition of the heteronormative context of schooling and sexuality education also helped to illuminate how transgender perspectives and gender diverse students' experiences of sexuality and desire are invisible in schools (Brömdal et al., 2017). In fact, it can be argued they are more invisible than LGB identities and perspectives, as research newly emerges in the field. A recent example is Riggs and Bartholomaeus' (2017) work that reveals sexuality education frequently teaches anatomy in terms of cis-gendered genital representations, separates content in terms of 'girls' and 'boys' and offers pregnancy prevention messages only in cis-heteronormative terms. Teaching about bodies and intimacy only through the lens of normative genders and anatomies fails to affirm and include transgendered students' sexualities, let alone recognize their desires and pleasures. Therefore, while a heterosexual discourse of desire has been traced as missing from sexuality education, especially for females, that silence is doubly amplified for transgender and gender diverse students. The absence of nonconforming gender identities from the curriculum leaves little hope for the acknowledgment and exploration of queer desires and pleasures in this context. This situation creates a knowledge gap in many current programs, casting non-conforming gender identities and their expressions of sexuality as 'abnormal' or 'inferior.'

Desire and Pleasure's Reconfiguration of Sexual Health

One effect of the critique of a missing discourse of desire in sexuality education has been a reassessment of what constitutes sexual health. The purpose of sexuality education is often framed as the "regulatory management of social risk" (Beasley, 2008, p. 159). That is, at a policy level, its key objectives and justification for its existence are to reduce costly social and health outcomes. When sexuality education is concerned with, and evaluated through, a public health framework, sexual activity is something to be regulated and controlled to reduce unplanned pregnancies and sexually transmitted infections (STIs) (Ingham, 2005). Its logic follows that providing information to individuals about how to avoid these risks will reduce their incidence overall. For example, the United Kingdom's 2014 updated guidelines for sexuality and relationships education continue to focus on the avoidance of pregnancy and sexual disease through delaying sexual activity. The educational emphasis is on risk, teenage pregnancy, and safeguarding against the personal choices that lead to such 'undesirable' outcomes (Ringrose, 2016). As Beasley (2008) notes, when we understand sexuality through a medicalized lens, sexual health becomes aligned with 'danger' and 'risk' emphasizing sexual 'problems' that are framed in biomedical terms.

Prompted by feminist critiques of the sex-negative emphasis on danger and risk in sexuality education, attempts have been made to reconceptualize sexual health positively and holistically beyond the absence of disease. Aggleton and Campbell (2000) note that while avoidance of STIs and unplanned pregnancy might be preconditions for achieving sexual health, our vision must go further to include sexual expression beyond procreative relationships and integrate individual and collective needs, rights, and responsibilities. This orientation to sexual health is evident in the World Health Organization's definition:

> sexual health is a state of physical, emotional, mental and social well-being related to sexuality; it is not merely the absence of disease, dysfunction or infirmity. Sexual health requires a positive and respectful approach to sexuality and sexual relationships, as well as the possibility of having pleasurable and safe sexual experiences, free of coercion, discrimination and violence. For sexual health to be attained and maintained, the sexual rights of all persons must be respected, protected and fulfilled. (World Health Organization, 2002, p. 5)

Such definitions of sexual health are more holistic and sex positive and can, as the World Health Organization does here, explicitly recognize a right to pleasure devoid of discrimination and coercion. While, in some pockets of the globe, rhetoric around sexual health might be changing, what this means for the teaching and practice of sexuality education remains unclear.

This is partly because the terms 'pleasure' and 'desire' are not uncontroversial or without their own politics (Allen et al., 2014). Not everyone believes desire and pleasure should be included within sexuality education and may oppose it on religious, cultural, or other grounds (see Hirst, 2014). Others warn that its inclusion will not necessarily engender positive or progressive outcomes in the way feminists and other proponents have initially envisaged. In *The History of Sexuality*, Foucault suggested moving away from the notions of sex and desire in favor of a movement toward bodies and pleasures instead (Rasmussen, 2004). Foucault's preference for the use of pleasure derives from desire being associated with a sense of identity, which excludes those placed outside a norm and inhibits it from being reconfigured in new ways (Allen & Carmody, 2012). Pleasure on the other hand "is an experience that can be divorced from the subject with the potential to reconfigure it" (Allen & Carmody, 2012, p. 464). Others use the term 'erotics' as a way of capturing both pleasure and desire but being broader than both (Allen & Carmody, 2012).

Problematizing Pleasure and Desire

As recent literature attests (Allen et al., 2014; McGeeney, 2017; McGeeney & Kehily, 2016) a discourse of female desire is still missing from many official school discourses. However, female desire is certainly not absent in media or popular culture (Levy, 2005; Ringrose, 2016). Silence around female sexual desire has been replaced with a "virtual racket" (Tolman, 2012, p. 747), where narrow depictions of sexualized girls pervade everyday life (Gill, 2009) and empowerment has often become problematically aligned with consumerism, media, pornography, and heterosexism (Lamb & Peterson, 2011). Popular media is highly sexualized, eroticized, and commodified and particular narratives of sexual pleasure are readily available through the medium of online pornography.

Social anxieties about the sexualization of childhood and girlhood in particular, have provoked a retreat within social understandings of young women, to a narrative of childhood innocence that evokes sexual protectionism (Kehily, 2012). Socially and historically located age-defined categories of citizenship come to justify protectionism and regulation of children's lives by adults (McClelland & Hunter, 2013) and the school is an important site of governance in which adults define and police these terms of being (Lesko, 2012). Sex and sexuality often represent a key signifier of the division between childhood and adulthood, with the construct of the innocent child underlying moral panic that obstructs openly addressing sexuality in schools (Alldred & David, 2007; Irvine, 2002; McClelland & Hunter, 2013). This has been the recent context in which the inclusion of desire and pleasure in sexuality education have been debated, and by which such discussion has been shaped.

If the purpose of sexuality education is a form of protection from the harms of sexuality, this leaves little space for teaching about its positive potential. Some researchers have argued that if sexuality education teaches young people only how to resist sex then the realm of pleasure is left to privatized (or pornified) voices and the opportunity to teach equal sexual relations through education is missed (Beasley, 2008). That is, unlike easily accessible commercial sources of information about sexuality and sexual pleasure, education represents a space that can offer an alternative discourse to pornography in ways that emphasize not only sexual health but sexual citizenship. It is argued that if pleasure is integrated into sexuality education, it might offer an alternative discourse about pleasurable sexuality that, unlike mainstream pornography, is based on a goal of safe, consensual, equal, and mutual sexual experiences (Allen, 2004).

In recognition of the complexities that notions of sexualization lend to the inclusion of female sexual desire and pleasure in sexuality education, several authors have revisited its politics. In their "historic revision to the missing discourse of desire," Fine and McClelland's (2006, p. 300) call for a framework of sexual health that recognizes "how macro-structures, public institutions, practices and relationships affect 'personal decisions'" (p. 328). Using a human rights paradigm, the authors develop the notion of 'thick desire' to address their concerns over the unevenly distributed consequences of the Abstinence Only Until Marriage campaign in the United States. Thick desire is an attempt to conceptualize sexual health and well-being not only as an individual property but as situated within social and economic structural contexts. Fine and McClelland (2006) argue that government policy in the United States constructs vulnerable youth, such as youth of color and the working class, as irresponsible and more likely to make 'bad choices' that result in poor sexual health.

This individualistic understanding of pleasure has been queried in feminist debates about girls' empowerment, where some feminists conflate experiencing pleasure with sexual subjectivity and agency (Lamb & Peterson, 2011). Others contend that theoretically and politically complex concepts of desire have "been hollowed by a neoliberal psychological interpretation that reduces desire only to the property of an individual girl" (Tolman, 2012, p. 751). Speaking to the assumption of women's pleasure as equated with empowerment, Gavey (2012) suggests it may be more productive to critique the "cultural conditions of possibility" (p. 718) for sexual empowerment, given that the term itself has been "co-opted and depoliticised within neoliberal post-feminist discourse" (p. 718). These debates highlight that the meaning and effects of pleasure are not static or self-evident. Female sexual pleasure is a political, contextual, and shifting phenomenon. While it has been variously offered up as "a pedagogical tool that in its different forms is informative, political, liberatory, transgressive and regulatory"

(McGeeney & Kehily, 2016, p. 253), its educational trajectory is by no means fixed or extinguished.

Pleasure and Desire's Normalizing Effects

Since Fine's pivotal article and the global research it inspired, some researchers have taken pause to reflect on the effects of this discourse and its materialization in schooling. The ways pleasure has been operationalized in sexuality education are not necessarily as its proponents initially intended (Allen & Carmody, 2012). Some feminists have considered the trajectory female desire has taken and lamented its form and effects. Fine herself reflected in a 2005 special issue of *Feminism & Psychology* how in her original work desire had "been mediated and colonised by global capital, medicalisation, privatisation and the imperial presence of the state" (p. 56).

The way in which pleasure has been theoretically conceived may inhibit its productive potential in sexuality education (Allen & Carmody, 2012). Reflecting on the potential for a specific set of pleasures to become problematically normalized, Allen and Carmody refine the call for pleasure's inclusion to one that allows "spaces for the possibility of ethical pleasures, in forms that are not pre-conceived, heteronormative or mandatory" (p. 457). Concerns have been raised that the call for pleasure's inclusion has resulted in the promotion of a *pleasure imperative*, rather than a basis for legitimating young people's right to and interest in pleasure (Allen & Carmody, 2012). Others have warned of the regulatory effects of equating the attainment of sexual pleasure with empowerment (Jagose, 2010), sexual health, or any other political end.

Like pinning pleasure to agency, this concept can become equally problematic when its meaning is tied to specific "corporeal sensations, heteronormative configurations and bodily acts" (Allen & Carmody, 2012, p. 465). Allen and Carmody argue that if pleasure becomes prescribed curriculum content, where young people are meant to achieve or strive for pleasure in their sexual experiences, it mutates into a normative expectation losing its transformative potential. They warn that educators should "resist attempts to reduce discourses of erotics to, 'a pleasure imperative' where students learn the recipe for how to gain it, and maybe, even, how to give it" (p. 465). The potential of pleasure in sexuality education is not in its capacity as a static set of knowledge but in evoking a conceptual space that might have transformative potential in ways that cannot be preempted.

Additionally, this substantive body of research itself may have had normative effects on the collective feminist conscious. Allen (2013) suggests that a possible unintended effect of feminist research following Fine, was that it reinscribed girls' desire as absent and problematic. This orientation to the issues of desire and pleasure may have inhibited research that recognizes desire as an everyday presence in schooling and a site of possibility. As a counter measure to this tendency,

Allen's (2013) study employs visual methods to position the girls in her research as desiring subjects who frame young men as desired objects in photos.

The Practice of Desire and Pleasure in Sexuality Education

While many educators, researchers, and students still face prohibitions in the "fraught process" of openly addressing pleasure in the formal curricula of schooling (Rasmussen, 2004, p. 451), pleasure has gained a presence in education programs in some parts of the globe. It is important to note that sexuality education is still not a mandatory component of the curriculum in countries like Russia and Greece, where the possibility of desire and pleasure's inclusion is a redundant consideration. For countries where sexuality education is an entrenched element of the schooling curriculum and pandemics such as HIV/AIDS have receded, desire and pleasure are more likely to be addressed. The challenges and outcomes of these inclusions that move the push for pleasure beyond the theoretical realm and into the classroom, have created particular issues for pedagogy and teacher training.

British research by McGeeney (2015) demonstrates there are real practical challenges to getting young people to discuss pleasure among their peers. Her focus groups with disadvantaged young men in the United Kingdom demonstrate that what it is possible to say about sex and pleasure is shaped by social expectations of peers and professionals. This work highlights that creating spaces for exploring sexual pleasure that involve diverse and equal expressions of gender and sexuality might be hampered by expectations of hypermasculinity (McGeeney, 2015). That is, social norms around gender and sexuality might be reinforced, rather than challenged, through peer talk about pleasure. McGeeney's work also highlights that spaces that are devised to allow young people to critically discuss sexual pleasure are inevitably shaped by their adult presence. What is able to be said will be shaped by their presence, and educators might face challenges in trying to ensure these are safe spaces that maintain confidentiality and respectful language.

An analysis of US curricula by Lamb et al. (2013) found that, when pleasure and desire are acknowledged in sex education curricula, they are often linked to the negative consequence of STIs and pregnancy. This study found that, while pleasure is no longer absent or missing, its integration is often heterosexist and portrayed as an uncontrollable force that produces risks and negative outcomes. Therefore, instead of girls being taught to avoid the desires of predatory males, they are taught about the need to stay safe from the passions of desire, including their own. In this reiteration of the discourse of victimization, pleasure is again equated with danger and students are taught that seeking sex for pleasure will result in harm.

In the Australian context, Ollis (2016) has described the challenges of educating 42 pre-service health and physical education teachers about how to include issues of desire and pleasure in sexuality lessons. Part of this difficulty stems from how pedagogies of pleasure sit in tension with the current sex-negative approach that has historically pervaded sexuality education. This context renders a "focus on pleasure risky business for teachers" (Ollis, 2016, p. 321) evidenced in teachers' discomfort in watching the visual resource, *Sex on the Map*. As part of their training, teachers were shown this cartoon film designed to explore in a sex-positive and explicit way, issues of sexual practice, desire, and intimacy with year 9 and 10 students (aged 13–15). The film, which shows masturbation, sexual arousal, and orgasm, shocked some teachers with one commenting that, "I felt like I was in a way watching porn" (Ollis, 2016, p. 316). Ollis' research highlights the challenge of moving to a sex-positive approach in teaching sexuality education, given the sex-negative history of this subject. This shift necessitates teachers "develop comfort and confidence required to teach about sexual pleasure in a context where there is little opportunity to reflect, explore and engage in pedagogies of pleasure and even fewer resources to support this work" (Ollis, 2016, p. 320). How to train teachers effectively in this regard, represents a challenge for the practical implementation of a discourse of pleasure in sexuality education.

Culture, Religion, and the Future of Pleasure in Schools

As the earlier-mentioned literature demonstrates, there has been no shortage of critique of pleasure being missing from sexuality education. However, until recently, varied understandings of pleasure and its place in relation to sexuality for different religious, ethnic, and cultural communities have garnered minimal attention. Because if its feminist origins, the political push for pleasure's inclusion in sexuality education has been premised on a desired end of gender equity. Inadvertently, this has foreclosed exploration of how other issues that intersect with pleasure and desire, such as social class and ethnicity might configure its place in programs differently (Allen, 2012). McClelland and Fine (2014) note that an assumption of a strong positive association between "pleasure, agency, and justice" (p. 29) underpins pleasure and desire's wide uptake in feminist research, and this has begun to be challenged. Allen (2012) reflects that advocating for a discourse of pleasure in sexuality education is premised on values including gender equality, personal pleasure, and the desire to promote "less restrictive non-heteronormative ways of doing masculinities and femininities" (p. 461). She then critically interrogates whose interests and what understandings these particular conceptualizations of "social/sexual justice" (p. 461) have sought to serve, and whose interests they may unintentionally elide. Indeed, the feminist origins of the identification of the missing discourse of desire privileges a certain sort of 'justice' that, in foregrounding female sexuality, will have simultaneously silenced other sexualities. This is one issue that sexuality education has failed to acknowledge, and must effectively grapple with in the future.

In her contribution to this discussion Rasmussen (2012) notes advocating for pleasure and desire in sexuality education is premised on secular assumptions.

These contain their own form of moralizing that remain largely unscrutinized within the research field and risk alienating religious or culturally diverse youth. Rasmussen's critical reflexivity is a reminder that a value-free sexuality education is an impossibility, and even factual or secular positioning of sexuality education that seeks to offer unbiased information will deploy a certain version of morality. She urges us to recognize that ideals associated with secularism such as autonomy, pleasure, and sexual freedom must be subjected to the same scrutiny applied in other 'progressive' critiques of sexuality education. Her argument is that thick desire embeds a "sexularism" (p. 471) that conceals its own morality by positioning itself as a reasoned critique of neoliberal or fundamentalist moralising. A secular, health-focused sexuality education (often pitted against abstinence-only approaches in research) is often unreflexively aligned with ideals of autonomy, liberation, sexual freedom, and reason. Through this logic, religious, cultural, spiritual, or ethical influences on young people's sexualities can be excluded or deemed less valid, while pleasure is simultaneously uncritically normalized (Rasmussen, 2012).

In recent scholarship, researchers have begun to critique the way pleasure is often conceptualized in opposition to cultural and religious beliefs (Sanjakdar, 2014). Sanjakdar (2014) argues that contrary to popular dismissals in the literature and existing sexuality education, a discourse of pleasure is not missing from Islamic religion. In her research in Australian Islamic schools, Sanjakdar (2014) observes many sexuality education programs "promote a narrow kind of sexual subjectivity, which obscures sexual pleasure and desire" (p. 107), despite sexuality's pronounced importance in Islamic scriptures. She highlights that, like feminist hopes for sexuality education, pleasure should be honored for Muslim students rather than negatively focusing on sexuality's risks. Her justification is that the place of female pleasure is documented in the Qur'an and other religious scriptures in the context of heterosexual marriage. Sanjakdar writes that, "the 'sex education' available in these texts emphasises the importance of artful lovemaking and refining pleasure, that it is a learned art, and people should be encouraged to learn to venerate the flesh, to attend to the preliminaries of lovemaking, to sexual play, and to fantasy" (p. 104). However, she argues that Islamic understandings of sexuality are not yet legitimatized as important sources of knowledge that should have a place in sexuality education curricula for Muslim students.

Sanjakdar notes that, while a feminist viewpoint on pleasure is premised around inequalities associated with division of gender, "Islam argues that gender roles should seek to be complementary rather than the same" (p. 103). Islam offers a critique of heterosexuality that is not based on hegemonic and subordinate forms of sexuality, but is focused on how male and female roles are lived complementarily in relation to giving and seeking pleasure. Her proposal is that learning about sexuality and pleasure from an Islamic perspective should be openly addressed in schools so that this knowledge can "bring the student closer to the understanding of tawhid, the oneness of God" (p. 105). This call raises another issue for the future inclusion of desire and pleasure in sexuality education. How to acknowledge and respect Islamic gendered portrayals of pleasure in heterosexual marriage, and, at the same time, acknowledge and respect the discourses of other diverse groups that fall outside this configuration.

Despite the fact Fine (1988) introduced the possibility of a discourse of desire in sexuality education 30 years ago, it remains an issue that is controversial and unresolved. In the decades since Fine's article, the conversation around pleasure in sexuality education has broadened beyond questions of its absence, to analyses of how pleasure can, or is, being utilized in learning contexts, and what possibilities it holds for education (McGeeney & Kehily, 2016). These discussions have involved an interrogation of pleasure and desire's politics, which reveal that *if* they are included in sexuality education and how, is *always* political. Future engagements with pleasure and desire will be influenced by current critique of the normalizing and regulating effects of their current conceptualizations. While these hold the potential for opening up their ontological and epistemological foundations, whether or not this is realized at the level of program practice is uncertain. History in the field of sexuality education suggests that changes in this regard are slow and easily recouped. One thing that is perhaps more likely, however, is that the centrality of desire and pleasure to social experiences and conceptualizations of sexuality and gender ensure that this discussion will endure.

References

Aggleton, P. & Campbell, C. (2000). Working with Young People: Towards an Agenda for Sexual Health. *Sexual and Relationship Therapy*, *15*(3), 283–296.

Alldred, M. & David, M. E. (2007). *Get Real about Sex: The Politics and Practice of Sex Education*. Maidenhead: Open University Press.

Allen, L. (2004). Beyond the Birds and the Bees: Constituting a Discourse of Erotics in Sexuality Education. *Gender & Education*, *16*(2), 151–167.

(2007). Denying the Sexual Subject: Schools' Regulation of Student Sexuality. *British Educational Research Journal*, *33*(2), 221–234.

(2012). Pleasure's Perils? Critically Reflecting on Pleasure's Inclusion in Sexuality Education. *Sexualities*, *15*(3/4), 455–471.

(2013). Girls' Portraits of Desire: Picturing a Missing Discourse. *Gender and Education*, *25*(3), 295–310.

Allen, L. & Carmody, M. (2012). Pleasure Has No Passport: Re-Visiting the Potential of Pleasure in Sexuality Education. *Sex Education*, *12*(4), 455–468.

Allen, L., Rasmussen, M. L., & Quinlivan, K. (2014). *The Politics of Pleasure in Sexuality Education: Pleasure Bound*. New York: Routledge.

Beasley, C. (2008). The Challenge of Pleasure: Re-Imagining Sexuality and Sexual Health. *Health Sociology Review*, *17*(2), 151–163.

Brömdal, N., Rasmussen, M., Sanjakdar, F., Allen, L., & Quinlivan, K. (2017). Intersex Bodies in Sexuality Education: On the Edge of Cultural Difference. In Allen, L. & Rasmussen, M. (Eds.), *The Palgrave Handbook of Sexuality Education* (369–390). London: Palgrave, Springer Nature.

Butler, J. (1999). *Gender Trouble: Feminism and the Subversion of Identity, 10th anniversary edn*. New York: Routledge.

Carmody, M. (2009). *Sex and Ethics: Young People and Ethical Sex*. Melbourne: Palgrave Macmillan.

Connell, R. & Messerschmidt, J. (2005). Hegemonic Masculinity Rethinking the Concept. *Gender and Society*, *19*(6), 829–859.

Elia, J. P. & Eliason, M. (2010). Discourses of Exclusion: Sexuality Education's Silencing of Sexual Others. *Journal of LGBT Youth*, *7*, 29–48.

Epstein, D. & Johnson, R. (1998). *Schooling Sexualities*. Buckingham: Open University Press.

Epstein, D., O'Flynn, S., & Telford, D. (2003). *Silenced Sexualities in Schools and Universities*. Oakhill: Trentham.

Ferfolja, T. (2007). Schooling Cultures: Institutionalizing Heteronormativity and Heterosexism. *International Journal of Inclusive Education*, *11*(2), 147–162.

Fine, M. (1988). Sexuality, Schooling, and Adolescent Females: The Missing Discourse of Desire. *Harvard Educational Review*, *58*, 29–53.

(1992). *Disruptive Voices: The Possibilities of Feminist Research*. Ann Arbor: University of Michigan Press.

(2005). Desire: The Morning (and 15 Years) After. *Feminism & Psychology*, *15*(1), 54–60.

Fine, M. & McClelland, S. (2006). Sexuality Education and Desire: Still Missing after All These Years. *Harvard Educational Review*, *76*(3), 297–437.

Gavey, N. (2012). Beyond "Empowerment"? Sexuality in a Sexist World. *Sex Roles*, *66*(11–12), 718–724.

Gill, R. (2009). Beyond the 'Sexualization of Culture' Thesis: An Intersectional Analysis of 'Sixpacks, 'Midriffs' and 'Hot Lesbians' in Advertising. *Sexualities*, *12*(2), 137–160.

Harrison, L., Hillier, L., & Walsh, J. (1996). Teaching for a Positive Sexuality: Sounds Good, but What about Fear, Embarrassment, Risk and the 'Forbidden' Discourse of Desire. In Laskey, L. & Beavis, C. (Eds.), *Schooling and Sexualities: Teaching for a Positive Sexuality* (68–92). Geelong: Deakin Centre for Education and Change.

Harrison, L. & Ollis, D. (2015). Stepping Out of Our Comfort Zones: Pre-Service Teachers' Responses to a Critical Analysis of Gender/Power Relations in Sexuality Education. *Sex Education*, *15*(3), 318–331.

Hillier, L., Harrison, L., & Dempsey, D. (1999). Whatever Happened to Duty of Care? Same-Sex Attracted Young People's Stories of Schooling and Violence. *Melbourne Studies in Education*, *40*(2), 59–74.

Hirst, J. (2004). Researching Young People's Sexuality and Learning about Sex: Experience, Need, and Sex and Relationship Education. *Culture, Health & Sexuality*, *6*(2), 115–129.

(2013). 'It's Got to Be about Enjoying Yourself ': Young People, Sexual Pleasure, and Sex and Relationships Education. *Sex Education*, *13*(4), 423–436.

(2014). 'Get Some Rhythm Round the Clitoris': Addressing Sexual Pleasure in Sexuality Education in Schools and Other Youth Settings. In Allen, L., Rasmussen, M. & Quinlivan, K. (Eds.), *The Politics of Pleasure in Sexuality Education: Pleasure Bound* (35–56). New York: Routledge.

Holland, J., Ramazanoglu, C., Scott, S., Sharpe, S., & Thomson, R. (1992). Risk, Power and the Possibility of Pleasure: Young Women and Safer Sex. *AIDS Care: Psychological and Socio-medical Aspects of AIDS/HIV, 4*(3), 273–283.

Ingham, R. (2005). "We Didn't Cover That at School": Education against Pleasure or Education for Pleasure? *Sex Education, 5*(4), 375–388.

Irvine, J. (2002). *Talk about Sex: The Battles over Sex Education in the United States*. Los Angeles: University of California Press.

Jackson, S. & Weatherall, A. (2010). The (Im)possibilities of Feminist School Based Sexuality Education. *Feminism & Psychology, 20*(2), 166–185.

Jagose, A. (2010). Counterfeit Pleasures: Fake Orgasm and Queer Agency. *Textual Practice 24*(3), 517–539.

Kehily, M. J. (2012) Contextualising the Sexualisation of Girls Debate: Innocence, Experience and Young Female Sexuality. *Gender and Education*, 24(3), 255–268.

Kiely, E. (2005). Where Is the Discourse of Desire? Deconstructing the Irish Relationships and Sexuality Education (RSE) Resource Materials. *Irish Educational Studies 24*(2–3), 253–266.

Lamb, S. (2010). Feminist Ideals for a Healthy Female Adolescent Sexuality: A Critique. *Sex Roles, 62*(5), 294–306.

(2013). *Sex Ed for Caring Schools: Creating an Ethics Based Curriculum*. New York: Teachers College Press.

Lamb, S., Lustig, K., & Graling, K. (2013). The Use and Misuse of Pleasure in Sex Education Curricula. *Sex Education, 13*(3), 305–318.

Lamb, S. & Peterson, Z. (2011). Adolescent Girls' Sexual Empowerment: Two Feminists Explore the Concept. *Sex Roles, 66*, 703–712.

Lenskyj, H. (1990). Beyond Plumbing and Prevention: Feminist Approaches to Sex Education. *Gender and Education 2*(2), 217–230.

Lesko, N. (2012). *Act Your Age! A Cultural Construction of Adolescence*. New York: Routledge.

Letts, W. & Sears, J. (1999). *Queering Elementary Education: Advancing the Dialogue about Sexualities and Schooling.* Lanhan: Roman and Littlefield Publishers.

Levy, A. (2005). *Female Chauvinist Pigs: Women and the Rise of Raunch Culture*. New York: Free Press.

McClelland, S. I. & Fine, M. (2014). Over-Sexed and Under Surveillance: Adolescent Sexualities, Cultural Anxieties, and Thick Desire. In Allen, L., Rasmussen, M. L., & Quinlivan, K. (Eds.), *The Politics of Pleasure in Sexuality Education: Pleasure Bound* (12–34). New York: Routledge.

McClelland, S.I. & Hunter, L.E. (2013). Bodies That Are Always Out of Line: A Closer Look at "Age Appropriate Sexuality." In Fahs, B., Dudy, M. L., & Stage, S. (Eds.), *The Moral Panics of Sexuality* (59–76). New York: Palgrave Macmillan.

McGeeney, E. (2015) A Focus on Pleasure? Desire and Disgust in Group Work with Young Men. *Culture, Health & Sexuality, 17*(2), 223–237.

McGeeney, E. (2017). Possibilities for Pleasure: A Creative Approach to Including Pleasure in Sexuality Education. In Allen, L. & Rasmussen, M. (Eds.), *The Palgrave Handbook of Sexuality Education* (571–590). London: Springer Nature.

McGeeney, E. & Kehily, M. J. (2016). Young People and Sexual Pleasure – Where Are We Now? *Sex Education, 16*(3), 235–239.

Measor, L., Tiffin, C., & Miller, K. (2000). *Young People's Views on Sex Education*. London: RoutledgeFalmer.

Ollis, D. (2016). "I Felt Like I Was Watching Porn": The Reality of Preparing Pre-service Teachers to Teach about Sexual Pleasure. *Sex Education*, *16*(3), 308–323.

Rasmussen, M. (2004). Wounded Identities, Sex and Pleasure: "Doing it" at School. NOT!. *Discourse: Studies in the Cultural Politics of Education*, *25*(4), 445–458.

(2012). Pleasure/Desire, Sexularism and Sexuality Education. *Sex Education*, *12*(4), 469–481.

Rasmussen, M., Rofes, E., & Talburt, S. (2004). *Youth and Sexualities: Pleasure, Subversion and Insubordination In and Out of Schools*. Houndsmill: Palgrave Macmillan.

Riggs, D. W. & Bartholomaeus, C. (2017). Transgender Young People's Narratives of Intimacy and Sexual Health: Implications for Sexuality Education. *Sex Education*, 18(4), 376–390. doi:10.1080/14681811.2017.1355299.

Ringrose, J. (2016). Postfeminist Media Panics over Girls' 'Sexualisation': Implications for UK Sex and Relationship Guidance and Curriculum. In Sundaram, V. & Sauntson, H. (Eds.), *Global Perspectives and Key Debates in Sex and Relationships Education: Addressing Issues of Gender, Sexuality, Plurality and Power* (30–47). Basingstoke: Palgrave Macmillan.

Sanjakdar, F. (2014). Sacred Pleasure: Exploring Dimensions of Sexual Pleasure and Desire from an Islamic Perspective. In Allen, L., Rasmussen, M., & Quinlivan, K. (Eds.), *The Politics of Pleasure in Sexuality Education: Pleasure Bound* (95–114). New York: Routledge.

Schalet, A. (2010). Sexual Subjectivity Revisited: The Significance of Relationships in Dutch and American Girls' Experiences of Sexuality. *Gender & Society 24*(3), 304–329.

Sundaram, V. & Sauntson, H. (2016). Discursive Silences: Using Critical Linguistic and Qualitative Analysis to Explore the Continued Absence of Pleasure in Sex and Relationships Education in England. *Sex Education*, *16*(3), 240–254.

Thomson, R. & Holland, J. (1994). Young Women and Safer (Hetero)sex: Context, Constraints and Strategies. In Wilkinson, S. & Kitzinger, C. (Eds.), *Women and Health: Feminist Perspectives* (13–32). London: Taylor & Francis.

Thorogood, N. (2000). Sex Education as Disciplinary Technique: Policy and Practice in England and Wales. *Sexualities*, *3*, 425–438.

Tolman, D. (1994). Doing Desire: Adolescent Girls' Struggles for/with Sexuality. *Gender and Society*, *8*(3), 324–342.

(2002). *Dilemmas of Desire: Teenage Girls Talk about Sexuality*. Cambridge, MA: Harvard University Press.

(2012). Female Adolescents, Sexual Empowerment and Desire: A Missing Discourse of Gender Inequity. *Sex Roles*, *66*, 746–757.

Tolman, D. L., Striepe, M. I., & Harmon, T. (2010). Gender Matters: Constructing a Model of Adolescent Sexual Health. *The Journal of Sex Research*, *40*(1), 4–12.

World Health Organization. (2002). *Defining Sexual Health: Report of a Technical Consultation on Sexual Health, 28–31 January 2002*. Geneva: WHO.

27 Norm-Critical Sex Education in Sweden

Tensions within a Progressive Approach

Anna Bredström, Eva Bolander, and Jenny Bengtsson

Introduction

Imagine a sex education built upon queer feminist and anti-racist perspectives – a sex education that seeks to challenge discriminatory structures, empower the underprivileged, and challenge hierarchies and social dominance. To many of us critically engaged in researching and problematizing mainstream sex education, such a scenario only exists in an ideal world. It is therefore with some caution that this chapter has been written, and should equally be read, as our basic ambition is to tease out the inherent tensions in such a desirable approach.

The chapter draws upon a research project carried out by the authors between the years 2012 and 2016, financed by the Swedish Research Council (2011–5850). The project, *Young People and Sexual Risk-Taking: An Intersectional Analysis of Representations, Knowledge and Experiences*, included extensive field work observing sex education in different school settings, interviewing teachers and other key actors, and critical analyses of sex educational materials including textbooks, films, websites, and manuals.

Initially, the project set out to explore how different masculinities and femininities are linked to risk and safety in discourses, practices, and experiences of safer sex among young people in Sweden. In doing so, we aimed to explain how normative understandings of class, gender, sexuality, race, and ethnicity tie into understandings of risk and responsibility, and how, in turn, different intersections of these identity categories either enable or obstruct young people's safer sex practices (Bredström, 2008, 2011). Of particular interest for us were the ways in which sex education strategies dealt with social hierarchies and power relations among youth. During our field research we became increasingly interested in progressive teachers and policy makers who were pursuing a queer feminist, anti-discriminatory, and *norm-critical* sex education, and thus seemed to be in line with our thinking. We learned that not only had such perspectives gained ground in many of the classrooms we visited but the norm-critical approach had also been adopted by recent sex educational policy (Swedish National Agency for Education, 2013a, 2013b, 2013c).

This chapter is an attempt to follow the trail of the proponents of the norm-critical approach and to critically discuss sex education efforts that aim to be progressive and anti-oppressive. This is a sex education that both relies on a social and cultural critique of 'norms' – that is, cultural perceptions of normality with reference to gender, sexual identity, race, ethnicity, class, able-bodiedness, age, and other categories of differences (Bromseth & Darj, 2010; Martinsson & Reimers, 2014) – and tries to teach and develop pedagogies that enable young people to move beyond such constraints.

Our chapter will begin with an extensive background of the norm-critical approach situated in the historical and sex educational context of Sweden, as well as a broader discussion of progressive sex education that is more contemporary and international in scope. We then use three examples from our research project – field notes from our research in a classroom situation, an educational film, and a written teaching material – to problematize the norm-critical approach and point to some inherent tensions. The tensions are: (1) the ways in which the norm-critical approach focuses on privileged identities, and the contradictions it involves when being applied in a heterogeneous school context; (2) the challenge of being all-inclusive as regards to different power structures and identities; and (3) the neglect of potentially colliding values, and how the norm-critical ambition is – despite its intentions – caught up in a neo-assimilatory framework where certain sexual values are promoted as universal and uncontested. In doing so, we will show that young peoples' sexual development, as it is portrayed in norm-critical education, remains a national project that does not escape the norms of Swedishness and 'otherness.' By way of conclusion, we will summarize our main points and discuss how a norm-critical approach could be further developed in order to move beyond these constraints.

The Historical Context of Swedish Sex Education

When it comes to sex education, Sweden – the small Nordic country with its insignificant population of nine million people – stands out internationally as exemplary, in particular for those interested in the intersection between sex education, welfare, and health. Sweden is well known for its inclusive welfare state, and celebrated for liberal views on sexuality and gender equality. Yet, there is also a darker side to the story. For instance, during the *folkhem* period (circa 1930–1960), sexual information – pivotal for improving the well-being of the poor working class – was concurrently embedded in eugenic philosophies and ideas about racial differences (Svendsen, 2017).

Modern sex education in Sweden grew out of feminist struggles for women's rights and the quest for sexual liberation. The establishment of medical sexology also played an important role. In late nineteenth century, the first female physician and renowned feminist Karolina Widerström (1907) taught 'sexual hygiene' to schoolmistresses in Stockholm. Widerström further advocated that both boys and girls should receive sex education, but her ideas were met with wide resistance. The then general sentiment about providing sex education for boys seemed to be, as the saying goes, 'better to let sleeping dogs lie'[1] (Lennerhed, 2012; Sandström, 1995, p. 10), and thus it remained scarce.

Gradually, the drive for sex education targeting both boys and girls met wider acceptance. The Swedish Association for Sex Education (RFSU) was here an important actor. Established in 1933 by the journalist Elise Ottesen-Jensen together with a group of socialist physicians and trade union representatives, the RFSU's main objective during this period was to pursue the right to inform the public about contraceptives (which were illegal between the years 1910 and 1938) and to argue for mandatory school-based sex education, women's rights to abortion and sterilization, and the decriminalization of homosexuality (Lennerhed, 2002, pp. 9–10).

As the Swedish welfare state took shape, sex education was increasingly subjected to governmental regulation (Hirdman, 1989). In 1945, the first guidelines for sex education in elementary school were published, followed in 1949 by directives for senior students (Lennerhed, 2012), and in 1955, sex education became mandatory in order to guarantee that all young people would be well informed on the biological, social, and moral aspects of sexuality. The decision to make sex education mandatory reflected an incipient shift in society toward a more liberal attitude regarding sex, in general, and youth sexuality, in particular. Lennerhed (1994) points to the influence of noteworthy studies on human sexual behaviors such as the American Kinsey report on male sexuality (Kinsey et al., 1948) and Gustav Jonsson's study on sexual behavior among Swedish youth, completed in 1947 and published in a Swedish Government Official Report (SOU, 1951). Both studies showed that a majority of those interviewed had had their sexual 'debut' (defined as heterosexual vaginal intercourse) prior to marriage, and that the age of debut was lower than anticipated (Lennerhed, 1994, pp. 67–68). Such facts were subsequently put forward in a Swedish Government Official Report as an argument in favor of mandatory sex education reflecting "the reality young people meet outside school" (SOU, 1951, pp. 107 & 113).

The resulting national guidelines for sex education from 1956 covered sex education from preschool ages up to 17–20 year olds and stated that the education should include, among other things, 'differences between the sexes,' the function of the genitals, puberty, menstruation, masturbation, pregnancy, childbirth, abortion, 'illegitimate children,' venereal diseases, contraceptives, sterilization, menopause, and 'sex drive deviations' (Skolöverstyrelsen, 1956). The guidelines also favored abstinence until marriage, but, at the same time, pointed out the need to be *preventive* (p. 15, italics in original) with reference to Kinsey et al.'s (1948) and Jonsson's (1951) findings about peoples' sexual habits. Mandatory sex education thus served as a pragmatic tool for fostering a healthy development among the

[1] Literally, in Swedish 'not wake the sleeping bear' ('Inte väcka den björn som sover').

Swedish population and particularly the Swedish youth, whose "characters would be strengthened through access to factual information" (pp. 7 & 10).

The vivid public debate on sexuality in the 1960s formed the basis for a more affirmative attitude toward youth sexuality that characterized sex education in the 1970s (Lennerhed, 1994; Sandström, 2001). Here the ideal of abstinence until marriage was abandoned in sex education guidelines. However, in order to regain some control over Swedish youth, the guidelines articulated sexual responsibility in terms of *love*. Sexual desires and pleasure were to be treated in an affirmative way, but only if they took place within a loving relationship (Sandström, 2001). Since then, sex educators have gradually distanced themselves from the morals of such 'love ideology,' largely because of its role in maintaining gendered double standards, where girls are expected to, for instance, express feelings of love in order to justify (casual) sex (Frisell, 1996). Instead, contemporary sex educators in Sweden put forward a sex-positive and pleasure-oriented rationale, with *lust* as a key word and motive for sexual acts (Bäckman, 2003). We will return to the present-day agenda later, but first we will describe the norm-critical turn in more detail.

The Development and Impact of Norm-Critical Pedagogy in Sweden

Sex education has never been a separate school subject in Sweden, that is, there has never been a national syllabus specifically for sex education; rather, it has been considered a theme that should be integrated across different school subjects. Until recently, however, sex education was mostly dealt with in biology classes. This was problematized both by the Swedish National Agency for Education (2000) as well as by scholars arguing that when positioned within biology curricula, sex education tends to focus too much on reproduction and the body, leaving out social aspects of coexistence and sexual relationships (Bolander, 2009; Larsson & Rosén, 2006). Recent policy in the field attempts to amend this by strategically emphasizing sexuality (in addition to related concepts such as gender norms, identity, belonging, and power structures) in syllabi for subjects such as English, History, Social Science, Swedish language, Religion, Physical Education, and Health to ensure that sex education is being addressed in a more interdisciplinary and subject-integrated way (Swedish National Agency for Education, 2011a, 2011b). For instance, in History, the Agency points to including topics such as family and abortion policy, suffrage, and the 'discovery of HIV and AIDS' (Swedish National Agency for Education, 2013c). Correspondingly, statistics on gender equality or the prevalence of sexually transmitted infections among youth may be used in Mathematics (ibid.).

Another recent shift in policy has been the promotion of a *norm-critical approach* in sex education (Swedish National Agency for Education 2013a, 2013b, 2013c). The term norm-critical pedagogy was coined in 2007 by a queer pedagogical network that gathered researchers, practitioners, and activists together (Bromseth & Darj, 2010). The network was highly influenced by Kevin Kumashiro's (2002) anti-oppressive pedagogy, which combines critical pedagogy with the poststructuralist views on power and identity that inform queer pedagogy.

A poststructuralist view on power and identity sees identities as unstable and shaped by the context in which they are lived and expressed. Identities are thus subjected to change depending upon time and place, but temporarily stabilized by norms that uphold boundaries for proper and comprehensible behavior (Butler, 2004). Accordingly, norms shape the identities and lived experiences of different groups of people rewarding some expressions and life scripts over others. In this perspective, which draws on Michel Foucault's theories of power (1976), knowledge, and discursive 'truth claims' are considered forms of power that recognize only some identities (or subjectivities) as intelligible.

Translated into pedagogy, the norm-critical approach acknowledges and troubles such truth claims. A norm-critical approach also poses a challenge to so-called tolerance education. Tolerance education focuses on producing sympathy, acceptance, and understanding toward that or those who depart from the putatively normal. The ways in which sex education has accommodated LGBTQ identities is illustrative of this critique. Since 1977, educational policy in Sweden has officially declared that sex education should counter discrimination based on homosexuality and challenge homophobic attitudes among youth (Centerwall, 1995; Skolöverstyrelsen, 1977, p. 19). However, despite good intentions, research has shown that education on homosexuality has often had the opposite effect. Around the millennium, Nordic researchers conceptualized the school as a 'hetero factory,' that is, as a site where mandatory heterosexuality was produced (Rossi, 2003, 2010). Drawing upon queer theory and its emphasis on heterosexuality as a social and normative construction (Butler, 1990), Nordic researchers problematized the ways in which schools take heterosexuality for granted, treating homosexuality as a separate issue and a phenomenon that the presumed heterosexual student should learn to accept and tolerate. Similar critiques were also put forward by authorities as well as by nongovernmental organizations (NGOs). For instance, the education administration evaluated Biology, History, Religion, and Civics teaching materials produced during the years 2000 to 2005 and claimed that, while the material tried to depict homosexuality and other queer sexualities in an unbiased way, it nevertheless created a distinction between 'us' and 'them,' and thereby maintained heterosexuality as norm (Larsson & Rosén, 2006). The report also showed that education on homosexuality in general is problem oriented and that homosexuality is constructed as something that presumably 'worries' young people. Students are encouraged to discuss pro and con sides of LGBTQ rights (e.g., adoption and marriage), whereas corresponding rights for heterosexuals simply seem self-evident (Larsson & Rosén, 2006).

Conceptualized as 'homo-tolerance' (Reimers, 2007, 2010; Røthing, 2008), Nordic researchers have shown that tolerance education is common in both elementary schooling and in teacher training programs on issues related to homosexuality. Some of these studies also reveal how sexuality cannot be separated from other social categories and axes of power. Reimers (2007) points out, for instance, that in sex education homophobia is repeatedly projected onto 'others,' that is, migrants and people belonging to 'other cultures,' while simultaneously portraying 'Swedes' as broadminded and equal. This shows how the construction of the gender-equal and sexually liberal Swedish nation relies on marking as other those who are perceived of as lacking such values. Thus, homo-tolerance contributes not only to gendered and sexualized boundaries but also to racist and islamophobic discourses (Røthing & Svendsen, 2010, 2011).

Being aware of such connections, the norm-critical network deliberately chose to talk of norm-critical pedagogy – using the general noun norm instead of, for instance, queer pedagogy (Bromseth & Darj, 2010). A norm-critical approach thus seeks to trouble not only gender and heteronormativity but to approach norms from an *intersectional* perspective. The concept of intersectionality was coined by Black feminist Law Professor Kimberlé Crenshaw (1989, 1991, Lutz et al. 2011) as a way to conceptualize how different social categories are intertwined with each other. In her early work on this matter, Crenshaw wrote about how race, gender, and class intersect, using policy against gender and racial discrimination and violence against women as illustrative examples. She argued that anti-discrimination legislation does not adequately capture the complexity of discrimination against Black women, who have to choose if they are discriminated against on the basis of gender *or* race, while in fact their gendered experiences are shaped by race and *vice versa*. Moreover, in her analyses of violence against women, Crenshaw argues that feminist analyses that locate violence against women as primarily linked to gender power do not grasp the importance of poverty and marginalization.

The shift from queer pedagogy to norm-critical pedagogy was thus a strategic move. The ways in which it incorporates several different power structures simultaneously also explains why the approach has been so successful – it is seen by educators and policy makers as a useful tool to come to terms with all kinds of inequality and discrimination (Langmann & Månsson, 2016). Following Swedish legislation, education providers took active measures to combat discrimination and promote equal treatment in schools (SFS, 2008, 567). Several reports from the Education administration and from different NGOs have criticized other frequently used anti-bullying methods as insufficient. For instance, a review made by the anti-bullying organization Friends and the Swedish Youth Federation for LGBTQ Rights (RFSL Ungdom) shows how popular anti-bullying methods are built upon heteronormative presumptions, which are reinforced through the use of compensatory and gendered strategies, that is, anti-bullying strategies that seek to empower girls and teach them to fend off sexual harassment (Bromseth & Wildow, 2007). As a better alternative, the organizations suggest norm-critical pedagogy.

These organizations are also critical toward standardized user guides, as these tend to focus on the individual level instead of underlying structures (Bromseth & Wildow, 2007, see also Swedish National Agency for Education, 2009). Paradoxically, the wide dispersion of the norm-critical approach as a useful way to combat discrimination has led to numerous ready-made methods and courses, as well as an array of related concepts such as 'norm-awareness' and 'norm-creativity.' Later, we will look into some of these initiatives, but first we will situate the norm-critical approach in a broader international research context.

The Norm-Critical Approach in an International Research Context

The arguments put forward by proponents of the norm-critical approach to sex education are not unique to the Swedish and Nordic context. Rather, they echo calls for more critical sex education in other (Western) countries. Key issues that are included in such calls are for sex education to be more inclusive and to address questions of social inequality and diversity, in general, and critical perspectives on gender, sexuality, race, and ethnicity, in particular (Fields, 2008; Lamb, 2010; Lamb & Randazzo, 2016; Sanjakdar et al. 2015; Sundaram & Sauntson, 2016). Many of these scholars suggest that sex education should make use of critical thinking and critical pedagogy, following Freire (1972). Martos (2016), for instance, argues for a critical pedagogy in sexual health education targeting young men who have sex with men that sets out from the young men's own experiences and that aims for empowerment. Sanjakdar et al. (2015, p. 56) propose critical pedagogy as a way to disrupt hegemonic and oppressive pedagogies within sex education, and they highlight key words such as participatory, democratic, critical, and reflective. Fields (2008) argues that a critical approach to teaching and learning where students and teachers explore topics together is a fruitful way to transform social inequalities.

Within the international debate on progressive sex education, two discussions are of particular interest for our argument in this chapter. The first is the basic critique of how social differences in sex education are dealt with as 'add-ons' (Haggis & Mullholland, 2014), leaving normative subjectivities unchallenged. Here, the aforementioned anti-oppressive pedagogy put forward by Kumashiro is relevant. Kumashiro (2002) describes different strategies used by educators to challenge oppression in terms of heterosexism, racism, classism, and sexism. These include 'education for the Other,' which targets marginalized groups with consciousness raising and empowerment as goals, as well as 'education about the Other,' which targets the majority population to teach them to accept and tolerate the minority. Kumashiro further addresses education that criticizes the privilege and normative status of certain groups as an anti-oppressive alternative, as well as education that seeks transformative change on both individual and societal level (Kumashiro, 2002).

Kumashiro's main point is that education that targets minorities either directly (i.e., for the other) or indirectly (i.e., about the other) is insufficient when it comes to equalizing power differences. Even though it may be valuable for privileged groups to learn about minorities given that such knowledge often is silenced in dominant majority cultures – and even though minorities may experience emancipation to some degree – strategies focusing on minorities only reach as far as the underlying structure where the 'other' is normalized and the 'normal' is privileged will nevertheless be sustained (Kumashiro, 2002, p. 37).

In order to effectively challenge the *status quo*, Kumashiro argues for a shift in focus. Instead of focusing on minorities, education should enable those in privileged positions to go through a soul-searching examination of their privileges. By doing so they can be subjected to a changeover, conceptualized by Kumashiro as 'learning through crisis' (Kumashiro, 2002, p. 64). In our first analytical section, we will discuss how such an approach played out in a classroom setting in a Swedish upper secondary school, and discuss its potentials and pitfalls.

Another issue raised among scholars engaged in progressive sex education is how to address several norms simultaneously, or perhaps the difficulty inherent in doing so. In this regard, scholars have argued that critical thinking about race, ethnicity, and faith constitute an underdeveloped area in progressive approaches (Allen et al., 2014). For instance, Whitten and Sethna (2014) show how sex education policy in Canada includes sexual diversity but completely leaves out anti-racism. Scholars have also argued that progressive ideals (e.g., encouraging girls and women to explore their sexuality and the sex-positive focus on sexual pleasure) have been linked to secularity, thus marking religion and faith as less progressive and backward (Rasmussen, 2016). Rasmussen emphasizes that secularity is not neutral but an ideology among others (Rasmussen, 2016). Other scholars argue on similar grounds that religion should have its space within progressive sex education. Instead of being looked upon as a hindrance or as necessarily sex negative, religion may just as well enable critical thinking, Sanjakdar (2016) argues, and adds that there need to be room for religious and cultural diversity in any progressive approach to sex education. In our second and third examples, we discuss how norm-critical teaching materials address diversity in the Swedish context, using the examples of a film and a text-based teaching resource, both of which are intended to be used in class. In these sections, we will return to the intersections of sexuality, gender, race, and secularity and show how norm-critical sex education is intertwined with discourses of 'Swedishness,' and how youth sexual development remains caught up in a nationalist framework even when it is approached by progressive educators. First, however, we will start by pointing to some inherent difficulties when the norm-critical approach is translated into concrete educational practice.

Critical Learning for Whom?

In the following, we draw upon our research on contemporary sex education in Sweden and use three examples to illuminate what we conceptualize as *tensions* within the norm-critical approach. These examples also reflect the wide scope of sex education in Sweden. The first example focuses on the practical use of norm-critical exercises, and we argue that rather than challenging existing power structures, the idea of 'learning through crisis' – which, naturally, is a painful process and involves both guilt and shame – could, in some contexts, turn into violent practice.

As mentioned earlier, the broad impact and popularization of norm-critical methods in education has resulted in the availability of large quantities of pre-formulated exercises; these are distributed by well-known NGOs as well as public authorities such as the Swedish National Agency for Education. In sex education contexts, such exercises are used as a way to address questions of inequalities, oppression, and power, which are seen as important for young people's well-being and sexual health. Educational policy states that sex education should be approached as an interdisciplinary subject, merged into different curricula, and cover a broad range of topics. It is fairly common for schools to incorporate sex education by addressing a specific theme from several perspectives during a short period of time and by inviting external guests with a particular expertise (see, e.g., Swedish National Agency for Education, 2014, p. 7). It is on such an occasion that the following observation took place.

It was late fall and two of the authors were attending an upper secondary school in a segregated Swedish suburb where a large majority have a migrant background. The school had organized a theme week on 'love, relationships and democracy' during which students were assigned to participate in different workshops. At one workshop, a local NGO had been invited to carry out a norm-critical exercise called 'One step forward,' as described in our field notes:

> About 30 students, aged 16 and 17 years, are gathered in the assembly hall with two NGO representatives that will lead the exercise. The session starts with the leaders handing out sheets with descriptions of different characters to all participants. On each sheet it says, for instance, that "I am a 30-year-old, white, heterosexual woman who works as a nurse"; "I am a 12-year-old boy who was born in Iraq and wants to go to medical school"; "I am a homosexual man from a small city in the north of Sweden"; and "I live in a segregated suburb and my mother is a cleaner".
>
> The participants are asked to shortly reflect on their allocated character in silence. Standing side-by-side, facing the leaders, they are subsequently told to pay attention to different statements read out loud by one of the leaders, and, to take one step forward if the statement concerns their character. The leader begins with the following statements: "I have close contact with my family"; "I have no trouble getting a loan from the bank"; "I can walk hand in hand with my partner without people staring"; and "I have lots of options on the labour market".
>
> There are many students attending the workshop and the students seem a bit confused over when to move forward, and when to stand still. There are also some students with disabilities that need help from their assistants in order to move at all. The leaders explain the setup again, and continue proposing different statements. Gradually, the exercise begins to run more smoothly and the students move forward, some more than others.
>
> After a while, the leaders stop proposing statements and open up for reflections on the different characters, and their ability to move forward. Most of the students seem to have a rather positive view on their character's opportunities. One of the characters that has moved furthest is the Iraqi born boy. The leaders seem frustrated; it was obviously not what they had in mind. An Iraqi boy does not have

> the privileges that the student gives him by moving forward. A heated debate arises where the leaders try to convince the audience of the difficulties that young migrant men experience in Swedish society. The students, on the other hand, refuse to accept that one is destined by one's ethnic background, and one student states triumphantly that this particular boy has a bright future ahead; he is clearly an ambitious individual as he aims to go to medical school!
>
> The exercise ends in turmoil and the leaders announce a break. (Field notes, upper secondary school)

This particular exercise, 'One step forward,' is also called 'Walk of privileges' and is recommended by the Swedish National Agency for Education (2013a). The origin of this exercise is an influential essay on White privilege, where American feminist Peggy McIntosh (1989) listed a number of privileges White people enjoy in their everyday life. The concept has been taken up by various groups in diversity work and developed into an exercise. In the Swedish version, functionality, class, ethnicity, gender, sexuality, and the privileges that heterosexuals experience are included; these are reflected in some of the characters' identities and in the statements described earlier.

The core tactic of the exercise is to uncover norms by visualizing and engaging bodies and emotions (see also Leahy, 2014). The exercise is intended to be used in all student populations, but teachers are encouraged to adjust it to the specific student group, for instance by choosing appropriate characters and statements (Swedish National Agency of Education, 2013a). Other examples of widely accessible norm-critical activities include exercises such as the 'self-assessment-test' (also called the 'Non-stick-test') and 'the exercise of tolerance.' In the self-assessment test, the participants estimate the level of friction in relation to their gender, sexuality, ethnicity, age, and so on by color-marking different columns. When finished, a visual image of how they are affected by different norms emerges and they may reflect upon the ways that they are privileged or not privileged (see Andersson, 2010). The 'exercise of tolerance' involves face-to-face dialogues between two individuals. The dialogue begins with the first person saying "I tolerate you for (for instance) wearing glasses," whereby the second person says "thank you" in a grateful manner. The exercise could be conceptualized as affect-oriented pedagogy as it aims to let people experience how it feels to express gratitude toward an oppressor (see, for instance, Edemo & Rindå, 2004). It thus shows the limits of the tolerance approach, against which the norm-critical pedagogy distance itself.

The exercise that we witnessed is illustrative of how norm-critical pedagogy is presented as a strategy to challenge inequality and mechanisms of exclusion by turning attention to the norm itself. It also shows that it is quite complicated to put this ideal into practice. The exercise is clearly designed to make people aware of privileges and where they lead us in life. The complexity at hand, however, is that the exercise was used in a school setting in a segregated part of the city with a multi-ethnic and inter-religious group of students, and one may imagine that there is a difference in being exposed to one's own privileges compared with the privileges of others. One interpretation that felt accurate at the time was to understand the emotionally charged situation as a protest against the privileged White NGO representatives that limited the students' possibilities of a bright future. That is to say, the fictional characters felt personal to the students (just as intended) but this personal connection did not result in a 'learning crisis' about their own privileges, mainly because they were not a particularly privileged group of students. Instead of learning about norms, or the complexity of privileges and oppression, the student learnt that there was no chance of hope or change, and the leaders – who struggled hard to make the exercise work 'as intended' – dismissed any possibility of resistance.

A related interpretation is that the exercise encourages only one way of being reflexive. By visualizing and engaging bodies in the room, the exercise aimed to make norms seem material to the students. Yet, it was only if the students reflected upon norms in a particular manner that the exercise was considered successful. Our observation is thus illustrative of the slippery line between *exposing* norms and *reinstating* them. It also points to the notion that exercises such as these may, in the long run, construct reflexivity and transgression as something that is associated with White, privileged identities more so than with non-privileged identities, as apparently migrant and disabled students were not able to achieve the exercise's goal. It should be stressed that the resistance that the student expressed so vividly could, of course, be understood as subversive; yet, this student was not ascribed a *reflexive* subjectivity.

An Apolitical Diversity?

In our next example, we will turn to an adjacent topic: how norm-critical approaches deal with difference. Here we will argue that while the norm-critical approach aspires to plurality, its approach to difference only reaches so far, and there is within it a strong underlying current promoting certain sexual values as more worthy than others.

This time we turn to an animated film, called *Sex on the Map*, produced by The Swedish Association for Sexuality Education (RFSU) and the Swedish Educational Broadcasting Company in 2011. It is based on questions about sexuality that young people have posed to the RFSU, and its target audience is 13–16-year-old students. The film is available in Swedish with subtitles in ten languages and is accompanied with a teacher's guide (RFSU, 2012) that includes both informative texts on norm-critical perspectives on sexuality and examples of different methods to be used in class.

The film plays out in a school setting. The main plot is a group of students that have gathered for a supplementary class in math, but the math teacher never shows. Instead one of the main characters, Jao, enters and gives them a class in sex education. The room is filled with sexual tensions and allusions, and the film scenery alternates between the classroom location, individual thoughts and feelings among the youngsters, and a sexual meeting between two of the students that recently took place at a rehearsal hall.

The key message in the film is that teenagers *should* feel encouraged to explore their sexuality. "Nothing is wrong as long as it feels good for yourself and others," Jao explains while pulling down a map where he, together with the students, starts to draw "everything that one may do while having sex." Bit by bit, the map gets filled with animated people that "make out," "fuck," "suck," and "lick" various body parts. Jao emphasizes once again that anything goes, just as long as it "makes you horny," and the students suggest "hugging and kissing," as well as "threesomes," "watching porn," and "anal intercourse" as sexual practices to be included on the map. Eventually, the map is filled with numerous and various bodies that have sex in different positions and constellations.

This permissive attitude toward sexuality is combined with a more medicalized depiction with detailed pictures of intimate body parts and illustrative portrayals of sperm production, ovulation, and menstruation. Altogether, the film comes out as explicit and liberal, and it has been criticized for being too open, provocative and even pornographic (see, e.g., Ollis, 2016). It has also been considered inappropriate for the intended target group, in general, and for a mandatory school situation, in particular (Björklund, 2014). Nevertheless, the film was widely acclaimed by critics, and, to our knowledge, is generally well appreciated among norm-critical educators.

Of particular interest, for our purpose, is how the film keeps referring to *similarities* rather than differences. When describing male and female genitals and arousal, for instance, Jao highlight that "both cocks and twats consist of swell organs" and that "both men and women can ejaculate." Also, while adding sexual activities to the map, Jao explains that sexual identity has "nothing to do with sexual practice," "it only tells you with whom you have sex"; and, similarly, trans *identity* is defined as "who you feel like you are" and does not, Jao claims, affect what you do.

Let us dwell some more upon this idea of similarity, which, as will be seen, permeates the film's message in additional ways. As mentioned earlier, appropriating the noun norm was a way for the queer pedagogical network to adopt a more intersectional approach and take into account the simultaneousness of different power relations when considering how norms affect people's lives (Bromseth & Sörensdotter, 2012, pp. 44–45). However, in doing so, norm-critical proponents also imply that, on some level, different power relations work the same. Yet, this does not mean advocates of the norm-critical approach ignore difference. To the contrary, norm-critical educators are well aware of the importance of being inclusive. Returning to *Sex on the Map* as an example, differences *proliferate* through the way the film embraces a wide diversity of characters, bodies, and acts. Even if the map could be accused for being conspicuously White[2] and in other ways

[2] The 'White' characters on the map could also be interpreted as an attempt to transcend race (Gazi, 2017).

'bodily normative' – save for the occasional person in a wheel chair – the moviemakers addresses heterogeneity through having both a young, White lesbian (perhaps of working-class background) and a Black young man with a Muslim name among the main characters in the film.

Key here, however, is that this diversity of characters in the film does not seem to matter much when it comes to sexual values and practices. Rather, like the trans identities Jao referred to earlier, differences seemingly appear only at surface level. That is to say, we appear different but, beneath the surface, we all are presumed to share the same values. In this way, diversity in *Sex on the Map* resembles the discourse of diversity management, which has been criticized for addressing diversity in an apolitical and often stereotypical manner (de los Reyes, 2001). Building on ideas of human capital rather than social justice, diversity management discourses occur, for instance, in market driven corporate businesses (Schierup, 2010). Diversity programs have also been important policy instruments in the public sector, and are often seen as a way to proactively prevent discrimination. However, critics have argued that without a deeper understanding of social structures and power relations, diversity programs will not necessarily challenge *status quo* (de los Reyes, 2005). In fact, analyses of diversity programs have shown that they sometimes reproduce rather than challenge dominant norms by, for instance, resting upon heteronormative assumptions of men and women or culturally essentialist understandings of people with migrant backgrounds (de los Reyes, 2005).

Obviously, diversity discourses in a norm-critical context are more complex. For one, norm-critical pedagogies have the explicit ambition to challenge stereotypical representations. One common norm-critical strategy is to pay careful attention to language use, and during the past decade the Swedish language has been provided with a range of new words such as the gender-neutral pronoun 'hen' (Wojahn, 2015). Another strategy is to always include non-normative sexualities and gender identities in lesson plans and teaching materials.

Even if the norm-critical approach to diversity does not necessarily fall prey to stereotypes, *plurality* remains a delicate issue. The ways in which *Sex on the Map* stresses similarities and sameness risks turning some characters in the film into mere tokens, as the values represented by the film are clearly not attached to them. Addressing differences as if they do not really matter also disguises the notion that the norm-critical approach also has a normative agenda. In fact, *Sex on the Map* clearly selects some norms as more important than others.

Zooming in on the ideal values, *Sex on the Map* has a very explicit message that states that a *good* youth sexuality is mutual, sex positive, and pleasure oriented. As mentioned earlier, the film concludes that anything goes as long as it "feels right." Obviously, there are limits to this broadmindedness: the film does not, for instance, venture into the terrain of sexual acts that are considered illegal such as intergenerational sex involving under-aged children or sex work. Neither does it bring up the age of consent, which is interesting, given the age of its target group and the fact that since the 2005 amendments, the Sexual Crime Act in Sweden considers sex with a person below 15 years to be rape (SFS, 2005:90).

The film breaks with gender norms of masculine heterosexuality as active and irresponsible, and feminine heterosexuality as necessarily oriented toward his pleasure (Holland et al., 2004). As such, it emphasizes men's and women's shared responsibility for sexual safety: the intimate portrayal of a sexual meeting between two of the students, 'Abdu' and 'Melody,' shows how they explore each other carefully and give room for both his feelings of insecurity and her pleasure. The film also departs from *the coital imperative*, the idea that 'real sex' equals penile–vaginal penetration (Jackson, 1984; McPhillips et al., 2001). Accordingly, Melody and Abdu do not engage in vaginal intercourse, but, with the help of Jao's lecture, Melody concludes that her experience still 'counts as sex' and she ticks off 'done *it*' on her private 'to-do list.'

Accordingly, the film presents gender and heteronormativity as crucial power structures to challenge, and produces a normative agenda that corresponds to a queer feminist theoretical understanding that sees gender and heterosexuality as socially constructed, produced thorough discourses of normality and desirability (Butler, 1990, 2004). Yet, potential conflicts between, for instance, feminist critiques of male dominance and queer critiques of the social categories of men and women are not brought to the surface. Rather, *Sex on the Map* seems to be oriented toward the latter. In other words, the emphasis on similarities between men and women does not give much room for a critical discussion on any imbalance between (heterosexual) men's and women's possibilities for pursuing their sexual desires.

The teachers' manual that accompanies the film points out that norms of gender and sexuality are prioritized by the RFSU. The manual discusses concepts such as heteronormativity, LGBTQ identities, and different understandings of gender in detail, but does not even mention class, ethnicity, or able-bodiedness. The latter categories, thus, seem to be too troublesome to include in a progressive approach. Alternatively, are they understood as irrelevant when it comes to sexual values?

While we are aware of the impossibility of covering all social categories and power relations, we still believe that it is necessary to be more reflexive upon the values that are favored. In our final example, we will go deeper into this issue by focusing on what happens with the norm-critical approach when it is exposed to multiple values concerning gender and sexual relations among youth.

Colliding Values?

As we have argued thus far, norm-critical sex education aspires to be all-inclusive in terms of different identities and norms, and yet it prioritizes certain norms as more essential for sex education; that is to say, norm-critical sex education pursues a normative agenda and construes some sexual values as more desirable than others.

As our final example, we have chosen a norm-critical sex education teaching resource that stands out in several ways. While most norm-critical materials focus on gender and heteronormativity and de-emphasize other power axes or categories of differences, our final example, by contrast, deals explicitly with norms of race and ethnicity. It also explicitly targets a non-privileged group in Swedish society, newly arrived migrants. It is thus a suitable example for investigating in more depth how norm-critical approaches may harbor potentially colliding views of sexual values and practices.

The resource is called *Sexual Education in Easy Swedish (Sexualundervisning på lättare svenska)*, and consists of two books, one teacher's manual (RFSU, 2013a) and a workbook (RFSU, 2013b) with different exercises for students. It was produced by the RFSU in 2013, and updated editions are available for download online.[3]

The material is intended to be used in introductory education programs for 16–20 year olds, as well as in introductory education for adults (so-called Swedish for immigrant classes). The books are grand in scale, colorful, and explicit; the deliberately naive, exaggerated, and lifelike drawings illustrate bodies and body parts (foremost genitals) in different shapes and sizes, and arrows and plus signs are used to illustrate how bodies may come together in various ways. The material also provides the reader with a diversity of bodies and identities in terms of color, size, gender, religion, and ethnicity. The self-reflexive approach mentioned earlier is present as well, but it is mainly the educators – and not the students – who are encouraged to do personal soul searching. (The manual states that it would be unethical to pressure students to talk about personal intimate matters in a classroom context (RFSU, 2013a, p. 60).) The teacher manual includes several exercises that aim to make the educators aware of their prejudices. For instance, educators are to imagine sexual values and experiences among their students in order to make them aware of how they themselves are informed by dominant discourses. This indicates that the RFSU presumes that their educators are White and Swedish, and, like in the norm-critical exercise described earlier, it is suggestive of who this material construes as a reflexive subject.

Students are also asked to reflect upon norms, but to address issues in a more general rather than personal mode. On the topic of sex and relationships, the workbook presents several cases that point to frictions regarding different norms. For instance, in one case there is a picture of two men with a mutual dream bubble that has two rings and a heart in it (RFSU, 2013b, p. 195). The text reads: "Panos and his boyfriend are 18 years old. They want to get married. Their parents think that they should wait until they are older. Should Panoz and his boyfriend get married?" Through such examples, *Sexual Education in Easy Swedish* urges the students to reflect upon heteronormativity, age, and parent–child relations. The books similarly encourage students to reflect upon the meaning of gender, rather than taking it for granted. When it is not necessary to address heteronormativity and

3 www.rfsu.se/sv/Sexualundervisning/Sexualundervisning-pa-lattare-svenska/.

homophobia – as it is in the case of Panoz and his boyfriend – pictures and practices intentionally use gender-neutral names.

In terms of values, *Sexual Education in Easy Swedish* is just as informed by a sex-positive ideology as *Sex on the Map*. The manual highlights the benefits of an affirmative instead of a risk-oriented approach, and it gives little room for asexuality, or lack of sexual desire. The manual also stresses that the RFSU favor norms such as *mutuality* and *equality* (RFSU, 2013a, p. 29).

Obviously, the manual pays much attention to gender and heteronormativity as important norms regulating sexuality. However, given its explicit focus on race and ethnicity, and its target group (newly arrived migrants*), Sexual Education in Easy Swedish* also problematizes Swedishness and Whiteness as norms. The manual explains that "It is a norm to be 'Swedish' and white in our society, and there are different expectations and perceptions about Swedes and about those considered non-Swedes" (RFSU, 2013a, p. 32). It also explains that these norms rest upon notions of "culture and religion as something neatly defined, static and uniform, and that determines people's behaviours" (RFSU, 2013a, p. 32).

In order to be norm critical in this respect, the manual concludes that educators must defy such static notions of culture and religion. The manual also acknowledges that gender and sexuality are often at the centre of racialized discourses, and refer to scholars such as Reimers (2007) and Bredström (2008) who have revealed that mainstream discourses construct Swedes as gender equal and LBGTQ friendly, whereas non-Swedes are seen as much more patriarchal and homophobic with reference to their putative culture or religion. Thus, *Sexual Education in Easy Swedish* interprets being norm critical as refusing to link any particular cultural value (e.g., gender equality) to a specific race, ethnicity, or nationality. As written in the manual:

> Be open to [the fact] that participants may have different views on gender and sexuality, even when they do not follow prevailing understandings of culture and religion. Have an open mind when you discuss values and experiences, and do not see students or yourself as representatives of a particular culture. (RFSU, 2013a p. 44)

However, while it is stressed in the material that educators should meet differences with an open mind, very little is said about how potential conflicts can be dealt with. That is to say, the text mentions that there may be different views, but the possibility of conflicting values – for instance, between collectivistic versus individual oriented views, or secular versus religious views – is more or less silenced. Instead, educators are encouraged to guide participants toward some interpretations rather than others: that is, if they express views that the educators think are reproducing norms on, for instance, gender or heteronormativity, the educator is asked to rephrase questions or suggest different interpretations. That conflicts would arise as a protest of educators imposing 'Swedish' values upon non-Swedish students, or as a reaction toward being forced into talking about sex in a class on Swedish language (and to participate in practices discussing detailed pictures of intimate body parts), is not addressed at all. Instead, the main message is that anyone – regardless of ethnic identification – may represent the sexual values promoted by the RFSU.

In a paradoxical way then, the RFSU keeps their normative agenda, favoring some values over others, even in a teaching resource that explicitly addresses differences and urges users to be open-minded. The reason for this, we argue, is because these values are not seen as values but rather as *universal rights*. On the few occasions when conflicting positions are addressed, the RFSU turns to the right of the individual to, for instance, choose freely. Thus, the sexual values proposed as norm critical are constructed as *culture free*. By doing so, the RFSU aspires to a liberal notion of an abstract sovereign subject that is free to choose their path in life (Rasmussen, 2016), a subject that, paradoxically, would not have to be *norm critical* to begin with.

Conclusion

In times like these, where reactionary and conservative powers are gaining ground and challenge the future of sex education, being critical of social justice-oriented, anti-discriminatory, and sex-positive initiatives feels uncomfortable. Indeed, much of the work that the RFSU and other norm-critical advocates do is cutting edge, and should be acknowledged as such. However, even progressive ideas need to be continuously developed, and our ambition with this chapter is to point to some tensions in order to advance the norm-critical agenda.

In the chapter, we have pointed to the need for education to be sensitive to specific situations and contexts and to adopt teaching exercises that carefully consider diversity among their presumed audiences. Our study thus contributes to research that has problematized the *what, how*, and *for whom* knowledge and action appear in critical approaches (e.g., Ellsworth, 1989; Kumashiro, 2002; McLaren & Kincheloe, 2007). Our research has shown that the push to uncover privileged structures and norms does not always work as intended, and that anti-discriminatory acts may in fact reinforce the very norms they seek to challenge. Here, we see it as particularly important to be critical of how different subject positions are articulated in norm-critical discourses, constructing, for instance, some as more able to meet the call to be self-reflexive and transgressive than others.

In the chapter, we have also shown that the strategy of focusing on similarities rather than on differences in norm-critical approaches signals a liberal and individual-oriented discourse that inevitably will have difficulties of incorporating, for instance, collectiveness and faith-based sexual values. Last, but not least, our analysis shows the need to further interrogate the implication that norm-critical sex education can't seem to work beyond promoting and leaning on some values as universal and non-negotiable. Not only will such an approach run into difficulties when coming across values that do not fit the universal framework, that is, values that challenge the queer, sameness, and individual-oriented sex-positive agenda, but, more fundamentally, such an approach will miss that their claim to universal values is too similar to contemporary neo-assimilatory racism (Bredström & Bolander, forthcoming). To truly detach young people's sexual development from nationalist discourses thus seems to be a tricky affair. That is to say, despite the norm-critical approach's attempt to delink sexual values from specific cultures or ethnic backgrounds, the call for universal sexual norms is nevertheless an expression of an ethnicized viewpoint, be it Western, European, or Swedish. This, we argue, is the fundamental challenge that a norm-critical sex education needs to take on in order to truly come up with a sex education for all – or, at least, to truly acknowledge the difficulties of such ambition and welcome more open-endedness (Youdell, 2011) of sex education practices.

References

Allen, L., Rasmussen, M. L., & Quinlivan, K. (Eds.) (2014). *The Politics of Pleasure in Sexuality Education*. New York: Routledge.

Andersson, L. (2010). Tricky Business! In Bromseth, J. & Darj, F. (Eds.) *Normkritisk Pedagogik – Makt, Lärande Och Strategier För Förändring*. Uppsala: Centrum för genusvetenskap.

Björklund, E. (2014). Statlig sexpropaganda? UR: soch RFSU: S sexualupplysningsfilm sex på kartan. In Hedling, E. & Wallengren, A. (Eds.) *Den Nya Svenska Filmen: Kultur, Kriminalitet Och Kakafoni* (245–268). Stockholm: Atlantis.

Bolander, E. (2009). *Risk och bejakande. Sexualitet och genus i sexualupplysning och sexualundervisning i Tv.* (Doctoral dissertation). Linköping: Linköping University.

Bredström, A. (2008). *Safe Sex, Unsafe Identities: Intersections of 'Race', Gender and Sexuality in Swedish HIV/AIDS Policy*. Linköping: Linköping University.

(2011). *Alkohol, unga och sexuellt risktagande*. Stockholm: Smittskyddsinstitutet.

Bredström, A. & Bolander, E. (2018, in press). Beyond Cultural Racism: Challenges for an Anti-Racist Sex Education for Youth. In Aggleton, P., Cover, R., Leahy, D., Marshall, D., & Rasmussen, M. L. (Eds.), *Youth and Sexual Citizenship* (71–85). London: Routledge.

Bromseth, J. & Darj, F. (2010). *Normkritisk pedagogik – Makt, lärande och strategier för förändring*. Uppsala: Centrum för genusvetenskap.

Bromseth, J. & Sörensdotter, R. (2012). Normkritisk pedagogik: En möjlighet att förändra undervisningen. In Lundberg, A. & Werner A. (Eds.), *Genusvetenskapens pedagogik och didaktik.* (43–57). Göteborg: Nationella sekretariatet för genusforskning.

Bromseth, J. & Wildow, H. (2007). *"Man kan ju inte läsa om bögar i nån historiebok": Skolors förändringsarbeten med fokus på jämställdhet, genus och sexualitet.* Stockholm: Stiftelsen Friends.

Butler, J. (1990). *Gender Trouble. Feminism and the Subversion of Identity.* London: Routledge.

(2004). *Undoing Gender.* New York & London: Routledge.

Bäckman, M. (2003). *Kön och känsla: Samlevnadsundervisning och ungdomars tankar om sexualitet.* (Doctoral dissertation). Stockholm: Makadam.

Centerwall, E. (1995). *'Kärlek känns! Förstår du': Samtal om sexualitet och samlevnad i skolan: ett referensmaterial från skolverket*. Stockholm: Statens skolverk.

Crenshaw, K. (1989). Demarginalizing the Intersection of Race and Sex: A Black Feminist Critique of Antidiscrimination Doctrine, Feminist Theory and Antiracist Politics. *University of Chicago Legal Forum*, 139–167.

(1991). Mapping the Margins: Intersectionality, Identity Politics, and Violence against Women of Color. *Stanford Law Review, 43*(6), 1241–1299.

de los Reyes, P. (2001). *Mångfald och differentiering: Diskurs, olikhet och normbildning inom svensk forskning och samhällsdebatt*. Solna: SALTSA.

(2005). Intersektionalitet, makt och strukturell diskriminering. In *Bortom vi och dom: teoretiska reflektioner om makt, integration och strukturell diskriminering: SOU-rapport.* Stockholm: Fritzes offentliga publikationer.

Edemo, G. & Rindå, J. (2004). *Någonstans går gränsen: En lärarhandledning om kön, sexualitet och normer i unga människors liv.* Stockholm: RFSL.

Ellsworth, E. (1989). Why Doesn't This Feel Empowering? Working through the Repressive Myths of Critical Pedagogy. *Harvard Educational Review, 59*(3), 297–325.

Fields, J. (2008). *Risky Lessons. Sex Education and Social Inequality.* New Brunswick: Rutgers University Press.

Foucault, M. (1976/1990). *The History of Sexuality. Vol. 1, The Will to Knowledge.* Harmondsworth: Penguin.

Freire, P. (1972). *Pedagogy of the Oppressed.* Harmondsworth: Penguin Books.

Frisell, A. (1996). *Kärlek utan sex går an: Men inte sex utan kärlek: om gymnasieflickors tankar kring kärlek och sexualitet.* Tumba: Mångkulturellt centrum i samarbete med Folkhälsoinstitutet.

Gazi, J. (2017). De/facing Race: Towards a Model for a Universal World Comics, *Journal of Graphic Novels and Comics*, *8*(2), 119–138.

Haggis, J. & Mullholland, M. (2014). Rethinking Difference and Sex Education: From Cultural Inclusivity to Normative Diversity. *Sex Education, 14*(1), 57–66.

Hirdman, Y. (1989). *Att lägga livet tillrätta: Studier i svensk folkhemspolitik*. Stockholm: Carlsson.

Holland, J., Ramazanoglu, C., Sharpe, S., & Thomson, R. (2004). *The Male in the Head: Young People, Heterosexuality and Power, 2nd edn.* London: Tufnell.

Jackson, M. (1984). Sex Research and the Construction of Sexuality: A Tool of Male Supremacy? *Women's Studies International Forum*, *7*(1), 43–51.

Jonsson, G. (1951). *Sexualvanor Hos Svensk Ungdom*. Statens offentliga utredningar, 1951:41. Ungdomsvårdskommittén, Ungdomen möter samhället: Ungdomsvårdskommitténs slutbetänkande. Stockholm: Statens offentliga utredningar, 0375-250X; 1951:41.

Kinsey, A., Pomeroy, W., & Martin, C. (1948). *Sexual Behavior in the Human Male*. Philadelphia: Saunders.

Kumashiro, K. K. (2002). *Troubling Education: Queer Activism and Antioppressive Pedagogy.* New York: Routledge.

Lamb, S. (2010). Toward a Sexual Ethics Curriculum: Bringing Philosophy and Society to Bear on Individual Development. *Harvard Educational Review, 80*(1), 81–106.

Lamb, S. & Randazzo, R. (2016). From I to e: Sex Education as a Form of Civics Education in a Neoliberal Context. *Curriculum Inquiry, 46*(2), 148–167.

Langmann, E. & Månsson, N. (2016). Att vända blicken mot sig själv: En problematisering av den normkritiska pedagogiken. *Pedagogisk forskning i Sverige*, *21*(1–2), 79–100.

Larsson, H. & Rosén, M. (2006). Vem har en sexuell läggning? Heteronormativitet och välvilja i läroböcker. In *I enlighet med skolans värdegrund?* Stockholm: The Swedish National Agency for Education.

Leahy, D. (2014). Assembling a Health[y] Subject: Risky and Shameful Pedagogies in Health Education. *Critical Public Health*, *24*(2), 171–181.

Lennerhed, L. (1994). Frihet Att Njuta. Sexualdebatten i Sverige På 1960-Talet. (Doctoral dissertation.) Stockholm: Norstedts.

(2002). *Sex i folkhemmet: RFSU: Stidiga historia*. Hedemora: Gidlund.

(2012). Taking the Middle Way. Sex Education Debates in Sweden in the Early Twentieth Century. In Sauerteig, L. & Davidson, R. (Eds.) *Shaping Sexual Knowledge: A Cultural History of Sex Education in Twentieth Century Europe* (55–70). London: Routledge.

Lutz, H., Herrera Vivar, M. T., & Supik, L. (Eds.) (2011). *Framing Intersectionality: Debates on a Multi-faceted Concept in Gender Studies*. Farnham: Ashgate.

Martinsson, L. & Reimers, E. (Eds.) (2014). *Skola i normer, 2nd edn*. Malmö: Gleerups.

Martos, A. J. (2016). Vernacular Knowledge and Critical Pedagogy: Conceptualising Sexual Health Education for Young Men Who Have Sex with Men. *Sex Education*, *16*(2), 184–198.

McIntosh, P. (1989). White Privilege: Unpacking the Invisible Knapsack, *Independent School*, *49*(2), 31–35.

McLaren, P. & Kincheloe, J. L. (Eds.) (2007). *Critical Pedagogy: Where Are We Now?* New York: Peter Lang.

McPhillips, K. Braun, V., & Gavey, N. (2001). Defining (Hetero)sex. How Imperative Is the 'Coital Imperative'? *Womens's Studies International Forum*, *24*(2), 229–240.

Ollis, D. (2016) "I Felt Like I Was Watching Porn": The Reality of Preparing Pre-service Teachers to Teach about Sexual Pleasure. *Sex Education Sexuality, Society and Learning*, *16*(31), 308–323.

Rasmussen, M. L. (2016). *Progressive Sexuality Education: The Conceits of Secularism*. New York: Routledge.

Reimers, E. (2007). Always Somewhere Else – Heteronormativity in Swedish Teacher Training. In Martinsson, L., Reimers, E., Reingardė, J., & Lundgren A. S. (Eds.), *Norms at Work: Challenging Homophobia and Heteronormativity*. Stockholm: Transnational Cooperation for Equality.

(2010). Homotolerance or Queer Pedagogy? In Martinsson, L. & Reimers, E. (Eds.), *Norm-struggles: Sexualities in Contentions* (14–28). Newcastle: Cambridge Scholars.

RFSU (2012). *Teaching Notes for Sex on the Map*. Stockholm: Riksförbundet för sexuell upplysning (RFSU).

(2013a). *Sexualundervisning på lättare svenska. Lärarhandledning och metoder*. Stockholm: Riksförbundet för sexuell upplysning, author Agnes Dahné.

(2013b). *Sexualundervisning på lättare svenska. lektionsunderlag*. Stockholm: Riksförbundet för sexuell upplysning.

Rossi, L-M. (2003). *Heterotehdas. Televisiomainonta sukupuolituotantona*, Helsinki: Gaudeamus.

(2010). How to Make (Visual) Trouble Inside the Hetero Factory. In Martinsson, L. & Reimers, E. (Eds.), *Norm-struggles: Sexualities in Contentions*, 83–97. Newcastle: Cambridge Scholars.

Røthing, Å. (2008). Homotolerance and Heteronormativity in Norwegian Classrooms. *Gender and Education*, *20*(3), 253–266.

Røthing, Å. & Svendsen Bang, S. H. (2010). Homotolerance and Heterosexuality as Norwegian Values. *Journal of LGBT Youth*, 7(2), 147–166.

(2011) Sexuality in Norwegian Textbooks: Constructing and Controlling Ethnic Borders?, *Ethnic and Racial Studies*, *34*(11), 1953–1973.

Sandström, B. (1995). *Ungdomssexualitet som undervisningsämne och forskningsområde*. Stockholm: Hälsohögskolan.

(2001). Den välplanerade sexualiteten: Frihet och kontroll i 1970-talets svenska sexualpolitik. (Doctoral dissertation). Stockholm: Stockholm University.

Sanjakdar, F. (2016), Can Difference Make a Difference?: A Critical Theory Discussion of Religion in Sexuality Education. *Discourse: Studies in the Cultural Politics of Education*, *39*(3), 1–15.

Sanjakdar, F., Allen, L., Rasmussen, M. L., Quinlivan, K., Brömdal, A., & Aspin, C. (2015). In Search of Critical Pedagogy in Sexuality Education: Visions, Imaginations, and Paradoxes. *Review of Education, Pedagogy and Cultural Studies*, *37*(1), 53–70.

Schierup, C.-U. (2010). *'Diversity' and Social Exclusion in Third Way Sweden: The 'Swedish Model' in Transition, 1975–2005*. Themes working paper nr 35. Linköping: REMESO.

Skolöverstyrelsen (1956). *Handledning i sexualundervisning*. Stockholm: Skolöverstyrelsen.

(1977). *Samlevnadsundervisning*. Stockholm: Liber Läromedel

SOU 1951:41 Ungdomsvårdskommittén (1951). *Ungdomen möter samhället: Ungdomsvårdskommitténs slutbetänkande*. Stockholm: Statens offentliga utredningar 0375-250X; 1951:41.

Sundaram, V. & Sauntson, H. (Eds.) (2016). *Global Perspectives and Key Debates in Sex and Relationships Education: Addressing Issues of Gender, Sexuality, Plurality and Power*. New York: Palgrave Macmillan.

Svendsen, S. (2017). The Cultural Politics of Sex Education in the Nordics. In Allen, L & Rasmussen, M. L. (Eds.), *The Palgrave Handbook of Sexuality Education*, 137–153. New York: Palgrave Macmillan.

Svensk författningssamling (SFS) (2005:90). Lag om ändring i brottsbalken.

Svensk författningssamling (SFS) (2008:567). Diskrimineringslagen.

Swedish National Agency for Education (2000). *Nationella kvalitetsgranskningar 1999*. [National Quality Audits 1999]. Stockholm: Swedish National Agency for Education.

(2009). *Diskriminerad, trakasserad, kränkt? Barns, elevers och studerandes uppfattningar om diskriminering och trakasserier*. Stockholm: Swedish National Agency for Education.

(2011a). *Läroplan för gymnasieskolan*. Stockholm: Swedish National Agency for Education.

(2011b). *Läroplan för grundskolan, förskoleklassen och fritidshemmet*. Stockholm: Swedish National Agency for Education.

(2013a). *Förskolans och skolans värdegrund: Förhållningssätt, verktyg och metoder*. Stockholm: Swedish National Agency for Education.

(2013b). *Sex- och samlevnadsundervisning i grundskolans senare år: Jämställdhet, sexualitet och relationer i ämnesundervisningen: Årskurserna 7–9*. Stockholm: Swedish National Agency for Education.

(2013c). *Sex- och samlevnadsundervisning i gymnasieskolan: Sexualitet, relationer och jämställdhet i de gymnasiegemensamma ämnena*. Stockholm: Swedish National Agency for Education.

(2014). *Sex Education. Gender equality, sexuality and human relationships in the Swedish Curricula*. Stockholm: Swedish National Agency for Education.

Whitten, A. & Sethna, C. (2014). What's Missing? Anti-Racist Sex Education! *Sex Education*, *14*(4), 414–429.

Widerström, K. (1907). *Uppfostran och sexuell hygien: Föredrag hållet vid sommarkurserna i stockholm 1907 samt (i något ändrad form) vid anitalkoholkongressen s. å.* Uppsala: Almkvist och Wiksell.

Wojahn, D. (2015). *Språkaktivism: Diskussioner om feministiska språkförändringar i sverige från 1960-talet till 2015*. (Doctoral dissertation.) Uppsala: Uppsala University.

Youdell, D. (2011). *School Trouble: Identity, Power and Politics in Education*. Abingdon: Routledge.

28 Robot Babies, Young People, and Pregnancy Prevention

Alternative Imaginings of Sexual Futures

Mary Lou Rasmussen and Aoife Neary

The principal focus of sexuality education continues to be prophylactic – designed to prevent harm or disease. Adults and young people associate sexuality education with prevention – prevention of unintended pregnancy, gender-based violence, child abuse, homophobia, HIV, and sexually transmitted infections. While all of these issues are important concerns of sexuality educators, they are also embedded in the understanding that sexuality education of young people is essentially a problem of constraint. This longstanding prophylactic focus has been reinforced by chrononormative understandings of sexuality and development. These are norms that prescribe that young people must follow certain chronological temporal/time-oriented scripts in relation to sex, reproduction, sexuality, and gender. In this discussion of young people and sexuality education, our focus is on disrupting these taken-for-granted, state-sponsored temporal arrangements and looking to alternative ways of imagining young people's sexual futures. We consider how researchers, corporations, and pedagogical programs seek to influence and orchestrate children and young people's sexual development in relation to pregnancy and related questions of kinship arrangements. How might sexuality education work with young people to imagine different types of sexual futures outside an emphasis on prophylactics? What might such a sexuality education look like and in what ways might it upset the strictures of prevention? In what spaces might it flourish? Inspired by Elizabeth Freeman's *Time Binds: Queer Temporalities, Queer Histories*, (2010, p. xv), our focus in this chapter is on futurities which are "out of synch with state-sponsored narratives of belonging and becoming" and "speculating futures" in ways that counter the chrononormative "present tense" of young people and sexuality education.

Chrononormativity, Sexual Development, and Sexuality Education

Elizabeth Freeman's (2010) concept of chrononormativity is crucial to how we are seeking to disrupt everyday understandings of sexual development. Freeman (2010, p. 3) uses the term chrononormativity to denote the ways in which time is used to bind people together with regard to gender and sexuality to make "them feel coherently collective, through particular orchestrations of time." Luciano (cited in Freeman, 2010, p. 3) has termed this chronobiopolitics or "the sexual arrangement of the time of life of entire populations." This means that young people whose sex, sexuality, and gender fails to conform with these orchestrations are often made to feel excluded. For instance, young people who are pregnant and parenting may be forced to leave school or to enroll in a different educational institution because of the example they are seen to set to peers. The very idea that young people may be parenting while at school continues to be understood as very queer in most education contexts. We use the term queer here to denote a practice related to sexuality and gender that somehow deviates from expected sexual arrangements for teens. The default position in most secondary contexts is that high school is not the time of life for reproduction, and education institutions that admit this possibility tend to be outside of mainstream education[1]. This means that young people, especially young women, who are dealing with the challenges faced by all new parents, must generally find a way to manage this significant change in education contexts that are unfamiliar to them, and therefore removed from existing support structures that they might have cultivated in relation to teachers and peers.

Dana Luciano's work on chrononbiopolitics is concerned with the ways in which people's subjectivity, their understanding of themselves, is shaped over time through "culturally enforced rhythms, or timings, shap[ing] flesh into legible, acceptable embodiment" (Luciano cited in Freeman, 2010, p. 4). This idea of chronobiopolitics informs Freeman's work on chrononormativity. For the purposes of our analysis, these ideas help us understand how young people who are pregnant and parenting develop understandings of themselves that would likely translate into feelings of unacceptable embodiment – pregnant teenage bodies at school are illegible because they go against culturally enforced rhythms. While this affects individual young people who are pregnant and parenting while at school, it also has much wider impact. This is because, as Freeman notes, bodies aren't just shaped at the level of the individual, but the temporality of sexuality "extends beyond individual anatomies to encompass the management of entire populations ... [shaping] teleological schemes of events or strategies for living" that craft socially, economically, and politically acceptable moments at which to engage in sexuality, to marry, and to reproduce (Freeman, 2010, p. 4).

Bodily temporalities associated with sexuality and development don't only impact young people, they also shape the perceptions and understandings of teachers, parents, and researchers regarding pregnancy and adolescence. Through these temporalities we come to understand young people as fecund, desirous of intimacy, endlessly curious about sex, and, therefore, predisposed to having lots of sex. Such assumptions drive the prophylactic rationale that underpins sexuality education. These temporalities also teach us that reproductive sexuality is ideally

[1] See www.abc.net.au/news/2015–12-11/teen-mothers-find-alternative-classroom-to-complete-education/7018102

married to specific conditions and future selves; to a time when one's material conditions afford independent housing, secure employment, and a stable, monogamous, relationship. These same temporalities shape developmental discourses that continue to result in educational exclusion and pathologization of young people who are pregnant and parenting. It is important to focus on how these chrononormative ideas might shape young people, schools, and teachers – such an understanding may be the basis for crafting alternative imaginings of adolescent sexuality. It can also inform the production of pedagogies that incorporate less/non-chrononormative conceptualizations of pregnancy, parenting, and education.

Sexuality education is always already crafted so as to assume specific types of sexual practices and futures predicated on particular relationships between temporality, sexuality, race, class, ability, production, and reproduction. Freeman's (2010, p. 4) chronormativity traces how the state and institutions like schools

> link properly temporalized bodies to narratives of movement and change. These are teleological schemes of events or strategies for living such as marriage, accumulation of health and wealth for the future, reproduction, childrearing, and death and its attendant rituals . . . This timeline tends to serve a nation's economic interests . . .

Education, more broadly, and sexuality education, specifically, can thus be understood as part of the project of properly temporalizing bodies – crafting specific types of sexual futures that serve the nation's economic interests.

Like pregnancy and parenting, the timing of non-reproductive sexual pleasures may be constituted as part of young people's sexual futures. In this manner, strong prohibitions on sexuality and reproduction also affirm abstinence pedagogies. Katherine Franke coined the term repronormativity (2001) to draw attention to the ways in which norms around reproduction obscure a focus on non-reproductive sexuality. Just as teenage pregnancies are construed as out of time within normative frames of sexual development; sexual futures that are focused on sexual pleasure, not pregnancy, are absent within the frame of sexuality education. To make it plain, there is often an assumption within sexuality education that sexuality is principally associated with reproduction. Depending on one's time of life, you might be preoccupied with avoiding pregnancy, or, increasingly, maximizing your fertility. How might a move away from this style of thought and imagining open up different types of conversations between young people, and their educators, about their sexual futures. For instance, we know now that in Australia one in four women will not reproduce. How might young people begin to conceive of themselves inhabiting the space of non-parenting or co-parenting in worlds that assume women will reproduce?

As Franke's (2001) discussion of repronormativity underscores, how and when young people should be educated about sex, sexuality, and gender is intertwined with the production of nation states. Sexuality education is, we argue, thus wedded to broader visions of the future of the nation and its economic prosperity. Franke and Freeman's focus on the intersections between sexuality and economic development compellingly illustrates how discourses of sexual development leak beyond the domains of biology and psychology to be implicated in the health of the population – and thus tied to assumptions of reproduction. In this framing, sexuality education is developmentally appropriate only when it can be construed as serving nations' economic interests and young people's health and well-being. However, in this way of seeing, not only do alternative sexual futures become obscured but sexuality education devised for young people inevitably becomes wedded to a focus on prophylactics as this is seen to best serve the interests of the state and young people themselves. Freeman (2010, p. 3) apprehends how manipulations of sexual time transform "regimes of asymmetrical power into seemingly ordinary bodily tempos and routines, which in turn organize the value and meaning of time." Inspired by Freeman, we want readers to apprehend how seemingly ordinary bodily tempos and routines are embedded in the provision of developmentally appropriate sexuality education.

Alys Weinbaum's (2004) study of reproduction is also useful here in making the link between education about reproduction and larger questions of nation building. She urges readers to think about reproduction beyond "women's bodies and the domestic realm" to include "politically charged issues of racism, nation building and imperial expansion" (2004, p. 3). Both Weinbaum and Freeman think about race and reproduction as intertwined; neither believes that sexuality and the nation can be easily untethered. Weinbaum speaks specifically to the strength of the entanglement of reproduction of racist economies within modern sexual economies:

> Although the sexual economy of reproduction has begun to budge (for example, the increasing number of lesbian and queer families, single, heterosexual and older women using reproductive technologies to produce unconventional households), the racial economy of the new reproduction . . . remains quite static. *The pervasive disinclination to conceive of and to practice reproduction differently – and this despite the availability of knowledges and technologies that would make this possible . . .* (Weinbaum, 2004, p. 232) [our emphasis]

Such an analysis calls those involved in sexuality education conception and provision to go beyond the interrogation of sexuality and development as something intrinsic to biology and or psychology. Weinbaum speaks to the technological capacity to think differently about economies of reproduction, but also illustrates how changing technological capacities are not matched by different practices and pedagogies of reproduction. Sexuality education that is alive to the role of reproduction in nation building and in the reproduction of racist economies of development, might call on young people to interrogate their assumptions about who lives and sleeps with whom, in what types of domestic arrangements, and at what age. Such an approach calls on us to think through how assumptions about teen pregnancy and sexual activity are governed by perceptions of time and reproduction that are embedded in education curricula. It also alerts to how education about sexuality is underpinned by broader repronormative discourses, where sex is timely when it is consistent with the reproduction of Whiteness and heterosexuality.

Indeed, we are carefully taught from a young age about the temporalities of proper sexual development. Such bodily tempos and routines organize the value and meaning of sexual time – and they also attach worth to different types of bodies, routines, and tempos. Our focus on queer temporalities alerts to how sexual futures, in the service of the nation, structure how sexuality education is imagined and delivered. Grasping the relationship between sexuality education, temporality, and nation building is important for thinking about sexuality education otherwise and for making apparent the ways in which existing approaches to sexuality education may be linked to broader imaginings of reproduction. We are not suggesting that norms related to gender and sexual development can be completely undone, or that this would be desirable even if it were possible. We suggest that education about sex, gender, and sexuality might be capacious enough to grasp the complexities of young people's lives in ways that don't endanger young people but, at the same time, adequately reflect the messiness of their current and future realities. To elaborate this claim, we interrogate the association between sexuality education and chrononormative understandings of teen pregnancy via an investigation of an international virtual infant parenting program.

"Untimely" Teen Pregnancy and the "Natural Adolescent"

There is much research that links economic disadvantage with teenage pregnancy. For Wanda Pillow (2004), chrononormative conceptions of teenage pregnancy as pathological (both the result of childhood trauma and likely the inflictor of more trauma on young mothers and their children) can have grave effects on young people, especially young women. Attending to how temporality, sexuality, and social policy marks certain bodies as in deficit, Pillow (2004, 2015) explains how the "teen mother" is understood to be "out of time." But, she asks: "what if we began to question what lies behind such static conceptions of time? What if we rethink and reimagine policy-time as broken, as 'out of joint'?" (Pillow, 2015, p. 55). Pillow's analysis builds on Nancy Lesko's (2012) influential tracing of traditional chronologies of adolescence and sexuality, highlighting how relationships between the nation state, social order, and adolescence are interwoven to produce the presumed "natural adolescent." Pillow (2015) also draws attention to how the "natural adolescent" within discourses of sexuality education is not only temporalized but also classed and racialized.

The question of when it is timely for young people, especially young women, to think about having children has long been the focus of much state interest in sexuality education. In Australia, births to mothers aged 19 years and younger is in a continuing pattern of decline both in number (8,574 in 2016) and proportion of all births (2.8 percent)[2]. Yet teen pregnancy prevention is a goal that continues to attract the enthusiastic support of advocates of comprehensive and abstinence-based approaches to sexuality. In undertaking education about pregnancy prevention, sexuality education is decidedly prophylactic and regulatory. Following this chapter's aim to imagine existing chrononormative understandings of sexual development otherwise, we are interested in how such prophylactic framings of teen pregnancy may constrain young people's conversations, imaginings, and speculations about their sexual futures and the place that children might play in their present or future lives. The idea that there is a right time for motherhood is not a new insight; many researchers have pointed to the ways in which teenagers are construed as out of time when they have children (Perrier, 2013; Pillow, 2015). Maud Perrier (2013) studies how normative ideas about the right time for reproduction impact the lives of mothers who are seen as too young or too old. She notes judgments made about the right time for pregnancy are predicated on the "illusion that women can exercise complete control over their reproductive capacities" (2013, p. 71).

Catriona Macleod (2003) has traced the relationship between developmental discourses and dominant understandings of teen pregnancy in South Africa. She argues that the problem of teen pregnancy is closely linked to beliefs about teenagers living lives that are in transition. She argues that in this developmental framing, teenagers are fundamentally no longer children, but also not adults. When adolescence is "accepted as a separable stage of development, as an identifiable phase in the life span" (2013, p. 420), it can then become the target of tailored education programs that are considered appropriate to this sexual age and stage. Following on from this classification of teenage pregnancy as discrete, based on developmental ideas about adolescence, Macleod observes that:

> Researchers and service providers [are able to] express humanitarian concern for teen mothers and their children because the consequences of early reproduction are depicted as deleterious. This is partially to do with the 'untimely' nature of the activity. Teenage pregnancy, it is argued, leads, inter alia, to: a disruption of schooling; poor obstetric outcomes owing to the teenager's biological immaturity; and inadequate mothering, including neglect, maltreatment and abuse, owing to the teenager's emotional immaturity. (Macleod, 2003, p. 419)

In a recent literature review of Australian health discourses pertaining to young mothers, Brand et al. (2014, p. 175) also critique the persistent and dominant discourses of teen pregnancy as perverse and untimely. They are critical of research related to young mothers that affirms them "as the cause and consequence of poverty and welfare dependency . . . as deviant for making the 'wrong' choice, a choice that does not follow the 'normal' life trajectory (i.e. finish school, get a job, marry and have children)." Brand et al., Macleod, and Pillow's research that seeks to problematize dominant developmental understandings of teen pregnancy is set

[2] See www.abs.gov.au/ausstats%5Cabs@.nsf/0/8668A9A0D4B0156CCA25792F0016186A?Opendocument.

against a huge body of literature that makes the case that children born of teenagers suffer developmentally because of their untimely birth.

For instance, in a chapter entitled "Adolescent Pregnancy in Australia," in the *International Handbook of Adolescent Pregnancy*, Lucy Lewis and Rachel Skinner make the case that:

> adolescent mothers are more likely to be: single, smoke, have high levels of illicit and licit substance use, live in an area of socioeconomic disadvantage, have pregnancies with uncertain dates, have partners at increased risk of exposure to domestic violence and family dysfunction as children, and partners who are often involved with illegal activities especially illicit drugs. (Lewis & Skinner, 2014, p. 191)

Such research clearly affirms associations drawn between young mothers, dysfunction, and degeneration. This type of research, that affirms the problems and risks associated with teen pregnancy, provides a strong rationale for the provision of pregnancy prevention programs aimed at teenagers. Teenage sexuality is not only constructed as untimely in relation to developmental discourses, it is also problematized because of associations made between race, class, and teen pregnancy (Fields, 2005; Kaplan, 1997; Pillow, 2015).

Juana Maria Rodríguez (2014), in her book, *Sexual Futures, Queer Gestures, and Other Latina Longings,* attends to the ways in which race, class, and sexuality intersect with normalizing conceptions of temporality and reproduction. Rodríguez (2014, pp. 36–37) speaks to the ways in which some young people – such as queer young people of color who are pregnant, parenting, and cohabiting with extended family – are "marked by 'the unruly excessiveness' of difference." They "fall outside the model of proper adulthood [but] also fall out of the political agendas of mainstream LGBT activists" who seek marriage reform (ibid.). This is why imaginings of sexual futures needs to be focused on much more than normative visions of reproductive adulthood.

Dana Luciano notes, queerness is not merely determined "by the gender of object-choice but by a perceived 'mistiming' of desire, a lack of synchronicity with the reproductive-generational order" (Luciano, 2007, pp. 260–261). As a consequence, young people of color who are pregnant and parenting, whether or not they identify as LGBTI, may be constituted as out of time. But young people of color who are queer, pregnant, and parenting are constituted as particularly excessive because:

> . . . social legibility . . . based on a discourse of parental rights, racial inheritance, sustained monogamy, and the promotion of linear developmental narratives of familial and national relations demands that queers cross the imaginary border from pleasure-seeking perverts to sanitized sexless adult guardians, committed self-sacrificing partners and parents. For queers who are not white, middle-class, able-bodied, coupled, or normatively gendered, choosing to parent can actually make us appear more, rather than less, perverse. (Rodríguez, 2014, p. 53)

All young people who are pregnant and choose to parent draw attention to their own perversity; a perversity that is continuously reinforced by research, social policy, and the prevalence of developmental thinking in education, psychology, and health. But this perversity is compounded by their perceived distance from the reproductive–racialized–generational order. Evidence of this perceived perversity is apparent in the lack of structural support for young people who are pregnant and parenting. For instance, in Australia, currently only one state (the Australian Capital Territory) has a comprehensive education program to support young people who are pregnant and parenting. At the same time that education of young people who are pregnant and parenting is woefully inadequate; persistent beliefs about child sexual development, pregnancy, and parenting mean that governments continue fund to educational initiatives like the robot babies.

Robot Babies, Chrononormativity, and "the Traumatized Adolescent Brain"

Here we take a closer look at the robot babies program and two critiques of the program published in the prestigious medical journal, *The Lancet.* Robot babies was devised by Realityworks,[3] a private US company that largely controls the international market on robot babies. The principal pedagogical purpose of the program is to discourage teen pregnancy because of the "unforgettable lessons" (www.realityworks.com) the program provides about the amount of care and attention babies require. Realityworks has designed an extensive curriculum that it recommends for use in concert with the robot babies being taken home by high school students for 48 hours. During this time, the robot babies mimic the needs and behaviors of real babies, complete with randomly programmed crying, along with the need for comfort, sleep, and nappy changes. Robot babies have "become staples of American education, reaching more than 6 million students at 17,000 schools . . . 91 countries around the world" (Deprez, 2016) and have proven to be a persuasive element of sexuality education programs internationally. Julie Quinlivan provides a persuasive account of why the robot babies have been so popular internationally:

> If a teenage girl cared for a simulated baby, the experience would be sufficiently profound and challenging to act as a reality check against the perils of teenage pregnancy. Combine the experience with an educational intervention, and you had a programme worthy of public funds. Educators were charmed. Students excited. The magic dolls were fun. The expensive infant simulators represented a brave new world. Governments could safely tick a box in a controversial area. (Quinlivan,2016)

Quinlivan's observations speak to the complexities of educating young people about sexuality and the desire for solutions to the "perils of teenage pregnancy"; specifically, the desire for solutions that show that governments are acting, without inflaming teenage sexual desire. Quinlivan is clearly critical of the robot babies

[3] According to the organization's website Realityworks program runs in over 90 countries – see http://realityworks.com/distributors.

program, but, as we demonstrate later, her critique is underpinned by her frustration that such programs might unintentionally incite pregnancy, rather than playing a deterrent role.

The prophylactic efficacy of robot babies was the subject of a recent study conducted by Brinkman et al. (2016). They evaluated the program via a randomized control trial that focused on pregnancy outcomes (birth and induced abortion). This study was conducted with over 3,000 schoolgirls aged 13–15 in the state of Western Australia. They concluded that the infant simulator-based virtual infant parenting (VIP) program did not achieve its aim of reducing teenage pregnancy, finding that "Girls in the intervention group were more likely to experience a birth or an induced abortion than those in the control group before they reached twenty years of age" (2016, p. 1). These findings were widely reported in a range of media after they were published in an article in *The Lancet*[4]. The study and the media reporting related to their findings regarding robot babies continue to reinforce teenage pregnancy as pathological and, unquestionably, an undesirable education outcome. This story is instructive in the context of this chapter because it helps to underscore how chronormative ideas about young people, development, and sexuality emerge in the design and evaluation of educational programs designed to prevent teen pregnancy.

In a commentary on Brinkman's research in *The Lancet*, Quinlivan advises readers that pregnant "teenagers themselves often fail to fulfil their educational, occupational, and economic potential" (Quinlivan, 2016, p. 1). She draws on a breadth of research to demonstrate that teenage pregnancy is not only traumatic and pathological but also deleterious economically. Quinlivan further suggests there is evidence that teen pregnancy is linked to adversity in early childhood such that "[b]y the time a child reaches secondary education, *the traumatised adolescent brain might have already evolved towards a desire for early childbearing to address subconscious evolutionary fears*" (2016, p. 1) [our emphasis]. She also suggests that teenage pregnancy is linked to an idealized version of parenthood. For Quinlivan, the intervention's "brief exposure [of susceptible teenagers] to a doll [robot baby] reinforces idealization [while] negative consequences of teenage pregnancy are diminished" (Quinlivan, 2016). So, for Quinlivan, specific groups of young adolescent women are already more likely to desire early childbearing because of trauma they experienced as part of their own development; the robot babies are problematic for Quinlivan because they further inflame this desire.

At the same time as Quinlivan (2016) is eager to ensure that teenage pregnancy interventions are robust, she also emphasizes the primacy of structural disadvantage in the lives of young women, regardless of whether they become mothers. She writes:

[4] Realityworks refuted Brinkman's findings in a blog post on its own website. See www.realityworks.com/blog/our-response-to-a-recent-study/. See www.thelancet.com/journals/lancet/article/PIIS0140-6736(16)30384-1/abstract.

> *teenage pregnancy, although often labelled as a cause of social and economic burden, is more likely an association.* Cohort studies following disadvantaged women have found little economic difference between sisters from disadvantaged backgrounds where one gave birth as a teenager and the other sister did not. *The crucial causal factor is disadvantage, be it socioeconomic, educational, or environmental.* (Quinlivan, 2016) [our emphasis]

Quinlivan, recognizes that brighter futures for young women are not adversely affected by pregnancy alone but by how pregnancy further compounds structural disadvantage through the exclusion of young women from education, peers, and employments options. Based on this analysis, and as an alternative to robot babies, Quinlivan (2016) suggests that pregnancy prevention "*Programmes need to start in infancy.* Investment in vulnerable children is needed to entice these adolescents from the path of premature parenthood *into brighter futures*" [our emphasis]. For Quinlivan (2016), brighter sexual futures clearly means the absence of pregnancy, even though young women who experience economic and social disadvantage are likely to be profoundly impacted by this, regardless of whether they become parents.

Brand et al. (2014, p. 175) have a different take to Quinlivan. All share the observation that structural disadvantage adversely impacts young people's futures. Brand et al. argue against interventionist approaches in health:

> Whether the 'problem' of 'teenage motherhood' is portrayed as a moral, social or economic one, it further legitimises the 'at risk' concept that requires a public health response. The health system reaction has positioned its response accordingly tending to focus on targeted, interventionist responses rather the acknowledging the bigger picture and honouring the complexity of young people's lives and the social conditions in which they live. This reaction has caused fragmented and inadequate youth health services in Australia.

Brand et al.'s (2014) focus is on health interventions related to "teenage motherhood." In this chapter we are tracing the ways in which notions of intervention and the problematization of teenage motherhood underscore the approach of researchers such as Brinkman and Quinlivan in their evaluation of programs like robot babies. The dominance of interventionist responses in addressing issues related to "teenage motherhood" is evidenced by the fact that both supporters and critics of the robot babies program agree that teenage pregnancy is a problem; where they differ is on the efficacy of the intervention program. Our intention in studying the robot babies program is quite different; we are interested in the ways that programs like the robot babies might misfire and open up the potential for young people to think about their present and future sexual lives in ways that aren't predicated upon the problematization of teenage motherhood.

Young people who are pregnant and parenting will be perceived as out of time as long as the teenage years are perceived as a time when young people need to learn about contraception and safe sex, not about sexual pleasure, parenting, or desires for family formation. Turning such thinking around requires an acknowledgment of the pedagogical possibilities that might be afforded by sexuality education that offers young people the chance to think about themselves as future parents, people who might enjoy sex but defer parenting, people who may enjoy sex but choose not to parent, people who might be parenting in their teens, or people who might eschew sex and parenting. Later we think about other pedagogical possibilities that might be associated with robot babies.

"Do Robot Babies Make Teens Want Real Babies?": Reimagining Sexual Futures with the Robot Babies

Here we study robot babies, or the VIP program, from a different angle. As indicated earlier, we are less concerned with robot babies' prophylactic capacities and more interested in their capacity to provide young people with opportunities to think about their sexual futures and family formations in open-ended ways. Such openings proffer the potential for young people to consider a myriad of sexual selves and family formations, and, to our minds, this is a significant benefit of the program. However, as is already evident, because of the developmental emphasis within sexuality education on pregnancy prevention, this is not seen as a benefit in research regarding the efficacy of the programs.

In a piece entitled *Do Robot Babies Make Teens Want Real Babies?*, produced for the US public radio program, 'This American Life,' in August 2016, Hilary Frank interviews Paige and Rachel. These young women, high school seniors from Glen Ridge, New Jersey, cared for robot babies for 48 hours. Frank was curious about how this experience made them think about their sexual futures. She notes:

> The students couldn't have been more different. Paige was devoutly Christian, conservative, dreamed of meeting a man in college, getting married, and having kids young. Rachel identified as bisexual, liberal, and no way did she want kids until she'd started a fulfilling career and had plenty of adventures. Of course, I figured Paige would love playing mom, and Rachel would see it as . . . just another weird high school adventure . . . After two nights with her robot baby, Paige was a wreck. She said she couldn't imagine ever doing this in real life . . . Rachel, though. She bonded with her baby . . . She told me that her experience with this hunk of plastic actually made her feel more prepared for unintended pregnancy. "If I have a baby really young, I feel like I would keep the baby," she told me. I was shocked. *Rachel's response to the robot baby was exactly the opposite of what you were supposed to have after going through this program. You were supposed to feel like Paige.* (Frank, 2016) (our emphasis)

For Brinkman et al. (2016) and Quinlivan (2016), the program's primary pedagogical intent was to teach young people that they are not yet ready for parenting. We wonder whether sexuality education involving robot simulators might be seen as a valuable addition to sexuality education, not because of its prophylactic qualities but because of its capacity to affect and challenge young people's imaginings of themselves as future parents. Frank (2016) observes that, while the correct lesson of the program is that young women should find that they are not ready for parenting, through participation in this program one of these young women questioned her dream of marrying young and starting a family, while the other felt less daunted by the prospect of an unplanned pregnancy as a result of her participation in the program. Part of what we are contemplating in this chapter is the production of an approach to sexuality education that queers assumptions about and imaginings of sexual futures. We use the term queer here not to indicate a sexuality education program that might make people gay (although this is still clearly a concern of many opposed to sexuality education about gender and sexuality diversity). Rather, we deploy the term queer to encompass understandings of young people, sexuality, and temporality where young people who don't conform might be seen as "figures for and bearers of new corporeal sensations, including those of a certain counterpoint between now and then, and of occasional disruptions to the sped-up and hyperregulated time of industry" (Freeman, 2010, p.7).

In thinking about the relationship between education and young people's sexual futures, we are hoping to prompt conversations about reproduction and education for a number of purposes. We want to point to the ways in which chrononormativity continues to profoundly shape young people's access to and experience of education. Why do schools continue to be so reluctant to embrace young people who are pregnant and parenting? Why are these young people deemed to be so out of time? Why might a program that engages young people in imaginings of parenting be deemed a pedagogical failure? Young people who are pregnant and parenting continue to be perceived as "failures or refusals to inhabit middle- and upper-middle-class habitus appear as precisely, asynchrony, or time out of joint" (Freeman, 2010, p.19). But it is not only the failures and refusals that are pertinent here; the value of bringing together analyses of queer futures and young reproductive bodies and associated pedagogies is an understanding of how these positions sometimes, *but not always*, overlap, even as they *may* experience different positions of power in relation to class and race (Freeman, 2010, p.19).

Embracing Sexual Futures that Are "Out of Joint"

In this chapter, we have wondered about how robot babies are already unbinding normative relationships, between temporality, reproduction, and production. Following on from Juana Maria Rodríguez and her queering of parenting discourses, we are trying to envisage how sexuality education might think differently about sexual development in order to ensure that young people, especially young people "who are not white, middle-class, able-bodied, coupled, or normatively gendered" (Rodríguez, 2014, p. 53), can become legible both as students and as parents via interventions in policy and pedagogy in education. Such imaginings, we argue, should not be deferred until schooling is finished. There is a mosaic of educational programs that support young people who are pregnant and parenting in Australia but *Canberra College Cares* is still, to our knowledge, Australia's only purpose-built educational facility to comprehensively support young people who are pregnant and parenting in the pursuit of their education. The absence of young people who are pregnant and parenting in schools, which is no doubt materially related to the absence of programs to support these young people to stay in school, is a question of justice in education that needs to be asked and answered.

It is possible to imagine how young people's experiences of reproduction and sexuality might be incorporated into education in ways that are other than prophylactic. Could the robot babies program be adapted so it invites young women who are pregnant or looking after a child and imagining themselves pursuing an education simultaneously? Might secondary schools move from nurseries for robot babies to nurseries for real babies, buoyed by young people's enthusiasm for education and parenthood? Frank's treatment of robot babies on 'This American Life' demonstrates how shifts in terms of sexual futures can be opened up by programs that prompt young people to imagine themselves as reproductive. This shouldn't be read as a developmental turn that insists on reproductive futures but rather recognition that sexuality and development are related and pertinent in the lives of young people, but not in ways that are predictable. Robot babies have caught our interest because of their unpredictability. Their misfires revealed and enabled some resistances to ordinary tempos and routines that privilege particular bodies and lives. The affective engagements in which young people involved in the program become entangled invite speculation about reproductive futures, but not in a way that might be predicted at the outset. So, robot babies can also help young people who aren't pregnant or parenting to begin contemplating the types of kinship and support networks that they may imagine for their future selves. The program prompts them to at least question whether their sexual future will be reproductive or non-reproductive. We believe this is something that is worth asking young people to start pondering while in school.

To further imagine unbinding of normative relationships between temporality, reproduction, and production we look to Japan, one of several Western countries that has a perceived 'crisis' in fertility. In Japan's case, this crisis is fueled, in part, by a longstanding refusal to look to immigration in order to address low population growth (White, 2015)[5]. In Japan, the relevance of Alys Weinbaum's discussion of the "pervasive disinclination to conceive of and to practice reproduction differently" means that the its elderly population is starting to outpace its young population. According to UN reports, "by 2050 there will be about double the number of people living in Japan in the 70-plus age range compared to those aged 15–30."[6] In

[5] See www.reuters.com/article/us-japan-economy-population/japan-targets-boosting-birth-rate-to-increase-growth-idUSKCN0T113A20151112.

[6] See 'Robot babies from Japan raise all sorts of questions about how parents bond with AI'https://theconversation.com/robot-babies-from-japan-raise-all-sorts-of-questions-about-how-parents-bond-with-ai-66815.

the context of this study of normative sexual development, it is possible to see how norms regarding sexual development and childbearing can come to have perverse effects at the level of the individual and the nation. In 2015, the *Japan Times* reported a misguided attempt to bring about a reversal in these population figures by the Japanese Ministry of Education. The Ministry was pilloried for distributing information to school students suggesting that young women's fertility began to massively decline at age 22. *The Japan Times* speculates that the decision was no doubt motivated by the desire to address the nation's continued low birth rate.[7]

In a piece in *The Conversation*, Mark Anderson, an expert in computing and information systems from the United Kingdom, touches on Japan's fertility 'crisis.' Anderson looks to Brinkman's research on robot babies to consider the possibility of using this technology to encourage young people to reproduce in order to address falling rates of fertility. Anderson is cautious in recommending this approach too enthusiastically, warning that it is "too simplistic" to say that "all adopters of robotic babies" would be moved to have children by exposure to the dolls. What is interesting about Anderson's observations in the context of this chapter is how the robot babies are employed toward differing ends with intended and unintended effects. The idea that, in countries where the desire to parent is on the decline, the purpose of robot babies might be to engender the desire to parent points to the ways in which normative ideas about sexual development might become contested. Such contestations have the potential to reveal how normative sexuality is driven by and intertwined with economic or national survival, rather than psychological or medical norms of development.

In an editorial in *The Economist* entitled "Sex education in Japan: Tiptoeing around," they reported on a controversy within the country about the purpose of sex education. Ryoichi Mori, from the Ministry of Education is reported as saying that: "hitherto the main goal has been to prevent STDs, but that Japan's shrinking population has started a debate about whether the aim should be, in part, to encourage childbearing[8]" (2016). To be clear, our aim is not to enthusiastically embrace a natalist approach to development which calls for the birth of more babies in order to build economic prosperity. Although, we have pointed to the ways in which developmental discourses within sexuality education can't be separated from concerns about the nation. Evidence of shifting and competing developmental discourses associated with development and sexuality education are appearing on the horizon in several developed countries (Singapore, Denmark, Sweden, Germany) with concerns about declining rates of fertility[9]. The impact of such concerns on the production of developmental norms in sexuality education have yet to overtake prophylactic imperatives, but a swing in the other direction would likely be just as concerning for young people and those

[7] See www.japantimes.co.jp/opinion/2015/10/10/editorials/sex-education-propaganda/#.Wcl-r5MjFPU.

[8] See www.economist.com/news/asia/21709599-better-learn-about-sex-school-pornographic-comics-tiptoeing-around.

[9] See www.theatlantic.com/sexes/archive/2013/01/robot-babies-no-kids-tax-and-other-ways-nations-try-to-up-the-birth-rate/267203/.

responsible for developing sexuality education. The possibility of such a turn might also beg the question of why there isn't more concern about the current developmental emphasis on prophylactic sexuality education, given the consequences it has on educational access for young people who are currently pregnant and parenting.

Conclusion

Everyday conceptualizations of sexual development are underpinned by taken-for-granted temporal logics that give value and worth to certain individual bodies over others. But normative sexual development is not only about individual young people and their sexual futures, it is also about broader society and the ways in which gender, sexuality, race, and class are entwined in particular imaginings of the nation and its sexual citizens. In this chapter, through our exploration of robot babies we have made visible some of the ways that researchers and pedagogical programs attempt to influence normative timelines of sexual development and kinship with ambivalent effects. Robot babies are designed to heavily enforce an acceptable, proper timeline of sexual development such that particular bodies who reproduce "out of time" are marked as deficit with particularly costly effects for young people who are economically disadvantaged and young people of color. However, while intending to persuade young people of the perils of teen pregnancy, the use of robot babies misfired. Furthermore, the consideration of robot babies as a potential mechanism for the converse aim of increasing birth rates underlines the unpredictability of such technologies.

It is the very unpredictability of the robot babies that has caught our attention. Their misfires, unintended uses and effects signal the potential in using technologies such as robot babies in an open-ended pedagogical way in sex education. A critical dialogue with young people might interrogate the robot babies themselves – their original function, how they have been mobilized in different contexts, and how they have misfired – enabling a visibilizing of the temporal arrangements related to sexual development and interrogation of their classed and racialized effects. In this way, the robot babies might be used, not with particular ends and outcomes in mind, but as an aid for facilitating young people to contemplate and imagine sexual futures and family formations in a less prescriptive, more open ended and ethical way.

References

Brand, G., Morrison, P., & Down, B. (2014). How Do Health Professionals Support Pregnant and Young Mothers in the Community? A Selective Review of the Research Literature. *Women and Birth*, *27*(3), 174–178.

Brinkman, S. A., Johnson, S. E., Codde, J. P., et al. (2016). Efficacy of Infant Simulator Programmes to Prevent Teenage Pregnancy: A School-Based Cluster Randomised Controlled Trial in Western Australia. *The Lancet*, *388*(10057), 2264–2271.

Deprez, E. (2016, December 22). Those robot babies meant to scare teens out of having kids might not work. *Bloomberg*. www.bloomberg.com/news/features/2016–12-22/robot-babies-meant-to-scare-teens-out-of-having-kids-aren-t-working.

Fields, J. (2005). "Children Having Children": Race, Innocence, and Sexuality Education. *Social Problems*, *52*(4), 549–571.

Frank, H. (2016, August 25) Do robot babies make teens want real babies. *This American Life*. http://hw4.thisamericanlife.org/extras/do-robot-babies-make-teens-want-real-babies.

Franke, K. M. (2001), Theorizing Yes: An Essay on Feminism, Law, and Desire. *Columbia Law Review 101*, 181–208.

Freeman, E. (2010). *Time Binds: Queer Temporalities, Queer Histories*. Durham, NC: Duke University Press.

Kaplan, E. B. (1997). *Not Our Kind of Girl: Unraveling the Myths of Black Teenage Motherhood*. Berkeley: University of California Press.

Lesko, N. (2012). *Act Your Age! A Cultural Construction of Adolescence*. New York: Routledge.

Lewis, L. N. & Skinner, S. R. (2014). Adolescent Pregnancy in Australia. In Cherry, A. L. & Dillon, M. E. (Eds.). *International Handbook of Adolescent Pregnancy* (191–203). Boston: Springer.

Luciano, D. (2007). Coming Around Again: The Queer Momentum of Far from Heaven. *GLQ: A Journal of Lesbian and Gay Studies*, *13*(2), 249–272.

Macleod, C. (2003). "Teenage Pregnancy and the Construction of Adolescence: Scientific Literature in South Africa", *Childhood*, *10*(4), 419–437.

Perrier, M. (2013). No Right Time: The Significance of Reproductive Timing for Younger and Older Mothers' Moralities. *The Sociological Review*, *61*(1), 69–87.

Pillow, W. S. (2004). *Unfit Subjects: Educational Policy and the Teen Mother*. New York, London: Routledge.

(2015). Policy Temporality and Marked Bodies: Feminist Praxis amongst the Ruins. *Critical Studies in Education*, *56*(1), 55–70.

Quinlivan, J. A. (2016). Magic Dolls: No Quick Fix for Teenage Pregnancy. *The Lancet*, *388*(10057), 2214–2215.

Rodríguez, J. M. (2014). *Sexual Futures, Queer Gestures, and Other Latina Longings*. New York: New York University Press.

Weinbaum, A. (2004). *Wayward Reproductions: Genealogies of Race and Nation in Modern Transatlantic Thought*. Durham, NC: Duke University Press.

White, S. (2015, November 12). Japan targets boosting birth rate to increase growth. *Reuters* (US edition).

Index